3rd Workshop on Statistical Machine Translation 2008

(WMT 08)

Held in conjunction with ACL-HLT 2008

Columbus, Ohio, USA
19 June 2008

ISBN: 978-1-61738-550-6

Printed from e-media with permission by:

Curran Associates, Inc.
57 Morehouse Lane
Red Hook, NY 12571

Some format issues inherent in the e-media version may also appear in this print version.

Printed by Curran Associates, Inc. (2010)

For permission requests, please contact the Association for Computational Linguistics at the address below.

Association for Computational Linguistics
209 N. Eighth Street
Stroudsburg, Pennsylvania 18360

Phone: 1-570-476-8006
Fax: 1-570-476-0860

acl@aclweb.org

Additional copies of this publication are available from:

Curran Associates, Inc.
57 Morehouse Lane
Red Hook, NY 12571 USA
Phone: 845-758-0400
Fax: 845-758-2634
Email: curran@proceedings.com
Web: www.proceedings.com

Introduction

The ACL 2008 Workshop on Statistical Machine Translation (WMT-08) took place on Thursday, June 19 in Columbus, Ohio, United States, immediately following the annual meeting of the Association for Computational Linguistics, which was hosted by the Ohio State University.

This is the third time this workshop has been held. It has its root in the ACL 2005 Workshop on Building and Using Parallel Texts In the following years the Workshop on Statistical Machine Translation was held at HLT-NAACL 2006 in New York City, US, and at ACL 2007 in Prague, Czech Republic.

The focus of our workshop was to use parallel corpora for machine translation. Recent experimentation has shown that the performance of SMT systems varies greatly with the source language. In this workshop we encouraged researchers to investigate ways to improve the performance of SMT systems for diverse languages, including morphologically more complex languages and languages with partial free word order.

Prior to the workshop, in addition to soliciting relevant papers for review and possible presentation we conducted a shared task that brought together machine translation systems for an evaluation on previously unseen data. This year's task resembled the shared tasks of previous years in many ways, but also included Hungarian-English and Spanish-German as new language pairs. In addition, we evaluated submitted systems against new test sets from the newswire domain.

The results of the shared task were announced at the workshop, and these proceedings also include an overview paper for the shared task that summarizes the results, as well as provides information about the data used and any procedures that were followed in conducting or scoring the task. In addition, there are short papers from each participating team that describe their underlying system in some detail.

Due to the large number of high quality submission for the full paper track, shared task submissions were presented as posters. The poster session was held in the afternoon and gave participants of the shared task the opportunity to present their approaches. The rest of the day was devoted to oral paper presentations and Daniel Marcu's invited talk in the afternoon.

Like in previous years, we have received a far larger number of submission than we could accept for presentation. This year we have received 18 full paper submissions and 26 shared task submissions. In total WMT-08 featured 12 full paper oral presentations and 25 shared task poster presentations. The invited talk was given by Daniel Marcu of the Information Sciences Institute at the University of Southern California.

We would like to thank the members of the Program Committee for their timely reviews. We also would like to thank the participants of the shared task and all the other volunteers who helped with the manual evaluations. We also acknowledge the financial support of the shared task by the EuroMatrix project funded by the European Commission (6th Framework Programme).

Chris Callison-Burch, Philipp Koehn, Christof Monz, Josh Schroeder, and Cameron Shaw Fordyce

Co-Organizers

Organizers:

Chris Callison-Burch (Johns Hopkins University)
Philipp Koehn (University of Edinburgh)
Christof Monz (University of London)
Josh Schroeder (University of Edinburgh)
Cameron Shaw Fordyce

Program Committee:

Lars Ahrenberg (Linköping University)
Yaser Al-Onaizan (IBM Research)
Oliver Bender (RWTH Aachen)
Chris Brockett (Microsoft Research)
Bill Byrne (Cambridge University)
Francisco Casacuberta (University of Valencia)
Colin Cherry (Microsoft Research)
Stephen Clark (Oxford University)
Trevor Cohn (Edinburgh University)
Mona Diab (Columbia University)
Hal Daume (University of Utah)
Chris Dyer (University of Maryland)
Andreas Eisele (University Saarbrücken)
Marcello Federico (ITC-IRST)
George Foster (Canada National Research Council)
Alex Fraser (University of Stuttgart)
Ulrich Germann (University of Toronto)
Nizar Habash (Columbia University)
Jan Hajic (Charles University)
Keith Hall (Google)
John Henderson (MITRE)
Rebecca Hwa (University of Pittsburgh)
Doug Jones (Lincoln Labs MIT)
Damianos Karakos (Johns Hopkins University)
Kevin Knight (ISI/University of Southern California)
Shankar Kumar (Google)
Philippe Langlais (University of Montreal)
Alon Lavie (Carnegie Melon University)
Adam Lopez (Edinburgh University)
Daniel Marcu (ISI/University of Southern California)
Lambert Mathias (Johns Hopkins University)
Arul Menezes (Microsoft Research)
Bob Moore (Microsoft Research)

Miles Osborne (University of Edinburgh)
Kay Peterson (NIST)
Mark Przybocki (NIST)
Chris Quirk (Microsoft Research)
Philip Resnik (University of Maryland)
Michel Simard (National Research Council Canada)
Libin Shen (BBN Technologies)
Wade Shen (Lincoln Labs MIT)
Eiichiro Sumita (NICT/ATR)
David Talbot (Edinburgh University)
Jörg Tiedemann (University of Groningen)
Christoph Tillmann (IBM Research)
Kristina Toutanova (Microsoft Research)
Nicola Ueffing (National Research Council Canada)
Clare Voss (Army Research Labs)
Taro Watanabe (NTT)
Dekai Wu (HKUST)
Richard Zens (Google)

Additional Reviewers:

Mahmoud Ghoneim
Jeffrey Micher

Invited Speaker:

Daniel Marcu (ISI/University of Southern California)

Table of Contents

Workshop Program

Thursday, June 19, 2008

Thursday, June 19, 2008 (continued)

12:40-2:00 Lunch

Session 3: Shared Task

2:00-2:30 *Further Meta-Evaluation of Machine Translation*
Chris Callison-Burch, Cameron Fordyce, Philipp Koehn, Christof Monz and Josh Schroeder

2:30–2:40 *Limsi's Statistical Translation Systems for WMT'08*
Daniel Déchelotte, Gilles Adda, Alexandre Allauzen, Hélène Bonneau-Maynard, Olivier Galibert, Jean-Luc Gauvain, Philippe Langlais and François Yvon

2:40–2:50 *The MetaMorpho Translation System*
Attila Novák, László Tihanyi and Gábor Prószéky

2:50–3:00 *Meteor, M-BLEU and M-TER: Evaluation Metrics for High-Correlation with Human Rankings of Machine Translation Output*
Abhaya Agarwal and Alon Lavie

3:00-3:30 Booster Session: Shared Task

Shared Translaton Task

First Steps towards a General Purpose French/English Statistical Machine Translation System
Holger Schwenk, Jean-Baptiste Fouet and Jean Senellart

The University of Washington Machine Translation System for ACL WMT 2008
Amittai Axelrod, Mei Yang, Kevin Duh and Katrin Kirchhoff

The TALP-UPC Ngram-Based Statistical Machine Translation System for ACL-WMT 2008
Maxim Khalilov, Adolfo Hernández H., Marta R. Costa-jussà, Josep M. Crego, Carlos A. Henríquez Q., Patrik Lambert, José A. R. Fonollosa, José B. Mariño and Rafael E. Banchs

European Language Translation with Weighted Finite State Transducers: The CUED MT System for the 2008 ACL Workshop on SMT
Graeme Blackwood, Adrià de Gispert, Jamie Brunning and William Byrne

Effects of Morphological Analysis in Translation between German and English
Sara Stymne, Maria Holmqvist and Lars Ahrenberg

Towards better Machine Translation Quality for the German-English Language Pairs
Philipp Koehn, Abhishek Arun and Hieu Hoang

Thursday, June 19, 2008 (continued)

Shared Evaluation Task

The Role of Pseudo References in MT Evaluation
Joshua Albrecht and Rebecca Hwa

Ranking vs. Regression in Machine Translation Evaluation
Kevin Duh

A Smorgasbord of Features for Automatic MT Evaluation
Jesús Giménez and Lluís Màrquez

3:30-4:40 Coffee Break and Poster Session

Session 4: Full Papers

4:40–5:00 *Fast, Easy, and Cheap: Construction of Statistical Machine Translation Models with MapReduce*
Chris Dyer, Aaron Cordova, Alex Mont and Jimmy Lin

5:00–5:20 *Dynamic Model Interpolation for Statistical Machine Translation*
Andrew Finch and Eiichiro Sumita

5:20–5:40 *Improved Statistical Machine Translation by Multiple Chinese Word Segmentation*
Ruiqiang Zhang, Keiji Yasuda and Eiichiro Sumita

5:40–6:00 *Optimizing Chinese Word Segmentation for Machine Translation Performance*
Pi-Chuan Chang, Michel Galley and Christopher D. Manning

An Empirical Study in Source Word Deletion for Phrase-based Statistical Machine Translation

Chi-Ho Li, Dongdong Zhang, Mu Li, Ming Zhou
Microsoft Research Asia
Beijing, China
chl, dozhang@microsoft.com
muli, mingzhou@microsoft.com

Hailei Zhang
Northeastern University of China
Shenyang, China
hailei.zh@gmail.com

Abstract

The treatment of 'spurious' words of source language is an important problem but often ignored in the discussion on phrase-based SMT. This paper explains why it is important and why it is not a trivial problem, and proposes three models to handle spurious source words. Experiments show that any source word deletion model can improve a phrase-based system by at least 1.6 BLEU points and the most sophisticated model improves by nearly 2 BLEU points. This paper also explores the impact of training data size and training data domain/genre on source word deletion.

1 Introduction

It is widely known that translation is by no means word-to-word conversion. Not only because sometimes a word in some language translates as more than one word in another language, also every language has some 'spurious' words which do not have any counterpart in other languages. Consequently, an MT system should be able to identify the spurious words of the source language and not translate them, as well as to generate the spurious words of the target language. This paper focuses on the first task and studies how it can be handled in phrase-based SMT.

An immediate reaction to the proposal of investigating source word deletion (henceforth SWD) is: Is SWD itself worth our attention? Isn't it a trivial task that can be handled easily by existing techniques? One of the reasons why we need to pay attention to SWD is its significant improvement to translation performance, which will be shown by the experiments results in section 4.2. Another reason is that SWD is not a trivial task. While some researchers think that the spurious words of a language are merely function words or grammatical particles, which can be handled by some simple heuristics or statistical means, there are in fact some tricky cases of SWD which need sophisticated solution. Consider the following example in Chinese-to-English translation: in English we have the subordinate clause "according to NP", where NP refers to some source of information. The Chinese equivalent of this clause can sometimes be "ACCORDING-TO/根据 NP EXPRESS/表示"; that is, in Chinese we could have a clause rather than a noun phrase following the preposition ACCORDING-TO/根据. Therefore, when translating Chinese into English, the content word EXPRESS/表示 should be considered spurious and not to be translated. Of course, the verb EXPRESS/表示 is not spurious in other contexts. It is an example that SWD is not only about a few function words, and that the solution to SWD has to take context-sensitive factors into account. Moreover, the solution needed for such tricky cases seems to be beyond the scope of current phrase-based SMT, unless we have a very large amount of training data which covers all possible variations of the Chinese pattern "ACCORDING-TO/根据 NP EXPRESS/表示".

Despite the obvious need for handling spurious source words, it is surprising that phrase-based SMT, which is a major approach to SMT, does not well address the problem. There are two possible ways for a phrase-based system to deal with SWD. The first one is to allow a source

Proceedings of the Third Workshop on Statistical Machine Translation, pages 1–8,
Columbus, Ohio, USA, June 2008.

language phrase to translate to nothing. However, no existing literature has mentioned such a possibility and discussed the modifications required by such an extension. The second way is to capture SWD within the phrase pairs in translation table. That is, suppose there is a foreign phrase $\tilde{F} = (f_A f_B f_C)$ and an English phrase $\tilde{E} = (e_A e_C)$, where f_A is aligned to e_A and f_C to e_C, then the phrase pair $(\tilde{F}, \tilde{E})$ tacitly deletes the spurious word f_B. Such a SWD mechanism fails when data sparseness becomes a problem. If the training data does not have any word sequence containing f_B, then the spurious f_B cannot associate with other words to form a phrase pair, and therefore cannot be deleted tacitly in some phrase pair. Rather, the decoder can only give a phrase segmentation that treats f_B itself as a phrase, and this phrase cannot translate into nothing, as far as the SMT training and decoding procedure reported by existing literature are used. In sum, the current mechanism of phrase-based SMT is not capable of handling all cases of SWD.

In this paper, we will present, in section 3, three SWD models and elaborate how to apply each of them to phrase-based SMT. Experiment settings are described in section 4.1, followed by the report and analysis of experiment results, using BLEU as evaluation metric, in section 4.2, which also discusses the impact of training data size and training data domain on SWD models. Before making our conclusions, the effect of SWD on another evaluation metric, viz. METEOR, is examined in section 5.

2 Literature Review

Research work in SMT seldom treats SWD as a problem separated from other factors in translation. However, it can be found in different SMT paradigms the mechanism of handling SWD. As to the pioneering IBM word-based SMT models (Brown et al., 1990), IBM models 3, 4 and 5 handle spurious source words by considering them as corresponding to a particular EMPTY word token on the English side, and by the fertility model which allows the English EMPTY to generate a certain number of foreign words.

As to the hierarchical phrase-based approach (Chiang, 2007), its hierarchical rules are more powerful in SWD than the phrase pairs in conventional phrase-based approach. For instance, the "ACCORDING-TO/根据 NP EXPRESS/表示" example in the last section can be handled easily by the hierarchical rule

$$X \rightarrow <\text{根据 X 表示, according to X}> .$$

In general, if the deletion of a source word depends on some context cues, then the hierarchical approach is, at least in principle, capable of handling it correctly. However, it is still confronted by the same problem as the conventional phrase-based approach regarding those words whose 'spuriousness' does not depend on any context.

3 Source Word Deletion Models

This section presents a number of solutions to the problem of SWD. These solutions share the same property that a specific empty symbol ϵ on the target language side is posited and any source word is allowed to translate into ϵ. This symbol is invisible in every module of the decoder except the translation model. That is, ϵ is not counted when calculating language model score, word penalty and any other feature values, and it is omitted in the final output of the decoder. It is only used to delete spurious source words and refine translation model scores accordingly.

It must be noted that in our approach phrases comprising more than one source word are not allowed to translate into ϵ. This constraint is based on our subjective evaluation of alignment matrix, which indicates that the un-alignment of a continuous sequence of two or more source words is far less accurate than the un-alignment of a single source word lying within aligned neighbors. Consequently, in order to treat a source word as spurious, the decoder must give a phrase segmentation that treats the word itself as a phrase.

Another important modification to the phrase-based architecture is a new feature added to the log-linear model. The new feature, ϵ-penalty, represents how many source words translate into ϵ. The purpose of this feature is the same as that of the feature of word penalty. As many features used in the log-linear model have values of logarithm of probability, candidate translations with more words have, in general, lower scores, and

Model 1	$P(\epsilon)$
Model 2	$P(\epsilon\|f)$
Model 3	$P_{CRF}(\epsilon\|\vec{F}(f))$

Table 1: Summary of the Three SWD Models

therefore the decoder has a bias towards shorter translations. Word penalty (in fact, it should be renamed as word *reward*) is used to neutralize this bias. Similarly, the more source words translate into ϵ, the shorter the translation will be, and therefore the higher score the translation will have. The ϵ-penalty is proposed to neutralize the bias towards shorter translations.

The core of the solutions is the SWD model, which calculates $P(\epsilon|f)$, the probability distribution of translating some source word f to ϵ. Three SWD models will be elaborated in the following subsections. They differ from each other by the conditions of the probability distribution, as summarized in Table 1. Model 1 is a uniform probability distribution that does not take the source word f into account. Model 2 is a simple probability distribution conditioned on the lexical form of f only. Model 3 is a more complicated distribution conditioned on a feature vector of f, and the distribution is estimated by the method of Conditional Random Field.

3.1 Model 1: Uniform Probability

The first model assumes a uniform probability of translation to ϵ. This model is inspired by the HMM-based alignment model (Och and Ney, 2000a), which posits a probability P_0 for alignment of some source word to the empty word on the target language side, and weighs all other alignment probabilities by the factor $1 - P_0$. In the same style, SWD model 1 posits a probability $P(\epsilon)$ for the translation of any source word to ϵ. The probabilities of normal phrase pairs should be weighed accordingly. For a source phrase containing only one word, its weight is simply $P(\bar{\epsilon}) = 1 - P(\epsilon)$. As to a source phrase containing more than one word, it implies that every word in the phrase does not translate into ϵ, and therefore the weighing factor $P(\bar{\epsilon})$ should be multiplied as many times as the number of words in the source phrase. In sum, for any phrase pair $< \tilde{F}, \tilde{E} >$, its probability is

$$P(\tilde{E}|\tilde{F}) = \begin{cases} P(\epsilon) & if \tilde{E} = (\epsilon) \\ P(\bar{\epsilon})^{|\tilde{F}|} P_T(\tilde{E}|\tilde{F}) & otherwise \end{cases}$$

where $P_T(\tilde{E}|\tilde{F})$ is the probability of the phrase pair as registered in the translation table, and $|\tilde{F}|$ is the length of the phrase $\tilde{F}$. The estimation of $P(\epsilon)$ is done by MLE:

$$P(\epsilon) = \frac{\text{number of unaligned source word tokens}}{\text{number of source word tokens}}.$$

3.2 Model 2: EMPTY as Normal Word

Model 1 assumes that every word is as likely to be spurious as any other word. Definitely this is not a reasonable assumption, since certain function words and grammatical particles are more likely to be spurious than other words. Therefore, in our second SWD model the probability of translating a source word f to ϵ is conditioned on f itself.

This probability, $P(\epsilon|f)$, is in the same form as the probability of a normal phrase pair, $P(\tilde{E}|\tilde{F})$, if we consider ϵ as some special phrase of the target language and f as a source language phrase on its own. Thus $P(\epsilon|f)$ can be estimated and recorded in the same way as the probability of normal phrase pairs. During the phase of phrase enumeration, in addition to enumerating all normal phrase pairs, we also enumerate all unaligned source words f and add phrase pairs of the form $< (f), (\epsilon) >$. These special phrase pairs, TO-EMPTY phrase pairs, are fed to the module of phrase scoring along with the normal phrase pairs. Both types of phrase pairs are then stored in the translation table with corresponding phrase translation probabilities. It can be seen that, since the probabilities of normal phrase pairs are estimated in the same procedure as those of TO-EMPTY phrase pairs, they do not need re-weighing as in the case of SWD model 1.

3.3 Model 3: Context-sensitive Model

Although model 2 is much more informative than model 1, it is still unsatisfactory if we consider the problem of SWD as a problem of *tagging*. The decoder can be conceived as if it carries out a tagging task over the source language sentence: each source word is tagged either as "spurious" or "non-spurious". Under such a perspective, SWD model 2 is merely a unigram tagging model, and it uses only one feature template, viz. the lexical form of the source word in hand. Such a model can by no means encode any contextual information, and therefore it cannot handle the "ACCORDING-TO/根据 NP EXPRESS/表示" example in section 1.

An obvious solution to this limitation is a more powerful tagging model augmented with context-sensitive feature templates. Inspired by research work like (Lafferty et al., 2001) and (Sha and Pereira, 2003), our SWD model 3 uses first-order Conditional Random Field (CRF) to tackle the tagging task.[1] The CRF model uses the following feature templates:

1. the lexical form and the POS of the foreign word f itself;

2. the lexical forms and the POSs of f_{-2}, f_{-1}, f_{+1}, and f_{+2}, where f_{-2} and f_{-1} are the two words to the left of f, and f_{+1} and f_{+2} are the two words to the right of f;

3. the lexical form and the POS of the *head* word of f;

4. the lexical forms and the POSs of the *dependent* words of f.

The lexical forms are the major source of information whereas the POSs are employed to alleviate data sparseness. The neighboring words are used to capture local context information. For example, in Chinese there is often a comma after verbs like "*said*" or "*stated*", and such a comma is not translated to any word or punctuation in English. These spurious commas are therefore identified by their immediate left neighbors. The head and dependent words are employed to capture non-local context information found by some dependency parser. For the "ACCORDING-TO/根据 NP EXPRESS/表示" example in section 1, the Chinese word ACCORDING-TO/根据 is the head word of EXPRESS/表示. The spurious token of EXPRESS/表示 in this pattern can be distinguished from the non-spurious tokens through the feature template of head word.

[1]Maximum Entropy was also tried in our experiments but its performance is not as good as CRF.

The training data for the CRF model comprises the alignment matrices of the bilingual training data for the MT system. A source word (token) in the training data is tagged as "non-spurious" if it is aligned to some target word(s), otherwise it is tagged as "spurious". The sentences in the training data are also POS-tagged and parsed by some dependency parser, so that each word can be assigned values for the POS-based feature templates as well as the feature templates of head word and dependency words.

The trained CRF model can then be used to augment the decoder to tackle the SWD problem. An input source sentence should first be POS-tagged and parsed for assigning feature values. The probability for f being spurious, $P(\epsilon|f)$, is then calculated by the trained CRF model as

$$P_{CRF}(\text{spurious}|\vec{F}(f)).$$

The probability for f being non-spurious is simply $1 - P(\epsilon|f)$. For a normal phrase pair $< \tilde{F}, \tilde{E} >$ recorded in the translation table, its phrase translation probability and the lexical weight should be re-weighed by the probabilities of non-spuriousness. The weighing factor is

$$\prod_{f_i \epsilon \tilde{F}} (1 - P(\epsilon|f_i)),$$

since the translation of $\tilde{F}$ into $\tilde{E}$ means the decoder considers every word in $\tilde{F}$ as non-spurious.

4 Experiments

4.1 Experiment Settings

A series of experiments were run to compare the performance of the three SWD models against the baseline, which is the standard phrase-based approach to SMT as elaborated in (Koehn et al., 2003). The experiments are about Chinese-to-English translation. The bilingual training data is the one for NIST MT-2006. The GIGAWORD corpus is used for training language model. The development/test corpora are based on the test sets for NIST MT-2005/6.

The alignment matrices of the training data are produced by the GIZA++ (Och and Ney, 2000b) word alignment package with its default settings. The subsequent construction of translation table was done in exactly the same way as explained in (Koehn et al., 2003). For SWD model 2, the phrase enumeration step is modified as described in section 3.2. We used the Stanford parser (Klein and Manning, 2003) with its default Chinese grammar for its POS-tagging as well as finding the head/dependent words of all source words. The CRF toolkit used for model 3 is CRF++[2]. The training data for the CRF model should be the same as that for translation table construction. However, since there are too many instances (every single word in the training data is an instance) with a huge feature space, no publicly available CRF toolkit can handle the entire training set of NIST MT-2006.[3] Therefore, we can use at most only about one-third of the NIST training set (comprising the FBIS, B1, and T10 sections) for CRF training.

The decoder in the experiments is our re-implementation of HIERO (Chiang, 2007), augmented with a 5-gram language model and a reordering model based on (Zhang et al., 2007). Note that no hierarchical rule is used with the decoder; the phrase pairs used are still those used in conventional phrase-based SMT. Note also that the decoder does not translate OOV at all even in the baseline case, and thus the SWD models do not improve performance simply by removing OOVs.

In order to test the effect of training data size on the performance of the SWD models, three variations of training data were used:

FBIS Only the FBIS section of the NIST training set is used as training data (for both translation table and the CRF model in model 3). This section constitutes about 10% of the entire NIST training set. The purpose of this variation is to test the performance of each model when very small amount of data are available.

BFT Only the B1, FBIS, and T10 sections of the NIST training set are used as training data. These sections are about one-third of the entire NIST training set. The purpose of this variation is to test each model when medium size of data are available.[4]

NIST All the sections of the NIST training set are used. The purpose of this variation is to test each model when a large amount of data are available.

Data	baseline	model 1	model 2	model 3
FBIS	28.01	29.71	29.48	29.64
BFT	29.82	31.55	31.61	31.75
NIST	29.77	31.39	31.33	31.71

Table 2: BLEU scores in Experiment 1: NIST'05 as dev and NIST'06 as test

(Case-insensitive) BLEU-4 (Papineni et al., 2002) is used as the evaluation metric. In each test in our experiments, maximum BLEU training were run 10 times, and thus there are 10 BLEU scores for the test set. In the following we will report the mean scores only.

4.2 Experiment Results and Analysis

Table 2 shows the results of the first experiment, which uses the NIST MT-2005 test set as development data and the NIST MT-2006 test set as test data. The most obvious observation is that any SWD model achieves much higher BLEU score than the baseline, as there is at least 1.6 BLEU point improvement in each case, and in some case the improvement of using SWD is nearly 2 BLEU points. This clearly proves the importance of SWD in phrase-based SMT.

The difference between the performance of the various SWD models is much smaller. Yet there are still some noticeable facts. The first one is that model 1 gives the best result in the case of using only FBIS as training data but it fails to do so when more training data is available. This phenomenon is not strange since model 2 and model 3 are conditioned on more information and therefore they need more training data.

The second observation is about the strength of SWD model 3, which achieves the best BLEU score in both the BFT and NIST cases. While its improvement over models 1 and 2 is marginal in the case of BFT, its performance in the NIST

[2] http://crfpp.sourceforge.net/

[3] Apart from CRF++, we also tried FLEX-CRF (http://flexcrfs.sourceforge.net) and MALLET (http://mallet.cs.umass.edu).

[4] Note also that the BFT data set is the largest training data that the CRF model in model 3 can handle.

case is remarkable. A suspicion to the strength of model 3 is that in the NIST case both models 1 and 2 use the entire NIST training set for estimating $P(\epsilon)$, while model 3 uses only the BFT sections to train its CRF model. It may be that the BFT sections are more consistent with the test data set than the other NIST sections, and therefore a SWD model trained on BFT sections only is better than that trained on the entire NIST. This conjecture is supported by the fact that in all four settings the BLEU scores in the NIST case are lower than those in the BFT case, which suggests that other NIST sections are noisy. While it is impossible to test model 3 with the entire NIST, it is possible to restrict the data for the estimation of $P(\epsilon|f)$ in model 1 to the BFT sections only and check if such a restriction helps.[5] We estimated the uniform probability $P(\epsilon)$ from only the BFT sections and used it with the translation table constructed from the complete NIST training set. The BLEU score thus obtained is 31.24, which is even lower than the score (31.39) of the original case of using the entire NIST for both translation table and $P(\epsilon|f)$ estimation. In sum, the strength of model 3 is not simply due to the choice of training data.

The test set used in Experiment 1 distinguishes itself from the development data and the training data by its characteristics of combining text from different *genres*. There are three sources of the NIST MT-2006 test set, viz. "newswire", "newsgroup", and "broadcast news", while our development data and the NIST training set comprises only newswire text and text of similar style. It is an interesting question whether SWD only works for some genres (say, newswire) but not for other genres. In fact, it is dubious whether SWD fits the test set to the same extent as it fits the development set. That is, perhaps SWD contributes to the improvement in Experiment 1 simply by improving the translation of the development set which is composed of newswire text only, and SWD may not benefit the translation of the test data at all. In order to test this conjecture, we ran Experiment 2, in which the SWD models were still applied to the development data during training, but all SWD models stopped working when translating the test data with the trained parameters. The results are shown in Table 3. These results are very discouraging if we compare each cell in Table 3 against the corresponding cell in Table 2: in all cases SWD seems harmful to the translation of the test data. It is tempting to accept the conclusion that SWD works for newswire text only.

Data	model 1	model 2	model 3
FBIS	29.85	29.91	29.95
BFT	31.73	31.84	32.08
NIST	31.70	31.82	32.05

Table 3: BLEU scores in Experiment 2, which is the same as Experiment 1 but no word is deleted for test corpus. Note: the baseline scores are the same as the baselines in Experiment 1 (Table 2).

To scrutinize the problem, we split up the test data set into two parts, viz. the newswire section and the non-newswire section, and ran experiments separately. Table 4 shows the results of Experiment 3, in which the development data is still the NIST MT-2005 test set and the test data is the newswire section of NIST MT-2006 test set. It is confirmed that if test data shares the same genre as the training/development data, then SWD does improve translation performance a lot. It is also observed that more sophisticated SWD models perform better when provided with sufficient training data, and that model 3 exhibits remarkable improvement when it comes to the NIST case.

Of course, the figures in Table 5, which shows the results of Experiment 4 where the non-newswire section of NIST MT-2006 test set is used as test data, still leave us the doubt that SWD is useful for a particular genre only. After all, it is reasonable to assume that a model trained from data of a particular domain can give good performance only to data of the same domain. On the other hand, the language model is another cause of the poor performance, as the GIGAWORD corpus is also of the newswire style.

While we cannot prove the value of SWD with respect to training data of other genres in the mean time, we could test the effect of using development data of other genres. In our last experiment, the first halves of both the newswire

[5]Unfortunately this way does not work for model 2 as the estimation of $P(\epsilon|f)$ and the construction of translation table are tied together.

	apply SWD for test set			no SWD for test set		
Data	model 1	model 2	model 3	model 1	model 2	model 3
FBIS	30.81	30.81	30.68	29.23	29.61	29.46
BFT	33.57	33.74	33.71	31.88	31.87	32.25
NIST	33.65	34.01	34.42	32.14	32.59	32.87

Table 4: BLEU scores in Experiment 3, which is the same as Experiments 1 and 2 but only the **newswire** section of NIST'06 test set is used. Note: the baseline scores are the same as the baselines in Experiment 1 (Table 2).

	apply SWD for test set			no SWD for test set		
Data	model 1	model 2	model 3	model 1	model 2	model 3
FBIS	29.19	28.86	29.16	30.07	29.67	30.08
BFT	30.62	30.64	30.86	31.66	31.83	32.00
NIST	30.34	30.10	30.46	31.50	31.45	31.66

Table 5: BLEU scores in Experiment 4, which is the same as Experiments 1 and 2 but only the **non-newswire** section of NIST'06 test set is used. Note: the baseline scores are the same as the baselines in Experiment 1 (Table 2).

Data	baseline	model 1	model 2	model 3
FBIS	26.87	27.79	27.51	27.61
BFT	29.11	30.38	30.49	30.41
NIST	29.34	30.63	30.95	31.00

Table 6: BLEU scores in Experiment 5: which is the same as Experiment 1 but uses half of NIST'06 as development set and another half of NIST'06 as test set.

and non-newswire sections of NIST MT-2006 test set are combined to form the new development data, and the second halves of the two sections are combined to form the new test data. The new development data is therefore consistent with the new test data. If SWD, or at least a SWD model from newswire, is harmful to the non-newswire section, which constitutes about 60% of the development/test data, then it will be either that the parameter training process minimizes the impact of SWD, or that the SWD model will make the parameter training process fail to search for good parameter values. The consequence of either case is that the baseline setting should produce similar or even higher BLEU score than the settings that employ some SWD model. Experiment results, as shown in Table 6, illustrate that SWD is still very useful even when both development and test sets contain texts of different genres from the training text. It is also observed, however, that the three SWD models give rise to roughly the same BLEU scores, indicating that the SWD training data do not fit the test/development data very well as even the more sophisticated models are not benefited from more data.

5 Experiments using METEOR

The results in the last section are all evaluated using the BLEU metric only. It is dubious whether SWD is useful regarding recall-oriented metrics like METEOR (Banerjee and Lavie, 2005), since SWD removes information in source sentences. This suspicion is to certain extent confirmed by our application of METEOR to the translation outputs of Experiment 1 (c.f. Table 7), which shows that all SWD models achieve lower METEOR scores than the baseline. However, SWD is not entirely harmful to METEOR: if SWD is applied to parameter tuning only but not for the test set, (i.e. Experiment 2), even higher METEOR scores can be obtained. This puzzling observation may be because the parameters of the decoder are optimized with respect to BLEU score, and SWD benefits parameter tuning by improving BLEU score. In future experiments, maximum METEOR training should be used instead of maximum BLEU training so as to examine if SWD is really useful for parameter tuning.

	Experiment 1 SWD for both dev/test				Experiment 2 SWD for dev only		
Data	baseline	model 1	model 2	model 3	model 1	model 2	model 3
FBIS	50.07	47.90	49.83	49.34	51.58	51.08	51.17
BFT	52.47	50.55	51.89	52.10	54.72	54.43	54.30
NIST	52.12	49.86	50.97	51.59	54.14	53.82	54.01

Table 7: METEOR scores in Experiments 1 and 2

6 Conclusion and Future Work

In this paper, we have explained why the handling of spurious source words is not a trivial problem and how important it is. Three solutions, with increasing sophistication, to the problem of SWD are presented. Experiment results show that, in our setting of using NIST MT-2006 test set, any SWD model leads to an improvement of at least 1.6 BLEU points, and SWD model 3, which makes use of contextual information, can improve up to nearly 2 BLEU points. If only the newswire section of the test set is considered, SWD model 3 is even more superior to the other two SWD models.

The effect of training data size on SWD has also been examined, and it is found that more sophisticated SWD models do not outperform unless they are provided with sufficient amount of data. As to the effect of training data domain/genre on SWD, it is clear that SWD models trained on text of certain genre perform the best when applied to text of the same genre. While it is infeasible for the time being to test if SWD works well for non-newswire style of training data, we managed to illustrate that SWD based on newswire text still to certain extent benefits the training and translation of non-newswire text.

In future, two extensions of our system are needed for further examination of SWD. The first one is already mentioned in the last section: maximum METEOR training should be implemented in order to fully test the effect of SWD regarding METEOR. The second extension is about the weighing factor in models 1 and 3. The current implementation assumes that all source words in a normal phrase pair need to be weighed by $1 - P(\epsilon)$. However, in fact some source words in a source phrase are tacitly deleted (as explained in the Introduction). Thus the word alignment information within phrase pairs need to be recorded and the weighing of a normal phrase pair should be done in accordance with such alignment information.

References

Brown, P., J. Cocke, S. Della Pietra, V. Della Pietra, F. Jelinek, J. Lafferty, R. Mercer, and P. Roossin. 1990. A Statistical Approach to Machine Translation *Computational Linguistics, 16(2).*

Satanjeev Banerjee and Alon Lavie. 2005. METEOR: An Automatic Metric for MT Evaluation with Improved Correlation with Human Judgments. *Proceedings of Workshop on Evaluation Measures for MT and/or Summarization at ACL 2005.*

David Chiang. 2007. Hierarchical Phrase-based Translation. *Computational Linguistics, 33(2).*

Dan Klein and Christopher D. Manning. 2003. Accurate Unlexicalized Parsing. *Proceedings for ACL 2003.*

Philipp Koehn, Franz J. Och, and Daniel Marcu. 2003. Statistical Phrase-based Translation. *Proceedings for HLT-NAACL 2003.*

John Lafferty, Andrew McCallum, and Fernando Pereira 2001. Conditional Random Fields: Probabilistic Models for Segmenting and Labeling Sequence Data. *Proceedings for 18th International Conf. on Machine Learning.*

Franz J. Och, and Hermann Ney. 2000. A comparison of alignment models for statistical machine translation. *Proceedings of COLING 2000.*

Franz J. Och, and Hermann Ney. 2000. Improved Statistical Alignment Models. *Proceedings for ACL 2000.*

Kishore Papineni, Salim Roukos, Todd Ward, and Wei-Jing Zhu. 2002. BLEU: a Method for Automatic Evaluation of Machine Translation. *Proceedings for ACL 2002.*

Fei Sha, Fernando Pereira. 2003. Shallow parsing with conditional random fields. *Proceedings of NAACL 2003.*

Dongdong Zhang, Mu Li, Chi-Ho Li and Ming Zhou. 2007. Phrase Reordering Model Integrating Syntactic Knowledge for SMT. *Proceedings for EMNLP 2007.*

Rich Source-Side Context for Statistical Machine Translation

Kevin Gimpel and **Noah A. Smith**
Language Technologies Institute
School of Computer Science
Carnegie Mellon University
Pittsburgh, PA 15213, USA
{kgimpel,nasmith}@cs.cmu.edu

Abstract

We explore the augmentation of statistical machine translation models with features of the *context* of each phrase to be translated. This work extends several existing threads of research in statistical MT, including the use of context in example-based machine translation (Carl and Way, 2003) and the incorporation of word sense disambiguation into a translation model (Chan et al., 2007). The context features we consider use surrounding words and part-of-speech tags, local syntactic structure, and other properties of the source language sentence to help predict each phrase's translation. Our approach requires very little computation beyond the standard phrase extraction algorithm and scales well to large data scenarios. We report significant improvements in automatic evaluation scores for Chinese-to-English and English-to-German translation, and also describe our entry in the WMT-08 shared task based on this approach.

1 Introduction

Machine translation (MT) by statistical modeling of bilingual phrases is one of the most successful approaches in the past few years. Phrase-based MT systems are straightforward to train from parallel corpora (Koehn et al., 2003) and, like the original IBM models (Brown et al., 1990), benefit from standard language models built on large monolingual, target-language corpora (Brants et al., 2007). Many of these systems perform well in competitive evaluations and scale well to large-data situations (NIST, 2006; Callison-Burch et al., 2007). End-to-end phrase-based MT systems can be built entirely from freely-available tools (Koehn et al., 2007).

We follow the approach of Koehn et al. (2003), in which we translate a source-language sentence $\boldsymbol{f}$ into the target-language sentence $\hat{\mathbf{e}}$ that maximizes a linear combination of features and weights:[1]

$$\langle \hat{\boldsymbol{e}}, \hat{\boldsymbol{a}} \rangle = \underset{\langle \boldsymbol{e}, \boldsymbol{a} \rangle}{\operatorname{argmax}} \operatorname{score}(\boldsymbol{e}, \boldsymbol{a}, \boldsymbol{f}) \quad (1)$$

$$= \underset{\langle \boldsymbol{e}, \boldsymbol{a} \rangle}{\operatorname{argmax}} \sum_{m=1}^{M} \lambda_m h_m(\boldsymbol{e}, \boldsymbol{a}, \boldsymbol{f}) \quad (2)$$

where $\boldsymbol{a}$ represents the segmentation of $\boldsymbol{e}$ and $\boldsymbol{f}$ into phrases and a correspondence between phrases, and each h_m is a $\mathbb{R}$-valued feature with learned weight λ_m. The translation is typically found using beam search (Koehn et al., 2003). The weights $\langle \lambda_1, ..., \lambda_M \rangle$ are typically learned to directly minimize a standard evaluation criterion on development data (e.g., the BLEU score; Papineni et al., (2002)) using numerical search (Och, 2003).

Many features are used in phrase-based MT, but nearly ubiquitous are estimates of the conditional translation probabilities $p(\boldsymbol{e}_i^j \mid \boldsymbol{f}_k^\ell)$ and $p(\boldsymbol{f}_k^\ell \mid \boldsymbol{e}_i^j)$ for each phrase pair $\langle \boldsymbol{e}_i^j, \boldsymbol{f}_k^l \rangle$ in the candidate sentence pair.[2] In this paper, we add and evaluate fea-

[1] In the statistical MT literature, this is often referred to as a "log-linear model," but since the score is normalized during neither parameter training nor decoding, and is never interpreted as a log-probability, it is essentially a linear combination of feature functions. Since many of the features are actually probabilities, this linear combination is closer to a *mixture model*.

[2] We will use $\boldsymbol{x}_i^j$ to denote the subsequence of $\boldsymbol{x}$ containing the ith through jth elements of $\boldsymbol{x}$, inclusive.

Proceedings of the Third Workshop on Statistical Machine Translation, pages 9–17,
Columbus, Ohio, USA, June 2008.

tures that condition on additional context features on the *source* ($\boldsymbol{f}$) side:

$$p(\boldsymbol{e}_i^j \mid \mathit{Phrase} = \boldsymbol{f}_k^\ell, \mathit{Context} = \langle \boldsymbol{f}_1^{k-1}, \boldsymbol{f}_{\ell+1}^F, \ldots \rangle)$$

The advantage of considering context is well-known and exploited in the example-based MT community (Carl and Way, 2003). Recently researchers have begun to use source phrase context information in statistical MT systems (Stroppa et al., 2007). Statistical NLP researchers understand that conditioning a probability model on more information is helpful only if there are sufficient training data to accurately *estimate* the context probabilities.[3] Sparse data are often the death of elaborate models, though this can be remedied through careful smoothing.

In this paper we leverage the existing linear model (Equation 2) to bring source-side context into phrase-based MT in a way that is robust to data sparseness. We interpret the linear model as a mixture of many probability estimates based on different context features, some of which may be very sparse. The mixture coefficients are trained in the usual way ("minimum error-rate training," Och, 2003), so that the additional context is exploited when it is useful and ignored when it isn't.

The paper proceeds as follows. We first review related work that enriches statistical translation models using context (§2). We then propose a set of source-side features to be incorporated into the translation model, including the novel use of syntactic context from source-side parse trees and global position within $\boldsymbol{f}$ (§3). We explain why analogous *target*-side features pose a computational challenge (§4). Specific modifications to the standard training and evaluation paradigm are presented in §5. Experimental results are reported in §6.

2 Related Work

Stroppa et al. (2007) added souce-side context features to a phrase-based translation system, including conditional probabilities of the same form that we use. They consider up to two words and/or POS tags of context on either side. Because of the aforementioned data sparseness problem, they use a decision-tree classifier that implicitly smooths relative frequency estimates. The method improved over a standard phrase-based baseline trained on small amounts of data ($<$ 50K sentence pairs) for Italian $\rightarrow$ English and Chinese $\rightarrow$ English. We explore a significantly larger space of context features, a smoothing method that more naturally fits into the widely used, error-driven linear model, and report a more comprehensive experimental evaluation (including feature comparison and scaling up to very large datasets).

Recent research on the use of word-sense disambiguation in machine translation also points toward our approach. For example, Vickrey et al. (2005) built classifiers inspired by those used in word sense disambiguation to fill in blanks in a partially-completed translation. Giménez and Màrquez (2007) extended the work by considering phrases and moved to full translation instead of filling in target-side blanks. They trained an SVM for each source language phrase using local features of the sentences in which the phrases appear. Carpuat and Wu (2007) and Chan et al. (2007) embedded state-of-the-art word sense disambiguation modules into statistical MT systems, achieving performance improvements under several automatic measures for Chinese $\rightarrow$ English translation.

Our approach is also reminiscent of example-based machine translation (Nagao, 1984; Somers, 1999; Carl and Way, 2003), which has for many years emphasized use of the context in which source phrases appear when translating them. Indeed, like the example-based community, we do not begin with any set of assumptions about *which kinds* of phrases require additional disambiguation (cf. the application of word-sense disambiguation, which is motivated by lexical ambiguity). Our feature-rich approach is omnivorous and can exploit *any* linguistic analysis of an input sentence.

3 Source-Side Context Features

Adding features to the linear model (Equation 2) that consider more of the source sentence requires changing the decoder very little, if at all. The reason is that the source sentence is fully observed, so the information to be predicted is the same as before—the difference is that we are using more clues to carry out the prediction.

[3] An illustrative example is the debate over the use of bilexicalized grammar rules in statistical parsing (Gildea, 2001; Bikel, 2004).

We see this as an opportunity to include many more features in phrase-based MT without increasing the cost of decoding at runtime. This discussion is reminiscent of an advantage gained by moving from hidden Markov models to conditional random fields for sequence labeling tasks. While the same core algorithm is used for decoding with both models, a CRF allows inclusion of features that consider the *entire* observed sequence—i.e., more of the observable context of each label to be predicted. Although this same advantage was already obtained in statistical MT through the transition from "noisy channel" translation models to (log-)linear models, the customary set of features used in most phrase-based systems does not take full advantage of the observed data.

The standard approach to estimating the phrase translation conditional probability features is via relative frequencies (here $\boldsymbol{e}$ and $\boldsymbol{f}$ are phrases):

$$p(\boldsymbol{e} \mid \boldsymbol{f}) = \frac{count(\boldsymbol{e}, \boldsymbol{f})}{\sum_{\boldsymbol{e}'} count(\boldsymbol{e}', \boldsymbol{f})}$$

Our new features all take the form $p(\boldsymbol{e} \mid \boldsymbol{f}, \boldsymbol{f}_{context})$, where $\boldsymbol{e}$ is the target language phrase, $\boldsymbol{f}$ is the source language phrase, and $\boldsymbol{f}_{context}$ is the context of the source language phrase in the sentence in which it was observed. Like the context-bare conditional probabilities, we estimate probability features using relative frequencies:

$$p(\boldsymbol{e} \mid \boldsymbol{f}, \boldsymbol{f}_{context}) = \frac{count(\boldsymbol{e}, \boldsymbol{f}, \boldsymbol{f}_{context})}{\sum_{\boldsymbol{e}'} count(\boldsymbol{e}', \boldsymbol{f}, \boldsymbol{f}_{context})}$$

Since we expect that adding conditioning variables will lead to sparser counts and therefore more zero estimates, we compute features for many different types of context. To combine the many differently-conditioned features into a single model, we provide them as features to the linear model (Equation 2) and use minimum error-rate training (Och, 2003) to obtain interpolation weights λ_m. This is similar to an interpolation of backed-off estimates, if we imagine that all of the different contexts are differently-backed off estimates of the *complete* context. The error-driven weight training effectively smooths one implicit context-rich estimate $p(\boldsymbol{e} \mid \boldsymbol{f}, \boldsymbol{f}_{context})$ so that all of the backed-off estimates are taken into account, including the original $p(\boldsymbol{e} \mid \boldsymbol{f})$. Our approach is asymmetrical; we have not, for example, estimated features of the form $p(\boldsymbol{f}, \boldsymbol{f}_{context} \mid \boldsymbol{e})$.

We next discuss the specific source-side context features used in our model.

3.1 Lexical Context Features

The most obvious kind of context of a source phrase $\boldsymbol{f}_k^\ell$ is the m-length sequence before it ($\boldsymbol{f}_{k-m}^{k-1}$) and the m-length sequence after it ($\boldsymbol{f}_{\ell+1}^{\ell+m}$). We include context features for $m \in \{1, 2\}$, padding sentences with m special symbols at the beginning and at the end. For each value of m, we include three features:

- $p(\boldsymbol{e} \mid \boldsymbol{f}, \boldsymbol{f}_{k-m}^{k-1})$, the left lexical context;
- $p(\boldsymbol{e} \mid \boldsymbol{f}, \boldsymbol{f}_{\ell+1}^{\ell+m})$, the right lexical context;
- $p(\boldsymbol{e} \mid \boldsymbol{f}, \boldsymbol{f}_{k-m}^{k-1}, \boldsymbol{f}_{\ell+1}^{\ell+m})$, both sides.

3.2 Shallow Syntactic Features

Lexical context features, especially when $m > 1$, are expected to be sparse. Representing the context by part-of-speech (POS) tags is one way to overcome that sparseness. We used the same set of the lexical context features described above, but with POS tags replacing words in the context. We also include a feature which conditions on the POS tag sequence of the actual phrase being translated.

3.3 Syntactic Features

If a robust parser is available for the source language, we can include context features from parse trees. We used the following parse tree features:

- Is the phrase (exactly) a constituent?
- What is the nonterminal label of the lowest node in the parse tree that covers the phrase?
- What is the nonterminal label or POS of the highest nonterminal node that ends immediately before the phrase? Begins immediately after the phrase?
- Is the phrase strictly to the left of the root word, does it contain the root word, or is it strictly to the right of the root word? (Requires a parse with head annotations.)

We also used a feature that conditions on both features in the third bullet point above.

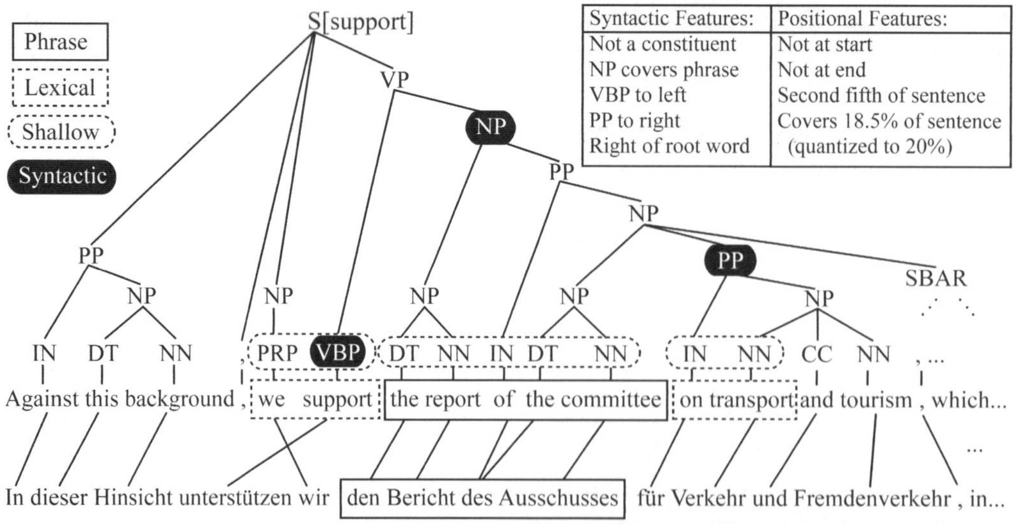

Figure 1: A (partial) sentence pair from the WMT-07 Europarl training corpus. Processing of the data (parsing, word alignment) was done as discussed in §6. The phrase pair of interest is boxed and context features are shown in dotted shapes. The context features help determine whether the phrase should be translated as "der Bericht des Ausschusses" (nominative case) or "den Bericht des Ausschusses" (accusative case). See text for details.

3.4 Positional Features

We include features based on the position of the phrase in the source sentence, the phrase length, and the sentence length. These features use information from the entire source sentence, but are not syntactic. For a phrase $\boldsymbol{f}_k^\ell$ in a sentence $\boldsymbol{f}$ of length n:

- Is the phrase at the start of the sentence ($k = 1$)?
- Is the phrase at the end of the sentence ($\ell = n$)?
- A quantization of $r = \frac{k+\frac{\ell-k+1}{2}}{n}$, the relative position in $(0, 1)$ of the phrase's midpoint within $\boldsymbol{f}$. We choose the smallest $q \in \{0.2, 0.4, 0.6, 0.8, 1\}$ such that $q > r$.
- A quantization of $c = \frac{\ell-k+1}{n}$, the fraction of the words in $\boldsymbol{f}$ that are covered by the phrase. We choose the smallest $q \in \{\frac{1}{40}, \frac{1}{20}, \frac{1}{10}, \frac{1}{5}, \frac{1}{3}, 1\}$ such that $q > c$.

An illustration of the context features is shown in Fig. 1. Consider the phrase pair "the report of the committee"/"den Bericht des Ausschusses" extracted by our English → German baseline MT system (described in §6.3). The German word "Bericht" is a masculine noun; therefore, it takes the article "der" in the nominative case, "den" in the accusative case, and "dem" in the dative case. These three translations are indeed available in the phrase table for "the report of the committee" (see Table 1, "no context" column), with relatively high entropy. The choice between "den" and "der" must be made by the language model alone.

Knowing that the phrase follows a verb, or appears to the right of the sentence's root word, or within the second fifth of the sentence should help. Indeed, a probability distribution that conditions on context features gives more peaked distributions that give higher probability to the correct translation, given *this* context, and lower probability given some *other* contexts (see Table 1).

4 Why Not Target-Side Context?

While source context is straightforward to exploit in a model, including target-side context features breaks one of the key independence assumptions made by phrase-based translation models: the translations of the source-side phrases are conditionally *independent* of each other, given $\boldsymbol{f}$, thereby requiring new algorithms for decoding (Marino et al., 2006).

We suggest that target-side context may already be well accounted for in current MT systems. Indeed, *language models* pay attention to the local context of phrases, as do reordering models. The recent emphasis on improving these components of a translation system (Brants et al., 2007) is likely due in part to the widespread availability of NLP tools for the language that is most frequently the target: English. We will demonstrate that NLP tools (tag-

g	no context	Shallow: 2 POS on left		Syntax: _ of root		Positional: rel. pos.	
		*"PRP VBP"	"VBN IN"	*right	left	*2nd fifth	1st fifth
den bericht des ausschusses	0.3125	**1.0000**	0.3333	**0.5000**	0.0000	**0.6000**	0.0000
der bericht des ausschusses	0.3125	0.0000	0.0000	0.1000	**0.6667**	0.2000	**0.6667**
dem bericht des ausschusses	0.2500	0.0000	**0.6667**	0.3000	0.1667	0.0000	0.1667

Table 1: Phrase table entries for "the report of the committee" and their scores under different contexts. These are the top three phrases in the baseline English → German system ("no context" column). Contexts from the source sentence in Fig. 1 (starred) predict correctly; we show also alternative contexts that give very different distributions.

gers and parsers) for the *source* side can be used to improve the translation model, exploiting analysis tools for other languages.

5 Implementation

The additional data required to compute the context features is extracted along with the phrase pairs during execution of the standard phrase extraction algorithm, affecting phrase extraction and scoring time by a constant factor. We avoid the need to modify the standard phrase-based decoder to handle context features by appending a unique identifier to each token in the sentences to be translated. Then, we precompute a phrase table for the phrases in these sentences according to the phrase contexts. To avoid extremely long lists of translations of common tokens, we filter the generated phrase tables, removing entries for which the estimate of $p(e \mid \boldsymbol{f}) < c$, for some small c. In our experiments, we fixed $c = 0.0002$. This filtering reduced time for experimentation dramatically and had no apparent effect on the translation output. We did not perform any filtering for the baseline system.

6 Experiments

In this section we present experimental results using our context-endowed phrase translation model with a variety of different context features, on Chinese → English, German → English, and English → German translation tasks. Dataset details are given in Appendices A (Chinese) and B (German).

Context features	Chinese → English (UN) BLEU	NIST	METEOR
None	0.3715	7.918	0.6486
Lexical	**0.4030**	**8.367**	**0.6716**
Shallow	**0.3807**	**7.981**	**0.6523**
Lexical + Shallow	**0.4030**	**8.403**	**0.6703**
Syntactic	**0.3823**	**7.992**	**0.6531**
Positional	**0.3775**	7.958	**0.6510**

Table 2: Chinese → English experiments: training and testing on UN data. Boldface marks scores significantly higher than "None."

Baseline We use the Moses MT system (Koehn et al., 2007) as a baseline and closely follow the example training procedure given for the WMT-07 and WMT-08 shared tasks.[4] In particular, we perform word alignment in each direction using GIZA++ (Och and Ney, 2003), apply the "grow-diag-final-and" heuristic for symmetrization and use a maximum phrase length of 7. In addition to the two phrase translation conditionals $p(e \mid \boldsymbol{f})$ and $p(\boldsymbol{f} \mid \boldsymbol{e})$, we use lexical translation probabilities in each direction, a word penalty, a phrase penalty, a length-based reordering model, a lexicalized reordering model, and an n-gram language model, SRILM implementation (Stolcke, 2002) with modified Kneser-Ney smoothing (Chen and Goodman, 1998). Minimum error-rate (MER) training (Och, 2003) was applied to obtain weights (λ_m in Equation 2) for these features. A recaser is trained on the target side of the parallel corpus using the script provided with Moses. All output is recased and detokenized prior to evaluation.

Evaluation We evaluate translation output using three automatic evaluation measures: BLEU (Papineni et al., 2002), NIST (Doddington, 2002), and METEOR (Banerjee and Lavie, 2005, version 0.6).[5] All measures used were the case-sensitive, corpus-level versions. The version of BLEU used was that provided by NIST. Significance was tested using a paired bootstrap (Koehn, 2004) with 1000 samples ($p < 0.05$).[6]

[4] http://www.statmt.org/wmt08

[5] METEOR details: For English, we use exact matching, Porter stemming, and WordNet synonym matching. For German, we use exact matching and Porter stemming. These are the same settings that were used to evaluate systems for the WMT-07 shared task.

[6] Code implementing this test for these metrics can be freely downloaded at http://www.ark.cs.cmu.edu/MT.

	Chinese → English					
	Testing on UN			Testing on News (NIST 2005)		
Context features	BLEU	NIST	METEOR	BLEU	NIST	METEOR
Training on in-domain data only:						
None	0.3715	7.918	0.6486	0.2700	7.986	0.5314
Training on all data:						
None	0.3615	7.797	0.6414	0.2593	7.697	0.5200
Lexical	**0.3898**	**8.231**	**0.6697**	0.2522	7.852	0.5273
Shallow: ≤ 1 POS tag	0.3611	7.713	0.6430	0.2669	**8.243**	**0.5526**
Shallow: ≤ 2 POS tags	0.3657	7.808	0.6455	0.2591	7.843	0.5288
Lexical + Shallow	**0.3886**	**8.245**	**0.6675**	0.2628	7.881	0.5290
Syntactic	0.3717	7.899	**0.6531**	0.2653	**8.123**	**0.5403**
Lexical + Syntactic	**0.3926**	**8.224**	**0.6636**	0.2572	7.774	0.5234
Positional	0.3647	7.766	0.6469	0.2648	7.891	0.5275
All	**0.3772**	**8.176**	**0.6582**	0.2566	7.775	0.5225
Feature selection (see Sec. 6.4)	**0.3843**	**8.079**	**0.6594**	0.2730	8.059	0.5343

Table 3: Chinese → English experiments: first row shows baseline performance when training only on in-domain data for each task; all other rows show results when training on *all* data (UN and News). Left half shows results when tuning and testing on UN test sets; right half shows results when tuning on NIST 2004 News test set and testing on NIST 2005. For feature selection, an additional set of unseen data was used: 2000 held-out sentences from the UN data for the left half and the NIST 2003 test set for the right half. Boldface marks scores that are significantly higher than the first row, in-domain baseline.

6.1 Chinese → English

For our Chinese → English experiments, two kinds of data were used: UN proceedings, and newswire as used in NIST evaluations.

UN Data UN data results are reported in Table 2. Significant improvements are obtained on all three evaluation measures—e.g., more than 3 BLEU points—using lexical or lexical and shallow features. While improvements are smaller for other features and feature combinations, performance is not *harmed* by conditioning on context features. Note that using syntactic features gave 1 BLEU point of improvement.

News Data In News data experiments, none of our features obtained BLEU performance statistically distinguishable from the baseline of 0.2700 BLEU (neither better, nor worse). The News training corpus is less than half the size of the UN training corpus (in words); unsurprisingly, the context features were too sparse to be helpful. Further, newswire are less formulaic and repetitive than UN proceedings, so contexts do not generalize as well from training to test data. Fortunately, our "error-minimizing mixture" approach protects the BLEU score, which the λ_m are tuned to optimize.

Combined UN + News Data Our next experiment used *all* of the available training data ($>$ 200M words on each side) to train the models, in-domain λ_m tuning, and testing for each domain separately; see Table 3. Without context features, training on mixed-domain data consistently *harms* performance. With contexts that include lexical features, the mixed-domain model significantly outperforms the *in-domain* baseline for UN data. These results suggest that context features enable better use of out-of-domain data, an important advantage for statistical MT since parallel data often arise from very different sources than those of "real-world" translation scenarios. On News data, context features did not give a significant advantage on the BLEU score, though syntactic and ≤ 1 POS contexts did give significant NIST and METEOR improvements over the in-domain baseline.

6.2 German → English

We do not report full results for this task, because the context features neither helped nor hurt performance significantly. We believe this is due to data sparseness resulting from the size of the training corpus (26M German words), German's relatively rich morphology, and the challenges of German parsing.

Context features	English → German BLEU	NIST	METEOR
None	0.2069	6.020	0.2811
Lexical	0.2018	6.031	0.2772
Shallow	0.2017	5.911	0.2748
Syntactic	0.2077	6.049	0.2829
Positional	0.2045	5.930	0.2772
Lex. + Shal. + Syn.	0.2045	**6.061**	0.2817
All	0.2053	6.009	0.2797
Feature selection	0.2080	6.009	0.2807

Table 4: English → German experiments: training and testing on Europarl data. WMT-07 Europarl parallel training data was used for training, dev06 was used for tuning, devtest06 was used for feature selection and developmental testing, and test07 was used for final testing. Boldface marks scores significantly higher than "None."

6.3 English → German

English → German results are shown in Table 4. The baseline system here is highly competitive, having scored higher on automatic evaluation measures than any other system in the WMT-07 shared task (Callison-Burch et al., 2007). Though most results are not statistically significant, small improvements do tend to come from *syntactic* context features. Comparing with the German → English experiment, we attribute this effect to the high accuracy of the English parser compared to the German parser.

6.4 Feature Selection

Translation performance does not always increase when features are added to the model. This motivates the use of feature selection algorithms to choose a subset of features to optimize performance. We experimented with several feature selection algorithms based on information-theoretic quantities computed among the source phrase, the target phrase, and the context, but found that a simple forward variable selection algorithm (Guyon and Elisseeff, 2003) worked best. In this procedure, we start with no context features and, at each iteration, add the single feature that results in the largest increase in BLEU score on an unseen development set after λ_m tuning. The algorithm terminates if no features are left or if none result in an increase in BLEU. We ran this algorithm to completion for the two Chinese → English tune/test sets (training on *all* data in each case) and the English → German task; see Tables 3 and 4. In all cases, the algorithm finishes after ≤ 4 iterations.

Feature selection for Chinese → English (UN) first chose the lexical feature "1 word on each side," then the positional feature indicating which fifth of the sentence contains the phrase, and finally the lexical feature "1 word on right." For News, the features chosen were the shallow syntactic feature "1 POS on each side," then the positional beginning-of-sentence feature, then the position relative to the root (a syntactic feature). For English → German, the shallow syntactic feature "2 POS on left," then the lexical feature "1 word on right" were selected.

In the case where context features were most helpful (Chinese → English UN data), we found feature selection to be competitive at 2.28 BLEU points above the no-context baseline, but not the best achieved. In the other two cases (Chinese → English News and English → German Europarl), our best results were achieved using these automatically selected features, and in the Chinese → English News case, improvements on all three scores (including 1.37 BLEU points) are significant compared to the no-context baseline trained on the same data.

6.5 WMT-08 Shared Task: English → German

Since we began this research before the release of the data for the WMT-08 shared task, we performed the majority of our experiments using the data released for the WMT-07 shared task (see Appendix B). To prepare our entry for the 2008 shared task, we trained a baseline system on the 2008 data using a nearly identical configuration.[7] Table 5 compares performance of the baseline system (with no context features) to performance with the two context features chosen automatically as described in §6.4. In addition to the devtest06 data, we report results on the 2007 and 2008 Europarl test sets. Most improvements were statistically significant.

7 Future Work

In future work, we plan to apply more sophisticated learning algorithms to rich-feature phrase table estimation. Context features can also be used as conditioning variables in other components of translation

[7]The only differences were the use of a larger max sentence length threshold of 55 tokens instead of 50, and the use of the better-performing "englishFactored" Stanford parser model.

	devtest06			test07			test08		
System	BLEU	NIST	METEOR	BLEU	NIST	METEOR	BLEU	NIST	METEOR
Baseline	0.2009	5.866	0.2719	0.2051	5.957	0.2782	0.2003	5.889	0.2720
Context	**0.2039**	**5.941**	**0.2784**	**0.2088**	**6.036**	**0.2826**	0.2016	**5.956**	**0.2772**

Table 5: English → German shared task system results using WMT-08 Europarl parallel data for training, dev06 for tuning, and three test sets, including the final 2008 test set. The row labeled "Context" uses the top-performing feature set {2 POS on left, 1 word on right}. Boldface marks scores that are significantly higher than the baseline.

models, including the lexicalized reordering model and the lexical translation model in the Moses MT system, or hierarchical or syntactic models (Chiang, 2005). Additional linguistic analysis (e.g., morphological disambiguation, named entity recognition, semantic role labeling) can be used to define new context features.

8 Conclusion

We have described a straightforward, scalable method for improving phrase translation models by modeling features of a phrase's source-side context. Our method allows incorporation of features from any kind of source-side annotation and barely affects the decoding algorithm. Experiments show performance rivaling or exceeding strong, state-of-the-art baselines on standard translation tasks. Automatic feature selection can be used to achieve performance gains with just two or three context features. Performance is strongest when large in-domain training sets and high-accuracy NLP tools for the source language are available.

Acknowledgments

This research was supported in part by an ARCS award to the first author, NSF IIS-0713265, supercomputing resources provided by Yahoo, and a Google grant. We thank Abhaya Agarwal, Ashish Venugopal, and Andreas Zollmann for helpful conversations and Joy Zhang for his Chinese segmenter. We also thank the anonymous reviewers for helpful comments.

A Dataset Details (Chinese-English)

We trained on data from the NIST MT 2008 constrained Chinese-English track: Hong Kong Hansards and news (LDC2004T08), Sinorama (LDC2005T10), FBIS (LDC2003E14), Xinhua (LDC2002E18), and financial news (LDC2006E26)—total 2.5M sents., 66M Chinese words, 68M English. For news experiments, the newswire portion of the NIST 2004 test set was used for tuning, the full NIST 2003 test set was used for developmental testing and feature selection, and the NIST 2005 test set was used for testing (900-1000 sents. each). We also used the United Nations parallel text (LDC2004E12), divided into training (4.7M sents.; words: 136M Chinese, 144M English), tuning (2K sents.), and test sets (2K sents.). We removed sentence pairs where either side was longer than 80 words, segmented all Chinese text automatically,[8] and parsed/tagged using the Stanford parser with the pre-trained "xinhuaPCFG" model (Klein and Manning, 2003). Trigram language models were trained on the English side of the parallel corpus along with approximately 115M words from the Xinhua section of the English Gigaword corpus (LDC2005T12), years 1995–2000 (total 326M words).

B Dataset Details (German-English)

For German ↔ English experiments, we used data provided for the WMT-07 shared task (1.1M sents., 26M German words, 27M English). We used dev06 for tuning, devtest06 for feature selection and developmental testing, and test07 for final testing (2K sents. each). We removed sentence pairs where either side was longer than 50 words and parsed/tagged the German and English data using the Stanford parser (Klein and Manning, 2003) (with pre-trained "germanFactored" and "englishPCFG" models). 5-gram language models were trained on the entire target side of the parallel corpus (37M German words, 38M English).

[8] Available at `http://projectile.is.cs.cmu.edu/research/public/tools/segmentation/lrsegmenter/lrSegmenter.perl`.

References

S. Banerjee and A. Lavie. 2005. METEOR: An automatic metric for MT evaluation with improved correlation with human judgments. In *Proc. of ACL Workshop on Intrinsic and Extrinsic Evaluation Measures for MT and/or Summarization*.

D. M. Bikel. 2004. A distributional analysis of a lexicalized statistical parsing model. In *Proc. of EMNLP*.

T. Brants, A. C. Popat, P. Xu, F. J. Och, and J. Dean. 2007. Large language models in machine translation. In *Proc. of EMNLP-CoNLL*.

P. F. Brown, J. Cocke, S. A. Della Pietra, V. J. Della Pietra, F. Jelinek, J. D. Lafferty, R. L. Mercer, and P. S. Roossin. 1990. A statistical approach to machine translation. *Computational Linguistics*, 16(2):79–85.

C. Callison-Burch, P. Koehn, C. Fordyce, and C. Monz, editors. 2007. *Proc. of the 2nd Workshop on Statistical Machine Translation*.

M. Carl and A. Way. 2003. *Recent Advances in Example-Based Machine Translation*. Kluwer Academic.

M. Carpuat and D. Wu. 2007. Improving statistical machine translation using word sense disambiguation. In *Proc. of EMNLP-CoNLL*.

Y. Chan, H. Ng, and D. Chiang. 2007. Word sense disambiguation improves statistical machine translation. In *Proc. of ACL*.

S. Chen and J. Goodman. 1998. An empirical study of smoothing techniques for language modeling. Technical report 10-98, Harvard University.

D. Chiang. 2005. A hierarchical phrase-based model for statistical machine translation. In *Proc. of ACL*.

G. Doddington. 2002. Automatic evaluation of machine translation quality using n-gram co-occurrence statistics. In *Proc. of HLT*.

D. Gildea. 2001. Corpus variation and parser performance. In *Proc. of EMNLP*.

J. Giménez and L. Màrquez. 2007. Context-aware discriminative phrase selection for statistical machine translation. In *Proc. of the 2nd Workshop on Statistical Machine Translation*.

I. Guyon and A. Elisseeff. 2003. An introduction to variable and feature selection. *Journal of Machine Learning Research*, 3:1157–1182.

D. Klein and C. D. Manning. 2003. Fast exact inference with a factored model for natural language parsing. In *Advances in NIPS 15*.

P. Koehn, F. J. Och, and D. Marcu. 2003. Statistical phrase-based translation. In *Proc. of HLT-NAACL*, pages 127–133.

P. Koehn, H. Hoang, A. Birch, C. Callison-Burch, M. Federico, N. Bertoldi, B. Cowan, W. Shen, C. Moran, R. Zens, C. Dyer, O. Bojar, A. Constantin, and E. Herbst. 2007. Moses: Open source toolkit for statistical machine translation. In *ACL demonstration session*.

P. Koehn. 2004. Statistical significance tests for machine translation evaluation. In *Proc. of EMNLP*.

José B. Marino, Rafael E. Banchs, Josep M. Crego, Adrià de Gispert, Patrik Lambert, José A. R. Fonollosa, and Marta R. Costa-jussà. 2006. N-gram-based machine translation. *Computational Linguistics*, 32(4):527–549.

M. Nagao. 1984. A framework of a mechanical translation between Japanese and English by analogy principle. In *Proc. of the International NATO Symposium on Artificial and Human Intelligence*. Elsevier North-Holland, Inc.

NIST. 2006. NIST 2006 machine translation evaluation official results.

F. Och and H. Ney. 2003. A systematic comparison of various statistical alignment models. *Computational Linguistics*, 29(1).

F. J. Och. 2003. Minimum error rate training for statistical machine translation. In *Proc. of ACL*, pages 160–167.

K. Papineni, S. Roukos, T. Ward, and W.-J. Zhu. 2002. BLEU: a method for automatic evaluation of machine translation. In *Proc. of ACL*.

H. Somers. 1999. Review article: Example-based machine translation. *Machine Translation*, 14(2).

A. Stolcke. 2002. SRILM—an extensible language modeling toolkit. In *Proc. of ICSLP*.

N. Stroppa, A. van den Bosch, and A. Way. 2007. Exploiting source similarity for SMT using context-informed features. In *Proc. of TMI*.

D. Vickrey, L. Biewald, M. Teyssier, and D. Koller. 2005. Word-sense disambiguation for machine translation. In *Proc. of HLT-EMNLP*.

Discriminative Word Alignment via Alignment Matrix Modeling

Jan Niehues
Institut für Theoretische Informatik
Universität Karlsruhe (TH)
Karlsruhe, Germany
jniehues@ira.uka.de

Stephan Vogel
Language Technologies Institute
Carnegie Mellon University
Pittsburgh, PA, 15213, USA
stephan.vogel@cs.cmu.edu

Abstract

In this paper a new discriminative word alignment method is presented. This approach models directly the alignment matrix by a conditional random field (CRF) and so no restrictions to the alignments have to be made. Furthermore, it is easy to add features and so all available information can be used. Since the structure of the CRFs can get complex, the inference can only be done approximately and the standard algorithms had to be adapted. In addition, different methods to train the model have been developed. Using this approach the alignment quality could be improved by up to 23 percent for 3 different language pairs compared to a combination of both IBM4-alignments. Furthermore the word alignment was used to generate new phrase tables. These could improve the translation quality significantly.

1 Introduction

In machine translation parallel corpora are one very important knowledge source. These corpora are often aligned at the sentence level, but to use them in the systems in most cases a word alignment is needed. Therefore, for a given source sentence f_1^J and a given target sentence e_1^I a set of links (j, i) has to be found, which describes which source word f_j is translated into which target word e_i.

Most SMT systems use the freely available GIZA++-Toolkit to generate the word alignment. This toolkit implements the IBM- and HMM-models introduced in (Brown et al., 1993; Vogel et al., 1996). They have the advantage that they are trained unsupervised and are well suited for a noisy-channel approach. But it is difficult to include additional features into these models.

In recent years several authors (Moore et al., 2006; Lacoste-Julien et al., 2006; Blunsom and Cohn, 2006) proposed discriminative word alignment frameworks and showed that this leads to improved alignment quality. In contrast to generative models, these models need a small amount of hand-aligned data. But it is easy to add features to these models, so all available knowledge sources can be used to find the best alignment.

The discriminative model presented in this paper uses a conditional random field (CRF) to model the alignment matrix. By modeling the matrix no restrictions to the alignment are required and even n:m alignments can be generated. Furthermore, this makes the model symmetric, so the model will produce the same alignment no matter which language is selected as source and which as target language. In contrast, in generative models the alignment is a function where a source word aligns to at most one target word. So the alignment is asymmetric.

The training of this discriminative model has to be done on hand-aligned data. Different methods were tested. First, the common maximum-likelihood approach was used. In addition to this, a method to optimize the weights directly towards a word alignment metric was developed.

The paper is structured as follows: Section 2 and 3 present the model and the training. In Section 4 the model is evaluated in the word alignment task as well as in the translation task. The related work and the conclusion are given in Sections 5 and 6.

Proceedings of the Third Workshop on Statistical Machine Translation, pages 18–25,
Columbus, Ohio, USA, June 2008.

Figure 1: Alignment Example

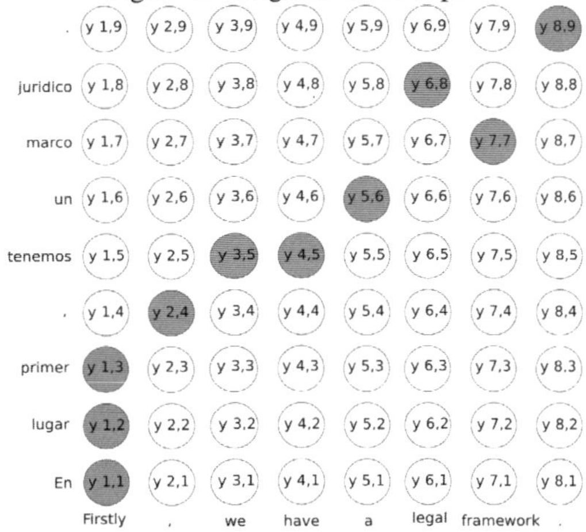

2 The Model

In the approach presented here the word alignment matrix is modeled by a conditional random field (CRF). A CRF is an unidirectional graphical model. It models the conditional distribution over random variables. In most applications like (Tseng et al., 2005; Sha and Pereira, 2003), a sequential model is used. But to model the alignment matrix the graphical structure of the model is more complex.

The alignment matrix is described by a random variable y_{ji} for every source and target word pair (f_j, e_i). These variables can have two values, 0 and 1, indicating whether these words are translations of each other or not. An example is shown in Figure 1. Gray circles represent variables with value 1, white circles stand for variables with value 0. Consequently, a word with zero fertility is indirectly modeled by setting all associated random variables to a value of 0.

The structure of the CRF is described by a factored graph like it was done, for example, in (Lan et al., 2006). In this bipartite graph there are two different types of nodes. First, there are hidden nodes, which correspond to the random variables. The second type of nodes are the factored nodes c . These are not drawn in Figure 1 to keep the picture clear, but they are shown in Figure 2. They define a potential Φ_c on the random variables V_c they are connected to. This potential is used to describe the probability of an alignment based on the information encoded in the features. This potential is a log-linear combination of some features $F_c(V_c) = (f_1(V_c), \ldots, f_n(V_c))$ and it can be written as:

$$\Phi_c(V_c) = exp(\Theta * F_c(V_c)) = exp(\sum_k \theta_k * f_k(V_c)) \quad (1)$$

with the weights Θ. Then the probability of an assignment of the random variables, which corresponds to a word alignment, can be expressed as:

$$p_\Theta(y|e,f) = \frac{1}{Z(e,f)} \prod_{c \in V_{FN}} \Phi_c(V_c) \quad (2)$$

with V_{FN} the set of all factored nodes in the graph, and the normalization factor $Z(e,f)$ defined as:

$$Z(e,f) = \sum_Y \prod_{c \in V_{FN}} \Phi_c(V_c) \quad (3)$$

where Y is the set of all possible alignments.

In the presented model there are four different types of factored nodes corresponding to four groups of features.

2.1 Features

One main advantage of the discriminative framework is the ability to use all available knowledge sources by introducing additional features. Different features have been developed to capture different aspects of the word-alignment.

The first group of features are those that depend only on the source and target words and may therefore be called local features. Consequently, the factored node corresponding to such a feature is connected to one random variable only (see Figure 2(a)). The lexical features, which represent the lexical translation probability of the words belong to this group. In our experiments the IBM4-lexica in both directions were used. Furthermore, there are source and target normalized lexical features for every lexicon. The source normalized feature, for example, is normalized in a way, that all translation probabilities of one source word to target words in the sentences sum up to one as shown in equation 4.

$$p_{sourceN}(f_j, e_i) = \frac{p_{lex}(f_j, e_i)}{\sum_{1 \le j \le J} p_{lex}(f_j, e_i)} \quad (4)$$

$$p_{targetN}(f_j, e_i) = \frac{p_{lex}(f_j, e_i)}{\sum_{1 \le i \le I} p_{lex}(f_j, e_i)} \quad (5)$$

Figure 2: Different features

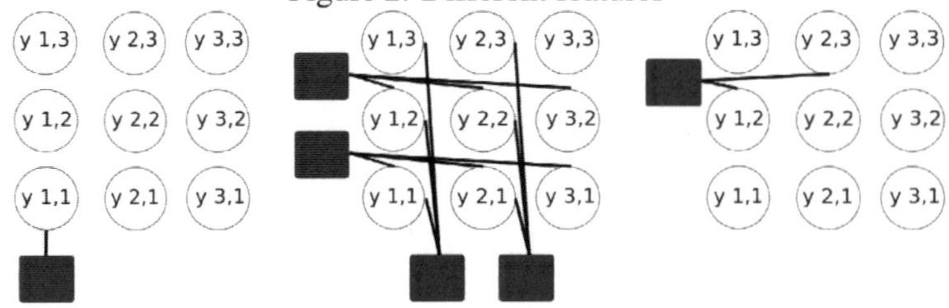

(a) Local features (b) Fertility features (c) First order features

They compare the possible translations in one sentence similar to the rank feature used in the approach presented by Moore (2006). In addition, the following local features are used: The relative distance of the sentence positions of both words. This should help to aligned words that occur several times in the sentence. The relative edit distance between source and target word was used to improve the alignment of cognates. Furthermore a feature indicating if source and target words are identical was added to the system. This helps to align dates, numbers and names, which are quite difficult to align using only lexical features since they occur quite rarely. In some of our experiments the links of the IBM4-alignments are used as an additional local feature. In the experiments this leads to 22 features. Lastly, there are indicator features for every possible combination of Parts-of-Speech(POS)-tags and for N_w high frequency words. In the experiments the 50 most frequent words were used, which lead to 2500 features and around 1440 POS-based features were used. The POS-feature can help to align words, for which the lexical features are weak.

The next group of features are the fertility features. They model the probability that a word translates into one, two, three or more words, or does not have any translation at all. The corresponding factored node for a source word is connected to all I random variables representing the links to the target words, and the node for a target word is connected to all the J nodes for the links to source words (s. Figure 2(b)). In this group of features there are two different types. First, there are indicator features for the different fertilities. To reduce the complexity of the calculation this is only done up to a given maximal fertility N_f and there is an additional indicator feature for all fertilities larger than N_f. This is an extension of the empty word indicator feature used in other discriminative word alignment models. Furthermore, there is a real-valued feature, which can use the GIZA++ probabilities for the different fertilities. This has the advantage compared to the indicator feature that the fertility probabilities are not the same for all words. But here again, all fertilities larger than a given N_f are not considered separately. In the evaluation $N_f = 3$ was selected. So 12 fertility features were used in the experiments.

The first-order features model the first-order dependencies between the different links. They are grouped into different directions. The factored node for the direction (s, t) is connected to the variable nodes y_{ji} and $y_{(j+s)(i+t)}$. For example, the most common direction is $(1, 1)$, which describes the situation that if the words at positions j and i are aligned, also the immediate successor words in both sentences are aligned as shown in Figure 2(c). In the default configuration the directions $(1, 1)$, $(2, 1)$, $(1, 2)$ and $(1, -1)$ are used. So this feature is able to explicitly model short jumps in the alignment, like in the directions $(2, 1)$ and $(1, 2)$ as well as crossing links like in the directions $(1, -1)$. Furthermore, it can be used to improve the fertility modeling. If a word has got a fertility of two, it is often aligned to two consecutive words. Therefore, for example in the Chinese-English system the directions $(1, 0)$ and $(0, 1)$ were used in addition. This does not mean, that other directions in the alignment are not possible, but other jumps in the alignment do not improve the probability of the alignment. For every direction, an indicator feature that both links are active and an additional one, which also depends on the POS-pair of the first word pair is used. For a configuration with 4 directions this leads to 4 indicator features and, for example, 5760 POS-based features.

The last group of features are phrase features, which are introduced to model context dependencies. First a training corpus is aligned. Then, groups of source and target words are extracted. Words build a group, if all source words in the group are aligned to all target words. The relative frequency of this alignment is used as the feature and indicator features for $1:1$, $1:n$, $n:1$ and $n:m$ alignments. The corresponding factored node is connected to all links that are important for this group.

2.2 Alignment

The structure of the described CRF is quite complex and there are many loops in the graphical structure, so the inference cannot be done exactly. For example, the random variables $y_{(1,1)}$ and $y_{(1,2)}$ as well as $y_{(2,1)}$ and $y_{(2,2)}$ are connected by the source fertility nodes of the words f_1 and f_2. Furthermore the variables $y_{(1,1)}$ and $y_{(2,1)}$ as well as $y_{(1,2)}$ and $y_{(2,2)}$ are connected by the target fertility nodes. So these nodes build a loop as shown in Figure 2(b). The first order feature nodes generate loops as well. Consequently an approximation algorithm has to be used. We use the belief propagation algorithm introduced in (Pearl, 1966). In this algorithm messages consisting of a pair of two values are passed along the edges between the factored and hidden nodes for several iterations. In each iterations first messages from the hidden nodes to the connected factored nodes are sent. These messages describe the belief about the value of the hidden node calculated from the incoming messages of the other connected factored nodes. Afterwards the messages from the factored nodes to the connected hidden nodes are send. They are calculated from the potential and the other incoming messages. This algorithm is not exact in loopy graphs and it is not even possible to prove that it converges, but in (Yedidia et al., 2003) it was shown, that this algorithm leads to good results.

The algorithm cannot be used directly, since the calculation of the message sent from a factored node to a random variable has an exponential runtime in the number of connected random variables. Although we limit the number of considered fertilities, the number of connected random variables can still be quite large for the fertility features and the phrase features, especially in long sentences. To reduce this complexity, we leverage the fact that the potential can only have a small number of different values. This will be shown for the fertility feature node. For a more detailed description we refer to (Niehues, 2007). The message sent from a factored node to a random variable is defined in the algorithm as:

$$m_{c\rightarrow(j,i)}(v) = \sum_{V_c/v} \Phi_c(V_c) \prod_{(j,i)'\in N(c)/(j,i)} n_{(j,i)'\rightarrow c}(v') \tag{6}$$

where V_c is the set of random variables connected to the factored node and $\sum_{V_c/v}$ is the sum over all possible values of V_c where the random variable y_{ji} has the the value v. So the value for the message is calculated by looking at every possible combination of the other incoming messages. Then the belief for this combination is multiplied with the potential of this combination. This can be rewritten, since the potential only depends on how many links are active, not on which ones are active.

$$\begin{aligned} m_{c\rightarrow(j,i)}(v) &= \sum_{n=0}^{N_f} \Phi_c(n+v) * \alpha(n) \\ &+ \Phi_c(N_f+1) * \alpha(N_f+1) \end{aligned} \tag{7}$$

with $\alpha(n)$ the belief for a fertility of n of the other connected nodes and $\alpha(N_f+1)$ the belief for a fertility bigger than N_f with $\Phi_c(N_f+1)$ the corresponding potential. The belief for a configuration of some random variables is calculated by the product over all out-going messages. So $\alpha(n)$ is calculated by the sum over all possible configurations that lead to a fertility of n over these products.

$$\begin{aligned} \alpha(n) &= \sum_{V_c/v:|V_c|=n} \prod_{(j,i)'\in V_c/(j,i)} n_{(j,i)'\rightarrow c}(v') \\ \alpha(N_f+1) &= \sum_{V_c/v:|V_c|>N_f} \prod_{(j,i)'\in V_c/(j,i)} n_{(j,i)'\rightarrow c}(v') \end{aligned}$$

The values of the sums can be calculated in linear time using dynamic programming.

3 Training

The weights of the CRFs are trained using a gradient descent for a fixed number of iterations, since this approach leads already to quite good results. In the experiments 200 iterations turned out to be a good number.

The default criteria to train CRFs is to maximize the log-likelihood of the correct solution, which is given by a manually created gold standard alignment. Therefore, the feature values of the gold standard alignment and the expectation values have to be calculated for every factored node. This can be done using again the belief propagation algorithm.

Often, this hand-aligned data is annotated with sure and possible links and it would be nice, if the training method could use this additional information. So we developed a method to optimize the CRFs towards the alignment error rate (AER) or the F-score with sure and possible links as introduced in (Fraser and Marcu, 2007). The advantage of the F-score is, that there is an additional parameter α, which allows to bias the metric more towards precision or more towards recall. To be able to use a gradient descent method to optimize the weights, the derivation of the word alignment metric with respect to these weights must be computed. This cannot be done for the mentioned metrics since they are not smooth functions. We follow (Gao et al., 2006; Suzuki et al., 2006) and approximate the metrics using the sigmoid function. The sigmoid function uses the probabilities for every link calculated by the belief propagation algorithm.

In our experiments we compared the maximum likelihood method and the optimization towards the AER. We also tested combinations of both. The best results were obtained when the weights were first trained using the ML method and the resulting factors were used as initial values for the AER optimization. Another problem is that the POS-based features and high frequency word features have a lot more parameters than all other features and with these two types of features overfitting seems to be a bigger problem. Therefore, these features are only used in a third optimization step, in which they are optimized towards the AER, keeping all other feature weights constant. Initial results using a Gaussian prior showed no improvement.

4 Evaluation

The word alignment quality of this approach was tested on three different language pairs. On the Spanish-English task the hand-aligned data provided by the TALP Research Center (Lambert et al., 2005) was used. As proposed, 100 sentences were used as development data and 400 as test data. The so called "Final Text Edition of the European Parliament Proceedings" consisting of 1.4 million sentences and this hand-aligned data was used as training corpus. The POS-tags were generated by the Brill-Tagger (Brill, 1995) and the FreeLing-Tagger (Asterias et al., 2006) for the English and the Spanish text respectively. To limit the number of different tags for Spanish we grouped them according to the first 2 characters in the tag names.

A second group of experiments was done on an English-French text. The data from the 2003 NAACL shared task (Mihalcea and Pedersen, 2003) was used. This data consists of 1.1 million sentences, a validation set of 37 sentences and a test set of 447 sentences, which have been hand-aligned (Och and Ney, 2003). For the English POS-tags again the Brill Tagger was used. For the French side, the TreeTagger (Schmid, 1994) was used.

Finally, to test our alignment approach with languages that differ more in structure a Chinese-English task was selected. As hand-aligned data 3160 sentences aligned only with sure links were used (LDC2006E93). This was split up into 2000 sentences of test data and 1160 sentences of development data. In some experiments only the first 200 sentences of the development data were used to speed up the training process. The FBIS-corpus was used as training corpus and all Chinese sentences were word segmented with the Stanford Segmenter (Tseng et al., 2005). The POS-tags for both sides were generated with the Stanford Parser (Klein and Manning, 2003).

4.1 Word alignment quality

The GIZA++-toolkit was used to train a baseline system. The models and alignment information were then used as additional knowledge source for the discriminative word alignment. For the first two tasks, all heuristics of the Pharaoh-Toolkit (Koehn et al., 2003) as well as the refined heuristic (Och and Ney, 2003) to combine both IBM4-alignments were tested and the best ones are shown in the tables. For the Chinese task only the grow-diag-final heuristic was used.

Table 1: AER-Results on EN-ES task

Name	Dev	Test
IBM4 Source-Target		21.49
IBM4 Target-Source		19.23
IBM4 grow-diag		16.48
DWA IBM1	15.26	20.82
+ IBM4	14.23	18.67
+ GIZA-fert.	13.28	18.02
+ Link feature	12.26	15.97
+ POS	9.21	15.36
+ Phrase feature	8.84	14.77

Table 2: AER-Results on EN-FR task

Name	Dev	Test
IBM4 Source-Target		8.6
IBM4 Target-Source		9.86
IBM4 intersection		5.38
DWA IBM1	5.54	6.37
+ HFRQ/POS	3.67	5.57
+ Link Feature	3.13	4.80
+ IBM4	3.60	4.60
+ Phrase feature	3.32	4.30

The results measured in AER of the discriminative word alignment for the English-Spanish task are shown in Table 1. In the experiments systems using different knowledge sources were evaluated. The first system used only the IBM1-lexica of both directions as well as the high frequent word features. Then the IBM4-lexica were used instead and in the next system the GIZA++-fertilities were added. As next knowledge source the links of both IBM4-alignments were added. Furthermore, the system could be improved by using also the POS-tags. For the last system, the whole EPPS-corpus was aligned with the previous system and the phrases were extracted. Using them as additional features, the best AER of 14.77 could be reached. This is an improvement of 1.71 AER points or 10% relative to the best baseline system.

Similar experiments have also been done for the English-French task. The results measured in AER are shown in Table 2. The IBM4 system uses the IBM4 lexica and links instead of the IBM1s and adds the GIZA++-fertilities. For the "phrase feature"-system the corpus was aligned with the "IBM4"-system and the phrases were extracted. This led to the best result with an AER of 4.30. This is 1.08 points or 20% relative improvement over the best generative system. One reason, why less knowledge sources are needed to be as good as the baseline system, may be that there are many possible links in the reference alignment and the discriminative framework can better adapt to this style. So a system using only features generated by the IBM1-model could already reach an AER of 4.80.

Table 3: AER-Results on CH-EN task

Name	Test
IBM4 Source-target	44.94
IBM4 Target-source	37.43
IBM4 Grow-diag-final	35.04
DWA IBM4	30.97
- similarity	30.24
+ Add. directions	27.96
+ Big dev	27.26
+ Phrase feature	27.00
+ Phrase feature(high P.)	26.90

In Table 3 results for the Chinese-English alignment task are shown[1]. The first system was only trained on the smaller development set and used the same knowledge source than the "IBM4"-systems in the last experiment. The system could be improved a little bit by removing the similarity feature and adding the directions $(0, 1)$ and $(1, 0)$ to the model. Then the same system was trained on the bigger development set. Again the parallel corpus was aligned with the discriminative word alignment system, once trained towards AER and once more towards precision, and phrases were extracted. Overall, an improvement by 8.14 points or 23% over the baseline system could be achieved.

These experiments show, that every knowledge source that is available should be used. For all languages pairs additional knowledge sources lead to an improvement in the word alignment quality. A problem of the discriminative framework is, that hand-aligned data is needed for training. So the

[1]For this task no results on the development task are given since different development sets were used

Table 4: Translation results for EN-ES

Name	Dev	Test
Baseline	40.04	47.73
DWA	**41.62**	**48.13**

Table 5: Translation results for CH-EN

Name	Dev	Test
Baseline	27.13	22.56
AER	**27.63**	23.85*
F0.3	26.34	22.35
F0.7	26.40	23.52*
Phrase feature AER	25.84	23.42*
Phrase feature F0.7	26.41	**23.92***

French-English dev set may be too small, since the best system on the development set does not correspond to the best system on the test set. And as shown in the Chinese-English task additional data can improve the alignment quality.

4.2 Translation quality

Since the main application of the word alignment is statistical machine translation, the aim was not only to generate better alignments measured in AER, but also to generate better translations. Therefore, the word alignment was used to extract phrases and use them then in the translation system. In all translation experiments the beam decoder as described in (Vogel, 2003) was used together with a 3-gram language model and the results are reported in the BLUE metric. For test set translations the statistical significance of the results was tested using the bootstrap technique as described in (Zhang and Vogel, 2004). The baseline system used the phrases build with the Pharaoh-Toolkit.

The new word alignment was tested on the English-Spanish translation task using the TC-Star 07 development and test data. The discriminative word alignment (DWA) used the configuration denoted by +POS system in Table 1. With this configuration it took around 4 hours to align 100K sentences. But, of course, generating the alignment can be parallelized to speed up the process. As shown in Table 4 the new word alignment could generate better translations as measured in BLEU scores.

For the Chinese-English task some experiments were made to study the effect of different training schemes. Results are shown in Table 5. The systems used the MT'03 eval set as development data and the NIST part of the MT'06 eval set was used as test set. Scores significantly better than the baseline system are mark by a *. The first three systems used a discriminative word alignment generated with the configuration as the one described as "+ big dev"-system in Table 3. The first one was optimized towards AER, the other two were trained towards the F-score with an α-value of 0.3 (recall-biased) and 0.7 (precision-biased) respectively. A higher precision word alignment generates fewer alignment links, but a larger phrase table. For this task, the precision seems to be more important. So the system trained towards the AER and the F-score with an α-value of 0.7 performed better than the other systems. The phrase features gave improved performance only when optimized towards the F-score, but not when optimized towards the AER.

5 Comparison to other work

Several discriminative word alignment approaches have been presented in recent years. The one most similar to ours is the one presented by Blunsom and Cohn (2006). They also used CRFs, but they used two linear-chain CRFs, one for every directions. Consequently, they could find the optimal solution for each individual CRF, but they still needed the heuristics to combine both alignments. They reached an AER of 5.29 using the IBM4-alignment on the English-French task (compared to 4.30 of our approach).

Lacoste-Julien et al. (2006) enriched the bipartite matching problem to model also larger fertilities and first-or der dependencies. They could reach an AER of 3.8 on the same task, but only if they also included the posteriors of the model of Liang et al. (2006). Using only the IBM4-alignment they generated an alignment with an AER of 4.5. But they did not use any POS-based features in their experiments.

Finally, Moore et al. (2006) used a log-linear model for the features and performed a beam search. They could reach an AER as low as 3.7 with both types of alignment information. But they presented no results using only the IBM4-alignment features.

6 Conclusion

In this paper a new discriminative word alignment model was presented. It uses a conditional random field to model directly the alignment matrix. Therefore, the algorithms used in the CRFs had to be adapted to be able to model dependencies between many random variables. Different methods to train the model have been developed. Optimizing the F-score allows to generate alignments focusing more on precision or on recall. For the model a multitude of features using the different knowledge sources have been developed. The experiments showed that the performance could be improved by using these additional knowledge sources. Furthermore, the use of a general machine learning framework like the CRFs enables this alignment approach to benefit from future improvements in CRFs in other areas.

Experiments on 3 different language pairs have shown that word alignment quality as well as translation quality could be improved. In the translation experiments it was shown that the improvement is significant at a significance level of 5%.

References

Atserias, J., B. Casas, E. Comelles, M. González, L. Padró and M. Padró. 2006. FreeLing 1.3: Syntactic and semantic services in an open-source NLP library. In *LREC'06*. Genoa, Italy.

P. Blunsom and T. Cohn. 2006. Discriminative word alignment with conditional random fields. In *ACL'06*, pp. 65-72. Sydney, Australia.

E. Brill. 1995. Transformation-based error-driven learning and natural language processing: A case study in part of speech tagging. *Computational Linguistics*, 21(4):543-565.

P.F. Brown, S. Della Pietra, V. J. Della Pietra, R. L. Mercer. 1993. The Mathematic of Statistical Machine Translation: Parameter Estimation. *Computational Linguistics*, 19(2):263-311.

A. Fraser, D. Marcu. 2007. Measuring Word Alignment Quality for Statistical Machine Translation *Computational Linguistics*, 33(3):293-303.

S. Gao, W. Wu, C. Lee, T. Chua. 2006. A maximal figure-of-merit (MFoM)-learning approach to robust classifier design for text categorization. *ACM Trans. Inf. Syst.*, 24(2):190-218.

D. Klein and C.D. Manning. 2003. Fast Exact Inference with a Factored Model for Natural Language Parsing. *Advances in Neural Information Processing Systems 15 (NIPS 2002)*, pp. 3-10.

P. Koehn, F. J. Och, D. Marcu. 2003. Statistical phrase-based translation. In *HTL-NAACL'03*, pp. 48-54. Morristown, New Jersey, USA.

S. Lacoste-Julien, B. Taskar, D. Klein, M. I. Jordan. 2006. Word alignment via quadratic assignment. In *HTL-NAACL'06*. New York, USA.

P. Lambert, A. de Gispert, R. Banchs and J. b. Marino. 2005. Guidelines for Word Alignment Evaluation and Manual Alignment. *Language Resources and Evaluation*, pp. 267-285, Springer.

X. Lan and S. Roth, D. P. Huttenlocher, M. J. Black. 2006. Efficient Belief Propagation with Learned Higher-Order Markov Random Fields. *ECCV (2), Lecture Notes in Computer Science*, pp. 269-282.

P. Liang, B. Taskar, D. Klein. 2006. Alignment by agreement. In *HTL-NAACL'06*, pp. 104-110. New York, USA.

R. Mihalcea, T. Pedersen. 2003. An Evaluation Exercise for Word Alignment. In *HLT-NAACL 2003 Workshop, Building and Using Parallel Texts: Data Driven Machine Translation and Beyond*, pp. 1-6. Edmonton,Canada.

R. C. Moore, W. Yih, A. Bode. 2006. Improved discriminative bilingual word alignment. In *ACL'06*, pp. 513-520. Sydney, Australia.

J. Niehues. 2007. Discriminative Word Alignment Models. Diplomarbeit at Universität Karlsruhe(TH).

F. J. Och and H. Ney. 2003. A Systematic Comparison of Various Statistical Alignment Models. *Computational Linguist*,29(1):19-51.

J. Pearl. 1988. *Probabilistic Reasoning in Intelligent Systems: Networks of Plausible Inference*.

H. Schmid. 1994. Probabilistic Part-of-Speech Tagging Using Decision Trees. In *NEMLAP'94*. Manchester, UK.

F. Sha and F. Pereira. 2003. Shallow parsing with conditional random fields. In *HLT-NAACL'03*, pp. 134–141. Edmonton, Canada.

J. Suzuki, E. McDermott, H. Isozaki. 2006. Training conditional random fields with multivariate evaluation measures In *ACL'06*, pp 217-224. Sydney, Australia.

H. Tseng, P. Chang, G. Andrew, D. Jurafsky and C. Manning. 2005. A Conditional Random Field Word Segmenter. In *SIGHAN-4*. Jeju, Korea.

S. Vogel, H. Ney, C. Tillmann. 1996. HMM-based word alignment in statistical translation. In *COLING'96*, pp. 836-841. Copenhagen, Denmark.

S. Vogel. 2003. SMT Decoder Dissected: Word Reordering. In *NLP-KE'03*. Bejing, China.

J. S. Yedidia, W. T. Freeman, Y. Weiss. 2003. Understanding belief propagation and its generalizations. *Exploring artificial intelligence in the new millennium*.

Y. Zhang and S. Vogel. 2004. Measuring Confidence Intervals for MT Evaluation Metrics. In *TMI 2004*. Baltimore, MD, USA.

Regularization and Search for Minimum Error Rate Training

Daniel Cer, **Daniel Jurafsky**, and **Christopher D. Manning**
Stanford University
Stanford, CA 94305
cerd,jurafsky,manning@stanford.edu

Abstract

Minimum error rate training (MERT) is a widely used learning procedure for statistical machine translation models. We contrast three search strategies for MERT: Powell's method, the variant of coordinate descent found in the Moses MERT utility, and a novel stochastic method. It is shown that the stochastic method obtains test set gains of +0.98 BLEU on MT03 and +0.61 BLEU on MT05. We also present a method for regularizing the MERT objective that achieves statistically significant gains when combined with both Powell's method and coordinate descent.

1 Introduction

Och (2003) introduced minimum error rate training (MERT) as an alternative training regime to the conditional likelihood objective previously used with log-linear translation models (Och & Ney, 2002). This approach attempts to improve translation quality by optimizing an automatic translation evaluation metric, such as the BLEU score (Papineni et al., 2002). This is accomplished by either directly walking the error surface provided by an evaluation metric w.r.t. the model weights or by using gradient-based techniques on a continuous approximation of such a surface. While the former is piecewise constant and thus cannot be optimized using gradient techniques, Och (2003) provides an approach that performs such training efficiently.

In this paper we explore a number of variations on MERT. First, it is shown that performance gains can be had by making use of a stochastic search strategy as compare to that obtained by Powell's method and coordinate descent. Subsequently, results are presented for two regularization strategies[1]. Both allow coordinate descent and Powell's method to achieve performance that is on par with stochastic search.

In what follows, we briefly review minimum error rate training, introduce our stochastic search and regularization strategies, and then present experimental results.

2 Minimum Error Rate Training

Let $\mathbf{F}$ be a collection of foreign sentences to be translated, with individual sentences $\mathbf{f}_0$, $\mathbf{f}_1$, ..., $\mathbf{f}_n$. For each $\mathbf{f}_i$, the surface form of an individual candidate translation is given by $\mathbf{e}_i$ with hidden state $\mathbf{h}_i$ associated with the derivation of $\mathbf{e}_i$ from $\mathbf{f}_i$. Each $\mathbf{e}_i$ is drawn from $\mathcal{E}$, which represents all possible strings our translation system can produce. The $(\mathbf{e}_i, \mathbf{h}_i, \mathbf{f}_i)$ triples are converted into vectors of m feature functions by $\Psi : \mathcal{E} \times \mathcal{H} \times \mathcal{F} \rightarrow \mathbb{R}^m$ whose dot product with the weight vector $\mathbf{w}$ assigns a score to each triple. The idealized translation process then is to find the highest scoring pair $(\mathbf{e}_i, \mathbf{h}_i)$ for each $\mathbf{f}_i$, or rather $(\mathbf{e}_i, \mathbf{h}_i) = \text{argmax}_{(\mathbf{e} \in \mathcal{E}, \mathbf{h} \in \mathcal{H})} \mathbf{w} \cdot \Psi(\mathbf{e}, \mathbf{h}, \mathbf{f})$.

The aggregate argmax for the entire data set $\mathbf{F}$ is given by equation (1)[2]. This gives $\mathbf{E_w}$ which represents the set of translations selected by the model for data set $\mathbf{F}$ when parameterized by the weight vector $\mathbf{w}$. Let's assume we have an automated measure of translation quality ℓ that maps the collec-

[1] While we prefer the term regularization, the strategies presented here could also be referred to as smoothing methods.

[2] Here, the translation of the entire data set is treated as a single structured prediction problem using the feature function vector $\Psi(\mathbf{E}, \mathbf{H}, \mathbf{F}) = \sum_i^n \Psi(\mathbf{e}_i, \mathbf{h}_i, \mathbf{f}_i)$

Proceedings of the Third Workshop on Statistical Machine Translation, pages 26–34,
Columbus, Ohio, USA, June 2008.

id	Translation	$\log(\mathbf{P_{TM}}(\mathbf{f}\|\mathbf{e}))$	$\log(\mathbf{P_{LM}}(\mathbf{e}))$	BLEU-2
$\mathbf{e}^1$	This is it	-1.2	-0.1	29.64
$\mathbf{e}^2$	This is small house	-0.2	-1.2	63.59
$\mathbf{e}^3$	This is miniscule building	-1.6	-0.9	31.79
$\mathbf{e}^4$	This is a small house	-0.1	-0.9	100.00
ref	This is a small house			

Table 1: Four hypothetical translations and their corresponding log model scores from a translation model $P_{TM}(f|e)$ and a language model $P_{LM}(e)$, along with their **BLEU-2** scores according to the given reference translation. The MERT error surface for these translations is given in figure 1.

tion of translations $\mathbf{E_w}$ onto some real valued loss, $\ell : \mathcal{E}^n \to \mathbb{R}$. For instance, in the experiments that follow, the loss corresponds to 1 minus the BLEU score assigned to $\mathbf{E_w}$ for a given collection of reference translations.

$$(\mathbf{E_w}, \mathbf{H_w}) = \underset{(\mathbf{E}\in\mathcal{E}^n, \mathbf{H}\in\mathcal{H}^n)}{\operatorname{argmax}} \mathbf{w} \cdot \Psi(\mathbf{E}, \mathbf{H}, \mathbf{F}) \quad (1)$$

Using n-best lists produced by a decoder to approximate $\mathcal{E}^n$ and $\mathcal{H}^n$, MERT searches for the weight vector $\mathbf{w}^*$ that minimizes the loss ℓ. Letting $\tilde{\mathbf{E}}_\mathbf{w}$ denote the result of the translation argmax w.r.t. the approximate hypothesis space, the MERT search is then expressed by equation (2). Notice the objective function being optimized is equivalent to the loss assigned by the automatic measure of translation quality, i.e. $\mathcal{O}(\mathbf{w}) = \ell(\tilde{\mathbf{E}}_\mathbf{w})$.

$$\mathbf{w}^* = \underset{\mathbf{w}}{\operatorname{argmin}}\, \ell(\tilde{\mathbf{E}}_\mathbf{w}) \quad (2)$$

After performing the parameter search, the decoder is then re-run using the weights $\mathbf{w}^*$ to produce a new set of n-best lists, which are then concatenated with the prior n-best lists in order to obtain a better approximation of $\mathcal{E}^n$ and $\mathcal{H}^n$. The parameter search given in (2) can then be performed over the improved approximation. This process repeats until either no novel entries are produced for the combined n-best lists or the weights change by less than some ϵ across iterations.

Unlike the objective functions associated with other popular learning algorithms, the objective $\mathcal{O}$ is piecewise constant over its entire domain. That is, while small perturbations in the weights, $\mathbf{w}$, will change the score assigned by $\mathbf{w} \cdot \Psi(\mathbf{e}, \mathbf{h}, \mathbf{f})$ to each triple, $(\mathbf{e}, \mathbf{h}, \mathbf{f})$, such perturbations will generally not change the ranking between the pair selected by the argmax, $(\mathbf{e}^*, \mathbf{h}^*) = \operatorname{argmax} \mathbf{w} \cdot \Psi(\mathbf{e}, \mathbf{h}, \mathbf{f})$, and any given competing pair $(\mathbf{e}', \mathbf{h}')$. However, at certain critical points, the score assigned to some competing pair $(\mathbf{e}', \mathbf{h}')$ will exceed that assigned to the prior winner $(\mathbf{e}^*_{w_{old}}, \mathbf{h}^*_{w_{old}})$. At this point, the pair returned by $\operatorname{argmax} \mathbf{w} \cdot \Psi(\mathbf{e}, \mathbf{h}, \mathbf{f})$ will change and loss ℓ will be evaluated using the newly selected $\mathbf{e}'$.

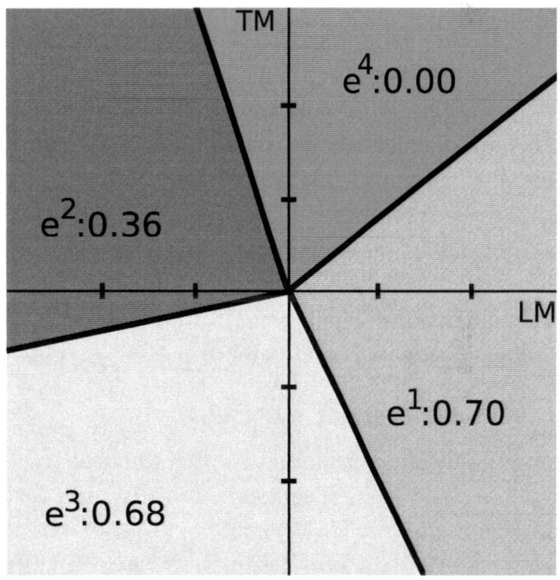

Figure 1: MERT objective for the translations given in table 1. Regions are labeled with the translation that dominates within it, i.e. $\operatorname{argmax} \mathbf{w} \cdot \Psi(\mathbf{e}, \mathbf{f})$, and with their corresponding objective values, $1 - \ell(\operatorname{argmax} \mathbf{w} \cdot \Psi(\mathbf{e}, \mathbf{f}))$.

This is illustrated in figure (1), which plots the MERT objective function for a simple model with two parameters, w_{tm} & w_{lm}, and for which the space of possible translations, $\mathcal{E}$, consists of the four sentences given in table 1[3]. Here, the loss ℓ is de-

[3]For this example, we ignore the latent variables, $\mathbf{h}$, associ-

fined as 1.0−BLEU-2(e). That is, ℓ is the difference between a perfect BLEU score and the BLEU score calculated for each translation using unigram and bi-gram counts.

The surface can be visualized as a collection of plateaus that all meet at the origin and then extend off into infinity. The latter property illustrates that the objective is scale invariant w.r.t. the weight vector $\mathbf{w}$. That is, since any vector $\mathbf{w}' = \lambda\mathbf{w}\ \forall_{\lambda>0}$ will still result in the same relative rankings of all possible translations according to $\mathbf{w} \cdot \Psi(\mathbf{e}, \mathbf{h}, \mathbf{f})$, such scaling will not change the translation selected by the argmax. At the boundaries between regions, the objective is undefined, as 2 or more candidates are assigned identical scores by the model. Thus, it is unclear what should be returned by the argmax for subsequent scoring by ℓ.

Since the objective is piecewise constant, it cannot be minimized using gradient descent or even the sub-gradient method. Two applicable methods include downhill simplex and Powell's method (Press et al., 2007). The former attempts to find a local minimum in an n dimensional space by iteratively shrinking or growing an $n + 1$ vertex simplex[4] based on the objective values of the current vertex points and select nearby points. In contrast, Powell's method operates by starting with a single point in weight space, and then performing a series of line minimizations until no more progress can be made. In this paper, we focus on line minimization based techniques, such as Powell's method.

2.1 Global minimum along a line

Even without gradient information, numerous methods can be used to find, or approximately find, local minima along a line. However, by exploiting the fact that the underlying scores assigned to competing hypotheses, $\mathbf{w} \cdot \Psi(\mathbf{e}, \mathbf{h}, \mathbf{f})$, vary linearly w.r.t. changes in the weight vector, $\mathbf{w}$, Och (2003) proposed a strategy for finding the global minimum along any given search direction.

The insight behind the algorithm is as follows. Let's assume we are examining two competing translation/derivation pairs, $(\mathbf{e}^1, \mathbf{h}^1)$ & $(\mathbf{e}^2, \mathbf{h}^2)$. Further, let's say the score assigned by the model to $(\mathbf{e}^1, \mathbf{h}^1)$ is greater than $(\mathbf{e}^2, \mathbf{h}^2)$, i.e. $\mathbf{w} \cdot \Psi(\mathbf{e}^1, \mathbf{h}^1, \mathbf{f}) > \mathbf{w} \cdot \Psi(\mathbf{e}^2, \mathbf{h}^2, \mathbf{f})$. Since the scores of the two vary linearly along any search direction, $\mathbf{d}$, we can find the point at which the model's relative preference for the competing pairs switches as $p = \frac{\mathbf{w}\cdot\Psi(\mathbf{e}^1,\mathbf{h}^1,\mathbf{f}) - \mathbf{w}\cdot\Psi(\mathbf{e}^2,\mathbf{h}^2,\mathbf{f})}{\mathbf{d}\cdot\Psi(\mathbf{e}^2,\mathbf{h}^2,\mathbf{f}) - \mathbf{d}\cdot\Psi(\mathbf{e}^1,\mathbf{h}^1,\mathbf{f})}$. At this particular point, we have the equality $(p\mathbf{d} + \mathbf{w}) \cdot \Psi(\mathbf{e}^1, \mathbf{h}^1, \mathbf{f}) = (p\mathbf{d} + \mathbf{w}) \cdot \Psi(\mathbf{e}^2, \mathbf{h}^2, \mathbf{f})$, or rather the point at which the scores assigned by the model to the candidates intersect along search direction $\mathbf{d}$[5]. Such points correspond to the boundaries between adjacent plateaus in the objective, as prior to the boundary the loss function ℓ is computed using the translation, $\mathbf{e}^1$, and after the boundary it is computed using $\mathbf{e}^2$.

To find the global minimum for a search direction $\mathbf{d}$, we move along $\mathbf{d}$ and for each plateau we

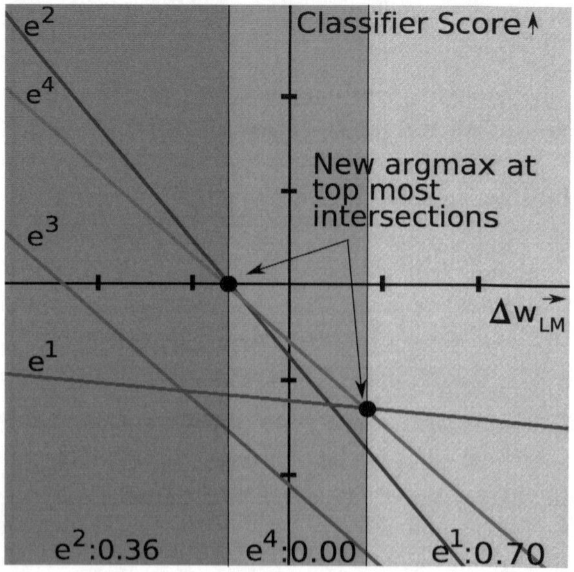

Figure 2: Illustration of how the model score assigned to each candidate translation varies during a line search along the coordinate direction w_{lm} with a starting point of $(w_{tm}, w_{lm}) = (1.0, 0.5)$. Each plotted line corresponds to the model score for one of the translation candidates. The vertical bands are labeled with the hypothesis that dominates in that region. The transitions between bands result from the dotted intersections between 1-best lines.

ated with the derivation of each $\mathbf{e}$ from the foreign sentence $\mathbf{f}$. If included, such variables would only change the graph in that multiple different derivations would be possible for each $\mathbf{e}^j$. If present, the graph could then include disjoint regions that all map to the same $\mathbf{e}^j$ and thus the same objective value.

[4]A simplex can be thought of as a generalization of a triangle to arbitrary dimensional spaces.

[5]Notice that, this point only exists if the slopes of the candidates' model scores along $\mathbf{d}$ are not equivalent, i.e. if $\mathbf{d} \cdot \Psi(\mathbf{e}^2, \mathbf{h}^2, \mathbf{f}) \neq \mathbf{d} \cdot \Psi(\mathbf{e}^1, \mathbf{h}^1, \mathbf{f})$.

Translation	m	b	1-best
e^1	-0.1	-1.25	(0.86,+∞]
e^2	-1.2	-0.8	(-0.83,0.88)
e^3	-0.9	-2.05	n/a
e^4	-0.9	-0.55	[−∞,-0.83]

Table 2: Slopes, m, intercepts, b, and 1-best ranges for the 4 translations given in table 1 during a line search along the coordinate w_{lm}, with a starting point of $(w_{tm}, w_{lm}) = (1.0, 0.5)$. This line search in illustrated in figure(2).

identify all the points at which the score assigned by the model to the current 1-best translation intersects the score assigned to competing translations. At the closest such intersection, we have a new 1-best translation. Moving to the plateau associated with this new 1-best, we then repeat the search for the nearest subsequent intersection. This continues until we know what the 1-best translations are for all points along $\mathbf{d}$. The global minimum can then be found by examining ℓ once for each of these.

Let's return briefly to our earlier example given in table 1. Starting at position $(w_{tm}, w_{lm}) = (1.0, 0.5)$ and searching along the w_{lm} coordinate, i.e. $(d_{tm}, d_{lm}) = (0.0, 1.0)$, table 2 gives the line search slopes, $m = \mathbf{d} \cdot \Psi(\mathbf{e}, \mathbf{h}, \mathbf{f})$, and intercepts, $b = \mathbf{w} \cdot \Psi(\mathbf{e}, \mathbf{h}, \mathbf{f})$, for each of the four candidate translations. Using the procedure just described, we can then find what range of values along $\mathbf{d}$ each candidate translation is assigned the highest relative model score. Figure 2 illustrates how the score assigned by the model to each of the translations changes as we move along $\mathbf{d}$. Each of the banded regions corresponds to a plateau in the objective, and each of the top most line intersections represents the transition from one plateau to the next. Note that, while the surface that is defined by the line segments with the highest classifier score for each region is convex, this is not a convex optimization problem as we are optimizing over the loss ℓ rather than classifier score.

Pseudocode for the line search is given in algorithm 1. Letting n denote the number of foreign sentences, $\mathbf{f}$, in a dataset, and having m denote the size of the individual n-best lists, $|l|$, the time complexity of the algorithm is given by $\mathcal{O}(nm^2)$. This is seen in that each time we check for the nearest intersection to the current 1-best for some n-best list l, we must calculate its intersection with all other candidate translations that have yet to be selected as the 1-best. And, for each of the n n-best lists, this may have to be done up to $m - 1$ times.

Algorithm 1 Och (2003)'s line search method to find the global minimum in the loss, ℓ, when starting at the point $\mathbf{w}$ and searching along the direction $\mathbf{d}$ using the candidate translations given in the collection of n-best lists $\mathcal{L}$.

```
Input: L, w, d, ℓ
I ⇐ {}
for l ∈ L do
  for e ∈ l do
    m{e} ⇐ e.features · d
    b{e} ⇐ e.features · w
  end for
  best_n ⇐ argmax_{e∈l} m{e} {b{e} breaks ties}
  loop
    best_{n+1} = argmin_{e∈l} max(0, (b{best_n} − b{e}) / (m{e} − m{best_n}))
    intercept ⇐ max(0, (b{best_n} − b{best_{n+1}}) / (m{best_{n+1}} − m{best_n}))
    if intercept > 0 then
      add(I, intercept)
    else
      break
    end if
  end loop
end for
add(I, max(I) + 2ε)
i_best = argmin_{i∈I} eval_ℓ(L, w + (i − ε) · d)
return w + (i_best − ε) · d
```

2.2 Search Strategies

In this section, we review two search strategies that, in conjunction with the line search just described, can be used to drive MERT. The first, Powell's method, was advocated by Och (2003) when MERT was first introduced for statistical machine translation. The second, which we call Koehn-coordinate descent (KCD)[6], is used by the MERT utility packaged with the popular Moses statistical machine translation system (Koehn et al., 2007).

[6] Moses uses David Chiang's CMERT package. Within the source file mert.c, the function that implements the overall search strategy, optimize_koehn(), is based on Philipp Koehn's Perl script for MERT optimization that was distributed with Pharaoh.

2.2.1 Powell's Method

Powell's method (Press et al., 2007) attempts to efficiently search the objective by constructing a set of mutually non-interfering search directions. The basic procedure is as follows: (i) A collection of search directions is initialized to be the coordinates of the space being searched; (ii) The objective is minimized by looping through the search directions and performing a line minimization for each; (iii) A new search direction is constructed that summarizes the cumulative direction of the progress made during step (ii) (i.e., $\mathbf{d}_{new} = \mathbf{w}_{pre_{ii}} - \mathbf{w}_{post_{ii}}$). After a line minimization is performed along $\mathbf{d}_{new}$, it is used to replace one of the existing search directions. (iv) The process repeats until no more progress can be made. For a quadratic function of n variables, this procedure comes with the guarantee that it will reach the minimum within n iterations of the outer loop. However, since Powell's method is usually applied to non-quadratic optimization problems, a typical implementation will forego the quadratic convergence guarantees in favor of a heuristic scheme that allows for better navigation of complex surfaces.

2.2.2 Koehn's Coordinate Descent

KCD is a variant of coordinate descent that, at each iteration, moves along the coordinate which allows for the most progress in the objective. In order to determine which coordinate this is, the routine performs a trial line minimization along each. It then updates the weight vector with the one that it found to be most successful. While much less sophisticated that Powell, our results indicate that this method may be marginally more effective at optimizing the MERT objective[7].

3 Extensions

In this section we present and motivate two novel extensions to MERT. The first is a stochastic alternative to the Powell and KCD search strategies, while the second is an efficient method for regularizing the objective.

[7] While we are not aware of any previously published results that demonstrate this, it is likely that we were not the first to make this discovery as even though Moses' MERT implementation includes a vestigial implementation of Powell's method, the code is hardwired to call optimize_koehn rather than the routine for Powell.

3.1 Random Search Directions

One significant advantage of Powell's algorithm over coordinate descent is that it can optimize along diagonal search directions in weight space. That is, given a model with a dozen or so features, it can explore gains that are to be had by simultaneously varying two or more of the feature weights. In general, the diagonals that Powell's method constructs allow it to walk objective functions more efficiently than coordinate descent (Press et al., 2007). However, given that we have a line search algorithm that will find the global minima along any given search direction, diagonal search may be of even more value. That is, similar to ridge phenomenon that arise in traditional hill climbing search, it is possible that there are points in the objective that are the global minimum along any given coordinate direction, but are not the global minimum along diagonal directions.

However, one substantial disadvantage for Powell is that the assumptions it uses to build up the diagonal search directions do not hold in the present context. Specifically, the search directions are built up under the assumption that near a minimum the surface looks approximately quadratic and that we are performing local line minimizations within such regions. However, since we are performing global line minimizations, it is possible for the algorithm to jump from the region around one minima to another. If Powell's method has already started to tune its search directions for the prior minima, it will likely be less effective in its efforts to search the new region. To this extent, coordinate descent will be more robust than Powell as it has no assumptions that are violated when such a jump occurs.

One way of salvaging Powell's algorithm in this context would be to incorporate additional heuristics that detect when the algorithm has jumped from the region around one minima to another. When this occurs, the search directions could be reset to the coordinates of the space. However, we opt for a simpler solution, which like Powell's algorithm performs searches along diagonals in the space, but that like coordinate descent is sufficiently simple that the algorithm will not be confused by sudden jumps between regions.

Specifically, the search procedure chooses directions at random such that each component

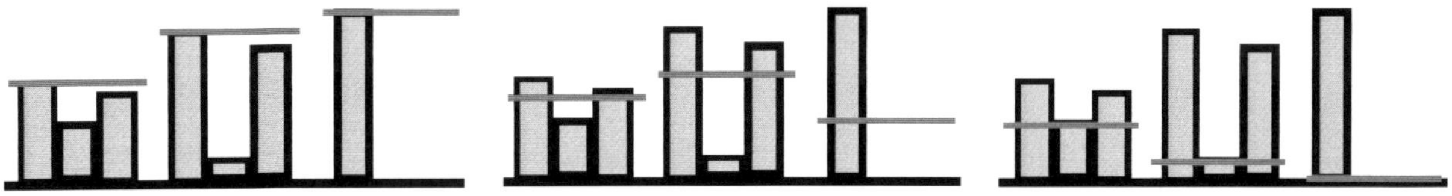

Figure 3: Regularization during line search - using, from left to right: (i) the maximum loss of adjacent plateaus, (ii) the average loss of adjacent plateaus, (iii) no regularization. Each set of bars represents adjacent plateaus along the line being searched, with the height of the bars representing their associated loss. The vertical lines indicate the surrogate loss values used for the center region under each of the schemes (i-iii).

is distributed according to a Gaussian[8], $\mathbf{d}$ s.t. $d_i \sim N(0, 1)$. This allows the procedure to minimize along diagonal search directions, while making essentially no assumptions regarding the characteristics of the objective or the relationship between a series of sequential line minimizations. In the results that follow, we show that, perhaps surprisingly, this simple procedure outperforms both KCD and Powell's method.

3.2 Regularization

One potential drawback of MERT, as it is typically implemented, is that it attempts to find the best possible set of parameters for a training set without making any explicit efforts to find a set of parameters that can be expected to generalize well. For example, let's say that for some objective there is a very deep but narrow minima that is surrounded on all sides by very bad objective values. That is, the BLEU score at the minima might be 39.1 while all surrounding plateaus have a BLEU score that is < 10. Intuitively, such a minima would be a very bad solution, as the resulting parameters would likely exhibit very poor generalization to other data sets. This could be avoided by regularizing the surface in order to eliminate such spurious minima.

One candidate for performing such regularization is the continuous approximation of the MERT objective, $\mathcal{O} = \mathbb{E}_{p_\mathbf{w}}(\ell)$. Och (2003) claimed that this approximation achieved essentially equivalent performance to that obtained when directly using the loss as the objective, $\mathcal{O} = \ell$. However, Zens et al. (2007) found that $\mathcal{O} = \mathbb{E}_{p_\mathbf{w}}(\ell)$ achieved substantially better test set performance than $\mathcal{O} = \ell$, even though it performs slightly worse on the data used to train the parameters. Similarly, Smith and Eisner (2006) reported test set gains for the related technique of minimum risk annealing, which incorporates a temperature parameter that trades off between the smoothness of the objective and the degree it reflects the underlying piecewise constant error surface. However, the most straightforward implementation of such methods requires a loss that can be applied at the sentence level. If the evaluation metric of interest does not have this property (e.g. BLEU), the loss must be approximated using some surrogate, with successful learning then being tied to how well the surrogate captures the critical properties of the underlying loss.

The techniques of Zens et al. (2007) & Smith and Eisner (2006) regularize by implicitly smoothing over nearby plateaus in the error surface. We propose an alternative scheme that operates directly on the piecewise constant objective and that mitigates the problem of spurious local minima by explicitly smoothing over adjacent plateaus during the line search. That is, when assessing the desirability of any given plateau, we examine a fixed window w of adjacent plateaus along the direction being searched and combine their evaluation scores. We explore two combination methods, max and $average$. The former, max, assigns each plateau an objective value that is equal to the maximum objective value in its surrounding window, while $average$ assigns a plateau an objective value that is equal to its window's average. Figure 3 illustrates both methods for regularizing the plateaus and contrasts them with the case where no regularization is used. Notice that, while both methods discount spurious pits in the objective, $average$ still does place some value on isolated deep plateaus, and max discounts them completely.

Note that one potential weakness of this scheme is the value assigned by the regularized objective to any given point differs depending on the direction being searched. As such, it has the potential to wreak havoc on methods such as Powell's, which effectively attempt to learn about the curvature of the

[8]However, we speculate that similar results could be obtained using a uniform distribution over $(-1, 1)$

objective from a sequence of line minimizations.

4 Experiments

Three sets of experiments were performed. For the first set, we compare the performance of Powell's method, KCD, and our novel stochastic search strategy. We then evaluate the performance of all three methods when the objective is regularized using the average of adjacent plateaus for window sizes varying from 3 to 7. Finally, we repeat the regularization experiment, but using the maximum objective value from the adjacent plateaus. These experiments were performed using the Chinese English evaluation data provided for NIST MT eval 2002, 2003, and 2005. MT02 was used as a dev set for MERT learning, while MT03 and MT05 were used as our test sets.

For all experiments, MERT training was performed using n-best lists from the decoder of size 100. During each iteration, the MERT search was performed once with a starting point of the weights used to generate the most recent set of n-best lists and then 5 more times using randomly selected starting points[9]. Of these, we retain the weights from the search that obtained the lowest objective value. Training continued until either decoding produced no novel entries for the combined n-best lists or none of the parameter values changed by more than 1e-5 across subsequent iterations.

4.1 System

Experiments were run using a right-to-left beam search decoder that achieves a matching BLEU score to Moses (Koehn et al., 2007) over a variety of data sets. Moreover, when using the same underlying model, the two decoders only produce translations that differ by one or more words 0.2% of the time. We made use of a stack size of 50 as it allowed for faster experiments while only performing modestly worse than a stack of 200. The distortion limit was set to 6. And, we retrieved 20 translation options for each unique source phrase.

Our phrase table was built using $1,140,693$ sentence pairs sampled from the GALE Y2 training data. The Chinese data was word segmented using the GALE Y2 retest release of the Stanford CRF segmenter (Tseng et al., 2005). Phrases were extracted using the typical approach described in Koehn et al. (2003) of running GIZA++ (Och & Ney, 2003) in both directions and then merging the alignments using the grow-diag-final heuristic. From the merged alignments we also extracted a bidirectional lexical reordering model conditioned on the source and the target phrases (Tillmann, 2004) (Koehn et al., 2007). A 5-gram language model was created using the SRI language modeling toolkit (Stolcke, 2002) and trained using the Gigaword corpus and English sentences from the parallel data.

Method	Dev MT02	Test MT03	Test MT05
KCD	30.967	30.778	29.580
Powell	30.638	30.692	29.780
Random	31.681	31.754	30.191

Table 3: BLEU scores obtained by models trained using the three different parameter search strategies: Powell's method, KCD, and stochastic search.

5 Results

As illustrated in table 3, Powell's method and KCD achieve a very similar level of performance, with KCD modestly outperforming Powell on the MT03 test set while Powell modestly outperforms coordinate descent on the MT05 test set. Moreover, the fact that Powell's algorithm did not perform better than KCD on the training data[10], and in fact actually performed modestly worse, suggests that Powell's additional search machinery does not provide much benefit for MERT objectives.

Similarly, the fact that the stochastic search obtains a much higher dev set score than either Powell or KCD indicates that it is doing a better job of optimizing the objective than either of the two alternatives. These gains suggest that stochastic search does make better use of the global minimum line search than the alternative methods. Or, alternatively, it strengthens the claim that the method succeeds at combining one of the critical strengths

[9]Only 5 random restarts were used due to time constraints. Ideally, a sizable number of random restarts should be used in order to minimize the degree to which the results are influenced by some runs receiving starting points that are better in general or perhaps better/worse w.r.t. their specific optimization strategy.

[10]This indicates that Powell failed to find a deeper minima in the objective, since recall that the unregularized objective is equivalent to the model's dev set performance.

Method	Window Avg	Dev MT02	Test MT03	Test MT05	Method	Window Max	Dev MT02	Test MT03	Test MT05
Coordinate	none	30.967	30.778	29.580	Coordinate	none	30.967	30.778	29.580
	3	31.665	**31.675**	**30.266**		3	31.536	**31.927**	**30.334**
	5	31.317	31.229	**30.182**		5	31.484	**31.702**	29.687
	7	31.205	**31.824**	30.149		7	31.627	31.294	**30.199**
Powell	none	30.638	30.692	29.780	Powell	none	30.638	30.692	29.780
	3	31.333	31.412	29.890		3	31.428	30.944	29.598
	5	31.748	**31.777**	**30.334**		5	31.407	**31.596**	30.090
	7	31.249	**31.571**	30.161		7	30.870	30.911	29.620
Random	none	31.681	31.754	30.191	Random	none	31.681	31.754	30.191
	3	31.548	31.778	30.263		3	31.179	30.898	29.529
	5	31.336	31.647	30.415		5	30.903	31.666	29.963
	7	30.501	29.336	28.372		7	31.920	31.906	30.674

Table 4: BLEU scores obtained when regularizing using the average loss of adjacent plateaus, left, and the maximum loss of adjacent plateaus, right. The none entry for each search strategy represents the baseline where no regularization is used. Statistically significant test set gains, $p < 0.01$, over the respective baselines are in bold face.

of Powell's method, diagonal search, with coordinate descent's robustness to the sudden jumps between regions that result from global line minimization. Using an approximate randomization test for statistical significance (Riezler & Maxwell, 2005), and with KCD as a baseline, the gains obtained by stochastic search on MT03 are statistically significant ($p = 0.002$), as are the gains on MT05 ($p = 0.005$).

Table 4 indicates that performing regularization by either averaging or taking the maximum of adjacent plateaus during the line search leads to gains for both Powell's method and KCD. However, no reliable additional gains appear to be had when stochastic search is combined with regularization.

It may seem surprising that the regularization gains for Powell & KCD are seen not only in the test sets but on the dev set as well. That is, in typical applications, regularization slightly decreases performance on the data used to train the model. However, this trend can in part be accounted for by the fact that during training, MERT is using n-best lists for objective evaluations rather than the more expensive process of running the decoder for each point that needs to be checked. As such, during each iteration of training, the decoding performance of the model actually represents its generalization performance relative to what was learned from the n-best lists created during prior iterations. Moreover, better generalization from the prior n-best lists can also help drive subsequent learning as there will then be more high quality translations on the n-best lists used for future iterations of learning. Additionally, regularization can reduce search errors by reducing the risk of getting stuck in spurious low loss pits that are in otherwise bad regions of the space.

6 Conclusions

We have presented two methods for improving the performance of MERT. The first is a novel stochastic search strategy that appears to make better use of Och (2003)'s algorithm for finding the global minimum along any given search direction than either coordinate descent or Powell's method. The second is a simple regularization scheme that leads to performance gains for both coordinate descent and Powell's method. However, no further gains are obtained by combining the stochastic search with regularization of the objective.

One quirk of the regularization scheme presented here is that the regularization applied to any given point in the objective varies depending upon what direction the point is approached from. We are currently looking at other similar regularization schemes that maintain consistent objective values regardless of the search direction.

Acknowledgments

We extend our thanks to our three anonymous reviewers,

particularly for the depth of analysis provided. This paper is based on work funded in part by the Defense Advanced Research Projects Agency through IBM.

References

Koehn, P., Hoang, H., Birch, A., Callison-Burch, C., Federico, M., Bertoldi, N., Cowan, B., Shen, W., Moran, C., Zens, R., Dyer, C., Bojar, O., Constantin, A., & Herbst, E. (2007). Moses: Open source toolkit for statistical machine translation. *In ACL.*

Koehn, P., Och, F. J., & Marcu, D. (2003). Statistical phrase-based translation. *In HLT-NAACL.*

Och, F.-J. (2003). Minimum error rate training in statistical machine translation. *In ACL.*

Och, F. J., & Ney, H. (2002). Discriminative training and maximum entropy models for statistical machine translation. *In ACL.*

Och, F. J., & Ney, H. (2003). A systematic comparison of various statistical alignment models. *Computational Linguistics*, *29*, 19–51.

Papineni, K., Roukos, S., Ward, T., & Zhu, W.-J. (2002). Bleu: a method for automatic evaluation of machine translation. *In ACL.*

Press, W. H., Teukolsky, S. A., Vetterling, W. T., & Flannery, B. P. (2007). *Numerical recipes 3rd edition: The art of scientific computing.* Cambridge University Press.

Riezler, S., & Maxwell, J. T. (2005). On some pitfalls in automatic evaluation and significance testing for mt. *In ACL.*

Smith, D. A., & Eisner, J. (2006). Minimum risk annealing for training log-linear models. *In ACL.*

Stolcke, A. (2002). Srilm – an extensible language modeling toolkit. *In ICSLP.*

Tillmann, C. (2004). A unigram orientation model for statistical machine translation. *In ACL.*

Tseng, H., Chang, P., Andrew, G., Jurafsky, D., & Manning, C. (2005). A conditional random field word segmenter for sighan bakeoff 2005. *In SIGHAN Workshop on Chinese Language Processing.*

Zens, R., Hasan, S., & Ney, H. (2007). A systematic comparison of training criteria for statistical machine translation. *In EMNLP.*

Learning Performance of a Machine Translation System: a Statistical and Computational Analysis

Marco Turchi **Tijl De Bie** **Nello Cristianini**
Dept. of Engineering Mathematics
University of Bristol,
Bristol, BS8 1TR, UK
{Marco.Turchi, Tijl.DeBie}@bristol.ac.uk
nello@support-vector.net

Abstract

We present an extensive experimental study of a Statistical Machine Translation system, Moses (Koehn et al., 2007), from the point of view of its learning capabilities. Very accurate learning curves are obtained, by using high-performance computing, and extrapolations are provided of the projected performance of the system under different conditions. We provide a discussion of learning curves, and we suggest that: 1) the representation power of the system is not currently a limitation to its performance, 2) the inference of its models from finite sets of i.i.d. data is responsible for current performance limitations, 3) it is unlikely that increasing dataset sizes will result in significant improvements (at least in traditional i.i.d. setting), 4) it is unlikely that novel statistical estimation methods will result in significant improvements. The current performance wall is mostly a consequence of Zipf's law, and this should be taken into account when designing a statistical machine translation system. A few possible research directions are discussed as a result of this investigation, most notably the integration of linguistic rules into the model inference phase, and the development of active learning procedures.

1 Introduction and Background

The performance of every learning system is the result of (at least) two combined effects: the representation power of the hypothesis class, determining how well the system can approximate the target behaviour; and statistical effects, determining how well the system can approximate the best element of the hypothesis class, based on finite and noisy training information. The two effects interact, with richer classes being better approximators of the target behaviour but requiring more training data to reliably identify the best hypothesis. The resulting trade-off, equally well known in statistics and in machine learning, can be expressed in terms of bias variance, capacity-control, or model selection. Various theories on learning curves have been proposed to deal with it, where a learning curve is a plot describing performance as a function of some parameters, typically training set size.

In the context of Statistical Machine Translation (SMT), where large bilingual corpora are used to train adaptive software to translate text, this task is further complicated by the peculiar distribution underlying the data, where the probability of encountering new words or expressions never vanishes. If we want to understand the potential and limitations of the current technology, we need to understand the interplay between these two factors affecting performance. In an age where the creation of intelligent behaviour is increasingly data driven, this is a question of great importance to all of Artificial Intelligence.

These observations lead us to an analysis of learning curves in machine translation, and to a number of related questions, including an analysis of the flexibility of the representation class used, an analysis of the stability of the models with respect to perturbations of the parameters, and an analysis of the computational resources needed to train these systems.

Using the open source package Moses (Koehn et

Proceedings of the Third Workshop on Statistical Machine Translation, pages 35–43,
Columbus, Ohio, USA, June 2008.

al., 2007) and the Spanish-English Europarl corpus (Koehn, 2005) we have performed a complete investigation of the influence of training set size on the quality of translations and on the cost of training; the influence of several design choices; the role of data sizes in training various components of the system. We use this data to inform a discussion about learning curves. An analysis of learning curves has previously been proposed by (Al-Onaizan et al., 1999). Recent advances in software, data availability and computing power have enabled us to undertake the present study, where very accurate curves are obtained on a large corpus.

Since our goal was to obtain high accuracy learning curves, that can be trusted both for comparing different system settings, and to extrapolate performance under unseen conditions, we conducted a large-scale series of tests, to reduce uncertainty in the estimations and to obtain the strongest possible signals. This was only possible, to the degree of accuracy needed by our analysis, by the extensive use of a high performance computer cluster over several weeks of computation.

One of our key findings is that the current performance is not limited by the representation power of the hypothesis class, but rather by model estimation from data. And that increasing of the size of the dataset is not likely to bridge that gap (at least not for realistic amounts in the i.i.d. setting), nor is the development of new parameter estimation principles. The main limitation seems to be a direct consequence of Zipf's law, and the introduction of constraints from linguistics seems to be an unavoidable step, to help the system in the identification of the optimal models without resorting to massive increases in training data, which would also result in significantly higher training times, and model sizes.

2 Statistical Machine Translation

What is the best function class to map Spanish documents into English documents? This is a question of linguistic nature, and has been the subject of a long debate. The de-facto answer came during the 1990's from the research community on Statistical Machine Translation, who made use of statistical tools based on a noisy channel model originally developed for speech recognition (Brown et al., 1994; Och and Weber, 1998; R.Zens et al., 2002; Och and Ney, 2001; Koehn et al., 2003). A Markovian language model, based on phrases rather than words, coupled with a phrase-to-phrase translation table are at the heart of most modern systems. Translating a text amounts to computing the most likely translation based on the available model parameters. Inferring the parameters of these models from bilingual corpora is a matter of statistics. By model inference we mean the task of extracting all tables, parameters and functions, from the corpus, that will be used to translate.

How far can this representation take us towards the target of achieving human-quality translations? Are the current limitations due to the approximation error of this representation, or to lack of sufficient training data? How much space for improvement is there, given new data or new statistical estimation methods or given different models with different complexities?

We investigate both the approximation and the estimation components of the error in machine translation systems. After analysing the two contributions, we focus on the role of various design choices in determining the statistical part of the error. We investigate learning curves, measuring both the role of the training set and the optimization set size, as well as the importance of accuracy in the numeric parameters.

We also address the trade-off between accuracy and computational cost. We perform a complete analysis of Moses as a learning system, assessing the various contributions to its performance and where improvements are more likely, and assessing computational and statistical aspects of the system.

A general discussion of learning curves in Moses-like systems and an extrapolation of performance are provided, showing that the estimation gap is unlikely to be closed by adding more data in realistic amounts.

3 Experimental Setup

We have performed a large number of detailed experiments. In this paper we report just a few, leaving the complete account of our benchmarking to a full journal version (Turchi et al., In preparation). Three experiments allow us to assess the most promising directions of research, from a machine learning point of view.

1. Learning curve showing translation performance as a function of training set size, where translation is performed on unseen sentences. The curves, describing the statistical part of the performance, are seen to grow very slowly with training set size.

2. Learning curve showing translation performance as a function of training set size, where translation is performed on known sentences. This was done to verify that the hypothesis class is indeed capable of representing high quality translations in the idealized case when all the necessary phrases have been observed in training phase. By limiting phrase length to 7 words, and using test sentences mostly longer than 20 words, we have ensured that this was a genuine task of decoding. We observed that translation in these idealized conditions is worse than human translation, but much better than machine translation of unseen sentences.

3. Plot of performance of a model when the numeric parameters are corrupted by an increasing amount of noise. This was done to simulate the effect of inaccurate parameter estimation algorithms (due either to imprecise objective functions, or to lack of sufficient statistics from the corpus). We were surprised to observe that accurate estimation of these parameters accounts for at most 10% of the final score. It is the actual list of phrases that forms the bulk of the knowledge in the system.

We conclude that the availability of the right models in the system would allow the system to have a much higher performance, but these models will not come from increased datasets or estimation procedures. Instead, they will come from the results of either the introduction of linguistic knowledge, or the introduction of query algorithms, themselves resulting necessarily from confidence estimation methods. Hence these appear to be the two most pressing questions in this research area.

3.1 Software

Moses (Koehn et al., 2007) is a complete translation toolkit for academic purposes. It provides all the components needed to create a machine translation system from one language to another. It contains different modules to preprocess data, train the language models and the translation models. These models can be tuned using minimum error rate training (Och, 2003). Moses uses standard external tools for some of these tasks, such as GIZA++ (Och and Ney, 2003) for word alignments and SRILM (Stolcke, 2002) for language modeling. Notice that Moses is a very sophisticated system, capable of learning translation tables, language models and decoding parameters from data. We analyse the contribution of each component to the overall score.

Given a parallel training corpus, Moses preprocesses it removing long sentences, lowercasing and tokenizing sentences. These sentences are used to train the language and translation models. This phase requires several steps as aligning words, computing the lexical translation, extracting phrases, scoring the phrases and creating the reordering model. When the models have been created, the development set is used to run the minimum error rate training algorithm to optimize their weights. We refer to that step as the optimization step in the rest of the paper. Test set is used to evaluate the quality of models on the data. The translated sentences are embedded in a sgm format, such that the quality of the translation can be evaluated using the most common machine translation scores. Moses provides BLEU (K.Papineni et al., 2001) and NIST (Doddington, 2002), but Meteor (Banerjee and Lavie, 2005; Lavie and Agarwal, 2007) and TER (Snover et al., 2006) can easily be used instead. NIST is used in this paper as evaluation score after we observed its high correlation to the other scores on the corpus (Turchi et al., In preparation).

All experiments have been run using the default parameter configuration of Moses. It means that Giza++ has used IBM model 1, 2, 3, and 4 with number of iterations for model 1 equal to 5, model 2 equal to 0, model 3 and 4 equal to 3; SRILM has used n-gram order equal to 3 and the Kneser-Ney smoothing algorithm; Mert has been run fixing to 100 the number of nbest target sentence for each develop sentence, and it stops when none of the weights changed more than 1e-05 or the nbest list does not change.

The training, development and test set sentences are tokenized and lowercased. The maximum number of tokens for each sentence in the training pair has been set to 50, whilst no limit is applied to the development or test set. TMs were limited to a phrase-length of 7 words and LMs were limited to 3.

3.2 Data

The Europarl Release v3 Spanish-English corpus has been used for the experiments. All the pairs of sentences are extracted from the proceedings of the European Parliament.

This dataset is made of three sets of pairs of sentences. Each of them has a different role: *training*, *development* and *test* set. The training set contains 1,259,914 pairs, while there are 2,000 pairs for development and test sets.

This work contains several experiments on different types and sizes of data set. To be consistent and to avoid anomalies due to overfitting or particular data combinations, each set of pairs of sentences have been randomly sampled. The number of pairs is fixed and a software selects them randomly from the whole original training, development or test set using a uniform distribution (bootstrap). Redundancy of pairs is allowed inside each subset.

3.3 Hardware

All the experiments have been run on a cluster machine, http://www.acrc.bris.ac.uk/acrc/hpc.htm. It includes 96 nodes each with two dual-core opteron processors, 8 GB of RAM memory per node (2 GB per core); 4 thick nodes each with four dual-core opteron processors, 32 GB of RAM memory per node (4 GB per core); ClearSpeed accelerator boards on the thick nodes; SilverStorm Infiniband high-speed connectivity throughout for parallel code message passing; General Parallel File System (GPFS) providing data access from all the nodes; storage - 11 terabytes. Each experiment has been run using one core and allocating 4Gb of RAM.

4 Experiments

4.1 Experiment 1: role of training set size on performance on new sentences

In this section we analyse how performance is affected by training set size, by creating learning curves (NIST score vs training set size).

We have created subsets of the complete corpus by sub-sampling sentences from a uniform distribution, with replacement. We have created 10 random subsets for each of the 20 chosen sizes, where each size represents 5%, 10%, etc of the complete corpus. For each subset a new instance of the SMT system has been created, for a total of 200 models. These have been optimized using a fixed size development set (of 2,000 sentences, not included in any other phase of the experiment). Two hundred experiments have then been run on an independent test set (of 2,000 sentences, also not included in any other phase of the experiment). This allowed us to calculate the mean and variance of NIST scores. This has been done for the models with and without the optimization step, hence producing the learning curves with error bars plotted in Figure 1, representing translation performance versus training set size, in the two cases.

The growth of the learning curve follows a typical pattern, growing fast at first, then slowing down (traditional learning curves are power laws, in theoretical models). In this case it appears to be growing even slower than a power law, which would be a surprise under traditional statistical learning theory models. In any case, the addition of massive amounts of data from the same distribution will result into smaller improvements in the performance. The small error bars that we have obtained also allow us to neatly observe the benefits of the optimization phase, which are small but clearly significant.

4.2 Experiment 2: role of training set size on performance on known sentences

The performance of a learning system depends both on the statistical estimation issues discussed in the previous subsection, and on functional approximation issues: how well can the function class reproduce the desired behaviour? In order to measure this quantity, we have performed an experiment much like the one described above, with one key differ-

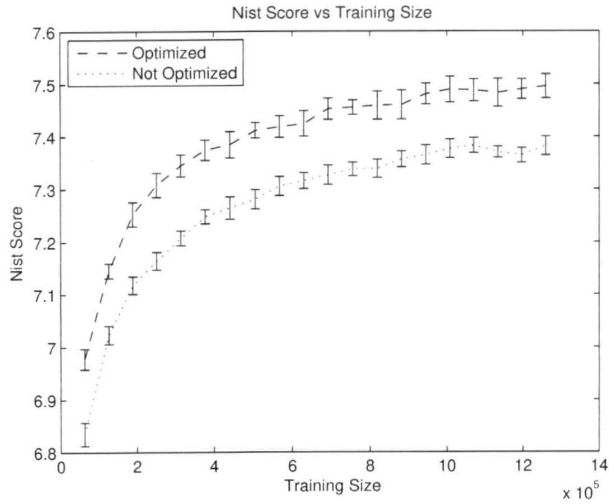

Figure 1: "Not Optimized" has been obtained using a fixed test set and no optimization phase. "Optimized" using a fixed test set and the optimization phase.

ence: the test set was selected randomly from the training set (after cleaning phase). In this way we are guaranteed that the system has seen all the necessary information in training phase, and we can assess its limitations in these very ideal conditions. We are aware this condition is extremely idealized and it will never happen in real life, but we wanted to have an upper bound on the performance achievable by this architecture if access to ideal data was not an issue. We also made sure that the performance on translating training sentences was not due to simple memorization of the entire sentence, verifying that the vast majority of the sentences were not present in the translation table (where the maximal phrase size was 7), not even in reduced form. Under these favourable conditions, the system obtained a NIST score of around 11, against a score of about 7.5 on unseen sentences. This suggests that the phrase-based Markov-chain representation is sufficiently rich to obtain a high score, if the necessary information is contained in the translation and language models.

For each model to be tested on known sentences, we have sampled ten subsets of 2,000 sentences each from the training set.

The "Optimized, Test on Training Set" learning curve, see figure 2, represents a possible upper bound on the best performance of this SMT system, since it has been computed in favourable conditions. It does suggest that this hypothesis class has the power of approximating the target behaviour more accurately than we could think based on performance on unseen sentences. If the right information has been seen, the system can reconstruct the sentences rather accurately. The NIST score computed using the reference sentences as target sentences is around 15, we identify the relative curve as "Human Translation". At this point, it seems likely that the process with which we learn the necessary tables representing the knowledge of the system is responsible for the performance limitations.

The gap between the "Optimized, Test on Training Set" and the "Optimized" curves is even more interesting if related to the slow growth rate in the previous learning curve: although the system can represent internally a good model of translation, it seems unlikely that this will ever be inferred by increasing the size of training datasets in realistic amounts.

The training step results in various forms of knowledge: translation table, language model and parameters from the optimization. The internal models learnt by the system are essentially lists of phrases, with probabilities associated to them. Which of these components is mostly responsible for performance limitations?

4.3 Experiment 3: effect on performance of increasing noise levels in parameters

Much research has focused on devising improved principles for the statistical estimation of the parameters in language and translation models. The introduction of discriminative graphical models has marked a departure from traditional maximum likelihood estimation principles, and various approaches have been proposed.

The question is: how much information is contained in the fine grain structure of the probabilities estimated by the model? Is the performance improving with more data because certain parameters are estimated better, or just because the lists are growing? In the second case, it is likely that more sophisticated statistical algorithms to improve the estimation of probabilities will have limited impact.

In order to simulate the effect of inaccurate estimation of the numeric parameters, we have added increasing amount of noise to them. This can either represent the effect of insufficient statistics in estimating them, or the use of imperfect parameter esti-

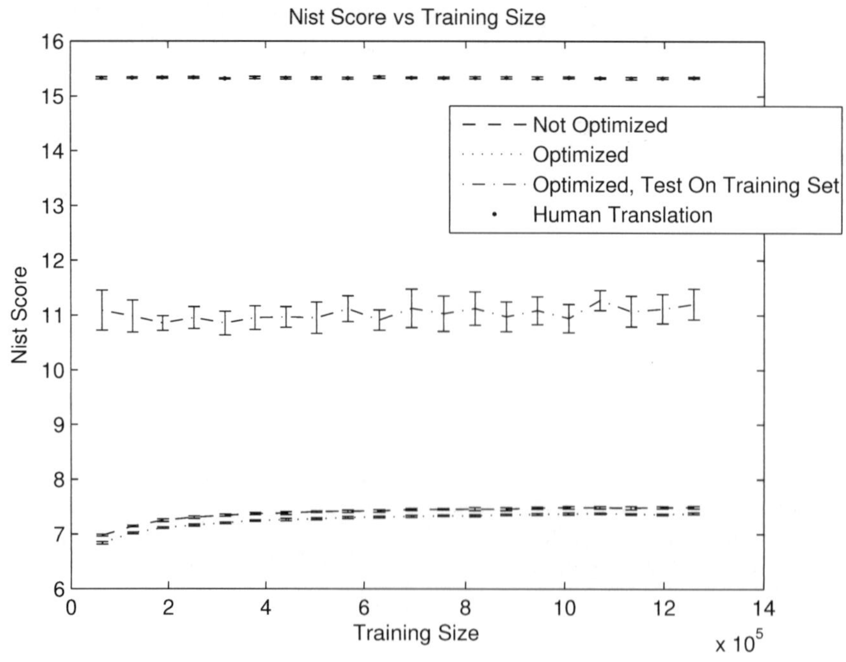

Figure 2: Four learning curves have been compared. "Not Optimized" has been obtained using a fixed test set and no optimization phase. "Optimized" using a fixed test set and the optimization phase. "Optimized Test On Training Set" a test set selected by the training set for each training set size and the optimization phase. "Human Translation" has been obtained by computing NIST using the reference English sentence of the test set as target sentences.

mation biases. We have corrupted the parameters in the language and translation models, by adding increasing levels of noise to them, and measured the effect of this on performance.

One model trained with 62,995 pairs of sentences has been chosen from the experiments in Section 4.1. A percentage of noise has been added to each probability in the language model, including conditional probability and back off, translation model, bidirectional translation probabilities and lexicalized weighting. Given a probability p and a percentage of noise, pn, a value has been randomly selected from the interval [$-x$,$+x$], where $x = p * pn$, and added to p. If this quantity is bigger than one it has been approximated to one. Different values of percentage have been used. For each value of pn, five experiment have been run. The optimization step has not been run.

We see from Figure 3 that the performance does not seem to depend crucially on the fine structure of the parameter vectors, and that even a large addition of noise (100%) produces a 10% decline in NIST score. This suggests that it is the list itself, rather

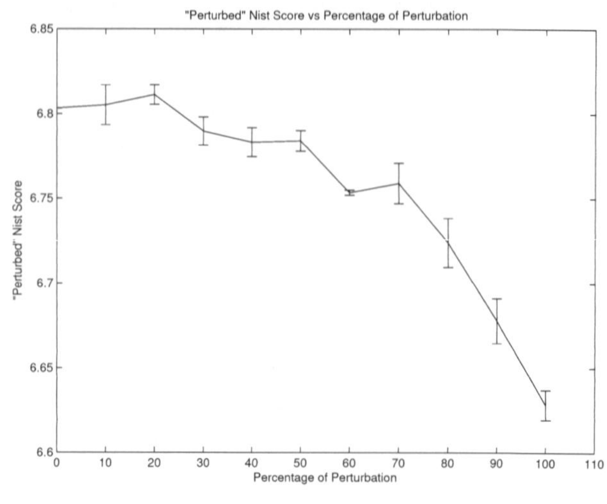

Figure 3: Each probability of the language and translation models has been perturbed adding a percentage of noise. This learning curve reports the not optimized NIST score versus the percentage of perturbation applied. These results have been obtained using a fixed training set size equal to 62,995 pairs of sentences.

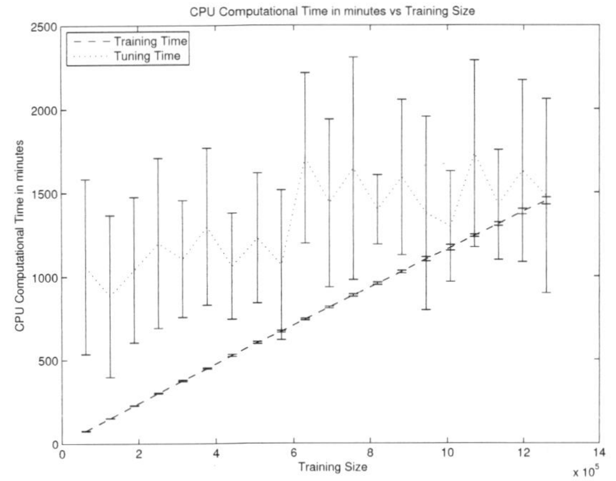

Figure 4: Training and tuning user time vs training set size. Time quantities are expressed in minutes.

than the probabilities in it, that controls the performance. Different estimation methods can produce different parameters, but this does not seem to matter very much. The creation of a more complete list of words, however, seems to be the key to improve the score. Combined with the previous findings, this would mean that neither more data nor better statistics will bridge the performance gap. The solution might have to be found elsewhere, and in our Discussion section we outline a few possible avenues.

5 Computational Cost

The computational cost of models creation and development-phase has been measured during the creation of the learning curves. Despite its efficiency in terms of data usage, the development phase has a high cost in computational terms, if compared with the cost of creating the complete language and translation models.

For each experiment, the user CPU time is computed as the sum of the user time of the main process and the user time of the children.

These quantities are collected for training, development, testing and evaluation phases. In figure 4, training and tuning user times are plotted as a function of the training set size. It is evident that increasing the training size causes an increase in training time in a roughly linear fashion.

It is hard to find a similar relationship for the tuning time of the development phase. In fact, the tuning time is strictly connected with the optimization algorithm and the sentences in the development set. We can also see in figure 4 that even a small development set size can require a large amount of tuning time. Each point of the tuning time curve has a big variance. The tuning phase involves translating the development set many times and hence its cost depends very weakly on the training set size, since a large training set leads to larger tables and these lead to slightly longer test times.

6 Discussion

The impressive capability of current machine translation systems is not only a testament to an incredibly productive and creative research community, but can also be seen as a paradigm for other Artificial Intelligence tasks. Data driven approaches to all main areas of AI currently deliver the state of the art performance, from summarization to speech recognition to machine vision to information retrieval. And statistical learning technology is central to all approaches to data driven AI.

Understanding how sophisticated behaviour can be learnt from data is hence not just a concern for machine learning, or to individual applied communities, such as Statistical Machine Translation, but rather a general concern for modern Artificial Intelligence. The analysis of learning curves, and the identification of the various limitations to performance is a crucial part of the machine learning method, and one where statistics and algorithmics interact closely.

In the case of Statistical Machine Translation, the analysis of Moses suggests that the current bottleneck is the lack of sufficient data, not the function class used for the representation of translation systems. The clear gap between performance on training and testing set, together with the rate of the learning curves, suggests that improvements may be possible but not by adding more data in i.i.d. way as done now. The perturbation analysis suggests that improved statistical principles are unlikely to make a big difference either.

Since it is unlikely that sufficient data will be available by simply sampling a distribution, one needs to address a few possible ways to transfer large amounts of knowledge into the system. All of them lead to open problems either in machine learning or in machine translation, most of them having been already identified by their respective communities as important questions. They are actively being worked on.

The gap between performances on training and on test sets is typically affected by model selection choices, ultimately controlling the trade off between overfitting and underfitting. In these experiments the system used phrases of length 7 or less. Changing this parameter might reflect on the gap and this is the focus of our current work.

A research programme naturally follows from our analysis. The first obvious approach is an effort to identify or produce datasets on demand (active learning, where the learning system can request translations of specific sentences, to satisfy its information needs). This is a classical machine learning question, that however comes with the need for further theoretical work, since it breaks the traditional i.i.d. assumptions on the origin of data. Furthermore, it would also require an effective way to do confidence estimation on translations, as traditional active learning approaches are effectively based on the identification (or generation) of instances where there is low confidence in the output (Blatz et al., 2004; Ueffing and Ney, 2004; Ueffing and Ney, 2005b; Ueffing and Ney, 2005a).

The second natural direction involves the introduction of significant domain knowledge in the form of linguistic rules, so to dramatically reduce the amount of data needed to essentially reconstruct them by using statistics. These rules could take the form of generation of artificial training data, based on existing training data, or a posteriori expansion of translation and language tables. Any way to enforce linguistic constraints will result in a reduced need for data, and ultimately in more complete models, given the same amount of data (Koehn and Hoang, 2007).

Obviously, it is always possible that the identification of radically different representations of language might introduce totally different constraints on both approximation and estimation error, and this might be worth considering.

What is not likely to work. It does not seem that the introduction of more data will change the situation significantly, as long as the data is sampled i.i.d. from the same distribution. It also does not seem that more flexible versions of Markov models would be likely to change the situation. Finally, it does not seem that new and different methods to estimate probabilities would make much of a difference. Our perturbation studies show that significant amounts of noise in the parameters result into very small variations in the performance. Note also that the current algorithm is not even working on refining the probability estimates, as the rate of growth of the tables suggests that new n-grams are constantly appearing, reducing the proportion of time spent refining probabilities of old n-grams.

It does seem that the control of the performance relies on the length of the translation and language tables. Ways are needed to make these tables grow much faster as a function of training set size; they can either involve active selection of documents to translate, or the incorporation of linguistic rules to expand the tables without using extra data.

It is important to note that many approaches suggested above are avenues currently being actively pursued, and this analysis might be useful to decide which one of them should be given priority.

7 Conclusions

We have started a series of extensive experimental evaluations of performance of Moses, using high performance computing, with the goal of understanding the system from a machine learning point of view, and use this information to identify weaknesses of the system that can lead to improvements. We have performed many more experiments that cannot be reported in this workshop paper, and will be published in a longer report (Turchi et al., In preparation). In general, our goal is to extrapolate the performance of the system under many conditions, to be able to decide which directions of research are most likely to deliver improvements in performance.

Acknowledgments

Marco Turchi is supported by the EU Project SMART. The authors thank Callum Wright, Bristol HPC Systems Administrator, and Moses mailing list.

References

Y. Al-Onaizan, J. Curin, M. Jahr, K. Knight, J. Lafferty, D. Melamed, F. J. Och, D. Purdy, N. A. Smith, and D. Yarowsky. 1999. Statistical machine translation: Final report. Technical report, Johns Hopkins University 1999 Summer Workshop on Language Engineering, Center for Speech and Language Processing.

S. Banerjee and A. Lavie. 2005. Meteor: An automatic metric for mt evaluation with improved correlation with human judgments. In *ACL '05: Proceedings of the 43rd Annual Meeting on Association for Computational Linguistics*, Morristown, NJ, USA. Association for Computational Linguistics.

J. Blatz, E. Fitzgerald, G. Foster, S. Gandrabur, C. Goutte, A. Kulesza, A. Sanchis, and N. Ueffing. 2004. Confidence estimation for machine translation. In *COLING '04: Proceedings of the 20th international conference on Computational Linguistics*, page 315, Morristown, NJ, USA. Association for Computational Linguistics.

P. F. Brown, S. Della Pietra, V.t J. Della Pietra, and R. L. Mercer. 1994. The mathematic of statistical machine translation: Parameter estimation. *Computational Linguistics*, 19(2):263–311.

G. Doddington. 2002. Automatic evaluation of machine translation quality using n-gram co-occurrence statistics. In *Proceedings of the second international conference on Human Language Technology Research*, pages 138–145, San Francisco, CA, USA. Morgan Kaufmann Publishers Inc.

P. Koehn and H. Hoang. 2007. Factored translation models. In *Proceedings of the 2007 Joint Conference on Empirical Methods in Natural Language Processing and Computational Natural Language Learning (EMNLP-CoNLL)*, pages 868–876.

P. Koehn, F. J. Och, and D. Marcu. 2003. Statistical phrase-based translation. In *NAACL '03: Proceedings of the 2003 Conference of the North American Chapter of the Association for Computational Linguistics on Human Language Technology*, pages 48–54, Morristown, NJ, USA. Association for Computational Linguistics.

P. Koehn, H. Hoang, A. Birch, C. Callison-Burch, M. Federico, N. Bertoldi, B. Cowan, W. Shen, C. Moran, R. Zens, C. Dyer, O. Bojar, A. Constantin, and E. Herbst. 2007. Moses: Open source toolkit for statistical machine translation. In *the Annual Meeting of the Association for Computational Linguistics, demonstration session.*

P. Koehn. 2005. Europarl: A parallel corpus for statistical machine translation. In *Machine Translation Summit X*, pages 79–86.

K.Papineni, S. Roukos, T. Ward, and W. J. Zhu. 2001. Bleu: a method for automatic evaluation of machine translation. In *Proceedings of ACL '02*, pages 311–318, Morristown, NJ, USA. Association for Computational Linguistics.

A. Lavie and A. Agarwal. 2007. Meteor: An automatic metric for mt evaluation with high levels of correlation with human judgments. In *ACL '07: Proceedings of 45th Annual Meeting of the Association for Computational Linguistics.* Association for Computational Linguistics.

F. J. Och and H. Ney. 2001. Discriminative training and maximum entropy models for statistical machine translation. In *Proceedings of ACL '02*, pages 295–302, Morristown, NJ, USA. Association for Computational Linguistics.

F. J. Och and H. Ney. 2003. A systematic comparison of various statistical alignment models. *Computational Linguistics*, 29(1):19–51.

F. J. Och and H. Weber. 1998. Improving statistical natural language translation with categories and rules. In *COLING-ACL*, pages 985–989.

F. J. Och. 2003. Minimum error rate training in statistical machine translation. In *Proceedings of ACL '03*, pages 160–167, Morristown, NJ, USA. Association for Computational Linguistics.

R.Zens, F. J.Och, and H. Ney. 2002. Phrase-based statistical machine translation. In *KI '02: Proceedings of the 25th Annual German Conference on AI*, pages 18–32, London, UK. Springer-Verlag.

M. Snover, B. Dorr, R. Schwartz, L. Micciulla, and J. Makhoul. 2006. A study of translation edit rate with targeted human annotation. In *Proceedings of the 7th Conference of the Association for Machine Translation in the Americas*, pages 223–231. Association for Machine Translation in the Americas.

A. Stolcke. 2002. Srilm – an extensible language modeling toolkit. In *Intl. Conf. on Spoken Language Processing.*

M. Turchi, T. De Bie, and N. Cristianini. In preparation. Learning analysis of a machine translation system.

N. Ueffing and H. Ney. 2004. Bayes decision rules and confidence measures for statistical machine translation. In *EsTAL-2004*, pages 70–81.

N. Ueffing and H. Ney. 2005a. Application of word-level confidence measures in interactive statistical machine translation. In *EAMT-2005*, pages 262–270.

N. Ueffing and H. Ney. 2005b. Word-level confidence estimation for machine translation using phrase-based translation models. In *Proceedings of HLT '05*, pages 763–770, Morristown, NJ, USA. Association for Computational Linguistics.

Using Syntax to Improve Word Alignment Precision for Syntax-Based Machine Translation

Victoria Fossum
Dept. of Computer Science
University of Michigan
Ann Arbor, MI 48104
vfossum@umich.edu

Kevin Knight
Information Sciences Institute
University of Southern California
Marina del Rey, CA 90292
knight@isi.edu

Steven Abney
Dept. of Linguistics
University of Michigan
Ann Arbor, MI 48104
abney@umich.edu

Abstract

Word alignments that violate syntactic correspondences interfere with the extraction of string-to-tree transducer rules for syntax-based machine translation. We present an algorithm for identifying and deleting incorrect word alignment links, using features of the extracted rules. We obtain gains in both alignment quality and translation quality in Chinese-English and Arabic-English translation experiments relative to a GIZA++ union baseline.

1 Introduction

1.1 Motivation

Word alignment typically constitutes the first stage of the statistical machine translation pipeline. GIZA++ (Och and Ney, 2003), an implementation of the IBM (Brown et al., 1993) and HMM (?) alignment models, is the most widely-used alignment system. GIZA++ *union* alignments have been used in the state-of-the-art syntax-based statistical MT system described in (Galley et al., 2006) and in the hierarchical phrase-based system Hiero (Chiang, 2007). GIZA++ *refined* alignments have been used in state-of-the-art phrase-based statistical MT systems such as (Och, 2004); variations on the refined heuristic have been used by (Koehn et al., 2003) (*diag* and *diag-and*) and by the phrase-based system Moses (*grow-diag-final*) (Koehn et al., 2007).

GIZA++ union alignments have high recall but low precision, while *intersection* or refined alignments have high precision but low recall.[1] There are two natural approaches to improving upon GIZA++ alignments, then: deleting links from union alignments, or adding links to intersection or refined alignments. In this work, we delete links from GIZA++ union alignments to improve precision.

The low precision of GIZA++ union alignments poses a particular problem for syntax-based rule extraction algorithms such as (Quirk et al., 2005; Galley et al., 2006; Huang et al., 2006; Liu et al., 2006): if the incorrect links violate syntactic correspondences, they force the rule extraction algorithm to extract rules that are large in size, few in number, and poor in generalization ability.

Figure 1 illustrates this problem: the dotted line represents an incorrect link in the GIZA++ union alignment. Using the rule extraction algorithm described in (Galley et al., 2004), we extract the rules shown in the leftmost column (R1–R4). Rule R1 is large and unlikely to generalize well. If we delete the incorrect link in Figure 1, we can extract the rules shown in the rightmost column (R2–R9): Rule R1, the largest rule from the initial set, disappears, and several smaller, more modular rules (R5–R9) replace it.

In this work, we present a supervised algorithm that uses these two features of the extracted rules (size of largest rule and total number of rules), as well as a handful of structural and lexical features, to automatically identify and delete incorrect links from GIZA++ union alignments. We show that link

[1] For a complete discussion of alignment symmetrization heuristics, including union, intersection, and refined, refer to (Och and Ney, 2003).

Proceedings of the Third Workshop on Statistical Machine Translation, pages 44–52,
Columbus, Ohio, USA, June 2008.

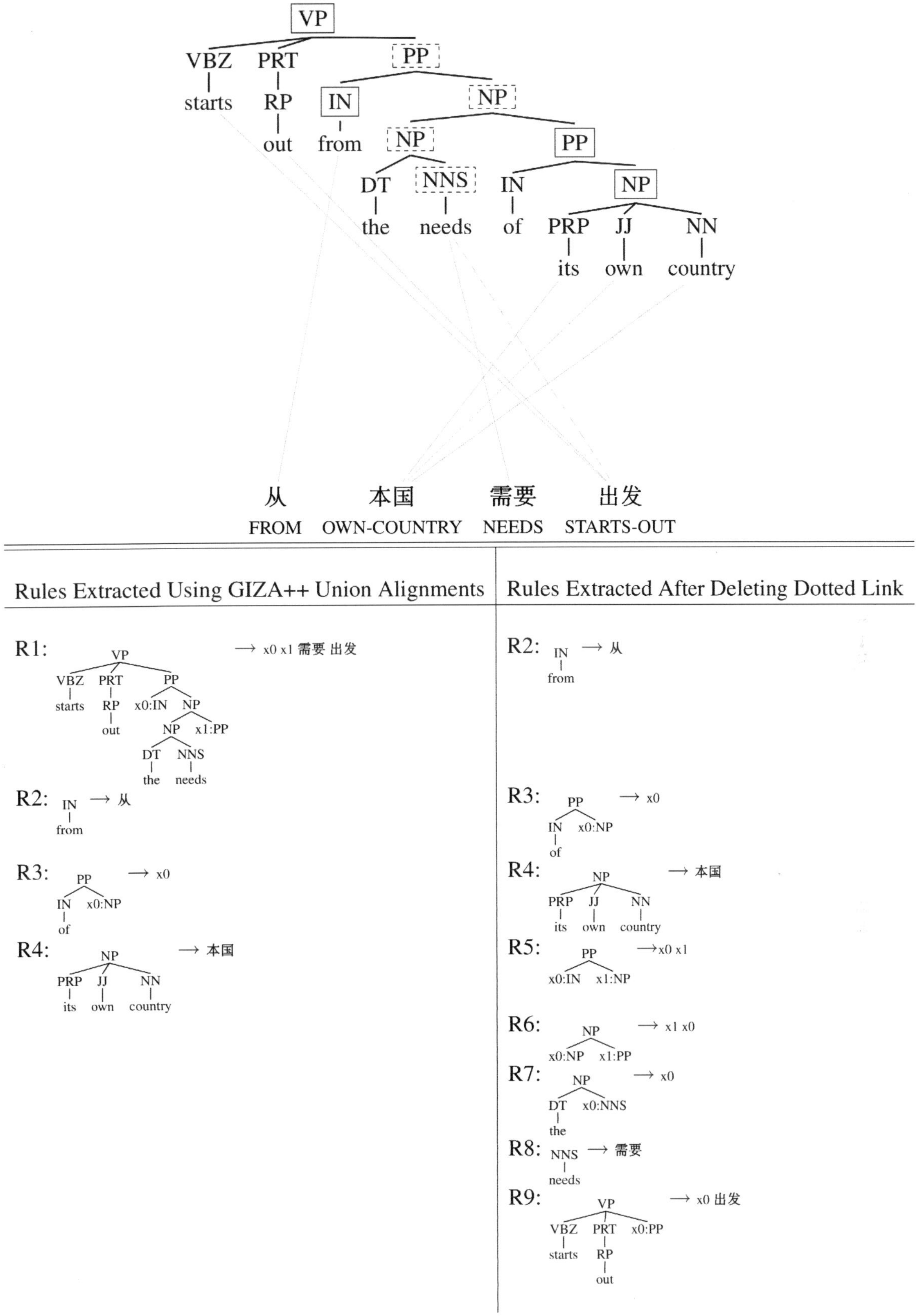

Figure 1: The impact of incorrect alignment links upon rule extraction. Using the original alignment (including all links shown) leads to the extraction of the tree-to-string transducer rules whose left hand sides are rooted at the solid boxed nodes in the parse tree (R1, R2, R3, and R4). Deleting the dotted alignment link leads to the omission of rule R1, the extraction of R9 in its place, the extraction of R2, R3, and R4 as before, and the extraction of additional rules whose left hand sides are rooted at the dotted boxed nodes in the parse tree (R5, R6, R7, R8).

deletion improves alignment quality and translation quality in Chinese-English and Arabic-English MT, relative to a strong baseline. Our link deletion algorithm is easy to implement, runs quickly, and has been used by a top-scoring MT system in the Chinese newswire track of the 2008 NIST evaluation.

1.2 Related Work

Recently, discriminative methods for alignment have rivaled the quality of IBM Model 4 alignments (Liu et al., 2005; Ittycheriah and Roukos, 2005; Taskar et al., 2005; Moore et al., 2006; Fraser and Marcu, 2007b). However, except for (Fraser and Marcu, 2007b), none of these advances in alignment quality has improved translation quality of a state-of-the-art system. We use a discriminatively trained model to identify and delete incorrect links, and demonstrate that these gains in alignment quality lead to gains in translation quality in a state-of-the-art syntax-based MT system. In contrast to the semi-supervised LEAF alignment algorithm of (Fraser and Marcu, 2007b), which requires 1,500-2,000 CPU *days* per iteration to align 8.4M Chinese-English sentences (anonymous, p.c.), link deletion requires only 450 CPU *hours* to re-align such a corpus (after initial alignment by GIZA++, which requires 20-24 CPU days).

Several recent works incorporate syntactic features into alignment. (May and Knight, 2007) use syntactic constraints to re-align a parallel corpus that has been aligned by GIZA++ as follows: they extract string-to-tree transducer rules from the corpus, the target parse trees, and the alignment; discard the initial alignment; use the extracted rules to construct a forest of possible string-to-tree derivations for each string/tree pair in the corpus; use EM to select the Viterbi derivation tree for each pair; and finally, induce a new alignment from the Viterbi derivations, using the re-aligned corpus to train a syntax-based MT system. (May and Knight, 2007) differs from our approach in two ways: first, the set of possible re-alignments they consider for each sentence pair is limited by the initial GIZA++ alignments seen over the training corpus, while we consider all alignments that can be reached by deleting links from the initial GIZA++ alignment for that sentence pair. Second, (May and Knight, 2007) use a time-intensive training algorithm to select the best re-alignment for each sentence pair, while we use a fast greedy search to determine which links to delete; in contrast to (May and Knight, 2007), who require 400 CPU hours to re-align 330k Chinese-English sentence pairs (anonymous, p.c), link deletion requires only 18 CPU hours to re-align such a corpus.

(Lopez and Resnik, 2005) and (Denero and Klein, 2007) modify the distortion model of the HMM alignment model (Vogel et al., 1996) to reflect tree distance rather than string distance; (Cherry and Lin, 2006) modify an ITG aligner by introducing a penalty for induced parses that violate syntactic bracketing constraints. Similarly to these approaches, we use syntactic bracketing to constrain alignment, but our work extends beyond improving alignment quality to improve translation quality as well.

2 Link Deletion

We propose an algorithm to re-align a parallel bitext that has been aligned by GIZA++ (IBM Model 4), then symmetrized using the union heuristic. We then train a syntax-based translation system on the re-aligned bitext, and evaluate whether the re-aligned bitext yields a better translation model than a baseline system trained on the GIZA++ union aligned bitext.

2.1 Link Deletion Algorithm

Our algorithm for re-alignment proceeds as follows. We make a single pass over the corpus. For each sentence pair, we initialize the alignment $A = A_{initial}$ (the GIZA++ union alignment for that sentence pair). We represent the score of A as a weighted linear combination of features h_i of the alignment A, the target parse tree $parse(e)$ (a phrase-structure syntactic representation of e), and the source string f:

$$score(A) = \sum_{i=0}^{n} \lambda_i \cdot h_i(A, parse(e), f)$$

We define a *branch* of links to be a *contiguous* 1-to-many alignment.[2] We define two alignments, A

[2]In Figure 1, the 1-to-many alignment formed by {本国-its, 本国- own,本国-country} constitutes a branch, but the 1-to-many alignment formed by {出发-starts,出发-out,出发-needs} does not.

and A', to be *neighbors* if they differ only by the deletion of a link or *branch* of links. We consider all alignments A' in the *neighborhood* of A, greedily deleting the link l or branch of links b maximizing the score of the resulting alignment $A' = A \setminus l$ or $A' = A \setminus b$. We delete links until no further increase in the score of A is possible.[3]

In section 2.2 we describe the features h_i, and in section 2.4 we describe how to set the weights λ_i.

2.2 Features

2.2.1 Syntactic Features

We use two features of the string-to-tree transducer rules extracted from A, $parse(e)$, and f according to the rule extraction algorithm described in (Galley et al., 2004):

ruleCount: Total number of rules extracted from A, $parse(e)$, and f. As Figure 1 illustrates, incorrect links violating syntactic brackets tend to decrease **ruleCount**; **ruleCount** increases from 4 to 8 after deleting the incorrect link.

sizeOfLargestRule: The size, measured in terms of internal nodes in the target parse tree, of the single largest rule extracted from A, $parse(e)$, and f. In Figure 1, the largest rules in the leftmost and rightmost columns are R1 (with 9 internal nodes) and R9 (with 4 internal nodes), respectively.

2.2.2 Structural Features

wordsUnaligned: Total number of unaligned words.

1-to-many Links: Total number of links for which one word is aligned to multiple words, in either direction. In Figure 1, the links {出发-starts,出发-out,出发-needs} represent a 1-to-many alignment. 1-to-many links appear more frequently in GIZA++ union alignments than in gold alignments, and are therefore good candidates for deletion. The category of 1-to-many links is further subdivided, depending on the degree of *contiguity* that the link exhibits with its neighbors.[4] Each link in a 1-to-many alignment can have 0, 1, or 2 neighbors, according to how many links are adjacent to it in the 1-to-many alignment:

zeroNeighbors: In Figure 1, the link 出发-needs has 0 neighbors.

oneNeighbor: In Figure 1, the links 出发-starts and 出发-out each have 1 neighbor–namely, each other.

twoNeighbors: In Figure 1, in the 1-to-many alignment formed by {本国-its,本国-own,本国-country}, the link 本国-own has 2 neighbors, namely 本国-it and 本国-country.

2.2.3 Lexical Features

highestLexProbRank: A link e_i-f_j is "max-probable from e_i to f_j" if $p(f_j|e_i) > p(f_{j'}|e_i)$ for all alternative words $f_{j'}$ with which e_i is aligned in $A_{initial}$. In Figure 1, $p(\text{需要}|needs) > p(\text{出发}|needs)$, so 需要-needs is max-probable for "needs". The definition of "max-probable from f_j to e_i" is analogous, and a link is max-probable (nondirectionally) if it is max-probable in either direction. The value of **highestLexProbRank** is the total number of max-probable links. The conditional lexical probabilities $p(e_i|f_j)$ and $p(f_j|e_i)$ are estimated using frequencies of aligned word pairs in the high-precision GIZA++ *intersection* alignments for the training corpus.

2.2.4 History Features

In addition to the above syntactic, structural, and lexical features of A, we also incorporate two features of the link deletion history itself into $Score(A)$:

linksDeleted: Total number of links deleted $A_{initial}$ thus far. At each iteration, either a link or a branch of links is deleted.

[3] While using a dynamic programming algorithm would likely improve search efficiency and allow link deletion to find an optimal solution, in practice, the greedy search runs quickly and improves alignment quality.

[4] (Deng and Byrne, 2005) observe that, in a manually aligned Chinese-English corpus, 82% of the Chinese words that are aligned to multiple English words are aligned to a *contiguous* block of English words; similarly, 88% of the English words that are aligned to multiple Chinese words are aligned to a *contiguous* block of Chinese words. Thus, if a Chinese word is correctly aligned to multiple English words, those English words are likely to be "neighbors" of each other, and if an English word is correctly aligned to multiple Chinese words, those Chinese words are likely to be "neighbors" of each other.

stepsTaken: Total number of iterations thus far in the search; at each iteration, either a link or a branch is deleted. This feature serves as a constant cost function per step taken during link deletion.

2.3 Constraints

Protecting Refined Links from Deletion: Since GIZA++ refined links have higher precision than union links[5], we do not consider any GIZA++ refined links for deletion.[6]

Stoplist: In our Chinese-English corpora, the 10 most common English words (excluding punctuation marks) include {a,in,to,of,and,the}, while the 10 most common Chinese words include {了,是,在,和,的}. Of these, {a,the} and {了,的} have no explicit translational equivalent in the other language. These words are aligned with each other frequently (and erroneously) by GIZA++ union, but rarely in the gold standard. We delete all links in the set {a, an, the} × {的, 了} from $A_{initial}$ as a preprocessing step.[7]

2.4 Perceptron Training

We set the feature weights λ using a modified version of averaged perceptron learning with structured outputs (Collins, 2002). Following (Moore, 2005), we initialize the value of our expected most informative feature (**ruleCount**) to 1.0, and initialize all other feature weights to 0. During each pass over the discriminative training set, we "decode" each sentence pair by greedily deleting links from $A_{initial}$ in order to maximize the score of the resulting alignment using the current settings of λ (for details, refer to section 2.1).

We construct a set of candidate alignments $A_{candidates}$ for use in reranking as follows. Starting with $A = A_{initial}$, we iteratively explore all alignments A' in the *neighborhood* of A, adding each *neighbor* to $A_{candidates}$, then selecting the *neighbor* that maximizes $Score(A')$. When it is no longer possible to increase $Score(A)$ by deleting any links, link deletion concludes and returns the highest-scoring alignment, $A_{1\text{-}best}$.

In general, $A_{gold} \notin A_{candidates}$; following (Collins, 2000) and (Charniak and Johnson, 2005) for parse reranking and (Liang et al., 2006) for translation reranking, we define A_{oracle} as alignment in $A_{candidates}$ that is most *similar* to A_{gold}.[8] We update each feature weight λ_i as follows: $\lambda_i = \lambda_i + h_i^{A_{oracle}} - h_i^{A_{1\text{-}best}}$.[9]

Following (Moore, 2005), after each training pass, we average all the feature weight vectors seen during the pass, and decode the discriminative training set using the vector of averaged feature weights. When alignment quality stops increasing on the discriminative training set, perceptron training ends.[10] The weight vector returned by perceptron training is the average over the training set of all weight vectors seen during all iterations; averaging reduces overfitting on the training set (Collins, 2002).

3 Experimental Setup

3.1 Data Sets

We evaluate the effect of link deletion upon alignment quality and translation quality for two Chinese-English data sets, and one Arabic-English data set. Each data set consists of newswire, and contains a small subset of manually aligned sentence pairs. We divide the manually aligned subset into a training set (used to discriminatively set the feature weights for link deletion) and a test set (used to evaluate the impact of link deletion upon alignment quality). Table 1 lists the source and the size of the manually aligned training and test sets used for each alignment task.

[5]On a 400-sentence-pair Chinese-English data set, GIZA++ union alignments have a precision of 77.32 while GIZA++ refined alignments have a precision of 85.26.

[6]To see how GIZA++ refined alignments compare to GIZA++ union alignments for syntax-based translation, we compare systems trained on each set of alignments for Chinese-English translation task A. Union alignments result in a test set BLEU score of 41.17, as compared to only 36.99 for refined.

[7]The impact upon alignment f-measure of deleting these stoplist links is small; on Chinese-English Data Set A, the f-measure of the baseline GIZA++ union alignments on the test set increases from 63.44 to 63.81 after deleting stoplist links, while the remaining increase in f-measure from 63.81 to 75.14 (shown in Table 3) is due to the link deletion algorithm itself.

[8]We discuss alignment similarity metrics in detail in Section 3.2.

[9](Liang et al., 2006) report that, for translation reranking, such *local* updates (towards the oracle) outperform *bold* updates (towards the gold standard).

[10]We discuss alignment quality metrics in detail in Section 3.2.

Using the feature weights learned on the manually aligned training set, we then apply link deletion to the remainder (non-manually aligned) of each bilingual data set, and train a full syntax-based statistical MT system on these sentence pairs. After maximum BLEU tuning (Och, 2003a) on a held-out tuning set, we evaluate translation quality on a held-out test set. Table 2 lists the source and the size of the training, tuning, and test sets used for each translation task.

3.2 Evaluation Metrics

AER (Alignment Error Rate) (Och and Ney, 2003) is the most widely used metric of alignment quality, but requires gold-standard alignments labelled with "sure/possible" annotations to compute; lacking such annotations, we can compute alignment f-measure instead.

However, (Fraser and Marcu, 2007a) show that, in phrase-based translation, improvements in AER or f-measure do not necessarily correlate with improvements in BLEU score. They propose two modifications to f-measure: varying the precision/recall tradeoff, and *fully-connecting* the alignment links before computing f-measure.[11]

Weighted Fully-Connected F-Measure Given a hypothesized set of alignment links H and a gold-standard set of alignment links G, we define $H^+ = fullyConnect(H)$ and $G^+ = fullyConnect(G)$, and then compute:

$$f\text{-}measure(H^+) = \frac{1}{\frac{\alpha}{precision(H^+)} + \frac{1-\alpha}{recall(H^+)}}$$

For phrase-based Chinese-English and Arabic-English translation tasks, (Fraser and Marcu, 2007a) obtain the closest correlation between weighted fully-connected alignment f-measure and BLEU score using α=0.5 and α=0.1, respectively. We use weighted fully-connected alignment f-measure as the training criterion for link deletion, and to evaluate alignment quality on training and test sets.

Rule F-Measure To evaluate the impact of link deletion upon rule quality, we compare the rule precision, recall, and f-measure of the rule set extracted from our hypothesized alignments and a Collins-style parser against the rule set extracted from gold alignments and gold parses.

BLEU For all translation tasks, we report case-insensitive NIST BLEU scores (Papineni et al., 2002) using 4 references per sentence.

Language	Train	Test
Chinese-English A	400	400
Chinese-English B	1500	1500
Arabic-English	1500	1500

Table 1: Size (sentence pairs) of data sets used in alignment link deletion tasks

3.3 Experiments

Starting with GIZA++ union (IBM Model 4) alignments, we use perceptron training to set the weights of each feature used in link deletion in order to optimize weighted fully-connected alignment f-measure (α=0.5 for Chinese-English and α=0.1 for Arabic-English) on a manually aligned discriminative training set. We report the (fully-connected) precision, recall, and weighted alignment f-measure on a held-out test set after running perceptron training, relative to the baseline GIZA++ union alignments. Using the learned feature weights, we then perform link deletion over the GIZA++ union alignments for the entire training corpus for each translation task. Using these alignments, which we refer to as "GIZA++ union + link deletion", we train a syntax-based translation system similar to that described in (Galley et al., 2006). After extracting string-to-tree translation rules from the aligned, parsed training corpus, the system assigns weights to each rule via frequency estimation with smoothing. The rule probabilities, as well as trigram language model probabilities and a handful of additional features of each rule, are used as features during decoding. The feature weights are tuned using minimum error rate training (Och and Ney, 2003) to optimize BLEU score on a held-out development set. We then compare the BLEU score of this system against a baseline system trained using GIZA++ union alignments.

To determine which value of α is most effective as a training criterion for link deletion, we set α=0.4 (favoring recall), 0.5, and 0.6 (favoring precision),

[11]In Figure 1, the fully-connected version of the alignments shown would include the links 需要-starts and 需要- out.

Language	Train	Tune	Test1	Test2
Chinese-English A	9.8M/newswire	25.9k/NIST02	29.0k/NIST03	–
Chinese-English B	12.3M/newswire	42.9k/newswire	42.1k/newswire	–
Arabic-English	174.8M/newswire	35.8k/NIST04-05	40.3k/NIST04-05	53.0k/newswire

Table 2: Size (English words) and source of data sets used in translation tasks

and compare the effect on translation quality for Chinese-English data set A.

4 Results

For each translation task, link deletion improves translation quality relative to a GIZA++ union baseline. For each alignment task, link deletion tends to improve fully-connected alignment precision more than it decreases fully-connected alignment recall, increasing weighted fully-connected alignment f-measure overall.

4.1 Chinese-English

On Chinese-English translation task A, link deletion increases BLEU score by 1.26 points on tuning and 0.76 points on test (Table 3); on Chinese-English translation task B, link deletion increases BLEU score by 1.38 points on tuning and 0.49 points on test (Table 3).

4.2 Arabic-English

On the Arabic-English translation task, link deletion improves BLEU score by 0.84 points on tuning, 0.18 points on test1, and 0.56 points on test2 (Table 3). Note that the training criterion for Arabic-English link deletion uses α=0.1; because this penalizes a loss in recall more heavily than it rewards an increase in precision, it is more difficult to increase weighted fully-connected alignment f-measure using link deletion for Arabic-English than for Chinese-English. This difference is reflected in the average number of links deleted per sentence: 4.19 for Chinese-English B (Table 3), but only 1.35 for Arabic-English (Table 3). Despite this difference, link deletion improves translation results for Arabic-English as well.

4.3 Varying α

On Chinese-English data set A, we explore the effect of varying α in the weighted fully-connected alignment f-measure used as the training criterion for link deletion. Using α=0.5 leads to a higher gain in BLEU score on the test set relative to the baseline (+0.76 points) than either α=0.4 (+0.70 points) or α=0.6 (+0.67 points).

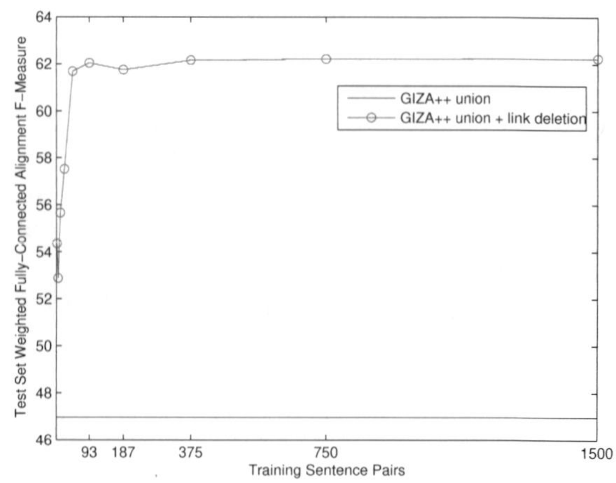

Figure 2: Effect of discriminative training set size on link deletion accuracy for Chinese-English B, α=0.5

4.4 Size of Discriminative Training Set

To examine how many manually aligned sentence pairs are required to set the feature weights reliably, we vary the size of the discriminative training set from 2-1500 sentence pairs while holding test set size constant at 1500 sentence pairs; run perceptron training; and record the resulting weighted fully-connected alignment f-measure on the test set. Figure 2 illustrates that using 100-200 manually aligned sentence pairs of training data is sufficient for Chinese-English; a similarly-sized training set is also sufficient for Arabic-English.

4.5 Effect of Link Deletion on Extracted Rules

Link deletion increases the *size* of the extracted grammar. To determine how the *quality* of the extracted grammar changes, we compute the rule pre-

Language	Alignment	Prec	Rec	α	F-measure	Links Del/ Sent	Grammar Size	BLEU Tune	BLEU Test1	BLEU Test2
Chi-Eng A	GIZA++ union	54.76	**75.38**	0.5	63.44	–	23.4M	41.80	41.17	–
Chi-Eng A	GIZA++ union + link deletion	**79.59**	71.16	0.5	**75.14**	4.77	59.7M	**43.06**	**41.93**	–
Chi-Eng B	GIZA++ union	36.61	**66.28**	0.5	47.16	–	28.9M	39.59	41.39	–
Chi-Eng B	GIZA++ union + link deletion	**65.52**	59.28	0.5	**62.24**	4.19	73.0M	**40.97**	**41.88**	–
Ara-Eng	GIZA++ union	35.34	**84.05**	0.1	73.87	–	52.4M	54.73	50.9	38.16
Ara-Eng	GIZA++ union + link deletion	**52.68**	79.75	0.1	**75.85**	1.35	64.9M	**55.57**	**51.08**	**38.72**

Table 3: Results of link deletion. Weighted fully-connected alignment f-measure is computed on alignment test sets (Table 1); BLEU score is computed on translation test sets (Table 2).

Alignment	Parse	Rule Precision	Rule Recall	Rule F-measure	Total Non-Unique
gold	gold	100.00	100.00	100.00	12,809
giza++ union	collins	**50.49**	44.23	47.15	11,021
giza++ union+link deletion, α=0.5	collins	47.51	53.20	**50.20**	13,987
giza++ refined	collins	44.20	**54.06**	48.64	15,182

Table 4: Rule precision, recall, and f-measure of rules extracted from 400 sentence pairs of Chinese-English data

cision, recall, and f-measure of the GIZA++ union alignments and various link deletion alignments on a held-out Chinese-English test set of 400 sentence pairs. Table 4 indicates the total (non-unique) number of rules extracted for each alignment/parse pairing, as well as the rule precision, recall, and f-measure of each pair. As more links are deleted, more rules are extracted–but of those, some are of good quality and others are of bad quality. Link-deleted alignments produce rule sets with higher rule f-measure than either GIZA++ union or GIZA++ refined.

5 Conclusion

We have presented a link deletion algorithm that improves the precision of GIZA++ union alignments without notably decreasing recall. In addition to lexical and structural features, we use features of the extracted syntax-based translation rules. Our method improves alignment quality and translation quality on Chinese-English and Arabic-English translation tasks, relative to a GIZA++ union baseline. The algorithm runs quickly, and is easily applicable to other language pairs with limited amounts (100-200 sentence pairs) of manually aligned data available.

Acknowledgments

We thank Steven DeNeefe and Wei Wang for assistance with experiments, and Alexander Fraser and Liang Huang for helpful discussions. This research was supported by DARPA (contract HR0011-06-C-0022) and by a fellowship from AT&T Labs.

References

Peter F. Brown, Stephen Della Pietra, Vincent J. Della Pietra, and Robert L. Mercer. *The Mathematics of Statistical Machine Translation: Parameter Estimation.* Computational Linguistics, Vol. 19, No. 2, 1993.

Eugene Charniak and Mark Johnson. *Coarse-to-fine n-best parsing and MaxEnt discriminative reranking.* Proceedings of ACL, 2005.

Colin Cherry and Dekang Lin. *Soft Syntactic Constraints for Word Alignment through Discriminative Training.* Proceedings of ACL (Poster), 2006.

David Chiang. *A Hierarchical Phrase-Based Model for Statistical Machine Translation.* Proceedings of ACL, 2005.

David Chiang. *Hierarchical phrase-based translation.* Computational Linguistics, 2007.

Michael Collins. *Discriminative Reranking for Natural Language Parsing.* Proceedings of ICML, 2000.

Michael Collins. *Discriminative training methods for hidden Markov models: theory and experiments with perceptron algorithms.* Proceedings of EMNLP, 2002.

John DeNero and Dan Klein. *Tailoring Word Alignments to Syntactic Machine Translation.* Proceedings of ACL, 2007.

Yonggang Deng and William Byrne. *HMM word and phrase alignment for statistical machine translation.* Proceedings of HLT/EMNLP, 2005.

Alexander Fraser and Daniel Marcu. *Measuring Word Alignment Quality for Statistical Machine Translation.* Computational Linguistics, Vol. 33, No. 3, 2007.

Alexander Fraser and Daniel Marcu. *Getting the Structure Right for Word Alignment: LEAF.* Proceedings of EMNLP, 2007.

Michel Galley, Mark Hopkins, Kevin Knight, and Daniel Marcu. *What's in a Translation Rule?* Proceedings of HLT/NAACL-04, 2004.

Michel Galley, Jonathan Graehl, Kevin Knight, Daniel Marcu, Steve DeNeefe, Wei Wang, and Ignacio Thayer. *Scalable Inference and Training of Context-Rich Syntactic Translation Models.* Proceedings of ACL, 2006.

Liang Huang, Kevin Knight, and Aravind Joshi. *Statistical Syntax-Directed Translation with Extended Domain of Locality.* Proceedings of AMTA, 2006.

Abraham Ittycheriah and Salim Roukos. *A Maximum Entropy Word Aligner for Arabic-English Machine Translation.* Proceedings of HLT/EMNLP, 2005.

Philipp Koehn, Franz Josef Och, and Daniel Marcu. *Statistical Phrase-Based Translation.* Proceedings of HLT/NAACL, 2003.

Philipp Koehn, Hieu Hoang, Alexandra Birch, Chris Callison-Burch, Marcello Federico, Nicola Bertoldi, Brooke Cowan, Wade Shen, Christine Moran, Richard Zens, Chris Dyer, Ondrej Bojar, Alexandra Constantin, Evan Herbst. *Moses: Open Source Toolkit for Statistical Machine Translation.* Proceedings of ACL (demo), 2007.

Percy Liang, Alexandre Bouchard-Cote, Dan Klein, and Ben Taskar. *An end-to-end discriminative approach to machine translation.* Proceedings of COLING/ACL, 2006.

Yang Liu, Qun Liu, and Shouxun Lin. *Log-linear Models for Word Alignment.* Proceedings of ACL, 2005.

Yang Liu, Qun Liu, and Shouxun Lin. *Tree-to-String Alignment Template for Statistical Machine Translation.* Proceedings of ACL, 2006.

Adam Lopez and Philip Resnik. *Improved HMM Alignment Models for Languages with Scarce Resources.* Proceedings of the ACL Workshop on Parallel Text, 2005.

Jonathan May and Kevin Knight. *Syntactic Re-Alignment Models for Machine Translation.* Proceedings of EMNLP-CoNLL, 2007.

Robert C. Moore. *A Discriminative Framework for Bilingual Word Alignment.* Proceedings of HLT/EMNLP, 2005.

Robert C. Moore, Wen-tau Yih, and Andreas Bode. *Improved discriminative bilingual word alignment.* Proceedings of ACL, 2006.

Franz Josef Och. *Minimum Error Rate Training in Statistical Machine Translation.* Proceedings of ACL, 2003.

Franz Josef Och and Hermann Ney. *A Systematic Comparison of Various Statistical Alignment Models.* Computational Linguistics, Vol. 29, No. 1, 2003.

Franz Josef Och and Hermann Ney. *The alignment template approach to statistical machine translation.* Computational Linguistics, 2004.

K. Papineni, S. Roukos, T. Ward, and W. J. Zhu. *BLEU: a Method for Automatic Evaluation of Machine Translation.* Proceedings of ACL, 2002.

Chris Quirk, Arul Menezes, and Colin Cherry. *Dependency Treelet Translation: Syntactically Informed Phrasal SMT.* Proceedings of ACL, 2005.

Ben Taskar, Simon Lacoste-Julien, and Dan Klein. *A Discriminative Matching Approach to Word Alignment.* Proceedings of HTL/EMNLP, 2005.

Stephan Vogel, Hermann Ney, and Christoph Tillmann. *HMM-Based Word Alignment in Statistical Translation* Proceedings of COLING, 1996.

Using Shallow Syntax Information to Improve Word Alignment and Reordering for SMT

Josep M. Crego
TALP Research Center
Universitat Politècnica de Catalunya
08034 Barcelona, Spain
jmcrego@gps.tsc.upc.edu

Nizar Habash
Center for Computational Learning Systems
Columbia University
New York, NY 10115, USA
habash@ccls.columbia.edu

Abstract

We describe two methods to improve SMT accuracy using shallow syntax information. First, we use chunks to refine the set of word alignments typically used as a starting point in SMT systems. Second, we extend an N-gram-based SMT system with chunk tags to better account for long-distance reorderings. Experiments are reported on an Arabic-English task showing significant improvements. A human error analysis indicates that long-distance reorderings are captured effectively.

1 Introduction

Much research has been done on using syntactic information in statistical machine translation (SMT). In this paper we use *chunks* (shallow syntax information) to improve an N-gram-based SMT system. We tackle both the alignment and reordering problems of a language pair with important differences in word order (Arabic-English). These differences lead to noisy word alignments, which lower the accuracy of the derived translation table. Additionally, word order differences, especially those spanning long distances and/or including multiple levels of reordering, are a challenge for SMT decoding.

Two improvements are presented here. First, we reduce the number of noisy alignments by using the idea that chunks, like raw words, have a translation correspondence in the source and target sentences. Hence, word links are constrained (i.e., noisy links are pruned) using chunk information. Second, we introduce rewrite rules which can handle both short/medium and long distance reorderings as well as different degrees of recursive application. We build our rules with two different linguistic annotations, (local) POS tags and (long-spanning) chunk tags. Despite employing an N-gram-based SMT system, the methods described here can also be applied to any phrase-based SMT system. Alignment and reordering are similarly used in both approaches.

In Section 2 we discuss previous related work. In Section 3, we discuss Arabic linguistic issues and motivate some of our decisions. In Section 4, we describe the N-gram based SMT system which we extend in this paper. Sections 5 and 6 detail the main contributions of this work. In Section 7, we carry out evaluation experiments reporting on the accuracy results and give details of a human evaluation error analysis.

2 Related Work

In the SMT community, it is widely accepted that there is a need for structural information to account for differences in word order between different language pairs. Structural information offers a greater potential to learn generalizations about relationships between languages than flat-structure models. The need for these '*mappings*' is specially relevant when handling language pairs with very different word order, such as Arabic-English or Chinese-English.

Many alternatives have been proposed on using syntactic information in SMT systems. They range from those aiming at harmonizing (monotonizing) the word order of the considered language pairs by means of a set of linguistically-motivated reordering patterns (Xia and McCord, 2004; Collins et al., 2005) to others considering translation a synchronous parsing process where reorderings introduced in the overall search are syntactically motivated (Galley et al., 2004; Quirk et al., 2005). The work presented here follows the word order harmonization strategy.

Proceedings of the Third Workshop on Statistical Machine Translation, pages 53–61,
Columbus, Ohio, USA, June 2008.

Collins et al. (2005) describe a technique for preprocessing German to look more like English syntactically. They used six transformations that are applied on German parsed text to reorder it before passing it on to a phrase-based system. They show a moderate statistically significant improvement. Our work differs from theirs crucially in that our preprocessing rules are learned automatically. Xia and McCord (2004) describe an approach for translation from French to English, where reordering rules are acquired automatically using source and target parses and word alignment. The reordering rules they use are in a context-free constituency representation with marked heads. The rules are mostly lexicalized. Xia and McCord (2004) use source and target parses to constrain word alignments used for rule extraction. Their results show that there is a positive effect on reordering when the decoder is run monotonically (i.e., without additional distortion-based reordering). The value of reordering is diminished if the decoder is run in a non-monotonic way.

Recently, Crego and Mariño (2007b) employ POS tags to automatically learn reorderings in training. They allow all possible learned reorderings to be used to create a lattice that is input to the decoder, which further improves translation accuracy. Similarly, Costa-jussà and Fonollosa (2006) use statistical word classes to generalize reorderings, which are learned/introduced in a translation process that transforms the source language into the target language word order. Zhang et al. (2007) describe a similar approach using unlexicalized context-free chunk tags (XPs) to learn reordering rules for Chinese-English SMT. Crego and Mariño (2007c) extend their previous work using syntax trees (dependency parsing) to learn reorderings on a Chinese-English task. Habash (2007) applies automatically-learned syntactic reordering rules (for Arabic-English SMT) to preprocess the input before passing it to a phrase-based SMT decoder.

As in (Zhang et al., 2007), (Costa-jussà and Fonollosa, 2006) and (Crego and Mariño, 2007b), we employ a word graph for a tight coupling between reordering and decoding. However, we differ on the language pair (Arabic-English) and the rules employed to learn reorderings. Rules are built using both POS tags and chunk tags in order to balance the higher generalization power of chunks with the higher accuracy of POS tags. Additionally, we introduce a method to use chunks for refining word alignments employed in the system.

3 Arabic Linguistic Issues

Arabic is a morpho-syntactically complex language with many differences from English. We describe here three prominent syntactic features of Arabic that are relevant to Arabic-English translation and that motivate some of our decisions in this work.

First, Arabic words are morphologically complex containing clitics whose translations are represented separately in English and sometimes in a different order. For instance, possessive pronominal enclitics are attached to the noun they modify in Arabic but their translation precedes the English translation of the noun: *kitAbu+hu*[1] *'book+his* $\rightarrow$ *his book'*. Other clitics include the definite article *Al+* *'the'*, the conjunction *w+* *'and'* and the preposition *l+* *'of/for'*, among others. We use the Penn Arabic Treebank tokenization scheme which splits three classes of clitics only. This scheme is compatible with the chunker we use (Diab et al., 2004).

Secondly, Arabic verb subjects may be: pro-dropped (verb conjugated), pre-verbal (SVO), or post-verbal (VSO). The VSO order is quite challenging in the context of translation to English. For small noun phrases (NP), small phrase pairs in a phrase table and some degree of distortion can easily move the verb to follow the NP. But this becomes much less likely with very long NPs that exceed the size of phrases in a phrase table.

Finally, Arabic adjectival modifiers typically follow their nouns (with a small exception of some superlative adjectives). For example, *rajul Tawiyl* (lit. man tall) translates as *'a tall man'*.

These three syntactic features of Arabic-English translation are not independent of each other. As we reorder the verb and the subject NP, we also have to reorder the NP's adjectival components. This brings new challenges to previous implementations of N-gram based SMT which had worked with language pairs that are more similar than Arabic and English, e.g., Spanish and English. Although Spanish is like Arabic in terms of its noun-adjective order; Spanish is similar to English in terms of its subject-verb order. Spanish morphology is more complex than English but not as complex as Arabic: Spanish is like Arabic in terms of being pro-drop but has a smaller

[1] All Arabic transliterations in this paper are provided in the Buckwalter transliteration scheme (Buckwalter, 2004).

number of clitics. We do not focus on morphology issues in this work. Table 1 illustrates these dimensions of variations. The more variations, the harder the translation.

	Morph.	Subj-Verb	Noun-Adj
AR	hard	VSO, SVO, pro-drop	N-A, A-N
ES	medium	SVO, pro-drop	N-A
EN	simple	SVO	A-N

Table 1: Arabic (AR), Spanish (ES) and English (EN) linguistic features.

4 N-gram-based SMT System

The **baseline** translation system described in this paper implements a log-linear combination of six models: a *translation model*, a *surface target language model*, a *target tag language model*, a *word bonus model*, a *source-to-target lexicon model*, and a *target-to-source lexicon model*. In contrast to standard phrase-based approaches, the translation model is expressed in **tuples**, bilingual translation units, and is estimated as an N-gram language model (Mariño et al., 2006).

4.1 Translation Units

Translation units (or tuples) are extracted after reordering source words following the **unfold** method for monotonizing word alignments (Crego et al., 2005). Figure 1 shows an example of tuple extraction with the original source-side word order resulting in one tuple (**regular**); and after reordering the source words resulting in three tuples (**unfold**).

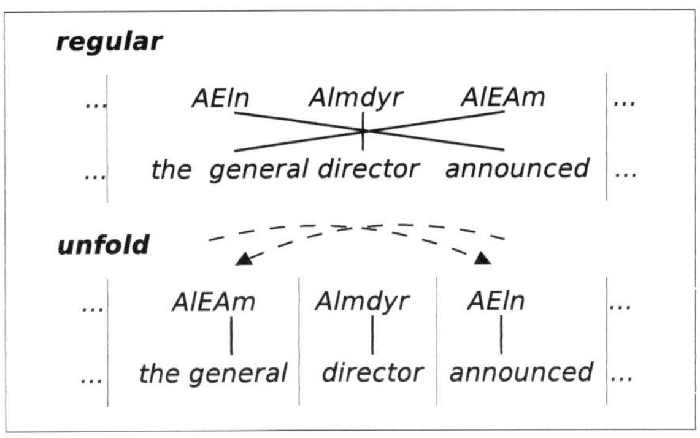

Figure 1: *Regular Vs. Unfold translation units.*

In general, the unfold extraction method outperforms the regular method because it produces smaller, less sparse and more reusable units, which is specially relevant for languages with very different word order. On the other hand, the unfold method needs the input source words to be reordered during decoding similarly to how source words were reordered in training. If monotonic decoding were used with unfolded units, translation hypotheses would follow the source language word order.

4.2 Reordering Framework

In training time, a set of reordering rules are automatically learned from word alignments. These rules are used in decoding time to provide the decoder with a set of reordering hypotheses in the form of a reordering input graph.

Rule Extraction

Following the **unfold** technique, source side reorderings are introduced into the training corpus in order to harmonize the word order of the source and target sentences. For each reordering produced in this step a record is taken in the form of a reordering rule: '$s_1, ..., s_n \rightarrow i_1, ..., i_n$', where '$s_1, ..., s_n$' is a sequence of of source words, and '$i_1, ..., i_n$' is a sequence of index positions into which the source words (left-hand side of the rule) are reordered. It is worth noticing that translation units and reordering rules are tightly coupled.

The reordering rules described so far can only handle reorderings of word sequences already seen in training. In order to improve the generalization power of these rules, linguistic classes (POS tags, chunks, syntax trees, *etc.*) can be used instead of raw words in the left-hand side of the rules. For example, the reordering introduced to unfold the alignments of the regular tuple '$AEln\ Almdyr\ AlEAm \rightarrow AlEAm\ Almdyr\ AEln$' in Figure 1 can produce the rule: '$VBD\ \ NN\ \ JJ \rightarrow 2\ \ 1\ \ 0$', where the left-hand side of the rule contains the sequence of POS tags ('*verb noun adjective*') belonging to the source words involved in reordering.

Search Graph Extension

In decoding, the input sentence is handled as a word graph. A monotonic search graph contains a single path, composed of arcs covering the input words in the original word order. To allow for reordering, the graph is extended with new arcs, covering the source words in the desired word order. For a given test sentence, any sequence of input tags fulfilling a left-hand side reordering rule leads to the

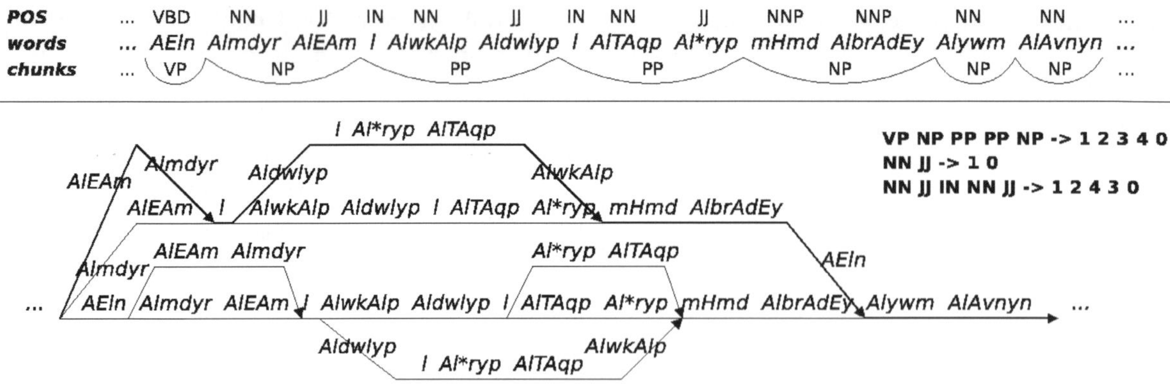

Figure 2: *Linguistic information, reordering graph and translation composition of an Arabic sentence.*

addition of a reordering path. Figure 2 shows an example of an input search graph extension (middle). The monotonic search graph is expanded following three different reordering rules.

5 Rules with Chunk Information

The generalization power of POS-based reordering rules is somehow limited to short rules (less sparse) which fail to capture many real examples. Longer rules are needed to model reorderings between full (linguistic) phrases, which are not restricted to any size. In order to capture such long-distance reorderings, we introduce rules with tags referring to arbitrary large sequences of words: chunk tags. Chunk-based rules allow the introduction of chunk tags in the left-hand side of the rule. For instance, the rule: '$VP \quad NP \rightarrow 1 \quad 0$' indicates that a verb phrase 'VP' preceding a noun phrase 'NP' are to be swapped. That is, the sequence of words composing the verb phrase are reordered at the end of the sequence of words composing the noun phrase.

In training, like POS-based rules, a record is taken in the form of a rule whenever a source reordering is introduced by the **unfold** technique. To account for chunk-based rules, a chunk tag is used instead of the corresponding POS tags when the words composing the phrase remain consecutive (not necessarily in the same order) after reordering. Notice that rules are built using POS tags as well as chunk tags. Since both approaches are based on the same reorderings introduced in training, both POS-based and chunk-based rules collect the same number of training rule instances.

Figure 3 illustrates the process of POS-based and chunk-based rule extraction. Here, the reordering

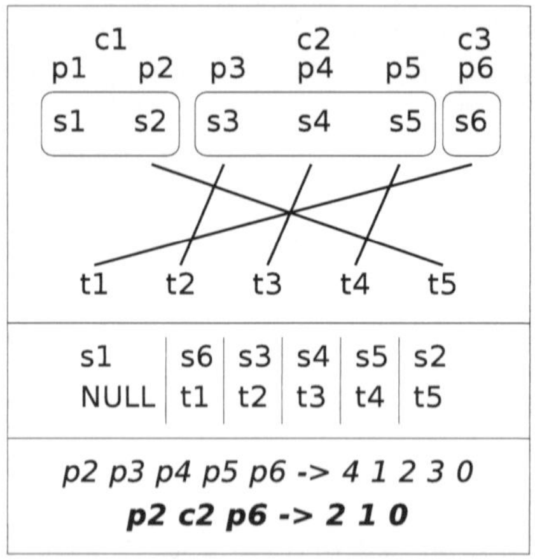

Figure 3: *POS-based and chunk-based Rule extraction: word-alignments, chunk and POS information (top), translation units (middle) and reordering rules (bottom) are shown.*

rule is applied over the sequence '$s_2\ s_3\ s_4\ s_5\ s_6$', which is transformed into '$s_6\ s_3\ s_4\ s_5\ s_2$'. As for the chunk rule, the POS tags '$p_3\ p_4\ p_5$' of the POS rule are replaced by the corresponding chunk tag 'c_2' since words within the phrase remain consecutive after being reordered. The vocabulary of chunk tags is typically smaller than that of POS tags. Hence, in order to increase the accuracy of the rules, we always use the POS tag instead of the chunk tag for single word chunks. In the example in Figure 3, the resulting chunk rule contains the POS tag 'p_6' instead of the corresponding chunk tag '$c3$'.

Any sequence of input POS/chunk tags fulfilling a left-hand side reordering rule entails the extension of the permutation graph with a new reordering path. Figure 2 shows the permutation graph (middle) computed for an Arabic sentence (top) after applying three reordering rules. The best path is drawn in bold arcs. It is important to notice that rules are *recursively* applied on top of sequences of already reordered words. Chunk rules are applied over phrases (sequences of words) which may need additional reorderings. Larger rules are applied before shorter ones in order to allow for an easy implementation of recursive reordering. Rules are allowed to match any path of the permutation graph consisting of a sequence of words in the original order. For example, the sequence *'Almdyr AlEAm'* is reordered into *'AlEAm Almdyr'* following the rule '$NN\ JJ \rightarrow 1\ 0$' on top of the monotonic path as well as on top of the path previously reordered by rule '$VP\ NP\ PP\ PP\ NP \rightarrow 1\ 2\ 3\ 4\ 0$'. In Figure 2, the best reordering path (bold arcs) could not be hypothesized without recursive reorderings.

6 Refinement of Word Alignments

As stated earlier, the Arabic-English language pair presents important word order disparities. These strong differences make word alignment a very difficult task, typically producing a large number of noisy (wrong) alignments. The N-gram-based SMT approach suffers highly from the presence of noisy alignments since translation units are extracted out of single alignment-based segmentations of training sentences. Noisy alignments lead to large translation units, which cause a loss of translation information and add to sparseness problems.

We propose an alignment refinement method to reduce the number of wrong alignments. The method employs two initial alignment sets: one with high precision, the other with high recall. We use the **Intersection** and **Union** (Och and Ney, 2000) of both alignment directions[2] as the high precision and high recall alignment sets, respectively. We will study the effect of various initial alignment sets (such as **grow-diag-final** instead of **Union**) in the future. The method is based on the fact that linguistic phrases (chunks), like raw words, have translation correspondences and can therefore be aligned. We use chunk information to reduce the number of allowed alignments for a given word. The simple idea that words in a source chunk are typically aligned to words in a single possible target chunk is used to discard alignments which link words from distant chunks. Since limiting alignments to one-to-one chunk links is perhaps too strict, we extend the number of allowed alignments by permitting words in a chunk to be aligned to words in a target range of words. This target range is computed as a projection of the source chunk under consideration. The resulting refined set contains all the Intersection alignments and some of the Union.

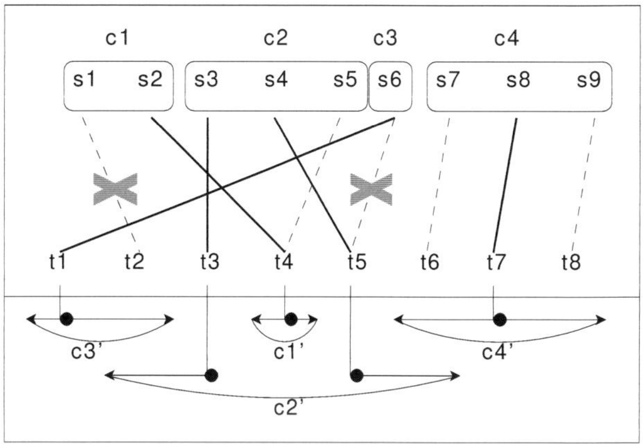

Figure 4: *Chunk projection: solid link are Intersection links and all links (solid and dashed) are Union links.*

We outline the algorithm next. The method can be decomposed in two steps. In the first step, using the Intersection set of alignments and source-side chunks, each chunk is projected into the target side. Figure 4 shows an example of word alignment refinement. The projection c'_k of the chunk c_k is composed of the sequence of consecutive target words $[t_{left}, t_{right}]$ which can be determined as follows:

- All target words t_j contained in Intersection links (s_i, t_j) with source word s_i within c_k are considered projection anchors. In the example in Figure 4, source words of chunk (c_2) are aligned into the target side by means of two Intersection alignments, (s_3, t_3) and (s_4, t_5), and producing two anchors (t_3 and t_5).

- For each source chunk c_k, t_{left}/t_{right} is set by extending its leftmost/rightmost anchor in the left/right direction up to the word before the next anchor (or the first/last word if at sentence edge). In the example in Figure 4, c'_1, c'_2, c'_3 and c'_4 are respectively $[t_4, t_4]$, $[t_2, t_6]$, $[t_1, t_2]$ and $[t_6, t_8]$.

In the second step, for every alignment of the Union set, the alignment is discarded if it links a

[2] We use IBM-1 to IBM-5 models (Brown et al., 1993) implemented with GIZA++ (Och and Ney, 2003).

source word s_i to a target word t_j that falls out of the projection of the chunk containing the source word. Notice that all the Intersection links are contained in the resulting refined set. In the example in Figure 4, the link (s_1, t_2) is discarded as t_2 falls out of the projection of chunk c_1 ($[t_4, t_4]$).

A further refinement can be done using the chunks of the target side. The same technique is applied by switching the role of source and target words/chunks in the algorithm described above and using the output of the basic source-based refinement (described above) as the high-recall alignment set, i.e., instead of Union.

7 Evaluation

7.1 Experimental Framework

All of the training data used here is available from the Linguistic Data Consortium (LDC).[3] We use an Arabic-English parallel corpus[4] consisting of 131K sentence pairs, with approximately 4.1M Arabic tokens and 4.4M English tokens. Word alignment is done with GIZA++ (Och and Ney, 2003). All evaluated systems use the same surface trigram language model, trained on approximately 340 million words of English newswire text from the English Gigaword corpus (LDC2003T05). Additionally, we use a 5-gram language model computed over the POS tagged English side of the training corpus. Language models are implemented using the SRILM toolkit (Stolcke, 2002).

For Arabic tokenization, we use the Arabic TreeBank tokenization scheme: 4-way normalized segments into conjunction, particle, word and pronominal clitic. For POS tagging, we use the collapsed tagset for PATB (24 tags). Tokenization and POS tagging are done using the publicly available Morphological Analysis and Disambiguation of Arabic (MADA) tool (Habash and Rambow, 2005). For chunking Arabic, we use the AMIRA (ASVMT) toolkit (Diab et al., 2004). English preprocessing simply included down-casing, separating punctuation from words and splitting off "'s". The English side is POS-tagged with TNT(Brants, 2000) and chunked with the freely available OpenNlp[5] tools.

We use the standard four-reference NIST MTEval data sets for the years 2003, 2004 and 2005 (henceforth MT03, MT04 and MT05, respectively) for testing and the 2002 data set for tuning.[6] BLEU-4 (Papineni et al., 2002), METEOR (Banerjee and Lavie, 2005) and multiple-reference Word Error Rate scores are reported. SMT decoding is done using MARIE,[7] a freely available N-gram-based decoder implementing a beam search strategy with distortion/reordering capabilities (Crego and Mariño, 2007a). Optimization is done with an in-house implementation of the SIMPLEX (Nelder and Mead, 1965) algorithm.

7.2 Results

In this section we assess the accuracy results of the techniques introduced in this paper for alignment refinement and word reordering.

Alignment Refinement Experiment

We contrast three systems built from different word alignments: (a.) the Union alignment set of both translation directions (U); (b.) the refined alignment set, detailed in Section 6, employing only source-side chunks (rS); (c.) the refined alignment set employing source as well as target-side chunks (rST). For this experiment, the system employs an n-gram bilingual translation model (TM) with $n = 3$ and $n = 4$. We also vary the use of a 5-gram target-tag language model (ttLM). The reordering graph is built using POS-based rules restricted to a maximum size of 6 tokens (POS tags in the left-hand side of the rule). The results are shown in Table 2.

Results from the refined alignment (rS) system clearly outperform the results from the alignment union (U) system. All measures agree in all test sets. Results further improve when we employ target-side chunks to refine the alignments (rST), although not statistically significantly. BLEU 95% confidence intervals for the best configuration (last row) are $\pm.0162$, $\pm.0210$ and $\pm.0135$ respectively for *MT03*, *MT04* and *MT05*.

As anticipated, the N-gram system suffers under high reordering needs when noisy alignments produce long (sparse) tuples. This can be seen by the increase in translation unit counts when refined links are used to alleviate the sparseness problem. The number of links of each alignment set over all

[3] http://www.ldc.upenn.edu

[4] The parallel text includes Arabic News (LDC2004T17), eTIRR (LDC2004E72), English translation of Arabic Treebank (LDC2005E46), and Ummah (LDC2004T18).

[5] http://opennlp.sourceforge.net/

[6] http://www.nist.gov/speech/tests/mt/

[7] http://gps-tsc.upc.es/veu/soft/soft/marie/

Align	TM	ttLM	BLEU	mWER	METEOR
MT03					
U	3	-	.4453	51.94	.6356
rS	3	-	.4586	50.67	.6401
rST	3	-	.4600	50.64	**.6416**
rST	4	-	.4610	50.20	.6401
rST	4	5	**.4689**	**49.36**	.6411
MT04					
U	3	-	.4244	50.12	.6055
rS	3	-	.4317	49.89	.6085
rST	3	-	**.4375**	49.69	**.6109**
rST	4	-	.4370	49.07	.6093
rST	4	5	.4366	**48.70**	.6092
MT05					
U	3	-	.4366	50.40	.6306
rS	3	-	.4447	49.77	.6353
rST	3	-	.4484	49.09	.6386
rST	4	-	.4521	48.69	.6377
rST	4	5	**.4561**	**48.07**	**.6401**

Table 2: *Evaluation results for experiments on translation units, alignment and modeling.*

training data is $5.5\,M$ (U), $4.9\,M$ (rS) and $4.6\,M$ (rST). Using the previous sets, the number of unique extracted translation units is $265.5\,K$ (U), $346.3\,K$ (rS) and $407.8\,K$ (rST). Extending the TM to order 4 and introducing the ttLM seems to further boost the accuracy results for all sets in terms of mWER and for MT03 and MT05 only in terms of BLEU.

Chunk Reordering Experiment

We compare POS-based reordering rules with chunk-based reordering rules under different maximum rule-size constraints. Results are obtained using TM $n = 4$, ttLM n=5 and rST refinement alignment. BLEU scores are shown in Table 3 for all test sets and rule sizes. Rule size $7R$ indicates that chunk rules are used with recursive reorderings.

BLEU	2	3	4	5	6	7	8	7R
MT03								
POS	.4364	.4581	.4656	**.4690**	.4689	.4686	.4685	-
Chunk	.4426	.4637	.4680	.4698	.4703	.4714	.4714	**.4725**
MT04								
POS	.4105	.4276	.4332	.4355	.4366	.4362	**.4368**	-
Chunk	.4125	.4316	.4358	**.4381**	.4373	.4372	.4373	.4364
MT05								
POS	.4206	.4465	.4532	.4549	.4561	.4562	**.4565**	-
Chunk	.4236	.4507	.4561	.4571	.4574	.4575	.4575	**.4579**

Table 3: *BLEU scores according to the maximum size of rules employed.*

Table 4 measures the impact of introducing reordering rules limited to a given size (Y axis) on the permutation graphs of input sentences from the MT03 data set (composed of 663 sentences containing 18,325 words). Column *Total* shows the number of additional (extended) paths introduced into the test set permutation graph (*i.e.*, 2,971 additional paths of size 3 POS tags were introduced). Columns 3 to 8 show the number of moves made in the 1-best translation output according to the size of the move in words (*i.e.*, 1,652 moves of size 2 words appeared when considering POS rules of up to size 3 words). The rows in Table 4 correspond to the columns associated with MT03 in Table 3. Notice that a chunk tag may refer to multiple words, which explains, for instance, how 42 moves of size 4 appear using chunk rules of size 2. Overall, short-size reorderings are far more abundant than larger ones.

Size	Total	2	3	4	[5,6]	[7,8]	[9,14]
POS rules							
2	8,142	2,129	-	-	-	-	-
3	+2,971	1,652	707	-	-	-	-
4	+1,628	1,563	631	230	-	-	-
5	+964	1,531	615	210	82	-	-
6	+730	1,510	604	200	123	-	-
7	+427	1,497	600	191	121	24	-
8	+159	1,497	599	191	120	26	-
Chunk rules							
2	9,201	2,036	118	42	20	1	0
3	+4,977	1,603	651	71	42	5	2
4	+1,855	1,542	593	200	73	7	0
5	+1,172	1,514	578	187	118	15	1
6	+760	1,495	573	178	130	20	5
7	+393	1,488	568	173	129	27	10
8	+112	1,488	568	173	129	27	10
$7R$	+393	1,405	546	179	152	54	25

Table 4: *Reorderings hypothesized and employed in the* 1*-best translation output according to their size.*

Differences in BLEU (Table 3) are very small across the alternative configurations (POS/chunk). It seems that larger reorderings, size 7 to 14, (shown in Table 4) introduce very small accuracy variations when measured using BLEU. POS rules are able to account for most of the necessary moves (size 2 to 6). However, the presence of the larger moves when considering chunk-based rules (together with accuracy improvements) show that long-size reorderings can only be captured by chunk rules. The largest moves taken by the decoder using POS rules consist of 2 sequences of 8 words (Table 4, column 7, row 9 minus row 8). The increase in the number of long moves when considering recursive chunks ($7R$) means that longer chunk rules provide only valid reordering paths if further (recursive) reorderings are also considered. The corresponding BLEU score (Table 3, last column) indicates that the new set of moves improves the resulting accuracy. The general lower scores and inconsistent behavior of MT04 compared to MT03/MT05 may be a result of MT04 being a mix of genres (newswire, speeches and editorials).

7.3 Error Analysis

We conducted a human error analysis by comparing the best results from the POS system to those of the best chunk system. We used a sample of 155 sentences from MT03. In this sample, 25 sentences (16%) were actually different between the two analyzed systems. The differences were determined to involve 30 differing reorderings. In all of these cases, the chunk system made a move, but the POS system only moved (from source word order) in 60% of the cases. We manually judged the relative quality of the move (or lack thereof). We found that 47% of the time, chunk moves were superior to POS choice. In 27% of the time POS moves were better. In the rest of the time, the two systems were equally good or bad. The main challenge for chunk reordering seems to be the lack of syntactic constraints: in many cases of errors the chunk reordering did not go far enough or went too far, breaking up NPs or passing multiple NPs, respectively. Additional syntactic features to constrain the reordering model may be needed.

8 Conclusions and Future Work

In this work we have described two methods to improve SMT accuracy using shallow syntax information. First, alignment quality has been improved (in terms of translation accuracy) by pruning out noisy links which do not respect a chunk-to-chunk alignment correspondence. Second, rewrite rules built with two different linguistic annotations, (local) POS tags and (long-spanning) chunk tags, can handle both short/medium and long distance reorderings as well as different degrees of recursive application. In order to better assess the suitability of chunk rules we carried out a human error analysis which confirmed that long reorderings were effectively captured by chunk rules. However, the error analysis also revealed that additional syntactic features to constrain the reordering model may be needed. In the future, we plan to introduce weights into the permutations graph to more accurately drive the search process as well as extend the rules with full syntactic information (parse trees).

Acknowledgments

The first author has been partially funded by the Spanish Government under the AVIVAVOZ project (TEC2006-13694-C03) the Catalan Government under BE-2007 grant and the Universitat Politècnica de Catalunya under UPC-RECERCA grant. The second author was funded under the DARPA GALE program, contract HR0011-06-C-0023.

References

S. Banerjee and A. Lavie. 2005. METEOR: An Automatic Metric for MT Evaluation with Improved Correlation with Human Judgments. In *Proceedings of the Association for Computational Linguistics (ACL) Workshop on Intrinsic and Extrinsic Evaluation Measures for Machine Translation and/or Summarization.*

T. Brants. 2000. TnT – a statistical part-of-speech tagger. In *Proceedings of the 6th Applied Natural Language Processing Conference (ANLP'2000).*

P. Brown, S. Della Pietra, V. Della Pietra, and R. Mercer. 1993. The mathematics of statistical machine translation: Parameter estimation. *Computational Linguistics*, 19(2):263–311.

T. Buckwalter. 2004. Buckwalter Arabic Morphological Analyzer Version 2.0. Linguistic Data Consortium, University of Pennsylvania, 2002. LDC Cat alog No.: LDC2004L02, ISBN 1-58563-324-0.

M. Collins, P. Koehn, and I. Kucerova. 2005. Clause Restructuring for Statistical Machine Translation. In *Proceedings of ACL'05.*

M.R. Costa-jussà and J.A.R. Fonollosa. 2006. Statistical machine reordering. *Proceedings of the 2006 Conference on Empirical Methods in Natural Language Processing (EMNLP).*

J.M. Crego and J.B. Mariño. 2007a. Extending marie: an n-gram-based smt decoder. *Proceedings of ACL'07).*

J.M. Crego and J.B. Mariño. 2007b. Improving statistical mt by coupling reordering and decoding. *Machine Translation*, 20(3):199–215.

J.M. Crego and J.B. Mariño. 2007c. Syntax-enhanced N-gram-based SMT. In *Proceedings of the Machine Translation Summit (MT SUMMIT XI).*

J.M. Crego, J.B. Mariño, and A. de Gispert. 2005. Reordered search and tuple unfolding for ngram-based smt. *Proceedings of MT Summit X.*

M. Diab, K. Hacioglu, and D. Jurafsky. 2004. Automatic tagging of arabic text: From raw text to base phrase chunks. In *Proceedings of HLT-NAACL'04.*

M. Galley, M. Hopkins, K. Knight, and D. Marcu. 2004. What's in a translation rule? In *Proceedings of HLT-NAACL'04.*

N. Habash and O. Rambow. 2005. Arabic Tokenization, Part-of-Speech Tagging and Morphological Disambiguation in One Fell Swoop. In *Proceedings of ACL'05.*

N. Habash. 2007. Syntactic Preprocessing for Statistical MT. In *Proceedings of MT SUMMIT XI.*

J.B. Mariño, R.E. Banchs, J.M. Crego, A. de Gispert, P. Lambert, J.A.R. Fonollosa, and M.R. Costa-jussà. 2006. N-gram based machine translation. *Computational Linguistics*, 32(4):527–549.

J.A. Nelder and R. Mead. 1965. A simplex method for function minimization. *The Computer Journal*, 7:308–313.

F. J. Och and H. Ney. 2000. Improved statistical alignment models. In *Proceedings of ACL.*

F. Och and H. Ney. 2003. A Systematic Comparison of Various Statistical Alignment Models. *Computational Linguistics*, 29(1):19–52.

K. Papineni, S. Roukos, T. Ward, and W. Zhu. 2002. BLEU: a Method for Automatic Evaluation of Machine Translation. In *Proceedings of ACL'02*

C. Quirk, A. Menezes, and C. Cherry. 2005. Dependency Treelet Translation: Syntactically Informed Phrasal SMT. In *Proceedings of ACL'05*

A. Stolcke. 2002. SRILM - an Extensible Language Modeling Toolkit. In *Proceedings of the International Conference on Spoken Language Processing (ICSLP).*

F. Xia and M. McCord. 2004. Improving a statistical mt system with automatically learned rewrite patterns. In *Proceedings of the 20th International Conference on Computational Linguistics (COLING 2004).*

Y. Zhang, R. Zens, and H. Ney. 2007. Chunk-level reordering of source language sentences with automatically learned rules for statistical machine translation. In *Proceedings of HLT-NAACL Workshop on Syntax and Structure in Statistical Translation.*

Improved Tree-to-string Transducer for Machine Translation

Ding Liu and **Daniel Gildea**
Department of Computer Science
University of Rochester
Rochester, NY 14627

Abstract

We propose three enhancements to the tree-to-string (TTS) transducer for machine translation: first-level expansion-based normalization for TTS templates, a syntactic alignment framework integrating the insertion of unaligned target words, and subtree-based n-gram model addressing the tree decomposition probability. Empirical results show that these methods improve the performance of a TTS transducer based on the standard BLEU-4 metric. We also experiment with semantic labels in a TTS transducer, and achieve improvement over our baseline system.

1 Introduction

Syntax-based statistical machine translation (SSMT) has achieved significant progress during recent years, with two threads developing simultaneously: the synchronous parsing-based SSMT (Galley et al., 2006; May and Knight, 2007) and the tree-to-string (TTS) transducer (Liu et al., 2006; Huang et al., 2006). Synchronous SSMT here denotes the systems which accept a source sentence as the input and generate the translation and the syntactic structure for both the source and the translation simultaneously. Such systems are sometimes also called TTS transducers, but in this paper, TTS transducer refers to the system which starts with the syntax tree of a source sentence and recursively transforms the tree to the target language based on TTS templates.

In synchronous SSMT, TTS templates are used similar to the context free grammar used in the standard CYK parser, thus the syntax is part of the output and can be thought of as a constraint on the translation process. In the TTS transducer, since the parse tree is given, syntax can be thought of as an additional feature of the input to be used in the translation. The idea of synchronous SSMT can be traced back to Wu (1997)'s Stochastic Inversion Transduction Grammars. A systematic method for extracting TTS templates from parallel corpora was proposed by Galley et al. (2004), and later binarized by Zhang et al. (2006) for high efficiency and accuracy. In the other track, the TTS transducer originated from the tree transducer proposed by Rounds (1970) and Thatcher (1970) independently. Graehl and Knight (2004) generalized the tree transducer to the TTS transducer and introduced an EM algorithm to estimate the probability of TTS templates based on a bilingual corpus with one side parsed. Liu et al. (2006) and Huang et al. (2006) then used the TTS transducer on the task of Chinese-to-English and English-to-Chinese translation, respectively, and achieved decent performance.

Despite the progress SSMT has achieved, it is still a developing field with many problems unsolved. For example, the word alignment computed by GIZA++ and used as a basis to extract the TTS templates in most SSMT systems has been observed to be a problem for SSMT (DeNero and Klein, 2007; May and Knight, 2007), due to the fact that the word-based alignment models are not aware of the syntactic structure of the sentences and could produce many syntax-violating word alignments. Approaches have been proposed recently towards getting better word alignment and thus better TTS templates, such as encoding syntactic structure information into the HMM-based word alignment model DeNero and Klein (2007), and build-

Proceedings of the Third Workshop on Statistical Machine Translation, pages 62–69,
Columbus, Ohio, USA, June 2008.

ing a syntax-based word alignment model May and Knight (2007) with TTS templates. Unfortunately, neither approach reports end-to-end MT performance based on the syntactic alignment. DeNero and Klein (2007) focus on alignment and do not present MT results, while May and Knight (2007) takes the syntactic re-alignment as an input to an EM algorithm where the unaligned target words are inserted into the templates and minimum templates are combined into bigger templates (Galley et al., 2006). Thus the improvement they reported is rather indirect, leading us to wonder how much improvement the syntactic alignment model can directly bring to a SSMT system. Some other issues of SSMT not fully addressed before are highlighted below:

1. Normalization of TTS templates. Galley et al. (2006) mentioned that with only the minimum templates extracted from GHKM (Galley et al., 2004), normalizing the template probability based on its tree pattern "can become extremely biased", due to the fact that bigger templates easily get high probabilities. They instead use a joint model where the templates are normalized based on the root of their tree patterns and show empirical results for that. There is no systematic comparison of different normalization methods.

2. Decomposition model of a TTS transducer (or syntactic language model in synchronous SSMT). There is no explicit modeling for the decomposition of a syntax tree in the TTS transducer (or the probability of the syntactic tree in a synchronous SSMT). Most systems simply use a uniform model (Liu et al., 2006; Huang et al., 2006) or implicitly consider it with a joint model producing both syntax trees and the translations (Galley et al., 2006).

3. Use of semantics. Using semantic features in a SSMT is a natural step along the way towards generating more refined models across languages. The statistical approach to semantic role labeling has been well studied (Xue and Palmer, 2004; Ward et al., 2004; Toutanova et al., 2005), but there is no work attempting to use such information in SSMT, to our limited knowledge.

This paper proposes novel methods towards solving these problems. Specifically, we compare three ways of normalizing the TTS templates based on the tree pattern, the root of the tree pattern, and the first-level expansion of the tree pattern respectively, in the context of hard counting and EM estimation; we present a syntactic alignment framework integrating both the template re-estimation and insertion of unaligned target words; we use a subtree-based n-gram model to address the decomposition of the syntax trees in TTS transducer (or the syntactic language model for synchronous SSMT); we use a statistical classifier to label the semantic roles defined by PropBank (Palmer et al., 2005) and try different ways of using the semantic features in a TTS transducer.

We chose the TTS transducer instead of synchronous SSMT for two reasons. First, the decoding algorithm for the TTS transducer has lower computational complexity, which makes it easier to integrate a complex decomposition model. Second, the TTS Transducer can be easily integrated with semantic role features since the syntax tree is present, and it's not clear how to do this in a synchronous SSMT system. The remainder of the paper will focus on introducing the improved TTS transducer and is organized as follows: Section 2 describes the implementation of a basic TTS transducer; Section 3 describes the components of the improved TTS transducer; Section 4 presents the empirical results and Section 5 gives the conclusion.

2 A Basic Tree-to-string Transducer for Machine Translation

The TTS transducer, as a generalization to the finite state transducer, receives a tree structure as its input and recursively applies TTS templates to generate the target string. For simplicity, usually only one state is used in the TTS transducer, i.e., a TTS template will always lead to the same outcome wherever it is used. A TTS template is composed of a left-hand side (LHS) and a right-hand side (RHS), where LHS is a subtree pattern and RHS is a sequence of the variables and translated words. The variables in the RHS of a template correspond to the bottom level non-terminals in the LHS's subtree pattern, and their relative order indicates the permutation desired at the point where the template is ap-

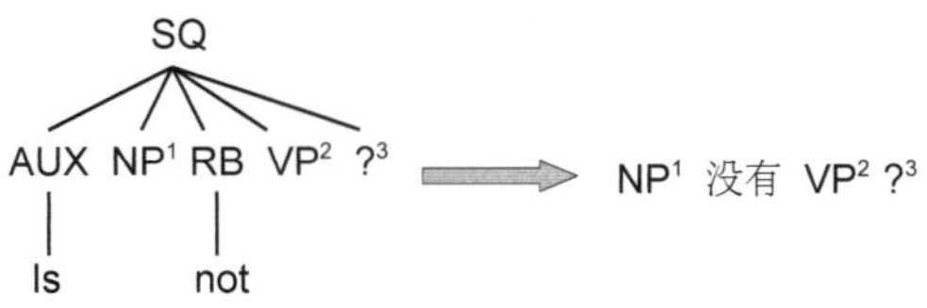

Figure 1: A TTS Template Example

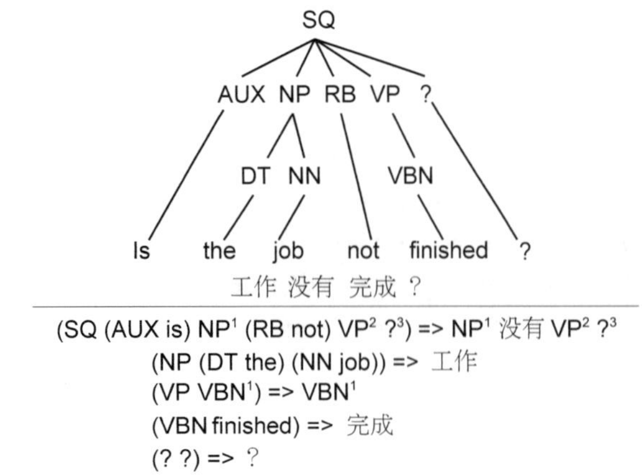

Figure 2: Derivation Example

plied to translate one language to another. The variables are further transformed and the recursive process goes on until there are no variables left. The formal description of a TTS transducer is described in Graehl and Knight (2004), and our baseline approach follows the *Extended Tree-to-String Transducer* defined in (Huang et al., 2006). Figure 1 gives an example of the English-to-Chinese TTS template, which shows how to translate a skeleton YES/NO question from English to Chinese. NP^1 and VP^2 are the variables whose relative position in the translation are determined by the template while their actual translations are still unknown and dependent on the subtrees rooted at them; and the English words *Is* and *not* are translated into the Chinese word *MeiYou* in the context of the template. The superscripts attached on the variables are used to distinguish the non-terminals with identical names (if there is any). Figure 2 shows the steps of transforming the English sentence *"Is the job not finished ?"* to the corresponding Chinese.

For a given derivation (decomposition) of a syntax tree, the translation probability is computed as the product of the templates which generate both the source syntax trees and the target translations. In theory, the translation model should sum over all possible derivations generating the target translation, but in practice, usually only the best derivation is considered:

$$Pr(S|T, D^*) = \prod_{t \in D^*} Weight(t)$$

Here, S denotes the target translation, T denotes the source syntax tree, and D^* denotes the best derivation of T. The implementation of a TTS transducer can be done either top down with memoization to the visited subtrees (Huang et al., 2006), or with a bottom-up dynamic programming (DP) algorithm (Liu et al., 2006). This paper uses the latter approach, and the algorithm is sketched in Figure 3. For the baseline approach, only the translation model and n-gram model for the target language are used:

$$S^* = \operatorname*{argmax}_S Pr(T|S) = \operatorname*{argmax}_S Pr(S)Pr(S|T)$$

Since the n-gram model tends to favor short translations, a penalty is added to the translation templates with fewer RHS symbols than LHS leaf symbols:

$$Penalty(t) = \exp(|t.RHS| - |t.LHSLeaf|)$$

where $|t.RHS|$ denotes the number of symbols in the RHS of t, and $|t.LHSLeaf|$ denotes the number of leaves in the LHS of t. The length penalty is analogous to the length feature widely used in log-linear models for MT (Huang et al., 2006; Liu et al., 2006; Och and Ney, 2004). Here we distribute the penalty into TTS templates for the convenience of DP, so that we don't have to generate the N-best list and do re-ranking. To speed up the decoding, standard beam search is used.

In Figure 3, $BinaryCombine$ denotes the target-size binarization (Huang et al., 2006) combination. The translation candidates of the template's variables, as well as its terminals, are combined pairwise in the order they appear in the RHS of the template. f_i denotes a combined translation, whose probability is equal to the product of the probabilities of the component translations, the probability of the rule, the n-gram probability of connecting the component translations, and the length penalty of

Match(v, t): the descendant tree nodes of v, which match the variables in template t
$v.sk$: the stack associated with tree node v
In(c_j, f_i): the translation candidate of c_j which is chosen to combine f_i

---

for all tree node v in bottom-up order **do**
  for all template t applicable at v **do**
    $\{c_1, c_2, ..., c_l\}$=Match(v, t);
    $\{f_1, f_2, ..., f_m\}$ = BinaryCombine($c_1.sk, c_2.sk, ..., c_n.sk, t$);
    for i=1:m **do**
      $Pr(f_i) = \prod_{j=1}^{l} Pr(In(c_j, f_i)) \cdot Weight(t)^{\beta} \cdot Lang(v, t, f_i)^{\gamma} \cdot Penalty(t)^{\alpha}$;
      Add $(f_i, Pr(f_i))$ to $v.sk$;
  Prune $v.sk$;

Figure 3: Decoding Algorithm

the template. α, β and γ are the weights of the length penalty, the translation model, and the n-gram language model, respectively. Each state in the DP chart denotes the best translation of a tree node with a certain *prefix* and *suffix*. The length of the *prefix* and the *suffix* is equal to the length of the n-gram model minus one. Without the beam pruning, the decoding algorithm runs in $O(N^{4(n-1)}RPQ)$, where N is the vocabulary size of the target language, n is the length of the n-gram model, R is the maximum number of templates applicable to one tree node, P is the maximum number of variables in a template, and Q is the number of tree nodes in the syntax tree. The DP algorithm works for most systems in the paper, and only needs to be slightly modified to encode the subtree-based n-gram model described in Section 3.3.

3 Improved Tree-to-string Transducer for Machine Translation

3.1 Normalization of TTS Templates

Given the story that translations are generated based on the source syntax trees, the weight of the template is computed as the probability of the target strings given the source subtree:

$$Weight(t) = \frac{\#(t)}{\#(t' : LHS(t') = LHS(t))}$$

Such normalization, denoted here as *TREE*, is used in most tree-to-string template-based MT systems (Liu et al., 2007; Liu et al., 2006; Huang et al., 2006). Galley et al. (2006) proposed an alteration in synchronous SSMT which addresses the probability of both the source subtree and the target string given the root of the source subtree:

$$Weight(t) = \frac{\#(t)}{\#(t' : root(t') = root(t))}$$

This method is denoted as *ROOT*. Here, we propose another modification:

$$Weight(t) = \frac{\#(t)}{\#(t' : cfg(t') = cfg(t))} \quad (1)$$

cfg in Equation 1 denotes the first level expansion of the source subtree and the method is denoted as *CFG*. *CFG* can be thought of as generating both the source subtree and the target string given the first level expansion of the source subtree. *TREE* focuses on the conditional probability of the target string given the source subtree, *ROOT* focuses on the joint probability of both the source subtree and the target string, while *CFG*, as something of a compromise between *TREE* and *ROOT*, hopefully can achieve a combined effect of both of them. Compared with *TREE*, *CFG* favors the one-level context-free grammar like templates and gives penalty to the templates bigger (in terms of the depth of the source subtree) than that. It makes sense considering that the big templates, due to their sparseness in the corpus, are often assigned unduly large probabilities by *TREE*.

3.2 Syntactic Word Alignment

The idea of building a syntax-based word alignment model has been explored by May and Knight (2007), with an algorithm working from the root tree node down to the leaves, recursively replacing the variables in the matched tree-to-string templates until there are no such variables left. The TTS templates they use are initially gathered using GHKM

1. Run GIZA++ to get the initial word alignment, use GHKM to gather translation templates, and compute the initial probability as their normalized frequency.
2. Collect all the one-level subtrees in the training corpus containing only non-terminals and create TTS templates addressing all the permutations of the subtrees' leaves if its spanning factor is not greater than four, or only the monotonic translation template if its spanning factor is greater than four. Collect all the terminal rules in the form of $A \rightarrow B$ where A is one source word, B is the consecutive target word sequence up to three words long, and A, B occurs in some sentence pairs. These extra templates are assigned a small probability 10^{-6}.
3. Run the EM algorithm described in (Graehl and Knight, 2004) with templates obtained in step 1 and step 2 to re-estimate their probabilities.
4. Use the templates from step 3 to compute the viterbi word alignment.
5. The templates not occurring in the viterbi derivation are ignored and the probability of the remaining ones are re-normalized based on their frequency in the viterbi derivation.

Figure 4: Steps generating the refined TTS templates

(Galley et al., 2004) with the word alignment computed by GIZA++ and re-estimated using EM, ignoring the alignment from Giza++. The refined word alignment is then fed to the expanded GHKM (Galley et al., 2006), where the TTS templates will be combined with the unaligned target words and re-estimated in another EM framework. The syntactic alignment proposed here shares the essence of May and Knight's approach, but combines the re-estimation of the TTS templates and insertion of the unaligned target words into a single EM framework. The process is described in Figure 4. The insertion of the unaligned target words is done implicitly as we include the extra terminal templates in Figure 4, and the extra non-terminal templates ensure that we can get a complete derivation forest in the EM training. The last viterbi alignment step may seem unnecessary given that we already have the EM-estimated templates, but in experiments we find that it produces better result by cutting off the noisy (usually very big) templates resulting from the poor alignments of GIZA++.

3.3 Tree Decomposition Model

A deficiency of the translation model for tree-to-string transducer is that it cannot fully address the decomposition probability of the source syntax trees. Though we can say that *ROOT/CFG* implicitly includes the decomposition model, a more direct and explicit modeling of the decomposition is still desired. Here we propose a novel n-gram-like model to solve this problem. The probability of a decomposition (derivation) of a syntax tree is computed as the product of the n-gram probability of the decomposed subtrees conditioned on their ascendant subtrees. The formal description of the model is in Equation 2, where D denotes the derivation and $PT(st)$ denotes the direct parent subtree of st.

$$Pr(D|T) = \prod_{\substack{\text{subtrees} \\ st \in D}} Pr(st|PT(st), PT(PT(st)), ...) \tag{2}$$

Now, with the decomposition model added in, the probability of the target string given the source syntax tree is computed as:

$$Pr(S|T) = Pr(D^*|T) \times Pr(S|T, D^*)$$

To encode this n-gram probability of the subtrees in the decoding process, we need to expand the state space of the dynamic programming algorithm in Figure 3, so that each state represents not only the prefix/suffix of the partial translation, but also the decomposition history of a tree node. For example, with a bigram tree model, the states should include the different subtrees in the LHS of the templates used to translate a tree node. With bigger n-grams, more complex history information should be encoded in the states, and this leads to higher computational complexity. In this paper, we only consider the tree n-gram up to size 2. It is not practical to search the full state space; instead, we modify the beam search algorithm in Figure 3 to encode the decomposition history information. The modified algorithm for the tree bigram creates a stack for each tree pattern occurring in the templates applicable to a tree node. This ensures that for each tree node, the decompositions headed with different subtrees have equal number of translation candidates surviving to the upper phase. The function

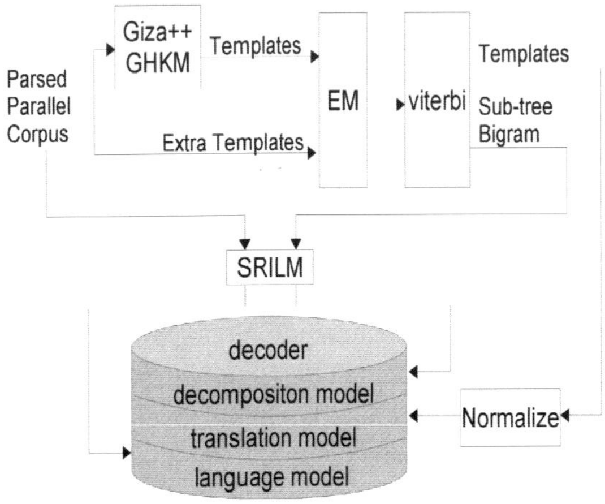

Figure 5: Flow graph of the system with all components integrated

$BinaryCombine$ is almost the same as in Figure 3, except that the translation candidates (states) of each tree node are grouped according to their associated subtrees. The bigram probabilities of the subtrees can be easily computed with the viterbi derivation in last subsection. Also, a weight should be assigned to this component. This tree n-gram model can be easily adapted and used in synchronous SSMT systems such as May and Knight (2007), Galley et al. (2006). The flow graph of the final system with all the components integrated is shown in Figure 5.

3.4 Use of Semantic Roles

Statistical approaches to MT have gone through word-based systems, phrase-based systems, and syntax-based systems. The next generation would seem to be semantic-based systems. We use PropBank (Palmer et al., 2005) as the semantic driver in our TTS transducer because it is built upon the same corpus (the Penn Treebank) used to train the statistical parser, and its shallow semantic roles are more easily integrated into a TTS transducer. A MaxEntropy classifier, with features following Xue and Palmer (2004) and Ward et al. (2004), is used to generate the semantic roles for each verb in the syntax trees. We then replace the syntactic labels with the semantic roles so that we have more general tree labels, or combine the semantic roles with the syntactic labels to generate more refined tree node labels. Though semantic roles are associated with the verbs, it is not feasible to differentiate the roles of different verbs due to the data sparseness problem. If some tree nodes are labeled different roles for different verbs, those semantic roles will be ignored.

	NP VP	VP NP
(S NP-agent VP)	0.983	0.017
(S NP-patient VP)	0.857	0.143

Table 1: The *TREE*-based weights of the skeleton templates with *NP* in different roles

A simple example demonstrating the need for semantics in the TTS transducer is that in English-Chinese translation, the *NP VP* skeleton phrase is more likely to be inverted when *NP* is in a *patient* role than when it is in an *agent* role. Table 1 shows the *TREE*-based weights of the 4 translation templates, computed based on our training corpus. This shows that the difference caused by the roles of *NP* is significant.

4 Experiment

We used 74,597 pairs of English and Chinese sentences in the FBIS data set as our experimental data, which are further divided into 500 test sentence pairs, 500 development sentence pairs and 73597 training sentence pairs. The test set and development set are selected as those sentences having fewer than 25 words on the Chinese side. The translation is from English to Chinese, and Charniak (2000)'s parser, trained on the Penn Treebank, is used to generate the syntax trees for the English side. The weights of the MT components are optimized based on the development set using a grid-based line search. The Chinese sentence from the selected pair is used as the single reference to tune and evaluate the MT system with word-based BLEU-4 (Papineni et al., 2002). Huang et al. (2006) used character-based BLEU as a way of normalizing inconsistent Chinese word segmentation, but we avoid this problem as the training, development, and test data are from the same source.

4.1 Syntax-Based System

The decoding algorithm described in Figure 3 is used with the different normalization methods described in Section 3.1 and the results are summarized in Table 2. The TTS templates are extracted using GHKM based on the many-to-one alignment

	Baseline		Syntactic Alignment		Subtree bigram	
	dev	test	dev	test	dev	test
TREE	12.29	8.90	13.25	9.65	14.84	10.61
ROOT	12.41	9.66	13.72	10.16	14.24	10.66
CFG	13.27	9.69	14.32	10.29	15.30	10.99
PHARAOH	9.04	7.84				

Table 2: BLEU-4 scores of various systems with the syntactic alignment and subtree bigram improvements added incrementally.

from Chinese to English obtained from GIZA++. We have tried using alignment in the reverse direction and the union of both directions, but neither of them is better than the Chinese-to-English alignment. The reason, based on the empirical result, is simply that the Chinese-to-English alignments lead to the maximum number of templates using GHKM. A modified Kneser-Ney bigram model of the Chinese sentence is trained using SRILM (Stolcke, 2002) using the training set. For comparison, results for Pharaoh (Koehn, 2004), trained and tuned under the same condition, are also shown in Table 2. The phrases used in Pharaoh are extracted as the pair of longest continuous spans in English and Chinese based on the union of the alignments in both direction. We tried using alignments of different directions with Pharaoh, and find that the union gives the maximum number of phrase pairs and the best BLEU scores. The results show that the TTS transducers all outperform Pharaoh, and among them, the one with *CFG* normalization works better than the other two.

We tried the three normalization methods in the syntactic alignment process in Figure 4, and found that the initialization (step 1) and viterbi alignment (step 3 and 4) based on the least biased model *ROOT* gave the best performance. Table 2 shows the results with the final template probability re-normalized (step 5) using *TREE*, *ROOT* and *CFG* respectively. We can see that the syntactic alignment brings a reasonable improvement for the TTS transducer no matter what normalization method is used. To test the effect of the subtree-based n-gram model, SRILM is used to compute a modified Kneser-Ney bigram model for the subtree patterns used in the viterbi alignment. The last 3 lines in Table 2 show the improved results by further incorporating the subtree-based bigram model. We can see that the difference of the three normalization methods is lessened and *TREE*, the weakest normalization in terms of addressing the decomposition probability, gets the biggest improvement with the subtree-based bigram model added in.

4.2 Semantic-Based System

Following the standard division, our max-entropy based SRL classifier is trained and tuned using sections 2-21 and section 24 of PropBank, respectively. The F-score we achieved on section 23 is 88.70%. We repeated the experiments in last section with the semantic labels generated by the SRL classifier. Table 3 shows the results, comparing the non-semantic-based systems with similar systems using the refined and general semantic labels, respectively. Unfortunately, semantic based systems do not always outperform the syntactic based systems. We can see that for the baseline systems based on *TREE* and *ROOT*, semantic labels improve the results, while for the other systems, they are not really better than the syntactic labels. Our approach to semantic roles is preliminary; possible improvements include associating role labels with verbs and backing off to the syntactic-label based models from semantic-label based TTS templates. In light of our results, we are optimistic that more sophisticated use of semantic features can further improve a TTS transducer's performance.

5 Conclusion

This paper first proposes three enhancements to the TTS transducer: first-level expansion-based normalization for TTS templates, a syntactic alignment framework integrating the insertion of unaligned target words, and a subtree-based n-gram model addressing the tree decomposition probability. The experiments show that the first-level expansion-based

	No Semantic Labels			Refined Labels			General Labels		
	Baseline	Syntactic Alignment	Subtree Bigram	Baseline	Syntactic Alignment	Subtree Bigram	Baseline	Syntactic Alignment	Subtree Bigram
TREE	8.90	9.65	10.61	9.40	10.25	10.42	9.40	10.02	10.47
ROOT	9.66	10.16	10.66	9.89	10.32	10.43	9.82	10.17	10.42
CFG	9.69	10.29	10.99	9.66	10.16	10.33	9.58	10.25	10.59

Table 3: BLEU-4 scores of semantic-based systems on test data. As in Table 2, the syntactic alignment and subtree bigram improvements are added incrementally within each condition.

normalization for TTS templates is better than the root-based one and the tree-based one; the syntactic alignment framework and the n-gram based tree decomposition model both improve a TTS transducer's performance. Our experiments using PropBank semantic roles in the TTS transducer show that the approach has potential, improving on our baseline system. However, adding semantic roles does not improve our best TTS system.

References

Eugene Charniak. 2000. A maximum-entropy-inspired parser. In *The Proceedings of the North American Chapter of the Association for Computational Linguistics*, pages 132–139.

John DeNero and Dan Klein. 2007. Tailoring word alignments to syntactic machine translation. In *Proceedings of ACL-07*, pages 17–24.

Michel Galley, Mark Hopkins, Kevin Knight, and Daniel Marcu. 2004. What's in a translation rule? In *Proceedings of NAACL-04*.

Michel Galley, Jonathan Graehl, Kevin Knight, Daniel Marcu, Steve DeNeefe, Wei Wang, and Ignacio Thayer. 2006. Scalable inference and training of context-rich syntactic translation models. In *Proceedings of COLING/ACL-06*, pages 961–968, July.

Jonathan Graehl and Kevin Knight. 2004. Training tree transducers. In *Proceedings of NAACL-04*.

Liang Huang, Kevin Knight, and Aravind Joshi. 2006. Statistical syntax-directed translation with extended domain of locality. In *Proceedings of the 7th Biennial Conference of the Association for Machine Translation in the Americas (AMTA)*, Boston, MA.

Philipp Koehn. 2004. Pharaoh: a beam search decoder for phrase-based statistical machine translation models. In *The Sixth Conference of the Association for Machine Translation in the Americas*, pages 115–124.

Yang Liu, Qun Liu, and Shouxun Lin. 2006. Tree-to-string alignment template for statistical machine translation. In *Proceedings of COLING/ACL-06*, Sydney, Australia, July.

Yang Liu, Yun Huang, Qun Liu, and Shouxun Lin. 2007. Forest-to-string statistical translation rules. In *Proceedings of ACL-07*, Prague.

J. May and K. Knight. 2007. Syntactic re-alignment models for machine translation. In *Proceedings of EMNLP*.

Franz Josef Och and Hermann Ney. 2004. The alignment template approach to statistical machine translation. *Computational Linguistics*, 30(4).

Martha Palmer, Daniel Gildea, and Paul Kingsbury. 2005. The Proposition Bank: An annotated corpus of semantic roles. *Computational Linguistics*, 31(1):71–106.

Kishore Papineni, Salim Roukos, Todd Ward, and Wei-Jing Zhu. 2002. BLEU: A method for automatic evaluation of machine translation. In *Proceedings of ACL-02*.

William C. Rounds. 1970. Mappings and grammars on trees. *Mathematical Systems Theory*, 4(3):257–287.

Andreas Stolcke. 2002. Srilm - an extensible language modeling toolkit. In *International Conference on Spoken Language Processing*, volume 2, pages 901–904.

J. W. Thatcher. 1970. Generalized^2 sequential machine maps. *J. Comput. System Sci.*, 4:339–367.

Kristina Toutanova, Aria Haghighi, and Christopher Manning. 2005. Joint learning improves semantic role labeling. In *Proceedings of ACL-05*, pages 589–596.

Wayne Ward, Kadri Hacioglu, James Martin, , and Dan Jurafsky. 2004. Shallow semantic parsing using support vector machines. In *Proceedings of EMNLP*.

Dekai Wu. 1997. Stochastic inversion transduction grammars and bilingual parsing of parallel corpora. *Computational Linguistics*, 23(3):377–403.

Nianwen Xue and Martha Palmer. 2004. Calibrating features for semantic role labeling. In *Proceedings of EMNLP*.

Hao Zhang, Liang Huang, Daniel Gildea, and Kevin Knight. 2006. Synchronous binarization for machine translation. In *Proceedings of NAACL-06*, pages 256–263.

Further Meta-Evaluation of Machine Translation

Chris Callison-Burch
Johns Hopkins University
ccb@cs.jhu.edu

Cameron Fordyce
camfordyce@gmail.com

Philipp Koehn
University of Edinburgh
pkoehn@inf.ed.ac.uk

Christof Monz
Queen Mary, University of London
christof@dcs.qmul.ac.uk

Josh Schroeder
University of Edinburgh
j.schroeder@ed.ac.uk

Abstract

This paper analyzes the translation quality of machine translation systems for 10 language pairs translating between Czech, English, French, German, Hungarian, and Spanish. We report the translation quality of over 30 diverse translation systems based on a large-scale manual evaluation involving hundreds of hours of effort. We use the human judgments of the systems to analyze automatic evaluation metrics for translation quality, and we report the strength of the correlation with human judgments at both the system-level and at the sentence-level. We validate our manual evaluation methodology by measuring intra- and inter-annotator agreement, and collecting timing information.

1 Introduction

This paper presents the results the shared tasks of the 2008 ACL Workshop on Statistical Machine Translation, which builds on two past workshops (Koehn and Monz, 2006; Callison-Burch et al., 2007). There were two shared tasks this year: a translation task which evaluated translation between 10 pairs of European languages, and an evaluation task which examines automatic evaluation metrics.

There were a number of differences between this year's workshop and last year's workshop:

- **Test set selection** – Instead of creating our test set by reserving a portion of the training data, we instead hired translators to translate a set of newspaper articles from a number of different sources. This out-of-domain test set contrasts with the in-domain Europarl test set.
- **New language pairs** – We evaluated the quality of Hungarian-English machine translation. Hungarian is a challenging language because it is agglutinative, has many cases and verb conjugations, and has freer word order. German-Spanish was our first language pair that did not include English, but was not manually evaluated since it attracted minimal participation.
- **System combination** – Saarland University entered a system combination over a number of rule-based MT systems, and provided their output, which were also treated as fully fledged entries in the manual evaluation. Three additional groups were invited to apply their system combination algorithms to all systems.
- **Refined manual evaluation** – Because last year's study indicated that fluency and adequacy judgments were slow and unreliable, we dropped them from manual evaluation. We replaced them with yes/no judgments about the acceptability of translations of shorter phrases.
- **Sentence-level correlation** – In addition to measuring the correlation of automatic evaluation metrics with human judgments at the system level, we also measured how consistent they were with the human rankings of individual sentences.

The remainder of this paper is organized as follows: Section 2 gives an overview of the shared

Proceedings of the Third Workshop on Statistical Machine Translation, pages 70–106,
Columbus, Ohio, USA, June 2008.

translation task, describing the test sets, the materials that were provided to participants, and a list of the groups who participated. Section 3 describes the manual evaluation of the translations, including information about the different types of judgments that were solicited and how much data was collected. Section 4 presents the results of the manual evaluation. Section 5 gives an overview of the shared evaluation task, describes which automatic metrics were submitted, and tells how they were evaluated. Section 6 presents the results of the evaluation task. Section 7 validates the manual evaluation methodology.

2 Overview of the shared translation task

The shared translation task consisted of 10 language pairs: English to German, German to English, English to Spanish, Spanish to English, English to French, French to English, English to Czech, Czech to English, Hungarian to English, and German to Spanish. Each language pair had two test sets drawn from the proceedings of the European parliament, or from newspaper articles.[1]

2.1 Test data

The test data for this year's task differed from previous years' data. Instead of only reserving a portion of the training data as the test set, we hired people to translate news articles that were drawn from a variety of sources during November and December of 2007. We refer to this as the News test set. A total of 90 articles were selected, 15 each from a variety of Czech-, English-, French-, German-, Hungarian- and Spanish-language news sites:[2]

Hungarian: Napi (3 documents), Index (2), Origo (5), Népszabadság (2), HVG (2), Uniospez (1)

Czech: Aktuálně (1), iHNed (4), Lidovky (7), Novinky (3)

French: Liberation (4), Le Figaro (4), Dernieres Nouvelles (2), Les Echos (3), Canoe (2)

[1]For Czech news editorials replaced the European parliament transcripts as the second test set, and for Hungarian the newspaper articles was the only test set.

[2]For more details see the XML test files. The `docid` tag gives the source and the date for each document in the test set, and the `origlang` tag indicates the original source language.

Original source language	avg. BLEU
Hungarian	8.8
German	11.0
Czech	15.2
Spanish	17.3
English	17.7
French	18.6

Table 1: Difficulty of the test set parts based on the original language. For each part, we average BLEU scores from the Edinburgh systems for 12 language pairs of the shared task.

Spanish: Cinco Dias (7), ABC.es (3), El Mundo (5)

English: BBC (3), Scotsman (3), Economist (3), Times (3), New York Times (3)

German: Financial Times Deutschland (3), Süddeutsche Zeitung (3), Welt (3), Frankfurter Allgemeine Zeitung (3), Spiegel (3)

The translations were created by the members of EuroMatrix consortium who hired a mix of professional and non-professional translators. All translators were fluent or native speakers of both languages, and all translations were proofread by a native speaker of the target language. All of the translations were done directly, and not via an intermediate language. So for instance, each of the 15 Hungarian articles were translated into Czech, English, French, German and Spanish. The total cost of creating the 6 test sets consisting of 2,051 sentences in each language was approximately 17,200 euros (around 26,500 dollars at current exchange rates, at slightly more than 10c/word).

Having a test set that is balanced in six different source languages and translated across six languages raises some interesting questions. For instance, is it easier, when the machine translation system translates in the same direction as the human translator? We found no conclusive evidence that shows this. What is striking, however, that the parts differ dramatically in difficulty, based on the original source language. For instance the Edinburgh French-English system has a BLEU score of 26.8 on the part that was originally Spanish, but a score of on 9.7 on the part that was originally Hungarian. For average scores for each original language, see Table 1.

In order to remain consistent with previous evaluations, we also created a Europarl test set. The Europarl test data was again drawn from the transcripts of EU parliamentary proceedings from the fourth quarter of 2000, which is excluded from the Europarl training data. Our rationale behind investing a considerable sum to create the News test set was that we believe that it more accurately represents the quality of systems' translations than when we simply hold out a portion of the training data as the test set, as with the Europarl set. For instance, statistical systems are heavily optimized to their training data, and do not perform as well on out-of-domain data (Koehn and Schroeder, 2007). Having both the News test set and the Europarl test set allows us to contrast the performance of systems on in-domain and out-of-domain data, and provides a fairer comparison between systems trained on the Europarl corpus and systems that were developed without it.

2.2 Provided materials

To lower the barrier of entry for newcomers to the field, we provided a complete baseline MT system, along with data resources. We provided:

- sentence-aligned training corpora
- language model data
- development and dev-test sets
- Moses open source toolkit for phrase-based statistical translation (Koehn et al., 2007)

The performance of this baseline system is similar to the best submissions in last year's shared task.

The training materials are described in Figure 1.

2.3 Submitted systems

We received submissions from 23 groups from 18 institutions, as listed in Table 2. We also evaluated seven additional commercial rule-based MT systems, bringing the total to 30 systems. This is a significant increase over last year's shared task, where there were submissions from 15 groups from 14 institutions. Of the 15 groups that participated in last year's shared task, 11 groups returned this year. One of the goals of the workshop was to attract submissions from newcomers to the field, and we are please to have attracted many smaller groups, some as small as a single graduate student and her adviser.

The 30 submitted systems represent a broad range of approaches to statistical machine translation. These include statistical phrase-based and rule-based (RBMT) systems (which together made up the bulk of the entries), and also hybrid machine translation, and statistical tree-based systems. For most language pairs, we assembled a solid representation of the state of the art in machine translation.

In addition to individual systems being entered, this year we also solicited a number of entries which combined the results of other systems. We invited researchers at BBN, Carnegie Mellon University, and the University of Edinburgh to apply their system combination algorithms to all of the systems submitted to shared translation task. We designated the translations of the Europarl set as the development data for combination techniques which weight each system.[3] CMU combined the French-English systems, BBN combined the French-English and German-English systems, and Edinburgh submitted combinations for the French-English and German-English systems as well as a multi-source system combination which combined all systems which translated from any language pair into English for the News test set. The University of Saarland also produced a system combination over six commercial RBMT systems (Eisele et al., 2008). Saarland graciously provided the output of these systems, which we manually evaluated alongside all other entries.

For more on the participating systems, please refer to the respective system descriptions in the proceedings of the workshop.

3 Human evaluation

As with last year's workshop, we placed greater emphasis on the human evaluation than on the automatic evaluation metric scores. It is our contention that automatic measures are an imperfect substitute for human assessment of translation quality. Therefore, rather than select an official automatic evaluation metric like the NIST Machine Translation Workshop does (Przybocki and Peterson, 2008), we define the manual evaluation to be primary, and use

[3]Since the performance of systems varied significantly between the Europarl and News test sets, such weighting might not be optimal. However this was a level playing field, since none of the individual systems had development data for the News set either.

Europarl Training Corpus

	Spanish ↔ English		French ↔ English		German ↔ English		German ↔ Spanish	
Sentences	1,258,778		1,288,074		1,266,520		1,237,537	
Words	36,424,186	35,060,653	38,784,144	36,046,219	33,404,503	35,259,758	32,652,649	35,780,165
Distinct words	149,159	96,746	119,437	97,571	301,006	96,802	298,040	148,206

News Commentary Training Corpus

	Spanish ↔ English		French ↔ English		German ↔ English		German ↔ Spanish	
Sentences	64,308		55,030		72,291		63,312	
Words	1,759,972	1,544,633	1,528,159	1,329,940	1,784,456	1,718,561	1,597,152	1,751,215
Distinct words	52,832	38,787	42,385	36,032	84,700	40,553	78,658	52,397

Hunglish Training Corpus

	Hungarian ↔ English	
Sentences	1,517,584	
Words	26,082,667	31,458,540
Distinct words	717,198	192,901

CzEng Training Corpus

	Czech ↔ English	
Sentences	1,096,940	
Words	15,336,783	17,909,979
Distinct words	339,683	129,176

Europarl Language Model Data

	English	Spanish	French	German
Sentence	1,412,546	1,426,427	1,438,435	1,467,291
Words	34,501,453	36,147,902	35,680,827	32,069,151
Distinct words	100,826	155,579	124,149	314,990

Europarl test set

	English	Spanish	French	German
Sentences	2,000			
Words	60,185	61,790	64,378	56,624
Distinct words	6,050	7,814	7,361	8,844

News Commentary test set

	English	Czech
Sentences	2,028	
Words	45,520	39,384
Distinct words	7,163	12,570

News Test Set

	English	Spanish	French	German	Czech	Hungarian
Sentences	2,051					
Words	43,482	47,155	46,183	41,175	36,359	35,513
Distinct words	7,807	8,973	8,898	10,569	12,732	13,144

Figure 1: Properties of the training and test sets used in the shared task. The training data is drawn from the Europarl corpus and from the Project Syndicate, a web site which collects political commentary in multiple languages. For Czech and Hungarian we use other available parallel corpora. Note that the number of words is computed based on the provided tokenizer and that the number of distinct words is the based on lowercased tokens.

ID	Participant
BBN-COMBO	BBN system combination (Rosti et al., 2008)
CMU-COMBO	Carnegie Mellon University system combination (Jayaraman and Lavie, 2005)
CMU-GIMPEL	Carnegie Mellon University Gimpel (Gimpel and Smith, 2008)
CMU-SMT	Carnegie Mellon University SMT (Bach et al., 2008)
CMU-STATXFER	Carnegie Mellon University Stat-XFER (Hanneman et al., 2008)
CU-TECTOMT	Charles University TectoMT (Zabokrtsky et al., 2008)
CU-BOJAR	Charles University Bojar (Bojar and Hajič, 2008)
CUED	Cambridge University (Blackwood et al., 2008)
DCU	Dublin City University (Tinsley et al., 2008)
LIMSI	LIMSI (Déchelotte et al., 2008)
LIU	Linköping University (Stymne et al., 2008)
LIUM-SYSTRAN	LIUM / Systran (Schwenk et al., 2008)
MLOGIC	Morphologic (Novák et al., 2008)
PCT	a commercial MT provider from the Czech Republic
RBMT1–6	Babelfish, Lingenio, Lucy, OpenLogos, ProMT, SDL (ordering anonymized)
SAAR	University of Saarbruecken (Eisele et al., 2008)
SYSTRAN	Systran (Dugast et al., 2008)
UCB	University of California at Berkeley (Nakov, 2008)
UCL	University College London (Wang and Shawe-Taylor, 2008)
UEDIN	University of Edinburgh (Koehn et al., 2008)
UEDIN-COMBO	University of Edinburgh system combination (Josh Schroeder)
UMD	University of Maryland (Dyer, 2007)
UPC	Universitat Politecnica de Catalunya, Barcelona (Khalilov et al., 2008)
UW	University of Washington (Axelrod et al., 2008)
XEROX	Xerox Research Centre Europe (Nikoulina and Dymetman, 2008)

Table 2: Participants in the shared translation task. Not all groups participated in all language pairs.

the human judgments to validate automatic metrics.

Manual evaluation is time consuming, and it requires a monumental effort to conduct it on the scale of our workshop. We distributed the workload across a number of people, including shared task participants, interested volunteers, and a small number of paid annotators. More than 100 people participated in the manual evaluation, with 75 people putting in more than an hour's worth of effort, and 25 putting in more than four hours. A collective total of 266 hours of labor was invested.

We wanted to ensure that we were using our annotators' time effectively, so we carefully designed the manual evaluation process. In our analysis of last year's manual evaluation we found that the NIST-style fluency and adequacy scores (LDC, 2005) were overly time consuming and inconsistent.[4] We therefore abandoned this method of evaluating the translations.

We asked people to evaluate the systems' output in three different ways:

- Ranking translated sentences relative to each other
- Ranking the translations of syntactic constituents drawn from the source sentence
- Assigning absolute yes or no judgments to the translations of the syntactic constituents.

The manual evaluation software asked for repeated judgments from the same individual, and had multiple people judge the same item, and logged the time it took to complete each judgment. This allowed us to measure intra- and inter-annotator agreement, and to analyze the average amount of time it takes to collect the different kinds of judgments. Our analysis is presented in Section 7.

3.1 Ranking translations of sentences

Ranking translations relative to each other is a relatively intuitive and straightforward task. We therefore kept the instructions simple. The instructions for this task were:

> Rank each whole sentence translation from Best to Worst relative to the other choices (ties are allowed).

Ranking several translations at a time is a variant of force choice judgments where a pair of systems is presented and an annotator is asked "Is A better than B, worse than B, or equal to B." In our experiments, annotators were shown five translations at a time, except for the Hungarian and Czech language pairs where there were fewer than five system submissions. In most cases there were more than 5 systems submissions. We did not attempt to get a complete ordering over the systems, and instead relied on random selection and a reasonably large sample size to make the comparisons fair.

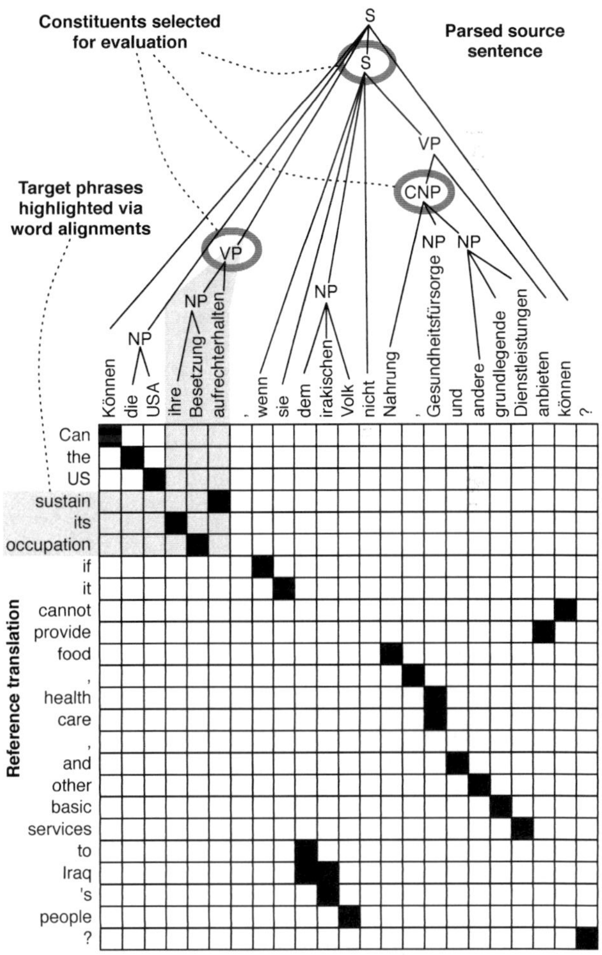

Figure 2: In constituent-based evaluation, the source sentence was parsed, and automatically aligned with the reference translation and systems' translations

[4]It took 26 seconds on average to assign fluency and adequacy scores to a single sentence, and the inter-annotator agreement had a Kappa of between .225–.25, meaning that annotators assigned the same scores to identical sentences less than 40% of the time.

Language Pair	Test Set	Constituent Rank	Yes/No Judgments	Sentence Ranking
English-German	Europarl	2,032	2,034	1,004
	News	2,170	2,221	1,115
German-English	Europarl	1,705	1,674	819
	News	1,938	1,881	1,944
English-Spanish	Europarl	1,200	1,247	615
	News	1,396	1,398	700
Spanish-English	Europarl	1,855	1,921	948
	News	2,063	1,939	1,896
English-French	Europarl	1,248	1,265	674
	News	1,741	1,734	843
French-English	Europarl	1,829	1,841	909
	News	2,467	2,500	2,671
English-Czech	News	2,069	2,070	1,045
	Commentary	1,840	1,815	932
Czech-English	News	0	0	1,400
	Commentary	0	0	1,731
Hungarian-English	News	0	0	937
All-English	News	0	0	4,868
	Totals	**25,553**	**25,540**	**25,051**

Table 3: The number of items that were judged for each task during the manual evaluation. The All-English judgments were reused in the News task for individual language pairs.

3.2 Ranking translations of syntactic constituents

We continued the constituent-based evaluation that we piloted last year, wherein we solicited judgments about the translations of short phrases within sentences rather than whole sentences. We parsed the source language sentence, selected syntactic constituents from the tree, and had people judge the translations of those syntactic phrases. In order to draw judges' attention to these regions, we highlighted the selected source phrases and the corresponding phrases in the translations. The corresponding phrases in the translations were located via automatic word alignments.

Figure 2 illustrates how the source and reference phrases are highlighted via automatic word alignments. The same is done for sentence and each of the system translations. The English, French, German and Spanish test sets were automatically parsed using high quality parsers for those languages (Bikel, 2002; Arun and Keller, 2005; Dubey, 2005; Bick, 2006).

The word alignments were created with Giza++ (Och and Ney, 2003) applied to a parallel corpus containing the complete Europarl training data, plus sets of 4,051 sentence pairs created by pairing the test sentences with the reference translations, and the test sentences paired with each of the system translations. The phrases in the translations were located using standard phrase extraction techniques (Koehn et al., 2003). Because the word-alignments were created automatically, and because the phrase extraction is heuristic, the phrases that were selected may not exactly correspond to the translations of the selected source phrase. We noted this in the instructions to judges:

> Rank each constituent translation from Best to Worst relative to the other choices (ties are allowed). Grade **only the highlighted part** of each translation.
>
> *Please note that segments are selected automatically, and they should be taken as an approximate guide. They might include extra words that are not in the actual alignment, or miss words on either end.*

The criteria that we used to select which constituents to evaluate were:

- The constituent could not be the whole source sentence
- The constituent had to be longer three words, and be no longer than 15 words
- The constituent had to have a corresponding phrase with a consistent word alignment in each of the translations

The final criterion helped reduce the number of alignment errors, but may have biased the sample to phrases that are more easily aligned.

3.3 Yes/No judgments for the translations of syntactic constituents

This year we introduced a variant on the constituent-based evaluation, where instead of asking judges to rank the translations of phrases relative to each other, we asked them to indicate which phrasal translations were acceptable and which were not.

> Decide if the **highlighted part** of each translation is acceptable, given the reference. This should not be a relative judgment against the other system translations.

The instructions also contained the same caveat about the automatic alignments as above. For each phrase the judges could click on "Yes", "No", or "Not Sure." The number of times people clicked on "Not Sure" varied by language pair and task. It was selected as few as 5% of the time for the English-Spanish News task to as many as 12.5% for the Czech-English News task.

3.4 Collecting judgments

We collected judgments using a web-based tool that presented judges with batches of each type of evaluation. We presented them with five screens of sentence rankings, ten screens of constituent rankings, and ten screen of yes/no judgments. The order of the types of evaluation were randomized.

In order to measure intra-annotator agreement 10% of the items were repeated and evaluated twice by each judge. In order to measure inter-annotator agreement 40% of the items were randomly drawn from a common pool that was shared across all annotators so that we would have items that were judged by multiple annotators.

Judges were allowed to select whichever data set they wanted, and to evaluate translations into whatever languages they were proficient in. Shared task participants were excluded from judging their own systems.

In addition to evaluation each language pair individually, we also combined all system translations into English for the News test set, taking advantage of the fact that our test sets were parallel across all languages. This allowed us to gather interesting data about the difficulty of translating from different languages into English.

Table 3 gives a summary of the number of judgments that we collected for translations of individual sentences. We evaluated 14 translation tasks with three different types of judgments for most of them, for a total of 46 different conditions. In total we collected over 75,000 judgments. Despite the large number of conditions we managed to collect between 1,000–2,000 judgments for the constituent-based evaluation, and several hundred to several thousand judgments for the sentence ranking tasks.

4 Translation task results

Tables 4, 5, and 6 summarize the results of the human evaluation of the quality of the machine translation systems. Table 4 gives the results for the manual evaluation which ranked the translations of sentences. It shows the average number of times that systems were judged to be better than or equal to any other system. Table 5 similarly summarizes the results for the manual evaluation which ranked the translations of syntactic constituents. Table 6 shows how many times on average a system's translated constituents were judged to be acceptable in the Yes/No evaluation. The bolded items indicate the system that performed the best for each task under that particular evaluate metric.

Table 7 summaries the results for the All-English task that we introduced this year. Appendix C gives an extremely detailed pairwise comparison between each of the systems, along with an indication of whether the differences are statistically significant.

The highest ranking entry for the All-English task

was the University of Edinburgh's system combination entry. It uses a technique similar to Rosti et al. (2007) to perform system combination. Like the other system combination entrants, it was tuned on the Europarl test set and tested on the News test set, using systems that submitted entries to both tasks.

The University of Edinburgh's system combination went beyond other approaches by combining output from multiple languages pairs (French-English, German-English and Spanish-English), resulting in 37 component systems. Rather than weighting individual systems, it incorporated weighted features that indicated which language the system was originally translating from. This entry was part of ongoing research in multi-lingual, multi-source translation. Since there was no official multi-lingual system combination track, this entry should be viewed only as a contrastive data point.

We analyzed the All-English judgments to see which source languages were preferred more often, thinking that this might be a good indication of how challenging it is for current MT systems to translate from each of the languages into English. For this analysis we collapsed all of the entries derived from one source language into an equivalence class, and judged them against the others. Therefore, all French systems were judged against all German systems, and so on. We found that French systems were judged to be better than or equal to other systems 69% of the time, Spanish systems 64% of the time, German systems 47% of the time, Czech systems 39% of the time, and Hungarian systems 29% of the time.

We performed a similar analysis by collapsing the RBMT systems into one equivalence class, and the other systems into another. We evaluated how well these two classes did on the sentence ranking task for each language pair and test set, and found that RBMT was a surprisingly good approach in many of the conditions. RBMT generally did better on the News test set and for translations into German, suggesting that SMT's forte is in test sets where it has appropriate tuning data and for language pairs with less reordering than between German and English.

	BBN-COMBO	CMU-COMBO	CMU-GIMPEL	CMU-SMT	CMU-STATXFER	CU-BOJAR	CU-TECTOMT	CUED	CUED-CONTR	DCU	LIMSI	LIU	LIUM-SYSTRAN	LIUM-SYS-CONTR	MORPHOLOGIC	PC-TRANSLATOR	RBMT2	RBMT3	RBMT4	RBMT5	RBMT6	SAAR	SAAR-CONTR	SYSTRAN	UCB	UCL	UEDIN	UEDIN-COMBO	UMD	UPC	UW	XEROX
Czech-English Commentary										**.745**														.445			.603		.717			
Czech-English News										**.675**																	.583		.646			
English-Czech Commentary						**.714**	.488									.663											.486					
English-Czech News						.634	.494									**.715**											.502					
English-French Europarl											**.791**		.775					.416	.608	.263	.436	.744	.786			.444	.766					
English-French News											.667		.655					.602	**.780**	.734	.657	.511	.573				.545					.317
English-German Europarl			.612								.584	.581					.615	.583	**.681**	.471	.432	.527				.386	.667					
English-German News											.361	.426					**.787**	.664	.752	.667	.555	.463					.444					
English-Spanish Europarl				.667							**.737**							.554	.560	.413	.436	.717				.500	.714			.593	.735	
English-Spanish News				.494							.537							.683	.674	**.724**	.715	.548			.586		.481			.601		
French-English Europarl					.415			.697		.642	.776		**.792**					.400	.504	.484	.323	.577	.753	.465		.524	.707					
French-English News	.659	.592			.379			.549	.643		.632		.660	**.693**				.581	.575	.654	.565	.540	.639				.614	.608				
German-English Europarl					.364						.485	.614					.627	.596	.610	.543	.537	.677				.416	**.679**					
German-English News	.514				.354						.518	.559					**.742**	.725	.731	.668	.590	.607	.649				.548	.441				
Hungarian-English News															**.853**												.321					
Spanish-English Europarl				.714				.676		.677	**.780**							.427	.488	.350	.470	.671				.425	.660			.687		
Spanish-English News				.567				.563	.674		.583							.667	**.768**	.577	.613	.669			.543		.561			.602		

Table 4: Summary results for the *sentence ranking* judgments. The numbers report the percent of time that each system was judged to be greater than or equal to any other system. Bold indicates the highest score for that task.

	BBN-COMBO	CMU-COMBO	CMU-GIMPEL	CMU-SMT	CMU-STATXFER	CU-BOJAR	CU-TECTOMT	CUED	CUED-CONTR	DCU	LIMSI	LIU	LIUM-SYSTRAN	LIUM-SYS-CONTR	MORPHOLOGIC	PC-TRANSLATOR	RBMT2	RBMT3	RBMT4	RBMT5	RBMT6	SAAR	SAAR-CONTR	SYSTRAN	UCB	UCL	UEDIN	UEDIN-COMBO	UMD	UPC	UW	XEROX
Czech-English Commentary																																
Czech-English News																																
English-Czech Commentary						**.594**	.427									.506											.409					
English-Czech News						**.540**	.422									.518											.441					
English-French Europarl											.745		**.843**					.490	.504	.442	.351	.701				.596	.750					
English-French News											.730		**.748**					.589	.593	.640	.576	.591	.586				.633					.302
English-German Europarl			.822								.794	.788					.692	.571	.665	.447	.466	.774				.611	**.849**					
English-German News											.559	.494					.689	.689	**.750**	.553	.598	.544					.518					
English-Spanish Europarl				.804							.872							.582	.598	.635	.600	.806				.714	.888			**.903**	.785	
English-Spanish News				.459							.532							.638	**.759**	.599	.623	.639			.568		.493			.366		
French-English Europarl					.612			.833		.876	.886		.891					.535	.620	.712	.540	.717	.860	.811		.734	**.910**					
French-English News					.554			.736	.788		**.805**		.789	.696				.628	.640	.762	.663	.638	.701				.718					
German-English Europarl					.534						.803	.831					.759	.744	.667	.633	.630	.823				.492	**.856**					
German-English News					.470						.725	.638					.717	.731	**.738**	.589	.684	.669	.716				.632					
Hungarian-English News																																
Spanish-English Europarl				.882				.857		.853	**.902**							.648	.562	.590	.550	.869				.730	.879			.857		
Spanish-English News				.635				.638	.694		.675							.610	.651	.594	.635	.697			.635		.622			**.707**		

Table 6: Summary results for the *Yes/No judgments for constituent translations* judgments. The numbers report the percent of each system's translations that were judged to be acceptable. Bold indicates the highest score for that task.

	BBN-COMBO	CMU-COMBO	CMU-GIMPEL	CMU-SMT	CMU-STATXFER	CU-BOJAR	CU-TECTOMT	CUED	CUED-CONTR	DCU	LIMSI	LIU	LIUM-SYSTRAN	LIUM-SYS-CONTR	MORPHOLOGIC	PC-TRANSLATOR	RBMT2	RBMT3	RBMT4	RBMT5	RBMT6	SAAR	SAAR-CONTR	SYSTRAN	UCB	UCL	UEDIN	UEDIN-COMBO	UMD	UPC	UW	XEROX
Czech-English Commentary																																
Czech-English News																																
English-Czech Commentary						**.732**	.538									.609											.614					
English-Czech News						.663	.615									**.674**											.610					
English-French Europarl											.876		**.881**					.561	.675	.546	.561	.807				.656	.870					
English-French News											.649		.760					.716	**.768**	.763	.671	.725	.746				.661					.437
English-German Europarl			.774								.750	.812					.577	.585	.582	.508	.518	.770				.690	**.822**					
English-German News											.649	.570					.720	.682	**.748**	.602	.563	.610					.556					
English-Spanish Europarl				.825							**.855**							.561	.592	.458	.573	.849				.592	.818			.775	.790	
English-Spanish News				.721							.694							.694	**.754**	.570	.644	.696			.653		.625			.595		
French-English Europarl					.626			.907		.854	.906		**.917**					.523	.648	.697	.517	.783	.865	.713		.741	.894					
French-English News					.506			.745	.787		**.801**		.765	.780				.652	.655	.726	.615	.640	.735				.773					
German-English Europarl					.554						.752	.795					.580	.640	.643	.579	.587	**.843**				.601	.832					
German-English News					.502						.715	.674					.772	.755	.740	.674	.640	.757	**.775**				.744					
Hungarian-English News																																
Spanish-English Europarl				.847				.846		.868	.854							.455	.561	.469	.567	**.893**				.646	.865			.870		
Spanish-English News				.715				.760	**.818**		.739							.644	.608	.699	.700	.760			.706		.758			.763		

Table 5: Summary results for the *constituent ranking* judgments. The numbers report the percent of time that each system was judged to be greater than or equal to any other system. Bold indicates the highest score for that task.

UEDIN-COMBO$_{xx}$	.717	SAAR$_{fr}$	.584
LIUM-SYSTRAN-C$_{fr}$	.708	SAAR-C$_{de}$	.574
RBMT5$_{fr}$	.706	RBMT4$_{de}$	.573
UEDIN-COMBO$_{fr}$	.704	CUED$_{es}$	.572
LIUM-SYSTRAN$_{fr}$	.702	RBMT3$_{de}$	.552
RBMT4$_{es}$	.699	CMU-SMT$_{es}$	.548
LIMSI$_{fr}$	.699	UCB$_{es}$	.547
BBN-COMBO$_{fr}$	.695	LIMSI$_{es}$	.537
SAAR$_{es}$	.678	RBMT6$_{de}$	.509
CUED-CONTRAST$_{es}$	.674	RBMT5$_{de}$	.493
CMU-COMBO$_{fr}$	.661	LIMSI$_{de}$	.469
UEDIN$_{es}$	.654	LIU$_{de}$	.447
CUED$_{fr}$	.652	SAAR$_{de}$	.445
CUED-CONTRAST$_{fr}$	.638	CMU-STATXFR$_{fr}$	.444
RBMT4$_{fr}$	.637	UMD$_{cz}$	.429
UPC$_{es}$	.633	BBN-COMBO$_{de}$	.407
RBMT3$_{es}$	.628	UEDIN$_{de}$	.402
RBMT2$_{de}$	.627	MORPHOLOGIC$_{hu}$	.387
SAAR-CONTRAST$_{fr}$	.624	DCU$_{cz}$	.380
UEDIN$_{fr}$	.616	UEDIN-COMBO$_{de}$	.327
RBMT6$_{fr}$	.615	UEDIN$_{cz}$	.293
RBMT6$_{es}$	.615	CMU-STATXFER$_{de}$	.280
RBMT3$_{fr}$	.612	UEDIN$_{hu}$	.188

Table 7: The average number of times that each system was judged to be better than or equal to all other systems in the sentence ranking task for the All-English condition. The subscript indicates the source language of the system.

5 Shared evaluation task overview

The manual evaluation data provides a rich source of information beyond simply analyzing the quality of translations produced by different systems. In particular, it is especially useful for validating the automatic metrics which are frequently used by the machine translation research community. We continued the shared task which we debuted last year, by examining how well various automatic metrics correlate with human judgments.

In addition to examining how well the automatic evaluation metrics predict human judgments at the system-level, this year we have also started to measure their ability to predict sentence-level judgments.

The automatic metrics that were evaluated in this year's shared task were the following:

- Bleu (Papineni et al., 2002)—Bleu remains the *de facto* standard in machine translation evaluation. It calculates n-gram precision and a brevity penalty, and can make use of multiple reference translations as a way of capturing some of the allowable variation in translation. We use a single reference translation in our experiments.

- Meteor (Agarwal and Lavie, 2008)—Meteor measures precision and recall for unigrams and applies a fragmentation penalty. It uses flexible word matching based on stemming and WordNet-synonymy. A number of variants are investigated here: meteor-baseline and meteor-ranking are optimized for correlation with adequacy and ranking judgments respectively. mbleu and mter are Bleu and TER computed using the flexible matching used in Meteor.

- Gimenez and Marquez (2008) measure overlapping grammatical dependency relationships (DP), semantic roles (SR), and discourse representations (DR). The authors further investigate combining these with other metrics including TER, Bleu, GTM, Rouge, and Meteor (ULC and ULCh).

- Popovic and Ney (2007) automatically evaluate translation quality by examining sequences of parts of speech, rather than words. They calculate Bleu (posbleu) and F-measure (pos4gramFmeasure) by matching part of speech 4grams in a hypothesis translation against the reference translation.

In addition to the above metrics, which scored the translations on both the system-level[5] and the sentence-level, there were a number of metrics which focused on the sentence-level:

- Albrecht and Hwa (2008) use support vector regression to score translations using past WMT manual assessment data as training examples. The metric uses features derived from target-side language models and machine-generated translations (svm-pseudo-ref) as well as reference human translations (svm-human-ref).

- Duh (2008) similarly used support vector machines to predict an ordering over a set of

[5]We provide the scores assigned to each system by these metrics in Appendix A.

system translations (svm-rank). Features included in Duh (2008)'s training were sentence-level BLEU scores and intra-set ranks computed from the entire set of translations.

- USaar's evaluation metric (alignment-prob) uses Giza++ to align outputs of multiple systems with the corresponding reference translations, with a bias towards identical one-to-one alignments through a suitably augmented corpus. The Model4 log probabilities in both directions are added and normalized to a scale between 0 and 1.

5.1 Measuring system-level correlation

To measure the correlation of the automatic metrics with the human judgments of translation quality at the system-level we used Spearman's rank correlation coefficient ρ. We converted the raw scores assigned each system into ranks. We assigned a ranking to the systems for each of the three types of manual evaluation based on:

- The percent of time that the sentences it produced were judged to be better than or equal to the translations of any other system.
- The percent of time that its constituent translations were judged to be better than or equal to the translations of any other system.
- The percent of time that its constituent translations were judged to be acceptable.

We calculated ρ three times for each automatic metric, comparing it to each type of human evaluation. Since there were no ties ρ can be calculated using the simplified equation:

$$\rho = 1 - \frac{6\sum d_i^2}{n(n^2-1)}$$

where d_i is the difference between the rank for system$_i$ and n is the number of systems. The possible values of ρ range between 1 (where all systems are ranked in the same order) and -1 (where the systems are ranked in the reverse order). Thus an automatic evaluation metric with a higher value for ρ is making predictions that are more similar to the human judgments than an automatic evaluation metric with a lower ρ.

	RANK	CONST	YES/NO	OVERALL
meteor-ranking	**.81**	.72	.77	**.76**
ULCh	.68	.79	.82	**.76**
meteor-baseline	.77	.75	.74	.75
posbleu	.77	**.8**	.66	.74
pos4gramFmeasure	.75	.62	.82	.73
ULC	.66	.67	**.84**	.72
DR	.79	.55	.76	.70
SR	.79	.53	.76	.69
DP	.57	.79	.65	.67
mbleu	.61	.77	.56	.65
mter	.47	.72	.68	.62
bleu	.61	.59	.44	.54
svm-rank	.21	.24	.35	.27

Table 8: Average system-level correlations for the automatic evaluation metrics on translations into English

5.2 Measuring consistency at the sentence-level

Measuring sentence-level correlation under our human evaluation framework was made complicated by the fact that we abandoned the fluency and adequacy judgments which are intended to be absolute scales. Some previous work has focused on developing automatic metrics which predict human ranking at the sentence-level (Kulesza and Shieber, 2004; Albrecht and Hwa, 2007a; Albrecht and Hwa, 2007b). Such work generally used the 5-point fluency and adequacy scales to combine the translations of all sentences into a single ranked list. This list could be compared against the scores assigned by automatic metrics and used to calculate correlation coefficients. We did not gather any absolute scores and thus cannot compare translations across different sentences. Given the seemingly unreliable fluency and adequacy assignments that people make even for translations of the same sentences, it may be dubious to assume that their scoring will be reliable across sentences.

The data points that we have available consist of a set of 6,400 human judgments each ranking the output of 5 systems. It's straightforward to construct a ranking of each of those 5 systems using the scores

	RANK	CONST	YES/NO	OVERALL
posbleu	.57	.78	**.80**	**.72**
bleu	.54	**.79**	.6	.64
meteor-ranking	.55	.74	.55	.61
meteor-baseline	.42	.78	.57	.59
pos4gramFmeasure	.37	.49	.79	.55
mter	.54	.50	.55	.53
svm-rank	.55	.56	.46	.52
mbleu	**.63**	.47	.43	.51

Table 9: Average system-level correlations for the automatic evaluation metrics on translations into French, German and Spanish

	RANK	CONST	YES/NO
DP	.514	.527	.536
DR	.500	.511	.530
SR	.498	.489	.511
ULC	.559	**.554**	**.561**
ULCh	**.562**	.542	.542
alignment-prob	.517	.538	.535
mbleu	.505	.516	.544
meteor-baseline	.512	.520	.542
meteor-ranking	.512	.517	.539
mter	.436	.471	.480
pos4gramFmeasure	.495	.517	.52
posbleu	.435	.43	.454
svm-human-ref	.542	.541	.552
svm-pseudo-ref	.538	.538	.543
svm-rank	.493	.499	.497

Table 10: The percent of time that each automatic metric was consistent with human judgments for translations into English

assigned to their translations of that sentence by the automatic evaluation metrics. When the automatic scores have been retrieved, we have 6,400 pairs of ranked lists containing 5 items. How best to treat these is an open discussion, and certainly warrants further thought. It does not seem like a good idea to calculate ρ for each pair of ranked list, because 5 items is an insufficient number to get a reliable correlation coefficient and its unclear if averaging over all 6,400 lists would make sense. Furthermore, many of the human judgments of 5 contained ties, further complicating matters.

Therefore rather than calculating a correlation coefficient at the sentence-level we instead ascertained how consistent the automatic metrics were with the human judgments. The way that we calculated consistency was the following: for every pairwise comparison of two systems on a single sentence by a person, we counted the automatic metric as being consistent if the relative scores were the same (i.e. the metric assigned a higher score to the higher ranked system). We divided this by the total number of pairwise comparisons to get a percentage. Because the systems generally assign real numbers as scores, we excluded pairs that the human annotators ranked as ties.

6 Evaluation task results

Tables 8 and 9 report the system-level ρ for each automatic evaluation metric, averaged over all translations directions into English and out of English[6] For the into English direction the Meteor score with its parameters tuned on adequacy judgments had the strongest correlation with ranking the translations of whole sentences. It was tied with the combined method of Gimenez and Marquez (2008) for the highest correlation over all three types of human judgments. Bleu was the second to lowest ranked overall, though this may have been due in part to the fact that we were using test sets which had only a single reference translation, since the cost of creating multiple references was prohibitively expensive (see Section 2.1).

In the reverse direction, for translations out of English into the other languages, Bleu does considerably better, placing second overall after the part-of-speech variant on it proposed by Popovic and Ney (2007). Yet another variant of Bleu which utilizes Meteor's flexible matching has the strongest correlation for sentence-level ranking. Appendix B gives a break down of the correlations for each of the lan-

[6]Tables 8 and 9 exclude the Spanish-English News Task, since it had a negative correlation with most of the automatic metrics. See Tables 19 and 20.

	RANK	CONST	YES/NO
mbleu	0.520	0.521	0.52
meteor-baseline	0.514	0.494	0.520
meteor-ranking	**0.522**	0.501	**0.534**
mter	0.454	0.441	0.457
pos4gramFmeasure	0.515	0.525	0.512
posbleu	0.436	0.446	0.416
svm-rank	0.514	**0.531**	0.51

Table 11: The percent of time that each automatic metric was consistent with human judgments for translations into other languages

guage pairs and test sets.

Tables 10 and 11 report the consistency of the automatic evaluation metrics with human judgments on a sentence-by-sentence basis, rather than on the system level. For the translations into English the ULC metric (which itself combines many other metrics) had the strongest correlation with human judgments, correctly predicting the human ranking of a each pair of system translations of a sentence more than half the time. This is dramatically higher than the chance baseline, which is not .5, since it must correctly rank a list of systems rather than a pair. For the reverse direction meteor-ranking performs very strongly. The svn-rank which had the lowest overall correlation at the system level does the best at consistently predicting the translations of syntactic constituents into other languages.

7 Validation and analysis of the manual evaluation

In addition to scoring the shared task entries, we also continued on our campaign for improving the process of manual evaluation.

7.1 Inter- and Intra-annotator agreement

We measured pairwise agreement among annotators using the kappa coefficient (K) which is widely used in computational linguistics for measuring agreement in category judgments (Carletta, 1996). It is defined as

$$K = \frac{P(A) - P(E)}{1 - P(E)}$$

Evaluation type	$P(A)$	$P(E)$	K
Sentence ranking	.578	.333	.367
Constituent ranking	.671	.333	.506
Constituent (w/identicals)	.678	.333	.517
Yes/No judgments	.821	.5	.642
Yes/No (w/identicals)	.825	.5	.649

Table 12: Kappa coefficient values representing the inter-annotator agreement for the different types of manual evaluation

Evaluation type	$P(A)$	$P(E)$	K
Sentence ranking	.691	.333	.537
Constituent ranking	.825	.333	.737
Constituent (w/identicals)	.832	.333	.748
Yes/No judgments	.928	.5	.855
Yes/No (w/identicals)	.930	.5	.861

Table 13: Kappa coefficient values for intra-annotator agreement for the different types of manual evaluation

where $P(A)$ is the proportion of times that the annotators agree, and $P(E)$ is the proportion of time that they would agree by chance. We define chance agreement for ranking tasks as $\frac{1}{3}$ since there are three possible outcomes when ranking the output of a pair of systems: $A > B$, $A = B$, $A < B$, and for the Yes/No judgments as $\frac{1}{2}$ since we ignored those items marked "Not Sure".

For inter-annotator agreement we calculated $P(A)$ for the yes/no judgments by examining all items that were annotated by two or more annotators, and calculating the proportion of time they assigned identical scores to the same items. For the ranking tasks we calculated $P(A)$ by examining all pairs of systems which had been judged by two or more judges, and calculated the proportion of time that they agreed that $A > B$, $A = B$, or $A < B$. For intra-annotator agreement we did similarly, but gathered items that were annotated on multiple occasions by a single annotator.

Table 12 gives K values for inter-annotator agreement, and Table 13 gives K values for intra-annotator agreement. These give an indication of how often different judges agree, and how often single judges are consistent for repeated judgments, respectively. The interpretation of Kappa varies, but according to Landis and Koch (1977), $0-.2$ is slight, $.2-.4$ is fair, $.4-.6$ is moderate, $.6-.8$ is substantial and the rest almost perfect. The inter-annotator agreement for the sentence ranking task was fair, for the constituent ranking it was moderate and for the yes/no judgments it was substantial.[7] For the intra-annotator agreement K indicated that people had moderate consistency with their previous judgments on the sentence ranking task, substantial consistency with their previous constituent ranking judgments, and nearly perfect consistency with their previous yes/no judgments.

These K values indicate that people are able to more reliably make simple yes/no judgments about the translations of short phrases than they are to rank phrases or whole sentences. While this is an interesting observation, we do not recommend doing away with the sentence ranking judgments. The higher agreement on the constituent-based evaluation may be influenced based on the selection criteria for which phrases were selected for evaluation (see Section 3.2). Additionally, the judgments of the short phrases are not a great substitute for sentence-level rankings, at least in the way we collected them. The average correlation coefficient between the constituent-based judgments with the sentence ranking judgments is only $\rho = 0.51$. Tables 19 and 20 give a detailed break down of the correlation of the different types of human judgments with each other on each translation task. It may be possible to select phrases in such a way that the constituent-based evaluations are a better substitute for the sentence-based ranking, for instance by selecting more of constituents from each sentence, or attempting to cover most of the words in each sentence in a phrase-by-phrase manner. This warrants further investigation. It might also be worthwhile to refine the instructions given to annotators about how to rank the translations of sentences to try to improve their agreement, which is currently lower than we would like it to be (although it is substantially better than the previous fluency and adequacy scores, which had a $K < .25$ in last year's evaluation).

[7]Note that for the constituent-based evaluations we verified that the high K was not trivially due to identical phrasal translations. We excluded screens where all five phrasal translations presented to the annotator were identical, and report both numbers.

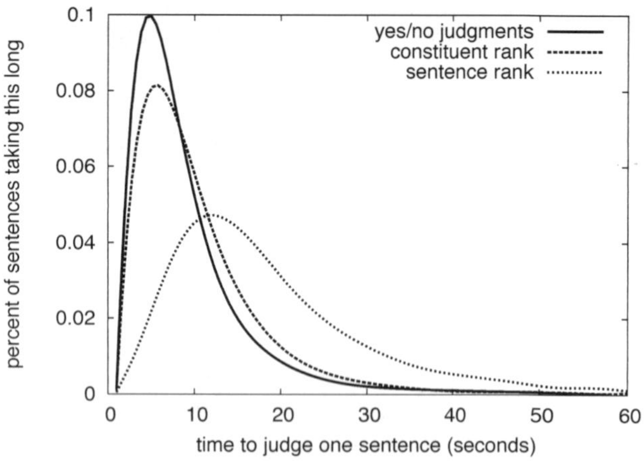

Figure 3: Distributions of the amount of time it took to judge single sentences for the three types of manual evaluation

7.2 Timing

We used the web interface to collect timing information. The server recorded the time when a set of sentences was given to a judge and the time when the judge returned the sentences. It took annotators an average of 18 seconds per sentence to rank a list of sentences.[8] It took an average of 10 seconds per sentence for them to rank constituents, and an average of 8.5 seconds per sentence for them to make yes/no judgments. Figure 3 shows the distribution of times for these tasks.

These timing figures indicate that the tasks which the annotators were the most reliable on (yes/no judgments and constituent ranking) were also much quicker to complete than the ones they were less reliable on (ranking sentences). Given that they are faster at judging short phrases, they can do proportionally more of them. For instance, we could collect 211 yes/no judgments in the same amount of time that it would take us to collect 100 sentence ranking judgments. However, this is partially offset by the fact that many of the translations of shorter phrases are identical, which means that we have to collect more judgments in order to distinguish between two systems.

[8]Sets which took longer than 5 minutes were excluded from these calculations, because there was a strong chance that annotators were interrupted while completing the task.

7.3 The potential for re-usability of human judgments

One strong advantage of the yes/no judgments over the ranking judgments is their potential for reuse. We have invested hundreds of hours worth of effort evaluating the output of the translation systems submitted to this year's workshop and last year's workshop. While the judgments that we collected provide a wealth of information for developing automatic evaluation metrics, we cannot not re-use them to evaluate our translation systems after we update their parameters or change their behavior in anyway. The reason for this is that altered systems will produce different translations than the ones that we have judged, so our relative rankings of sentences will no longer be applicable. However, the translations of short phrases are more likely to be repeated than the translations of whole sentences.

Therefore if we collect a large number of yes/no judgments for short phrases, we could build up a database that contains information about what fragmentary translations are acceptable for each sentence in our test corpus. When we change our system and want to evaluate it, we do not need to manually evaluate those segments that match against the database, and could instead have people evaluate only those phrasal translations which are new. Accumulating these judgments over time would give a very reliable idea of what alternative translations were allowable. This would be useful because it could alleviate the problems associated with Bleu failing to recognize allowable variation in translation when multiple reference translations are not available (Callison-Burch et al., 2006). A large database of human judgments might also be useful as an objective function for minimum error rate training (Och, 2003) or in other system development tasks.

8 Conclusions

Similar to previous editions of this workshop we carried out an extensive manual and automatic evaluation of machine translation performance for translating from European languages into English, and vice versa. One important aspect in which this year's shared task differed from previous years was the introduction of an additional newswire test set that was different in nature to the training data. We also added new language pairs to our evaluation: Hungarian-English and German-Spanish.

As in previous years we were pleased to notice an increase in the number of participants. This year we received submissions from 23 groups from 18 institutions. In addition, we evaluated seven commercial rule-based MT systems.

The goal of this shared-task is two-fold: First we want to compare state-of-the-art machine translation systems, and secondly we aim to measure to what extent different evaluation metrics can be used to assess MT quality.

With respect to MT quality we noticed that the introduction of test sets from a different domain did have an impact on the ranking of systems. We observed that rule-based systems generally did better on the News test set. Overall, it cannot be concluded that one approach clearly outperforms other approaches, as systems performed differently on the various translation tasks. One general observation is that for the tasks where statistical combination approaches participated, they tended to score relatively high, in particular with respect to Bleu.

With respect to measuring the correlation between automated evaluation metrics and human judgments we found that using Meteor and ULCh (which utilizes a variety of metrics, including Meteor) resulted in the highest Spearman correlation scores on average, when translating into English. When translating from English into French, German, and Spanish, Bleu and posbleu resulted in the highest correlations with human judgments.

Finally, we investigated inter- and intra-annotator agreement of human judgments using Kappa coefficients. We noticed that ranking whole sentences results in relatively low Kappa coefficients, meaning that there is only fair agreement between the assessors. Constituent ranking and acceptability judgments on the other hand show moderate and substantial inter-annotator agreement, respectively. Intra-annotator agreement was substantial to almost perfect, except for the sentence ranking assessment where agreement was only moderate. Although it is difficult to draw exact conclusions from this, one might wonder whether the sentence ranking task is simply too complex, involving too many aspects according to which translations can be ranked.

The huge wealth of the data generated by this

workshop, including the human judgments, system translations and automatic scores, is available at http://www.statmt.org/wmt08/ for other researchers to analyze.

Acknowledgments

This work was supported in parts by the EuroMatrix project funded by the European Commission (6th Framework Programme), the GALE program of the US Defense Advanced Research Projects Agency, Contract No. HR0011-06-C-0022, and the US National Science Foundation under grant IIS-0713448.

We are grateful to Abhaya Agarwal, John Henderson, Rebecca Hwa, Alon Lavie, Mark Przybocki, Stuart Shieber, and David Smith for discussing different possibilities for calculating the sentence-level correlation of automatic evaluation metrics with human judgments in absence of absolute scores. Any errors in design remain the responsibility of the authors.

Thank you to Eckhard Bick for parsing the Spanish test set. See http://beta.visl.sdu.dk for more information about the constraint-based parser. Thanks to Greg Hanneman and Antti-Veikko Rosti for applying their system combination algorithms to our data.

References

Abhaya Agarwal and Alon Lavie. 2008. Meteor, M-BLEU and M-TER: Evaluation metrics for high-correlation with human rankings of machine translation output. In *Proceedings of the Third Workshop on Statistical Machine Translation*, pages 115–118, Columbus, Ohio, June. Association for Computational Linguistics.

Joshua Albrecht and Rebecca Hwa. 2007a. A re-examination of machine learning approaches for sentence-level mt evaluation. In *Proceedings of the 45th Annual Meeting of the Association for Computational Linguistics (ACL-2007)*, Prague, Czech Republic.

Joshua Albrecht and Rebecca Hwa. 2007b. Regression for sentence-level mt evaluation with pseudo references. In *Proceedings of the 45th Annual Meeting of the Association for Computational Linguistics (ACL-2007)*, Prague, Czech Republic.

Joshua Albrecht and Rebecca Hwa. 2008. The role of pseudo references in MT evaluation. In *Proceedings of the Third Workshop on Statistical Machine Translation*, pages 187–190, Columbus, Ohio, June. Association for Computational Linguistics.

Abhishek Arun and Frank Keller. 2005. Lexicalization in crosslinguistic probabilistic parsing: The case of French. In *Proceedings of ACL*.

Amittai Axelrod, Mei Yang, Kevin Duh, and Katrin Kirchhoff. 2008. The University of Washington machine translation system for ACL WMT 2008. In *Proceedings of the Third Workshop on Statistical Machine Translation*, pages 123–126, Columbus, Ohio, June. Association for Computational Linguistics.

Nguyen Bach, Qin Gao, and Stephan Vogel. 2008. Improving word alignment with language model based confidence scores. In *Proceedings of the Third Workshop on Statistical Machine Translation*, pages 151–154, Columbus, Ohio, June. Association for Computational Linguistics.

Eckhard Bick. 2006. A constraint grammar-based parser for Spanish. In *Proceedings of the 4th Workshop on Information and Human Language Technology (TIL-2006)*, Ribeiro Preto, Brazil.

Dan Bikel. 2002. Design of a multi-lingual, parallel-processing statistical parsing engine. In *Proceedings of Second International Conference on Human Language Technology Research (HLT-02)*, San Diego, California.

Graeme Blackwood, Adrià de Gispert, Jamie Brunning, and William Byrne. 2008. European language translation with weighted finite state transducers: The CUED MT system for the 2008 ACL workshop on SMT. In *Proceedings of the Third Workshop on Statistical Machine Translation*, pages 131–134, Columbus, Ohio, June. Association for Computational Linguistics.

Ondřej Bojar and Jan Hajič. 2008. Phrase-based and deep syntactic English-to-Czech statistical machine translation. In *Proceedings of the Third Workshop on Statistical Machine Translation*, pages 143–146, Columbus, Ohio, June. Association for Computational Linguistics.

Chris Callison-Burch, Miles Osborne, and Philipp Koehn. 2006. Re-evaluating the role of Bleu in machine translation research. In *11th Conference of the European Chapter of the Association for Computational Linguistics (EACL-2006)*, Trento, Italy.

Chris Callison-Burch, Cameron Fordyce, Philipp Koehn, Christof Monz, and Josh Schroeder. 2007. (Meta-) evaluation of machine translation. In *Proceedings of the Second Workshop on Statistical Machine Translation*, pages 136–158, Prague, Czech Republic, June. Association for Computational Linguistics.

Jean Carletta. 1996. Assessing agreement on classification tasks: The kappa statistic. *Computational Linguistics*, 22(2):249–254.

Daniel Déchelotte, Gilles Adda, Alexandre Allauzen, Hélène Bonneau-Maynard, Olivier Galibert, Jean-Luc Gauvain, Philippe Langlais, and François Yvon. 2008. Limsi's statistical translation systems for WMT'08. In *Proceedings of the Third Workshop on Statistical Machine Translation*, pages 107–110, Columbus, Ohio, June. Association for Computational Linguistics.

Amit Dubey. 2005. What to do when lexicalization fails: parsing German with suffix analysis and smoothing. In *Proceedings of ACL*.

Loïc Dugast, Jean Senellart, and Philipp Koehn. 2008. Can we relearn an RBMT system? In *Proceedings of the Third Workshop on Statistical Machine Translation*, pages 175–178, Columbus, Ohio, June. Association for Computational Linguistics.

Kevin Duh. 2008. Ranking vs. regression in machine translation evaluation. In *Proceedings of the Third Workshop on Statistical Machine Translation*, pages 191–194, Columbus, Ohio, June. Association for Computational Linguistics.

Christopher J. Dyer. 2007. The 'noisier channel': translation from morphologically complex languages. In *Proceedings of the ACL-2007 Workshop on Statistcal Machine Translation (WMT-07)*, Prague, Czech Republic.

Andreas Eisele, Christian Federmann, Hervé Saint-Amand, Michael Jellinghaus, Teresa Herrmann, and Yu Chen. 2008. Using moses to integrate multiple rule-based machine translation engines into a hybrid system. In *Proceedings of the Third Workshop on Statistical Machine Translation*, pages 179–182, Columbus, Ohio, June. Association for Computational Linguistics.

Jesus Gimenez and Lluis Marquez. 2008. A smorgasbord of features for automatic MT evaluation. In *Proceedings of the Third Workshop on Statistical Machine Translation*, pages 195–198, Columbus, Ohio, June. Association for Computational Linguistics.

Kevin Gimpel and Noah A. Smith. 2008. Rich source-side context for statistical machine translation. In *Proceedings of the Third Workshop on Statistical Machine Translation*, pages 9–17, Columbus, Ohio, June. Association for Computational Linguistics.

Greg Hanneman, Edmund Huber, Abhaya Agarwal, Vamshi Ambati, Alok Parlikar, Erik Peterson, and Alon Lavie. 2008. Statistical transfer systems for French-English and German-English machine translation. In *Proceedings of the Third Workshop on Statistical Machine Translation*, pages 163–166, Columbus, Ohio, June. Association for Computational Linguistics.

Shyamsundar Jayaraman and Alon Lavie. 2005. Multi-engine machine translation guided by explicit word matching. In *Proceedings of the 10th Annual Conference of the European Association for Machine Translation*, pages 143–152, Budapest, Hungary, May.

Maxim Khalilov, Adolfo Hernández H., Marta R. Costa-jussà, Josep M. Crego, Carlos A. Henríquez Q., Patrik Lambert, José A. R. Fonollosa, José B. Mariño, and Rafael E. Banchs. 2008. The TALP-UPC Ngram-based statistical machine translation system for ACL-WMT 2008. In *Proceedings of the Third Workshop on Statistical Machine Translation*, pages 127–130, Columbus, Ohio, June. Association for Computational Linguistics.

Philipp Koehn and Christof Monz. 2006. Manual and automatic evaluation of machine translation between European languages. In *Proceedings of NAACL 2006 Workshop on Statistical Machine Translation*, New York, New York.

Philipp Koehn and Josh Schroeder. 2007. Experiments in domain adaptation for statistical machine translation. In *Proceedings of the ACL-2007 Workshop on Statistcal Machine Translation (WMT-07)*, Prague, Czech Republic.

Philipp Koehn, Franz Josef Och, and Daniel Marcu. 2003. Statistical phrase-based translation. In *Proceedings of the Human Language Technology Conference of the North American chapter of the Association for Computational Linguistics (HLT/NAACL-2003)*, Edmonton, Alberta.

Philipp Koehn, Nicola Bertoldi, Ondrej Bojar, Chris Callison-Burch, Alexandra Constantin, Brooke Cowan, Chris Dyer, Marcello Federico, Evan Herbst, Hieu Hoang, Christine Moran, Wade Shen, and Richard Zens. 2007. Open source toolkit for statistical machine translation: Factored translation models and confusion network decoding. CLSP Summer Workshop Final Report WS-2006, Johns Hopkins University.

Philipp Koehn, Abhishek Arun, and Hieu Hoang. 2008. Towards better machine translation quality for the German-English language pairs. In *Proceedings of the Third Workshop on Statistical Machine Translation*, pages 139–142, Columbus, Ohio, June. Association for Computational Linguistics.

Alex Kulesza and Stuart M. Shieber. 2004. A learning approach to improving sentence-level MT evaluation.

In *Proceedings of the 10th International Conference on Theoretical and Methodological Issues in Machine Translation*, Baltimore, MD, October 4–6.

J. R. Landis and G. G. Koch. 1977. The measurement of observer agreement for categorical data. *Biometrics*, 33:159–174.

LDC. 2005. Linguistic data annotation specification: Assessment of fluency and adequacy in translations. Revision 1.5.

Preslav Nakov. 2008. Improving English-Spanish statistical machine translation: Experiments in domain adaptation, sentence paraphrasing, tokenization, and recasing. In *Proceedings of the Third Workshop on Statistical Machine Translation*, pages 147–150, Columbus, Ohio, June. Association for Computational Linguistics.

Vassilina Nikoulina and Marc Dymetman. 2008. Using syntactic coupling features for discriminating phrase-based translations (wmt-08 shared translation task). In *Proceedings of the Third Workshop on Statistical Machine Translation*, pages 159–162, Columbus, Ohio, June. Association for Computational Linguistics.

Attila Novák, László Tihanyi, and Gábor Prószéky. 2008. The MetaMorpho translation system. In *Proceedings of the Third Workshop on Statistical Machine Translation*, pages 111–114, Columbus, Ohio, June. Association for Computational Linguistics.

Franz Josef Och and Hermann Ney. 2003. A systematic comparison of various statistical alignment models. *Computational Linguistics*, 29(1):19–51, March.

Franz Josef Och. 2003. Minimum error rate training for statistical machine translation. In *Proceedings of the 41st Annual Meeting of the Association for Computational Linguistics (ACL-2003)*, Sapporo, Japan.

Kishore Papineni, Salim Roukos, Todd Ward, and Wei-Jing Zhu. 2002. Bleu: A method for automatic evaluation of machine translation. In *Proceedings of the 40th Annual Meeting of the Association for Computational Linguistics (ACL-2002)*, Philadelphia, Pennsylvania.

Maja Popovic and Hermann Ney. 2007. Word error rates: Decomposition over POS classes and applications for error analysis. In *Proceedings of ACL Workshop on Machine Translation*, Prague, Czech Republic.

Mark Przybocki and Kay Peterson, editors. 2008. *Proceedings of the 2008 NIST Open Machine Translation Evaluation Workshop*. Arlington, Virginia, March.

Antti-Veikko Rosti, Spyros Matsoukas, and Richard Schwartz. 2007. Improved word-level system combination for machine translation. In *Proceedings of the 45th Annual Meeting of the Association for Computational Linguistics (ACL-2007)*, Prague, Czech Republic.

Antti-Veikko Rosti, Bing Zhang, Spyros Matsoukas, and Richard Schwartz. 2008. Incremental hypothesis alignment for building confusion networks with application to machine translation system combination. In *Proceedings of the Third Workshop on Statistical Machine Translation*, pages 183–186, Columbus, Ohio, June. Association for Computational Linguistics.

Holger Schwenk, Jean-Baptiste Fouet, and Jean Senellart. 2008. First steps towards a general purpose French/English statistical machine translation system. In *Proceedings of the Third Workshop on Statistical Machine Translation*, pages 119–122, Columbus, Ohio, June. Association for Computational Linguistics.

Sara Stymne, Maria Holmqvist, and Lars Ahrenberg. 2008. Effects of morphological analysis in translation between German and English. In *Proceedings of the Third Workshop on Statistical Machine Translation*, pages 135–138, Columbus, Ohio, June. Association for Computational Linguistics.

John Tinsley, Yanjun Ma, Sylwia Ozdowska, and Andy Way. 2008. MaTrEx: The DCU MT system for WMT 2008. In *Proceedings of the Third Workshop on Statistical Machine Translation*, pages 171–174, Columbus, Ohio, June. Association for Computational Linguistics.

Zhuoran Wang and John Shawe-Taylor. 2008. Kernel regression framework for machine translation: UCL system description for WMT 2008 shared translation task. In *Proceedings of the Third Workshop on Statistical Machine Translation*, pages 155–158, Columbus, Ohio, June. Association for Computational Linguistics.

Zdenek Zabokrtsky, Jan Ptacek, and Petr Pajas. 2008. TectoMT: Highly modular MT system with tectogrammatics used as transfer layer. In *Proceedings of the Third Workshop on Statistical Machine Translation*, pages 167–170, Columbus, Ohio, June. Association for Computational Linguistics.

A Automatic scores for each system

	BLEU	MBLEU	METEOR-BASELINE	METEOR-RANKING	MTER	SVM-RANK
English-Czech News Commentary Task						
CU-BOJAR	**0.15**	**0.21**	**0.43**	**0.35**	**0.28**	**4.57**
CU-BOJAR-CONTRAST-1	0.04	0.11	0.32	0.25	0.18	0.90
CU-BOJAR-CONTRAST-2	0.14	0.2	0.42	0.34	0.27	2.86
CU-TECTOMT	0.09	0.15	0.37	0.29	0.23	2.13
PC-TRANSLATOR	0.08	0.14	0.35	0.28	0.19	2.09
UEDIN	0.12	0.18	0.4	0.32	0.25	2.28
English-Czech News Task						
CU-BOJAR	**0.11**	**0.18**	**0.37**	**0.3**	**0.18**	**4.72**
CU-BOJAR-CONTRAST-1	0.02	0.10	0.26	0.2	0.12	0.80
CU-BOJAR-CONTRAST-2	0.09	0.16	0.35	0.28	0.15	2.65
CU-TECTOMT	0.06	0.13	0.32	0.25	0.16	2.14
PC-TRANSLATOR	0.08	0.14	0.33	0.26	0.14	2.40
UEDIN	0.08	0.15	0.34	0.27	0.15	2.13

Table 14: Automatic evaluation metric for translations into Czech

	BLEU	MBLEU	METEOR-B	METEOR-R	MTER	POSF4G-AM	POSF4G-GM	POSBLEU	SVM-RANK
English-French News Task									
LIMSI	0.2	0.26	0.16	0.34	0.33	0.48	0.44	0.43	**9.74**
LIUM-SYSTRAN	**0.20**	**0.26**	**0.16**	0.35	**0.34**	**0.49**	**0.44**	**0.44**	7.38
LIUM-SYSTRAN-CONTRAST	0.20	0.26	0.16	**0.35**	0.34	0.48	0.44	0.44	7.02
RBMT1	0.13	0.19	0.12	0.28	0.24	0.42	0.37	0.35	5.46
RBMT3	0.17	0.23	0.14	0.31	0.31	0.45	0.4	0.40	5.60
RBMT4	0.19	0.24	0.15	0.33	0.32	0.48	0.43	0.43	6.80
RBMT5	0.17	0.23	0.14	0.32	0.31	0.47	0.42	0.42	6.15
RBMT6	0.16	0.22	0.13	0.32	0.3	0.46	0.40	0.41	5.60
SAAR	0.15	0.22	0.15	0.33	0.28	0.46	0.41	0.42	6.12
SAAR-CONTRAST	0.17	0.23	0.15	0.33	0.30	0.47	0.42	0.41	5.50
UEDIN	0.16	0.23	0.14	0.32	0.32	0.44	0.39	0.38	4.79
XEROX	0.13	0.2	0.12	0.29	0.29	0.41	0.34	0.34	3.91
XEROX-CONTRAST	0.13	0.2	0.12	0.29	0.29	0.41	0.35	0.35	3.86
English-French Europarl Task									
LIMSI	0.32	0.36	0.24	0.42	0.44	0.56	0.53	0.53	**8.84**
LIUM-SYSTRAN	**0.32**	**0.36**	**0.24**	**0.42**	**0.45**	**0.56**	**0.53**	**0.53**	7.46
LIUM-SYSTRAN-CONTRAST	0.31	0.36	0.23	0.42	0.44	0.56	0.52	0.53	6.69
RBMT1	0.15	0.20	0.13	0.29	0.26	0.44	0.4	0.37	3.89
RBMT3	0.18	0.24	0.15	0.34	0.33	0.47	0.42	0.43	4.13
RBMT4	0.2	0.25	0.17	0.35	0.35	0.5	0.45	0.45	4.70
RBMT5	0.12	0.16	0.09	0.22	0.06	0.37	0.32	0.32	3.01
RBMT6	0.17	0.23	0.14	0.33	0.32	0.47	0.42	0.42	3.93
SAAR	0.26	0.29	0.21	0.41	0.34	0.53	0.49	0.48	7.75
SAAR-CONTRAST	0.28	0.32	0.23	0.41	0.39	0.55	0.51	0.52	6.45
UCL	0.24	0.28	0.19	0.37	0.41	0.49	0.44	0.42	4.16
UEDIN	0.30	0.35	0.23	0.42	0.43	0.54	0.51	0.51	6.56

Table 15: Automatic evaluation metric for translations into French

	BLEU	MBLEU	METEOR-BASELINE	METEOR-RANKING	MTER	POSF4GRAM-AM	POSF4GRAM-GM	POSBLEU	SVM-RANK
English-German News Task									
LIMSI	0.11	0.18	0.19	0.45	0.22	0.36	0.29	0.28	**7.83**
LIU	0.10	0.17	0.18	0.44	0.24	0.36	0.28	0.27	4.03
RBMT1	0.12	0.18	0.18	0.44	0.22	0.39	0.33	0.32	5.42
RBMT2	0.13	0.19	**0.20**	**0.46**	0.24	0.4	0.33	0.33	5.76
RBMT3	0.12	0.18	0.19	0.44	0.24	0.39	0.32	0.32	4.70
RBMT4	**0.14**	**0.19**	0.2	0.46	0.25	**0.41**	**0.35**	**0.34**	5.58
RBMT5	0.11	0.17	0.17	0.43	0.21	0.38	0.31	0.31	4.49
RBMT6	0.10	0.16	0.17	0.43	0.2	0.37	0.3	0.29	4.81
SAAR	0.13	0.19	0.19	0.44	**0.27**	0.38	0.31	0.3	4.04
SAAR-CONTRAST	0.12	0.18	0.18	0.43	0.26	0.37	0.3	0.28	3.71
UEDIN	0.12	0.17	0.18	0.45	0.23	0.37	0.30	0.29	4.37
English-German Europarl Task									
CMU-GIMPEL	0.20	0.24	0.27	**0.54**	0.32	0.43	0.37	0.37	**9.54**
LIMSI	0.20	0.24	0.27	0.53	0.32	0.43	0.37	0.37	6.97
LIU	0.2	0.24	0.27	0.53	**0.32**	0.43	0.38	0.37	6.95
RBMT1	0.11	0.16	0.16	0.42	0.19	0.38	0.32	0.32	5.01
RBMT2	0.12	0.17	0.19	0.46	0.21	0.39	0.32	0.31	5.93
RBMT3	0.11	0.16	0.17	0.43	0.21	0.38	0.31	0.30	4.75
RBMT4	0.12	0.17	0.18	0.45	0.22	0.41	0.34	0.33	5.42
RBMT5	0.1	0.14	0.16	0.42	0.19	0.39	0.32	0.31	4.42
RBMT6	0.09	0.14	0.15	0.42	0.18	0.38	0.30	0.29	4.40
SAAR	0.20	0.25	0.26	0.53	0.32	0.43	0.38	0.37	6.67
SAAR-CONTRAST	0.2	0.24	0.26	0.52	0.31	0.43	0.37	0.37	6.35
UCL	0.16	0.20	0.23	0.49	0.31	0.4	0.33	0.31	5.12
UEDIN	**0.21**	**0.25**	**0.27**	0.54	0.32	**0.44**	**0.38**	**0.38**	7.02
English-Spanish News Task									
CMU-SMT	0.19	0.24	0.25	0.34	0.32	0.32	0.25	0.26	**8.34**
LIMSI	0.19	0.25	0.26	0.34	0.34	0.33	0.26	0.26	5.92
RBMT1	0.16	0.22	0.23	0.32	0.30	0.31	0.23	0.23	5.36
RBMT3	0.19	0.24	0.25	0.33	0.34	0.33	0.26	0.26	5.42
RBMT4	**0.21**	0.26	**0.26**	0.34	0.35	0.34	0.28	**0.28**	6.36
RBMT5	0.18	0.24	0.25	0.33	0.32	0.33	0.26	0.26	5.84
RBMT6	0.19	0.24	0.24	0.33	0.33	0.32	0.25	0.26	5.42
SAAR	0.20	**0.27**	0.26	0.34	**0.37**	**0.34**	**0.28**	0.28	5.04
SAAR-CONTRAST	0.2	0.26	0.25	0.34	0.37	0.34	0.27	0.27	4.86
UCB	0.20	0.26	0.26	**0.34**	0.34	0.33	0.26	0.27	5.70
UEDIN	0.18	0.25	0.25	0.33	0.35	0.33	0.26	0.26	4.30
UPC	0.18	0.23	0.24	0.32	0.35	0.32	0.25	0.24	3.97
English-Spanish Europarl Task									
CMU-SMT	**0.32**	0.36	0.33	0.42	0.45	0.40	0.35	0.36	**0.10**
LIMSI	0.31	0.36	0.33	0.42	0.45	0.4	0.35	0.35	7.80
RBMT1	0.16	0.22	0.24	0.32	0.31	0.32	0.25	0.25	4.47
RBMT3	0.20	0.25	0.25	0.34	0.35	0.33	0.27	0.27	4.66
RBMT4	0.21	0.25	0.26	0.34	0.36	0.34	0.28	0.28	4.85
RBMT5	0.18	0.24	0.25	0.34	0.33	0.34	0.27	0.27	5.03
RBMT6	0.18	0.23	0.25	0.33	0.33	0.33	0.26	0.26	4.57
SAAR	0.31	0.35	0.33	0.41	0.44	0.40	0.35	0.35	7.59
SAAR-CONTRAST	0.30	0.34	0.33	0.41	0.44	0.4	0.34	0.35	7.42
UCL	0.25	0.29	0.29	0.37	0.43	0.36	0.29	0.29	4.67
UEDIN	0.32	**0.36**	0.33	0.42	0.45	0.40	0.35	0.35	7.25
UPC	0.30	0.34	0.32	0.40	**0.46**	0.4	0.35	0.34	6.18
UW	0.32	0.36	**0.33**	**0.42**	0.45	0.40	0.35	0.35	7.36
UW-CONTRAST	0.32	0.35	0.33	0.42	0.45	**0.40**	**0.35**	**0.36**	7.21

Table 16: Automatic evaluation metric for translations into German and Spanish

	DP	DR	SR	ULC	ULCH	BLEU	MBLEU	METEOR-BASELINE	METEOR-RANKING	MTER	POSF4GRAM-AM	POSF4GRAM-GM	POSBLEU	SVM-RANK
Spanish-English Europarl Task														
CMU-SMT	0.34	**0.44**	0.26	0.29	0.33	**0.33**	0.39	0.59	0.48	0.51	0.52	0.48	0.48	**9.72**
CUED	0.33	0.43	0.25	0.29	0.33	0.32	0.38	0.59	0.48	0.50	0.51	0.47	0.47	7.41
CUED-CONTRAST	0.34	0.44	0.26	0.29	0.33	0.33	0.39	0.59	0.48	0.51	0.52	0.48	0.48	7.00
DCU	0.34	0.43	0.25	0.29	0.33	0.32	0.38	0.59	0.48	0.50	0.51	0.47	0.48	6.78
LIMSI	**0.34**	0.44	0.26	**0.29**	**0.33**	0.33	**0.39**	**0.59**	**0.48**	**0.51**	0.52	0.48	**0.48**	6.73
RBMT3	0.26	0.37	0.19	0.22	0.27	0.19	0.26	0.51	0.41	0.36	0.45	0.4	0.39	5.46
RBMT4	0.26	0.37	0.19	0.22	0.27	0.18	0.26	0.52	0.42	0.36	0.45	0.39	0.38	5.57
RBMT5	0.25	0.36	0.18	0.22	0.27	0.18	0.25	0.51	0.41	0.36	0.44	0.39	0.38	4.74
RBMT6	0.24	0.34	0.18	0.21	0.26	0.17	0.25	0.51	0.41	0.36	0.44	0.38	0.37	4.71
SAAR	0.34	0.44	**0.26**	0.29	0.33	0.32	0.39	0.59	0.48	0.51	**0.52**	**0.49**	0.48	6.30
SAAR-CONTRAST	0.33	0.43	0.25	0.28	0.33	0.30	0.37	0.59	0.48	0.47	0.51	0.47	0.46	7.33
UCL	0.29	0.4	0.21	0.25	0.29	0.25	0.32	0.55	0.43	0.47	0.47	0.42	0.4	4.02
UEDIN	0.34	0.44	0.26	0.29	0.33	0.33	0.39	0.59	0.48	0.50	0.52	0.48	0.48	6.61
UPC	0.33	0.43	0.25	0.28	0.33	0.32	0.38	0.59	0.48	0.5	0.52	0.48	0.48	6.82
French-English News Task														
BBN-COMBO	**0.27**	0.37	**0.2**	**0.23**	**0.28**	0.21	n/a	n/a	n/a	n/a	n/a	n/a	n/a	n/a
CMU-COMBO	0.26	0.36	0.18	0.22	0.27	0.19	n/a	n/a	n/a	n/a	n/a	n/a	n/a	n/a
CMU-COMBO-CONTRAST	n/a	n/a	n/a	n/a	n/a	0.19	n/a	n/a	n/a	n/a	n/a	n/a	n/a	n/a
CMU-STATXFER	0.21	0.32	0.14	0.19	0.23	0.14	0.22	0.48	0.39	0.28	0.38	0.32	0.30	**9.91**
CMU-STATXFER-CONTRAST	0.21	0.30	0.14	0.18	0.23	0.14	0.21	0.47	0.38	0.26	0.38	0.31	0.29	6.47
CUED	0.25	0.35	0.17	0.21	0.26	0.18	0.27	0.51	0.41	0.37	0.41	0.35	0.34	6.34
CUED-CONTRAST	0.26	0.37	0.18	0.22	0.27	0.19	0.28	**0.52**	**0.42**	0.38	0.42	0.37	0.36	6.29
LIMSI	0.26	0.37	0.18	0.22	0.27	0.20	0.28	0.51	0.40	0.40	0.43	0.38	0.37	5.75
LIUM-SYSTRAN	0.27	**0.38**	0.19	0.23	0.27	0.21	0.29	0.51	0.41	0.41	**0.44**	**0.39**	**0.38**	6.32
LIUM-SYSTRAN-CONTRAST	0.27	0.38	0.19	0.23	0.28	**0.21**	**0.29**	0.51	0.41	**0.41**	0.44	0.39	0.38	5.93
RBMT3	0.24	0.36	0.17	0.21	0.26	0.16	0.24	0.49	0.40	0.29	0.42	0.36	0.34	7.61
RBMT4	0.25	0.37	0.17	0.21	0.26	0.17	0.25	0.49	0.4	0.33	0.42	0.36	0.35	6.17
RBMT5	0.25	0.37	0.18	0.22	0.27	0.18	0.25	0.51	0.41	0.33	0.43	0.37	0.36	6.97
RBMT6	0.24	0.36	0.17	0.21	0.26	0.16	0.24	0.49	0.39	0.30	0.41	0.35	0.34	6.51
SAAR	0.24	0.14	0.17	0.19	0.22	0.15	0.24	0.47	0.37	0.39	0.39	0.32	0.31	3.22
SAAR-CONTRAST	0.26	0.36	0.18	0.22	0.27	0.17	0.27	0.51	0.41	0.36	0.41	0.35	0.35	6.01
UEDIN	0.25	0.36	0.17	0.21	0.26	0.18	0.26	0.51	0.41	0.35	0.42	0.36	0.35	5.97
UEDIN-COMBO	0.26	0.36	0.18	0.23	0.27	n/a	n/a	n/a	n/a	n/a	n/a	n/a	n/a	n/a
French-English Europarl Task														
CMU-STATXFER	0.24	0.34	0.18	0.22	0.26	0.2	0.26	0.52	0.42	0.37	0.42	0.36	0.35	9.85
CMU-STATXFER-CONTRAST	0.25	0.34	0.19	0.22	0.26	0.2	0.26	0.53	0.42	0.38	0.42	0.36	0.35	7.10
CUED	0.34	0.44	0.26	0.29	0.33	0.32	0.38	0.59	0.48	0.50	0.51	0.47	0.47	**0.11**
CUED-CONTRAST	0.34	0.44	0.26	0.29	0.34	0.32	0.39	0.59	0.48	0.51	0.51	0.47	0.47	9.34
DCU	0.33	0.43	0.25	0.28	0.33	0.31	0.37	0.58	0.47	0.49	0.50	0.46	0.46	9.16
LIMSI	0.34	0.44	0.26	0.29	0.34	0.33	0.39	0.59	0.48	0.51	0.52	0.48	0.48	9.59
LIUM-SYSTRAN	**0.35**	**0.45**	**0.27**	**0.3**	**0.34**	**0.33**	**0.39**	**0.59**	**0.48**	**0.51**	**0.52**	**0.48**	**0.49**	9.75
LIUM-SYSTRAN-CONTRAST	0.34	0.44	0.26	0.29	0.34	0.33	0.39	0.59	0.48	0.50	0.52	0.48	0.48	9.23
RBMT3	0.25	0.36	0.10	0.20	0.24	0.17	0.25	0.51	0.41	0.35	0.43	0.37	0.36	7.36
RBMT4	0.27	0.36	0.19	0.22	0.27	0.18	0.26	0.51	0.41	0.37	0.43	0.38	0.37	5.92
RBMT5	0.27	0.38	0.21	0.23	0.28	0.20	0.28	0.53	0.43	0.4	0.45	0.4	0.39	7.20
RBMT6	0.24	0.35	0.18	0.21	0.26	0.16	0.24	0.5	0.40	0.35	0.42	0.36	0.35	5.96
SAAR	0.32	0.41	0.23	0.27	0.31	0.27	0.33	0.54	0.43	0.49	0.49	0.44	0.41	4.76
SAAR-CONTRAST	0.33	0.43	0.25	0.28	0.33	0.3	0.36	0.58	0.48	0.47	0.51	0.47	0.46	0.10
SYSTRAN	0.3	0.4	0.23	0.26	0.30	0.26	0.34	0.55	0.45	0.46	0.48	0.43	0.43	7.01
UCL	0.3	0.40	0.22	0.26	0.3	0.26	0.32	0.55	0.44	0.47	0.47	0.42	0.41	6.35
UEDIN	0.34	0.44	0.26	0.29	0.33	0.33	0.39	0.59	0.48	0.50	0.52	0.48	0.48	9.41

Table 17: Automatic evaluation metric for translations into English

	DP	DR	SR	ULC	ULCH	BLEU	MBLEU	METEOR-BASELINE	METEOR-RANKING	MTER	POSF4GRAM-AM	POSF4GRAM-GM	POSBLEU	SVM-RANK
Czech-English News Commentary Task														
DCU	0.25	**0.34**	0.18	0.22	0.27	0.21	0.29	0.54	0.44	0.42	0.42	0.36	0.36	**2.45**
SYSTRAN	0.19	0.28	0.12	0.17	0.21	0.15	0.23	0.45	0.36	0.34	0.36	0.29	0.29	0.76
UEDIN	0.24	0.31	0.16	0.21	0.25	0.22	0.30	0.54	0.44	0.43	0.41	0.35	0.35	1.37
UMD	**0.26**	**0.34**	**0.19**	**0.23**	**0.28**	**0.24**	**0.33**	**0.56**	**0.45**	**0.49**	**0.44**	**0.39**	**0.38**	1.41
Czech-English News Task														
DCU	0.19	**0.30**	**0.13**	0.17	**0.22**	0.12	**0.22**	**0.45**	**0.35**	0.32	0.36	0.28	**0.28**	**1.78**
UEDIN	0.19	0.28	0.12	0.17	0.21	0.12	0.21	0.44	0.34	0.32	0.35	0.27	0.27	0.65
UMD	**0.2**	0.29	0.12	**0.18**	0.22	**0.13**	0.22	0.44	0.34	**0.36**	**0.36**	**0.29**	0.27	0.52
German-English News Task														
BBN-COMBO	0.23	0.34	0.14	0.21	0.25	**0.18**	n/a	n/a	n/a	n/a	n/a	n/a	n/a	n/a
CMU-STATXFER	0.16	0.27	0.09	0.15	0.19	0.11	0.18	0.43	0.34	0.25	0.33	0.25	0.24	**7.84**
LIMSI	0.22	0.33	0.13	0.19	0.23	0.17	0.25	0.47	0.37	**0.36**	0.4	0.33	0.32	5.58
LIU	0.21	0.32	0.06	0.18	0.22	0.15	0.24	0.48	0.38	0.33	0.38	0.31	0.31	5.51
RBMT1	0.22	0.33	0.14	0.19	0.23	0.14	0.22	0.44	0.35	0.28	0.37	0.31	0.30	6.13
RBMT2	0.24	0.37	0.17	0.21	0.26	0.15	0.24	0.5	0.40	0.31	0.4	0.33	0.32	7.14
RBMT3	0.24	0.37	0.16	0.21	0.26	0.16	0.24	0.49	0.4	0.32	0.41	0.34	0.34	6.97
RBMT4	**0.25**	**0.38**	**0.17**	**0.21**	**0.27**	0.16	0.25	**0.50**	**0.40**	0.34	**0.41**	**0.35**	**0.34**	7.03
RBMT5	0.23	0.36	0.15	0.20	0.25	0.15	0.23	0.48	0.39	0.32	0.4	0.33	0.32	5.94
RBMT6	0.22	0.34	0.14	0.19	0.24	0.14	0.22	0.47	0.38	0.31	0.39	0.32	0.31	5.65
SAAR	0.22	0.33	0.14	0.2	0.24	0.15	0.24	0.47	0.37	0.36	0.39	0.32	0.31	4.67
SAAR-CONTRAST	0.24	0.35	0.16	0.21	0.25	0.17	**0.26**	0.5	0.4	0.36	0.4	0.33	0.33	5.80
SAAR-CONTRAST-2	0.21	0.33	0.14	0.19	0.23	0.15	0.24	0.47	0.37	0.36	0.39	0.32	0.31	4.80
UEDIN	0.23	0.34	0.09	0.19	0.23	0.16	0.25	0.48	0.39	0.35	0.4	0.33	0.33	5.72
German-English Europarl Task														
CMU-STATXFER	0.2	0.31	0.12	0.19	0.22	0.17	0.23	0.49	0.39	0.34	0.39	0.32	0.31	7.11
LIMSI	0.28	0.38	0.18	0.24	0.28	0.27	0.33	0.55	0.44	0.43	0.47	0.42	0.42	**8.04**
LIU	0.28	0.39	0.09	0.23	0.26	0.27	0.33	0.55	0.44	0.44	0.47	0.43	0.43	7.46
RBMT1	0.21	0.3	0.14	0.18	0.22	0.12	0.19	0.42	0.33	0.27	0.36	0.30	0.28	4.61
RBMT2	0.24	0.35	0.16	0.20	0.25	0.14	0.23	0.49	0.39	0.32	0.39	0.33	0.32	5.42
RBMT3	0.24	0.35	0.16	0.20	0.25	0.15	0.23	0.48	0.39	0.32	0.40	0.34	0.33	5.43
RBMT4	0.24	0.36	0.15	0.20	0.25	0.14	0.23	0.49	0.39	0.34	0.41	0.34	0.34	5.11
RBMT5	0.23	0.34	0.15	0.2	0.24	0.14	0.22	0.48	0.38	0.33	0.4	0.33	0.32	4.55
RBMT6	0.22	0.33	0.13	0.18	0.23	0.13	0.21	0.47	0.37	0.31	0.38	0.31	0.31	4.08
SAAR	0.29	0.39	0.19	0.25	0.28	0.27	0.33	0.55	0.44	0.43	0.47	0.42	0.42	7.32
SAAR-CONTRAST	0.28	0.37	0.18	0.24	0.28	0.26	0.32	0.54	0.43	0.43	0.47	0.42	0.42	6.77
UCL	0.24	0.36	0.16	0.22	0.25	0.2	0.25	0.49	0.39	0.41	0.42	0.35	0.32	4.26
UEDIN	**0.30**	**0.41**	**0.20**	**0.26**	**0.3**	**0.28**	**0.34**	**0.56**	**0.45**	**0.45**	**0.48**	**0.44**	**0.44**	7.96
Spanish-English News Task														
CMU-SMT	0.24	0.35	0.17	0.21	0.25	0.18	0.26	0.48	0.38	0.39	0.41	0.35	0.34	**8.00**
CUED	0.25	0.36	0.17	0.21	0.26	0.19	0.28	0.50	0.40	0.38	0.42	0.36	0.36	6.03
CUED-CONTRAST	0.26	0.37	0.18	0.22	0.27	**0.21**	**0.3**	**0.52**	0.42	0.39	0.44	0.38	**0.38**	6.27
LIMSI	0.26	0.37	0.18	0.22	0.27	0.20	0.28	0.50	0.4	**0.41**	0.43	0.38	0.37	4.93
RBMT3	0.25	0.38	0.17	0.22	0.27	0.18	0.26	0.50	0.41	0.32	0.43	0.38	0.36	7.54
RBMT4	0.26	**0.38**	0.18	0.22	0.27	0.18	0.26	0.51	**0.42**	0.32	**0.44**	**0.39**	0.37	7.81
RBMT5	0.26	0.38	0.08	0.20	0.25	0.2	0.27	0.51	0.42	0.33	0.44	0.38	0.37	6.89
RBMT6	0.25	0.36	0.17	0.21	0.26	0.18	0.25	0.51	0.41	0.33	0.43	0.37	0.36	6.83
SAAR	0.26	0.37	0.19	0.22	0.27	0.19	0.29	0.51	0.41	0.39	0.43	0.37	0.37	5.23
SAAR-CONTRAST	0.26	0.37	0.18	0.22	0.27	0.19	0.28	0.51	0.41	0.37	0.42	0.37	0.36	5.95
UCB	0.25	0.35	0.17	0.21	0.26	0.19	0.27	0.5	0.39	0.39	0.42	0.36	0.35	4.40
UEDIN	0.24	0.35	0.17	0.21	0.26	0.18	0.27	0.50	0.40	0.36	0.41	0.35	0.34	5.07
UEDIN-COMBO	**0.27**	0.36	**0.19**	**0.23**	**0.27**	n/a	n/a	n/a	n/a	n/a	n/a	n/a	n/a	n/a
UPC	0.25	0.36	0.17	0.21	0.26	0.19	0.26	0.49	0.39	0.4	0.43	0.37	0.36	4.38

Table 18: Automatic evaluation metric for translations into English

B Break down of correlation for each task

	RANK	CONST	YES/NO	DP	DR	SR	ULC	ULCH	BLEU	MBLEU	METEOR-BASELINE	METEOR-RANKING	MTER	POSF4GRAM-AM	POSF4GRAM-GM	POSBLEU	SVM-RANK
All-English News Task																	
RANK	1	n/a	n/a	0.83	0.73	0.83	0.83	**0.87**	0.71	0.7	0.82	0.79	0.41	0.79	0.8	0.80	0.25
French-English News Task																	
RANK	1	0.69	0.63	**0.92**	0.83	0.89	0.90	0.90	0.81	0.80	0.88	0.80	0.57	0.87	0.9	0.9	– *0.21*
CONST	—	1	0.81	0.83	0.52	0.81	0.86	0.81	**0.93**	0.9	0.76	0.64	0.73	0.69	0.72	0.85	– *0.52*
YES/NO	—	—	1	0.71	0.57	0.76	0.77	0.74	**0.79**	0.75	0.67	0.59	0.62	0.66	0.67	0.79	– *0.26*
French-English Europarl Task																	
RANK	1	0.95	0.9	0.94	0.95	0.93	**0.95**	0.93	0.92	0.90	0.88	0.87	0.92	0.94	0.94	0.91	0.50
CONST	—	1	0.91	0.97	0.97	**0.98**	0.98	0.97	0.97	0.96	0.97	0.95	0.96	0.97	0.97	0.96	0.56
YES/NO	—	—	1	0.94	0.94	0.94	0.96	0.96	0.96	**0.97**	0.92	0.93	0.92	0.95	0.95	0.97	0.47
German-English News Task																	
RANK	1	0.56	0.56	0.85	0.93	0.92	0.85	**0.95**	0.12	0.09	0.83	0.89	– *0.11*	0.63	0.60	0.58	0.36
CONST	—	1	0.48	0.54	0.48	0.59	**0.66**	0.57	0.64	0.65	0.61	0.55	0.51	0.57	0.63	0.56	– *0.02*
YES/NO	—	—	1	0.68	0.61	0.69	0.73	0.67	0.60	0.41	0.54	0.56	0.33	0.79	**0.83**	0.70	0.08
German-English Europarl Task																	
RANK	1	0.63	0.81	**0.76**	0.59	0.46	0.57	0.60	0.30	0.39	0.40	0.66	0.25	0.53	0.53	0.64	0.35
CONST	—	1	0.78	0.87	**0.92**	0.51	0.83	0.86	0.69	0.69	0.76	0.80	0.69	0.88	0.88	0.88	0.61
YES/NO	—	—	1	**0.88**	0.77	0.48	0.77	0.78	0.66	0.67	0.64	0.86	0.58	0.74	0.74	0.85	0.78
Spanish-English News Task																	
RANK	1	– *0.07*	0.44	0.75	0.76	0.68	0.71	**0.81**	0.19	0.01	0.66	0.63	– *0.12*	0.73	0.76	0.66	0.36
CONST	—	1	0.66	– *0.03*	– *0.44*	0.29	0.29	0.14	0.45	0.66	– *0.11*	– *0.33*	**0.77**	– *0.37*	– *0.34*	0.16	– *0.58*
YES/NO	—	—	1	0.29	0.05	**0.73**	0.64	0.55	0.48	0.47	0.09	– *0.11*	0.71	0.06	0.1	0.39	– *0.43*
Spanish-English Europarl Task																	
RANK	1	0.69	0.76	0.78	0.73	0.73	0.8	0.77	0.78	0.79	0.83	0.84	0.77	0.73	0.73	0.80	**0.87**
CONST	—	1	0.68	0.76	0.77	0.75	0.69	0.73	0.64	0.67	0.64	0.68	0.73	**0.78**	**0.78**	0.73	0.56
YES/NO	—	—	1	0.94	0.93	0.95	0.96	0.95	**0.98**	0.97	0.91	0.91	0.95	0.94	0.94	**0.98**	0.69

Table 19: Correlation of automatic evaluation metrics with the three types of human judgments for translation into English

	RANK	CONST	YES/NO	BLEU	MBLEU	METEOR-BASELINE	METEOR-RANKING	MTER	POSF4GRAM-AM	POSF4GRAM-GM	POSBLEU	SVM-RANK
English-French News Task												
RANK	1	0.55	0.48	**0.73**	0.62	0.3	0.47	0.56	0.69	0.69	0.66	0.72
CONST	—	1	0.35	0.49	0.47	0.39	0.49	0.24	**0.59**	**0.59**	0.58	0.45
YES/NO	—	—	1	0.81	**0.92**	0.71	0.73	0.78	0.73	0.73	0.76	0.76
English-French Europarl Task												
RANK	1	0.98	0.88	0.95	0.95	0.95	0.95	0.90	**0.97**	**0.97**	0.93	0.93
CONST	—	1	0.94	0.98	0.98	0.98	0.98	0.93	**1**	**1**	0.97	0.91
YES/NO	—	—	1	**0.97**	**0.97**	**0.97**	**0.97**	0.92	0.95	0.95	0.92	0.83
English-German News Task												
RANK	1	0.57	0.71	0.58	0.42	0.43	0.13	0.25	**0.90**	**0.90**	**0.90**	0.32
CONST	—	1	0.78	0.75	**0.83**	0.82	0.55	0.60	0.72	0.72	0.72	0.58
YES/NO	—	—	1	0.62	0.54	0.51	0.36	0.23	0.75	0.75	0.75	**0.76**
English-German Europarl Task												
RANK	1	0.28	0.57	0.36	0.36	0.42	0.39	0.26	0.38	0.38	0.50	**0.56**
CONST	—	1	0.87	0.88	0.88	0.91	0.90	**0.93**	0.88	0.88	0.80	0.85
YES/NO	—	—	1	0.89	0.89	0.96	0.96	0.84	0.86	0.86	0.87	**0.98**
English-Spanish News Task												
RANK	1	–	0.49	–	–	–	–	–	–	–	–	**0.02**
		0.30		*0.04*	*0.47*	*0.25*	*0.29*	*0.33*	*0.19*	*0.19*	*0.07*	
CONST	—	1	0.43	**0.79**	0.61	0.64	0.56	0.2	0.59	0.59	0.55	0.56
YES/NO	—	—	1	0.55	0.41	0.43	0.31	0.13	0.65	0.65	**0.72**	0.16
English-Spanish Europarl Task												
RANK	1	0.90	0.63	0.8	0.83	**0.84**	0.83	0.73	0.79	0.79	0.76	0.80
CONST	—	1	0.73	0.84	**0.86**	0.81	0.8	0.74	0.84	0.83	0.84	**0.86**
YES/NO	—	—	1	0.68	0.75	0.66	0.67	**0.90**	0.67	0.66	0.73	0.68

Table 20: Correlation of automatic evaluation metrics with the three types of human judgments for translation into other languages

C Pairwise system comparisons by human judges

The following tables show pairwise comparisons between systems for each language pair, test set, and manual evaluation type. The numbers in each of the tables' cells indicate the percent of that the system in that column was judged to be better than the system in that row. Bolding indicates the winner of the two systems. The difference between 100 and the sum of the complimentary cells is the percent of time that the two systems were judged to be equal.

Because there were so many systems and data conditions the significance of each pairwise comparison needs to be quantified. We applied the Sign Test to measure which comparisons indicate genuine differences (rather than differences that are attributable to chance). In the following tables $\star$ indicates statistical significance at $p <= 0.05$ and $\dagger$ indicates statistical significance at $p <= 0.01$, according to the Sign Test.

	BBN-CMB	CMU-CMB	CMU-XFR	CUED	CUED-C	LIMSI	LIUM-SYS	LIUM-SYS-C	RBMT3	RBMT4	RBMT5	RBMT6	SAAR	SAAR-C	UEDIN	UEDIN-CMB
BBN-CMB		0.32	$0.18^\dagger$	0.21	**0.42**	**0.37**	0.29	0.24	0.33	**0.48**	**0.48**	0.32	0.29	**0.44**	**0.48**	0.21
CMU-CMB	**0.50**		0.26	0.29	**0.42**	0.4	**0.44**	**0.48**	**0.49**	**0.38**	**0.45**	**0.55**	0.32	0.34	0.34	**0.46**
CMU-XFR	$\mathbf{0.67}^\dagger$	**0.44**		$\mathbf{0.60}^\star$	$\mathbf{0.75}^\dagger$	**0.58**	$\mathbf{0.73}^\dagger$	**0.62**	**0.59**	**0.54**	$\mathbf{0.77}^\dagger$	**0.48**	**0.54**	$\mathbf{0.65}^\star$	$\mathbf{0.71}^\dagger$	**0.58**
CUED	**0.46**	**0.41**	$0.20^\star$		**0.47**	**0.56**	**0.47**	$\mathbf{0.51}^\star$	**0.41**	**0.54**	**0.57**	**0.37**	**0.43**	**0.61**	0.39	0.15
CUED-C	0.27	0.22	$0.08^\dagger$	0.20		0.31	**0.54**	$\mathbf{0.52}^\star$	0.32	**0.52**	**0.50**	0.31	0.40	**0.38**	0.30	**0.52**
LIMSI	0.34	0.4	0.29	0.31	**0.41**		$0.23^\star$	**0.52**	0.38	**0.50**	**0.39**	**0.49**	0.42	0.32	0.26	0.30
LIUM-SYS	**0.37**	0.32	$0.13^\dagger$	0.39	0.27	$\mathbf{0.60}^\star$		0.24	**0.44**	0.46	**0.46**	0.33	$0.24^\star$	0.25	0.30	0.19
LI-SYS-C	**0.40**	0.26	0.24	$0.20^\star$	$0.13^\star$	0.30	0.24		**0.44**	0.42	0.43	0.35	$0.21^\star$	0.30	0.30	0.31
RBMT3	**0.46**	0.43	0.26	0.38	**0.46**	**0.48**	0.39	0.39		0.41	**0.44**	0.26	0.36	**0.50**	$\mathbf{0.68}^\star$	**0.44**
RBMT4	0.36	0.33	0.31	0.36	0.39	0.35	**0.50**	**0.45**	**0.45**		**0.49**	**0.40**	0.35	**0.57**	**0.51**	**0.53**
RBMT5	0.37	0.33	$0.12^\dagger$	0.32	0.33	0.33	0.39	**0.46**	0.25	0.22		0.21	0.37	**0.44**	**0.49**	**0.57**
RBMT6	**0.50**	0.33	0.37	0.34	**0.50**	0.39	**0.44**	**0.50**	**0.48**	0.37	**0.55**		**0.42**	**0.48**	0.41	0.41
SAAR	**0.50**	**0.46**	0.37	0.38	**0.44**	**0.52**	$\mathbf{0.6}^\star$	$\mathbf{0.54}^\star$	**0.44**	**0.53**	**0.44**	0.29		**0.34**	**0.52**	**0.50**
SAAR-C	0.31	**0.47**	$0.23^\star$	0.30	0.24	**0.51**	**0.50**	**0.47**	0.25	0.31	0.33	0.35	0.26		0.47	0.38
UED	0.35	**0.37**	$0.13^\dagger$	0.39	**0.55**	**0.50**	**0.50**	**0.43**	$0.24^\star$	0.37	0.36	0.41	0.31	0.47		0.36
UED-CMB	**0.57**	0.36	0.16	**0.46**	0.38	0.30	**0.63**	**0.39**	0.39	0.37	0.35	**0.53**	0.27	**0.48**	0.36	
> OTHERS	0.43	0.37	0.22	0.34	0.41	0.44	0.45	0.45	0.4	0.42	**0.47**	0.37	0.34	0.43	0.44	0.42
≥ OTHERS	0.66	0.59	0.38	0.55	0.64	0.63	0.66	**0.69**	0.58	0.58	0.65	0.57	0.54	0.64	0.61	0.61

Table 21: Sentence-level ranking for the French-English News Task.

	CMU-XFR	CUED	DCU	LIMSI	LIUM-SYS	RBMT3	RBMT4	RBMT5	RBMT6	SAAR	SAAR-C	SYSTRAN	UCL	UEDIN
CMU-XFR		**0.53**	**0.50**	$\mathbf{0.74}^\dagger$	$\mathbf{0.79}^\star$	**0.55**	0.46	**0.50**	0.36	**0.73**	$\mathbf{0.92}^\dagger$	0.36	**0.44**	$\mathbf{0.77}^\star$
CUED	0.29		**0.42**	**0.29**	**0.48**	$0.16^\dagger$	**0.53**	$0.16^\dagger$	$0.18^\dagger$	$0.18^\star$	**0.55**	$0.06^\dagger$	0.21	0.38
DCU	0.46	0.29		0.38	**0.47**	0.37	0.27	0.24	0.29	0.35	**0.55**	0.18	0.25	**0.50**
LIMSI	$0.11^\dagger$	0.21	**0.44**		0.11	$0.12^\dagger$	0.17	0.29	$0.05^\dagger$	0.30	0.32	0.19	0.29	0.33
LIUM-SYS	$0.14^\star$	0.16	0.24	**0.32**		$0.06^\dagger$	0.13	0.22	$0.12^\dagger$	$0.14^\dagger$	0.33	$0.20^\star$	0.26	0.32
RBMT3	0.36	$\mathbf{0.79}^\dagger$	**0.58**	$\mathbf{0.88}^\dagger$	$\mathbf{0.72}^\dagger$		0.40	**0.57**	0.21	**0.67**	$\mathbf{0.72}^\dagger$	**0.50**	**0.54**	**0.67**
RBMT4	**0.50**	0.40	**0.64**	**0.67**	**0.56**	0.40		0.42	$0.21^\dagger$	**0.52**	**0.67**	0.33	**0.47**	**0.75**
RBMT5	0.38	$\mathbf{0.79}^\dagger$	**0.60**	**0.57**	**0.56**	0.24	0.42		0.26	0.48	$\mathbf{0.72}^\dagger$	**0.50**	**0.46**	**0.60**
RBMT6	**0.54**	$\mathbf{0.79}^\dagger$	**0.67**	$\mathbf{0.77}^\dagger$	$\mathbf{0.82}^\dagger$	**0.47**	$\mathbf{0.79}^\dagger$	**0.53**		$\mathbf{0.71}^\star$	$\mathbf{0.83}^\dagger$	**0.56**	**0.47**	$\mathbf{0.77}^\dagger$
SAAR	0.27	$\mathbf{0.59}^\star$	**0.57**	**0.47**	$\mathbf{0.71}^\dagger$	0.22	0.29	0.48	$0.18^\star$		**0.50**	0.35	0.23	**0.50**
SAAR-C	$0.04^\dagger$	0.15	0.31	**0.39**	**0.48**	$0.14^\dagger$	0.24	$0.21^\dagger$	$0.08^\dagger$	0.21		$0.17^\dagger$	0.20	**0.57**
SYSTRAN	**0.50**	$\mathbf{0.81}^\dagger$	**0.65**	**0.52**	$\mathbf{0.64}^\star$	0.38	**0.62**	0.33	0.32	**0.41**	$\mathbf{0.71}^\dagger$		**0.56**	**0.55**
UCL	0.31	**0.64**	**0.56**	**0.57**	**0.47**	0.46	0.40	0.39	0.27	**0.55**	**0.60**	0.44		**0.47**
UED	$0.24^\star$	**0.43**	0.35	0.33	**0.42**	0.28	0.25	0.33	$0.15^\dagger$	0.29	0.26	0.25	0.27	
> OTHERS	0.32	0.50	0.5	0.54	0.55	0.28	0.4	0.35	0.21	0.41	**0.59**	0.32	0.35	0.55
≥ OTHERS	0.42	0.7	0.64	0.78	**0.79**	0.40	0.50	0.48	0.32	0.58	0.75	0.47	0.52	0.71

Table 22: Sentence-level ranking for the French-English Europarl Task.

	LIMSI	LIUM-SYS	RBMT3	RBMT4	RBMT5	RBMT6	SAAR	SAAR-C	UEDIN	XEROX
LIMSI		0.29	0.25	**0.60**†	**0.52**	**0.48**	0.13	0.30	0.13*	0.17*
LIUM-SYSTRAN	**0.36**		**0.41**	**0.51**	**0.41**	**0.53**	0.22	0.26	0.27	0.04†
RBMT3	**0.56**	0.34		**0.48**	**0.52**	**0.40**	0.31	**0.53**	0.37	0.11†
RBMT4	0.13†	0.36	0.31		0.29	0.19*	0.26	0.15†	0.17†	0.09†
RBMT5	0.33	0.35	0.29	**0.42**		0.26	0.17†	0.32	0.17†	0.12†
RBMT6	0.42	0.38	0.37	**0.43***	**0.44**		0.32	0.32	0.28	0.11†
SAAR	**0.56**	**0.52**	**0.51**	**0.56**	**0.69**†	**0.41**		**0.33**	**0.46**	0.3
SAAR-CONTRAST	**0.55**	**0.44**	0.33	**0.63**†	**0.56**	**0.46**	0.21		0.41	0.22*
UEDIN	**0.48***	**0.48**	**0.41**	**0.60**†	**0.65**†	**0.53**	0.41	**0.43**		0.09†
XEROX	**0.63***	**0.74**†	**0.78**†	**0.74**†	**0.71**†	**0.75**†	**0.44**	**0.64***	**0.63**†	
> OTHERS	0.44	0.43	0.41	**0.54**	0.53	0.43	0.28	0.37	0.32	0.13
≥ OTHERS	0.67	0.66	0.60	**0.78**	0.73	0.66	0.51	0.57	0.55	0.32

Table 23: Sentence-level ranking for the English-French News Task.

	LIMSI	LIUM-SYS	RBMT3	RBMT4	RBMT5	RBMT6	SAAR	SAAR-C	UCL	UEDIN
LIMSI		**0.23**	0.21*	0.32	0.10†	0.15†	0.35	0.27	0.15†	0.17
LIUM-SYSTRAN			0.28	**0.39**	0.11†	0.21*	0.22	0.40	0.19†	0.15
RBMT3	**0.75***	**0.59**		**0.38**	0.39	**0.49**	**0.70**†	**0.81**†	**0.47**	**0.81**†
RBMT4	**0.64**	0.36	0.28		0.24*	0.18	**0.61**	**0.48**	0.42	**0.50**
RBMT5	**0.85**†	**0.89**†	**0.49**	**0.62***		**0.67***	**0.78**†	**0.91**†	**0.63***	**0.93**†
RBMT6	**0.85**†	**0.62***	0.26	**0.42**	0.24*		**0.83**†	**0.82**†	**0.47**	**0.68**†
SAAR	**0.41**	**0.52**	0.17†	0.30	0.11†	0.06†		**0.41**	0.11†	**0.41**
SAAR-CONTRAST	**0.47**	0.40	0.11†	0.26	0.03†	0.06†	0.32		0.27	0.26
UCL	**0.80**†	**0.70**†	0.42	**0.47**	0.22*	0.44	**0.71**†	**0.61**		**0.78**†
UEDIN	**0.46**	**0.41**	0.11†	0.33	0.04†	0.15†	0.32	**0.36**	0.03†	
> OTHERS	**0.62**	0.54	0.26	0.4	0.17	0.27	0.56	0.6	0.32	0.54
≥ OTHERS	**0.79**	0.78	0.42	0.61	0.26	0.44	0.74	0.79	0.44	0.77

Table 24: Sentence-level ranking for the English-French Europarl Task.

	BBN-CMB	CMU-XFR	LIMSI	LIU	RBMT2	RBMT3	RBMT4	RBMT5	RBMT6	SAAR	SAAR-C	UEDIN	UEDIN-CMB
BBN-COMBO		0.1†	0.22	0.37	**0.62***	**0.69**†	**0.74***	**0.66**†	0.41	**0.63***	**0.60***	**0.35**	**0.40**
CMU-STATXFER	**0.71**†		**0.44**	**0.54**	**0.76**†	**0.79**†	**0.73**†	**0.74**†	**0.80**†	**0.62**†	**0.65**†	**0.54**†	0.37
LIMSI	**0.44**	0.24		**0.41**	**0.67***	**0.65**†	**0.69**†	**0.54**	**0.50**	**0.50**	**0.63**	0.38	0.22
LIU	0.37	0.27	0.34		**0.55***	**0.56**	**0.61**†	**0.50**	**0.45**	**0.48**	**0.56**	**0.32**	0.34
RBMT2	0.21*	0.14†	0.31*	0.20*		0.27	0.43	0.29	0.34	0.30	0.13†	0.25†	0.24*
RBMT3	0.18†	0.13†	0.19†	0.27	**0.56**		0.37	0.33	0.32	0.29	0.29	0.19†	0.17†
RBMT4	0.22*	0.12†	0.17†	0.18†	**0.46**	**0.51**		0.3	0.31	0.18†	0.26*	0.28	0.17†
RBMT5	0.22†	0.12†	0.32	0.36	**0.58**	**0.51**	**0.40**		0.29	0.23*	0.37	0.3	0.28
RBMT6	**0.55**	0.08†	0.40	0.4	**0.51**	**0.51**	**0.47**	**0.51**		**0.49**	**0.52**	0.22*	0.43
SAAR	0.23*	0.21†	0.40	0.39	**0.52**	**0.50**	**0.61**†	**0.53***	0.38		**0.50***	0.26*	0.13*
SAAR-CONTRAST	0.23*	0.19†	0.3	0.37	**0.71**†	**0.37**	**0.60***	0.37	0.33	0.17*		**0.48**	0.13*
UEDIN	0.23	0.13†	0.38	0.3	**0.68**†	**0.65**†	**0.55**	**0.59**	**0.64***	**0.67***	0.38		**0.42**
UEDIN-COMBO	0.35	**0.41**	**0.59**	**0.50**	**0.72***	**0.66**†	**0.83**†	**0.56**	**0.52**	**0.50***	**0.67***	0.38	
> OTHERS	0.32	0.17	0.34	0.35	**0.61**	0.56	0.57	0.49	0.45	0.41	0.46	0.33	0.28
≥ OTHERS	0.51	0.35	0.52	0.56	**0.74**	0.73	0.73	0.67	0.59	0.61	0.65	0.55	0.44

Table 25: Sentence-level ranking for the German-English News Task.

	CMU-XFR	LIMSI	LIU	RBMT2	RBMT3	RBMT4	RBMT5	RBMT6	SAAR	UCL	UEDIN
CMU-STATXFER		**0.57**⋆	**0.77**†	**0.53**	**0.71**†	**0.69**†	**0.50**	**0.58**	**0.82**†	**0.46**	**0.75**†
LIMSI	0.17⋆		0.35	**0.71**⋆	**0.63**	**0.76**⋆	**0.50**	**0.59**	**0.52**	0.23	**0.67**†
LIU	0.14†	0.35		**0.50**	0.29	**0.67**	0.3	0.42	**0.35**	0.27	**0.57**
RBMT2	0.27	0.24⋆	0.46		0.39	0.33	0.36	0.42	**0.50**	0.33	**0.46**
RBMT3	0.23†	0.3	**0.57**	**0.45**		0.40	0.31	0.38	**0.56**	0.32	**0.55**
RBMT4	0.22†	0.19⋆	0.29	**0.50**	**0.48**		0.39	**0.48**	0.41	0.32	**0.61**
RBMT5	0.40	0.40	**0.56**	**0.54**	**0.57**	**0.52**		0.3	**0.48**	0.29⋆	**0.54**
RBMT6	0.27	0.32	**0.48**	**0.46**	**0.53**	0.44	**0.51**		**0.55**	0.36	**0.61**
SAAR	0.12†	0.19	0.30	0.44	0.41	**0.48**	0.32	0.42		0.20†	0.40
UCL	0.35	**0.54**	**0.46**	**0.63**	**0.61**	**0.68**	**0.68**⋆	**0.61**	**0.63**†		**0.65**†
UEDIN	0.22†	0.17†	0.32	0.42	0.42	0.36	0.41	0.27	0.40	0.23†	
> OTHERS	0.24	0.32	0.46	0.51	0.51	0.53	0.43	0.43	0.53	0.30	**0.58**
≥ OTHERS	0.36	0.49	0.61	0.63	0.6	0.61	0.54	0.54	0.68	0.42	**0.68**

Table 26: Sentence-level ranking for the German-English Europarl Task.

	LIMSI	LIU	RBMT2	RBMT3	RBMT4	RBMT5	RBMT6	SAAR	UEDIN
LIMSI		**0.44**	**0.8**†	**0.67**†	**0.81**†	**0.76**†	**0.63**†	**0.53**	**0.47**⋆
LIU	0.29		**0.80**†	**0.68**†	**0.81**†	**0.62**†	**0.63**†	0.25	0.31
RBMT2	0.13†	0.07†		0.35	0.33	0.32⋆	0.20†	0.17†	0.09†
RBMT3	0.18†	0.27†	**0.50**		**0.52**	**0.45**	0.29†	0.26	0.21†
RBMT4	0.09†	0.12†	**0.47**	0.30		**0.42**	0.22†	0.15†	0.17†
RBMT5	0.12†	0.26†	**0.59**⋆	0.42	0.40		0.33	0.28	0.24†
RBMT6	0.25†	0.22†	**0.6**†	**0.61**†	**0.63**†	**0.50**		0.36	0.33
SAAR	0.28	**0.63**	**0.66**†	**0.56**	**0.7**†	**0.62**	**0.46**		**0.45**
UEDIN	0.24⋆	**0.42**	**0.75**†	**0.66**†	**0.73**†	**0.68**†	**0.51**	0.36	
> OTHERS	0.19	0.28	**0.64**	0.54	0.61	0.54	0.40	0.3	0.27
≥ OTHERS	0.36	0.43	**0.79**	0.66	0.75	0.67	0.56	0.46	0.44

Table 27: Sentence-level ranking for the English-German News Task.

	CMU-GIMPEL	LIMSI	LIU	RBMT2	RBMT3	RBMT4	RBMT5	RBMT6	SAAR	UCL	UEDIN
CMU-GIMPEL		0.29	0.28	0.41	**0.49**	**0.56**	0.44	0.24†	0.09⋆	0.24⋆	**0.52**
LIMSI	**0.45**		0.31	0.48	0.45	**0.54**	0.40	0.35	0.40	0.29⋆	**0.47**
LIU	**0.34**	**0.47**		**0.56**	0.44	**0.65**⋆	0.37	0.30	0.31	0.19†	**0.50**
RBMT2	**0.51**	0.48	0.41		0.41	**0.48**	0.22†	0.24⋆	**0.62**	0.26⋆	0.43
RBMT3	0.40	**0.50**	**0.47**	**0.47**		**0.60**	0.33	0.3⋆	0.11	0.26⋆	**0.50**
RBMT4	0.39	0.37	0.27⋆	0.41	0.35		0.22†	0.14†	0.25	0.33	0.46
RBMT5	**0.49**	**0.47**	**0.54**	**0.64**†	**0.60**	**0.64**†		0.32	0.47	0.45	**0.64**†
RBMT6	**0.71**†	**0.50**	**0.58**	**0.57**⋆	**0.65**⋆	**0.74**†	**0.46**		**0.41**	0.36	**0.60**
SAAR	**0.73**⋆	0.40	**0.39**	0.39	**0.78**	**0.58**	0.47	0.35		0.31	**0.50**
UCL	**0.61**⋆	**0.6**⋆	**0.67**†	**0.59**⋆	**0.68**⋆	**0.64**	**0.53**	**0.51**	**0.62**		**0.70**†
UEDIN	0.25	0.27	0.30	**0.52**	0.41	**0.49**	0.26†	0.31	0.25	0.23†	
> OTHERS	0.47	0.43	0.43	0.51	0.51	**0.59**	0.36	0.3	0.37	0.3	0.54
≥ OTHERS	0.61	0.58	0.58	0.62	0.58	**0.68**	0.47	0.43	0.53	0.39	0.67

Table 28: Sentence-level ranking for the English-German Europarl Task.

	CMU-SMT	CUED	CUED-C	LIMSI	RBMT3	RBMT4	RBMT5	RBMT6	SAAR	UCB	UEDIN	UPC
CMU-SMT		**0.41**	**0.62***	0.33	**0.54***	**0.57**†	**0.42**	**0.46**	**0.46**	0.29	0.34	**0.37**
CUED	0.29		0.24	0.27	**0.54***	**0.76**†	**0.61***	**0.50**	**0.39**	**0.46**	0.26	**0.42**
CUED-CONTRAST	0.19*	0.24		0.23	**0.47**	**0.48**	0.28	**0.41**	0.37	0.26	0.26	0.33
LIMSI	0.33	**0.30**	**0.51**		0.41	**0.56**†	**0.47**	**0.41**	**0.46**	0.33	**0.37**	**0.43**
RBMT3	0.19*	0.23*	0.37	**0.43**		**0.39**	0.28	0.3	0.33	0.39	0.30	**0.49**
RBMT4	0.19†	0.14†	0.27	0.21†	0.27		0.21†	0.30	0.27	0.17†	0.29*	0.23*
RBMT5	0.37	0.19*	**0.56**	0.35	**0.47**	**0.57**†		**0.56**	**0.43**	0.24*	0.35	**0.52**
RBMT6	0.41	0.30	0.29	0.39	**0.43**	**0.50**	0.25		**0.46**	0.34	**0.44**	**0.46**
SAAR	0.29	0.25	**0.43**	0.32	**0.50**	**0.42**	0.33	0.31		0.2*	0.26	0.3
UCB	0.29	0.36	**0.52**	**0.49**	**0.46**	**0.61**†	**0.6***	**0.41**	**0.56***		**0.39**	0.28
UEDIN	**0.39**	**0.37**	**0.52**	0.30	**0.50**	**0.61***	**0.58**	0.39	**0.46**	0.24		**0.44**
UPC	0.26	0.36	**0.47**	0.35	0.40	**0.59***	0.32	0.42	**0.46**	**0.33**	0.41	
> OTHERS	0.29	0.28	0.43	0.34	0.45	**0.55**	0.39	0.40	0.42	0.29	0.34	0.39
≥ OTHERS	0.57	0.56	0.67	0.58	0.67	**0.77**	0.58	0.61	0.67	0.54	0.56	0.60

Table 29: Sentence-level ranking for the Spanish-English News Task.

	CMU-SMT	CUED	DCU	LIMSI	RBMT3	RBMT4	RBMT5	RBMT6	SAAR	UCL	UEDIN	UPC
CMU-SMT		0.36	**0.38**	**0.37**	0.10†	0.20†	0.14†	0.32	0.39	0.22	0.25	0.38
CUED	**0.40**		0.38	**0.53**	0.33	0.30	0.30	0.20†	0.32	0.08†	0.36	0.29
DCU	0.34	0.38		**0.46**	0.32	0.19*	0.26*	0.21*	0.32	0.33	0.25	**0.46**
LIMSI	0.31	0.30	0.21		0.05†	0.09†	0.15†	0.18*	0.24	0.10†	0.19	**0.48**
RBMT3	**0.83**†	**0.62**	**0.58**	**0.73**†		**0.56**	0.25	0.37	**0.60**†	0.31	**0.66***	**0.78**†
RBMT4	**0.73**†	**0.54**	**0.76***	**0.74**†	0.28		0.38	0.24	**0.53**	0.29	**0.56**	**0.65***
RBMT5	**0.79**†	**0.55**	**0.67***	**0.75**†	**0.58**	**0.57**		**0.59***	**0.70**†	**0.44**	**0.71***	**0.67**
RBMT6	**0.52**	**0.77**†	**0.66***	**0.68***	**0.42**	**0.49**	0.18*		**0.55**	0.41	**0.54**	**0.71**
SAAR	**0.43**	**0.42**	**0.41**	**0.47**	0.20†	0.32	0.17†	0.30		0.22*	0.35	**0.32**
UCL	**0.56**	**0.71**†	**0.56**	**0.70**†	**0.42**	**0.57**	0.33	**0.44**	**0.59***		**0.81**†	**0.67**
UEDIN	**0.28**	**0.46**	**0.39**	**0.31**	0.29*	0.42	0.25*	0.39	0.35	0.15†		0.40
UPC	**0.44**	**0.39**	0.43	0.36	0.07†	0.23*	0.24	0.29	0.27	0.20	0.40	
> OTHERS	0.50	0.5	0.49	**0.53**	0.28	0.36	0.24	0.32	0.44	0.26	0.45	0.51
≥ OTHERS	0.71	0.68	0.68	**0.78**	0.43	0.49	0.35	0.47	0.67	0.43	0.66	0.69

Table 30: Sentence-level ranking for the Spanish-English Europarl Task.

	CMU-SMT	LIMSI	RBMT3	RBMT4	RBMT5	RBMT6	SAAR	UCB	UEDIN	UPC
CMU-SMT		0.39	**0.57**	**0.52***	**0.62**†	**0.56***	**0.50**	**0.41**	**0.42**	**0.56**†
LIMSI	**0.42**		**0.56**	**0.53**	**0.63***	**0.58**	0.32	0.39	0.35	0.35
RBMT3	0.23	0.3		0.34	**0.46**	**0.50**	0.39	0.17	0.21†	0.06*
RBMT4	0.25*	0.30	**0.47**		0.31	0.35	0.38	0.36	0.32	0.19
RBMT5	0.21†	0.20*	0.28	**0.42**		0.42	0.29*	0.24	0.17†	0.23
RBMT6	0.23*	0.23	0.31	**0.41**	0.42		0.23*	0.19	0.24*	0.24
SAAR	0.36	**0.52**	0.39	**0.43**	**0.67***	**0.54***		0.36	0.29	0.42
UCB	0.37	0.39	**0.52**	**0.39**	**0.49**	**0.52**	**0.46**		0.27	0.25
UEDIN	0.35	**0.48**	**0.62**†	**0.48**	**0.64**†	**0.61***	**0.50**	**0.47**		**0.53***
UPC	0.11†	**0.41**	**0.63***	**0.48**	**0.50**	**0.57**	0.42	**0.63**	0.06*	
> OTHERS	0.28	0.36	0.47	0.45	**0.52**	0.51	0.38	0.34	0.27	0.33
≥ OTHERS	0.49	0.54	0.68	0.67	**0.72**	0.72	0.55	0.59	0.48	0.60

Table 31: Sentence-level ranking for the English-Spanish News Task.

	CMU-SMT	LIMSI	RBMT3	RBMT4	RBMT5	RBMT6	SAAR	UCL	UEDIN	UPC	UW
CMU-SMT		0.28	**0.47**	0.33	0.17†	0.26	**0.50**	0.25	**0.48***	**0.44**	0.28
LIMSI	**0.38**		0.19*	0.33	0.16*	0.23	0.33	0.14†	0.14	0.35	0.32
RBMT3	0.42	**0.62***		0.42	0.36	0.29	**0.54**	0.28	0.39	0.50	**0.75**†
RBMT4	**0.46**	**0.47**	0.42		0.19	0.31	**0.61**	**0.50**	0.40	**0.50**	**0.57**
RBMT5	**0.70**†	**0.64***	**0.59**	**0.48**		0.35	**0.65***	**0.52**	**0.64**	**0.61**	**0.63***
RBMT6	**0.63**	**0.58**	**0.47**	**0.56**	**0.50**		**0.78**†	0.32	**0.58**	0.33	**0.71***
SAAR	0.33	**0.40**	0.33	0.30	0.23*	0.19†		0.20	0.27	0.24	0.33
UCL	**0.46**	**0.64**†	**0.41**	0.46	0.36	**0.41**	**0.60**		**0.65***	**0.42**	**0.57***
UEDIN	0.09*	**0.29**	**0.48**	**0.45**	0.28	0.27	**0.41**	0.19*		0.25	0.17
UPC	0.22	**0.40**	0.50	0.43	0.28	**0.40**	**0.52**	0.26	**0.56**		**0.58**
UW	**0.44**	0.32	0.06†	0.29	0.17*	0.21*	0.33	0.14*	**0.33**	0.33	
$>$ OTHERS	0.43	0.46	0.4	0.4	0.26	0.28	**0.53**	0.28	0.46	0.4	0.49
$\geq$ OTHERS	0.67	**0.74**	0.55	0.56	0.41	0.44	0.72	0.50	0.71	0.59	0.74

Table 32: Sentence-level ranking for the English-Spanish Europarl Task.

	DCU	UEDIN	UMD
DCU		0.26†	0.4
UEDIN	**0.37**†		**0.46**†
UMD	0.4	0.31†	
$>$ OTHERS	0.38	0.28	**0.43**
$\geq$ OTHERS	**0.68**	0.58	0.65

Table 33: Sentence-level ranking for the Czech-English News Task.

	DCU	SYSTRAN	UEDIN	UMD
DCU		0.21†	0.19†	0.37
SYSTRAN	**0.59**†		**0.47**†	**0.61**†
UEDIN	**0.42**†	0.27†		**0.50**†
UMD	**0.38**	0.18†	0.29†	
$>$ OTHERS	0.46	0.22	0.31	**0.49**
$\geq$ OTHERS	**0.75**	0.45	0.60	0.72

Table 34: Sentence-level ranking for the Czech-English Commentary Task.

	CU-BOJAR	CU-TECTOMT	PC-TRANSLATOR	UEDIN
CU-BOJAR		0.32†	**0.51**†	0.27†
CU-TECTOMT	**0.52**†		**0.58**†	**0.42**
PC-TRANSLATOR	0.35†	0.25†		0.26†
UEDIN	**0.5**†	0.40	**0.59**†	
$>$ OTHERS	0.45	0.32	**0.56**	0.32
$\geq$ OTHERS	0.63	0.49	**0.72**	0.50

Table 35: Sentence-level ranking for the English-Czech News Task.

	CU-BOJAR	CU-TECTOMT	PC-TRANSLATOR	UEDIN
CU-BOJAR		0.28†	0.38	0.19†
CU-TECTOMT	**0.58**†		**0.53**†	**0.43**
PC-TRANSLATOR	**0.45**	0.3†		0.26†
UEDIN	**0.60**†	0.37	**0.56**†	
$>$ OTHERS	**0.54**	0.32	0.49	0.29
$\geq$ OTHERS	**0.71**	0.49	0.66	0.49

Table 36: Sentence-level ranking for the English-Czech Commentary Task.

	MLOGIC	UEDIN
MORPHOLOGIC		0.15†
UEDIN	**0.68**†	
> OTHERS	**0.68**	0.15
≥ OTHERS	**0.85**	0.32

Table 37: Sentence-level ranking for the Hungarian-English News Task.

	CMU-XFR	CUED	CUED-C	LIMSI	LIUM-SYS	LIUM-SYS-C	RBMT3	RBMT4	RBMT5	RBMT6	SAAR	SAAR-C	UEDIN
CMU-XFR		**0.37**	**0.49**†	**0.62**†	**0.57**†	**0.61**†	**0.49**	**0.49**	**0.48**⋆	**0.41**	**0.56**†	**0.39**	**0.46**⋆
CUED	0.28		**0.21**	**0.30**	**0.30**	0.13	0.28	0.18	**0.27**	0.28	0.31	**0.34**	**0.18**
CUED-C	0.2†	0.11		**0.30**⋆	0.19	**0.33**	0.18†	0.21	0.24	0.2†	0.2⋆	0.17⋆	**0.24**
LIMSI	0.13†	0.20	0.13⋆		**0.27**	0.22	0.23	0.24	0.2	0.20⋆	0.16⋆	0.23	0.22
LIUM-SYS	0.18†	0.17	**0.27**	0.17		**0.20**	0.18⋆	**0.41**	**0.29**	0.24	0.26	0.22	0.26
LI-SYS-C	0.18†	**0.28**	0.24	**0.25**	0.07		0.33	0.2⋆	0.27	0.18†	0.23	0.25	0.19
RBMT3	0.28	**0.34**	**0.52**†	**0.28**	**0.40**⋆	**0.37**		0.27	**0.46**†	0.27	0.30	**0.39**	**0.34**
RBMT4	0.29	**0.40**	**0.34**	**0.31**	0.39	**0.43**⋆	**0.33**		**0.34**	**0.34**	0.27	**0.41**	**0.31**
RBMT5	0.22⋆	0.24	**0.34**	**0.3**	0.27	**0.43**	0.14†	0.24		0.13⋆	0.32	**0.32**	**0.32**
RBMT6	0.3	**0.41**	**0.50**†	**0.39**⋆	**0.33**	**0.58**†	**0.3**	0.33	**0.37**⋆		0.33	**0.52**⋆	**0.37**
SAAR	0.27†	**0.33**	**0.43**⋆	**0.37**⋆	**0.4**	**0.42**	**0.41**	**0.36**	0.32	**0.41**		**0.23**	**0.41**
SAAR-C	0.28	0.32	**0.38**⋆	**0.27**	**0.27**	**0.45**	0.23	0.21	0.20	0.23⋆	0.18		0.19
UED	0.19⋆	0.15	0.20	**0.25**	**0.29**	0.19	0.28	0.27	0.19	0.24	0.21	**0.26**	
> OTHERS	0.24	0.27	0.33	0.32	0.32	**0.37**	0.29	0.28	0.30	0.27	0.29	0.31	0.29
≥ OTHERS	0.51	0.75	0.79	**0.80**	0.77	0.78	0.65	0.66	0.73	0.62	0.64	0.74	0.77

Table 38: Constituent ranking for the French-English News Task

	CMU-XFR	CUED	DCU	LIMSI	LIUM-SYS	RBMT3	RBMT4	RBMT5	RBMT6	SAAR	SAAR-C	SYSTRAN	UCL	UEDIN
CMU-XFR		**0.42**†	**0.4**†	**0.37**⋆	**0.54**†	0.16⋆	0.21	**0.41**	0.23	**0.49**†	**0.42**†	0.34	**0.45**	**0.50**†
CUED	0.03†		**0.13**	**0.08**	0.14	0.13†	0.13†	0.08†	0.05†	0.08	0.04	0.15	0.11	0.07
DCU	0.09†	0.08		0.10	0.12	0.06†	0.20	**0.31**	0.16†	0.14	**0.22**	0.13	0.10	0.16
LIMSI	0.1⋆	0.05	**0.19**		0.05	0.04†	0.08†	0.19	0.11†	0.18	0.09	0.05†	0.05†	
LIUM-SYS	0.03†	0.14	**0.19**	**0.07**		0	0.08⋆	0.03†	0.05†	0.03†	0.09	0.15	0.14	0.08
RBMT3	**0.44**⋆	**0.61**†	**0.50**†	**0.58**†	**0.56**†		**0.41**⋆	**0.38**	**0.32**	**0.37**	**0.53**†	**0.44**	**0.50**⋆	**0.58**†
RBMT4	**0.39**	**0.44**†	**0.43**	**0.45**†	**0.35**⋆	0.12⋆		**0.31**	0.23	**0.42**	**0.39**	0.33	**0.32**	**0.35**
RBMT5	0.19	**0.47**†	0.29	**0.35**	**0.37**†	0.18	0.17		0.23	**0.35**	**0.33**	0.19	**0.46**	**0.40**
RBMT6	**0.36**	**0.65**†	**0.54**†	**0.48**†	**0.55**†	0.26	**0.40**	**0.50**		**0.50**†	**0.52**†	**0.47**⋆	**0.60**†	**0.44**
SAAR	0.07†	**0.25**	**0.24**	0.18	**0.37**†	0.23	0.36	0.23	0.12†		0.12	0.23	0.13	**0.37**⋆
SAAR-C	0.09†	**0.18**	0.12	**0.16**	**0.16**	0.09†	0.18	0.2	0.06†	0.12		0.09	0.14	**0.15**
SYSTRAN	0.34	**0.40**	**0.21**	**0.38**†	**0.23**	0.25	**0.36**	**0.22**	0.15⋆	0.23	**0.28**		0.31	**0.30**⋆
UCL	0.25	**0.34**	**0.28**	**0.31**†	**0.19**	0.11⋆	0.24	0.23	0.11†	**0.24**	**0.31**	**0.34**		**0.37**⋆
UED	0.10†	**0.10**	0.16	**0.05**	0.08	0.03†	0.15	0.14	0.18	0.07⋆	0.13	0.07⋆	0.11⋆	
> OTHERS	0.2	**0.32**	0.27	0.28	0.28	0.12	0.22	0.25	0.15	0.26	0.27	0.22	0.25	0.28
≥ OTHERS	0.63	0.91	0.85	0.91	**0.92**	0.52	0.65	0.7	0.52	0.78	0.87	0.71	0.74	0.89

Table 39: Constituent ranking for the French-English Europarl Task

	LIMSI	LIUM-SYS	RBMT3	RBMT4	RBMT5	RBMT6	SAAR	SAAR-C	UEDIN	XEROX
LIMSI		**0.27**	**0.43**	**0.43**	0.29	**0.53***	0.32	**0.37**	**0.30**	0.14†
LIUM-SYSTRAN	0.09		0.33	**0.36**	0.18	**0.35**	0.16*	0.25	0.22	0.13†
RBMT3	0.36	0.33		0.22	**0.31**	0.28	**0.4**	0.26	0.26*	0.20†
RBMT4	0.25	0.26	**0.30**		0.23	0.16†	0.28	0.26	0.24	0.13†
RBMT5	**0.31**	**0.33**	0.22	**0.28**		0.17	0.27	0.25	0.23	0.13†
RBMT6	0.26*	0.30	**0.31**	**0.38**†	**0.32**		**0.33**	0.36	0.39	0.25*
SAAR	0.32	**0.41***	0.35	**0.38**	**0.32**	0.28		**0.14**	0.23	0.11†
SAAR-CONTRAST	0.25	**0.26**	**0.36**	**0.30**	**0.33**	0.36	0.05		0.22	0.13†
UEDIN	0.29	**0.34**	**0.45***	**0.4**	**0.33**	**0.40**	**0.31**	**0.35**		0.13†
XEROX	**0.66**†	**0.55**†	**0.61**†	**0.65**†	**0.58**†	**0.51***	**0.53**†	**0.57**†	**0.45**†	
> OTHERS	0.31	0.34	0.38	**0.38**	0.33	0.33	0.3	0.31	0.29	0.15
≥ OTHERS	0.65	0.76	0.72	**0.77**	0.76	0.67	0.73	0.75	0.66	0.44

Table 40: Constituent ranking for the English-French News Task

	LIMSI	LIUM-SYS	RBMT3	RBMT4	RBMT5	RBMT6	SAAR	UCL	UEDIN
LIMSI		**0.14**	0.09†	0.10†	0.24	0.11†	0.13	0.08†	0.12
LIUM-SYSTRAN			0.19†	0.19*	0.15	0.12†	0.06	0.06†	0.09
RBMT3	**0.65**†	**0.59**†		**0.33**	**0.43**	0.32	**0.50***	**0.39**	**0.46**†
RBMT4	**0.53**†	**0.47***	0.19		0.27	0.18*	**0.33**	**0.38**	**0.39**
RBMT5	**0.48**	**0.38**	0.32	**0.48**		**0.47**	**0.55**†	**0.44**	**0.51**†
RBMT6	**0.54**†	**0.49**†	0.32	**0.41***	0.26		**0.52**†	**0.45**	**0.58**†
SAAR	**0.21**	**0.17**	0.23*	0.25	0.21†	0.17†		0.19	**0.13**
UCL	**0.37**†	**0.33**†	0.38	0.35	0.36	0.32	**0.34**		**0.31**†
UEDIN	0.12	**0.11**	0.17†	0.23	0.13†	0.13†	0.07	0.07†	
> OTHERS	**0.38**	0.36	0.25	0.30	0.26	0.24	0.33	0.27	0.34
≥ OTHERS	0.88	**0.88**	0.56	0.68	0.55	0.56	0.81	0.66	0.87

Table 41: Constituent ranking for the English-French Europarl Task

	CMU-XFER	LIMSI	LIU	RBMT2	RBMT3	RBMT4	RBMT5	RBMT6	SAAR	SAAR-C	UEDIN
CMU-STATXFER		**0.47**†	**0.44**	**0.52**†	**0.53**†	**0.57**†	**0.49***	**0.41**	**0.49**	**0.58**†	**0.49**†
LIMSI	0.17†		0.18	**0.35**	0.34	**0.40**	**0.33**	**0.43**	0.19	0.28	0.19
LIU	0.25	**0.3**		**0.37**	**0.35**	**0.44**	0.28	**0.40**	0.21	**0.33**	**0.32***
RBMT2	0.19†	0.26	0.30		0.19	**0.32**	0.16*	0.20	0.26	**0.23**	0.21
RBMT3	0.22†	**0.36**	0.26	**0.23**		0.24	0.23	0.14†	**0.15**	**0.28**	0.29
RBMT4	0.20†	0.35	0.23	0.21	0.24		0.22	0.19*	**0.36**	**0.32**	**0.31**
RBMT5	0.26*	0.28	**0.38**	**0.34***	**0.31**	**0.35**		0.26	**0.3**	**0.43**†	**0.35**
RBMT6	0.38	0.37	0.39	**0.34**	**0.44**†	**0.4***	**0.30**		**0.28**	0.26	**0.38**
SAAR	0.29	**0.22**	**0.37**	**0.29**	0.10	0.28	0.19	0.22		**0.26**	0.18
SAAR-CONTRAST	0.18†	**0.33**	0.29	0.19	0.22	0.24	0.15†	0.26	0.18		0.23
UEDIN	0.11†	**0.3**	0.13*	**0.23**	**0.35**	0.3	0.2	0.37	**0.30**	**0.31**	
> OTHERS	0.22	0.33	0.3	0.31	0.32	**0.35**	0.25	0.29	0.28	0.33	0.30
≥ OTHERS	0.50	0.72	0.67	0.77	0.76	0.74	0.67	0.64	0.76	**0.78**	0.74

Table 42: Constituent ranking for the German-English News Task

	CMU-XFR	LIMSI	LIU	RBMT2	RBMT3	RBMT4	RBMT5	RBMT6	SAAR	UCL	UEDIN
CMU-STATXFER		**0.51**†	**0.51**†	0.38	**0.38**	**0.41**	0.37	**0.44**	**0.48**†	**0.39**	**0.6**†
LIMSI	0.18†		0.22	0.3	0.30	0.23	0.22†	0.32	**0.27**	0.18*	**0.29**
LIU	0.14†	0.22		0.26*	0.32	0.22*	0.16†	0.31	**0.20**	0.08†	0.12
RBMT2	0.38	**0.51**	**0.52***		**0.40**	**0.32**	0.25	0.31	**0.51**	0.40	**0.7**†
RBMT3	0.32	**0.42**	**0.45**	0.28		**0.46**	0.16	0.20*	**0.56**†	0.38	**0.43**
RBMT4	0.32	**0.45**	**0.52***	0.31	0.24		0.13†	0.30	**0.49**†	**0.44**	**0.48***
RBMT5	**0.44**	**0.57**†	**0.53**†	**0.34**	**0.31**	**0.43**†		0.19	**0.54**†	0.39	**0.54**†
RBMT6	0.33	**0.51**	**0.48**	**0.33**	**0.47***	**0.33**	**0.33**		**0.47***	**0.42**	**0.51***
SAAR	0.12†	0.1	0.15	0.26	0.09†	0.19†	0.17†	0.23*		0.11†	0.14
UCL	0.30	**0.43***	**0.49**†	0.40	**0.40**	0.30	**0.41**	0.39	**0.38**†		**0.51**†
UEDIN	0.11†	0.16	0.12	0.18†	0.25	0.2*	0.18†	0.23*	0.14	0.12†	
> OTHERS	0.27	0.40	0.41	0.31	0.32	0.32	0.25	0.3	0.41	0.30	**0.44**
≥ OTHERS	0.55	0.75	0.8	0.58	0.64	0.64	0.58	0.59	**0.84**	0.60	0.83

Table 43: Constituent ranking for the German-English Europarl Task

	LIMSI	LIU	RBMT2	RBMT3	RBMT4	RBMT5	RBMT6	SAAR	UEDIN
LIMSI		0.29	**0.46**	**0.45**	**0.37**	0.36	0.29†	0.33	0.22
LIU	**0.32**		**0.53**†	**0.45***	**0.51**†	**0.5***	0.38	**0.31**	**0.36**
RBMT2	0.33	0.32†		0.29	0.29	0.20†	0.25†	0.28	0.28†
RBMT3	0.34	0.3*	**0.4**		**0.33**	0.3*	0.34	0.20*	0.27†
RBMT4	0.26	0.25†	**0.31**	0.3		0.23*	0.23†	0.20*	0.21†
RBMT5	**0.46**	0.33*	**0.55**†	**0.46***	**0.40***		0.32	0.32	0.29†
RBMT6	**0.52**†	**0.40**	**0.47**†	**0.44**	**0.53**†	**0.40**		0.27	0.37
SAAR	**0.38**	0.3	**0.39**	**0.42***	**0.44***	**0.40**	**0.44**		0.34
UEDIN	**0.30**	0.24	**0.53**†	**0.52**†	**0.51**†	**0.56**†	**0.45**	**0.36**	
> OTHERS	0.36	0.31	**0.46**	0.41	0.42	0.37	0.33	0.28	0.29
≥ OTHERS	0.65	0.57	0.72	0.68	**0.75**	0.60	0.56	0.61	0.56

Table 44: Constituent ranking for the English-German News Task

	CMU-GIMPEL	LIMSI	LIU	RBMT2	RBMT3	RBMT4	RBMT5	RBMT6	SAAR	UCL	UEDIN
CMU-GIMPEL		0.12	**0.27**	0.21†	0.30	0.21†	0.27*	0.21†	0.22	0.22	**0.23**
LIMSI	**0.22**		**0.22**	0.34	0.29*	0.29†	0.23†	0.29†	0.2	0.21	**0.19**
LIU	0.18	0.2		0.20†	0.25*	0.17†	0.16†	0.12†	**0.28**	0.21	0.18
RBMT2	**0.54**†	**0.41**	**0.62**†		0.28	0.33	0.35	0.28	**0.61***	**0.43**	**0.47**†
RBMT3	**0.47**	**0.47***	**0.47***	**0.4**		**0.33**	0.32	0.28	**0.56***	**0.47**	**0.48**†
RBMT4	**0.52**†	**0.57**†	**0.52**†	**0.42**	0.32		0.27*	0.28	**0.47**	**0.45**	**0.39**
RBMT5	**0.49***	**0.57**†	**0.65**†	**0.42**	**0.38**	**0.48***		0.31	**0.76**†	**0.51**	**0.52**†
RBMT6	**0.51**†	**0.54**†	**0.60**†	**0.41**	**0.39**	**0.40**	**0.41**		**0.51***	**0.53***	**0.51**†
SAAR	**0.24**	**0.29**	0.17	0.26*	0.22*	0.25	0.20†	0.21*		**0.31**	0.12
UCL	**0.28**	**0.32**	**0.29**	0.33	0.38	0.32	0.32	0.29*	0.19		**0.30**
UEDIN	0.1	0.13	**0.22**	0.2†	0.18†	0.22	0.21†	0.18†	**0.15**	0.17	
> OTHERS	0.37	0.37	**0.42**	0.32	0.30	0.31	0.28	0.25	0.39	0.35	0.35
≥ OTHERS	0.77	0.75	0.81	0.58	0.59	0.58	0.51	0.52	0.77	0.69	**0.82**

Table 45: Constituent ranking for the English-German Europarl Task

	CMU-SMT	CUED	CUED-C	LIMSI	RBMT3	RBMT4	RBMT5	RBMT6	SAAR	UCB	UEDIN	UPC
CMU-SMT		0.19	0.17	**0.26**	**0.38**	0.27	**0.45**	0.32	**0.35**	**0.27**	**0.26**	**0.2**
CUED	**0.21**		**0.21**	0.24	0.24	0.2	**0.34**	0.25	0.27	0.18	**0.26**	0.21
CUED-CONTRAST	0.17	0.08		0.12	0.24	0.23*	0.27	0.25	0.21	0.12	0.11	**0.26**
LIMSI	0.17	**0.25**	**0.26**		0.34	0.18†	0.33	0.33	**0.31**	0.17	**0.26**	**0.23**
RBMT3	0.29	**0.31**	**0.35**	**0.37**		0.21	**0.4**	**0.31**	**0.32**	**0.43**	**0.42**	**0.52***
RBMT4	**0.38**	**0.34**	**0.54***	**0.47**†	**0.35**		**0.24**	**0.32**	**0.46**†	**0.37**	**0.40**	**0.53**
RBMT5	0.24	0.31	**0.40**	0.33	0.25	0.18		**0.31**	**0.33**	0.32	0.28	0.38
RBMT6	**0.33**	**0.29**	**0.28**	0.33	0.26	0.27	0.16		**0.26**	0.3	**0.39**	**0.41**
SAAR	0.26	0.27	**0.33**	0.26	0.21	0.12†	0.25	0.24		0.20	**0.28**	0.20
UCB	0.25	**0.30**	**0.23**	**0.27**	0.31	0.27	**0.40**	**0.34**	**0.28**		**0.32**	0.26
UEDIN	0.19	0.20	**0.19**	0.24	0.27	0.33	**0.31**	0.27	0.21	0.21		**0.25**
UPC	0.1	0.21	0.17	0.2	0.22*	0.28	**0.4**	0.24	**0.29**	**0.30**	0.2	
$>$ OTHERS	0.24	0.25	0.28	0.28	0.28	0.23	**0.33**	0.29	0.3	0.26	0.3	0.32
$\geq$ OTHERS	0.72	0.76	**0.82**	0.74	0.64	0.61	0.7	0.70	0.76	0.71	0.76	0.76

Table 46: Constituent ranking for the Spanish-English News Task

	CMU-SMT	CUED	DCU	LIMSI	RBMT3	RBMT4	RBMT5	RBMT6	SAAR	UCL	UEDIN	UPC
CMU-SMT		**0.2**	**0.20**	**0.1**	0.1†	0.18†	0.04†	0.18†	**0.16**	0.17	**0.19**	0.19
CUED	0.18		0.13	**0.19**	0.14†	0.12†	0.1†	0.2*	**0.13**	0.12*	**0.22**	0.12
DCU	0.15	0.13		0.11	0.09†	0.10†	0.13†	0.09†	**0.19**	0.15*	0.14	0.15
LIMSI	0.03	0.15	**0.16**		0.19†	0.18†	0.15†	0.19†	**0.19**	0.08†	0.07	**0.22**
RBMT3	**0.7**†	**0.73**†	**0.59**†	**0.49**†		0.19	**0.36**	0.22	**0.62**†	**0.55***	**0.68**†	**0.73**†
RBMT4	**0.55**†	**0.62**†	**0.51**†	**0.55**†	**0.23**		0.22	0.17	**0.56**†	**0.43**	**0.56**†	**0.44***
RBMT5	**0.60**†	**0.61**†	**0.53**†	**0.61**†	0.32	**0.38**		**0.28**	**0.63**†	**0.53**	**0.7**†	**0.59**†
RBMT6	**0.52**†	**0.48***	**0.51**†	**0.49**†	**0.23**	**0.26**	0.19		**0.49**†	**0.53***	**0.52**†	**0.50**†
SAAR	0.14	0.10	0.12	0.15	0.10†	0.12†	0.05†	0.07†		0.14*	0.05	**0.18**
UCL	**0.38**	**0.37***	**0.46***	**0.45**†	0.28*	0.32	0.29	0.24*	**0.38***		**0.38***	**0.36**
UEDIN	0.06	0.14	0.14	**0.18**	0.15†	0.16†	0.05†	0.16†	**0.15**	0.10*		**0.21**
UPC	0.19	0.12	**0.20**	0.12	0.07†	0.17*	0.09†	0.14†	0.04	0.17	0.14	
$>$ OTHERS	0.32	0.33	0.32	0.32	0.17	0.2	0.15	0.17	0.33	0.28	0.34	**0.35**
$\geq$ OTHERS	0.85	0.85	0.87	0.85	0.46	0.56	0.47	0.57	**0.89**	0.65	0.87	0.87

Table 47: Constituent ranking for the Spanish-English Europarl Task

	CMU-SMT	LIMSI	RBMT3	RBMT4	RBMT5	RBMT6	SAAR	UCB	UEDIN	UPC
CMU-SMT		0.20	**0.36**	**0.37**	0.24†	0.36	0.32	0.21	0.17	0.27
LIMSI	**0.23**		**0.4**	**0.46***	0.33	**0.39**	0.31	0.23	0.17	0.18
RBMT3	0.33	0.35		0.22	0.19†	0.3	0.31	**0.49**	0.34	0.22
RBMT4	0.30	0.25*	**0.25**		0.17*	0.17*	0.24	0.19†	0.34	0.30
RBMT5	**0.53**†	**0.42**	**0.50**†	**0.41***		**0.35**	**0.50***	**0.44**	0.37	0.29
RBMT6	0.36	0.35	**0.34**	**0.39***	0.32		0.35	0.36	0.37	0.38
SAAR	**0.33**	**0.36**	**0.38**	**0.28**	0.24*	**0.38**		0.29	0.22*	0.24
UCB	**0.32**	**0.29**	0.35	**0.54**†	0.33	**0.45**	**0.31**		0.19	**0.29**
UEDIN	**0.29**	**0.33**	**0.36**	**0.42**	**0.42**	**0.39**	**0.45***	**0.30**		**0.44**
UPC	**0.36**	**0.42**	**0.50**	**0.49**	**0.42**	**0.44**	**0.51**	0.21	0.26	
$>$ OTHERS	0.34	0.33	0.38	**0.39**	0.29	0.35	0.36	0.31	0.27	0.29
$\geq$ OTHERS	0.72	0.69	0.69	**0.75**	0.57	0.64	0.7	0.65	0.63	0.6

Table 48: Constituent ranking for the English-Spanish News Task

	CMU-SMT	LIMSI	RBMT3	RBMT4	RBMT5	RBMT6	SAAR	UCL	UEDIN	UPC	UW
CMU-SMT		0.13	0.10†	0.21*	0.2†	0.2†	**0.26**	0.22	0.13	0.16	0.14
LIMSI	**0.17**		0.24	0.16†	0.20†	0.13†	**0.21**	0.06†	0.09	**0.14**	0.08
RBMT3	**0.64**†	**0.45**		0.24	0.30	0.21	**0.57**†	**0.56**	**0.58***	0.32	**0.58**†
RBMT4	**0.54***	**0.52**†	**0.42**		0.26	0.24	**0.50***	0.35	**0.43**	**0.47**	**0.44**
RBMT5	**0.61**†	**0.68**†	**0.46**	**0.44**		**0.37**	**0.64**†	**0.50**	**0.63**†	**0.62**†	**0.54**
RBMT6	**0.57**†	**0.48**†	**0.39**	**0.33**	0.25		**0.52**†	0.33	**0.54**†	**0.46**	**0.46**
SAAR	0.19	0.14	0.07†	0.19*	0.09†	0.14†		0.13†	0.17	0.26	0.18
UCL	**0.43**	**0.46**†	0.29	**0.37**	0.38	**0.42**	**0.49**†		**0.37***	**0.48**	**0.40**
UEDIN	**0.15**	**0.11**	0.24*	0.20	0.13†	0.17†	**0.30**	0.14*		0.20	0.20
UPC	**0.26**	0.05	**0.35**	0.25	0.16†	0.23	**0.34**	0.21	**0.23**		0.10
UW	0.14	**0.14**	0.17†	0.22	0.23	0.2	**0.32**	0.20	0.20	**0.35**	
$>$ OTHERS	0.37	0.32	0.28	0.26	0.22	0.23	**0.42**	0.27	0.35	0.35	0.33
$\geq$ OTHERS	0.83	**0.86**	0.56	0.59	0.46	0.57	0.85	0.59	0.82	0.78	0.79

Table 49: Constituent ranking for the English-Spanish Europarl Task

	CU-BOJAR	CU-TECTOMT	PC-TRANSLATOR	UEDIN
CU-BOJAR		0.33	**0.41**	0.28*
CU-TECTOMT	**0.37**		**0.42**†	0.36
PC-TRANSLATOR	0.34	0.31†		0.32†
UEDIN	**0.37***	**0.37**	**0.43**†	
$>$ OTHERS	0.36	0.34	**0.42**	0.32
$\geq$ OTHERS	0.66	0.62	**0.67**	0.61

Table 50: Constituent ranking for the English-Czech News Task

	CU-BOJAR	CU-TECTOMT	PC-TRANSLATOR	UEDIN
CU-BOJAR		0.25†	0.33†	0.22†
CU-TECTOMT	**0.50**†		**0.44**†	**0.45**
PC-TRANSLATOR	**0.47**†	0.3†		**0.40**
UEDIN	**0.39**†	0.37	0.39	
$>$ OTHERS	**0.45**	0.31	0.39	0.36
$\geq$ OTHERS	**0.73**	0.54	0.61	0.61

Table 51: Constituent ranking for the English-Czech Commentary Task

French–English

Europarl	YES	NO
CMU-XFR	0.61	0.39
CUED	0.83	0.17
DCU	0.88	0.12
LIMSI	0.89	0.11
LIUM-SYS	0.89	0.11
RBMT3	0.54	0.47
RBMT4	0.62	0.38
RBMT5	0.71	0.29
RBMT6	0.54	0.46
SAAR	0.72	0.28
SAAR-C	0.86	0.14
SYSTRAN	0.81	0.19
UCL	0.73	0.27
UEDIN	**0.91**	**0.09**

News	YES	NO
CMU-XFR	0.55	0.45
CUED	0.74	0.26
CUED-C	0.79	0.21
LIMSI	**0.81**	**0.2**
LIUM-SYS	0.79	0.21
LI-SYS-C	0.7	0.30
RBMT3	0.63	0.37
RBMT4	0.64	0.36
RBMT5	0.76	0.24
RBMT6	0.66	0.34
SAAR	0.64	0.36
SAAR-C	0.70	0.3
UEDIN	0.72	0.28

English–French

Europarl	YES	NO
LIMSI	0.75	0.26
LIUM-SYS	**0.84**	**0.16**
RBMT3	0.49	0.51
RBMT4	0.50	0.5
RBMT5	0.44	0.56
RBMT6	0.35	0.65
SAAR	0.70	0.3
UCL	0.6	0.40
UEDIN	0.75	0.25

News	YES	NO
LIMSI	0.73	0.27
LIUM-SYS	**0.75**	**0.25**
RBMT3	0.59	0.41
RBMT4	0.59	0.41
RBMT5	0.64	0.36
RBMT6	0.58	0.42
SAAR	0.59	0.41
SAAR-C	0.59	0.41
UEDIN	0.63	0.37
XEROX	0.30	0.7

German–English

Europarl	YES	NO
CMU-XFER	0.53	0.47
LIMSI	0.80	0.2
LIU	0.83	0.17
RBMT2	0.76	0.24
RBMT3	0.74	0.26
RBMT4	0.67	0.33
RBMT5	0.63	0.37
RBMT6	0.63	0.37
SAAR	0.82	0.18
UCL	0.49	0.51
UEDIN	**0.86**	**0.14**

News	YES	NO
CMU-XFER	0.47	0.53
LIMSI	0.73	0.28
LIU	0.64	0.36
RBMT2	0.72	0.28
RBMT3	0.73	0.27
RBMT4	**0.74**	**0.26**
RBMT5	0.59	0.41
RBMT6	0.68	0.32
SAAR	0.67	0.33
SAAR-C	0.72	0.28
UEDIN	0.63	0.37

English–German

Europarl	YES	NO
CMU-GIMPEL	0.82†	0.18
LIMSI	0.79†	0.21
LIU	0.79†	0.21
RBMT2	0.69†	0.31
RBMT3	0.57	0.43
RBMT4	0.67†	0.34
RBMT5	0.45	0.55
RBMT6	0.47	0.53
SAAR	0.77†	0.23
UCL	0.61†	0.39
UEDIN	**0.85**†	**0.15**

News	YES	NO
LIMSI	0.56	0.44
LIU	0.49	0.51
RBMT2	0.69	0.31
RBMT3	0.69	0.31
RBMT4	**0.75**	**0.25**
RBMT5	0.55	0.45
RBMT6	0.6	0.40
SAAR	0.54	0.46
UEDIN	0.52	0.48

Spanish–English

Europarl	YES	NO
CMU-SMT	0.88	0.12
CUED	0.86	0.14
DCU	0.85	0.15
LIMSI	**0.90**	**0.1**
RBMT3	0.65	0.35
RBMT4	0.56	0.44
RBMT5	0.59	0.41
RBMT6	0.55	0.45
SAAR	0.87	0.13
UCL	0.73	0.27
UEDIN	0.88	0.12
UPC	0.86	0.14

News	YES	NO
CMU-SMT	0.64	0.37
CUED	0.64	0.36
CUED-C	0.69	0.31
LIMSI	0.68	0.33
RBMT3	0.61	0.39
RBMT4	0.65	0.35
RBMT5	0.59	0.41
RBMT6	0.64	0.37
SAAR	0.7	0.30
UCB	0.64	0.37
UEDIN	0.62	0.38
UPC	**0.71**	**0.29**

English–Spanish

Europarl	YES	NO
CMU-SMT	0.80	0.2
LIMSI	0.87	0.13
RBMT3	0.58	0.42
RBMT4	0.6	0.40
RBMT5	0.64	0.37
RBMT6	0.60	0.40
SAAR	0.81	0.19
UCL	0.71	0.29
UEDIN	0.89	0.11
UPC	**0.90**	**0.1**
UW	0.79	0.22

News	YES	NO
CMU-SMT	0.46	0.54
LIMSI	0.53	0.47
RBMT3	0.64	0.36
RBMT4	**0.76**	**0.24**
RBMT5	0.6	0.40
RBMT6	0.62	0.38
SAAR	0.64	0.36
UCB	0.57	0.43
UEDIN	0.49	0.51
UPC	0.37	0.63

English–Czech

Commentary	YES	NO
CU-BOJAR	**0.59**	**0.41**
CU-TECTO	0.43	0.57
PC-TRANS	0.51	0.49
UEDIN	0.41	0.59

News	YES	NO
CU-BOJAR	**0.54**	**0.46**
CU-TECTO	0.42	0.58
PC-TRANS	0.52	0.48
UEDIN	0.44	0.56

Table 52: Yes/No Acceptability of Constituents

	BBN-CMB-DE	BBN-CMB-FR	CMU-CMB-FR	CMU-SMT-ES	CMU-XFR-DE	CMU-XFR-FR	CUED-C-ES	CUED-C-FR	CUED-ES	CUED-FR	DCU-CZ	LIMSI-DE	LIMSI-ES	LIMSI-FR	LIU-DE	LIUM-S-C-FR	LIUM-SYS-FR	MLOGIC-HU	RBMT2-DE	RBMT3-DE	RBMT3-ES	RBMT3-FR	RBMT4-DE	RBMT4-ES	RBMT4-FR	RBMT5-DE	RBMT5-ES	RBMT5-FR	RBMT6-DE	RBMT6-ES	RBMT6-FR	SAAR-C-DE	SAAR-C-FR	SAAR-DE	SAAR-ES	SAAR-FR	UCB-ES	UED-CMB-DE	UED-CMB-FR	UED-CMB-XX	UED-CZ	UED-DE	UED-ES	UED-FR	UED-HU	UMD-CZ	UPC-ES
BBN-CMB-DE		**.50**	.40	**1**	.20	.50	**1***	**.64**	**1**	**.73**	.31		**.69***	**.71**	.38	**.70**	**.60**	**.60**	**.80**	**.77***	**.60**	**.63**	**.89***	**1**	**.57**	**.62**	**.83**	**.60**	.17	**.57**	**.55**	.41	**.70**	**.58**	**.71**	**.82**	**.75**	**.40**	.33	**1**	.25	**.36**	**.85***	.50		.40	**.60**
BBN-CMB-FR	.38		.14	.38	.09*	.13*	.33	**.63**	.20	.25	.13	.13	**.60**	.31	.46	**.43**	.27	.13	**.67**	.25	.46	.33	.38	.22	**.43**	.07*	.33	.42	**.50**	.36	.25	.46	.40	.06†	.30	.33	**.50**			**.80**	.14*	.20	**.67**	.33	.25	.13	.42
CMU-CMB-FR	**.60**	**.71**		**.54**	.09*	**.60**	.29	.13	**.57**	**.33**	.23	.33	.33	**.46**	**.44**	**.58**	**.40**	.20	**.54**	.27	.50	**.67**	.11	.14	**.44**	.11	.25	**.60**	.09*	.40	.29		.29	.25	**.56**	.20	**.56**	.25	.14	.38	.11*	.11	.22			.36	.44
CMU-SMT-ES		**.50**	.31		.50	.17	**.75**	**.46**	**.64**	.43	.25	**.54**	**.60**	**.83***	.40	.50	.17	.14	.46	.50	**.64**	**.73**	**.80**	**.67**	**.64**	.33	**.33**	**.67**	**.46**	.50	**.57**	**.50**	.39	.36	**.64**	**.70**	.17		.50	.33	.14		.25	.33	.13	.38	**.43**
CMU-XFR-DE	**.60**	**.82***	**.91***	.50		**.78**	**.56**	**.89***	**.42**	**.73***	**.55**	.27	**.33**	**.88***	**.57**	**.73**†	**.92**†	**.75**	**.80**†	**.82**	**.75***	**.67**	**.75**	**.86**	**.78**	**.91***	**.89***	**.79***	**.81**†	**.80**	**.80***	**.67**	**.90**†	**.64**	**.73**†	**.80**	**.64**	.33	**1**	**.83**	.11	**.20**	**1**†	**.90**†	.33	.50	**.85***
CMU-XFR-FR	.50	**.75***		**.67**	.11		**.70**	**.80***	**.88***	**.71**	.50		**.75**	**.50**	**.60**	**.71**	**.67**	.50	**.67**	**.60**	.40	**.43**	**.60**	**.67**	.29	.25	**.64**	**.75**	.38	**.75**	.38	.50	**.67**	.18	**.57**	.44	**.73**	.33	**.50**	**.75**		**.80**	**.69**	**.64**	.50	.33	**1**
CUED-C-ES	0	**.56**	**.59**		.22	.20		.18	.21	.19	0	.29	.15	**.47**	.14	.39	.50	.25	.39	.36	**.43**	**.46**	.33	.31	**.56**	**.50**	.07†	**.73***	.31	**.42**	.42	.43	.50	.42	.40	.27	.18		.50	**.38**	.29	.10*	.22	.33		**.43**	.33
CUED-C-FR	.29	.13	**.38**	.39	.11*	.10*	**.73**		**.50**	.25	.36	**.57**	.40	.36	.11*	**.70***	**.60**	.40	**.58**	.36	**.56**	.20	.39	**.50**	**.60**	.10*	.50	**.50**	.30	**.55**		.46	.33	0	.17	.20	.39	.13	**.88**		0	.29	.39	.36	0	.40	**.50**
CUED-ES		**.80**	.29	.18	.25	0	**.29**	.38		**.64**	.25	.20	.14	**.78**	.25	.36	**.88**	.25	.36	**.39**	**.69**	**.71**	**.58**	**.83***	**.67**	.30	**.50**	**.60**	.47	**.67**	.43	.40	.20	.38	**.50**	.50	**.57**	.25	.50	.50	.08†	0		**.57**	.20	.50	**.67**
CUED-FR	.18	.25	.22	.43	.09*	.29	**.69**	**.38**	.27			.11	.10*	**.47**	.33	**.64**	.15	.50	.38	**.57**	.50	**.42**	**.43**	.33	**.50**	.22	.46	**.46**	.33	**.58**	**.43**	**.50**	**.56**	.18	.44	.25	.38		.20	.25	0	.33	.13	.44	0	.10*	**.50**
DCU-CZ	**.39**	**.75**	**.69**	**.67**	.36	.50	**.90**†	**.46**	**.58**	**1**		**.44**	.22	**.91***	**.56**	**.60**	**.85***	**1**	**.77***	**.78**	**.86**	**.75**	**.62**	**.57**	**.83***	.30	**.55**	**.80**	**.67**	**.77***	**.80***	**.79***	**.50**	.33	**.80***	**.89**†	**.73**	.17	**.50**	**.60**	**.50**	**.54**	**.78**	**.80**	.13	**.38**	.39
LIMSI-DE	**.17**	**.63**	**.67**	.39	.27	**1**	**.71**	.43	**.80**	**.78**	.38		.33	**.57**	**.50**	**.77***	**1***	.29	.50	**.78**	**.50**	**.67**	**.71**	**.88**	**.71***	.33	**.57**	**.89***	.30	**.60**	**.80**	.43	**.78***	.27	.36	.17	.44		**1**	**1**	.13	**.50**	**.67**	**.50**	.40	.30	.43
LIMSI-ES	.08*	.40	**.67**	.30	.17	.25	**.54**	**.60**	**.57**	**.80***	**.56**	**.50**		**.50**	.43	**.55**	**.50**	.33	**.43**	.10*	**.67**	**.50**	**.63**	**.39**	**.69**	.29	**.75**	**.50**	.29	**.60**	**.82**	**.63**	.20	.22	**.55**	.33	.29	.25	**1**	**.75**	.17	.25	**.57**	**.50**		**.64**	**.50**
LIMSI-FR	.14	**.38**	.18	.08*	0	.40	.27	.36	.11	.35	.09*	.29	.25		.23	**.63**	.30	.25	.38	**.56**	.36	.44	.22	.25	**.50**	.10*	.31	.20	.20	**.56**	.40	.17	.20	.38	.50	.36	.33	**1**	**.33**	**.50**	.25	.08†	.27	.24	.25	.29	.50
LIU-DE	**.50**	**.55**	.33	**.60**		.40	**.86**	**.89***	**.38**	**.44**	.22	.25	**.57**	**.54**		**.73***	**.80**	**1**	.22	**.55**	**.86**	**.83**	**.67**	**.67**	**.67**	.25	**.89***	**.71**	**.50**	**.60**	**.58**	**.60**	**.60**	**.60**	**.75**	**.71**	**.67**	.33	**1**	**1**	.22	.22	**.43**	**.67**		.40	**.69**
LIUM-S-C-FR	.20	.29	.17	.50	0	.14	**.46**	0	**.43**	.21	.20	.08*	.18	.13	.09*		.25	.11*	.18	.39	.50	.27	.27	.46	**.50**	.13*	.31	**.55**	.33	.46	**.50**	.42	.25	.33	**.59***	.33	.33	.33	.50			.25	.22	.18	0	.44	**.60**
LIUM-S-FR	.20	**.36**	.20	**.67**	.08†	.11	.50	.20	.13	**.62**	.15*	0	.38	**.50**	.20	.25		.14	.42	.36	.17	.43	.13	**.60**	.30	.25	.33	**.52**	.25	.18	.43	.39	.29	.20	.44	.16*	.44		**.50**	**.60**	.08*	.17*	.23	.17	0	.16†	.46
MLOGIC-HU	.40	**.75**	**.60**	**.71**	.25	.50	**.63**	**.60**	**.75**	.50		**.43**	**.67**	**.50**		**.89***	**.71**		**.88**	**.67**	.44	**.86***		**1***	.50	**.75**	**.67**	**.83**	**.63**	**.63**	**.54**	**.63**	**.67**	**.50**	**.86**	.33	**.63**	.33	**.75**	**1**	.40	**1**	**1**	.44	.25		**.80**
RBMT2-DE		.33	.39	.46	.07†	.33	**.46**	.33	**.64**	.38	.08*	.50	.36	**.50**	**.33**	**.55**	**.58**	.13		.17	**.67**	.38	.38	**.70**	**.55**	.22	**.46**	**.46**	**.46**	**.43**	.17	.10	.42	.43	**.67**	.29	.33	.40	.40	**1**	.10*	.31	**.54**	.36	.14	.07†	**.56**
RBMT3-DE	.08*	**.75**	**.64**	.50	.18	.20	**.64**	**.64**	.31	.43	.22	.11	**.80***	.44	.36	**.62**	**.64**	.33	**.67**		**.55**	**.46**	.35	**.90***	**.40**	.14	**.80***	.40	.38	.38	**.60**	.25	**.53**	.44	.31	**.56**	**.63**	.17	**.80**	**.60**		.22	**.55**	**.60**	.17	.20	**.67**
RBMT3-ES	.40	**.55**	.50	.18	.13*	**.50**	.36	.22	.23	.50	.14	.42	.33	**.50**	.14	.50	**.83**	.44	.33	.27		.39	**.64**	.50	.50		.36	.33	.31	.27	**.46**	.33	.09	**.43**	.23	**.50**	.46	.29	**.75**	**.75**	.25	.25	.36	.50	0	.20	**.78**
RBMT3-FR	.25	**.58**	.22	.27	.33	.29	.27	**.40**	.29	.33	.13	.33	.43	**.50**	.17	**.55**	**.50**	0	**.56**	.31	**.62**		**.75**	**.63**	.33	.13	.44	.38	.27	**.60**	.09*	**.57**	**.63**	.17	**.50**	.38	.40			**1**	.11	.25	**.73**	**.50**		.25	**.53**
RBMT4-DE	.11*	**.50**	**.78**	.20		.40	**.67**	**.62**	.25	.14	.15	.29	.13	**.78**	.25	**.73**	**.75**		**.50**	**.55**	.18			.22	.43	**.50**	**.57**	.29	.25	**.50**	**.63**	.42	.33	.25	**.67**	**.58**	.50		**.60**	**.67**	.14	.38	.50	**.75**	0	.22	**.63**
RBMT4-ES		**.44**	**.57**	.22	.14	.17	**.38**	.38	.08*	**.56**	.14	.13	.31	**.50**	.33	.46	.30	0	.10	.10*	.50	.38	**.56**		.29	.43	.25	.33	.38	.25	.25	.46	.33	.14	.09	.25	.33	.11	**1**	**1**	0	.09*	.39	**.50**	0	.38	.38
RBMT4-FR	.43	.29	.22	.27	.11	**.57**	.22	.27	.33	.33	.08*	.14*	.23	.33	.22	.25	**.60**	.50	.46	.30	.50	**.47**	**.57**	**.41**		**.67**	.46	**.58**	**.54**	.43	.38	.36	**.63**	.14	**.86**	.36			.25	**.60**	.39	**.50**	**.50**	.33	.20		.38
RBMT5-DE	.23	**.71***	**.67**	**.50**	.09*	**.50**	.38	**.80***	**.40**	**.56**	**.60**	**.44**	**.57**	**.80***	**.63**	**.75***	**.75**	.25	**.67**	**.43**	**.83**	**.75**	.29	**.57**	.17		**.50**	**1**†	.13	**.67**	**.53**	**.40**	**.71**	.20	**.67**	**.47**	.38		**.86**	.25	.27	.25	**.70**	**.67**	.20	.38	**.50**
RBMT5-ES	.17	**.67**	**.75**	.27	.11*	.27	**.73**†	.50	.13	.46	.27	.43		**.62**	.11*	**.62**	**.50**	.22	.36	.10*	**.43**	.44	.43	**.63**	.46	.36		**.50**	.29	**.44**	.17	**.57**	.27	.29	.25	**.60**	.11	.33	**.60**	**.67**	.44	0	.30	.43	.17	.25	**.58**
RBMT5-FR	.30	.42	.10	.11	.14*	.17	.09*	.42	.30	.39	.20	.11*	.33	**.50**	.21	.27	.29		.15	.40	**.67**	.38	**.71**	.33	.17	0	.40		.50	.40	.20	.25	**.56**	.07†	**.50**	.31	.14		**.50**		.22	.40	**.57**	**.54**			.29
RBMT6-DE	**.67**	.25	**.91***	.36	.06†	**.50**	**.54**	**.70**	.47	**.53**	.33	**.50**	**.57**	**.70**	.40	**.67**	**.58**	.25	.39	.38	**.69**	**.73**	**.50**	**.50**	.46	**.50**	**.43**	.50		.13	**.50**	**.46**	**.62**	**.50**	**.46**	.50	**.46**	.40	.33	**.80**	.29	.20	**.57**	**.50**		.29	**.86**
RBMT6-ES	.29	**.55**	**.60**	.50		.25	.25	.46	.22	.33	.08*	.40	.20	.44		**.55**	**.64**	.38	.29	**.63**	**.40**	.30	.30	.25	**.57**	.33	.22	**.60**	**.63**		**.67**	**.64**	.42	.38	**.67**	**.71**	.46	0		.50	.22	.25	.50	.33	0	.13	**.67**
RBMT6-FR	.36	**.63**	**.57**	.43	.20*	**.63**	**.50**	**.83**	.43	.36	.10*		.18	.40	.17	.43	**.50**	.39	**.67**	.30	.39	**.73***	.38	**.63**	.38	.27	**.83**	**.50**	.38	.17		.29	**.67**	.22	.40	.33	.38		.33	.50	.13	.25	**.63**	.33		.14	.25
SAAR-C-DE	.41	**.55**	**.67**	.30	.25	.50	**.50**	**.54**	**.60**	.40	.14*	**.57**	.25	**.83**	.30	**.50**	**.62**	.25	**.70**	**.50**	**.47**	.36	**.50**	.46	**.55**	.33	.14	**.75**	.36	.27	**.59**		.21	.13	**.50**	.36	.42	.33	**1**	.20	.33	**.54**	**.88**	**.69**		0	.44
SAAR-C-FR	.20	.40	**.50**	**.54**	0	.33	.50	.33	**.60**	.44	.38	0	**.60**	**.60**	.40	**.42**	**.43**	.17	**.50**	.33	**.64**	.13	**.67**	**.67**	.25		**.46**	.22	.31	.42	.27	**.79**		.18	**.56**	.18	.17		**.60**	.25	.09		**.86**	**.50**	.18	.44	.44
SAAR-DE	.33	**.77**†	**.63**	**.43**	.14	**.64**	**.50**	**.91**†	**.44**	**.82**	**.58**	**.73**	**.67**	**.50**	.40	**.67**	**.70**	.33	.43	.44	.36	**.67**	**.67**	**.86**	**.86**	**.60**	**.50**	**.86**†	.29	**.56**	**.44**	**.53**	**.73**		.33	**.83***	.31		**.67**	**.86***	.43	.33	**.83***	**.56**	.17	**.78**	**.55**
SAAR-ES	.29	**.60**	.44	.18	.07†	.29	.40	**.67**	.17	.44	.10*	**.46**	.27	.50	.13	.12*	**.50**	.14	.33	**.46**	**.62**	.36	.25	**.55**	.14	.17	.25	.40	.39	.17	**.50**	.42	.44	**.47**		**.50**	.11		.33		.11†	.33	**.39**	.18		.08	.33
SAAR-FR	.18	**.44**	**.60**	.30	.20	**.56**	**.73**	**.60**	.50	**.58**	0	**.50**	.33	**.64**	.29	**.42**	**.63***	**.67**	**.57**	.33	.25	.38	.42	**.58**	**.43**	.41	.30	**.54**	.50	.29	.33	.36	**.36**	.17*	.43		.33	.40	**.60**	.33	.27	.20	**.64***	.31		.25	**.58**
UCB-ES		.33	.44	**.33**	.18	.18	**.55**	**.62**	.14	**.63**	.18	.44	**.57**	**.44**	.33	**.67**	.44	.25	**.56**	.25	.46	**.60**	.50	**.56**	**.83**	**.63**	**.56**	**.57**	.36	.46	**.50**	**.50**	**.75**	**.50**	**.56**	**.58**		**.88**	**.71**	**.57**	.14		**.42**	**.67**		.44	.31
UED-CMB-DE	.20	**.67**	**.75**	**1**	**.67**	.33	**1**	**.88**	**.75**	**1**	**.83**	**.71**	**.75**		**.67**	**.67**	**1**	**.44**	**.60**	**.67**	**.57**	**1**	**1**	**.78**	**1**	**.67**	**.44**	**1**	**.60**	**1***	**1**	**.67**	**1**	**.83**	**1**	.40	.13		**.67**	**.75***	.25	.50	.40	**1**	.50	**.75**	.50
UED-CMB-FR	**.67**	**1**	**.57**	.50			.50	.13	.50	**.40**	.33					.50		.25	.40	.20	.25	**.50**	.40		**.50**	.14	.20	.33	.33	**1**	**.67**		.40	.33	.33		.29			.38					.33	.33	.50
UED-CMB-XX			**.50**	**.67**		.25	.13	**1**	.50	**.50**	.40		.25				.20			.40	.13		.33		.40	**.75**	.33	**1**		.50	.50	**.60**	**.50**	0	**.67**	**.56**	.14	0	.38		0				.33		.25
UED-CZ	**.75**	**.79***	**.89***	**.86**	**.56**	**.83**	**.71**	**.77**†	**.92**†	**1**†	.20	**.88**	**.67**	**.63**	**.67**	**1**	**.69***	**.60**	**.80***	**.80**	**.75**	**.67**	**.86**	**.75***	**.62**	**.46**	**.56**	**.67**	**.71**	**.78**	**.88**	**.67**	**.64**	.43	**.78**†	**.73**	**.86**	**.50**	**1**	**1***		**.55**	**1**†	**.80***	0	**.46**	**.90***
UED-DE	.27	**.80**	**.78**	**1**		.20	**.80***	**.71**	**1**†	**.67**	.31	.25	**.75**	**.92**†	**.56**	**.67**	**.83***		**.62**	**.44**	**.67**	**.67**	**.63**	**.82***	.25	**.75**	**1**†	.40	**.40**	**.75**	**.75**	.23	**1**	**.67**	**.67**	**.60**	**.57**	.50		**1**	.36		**.64**	**.67**	.11	.25	**.67**
UED-ES	.15*	.17	**.56**	**.42**	0	.31	**.56**	**.46**	**.50**	**.88**	.11	.33	.29	**.46**	.29	**.67**	**.69**		.31	.36	**.46**	.27	.50	**.54**	.33	.30	**.60**	.43	.29	.50	.38	.13	.14	.17*	.23	0	.17	.40	**.83**	**.80**	0	.27		.46	0	.13	
UED-FR	.50	**.56**	**.75**	**.67**	0	.18	**.56**	**.50**	.14	.44	.20	.17	.42	**.53**	.22	**.64**	**.58**	.44	**.57**	.30	.50	.38	.17	.42	**.50**	.22	**.57**	.31	.38	**.44**	**.42**	.23	.40	.33	**.46**	**.39**	.33		**.75**	**1**	.10*	.11	.46			.31	.38
UED-HU	**1**	**.75**	**.67**	**.88**	**.67**	.50	**.75**	**1***	**.80**	**1***	**.38**	**.60**	**.83**	**.75**	**1**	**1***	**.86***	**.50**	**.86**	**.75**	**1**†	**.80**	**1***	**1***	**.80**	**.80**	**.83**	**1**	**1**	**1***	**1**	**.80**	**.82**	**.67**	**1**	**1**	**.83**	.50	.33	**.67**	**.86***	**.67**	**1***	**1**		**.83**	.40
UMD-CZ	.40	**.50**	**.64**	**.50**	.50	**.67**	.29	**.50**	.50	**.80***	.25	**.40**	.27	**.71**	**.60**	.44	**.79**†		**.79**†	**.70**	**.80**	**.63**	**.67**	**.50**	**.63**	**.44**	**.63**	**.60**	**.43**	**.75**	**.64**	**.91**†	**.56**	.11	**.54**	**.67**	.44	.25	**.67**	**1**	.27	**.50**	**.88**	**.69**	.17		**.62**
UPC-ES	.40	.42	.44	.21	.15*		**.44**	.38	.25	.38	**.54**	.43	.30	.50	.23	.40	**.55**		.33	.33	.22	.47	.13	**.50**	**.50**	.38	.25	**.43**	.14	.33	**.63**	**.56**	.44	.36	**.53**	.25	**.39**	.50	.50	**.50**	.10*	.33	**.63**	**.50**	.40	.31	
> OTHERS	.29	.54	.51	.41	.15	.35	.51	.52	.43	.51	.25	.34	.39	.55	.33	.57	.57	.3	.5	.44	.52	.49	.48	.56	.50	.35	.46	.57	.39	.50	.49	.46	.49	.32	.51	.45	.4	.22	.56	**.58**	.19	.28	.53	.48	.11	.3	.52
≥ OTHERS	.41	.7	.66	.55	.28	.44	.67	.64	.57	.65	.38	.47	.54	.7	.45	.71	.70	.39	.63	.55	.63	.61	.57	.7	.64	.49	.60	.71	.51	.62	.62	.57	.62	.45	.68	.58	.55	.33	.70	**.72**	.29	.40	.65	.62	.19	.43	.63

Table 53: Sentence-level ranking for the All-English News Task.

LIMSI's statistical translation systems for WMT'08

Daniel Déchelotte, Gilles Adda, Alexandre Allauzen, Hélène Bonneau-Maynard,
Olivier Galibert, Jean-Luc Gauvain, Philippe Langlais* and **François Yvon**
LIMSI/CNRS
`firstname.lastname@limsi.fr`

Abstract

This paper describes our statistical machine translation systems based on the Moses toolkit for the WMT08 shared task. We address the Europarl and News conditions for the following language pairs: English with French, German and Spanish. For Europarl, n-best rescoring is performed using an enhanced n-gram or a neuronal language model; for the News condition, language models incorporate extra training data. We also report unconvincing results of experiments with factored models.

1 Introduction

This paper describes our statistical machine translation systems based on the Moses toolkit for the WMT 08 shared task. We address the Europarl and News conditions for the following language pairs: English with French, German and Spanish. For Europarl, n-best rescoring is performed using an enhanced n-gram or a neuronal language model, and for the News condition, language models are trained with extra training data. We also report unconvincing results of experiments with factored models.

2 Base System architecture

LIMSI took part in the evaluations on Europarl data and on News data, translating French, German and Spanish from and to English, amounting a total of twelve evaluation conditions. Figure 1 presents the generic overall architecture of LIMSI's translation systems. They are fairly standard phrase-based translation systems (Och and Ney, 2004; Koehn et al., 2003) and use Moses (Koehn et al., 2007) to search for the best target sentence. The search uses the following models: a phrase table, providing 4 scores and a phrase penalty, a *lexicalized* reordering model (7 scores), a language model score and a word penalty. These fourteen scores are weighted and linearly combined (Och and Ney, 2002; Och, 2003); their respective weights are learned on development data so as to maximize the BLEU score. In the following, we detail several aspects of our systems.

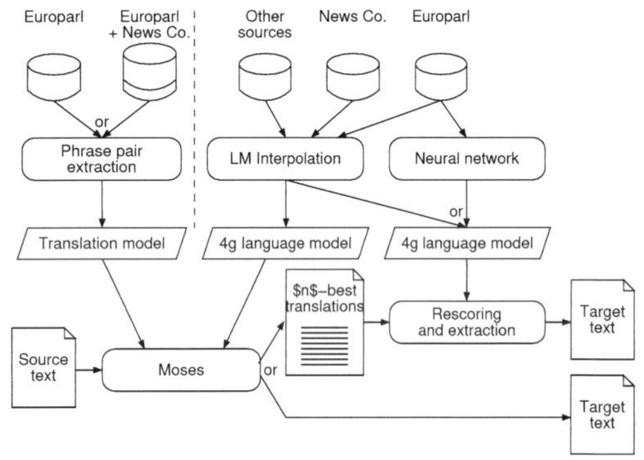

Figure 1: Generic architecture of LIMSI's SMT systems. Depending on the condition, the decoder generates either the final output or n-best lists. In the latter case, the rescoring incorporates the same translation features, except for a better target language model (see text).

2.1 Translation models

The translation models deployed in our systems for the europarl condition were trained on the provided Europarl parallel data only. For the news condition, they were trained on the Europarl data merged with

*Univ. Montréal, felipe@iro.umontreal.ca

Proceedings of the Third Workshop on Statistical Machine Translation, pages 107–110,
Columbus, Ohio, USA, June 2008.

the news-commentary parallel data, as depicted on Figure 1. This setup was found to be more favorable than training on Europarl data only (for obvious mismatching domain reasons) and than training on news-commentary data only, most probably because of a lack of coverage. Another, alternative way of benefitting from the coverage of the Europarl corpus *and* the relevance of the news-commentary corpus is to use two phrase-tables *in parallel*, an interesting feature of Moses. (Koehn and Schroeder, 2007) found that this was the best way to "adapt" a translation system to the news-commentary task. These results are corroborated in (Déchelotte, 2007)[1] , which adapts a "European Parliament" system using a "European and Spanish Parliaments" development set. However, we were not able to reproduce those findings for this evaluation. This might be caused by the increase of the number of feature functions, from 14 to 26, due to the duplication of the phrase table and the lexicalized reordering model.

2.2 Language Models

2.2.1 Europarl language models

The training of Europarl language models (LMs) was rather conventional: for all languages used in our systems, we used a 4-gram LM based on the entire Europarl vocabulary and trained only on the available Europarl training data. For French, for instance, this yielded a model with a 0.2 out-of-vocabulary (OOV) rate on our LM development set, and a perplexity of 44.9 on the development data. For French also, a more accurate n-gram LM was used to rescore the first pass translation; this larger model includes both Europarl and giga word corpus of newswire text, lowering the perplexity to 41.9 on the development data.

2.2.2 News language models

For this condition, we took advantage of the a priori information that the test text would be of newspaper/newswire genre and from the November-december 2007 period. We consequently built much larger LMs for translating both to French and to English, and optimized their combination on appropriate source of data. For French, we interpolated five different LMs trained on corpus containing respectively newspapers, newswire, news commentary and Europarl data, and tuned their combination with text downloaded from the Internet. Our best LM had an OOV rate of about 2.1% and a perplexity of 111.26 on the testset. English LMs were built in a similar manner, our largest model combining 4 LMs from various sources, which, altogether, represent about 850M words. Its perplexity on the 2008 test set was approximately 160, with an OOV rate of 2.7%.

2.2.3 Neural network language models

Neural-Network (NN) based continuous space LMs similar to the ones in (Schwenk, 2007) were also trained on Europarl data. These networks compute the probabilities of all the words in a 8192 word output vocabulary given a context in a larger, 65000-word vocabulary. Each word in the context is first associated with a numerical vector of dimension 500 by the input layer. The activity of the 500 neurons in the hidden layer is computed as the hyperbolic tangent of the weighted sum of these vectors, projecting the context into a $[-1, 1]$ hypercube of dimension 500. Final projection on a set of 8192 output neurons yields the final probabilities through a softmax-ed, weighted sum of the coordinates in the hypercube. The final NN-based model is interpolated with the main LM model in a 0.4-0.6 ratio, and yields a perplexity reduction of 9% relative with respect to the n-gram LM on development data.

2.3 Tuning procedure

We use MERT, distributed with the Moses decoder, to tune the first pass of the system. The weights were adjusted to maximize BLEU on the development data. For the baseline system, a dozen Moses runs are necessary for each MERT optimization, and several optimization runs were started and compared during the system's development. Tuning was performed using dev2006 for the Europarl task and on News commentary dev2007 for the news task.

2.4 Rescoring and post processing

For the Europarl condition, distinct 100 best translations from Moses were rescored with improved LMs: when translating to French, we used the French model described in section 2.2.1; when

[1](Déchelotte, 2007) further found that giving an increased weight to the small in-domain data could out-perform the setup with two phrase-tables in parallel. We haven't evaluated this idea for this evaluation.

	Es-En	En-Es	Fr-En	En-Fr
baseline	32.21	31.62	32.41	29.31
Limsi	32.49	31.23	32.62	30.27

Table 1: Comparison of two tokenization policies
All results on Europarl test2007

	CI system	CS system
En→Fr	27.23	27.55
Fr→En	30.96	30.98

Table 2: Effect of training on true case texts, for English to French (case INsensitive BLEU scores, untuned systems, results on test2006 dataset)

translating to English, we used the neuronal LM described in section 2.2.3.

For all the "lowcase" systems (see below), recaseing was finally performed using our own recaseing tool. Case is restored by creating a word graph allowing all possible forms of caseing for each word and each component of a compound word. This word graph is then decoded using a cased 4-gram LM to obtain the most likely form. In a final step, OOV words (with respect to the source language word list) are recased to match their original form.

3 Experiments with the base system

3.1 Word tokenization and case

We developed our own tokenizer for English, French and Spanish, and used the baseline tokenizer for German. Experiments on the 2007 test dataset for Europarl task show the impact of the tokenization on the BLEU scores, with 3-gram LMs. Results are always improved with our own tokenizer, except for English to Spanish (Table 1).

Our systems were initially trained on lowercase texts, similarly to the proposed baseline system. However, training on true case texts proved beneficial when translating from English to French, even when scoring in a case insensitive manner. Table 2 shows an approximate gain of 0.3 BLEU for that direction, and no impact on French to English performance. Our English-French systems are therefore case sensitive.

3.2 Language Models

For Europarl, we experimented with LMs of increasing orders: we found that using a 5-gram LM only yields an insignificant improvement over a 4-gram LM. As a result, we used 4-gram LMs for all our first pass decodings. For the second pass, the use of the Neural Network LMs, if used with an appropriate (tuned) weight, yields a small, yet consistent improvement of BLEU for all pairs.

Performance on the news task are harder to analyze, due to the lack of development data. Throwing in large set of in-domain data was obviously helpful, even though we are currently unable to adequately measure this effect.

4 Experiments with factored models

Even though these models were not used in our submissions, we feel it useful to comment here our (negative) experiments with factored models.

4.1 Overview

In this work, factored models (Koehn and Hoang, 2007) are experimented with three factors : the surface form, the lemma and the part of speech (POS). The translation process is composed of different mapping steps, which either translate input factors into output factors, or generate additional output factors from existing output factors. In this work, four mapping steps are used with two decoding paths. The first path corresponds to the standard and direct mapping of surface forms. The second decoding path consists in two translation steps for respectively POS tag and the lemmas, followed by a generation step which produces the surface form given the POS-lemma couple. The system also includes three reordering models.

4.2 Training

Factored models have been built to translate from English to French for the *news* task. To estimate the phrase and generation tables, the training texts are first processed in order to compute the lemmas and POS information. The English texts are tagged and lemmatized using the English version of the Treetagger[2]. For French, POS-tagging is carried out with a French version of the Brill's tagger trained

[2]http://www.ims.uni-stuttgart.de/projekte/corplex/TreeTagger

on the MULTITAG corpus (Allauzen and Bonneau-Maynard, 2008). Lemmatization is performed with a French version of the Treetagger.

Three phrase tables are estimated with the Moses utilities, one per factor. For the surface forms, the parallel corpus is the concatenation of the official training data for the tasks Europarl and News commentary, whereas only the parallel data of news commentary are used for lemmas and POS. For the generation step, the table built on the parallel texts of news commentary is augmented with a French dictionary of 280 000 forms. The LM is the largest LM available for French (see section 2.2.2).

4.3 Results and lessons learned

On the news test set of 2008, this system obtains a BLEU score of 20.2, which is worse than our "standard" system (20.9). A similar experiment on the Europarl task proved equally unsuccessful.

Using only models which ignore the surface form of input words yields a poor system. Therefore, including a model based on surface forms, as suggested (Koehn and Hoang, 2007), is also necessary. This indeed improved (+1.6 BLEU for Europarl) over using one single decoding path, but not enough to match our baseline system performance. These results may be explained by the use of automatic tools (POS tagger and lemmatizer) that are not entirely error free, and also, to a lesser extend, by the noise in the test data. We also think that more effort has to be put into the generation step.

Tuning is also a major issue for factored translation models. Dealing with 38 weights is an optimization challenge, which took MERT 129 iterations to converge. The necessary tradeoff between the huge memory requirements of these techniques and computation time is also detrimental to their use.

Although quantitative results were unsatisfactory, it is finally worth mentioning that a manual examination of the output revealed that the explicit usage of gender and number in our models (via POS tags) may actually be helpful when translating to French.

5 Conclusion

In this paper, we presented our statistical MT systems developed for the WMT 08 shared task. As expected, regarding the Europarl condition, our BLEU improvements over the best 2007 results are limited: paying attention to tokenization and caseing issues brought us a small pay-off; rescoring with better language models gave also some reward. The news condition was new, and more challenging: our satisfactory results can be attributed to the use of large, well tuned, language models. In comparison, our experiments with factored models proved disappointing, for reasons that remain to be clarified. On a more general note, we feel that the performance of MT systems for these tasks are somewhat shadowed by normalization issues (tokenization errors, inconsistent use of caseing, typos, etc), making it difficult to clearly analyze our systems' performance.

References

A. Allauzen and H. Bonneau-Maynard. 2008. Training and evaluation of POS taggers on the French multitag corpus. In *Proc. LREC'08, To appear.*

D. Déchelotte. 2007. *Traduction automatique de la parole par méthodes statistiques*. Ph.D. thesis, Univ. Paris XI, December.

P. Koehn and H. Hoang. 2007. Factored translation models. In *Proc. EMNLP-CoNLL*, pages 868–876.

P. Koehn and J. Schroeder. 2007. Experiments in domain adaptation for statistical machine translation. In *Proc. of the Workshop on Statistical Machine Translation*, pages 224–227, Prague, Czech Republic.

P. Koehn, F. J. Och, and D. Marcu. 2003. Statistical phrase-based translation. In *Proc. HLT-NAACL*, pages 127–133, Edmonton, Canada, May.

P. Koehn, H. Hoang, A. Birch, C. Callison-Burch, M. Federico, N. Bertoldi, B. Cowan, W. Shen, C. Moran, R. Zens, C. Dyer, O. Bojar, A. Constantin, and E. Herbst. 2007. Moses: Open source toolkit for statistical machine translation. In *ACL, demonstration session*, Prague, Czech Republic.

F.J. Och and H. Ney. 2002. Discriminative training and maximum entropy models for statistical machine translation. In *Proc. ACL*, pages 295–302.

Franz J. Och and Hermann Ney. 2004. The alignment template approach to statistical machine translation. *Computational Linguistics*, 30(4):417–449.

F. J. Och. 2003. Minimum error rate training in statistical machine translation. In *Proc. ACL*, Sapporo, Japan.

H. Schwenk. 2007. Continuous space language models. *Computer Speech and Language*, 21:492–518.

The MetaMorpho translation system

Attila Novák, László Tihanyi and Gábor Prószéky
MorphoLogic
Orbánhegyi út 5, Budapest 1126, Hungary
{novak,tihanyi,proszeky}@morphologic.hu

Abstract

In this article, we present MetaMorpho, a rule based machine translation system that was used to create MorphoLogic's submission to the WMT08 shared Hungarian to English translation task. The architecture of MetaMorpho does not fit easily into traditional categories of rule based systems: the building blocks of its grammar are pairs of rules that describe source and target language structures in a parallel fashion and translated structures are created while parsing the input.

1 Introduction

Three rule-based approaches to MT are traditionally distinguished: direct, interlingua and transfer. The direct method uses a primitive one-stage process in which words in the source language are replaced with words in the target language and then some rearrangement is done. The main idea behind the interlingua method is that the analysis of any source language should result in a language-independent representation. The target language is then generated from that language-neutral representation. The transfer method first parses the sentence of the source language. It then applies rules that map the lexical and grammatical segments of the source sentence to a representation in the target language.

The MetaMorpho machine translation system developed at MorphoLogic (Prószéky and Tihanyi, 2002), cannot be directly classified in either of the above categories, although it has the most in common with the transfer type architecture.

2 Translation via immediate transfer

In the MetaMorpho system, both productive rules of grammar and lexical entries are stored in the form of patterns, which are like context-free rules enriched with features. Patterns may contain more-or-less underspecified slots, ranging from general productive rules of grammar through more-or-less idiomatic phrases to fully lexicalized items. The majority of the patterns (a couple of hundreds of thousands in the case of our English grammar) represent partially lexicalized items.

The grammar operates with pairs of patterns that consist of one source pattern used during bottom-up parsing and one or more target patterns that are applied during top-down generation of the translation. While traditional transfer and interlingua based systems consist of separate parsing and generating rules, in a MetaMorpho grammar, each parsing rule has its associated generating counterpart. The translation of the parsed structures is already determined during parsing the source language input. The actual generation of the target language representations does not involve any additional transfer operations: target language structures corresponding to substructures of the source language parse tree are combined and the leaves of the resulting tree are interpreted by a morphological generator. We call this solution "immediate transfer" as it uses no separate transfer steps or target transformations.

The idea behind this architecture has much in common with the way semantic compositionality was formalized by Bach (1976) in the from of his rule-to-rule hypothesis, stating that to every rule of syntax that combines constituents into a phrase pertains a corresponding rule of semantics that

Proceedings of the Third Workshop on Statistical Machine Translation, pages 111–114,
Columbus, Ohio, USA, June 2008.

combines the meanings of the constituents. In the case of phrases with compositional meaning, the pair of rules of syntax and semantics are of a general nature, while in the case of idioms, the pair of rules is specific and arbitrary. The architecture implemented in the MetaMorpho system is based on essentially the same idea, except that the representation built during analysis of the input sentence is not expressed in a formal language of some semantic representation but directly in the human target language of the translation system.

3 System architecture

The analysis of the input is performed in three stages. First the text to be translated is segmented into sentences, and each sentence is broken up into a sequence of tokens. This token sequence is the actual input of the parser. Morphosyntactic annotation of the input word forms is performed by a morphological analyzer: it assigns morphosyntactic attribute vectors to word forms. We use the Humor morphological system (Prószéky and Kis, 1999; Prószéky and Novák, 2005) that performs an item-and-arrangement style morphological analysis. Morphological synthesis of the target language word forms is performed by the same morphological engine.

The system also accepts unknown elements: they are treated as strings to be inflected at the target side. The (potentially ambiguous) output of the morphological analyzer is fed into the syntactic parser called Moose (Prószéky, Tihanyi and Ugray, 2004), which analyzes this input sequence using the source language patterns and if it is recognized as a correct sentence, comes up with one or more root symbols on the source side.

Every terminal and non-terminal symbol in the syntactic tree under construction has a set of features. The number of features is normally up to a few dozen, depending on the category. These features can either take their values from a finite set of symbolic items (e.g., values of case can be `INS`, `ACC`, `DAT`, etc.), or represent a string (e.g., `lex="approach"`, the lexical form of a token). The formalism does not contain embedded feature structures. It is important to note that no structural or semantic information is amassed in the features of symbols: the interpretation of the input is contained in the syntactic tree itself, and not in the features of the node on the topmost level. Features are used to express constraints on the applicability of patterns and to store morphosyntactic valence and lexical information concerning the parsed input.

More specific patterns (e.g. *approach to*) can override more general ones (e.g. *approach*), in that case subtrees containing symbols that were created by the general pattern are deleted. Every symbol that is created and is not eliminated by an overriding pattern is retained even if it does not form part of a correct sentence's syntactic tree. Each pattern can explicitly override other rules: if the overriding rule covers a specific range of the input, it blocks the overridden ones over the same range. This method can be used to eliminate spurious ambiguities early during analysis.

When the whole input is processed and no applicable patterns remain, translation is generated in a top-down fashion by combining the target structures corresponding to the source patterns constituting the source language parse tree.

A source language pattern may have more than one associated target pattern. The selection of the target structure to apply relies on constraints on the actual values of features in the source pattern: the first target pattern whose conditions are satisfied is used for target structure generation. To handle complicated word-order changes, the target structure may need rearrangement of its elements within the scope of a single node and its children. There is another technique that can be used to handle word order differences between the source and the target language. A pointer to a subtree can be stored in a feature when applying a rule at parse time, and because this feature's value can percolate up the parse-tree and down the target tree, just like any other feature, a phrase swallowed somewhere in the source side can be expanded at a different location in the target tree. This technique can be used to handle both systematic word order differences (such as the different but fixed order of constituents in possessive constructions: *possession of possessor* in English versus *possessor possession + possessive suffix* in Hungarian) and accidental ones (such as the fixed order of subject verb and object in English, versus the "free" order of these constituents in Hungarian[1]).

Unlike in classical transfer-based systems, however, these rearrangement operations are al-

[1] In fact the order is determined by various factors other than grammatical function.

ready determined during parsing the source language input. During generation, the already determined rearranged structures are simply spelled out. The morphosyntactic feature vectors on the terminal level of the generated tree are interpreted by the morphological generator that synthesizes the corresponding target language word forms.

The morphological generator is not a simple inverse of the corresponding analyzer. It accepts many alternative equivalent morphological descriptions of each word form it can generate beside the one that the corresponding analyzer outputs.

4 The rule database

The rules used by the parser explicitly contain all the features of the daughter nodes to check, all the features to percolate to the mother node, all the features to set in the corresponding target structures and those to be checked on the source language structure to decide on the applicability of a target structure. The fact that all this redundant information is present in the run-time rule database makes the operation of the parser efficient in terms of speed. However, it would be very difficult for humans to create and maintain the rule database in this redundant format.

There is a high level version of the language: although it is not really different in terms of its syntax from the low-level one, it does not require default values and default correspondences to be explicitly listed. The rule database is maintained using this high level formalism. There is a rule converter for each language pair that extends the high-level rules with default information and may also create transformed rules (such as the passive version of verbal subcategorization frames) creating the rule database used by the parser.

Rule conversion is also necessary because in order to be able to parse a free word order language like Hungarian with a parser that uses context free rules, you need to use run time rules that essentially differ in the way they operate from what would be suggested by the rules they are derived from in the high level database. In Hungarian, arguments of a predicate may appear in many different orders in actual sentences and they also freely mix with sentence level adjuncts. This means that a verbal argument structure of the high level rule database with its normal context free rule interpretation would only cover a fraction of its real world realizations. Rule conversion effectively handles this problem by converting rules describing lexical items with argument structures expressed using a context free rule formalism into run time rules that do not actually combine constituents, but only check the saturation of valency frames. Constituents are combined by other more generic rules that take care of saturating the argument slots. This means that while the high level and the run time rules have a similar syntax, the semantics of some high level rules may be very different from similar rules in the low level rule database.

5 Handling sentences with no full parse

The system must not break down if the input sentence happens not to have a full parse (this inevitably happens in the case of real life texts). In that case, it reverts to using a heuristic process that constructs an output by combining the output of a selected set of partial structures covering the whole sentence stored during parsing the input. In the MetaMorpho terminology, this is called a “mosaic translation”. Mosaic translations are usually suboptimal, because in the absence of a full parse some structural information such as agreement is usually lost. There is much to improve on the current algorithm used to create mosaic translations: e.g. it does not currently utilize a statistical model of the target language, which has a negative effect on the fluency of the output. Augmenting the system with such a component would probably improve its performance considerably.

6 Motivation for the MetaMorpho architecture

An obvious drawback of the architecture described above compared to the interlingua and transfer based systems is that the grammar components of the system cannot be simply reused to build translation systems to new target languages without a major revision of the grammar. While in a classical transfer based system, the source language grammar may cover phenomena that the transfer component does not cover, in the MetaMorpho architecture, this is not possible. In a transfer based system, there is a relatively cheaper way to handle coverage issues partially by augmenting only the source grammar (and postponing creation of the corresponding transfer rules). This is not an option in the MetaMorpho architecture.

The main motivation for this system architecture was that it makes it possible to integrate machine translation and translation memories in a natural way and to make the system easily extensible by the user. There is a grammar writer's workbench component of MetaMorpho called Rule Builder. This makes it possible for users to add new, lexical or even syntactic patterns to the grammar in a controlled manner without the need to recompile the rest, using an SQL database for user added entries. The technology used in RuleBuilder can also be applied to create a special combination of the MetaMorpho machine translation tool and translation memories (Hodász, Grőbler and Kis 2004).

Moreover, existing bilingual lexical databases (dictionaries of idioms and collocations) are relatively easy to convert to the high level rule format of the system. The bulk of the grammar of the system was created based on such resources. Another rationale for developing language pair specific grammars directly is that this way distinctions in the grammar of the source language not relevant for the translation to the target language at hand need not be addressed.

7 Performance in the translation task

During development of the system and its grammar components, regression testing has been performed using a test set unknown to the developers measuring case insensitive BLEU with three human reference translations. Our usual test set for the system translating from Hungarian to English contains 274 sentences of newswire text. We had never used single reference BLEU before, because, although creating multiple translations is expensive, single reference BLEU is quite unreliable usually producing very low scores especially if the target language is morphologically rich, like Hungarian.

The current version of the MetaMorpho system translating from Hungarian to English has a BLEU score of 22.14 on our usual newswire test set with three references. Obtaining a BLEU score of 7.8 on the WMT08 shared Hungarian to English translation task test set was rather surprising, so we checked single reference BLEU on our usual test set: the scores are 13.02, 14.15 and 16.83 with the three reference translations respectively.

In the end, we decided to submit our results to the WMT08 shared translation task in spite of the low score. But we think, that these figures cast doubts on the quality of the texts and reference translations in the test set, especially in cases where both the English and the Hungarian text were translated from a third language, so we think that the scores on the WMT08 test set should be evaluated only relative to other systems' performance on the same data and the same language pair.

References

Emmon Bach. 1976. An extension of classical transformational grammar. In Saenz (ed.) *Problems of Linguistic Metatheory: Proceedings of the 1976 Conference,* 183–224. East Lansing, MI: Michigan State University.

Gábor Hodász, Tamás Grőbler and Balázs Kis. 2004. Translation memory as a robust example-based translation system. In Hutchins (ed.), 82–89.

John Hutchins (ed.) *Broadening horizons of machine translation and its applications.* Proceedings of the 9th EAMT Workshop, 26–27 April 2004. La Valletta: Foundation for International Studies.

Gábor Prószéky and Balázs Kis. 1999. Agglutinative and other (highly) inflectional languages. In Robert Dale & Kenneth W. Church (eds.) *Proceedings of the 37th Annual Meeting of the Association for Computational Linguistics*, 261–268. Morristown, NJ: Association for Computational Linguistics.

Gábor Prószéky and Attila Novák. 2005. Computational Morphologies for Small Uralic Languages. In: A. Arppe, L. Carlson, K. Lindén, J. Piitulainen, M. Suominen, M. Vainio, H. Westerlund, A. Yli-Jyrä (eds.): *Inquiries into Words, Constraints and Contexts Festschrift in the Honour of Kimmo Koskenniemi on his 60th Birthday,* 116–125. Gummerus Printing, Saarijärvi/CSLI Publications, Stanford.

Gábor Prószéky and László Tihanyi. 2002 MetaMorpho: A Pattern-Based Machine Translation System. In: *Proceedings of the 24th 'Translating and the Computer' Conference*, 19–24. ASLIB, London, United Kingdom.

Gábor Prószéky, László Tihanyi and Gábor Ugray. 2004. Moose: A robust high-performance parser and generator. In Hutchins (ed.), 138–142.

METEOR, M-BLEU and M-TER: Evaluation Metrics for High-Correlation with Human Rankings of Machine Translation Output

Abhaya Agarwal and **Alon Lavie**
Language Technologies Institute
Carnegie Mellon University
Pittsburgh, PA, 15213, USA
{abhayaa,alavie}@cs.cmu.edu

Abstract

This paper describes our submissions to the machine translation evaluation shared task in ACL WMT-08. Our primary submission is the METEOR metric tuned for optimizing correlation with human rankings of translation hypotheses. We show significant improvement in correlation as compared to the earlier version of metric which was tuned to optimized correlation with traditional adequacy and fluency judgments. We also describe M-BLEU and M-TER, enhanced versions of two other widely used metrics BLEU and TER respectively, which extend the exact word matching used in these metrics with the flexible matching based on stemming and Wordnet in METEOR .

1 Introduction

Automatic Metrics for MT evaluation have been receiving significant attention in recent years. Evaluating an MT system using such automatic metrics is much faster, easier and cheaper compared to human evaluations, which require trained bilingual evaluators. The most commonly used MT evaluation metric in recent years has been IBM's BLEU metric (Papineni et al., 2002). BLEU is fast and easy to run, and it can be used as a target function in parameter optimization training procedures that are commonly used in state-of-the-art statistical MT systems (Och, 2003). Various researchers have noted, however, various weaknesses in the metric. Most notably, BLEU does not produce very reliable sentence-level scores. METEOR , as well as several other proposed metrics such as GTM (Melamed et al., 2003), TER (Snover et al., 2006) and CDER (Leusch et al., 2006) aim to address some of these weaknesses.

METEOR , initially proposed and released in 2004 (Lavie et al., 2004) was explicitly designed to improve correlation with human judgments of MT quality at the segment level. Previous publications on METEOR (Lavie et al., 2004; Banerjee and Lavie, 2005; Lavie and Agarwal, 2007) have described the details underlying the metric and have extensively compared its performance with BLEU and several other MT evaluation metrics. In (Lavie and Agarwal, 2007), we described the process of tuning free parameters within the metric to optimize the correlation with human judgments and the extension of the metric for evaluating translations in languages other than English.

This paper provides a brief technical description of METEOR and describes our experiments in re-tuning the metric for improving correlation with the human rankings of translation hypotheses corresponding to a single source sentence. Our experiments show significant improvement in correlation as a result of re-tuning which shows the importance of having a metric tunable to different testing conditions. Also, in order to establish the usefulness of the flexible matching based on stemming and Wordnet, we extend two other widely used metrics BLEU and TER which use exact word matching, with the matcher module of METEOR .

2 The METEOR Metric

METEOR evaluates a translation by computing a score based on explicit word-to-word matches between the translation and a given reference translation. If more than one reference translation is available, the translation is scored against each reference independently, and the best scoring pair is used. Given a pair of strings to be compared, METEOR creates a *word alignment* between the two strings. An alignment is mapping between words, such that every word in each string maps to at most *one* word in the other string. This alignment is incrementally produced by a sequence of word-mapping modules. The "exact" module maps two words if they are exactly the same. The "porter stem" module maps two words if they are the same after they are stemmed us-

Proceedings of the Third Workshop on Statistical Machine Translation, pages 115–118,
Columbus, Ohio, USA, June 2008. ©2008 Association for Computational Linguistics

ing the Porter stemmer. The "WN synonymy" module maps two words if they are considered synonyms, based on the fact that they both belong to the same "synset" in WordNet.

The word-mapping modules initially identify all possible word matches between the pair of strings. We then identify the largest subset of these word mappings such that the resulting set constitutes an alignment as defined above. If more than one maximal cardinality alignment is found, METEOR selects the alignment for which the word order in the two strings is most similar (the mapping that has the least number of "crossing" unigram mappings). The order in which the modules are run reflects word-matching preferences. The default ordering is to first apply the "exact" mapping module, followed by "porter stemming" and then "WN synonymy".

Once a final alignment has been produced between the system translation and the reference translation, the METEOR score for this pairing is computed as follows. Based on the number of mapped unigrams found between the two strings (m), the total number of unigrams in the translation (t) and the total number of unigrams in the reference (r), we calculate unigram precision $P = m/t$ and unigram recall $R = m/r$. We then compute a parametrized harmonic mean of P and R (van Rijsbergen, 1979):

$$F_{mean} = \frac{P \cdot R}{\alpha \cdot P + (1 - \alpha) \cdot R}$$

Precision, recall and Fmean are based on single-word matches. To take into account the extent to which the matched unigrams in the two strings are in the same word order, METEOR computes a penalty for a given alignment as follows. First, the sequence of matched unigrams between the two strings is divided into the fewest possible number of "chunks" such that the matched unigrams in each chunk are adjacent (in both strings) and in identical word order. The number of chunks (ch) and the number of matches (m) is then used to calculate a fragmentation fraction: $frag = ch/m$. The penalty is then computed as:

$$Pen = \gamma \cdot frag^{\beta}$$

The value of γ determines the maximum penalty ($0 \leq \gamma \leq 1$). The value of β determines the functional relation between fragmentation and the penalty. Finally, the METEOR score for the alignment between the two strings is calculated as:

$$score = (1 - Pen) \cdot F_{mean}$$

The free parameters in the metric, α, β and γ are tuned to achieve maximum correlation with the human judgments as described in (Lavie and Agarwal, 2007).

3 Extending BLEU and TER with Flexible Matching

Many widely used metrics like BLEU (Papineni et al., 2002) and TER (Snover et al., 2006) are based on measuring string level similarity between the reference translation and translation hypothesis, just like METEOR . Most of them, however, depend on finding exact matches between the words in two strings. Many researchers (Banerjee and Lavie, 2005; Liu and Gildea, 2006), have observed consistent gains by using more flexible matching criteria. In the following experiments, we extend the BLEU and TER metrics to use the stemming and Wordnet based word mapping modules from METEOR .

Given a translation hypothesis and reference pair, we first align them using the word mapping modules from METEOR . We then rewrite the reference translation by replacing the matched words with the corresponding words in the translation hypothesis. We now compute BLEU and TER with these new references without changing anything inside the metrics.

To get meaningful BLEU scores at segment level, we compute smoothed BLEU as described in (Lin and Och, 2004).

4 Re-tuning METEOR for Rankings

(Callison-Burch et al., 2007) reported that the intercoder agreement on the task of assigning ranks to a given set of candidate hypotheses is much better than the intercoder agreement on the task of assigning a score to a hypothesis in isolation. Based on that finding, in WMT-08, only ranking judgments are being collected from the human judges.

The current version of METEOR uses parameters optimized towards maximizing the Pearson's correlation with human judgments of adequacy scores. It is not clear that the same parameters would be optimal for correlation with human rankings. So we would like to re-tune the parameters in the metric for maximizing the correlation with ranking judgments instead. This requires computing full rankings according to the metric and the humans and then computing a suitable correlation measure on those rankings.

4.1 Computing Full Rankings

METEOR assigns a score between 0 and 1 to every translation hypothesis. This score can be converted

Language	Judgments	
	Binary	Sentences
English	3978	365
German	2971	334
French	1903	208
Spanish	2588	284

Table 1: Corpus Statistics for Various Languages

to rankings trivially by assuming that a higher score indicates a better hypothesis.

In development data, human rankings are available as binary judgments indicating the preferred hypothesis between a given pair. There are also cases where both the hypotheses in the pair are judged to be equal. In order to convert these binary judgments into full rankings, we do the following:

1. Throw out all the equal judgments.
2. Construct a directed graph where nodes correspond to the translation hypotheses and every binary judgment is represented by a directed edge between the corresponding nodes.
3. Do a topological sort on the resulting graph and assign ranks in the sort order. The cycles in the graph are broken by assigning same rank to all the nodes in the cycle.

4.2 Measuring Correlation

Following (Ye et al., 2007), we first compute the Spearman correlation between the human rankings and METEOR rankings of the translation hypotheses corresponding to a single source sentence. Let N be the number of translation hypotheses and D be the difference in ranks assigned to a hypothesis by two rankings, then Spearman correlation is given by:

$$r = 1 - \frac{6 \sum D^2}{N(N^2 - 1)}$$

The final score for the metric is the average of the Spearman correlations for individual sentences.

5 Experiments

5.1 Data

We use the human judgment data from WMT-07 which was released as development data for the evaluation shared task. Amount of data available for various languages is shown in Table 1. Development data contains the majority judgments (not every hypotheses pair was judged by same number of judges) which means that in the cases where multiple judges judged the same pair of hypotheses, the judgment given by majority of the judges was considered.

	English	German	French	Spanish
α	0.95	0.9	0.9	0.9
β	0.5	3	0.5	0.5
γ	0.45	0.15	0.55	0.55

Table 2: Optimal Values of Tuned Parameters for Various Languages

	Original	Re-tuned
English	0.3813	0.4020
German	0.2166	0.2838
French	0.2992	0.3640
Spanish	0.2021	0.2186

Table 3: Average Spearman Correlation with Human Rankings for METEOR on Development Data

5.2 Methodology

We do an exhaustive grid search in the feasible ranges of parameter values, looking for parameters that maximize the average Spearman correlation over the training data. To get a fair estimate of performance, we use 3-fold cross validation on the development data. Final parameter values are chosen as the best performing set on the data pooled from all the folds.

5.3 Results

5.3.1 Re-tuning METEOR for Rankings

The re-tuned parameter values are shown in Table 2 while the average Spearman correlations for various languages with original and re-tuned parameters are shown in Table 3. We get significant improvements for all the languages. Gains are specially pronounced for German and French.

Interestingly, weight for recall becomes even higher than earlier parameters where it was already high. So it seems that ranking judgments are almost entirely driven by the recall in all the languages. Also the re-tuned parameters for all the languages except German are quite similar.

5.3.2 M-BLEU and M-TER

Table 4 shows the average Spearman correlations of M-BLEU and M-TER with human rankings. For English, both M-BLEU and M-TER show considerable improvements. For other languages, improvements in M-TER are smaller but consistent. M-BLEU , however, doesn't shows any improvements in this case. A possible reason for this behavior can be the lack of a "WN synonymy" module for languages other than English which results in fewer extra matches over the exact matching baseline. Additionally, French, German and Spanish have a richer morphology as compared to English. The morphemes in these languages

	Exact Match	Flexible Match
English: BLEU	0.2486	**0.2747**
TER	0.1598	**0.2033**
French: BLEU	**0.2906**	0.2889
TER	0.2472	**0.2604**
German: BLEU	**0.1829**	0.1806
TER	0.1509	**0.1668**
Spanish: BLEU	0.1804	**0.1847**
TER	0.1787	**0.1839**

Table 4: Average Spearman Correlation with Human Rankings for M-BLEU and M-TER

carry much more information and different forms of the same word may not be as freely replaceable as in English. A more fine grained strategy for matching words in these languages remains an area of further investigation.

6 Conclusions

In this paper, we described the re-tuning of METEOR parameters to better correlate with human rankings of translation hypotheses. Results on the development data indicate that the re-tuned version is significantly better at predicting ranking than the earlier version. We also presented enhanced BLEU and TER that use the flexible word matching module from Meteor and show that this results in better correlations as compared to the default exact matching versions. The new version of METEOR will be soon available on our website at: `http://www.cs.cmu.edu/~alavie/METEOR/` . This release will also include the flexible word matcher module which can be used to extend any metric with the flexible matching.

Acknowledgments

The work reported in this paper was supported by NSF Grant IIS-0534932.

References

Satanjeev Banerjee and Alon Lavie. 2005. METEOR: An Automatic Metric for MT Evaluation with Improved Correlation with Human Judgments. In *Proceedings of the ACL Workshop on Intrinsic and Extrinsic Evaluation Measures for Machine Translation and/or Summarization*, pages 65–72, Ann Arbor, Michigan, June.

Chris Callison-Burch, Cameron Fordyce, Philipp Koehn, Christof Monz, and Josh Schroeder. 2007. (meta-) evaluation of machine translation. In *Proceedings of the Second Workshop on Statistical Machine Translation*, pages 136–158, Prague, Czech Republic, June. Association for Computational Linguistics.

Alon Lavie and Abhaya Agarwal. 2007. METEOR: An Automatic Metric for MT Evaluation with High Levels of Correlation with Human Judgments. In *Proceedings of the Second ACL Workshop on Statistical Machine Translation*, pages 228–231, Prague, Czech Republic, June.

Alon Lavie, Kenji Sagae, and Shyamsundar Jayaraman. 2004. The Significance of Recall in Automatic Metrics for MT Evaluation. In *Proceedings of the 6th Conference of the Association for Machine Translation in the Americas (AMTA-2004)*, pages 134–143, Washington, DC, September.

Gregor Leusch, Nicola Ueffing, and Hermann Ney. 2006. CDER: Efficient MT Evaluation Using Block Movements. In *Proceedings of the Thirteenth Conference of the European Chapter of the Association for Computational Linguistics*.

Chin-Yew Lin and Franz Josef Och. 2004. Orange: a method for evaluating automatic evaluation metrics for machine translation. In *COLING '04: Proceedings of the 20th international conference on Computational Linguistics*, page 501, Morristown, NJ, USA. Association for Computational Linguistics.

Ding Liu and Daniel Gildea. 2006. Stochastic iterative alignment for machine translation evaluation. In *Proceedings of the COLING/ACL on Main conference poster sessions*, pages 539–546, Morristown, NJ, USA. Association for Computational Linguistics.

I. Dan Melamed, Ryan Green, and Joseph Turian. 2003. Precision and Recall of Machine Translation. In *Proceedings of the HLT-NAACL 2003 Conference: Short Papers*, pages 61–63, Edmonton, Alberta.

Franz Josef Och. 2003. Minimum Error Rate Training for Statistical Machine Translation. In *Proceedings of the 41st Annual Meeting of the Association for Computational Linguistics*.

Kishore Papineni, Salim Roukos, Todd Ward, and Wei-Jing Zhu. 2002. BLEU: a Method for Automatic Evaluation of Machine Translation. In *Proceedings of 40th Annual Meeting of the Association for Computational Linguistics (ACL)*, pages 311–318, Philadelphia, PA, July.

Matthew Snover, Bonnie Dorr, Richard Schwartz, Linnea Micciulla, and John Makhoul. 2006. A Study of Translation Edit Rate with Targeted Human Annotation. In *Proceedings of the 7th Conference of the Association for Machine Translation in the Americas (AMTA-2006)*, pages 223–231, Cambridge, MA, August.

C. van Rijsbergen, 1979. *Information Retrieval*. Butterworths, London, UK, 2nd edition.

Yang Ye, Ming Zhou, and Chin-Yew Lin. 2007. Sentence level machine translation evaluation as a ranking. In *Proceedings of the Second Workshop on Statistical Machine Translation*, pages 240–247, Prague, Czech Republic, June. Association for Computational Linguistics.

First Steps towards a general purpose French/English Statistical Machine Translation System

Holger Schwenk
LIUM, University of Le Mans
72085 Le Mans cedex 9
FRANCE
schwenk@lium.univ-lemans.fr

Jean-Baptiste Fouet **Jean Senellart**
SYSTRAN SA
92044 Paris La Défense cedex
FRANCE
fouet,senellart@systran.fr

Abstract

This paper describes an initial version of a general purpose French/English statistical machine translation system. The main features of this system are the open-source Moses decoder, the integration of a bilingual dictionary and a continuous space target language model. We analyze the performance of this system on the test data of the WMT'08 evaluation.

1 Introduction

Statistical machine translation (SMT) is today considered as a serious alternative to rule-based machine translation (RBMT). While RBMT systems rely on rules and linguistic resources built for that purpose, SMT systems can be developed without the need of any language knowledge and are only based on bilingual sentence-aligned and large monolingual data. However, while the monolingual data is usually available in large amounts, bilingual texts are a sparse resource for most of the language pairs. The largest SMT systems are currently build for the translation of Mandarin and Arabic to English, using more than 170M words of bitexts that are easily available from the LDC. Recent human evaluations of these systems seem to indicate that they have reached a level of performance allowing a human being to understand the automatic translations and to answer complicated questions on its content (Jones, 2008).

In a joint project between the University of Le Mans and the company SYSTRAN, we try to build similar general purpose SMT systems for European languages. In the final version, these systems will not only be trained on all available mono- and bilingual data, but also will include additional resources from SYSTRAN like high quality dictionaries, named entity transliteration and rule-based translation of expressions like numbers and dates. Our ultimate goal is to combine the power of data-driven approaches and the concentrated knowledge present in RBMT resources. In this paper, we describe an initial version of an French/English system and analyze its performance on the test corpora of the WMT'08 workshop.

2 Architecture of the system

The goal of statistical machine translation (SMT) is to produce a target sentence $\mathbf{e}$ from a source sentence $\mathbf{f}$. It is today common practice to use phrases as translation units (Koehn et al., 2003; Och and Ney, 2003) and a log linear framework in order to introduce several models explaining the translation process:

$$\begin{aligned} \mathbf{e}^* &= \arg\max p(\mathbf{e}|\mathbf{f}) \\ &= \arg\max_e \{exp(\sum_i \lambda_i h_i(\mathbf{e},\mathbf{f}))\} \end{aligned} \quad (1)$$

The feature functions h_i are the system models and the λ_i weights are typically optimized to maximize a scoring function on a development set (Och and Ney, 2002). In our system fourteen features functions were used, namely phrase and lexical translation probabilities in both directions, seven features for the lexicalized distortion model, a word and a phrase penalty and a target language model (LM).

The system is based on the Moses SMT toolkit (Koehn et al., 2007) and constructed as follows.

Proceedings of the Third Workshop on Statistical Machine Translation, pages 119–122,
Columbus, Ohio, USA, June 2008.

First, Giza++ is used to perform word alignments in both directions. Second, phrases and lexical reorderings are extracted using the default settings of the Moses SMT toolkit. A 4-gram target LM is then constructed as detailed in section 2.2. The translation itself is performed in two passes: first, Moses is run and a 1000-best list is generated for each sentence. The parameters of Moses are tuned on devtest2006 for the Europarl task and nc-devtest2007 for the news task, using the cmert tool. These 1000-best lists are then rescored with a continuous space 5-gram LM and the weights of the feature functions are optimized again using the numerical optimization toolkit Condor (Berghen and Bersini, 2005). Note that this step operates only on the 1000-best lists, no re-decoding is performed. This basic architecture of the system is identical to the one used in the 2007 WMT evaluation(Schwenk, 2007a).

2.1 Translation model

In the frame work of the 2008 WMT shared task, two parallel corpora were provided: the Europarl corpus (about 33M words) and the news-commentary corpus (about 1.2M words). It is known that the minutes of the debates of the European parliament use a particular jargon and these texts alone do not seem to be the appropriate to build a French/English SMT system for other texts. The more general news-commentary corpus is unfortunately rather small in size. Therefore, with the goal to build a general purpose system, we investigated whether more bilingual resources are available. Two corpora were identified: the proceedings of the Canadian parliament, also known as Hansard corpus (about 61M words), and data from the United nations (105M French and 89M English words). In the current version of our system only the Hansard bitexts are used.

In addition to these human generated bitexts, we investigated whether the translations of a high quality bilingual dictionary could be integrated into a SMT system. SYSTRAN provided this resource with more than 200 thousand entries, different forms of a verb or genres of an noun or adjective being counted as one entry. It is still an open research question how to best integrate a bilingual dictionary into a SMT system. At least two possibilities come to mind: add the entries directly to the phrase table or add the words and their translations to the bitexts. With the first solution one can be sure that the entries are added like there are and that they won't suffer any deformation due to imperfect alignment of multi-word expressions. However, it is not obvious how to obtain the phrase translation and lexical probabilities for each new phrase. The second solution has the potential advantage that the dictionary words could improve the alignments of these words when they also appear in the other bitexts. The calculation of the various scores of the phrase table is simplified too, since we can use the standard phrase extraction procedure. However, one has to be aware that all the translations that appear only in the dictionary will be equally likely which certainly does not correspond to the reality. In future work will try to improve these estimates using monolingual data.

For now, we used about ten thousand verbs and hundred thousand nouns from the dictionary. For each verb, we generated all the conjugations in the past, present, future and conditional tense; and for each noun the singular and plural form were generated. In total this resulted in 512k "new sentences" in the bitexts.

2.2 Language model

In comparison to bilingual texts which are needed for the translation model, it is much easier to find large quantities of monolingual data, in English as well as in French. In this work, the following resources were used for the language model:

- the monolingual parts of the Europarl, Hansard, UN and the news commentary corpus,
- the Gigaword corpus in French and English as provided by LDC (770M and 3261M words respectively),
- about 33M words of newspaper texts crawled from the WEB (French only)

Separate LMs were build on each data source with the SRI LM toolkit (Stolcke, 2002) and then linearly interpolated, optimizing the coefficients with an EM procedure. Note that we build two sets of LMs: a first set tuned on devtest2006, and a second one on nc-devtest2007. The perplexities of these LMs are

	French		English	
Data	Eparl	News	Eparl	News
Back-off 4-gram LM:				
Eparl+news	52.6	184.0	42.0	105.8
All	50.0	136.1	39.7	85.4
Continuous space 5-gram LM:				
All	42.0	118.9	34.1	75.0

Table 1: Perplexities on devtest2006 (Europarl) and nc-devtest2007 (news commentary) for various LMs.

given in Table 1. We were not able to obtain significantly better results with 5-gram back-off LMs.

It can be clearly seen that the additional LM data, despite its considerable size, achieves only a small decrease in perplexity for the Europarl data. This task is so particular that other out-of-domain data does not seem to be very useful. The system optimized on the more general news-commentary task, however, seems to benefit from the additional monolingual resources. Note however, that the test data newstest2008 is not of the same type and we may have a mismatch between development and test data.

We also used a so-called continuous space language model (CSLM). The basic idea of this approach is to project the word indices onto a continuous space and to use a probability estimator operating on this space (Bengio et al., 2003). Since the resulting probability functions are smooth functions of the word representation, better generalization to unknown n-grams can be expected. A neural network can be used to simultaneously learn the projection of the words onto the continuous space and to estimate the n-gram probabilities. This is still a n-gram approach, but the LM probabilities are "interpolated" for any possible context of length n-1 instead of backing-off to shorter contexts. This approach was successfully used in large vocabulary continuous speech recognition (Schwenk, 2007b) and in a phrase-based SMT systems (Schwenk et al., 2006; Déchelotte et al., 2007). Here, it is the first time trained on large amounts of data, more than 3G words for the English LM. This approach achieves an average perplexity reduction of almost 14% relative (see Table 1).

3 Experimental Evaluation

The shared evaluation task of the third workshop on statistical machine translation features two different test sets: test2008 and newstest2008. The first one contains data from the European parliament of the same type than the provided training and development data. Therefore good generalization performance can be expected. The second test set, however, is news type data from unknown sources. Scanning some of the sentences after the evaluation seems to indicate that this data is more general than the provided news-commentary training and development data – it contains for instance financial and public health news.

Given the particular jargon of the European parliament, we decided to build two different systems, one rather general system tuned in nc-devtest2007 and an Europarl system tuned on devtest2006. Both systems use the tokenization proposed by the Moses SMT toolkit and the case was preserved in the translation and language model. Therefore, in contrast to the official BLEU scores, we report here case sensitive BLEU scores as calculated by the NIST tool.

3.1 Europarl system

The results of the Europarl system are summarized in Table 2. The translation model was trained on the Europarl and the news-commentary data, augmented by parts of the dictionary. The LM was trained on all the data, but the additional out-of-domain data has probably little impact given the small improvements in perplexity (see Table 1).

	French/English		English/French	
Model	2007	2008	2007	2008
baseline	32.64	32.61	31.15	31.80
base+CSLM	32.98	33.08	31.63	32.37
base+dict	32.69	32.75	30.97	31.59
+CSLM	33.11	33.13	31.54	32.34

Table 2: Case sensitive BLEU scores for the Europarl system (test data)

When translating from French to English the CSLM achieves a improvement of about 0.4 points BLEU. Adding the dictionary had no significant impact, probably due to the jargon of the parliament proceedings. For the opposite translation direction, the dictionary even seems to worsen the performance. One reason for this observation could be the fact that the dictionary adds many French translations for one English word. These translation are not correctly weighted and we have to rely completely on the target LM to select the correct one. This may explain the large improvement achieved by the CSLM in this case (+0.75 BLEU).

3.2 News system

The results of the more generic news system are summarized in Table 3. The translation model was trained on the news-commentary, Europarl and Hansard bitexts as well as parts of the dictionary. The LM was again trained on all data.

	French/English		English/French	
Model/bitexts	2007	2008	2007	2008
news	29.31	17.98	28.60	17.51
news+dict	30.09	18.78	28.92	18.01
news+eparl	30.53	20.39	28.55	19.70
+dict	30.94	20.63	28.46	19.96
+Hansard	31.48	21.10	28.97	20.21
+CSLM	31.98	21.02	29.64	20.51

Table 3: Case sensitive BLEU scores of the news system (nc-test2007 and newstest2008)

First of all, we realize that the BLEU scores on the out-of-domain generic 2008 news data are much lower than on the nc-test2007 data. Adding more than 60M words of the Hansard bitexts gives an improvement of the BLEU score of about 0.5 for most of the test sets and translation directions. The dictionary is very interesting when only a limited amount of resources is available – a gain of up to 0.8 BLEU when only the news-commentary bitexts are used – but still useful when more data is available. As far as we know, this is the first time that adding a dictionary improved the translation quality of a very strong baseline. In previous works, results were only reported in a setting with limited resources (Vogel et al., 2003; Popović and Ney, 2006). However, we believe that he integration of the dictionary is not yet optimal, in particular with respect to the estimation of the translation probabilities. The only surprising result is the bad performance of the CSLM on the newstest2008 data for the translation from French to English. We are currently investigating this.

This work has been partially funded by the French Government under the project INSTAR (ANR JCJC06_143038).

References

Yoshua Bengio, Rejean Ducharme, Pascal Vincent, and Christian Jauvin. 2003. A neural probabilistic language model. *JMLR*, 3(2):1137–1155.

Frank Vanden Berghen and Hugues Bersini. 2005. CONDOR, a new parallel, constrained extension of powell's UOBYQA algorithm: Experimental results and comparison with the DFO algorithm. *Journal of Computational and Applied Mathematics*, 181:157–175.

Daniel Déchelotte, Holger Schwenk, Hélène Bonneau-Maynard, Alexandre Allauzen, and Gilles Adda. 2007. A state-of-the-art statistical machine translation system based on moses. In *MT Summit*, pages 127–133.

D. Jones. 2008. DLPT* MT comprehension test results, Oral presentation at the 2008 Nist MT Evaluation workshop, March 27.

Philipp Koehn, Franz Josef Och, and Daniel Marcu. 2003. Statistical phrased-based machine translation. In *HLT/NACL*, pages 127–133.

Philipp Koehn et al. 2007. Moses: Open source toolkit for statistical machine translation. In *ACL, demonstration session*.

Franz Josef Och and Hermann Ney. 2002. Discriminative training and maximum entropy models for statistical machine translation. In *ACL*, pages 295–302.

Franz Josef Och and Hermann Ney. 2003. A systematic comparison of various statistical alignement models. *Computational Linguistics*, 29(1):19–51.

Maja Popović and Hermann Ney. 2006. Statistical machine translation with a small amount of bilingual training data. In *LREC workshop on Minority Language*, pages 25–29.

Holger Schwenk, Marta R. Costa-jussà, and José A. R. Fonollosa. 2006. Continuous space language models for the IWSLT 2006 task. In *IWSLT*, pages 166–173, November.

Holger Schwenk. 2007a. Building a statistical machine translation system for French using the Europarl corpus. In *Second Workshop on SMT*, pages 189–192.

Holger Schwenk. 2007b. Continuous space language models. *Computer Speech and Language*, 21:492–518.

Andreas Stolcke. 2002. SRILM - an extensible language modeling toolkit. In *ICSLP*, pages II: 901–904.

Stephan Vogel, Ying Zhang, Fei Huang, Alicia Tribble, Ashish Venugopal, Bing Zhao, and Alex Waibel. 2003. The CMU statistical machine translation system. In *MT Summit*, pages 402–409.

The University of Washington Machine Translation System for ACL WMT 2008

Amittai Axelrod, Mei Yang, Kevin Duh, Katrin Kirchhoff
Department of Electrical Engineering
University of Washington
Seattle, WA 98195
{amittai,yangmei,kevinduh,katrin} @ee.washington.edu

Abstract

This paper present the University of Washington's submission to the 2008 ACL SMT shared machine translation task. Two systems, for English-to-Spanish and German-to-Spanish translation are described. Our main focus was on testing a novel boosting framework for N-best list reranking and on handling German morphology in the German-to-Spanish system. While boosted N-best list reranking did not yield any improvements for this task, simplifying German morphology as part of the preprocessing step did result in significant gains.

1 Introduction

The University of Washington submitted systems to two data tracks in the WMT 2008 shared task competition, English-to-Spanish and German-to-Spanish. In both cases, we focused on the in-domain test set only. Our main interest this year was on investigating an improved weight training scheme for N-best list reranking that had previously shown improvements on a smaller machine translation task. For German-to-Spanish translation we additionally investigated simplifications of German morphology, which is known to be fairly complex due to a large number of compounds and inflections. In the following sections we first describe the data, baseline system and postprocessing steps before describing boosted N-best list reranking and morphology-based preprocessing for German.

2 Data and Basic Preprocessing

We used the Europarl data as provided (version 3b, 1.25 million sentence pairs) for training the translation model for use in the shared task. The data was lowercased and tokenized with the auxiliary scripts provided, and filtered according to the ratio of the sentence lengths in order to eliminate mismatched sentence pairs. This resulted in about 965k parallel sentences for English-Spanish and 950k sentence pairs for German-Spanish. Additional preprocessing was applied to the German corpus, as described in Section 5. For language modeling, we additionally used about 82M words of Spanish newswire text from the Linguistic Data Consortium (LDC), dating from 1995 to 1998.

3 System Overview

3.1 Translation model

The system developed for this year's shared task is a state-of-the-art, two-pass phrase-based statistical machine translation system based on a log-linear translation model (Koehn et al, 2003). The translation models and training method follow the standard Moses (Koehn et al, 2007) setup distributed as part of the shared task. We used the training method suggested in the Moses documentation, with lexicalized reordering (the `msd-bidirectional-fe` option) enabled. The system was tuned via Minimum Error Rate Training (MERT) on the first 500 sentences of the `devtest2006` dataset.

Proceedings of the Third Workshop on Statistical Machine Translation, pages 123–126,
Columbus, Ohio, USA, June 2008.

3.2 Decoding

Our system used the Moses decoder to generate 2000 output hypotheses per input sentence during the first translation pass. For the second pass, the N-best lists were rescored with the additional language models described below. We re-optimized the model combination weights with a parallelized implementation of MERT over 16 model scores on the `test2007` dataset. Two of these model scores for each hypothesis were from the two language models used in our second-pass system, and the rest correspond to the 14 Moses model weights (for reordering, language model, translation model, and word penalty).

3.3 Language models

We built all of our language models using the SRILM toolkit (Stolcke, 2002) with modified Kneser-Ney discounting and interpolating all n-gram estimates of order > 1. For first-pass decoding we used a 4-gram language model trained on the Spanish side of the Europarl v3b data. The optimal n-gram order was determined by testing language models with varying orders (3 to 5) on `devtest2006`; BLEU scores obtained using the various language models are shown in Table 1. The 4-gram model performed best.

Table 1: LM ngram size vs. output BLEU on the dev sets.

order	devtest2006	test2007
3-gram	30.54	30.69
4-gram	31.03	30.94
5-gram	30.85	30.84

Two additional language models were used for second pass rescoring. First, we trained a large out-of-domain language model on Spanish newswire text obtained from the LDC, dating from 1995 to 1998.

We used a perplexity-filtering method to filter out the least relevant half of the out-of-domain text, in order to significantly reduce the training time of the large language model and accelerate the rescoring process. This was done by computing the perplexity of an in-domain language model on each newswire sentence, and then discarding all sentences with greater than average perplexity. This reduced the size of the training set from 5.8M sentences and 166M tokens to 2.8M sentences and 82M tokens. We then further restricted the vocabulary to the union of the vocabulary lists of the Spanish sides of the de-es and en-es parallel training corpora. The remaining text was used to train the language model.

The second language model used for rescoring was a 5-gram model over part-of-speech (POS) tags. This model was built using the Spanish side of the English-Spanish parallel training corpus. The POS tags were obtained from the corpus using Freeling v2.0 (Atserias et al, 2006).

We selected the language models for our translation system were selected based on performance on the English-to-Spanish task, and reused them for the German-to-Spanish task.

4 Boosted Reranking

We submitted an alternative system, based on a different re-ranking method, called BoostedMERT (Duh and Kirchhoff, 2008), for each task. BoostedMERT is a novel boosting algorithm that uses Minimum Error Rate Training (MERT) as a weak learner to build a re-ranker that is richer than the standard log-linear models. This is motivated by the observation that log-linear models, as trained by MERT, often do not attain the oracle BLEU scores of the N-best lists in the development set. While this may be due to a local optimum in MERT, we hypothesize that log-linear models based on our K re-ranking features are also not sufficiently expressive.

BoostedMERT is inspired by the idea of Boosting (for classification), which has been shown to achieve low training (and generalization) error due to classifier combination. In BoostedMERT, we maintain a weight for each N-best list in the development set. In each iteration, MERT is performed to find the best ranker on weighted data. Then, the weights are updated based on whether the current ranker achieves oracle BLEU. For N-best lists that achieve BLEU scores far lower than the oracle, the weights are increased so that they become the emphasis of next iteration's MERT. We currently use the factor e^{-r} to update the N-best list distribution, where r is the ratio of the oracle hypothesis' BLEU to the BLEU of the selected hypothesis. The final ranker is a weighted combination of many such rankers.

More precisely, let w_i be the weights trained by MERT at iteration i. Given any w_i, we can generate a ranking y_i over an N-best list where y_i is an N-dimensional vector of predicted ranks. The final ranking vector is a weighted sum: $y = \sum_{i=1}^{T} \alpha_i y_i$, where α_i are parameters estimated during the boosting process. These parameters are optimized for maximum BLEU score on the development set. The only user-specified parameter is T, the number of boosting iterations. Here, we choose T by dividing the dev set in half: dev1 and dev2. First, we train BoostedMERT on dev1 for 50 iterations, then pick the T with the best BLEU score on dev2. Second, we train BoostedMERT on dev2 and choose the optimal T from dev1. Following the philosophy of classifier combination, we sum the final rank vectors y from each of the dev1- and dev2-trained BoostedMERT to obtain our final ranking result.

5 German → Spanish Preprocessing

German is a morphologically complex language, characterized by a high number of noun compounds and rich inflectional paradigms. Simplification of morphology can produce better word alignment, and thus better phrasal translations, and can also significantly reduce the out-of-vocabulary rate. We therefore applied two operations: (a) splitting of compound words and (b) stemming.

After basic preprocessing, the German half of the training corpus was first tagged by the German version of TreeTagger (Schmid, 1994), to identify part-of-speech tags. All nouns were then collected into a noun list, which was used by a simple compound splitter, as described in (Yang and Kirchhoff, 2006). This splitter scans the compound word, hypothesizing segmentations, and selects the first segmentation that produces two nouns that occur individually in the corpus. After splitting the compound nouns in the filtered corpus, we used the TreeTagger again, only this time to lemmatize the (filtered) training corpus.

The stemmed version of the German text was used to train the translation system's word alignments (through the end of step 3 in the Moses training script). After training the alignments, they were projected back onto the unstemmed corpus. The parallel phrases were then extracted using the standard procedure. Stemming is only used during the training stage, in order to simplify word alignment. During the evaluation phase, only the compound-splitter is applied to the German input.

6 Results

6.1 English → Spanish

The unofficial results of our 2nd-pass system for the 2008 test set are shown in Table 2, for recased, untokenized output. We note that the basic second-pass model was better than the first-pass system on the 2008 task, but not on the 2007 task, whereas BoostedMERT provided a minor improvement in the 2007 task but not the 2008 task. This is contrary to previous results in the Arabic-English IWSLT 2007 task, where boosted MERT gave an appreciable improvement. This result is perhaps due to the difference in magnitude between the IWSLT and WMT translation tasks.

Table 2: En→Es system on the test2007 and test2008 sets.

System	test2007	test2008
First-Pass	30.95	31.83
Second-Pass	30.94	32.72
BoostedMERT	31.05	32.62

6.2 German → Spanish

As previously described, we trained two German-Spanish translation systems: one via the default method provided in the Moses scripts, and another using word stems to train the word alignments and then projecting these alignments onto the unstemmed corpus and finishing the training process in the standard manner. Table 3 demonstrates that the word alignments generated with word-stems markedly improved first-pass translation performance on the `dev2006` dataset. However, during the evaluation period, the worse of the two systems was accidentally used, resulting in a larger number of out-of-vocabulary words in the system output and hence a poorer score. Rerunning our German-Spanish translation system correctly yielded significantly better system results, also shown in Table 3.

Table 3: De→Es first-pass system on the development and 2008 test set.

System	dev2006	test2008
Baseline	23.9	21.2
Stemmed Alignments	26.3	24.4

6.3 Boosted MERT

BoostedMERT is still in an early stage of experimentation, and we were interested to see whether it improved over traditional MERT in re-ranking. As it turns out, the BLEU scores on test2008 and test2007 data for the En-Es track are very similar for both re-rankers. In our post-evaluation analysis, we attempt to understand the reasons for similar BLEU scores, since the weights w_i for both re-rankers are qualitatively different. We found that out of 2000 En-Es N-best lists, BoostedMERT and MERT differed on 1478 lists in terms of the final hypothesis that was chosen. However, although the rankers are choosing different hypotheses, the chosen strings appear very similar. The PER of BoostedMERT vs. MERT results is only 0.077, and manual observation indicates that the differences between the two are often single phrase differences in a sentence.

We also computed the sentence-level BLEU for each ranker with respect to the true reference. This is meant to check whether BoostedMERT improved over MERT in some sentences but not others: if the improvements and degradations occur in the same proportions, a similar corpus-level BLEU may be observed. However, this is not the case. For a majority of the 2000 sentences, the sentence-level BLEU for both systems are the same. Only 10% of sentences have absolute BLEU difference greater than 0.1, and the proportion of improvement/degradation is similar (each 5%). For BLEU differences greater than 0.2, the percentage drops to 4%.

Thus we conclude that although BoostedMERT and MERT choose different hypotheses quite often, the string differences between their hypotheses are negligible, leading to similar final BLEU scores. BoostedMERT has found yet another local optimum during training, but has not improved upon MERT in this dataset. We hypothesize that dividing up the original development set into halves may have hurt BoostedMERT.

7 Conclusion

We have presented the University of Washington systems for English-to-Spanish and German-to-Spanish for the 2008 WMT shared translation task. A novel method for reranking N-best lists based on boosted MERT training was tested, as was morphological simplification in the preprocessing component for the German-to-Spanish system. Our conclusions are that boosted MERT, though successful on other translation tasks, did not yield any improvement here. Morphological simplification, however, did result in significant improvements in translation quality.

Acknowledgements

This work was funded by NSF grants IIS-0308297 and IIS-0326276.

References

Atserias, J. et al. 2006. FreeLing 1.3: Syntactic and semantic services in an open-source NLP library. *Proceedings of the 5th International Conference on Language Resources and Evaluation (LREC 2006)*. Genoa, Italy.

Duh, K., and Kirchhoff, K. 2008. Beyond Log-Linear Models: Boosted Minimum Error Rate Training for MT Re-ranking. To appear, *Proceedings of the Association for Computational Linguistics (ACL)*. Columbus, Ohio.

Koehn, P. and Och, F.J. and Marcu, D. 2003. Statistical phrase-based translation. *Proceedings of the Human Language Technology Conference of the North American Chapter of the Association for Computational Linguistics, (HLT/NAACL)*. Edmonton, Canada.

Koehn, P. 2005. Europarl: A Parallel Corpus for Statistical Machine Translation *Proceedings of MT Summit*.

Koehn, P. et al. 2007. Moses: Open Source Toolkit for Statistical Machine Translation. *Annual Meeting of the Association for Computational Linguistics (ACL)*, demonstration session. Prague, Czech Republic.

Schmid, H. 1994. Probabilistic part-of-speech tagging using decision trees. *International Conference on New Methods in Language Processing*, Manchester, UK.

Stolcke, A. 2002. SRILM - An extensible language modeling toolkit. *Proceedings of ICSLP*.

Yang, M. and K. Kirchhoff. 2006. Phrase-based backoff models for machine translation of highly inflected languages. *Proceedings of the 11th Conference of the European Chapter of the Association for Computational Linguistics (EACL 2006)*. Trento, Italy.

The TALP-UPC Ngram-based statistical machine translation system for ACL-WMT 2008

Maxim Khalilov, Adolfo Hernández H., Marta R. Costa-jussà,
Josep M. Crego, Carlos A. Henríquez Q., Patrik Lambert,
José A. R. Fonollosa, José B. Mariño and **Rafael E. Banchs**
Department of Signal Theory and Communications
TALP Research Center (UPC)
Barcelona 08034, Spain
(khalilov, adolfohh, mruiz, jmcrego, carloshq, lambert, adrian, canton, rbanchs)@gps.tsc.upc.edu

Abstract

This paper reports on the participation of the TALP Research Center of the UPC (Universitat Politècnica de Catalunya) to the ACL WMT 2008 evaluation campaign.

This year's system is the evolution of the one we employed for the 2007 campaign. Main updates and extensions involve linguistically motivated word reordering based on the reordering patterns technique. In addition, this system introduces a target language model, based on linguistic classes (Part-of-Speech), morphology reduction for an inflectional language (Spanish) and an improved optimization procedure.

Results obtained over the development and test sets on Spanish to English (and the other way round) translations for both the traditional Europarl and a challenging News stories tasks are analyzed and commented.

1 Introduction

Over the past few years, the Statistical Machine Translation (SMT) group of the TALP-UPC has been developing the Ngram-based SMT system (Mariño et al., 2006). In previous evaluation campaigns the Ngram-based approach has proved to be comparable with the state-of-the-art phrase-based systems, as shown in Koehn and Monz(2006), Callison-Burch et al. (2007).

We present a summary of the TALP-UPC Ngram-based SMT system used for this shared task. We discuss the system configuration and novel features, namely linguistically motivated reordering technique, which is applied on the decoding step. Additionally, the reordering procedure is supported by an Ngram language model (LM) of reordered source Part-of-Speech tags (POS).

In this year's evaluation we submitted systems for Spanish-English and English-Spanish language pairs for the traditional (*Europarl*) and challenging (*News*) tasks. In each case, we used only the supplied data for each language pair for models training and optimization.

This paper is organized as follows. Section 2 briefly outlines the 2008 system, including tuple definition and extraction, translation model and additional feature models, decoding tool and optimization procedure. Section 3 describes the word reordering problem and presents the proposed technique of reordering patterns learning and application. Later on, Section 4 reports on the experimental setups of the WMT 2008 evaluation campaign. In Section 5 we sum up the main conclusions from the paper.

2 Ngram-based SMT System

Our translation system implements a log-linear model in which a foreign language sentence $f_1^J = f_1, f_2, ..., f_J$ is translated into another language $e_1^I = f_1, f_2, ..., e_I$ by searching for the translation hypothesis $\hat{e}_1^I$ maximizing a log-linear combination of several feature models (Brown et al., 1990):

$$\hat{e}_1^I = \arg\max_{e_1^I} \left\{ \sum_{m=1}^{M} \lambda_m h_m(e_1^I, f_1^J) \right\}$$

where the feature functions h_m refer to the system models and the set of λ_m refers to the weights corresponding to these models.

The core part of the system constructed in that way is a translation model, which is based on bilingual *n-grams*. It actually constitutes an Ngram-based LM of bilingual units (called tuples), which approximates the joint probability between the languages under consideration. The procedure of tuples extraction from a word-to-word alignment according to certain constraints is explained in detail in Mariño et al. (2006).

The Ngram-based approach differs from the phrase-based SMT mainly by distinct representating of the bilingual units defined by word alignment and using a higher

Proceedings of the Third Workshop on Statistical Machine Translation, pages 127–130,
Columbus, Ohio, USA, June 2008. ©2008 Association for Computational Linguistics

order HMM of the translation process. While regular phrase-based SMT considers context only for phrase reordering but not for translation, the N-gram based approach conditions translation decisions on previous translation decisions.

The TALP-UPC 2008 translation system, besides the bilingual translation model, which consists of a 4-*gram* LM of tuples with *Kneser-Ney discounting* (estimated with SRI Language Modeling Toolkit[1]), implements a log-linear combination of five additional feature models:

- a **target language model** (*a* 4-*gram* model of words, estimated with *Kneser-Ney smoothing*);
- a **POS target language model** (a 4-*gram* model of tags with *Good-Turing discounting* (TPOS));
- a **word bonus model**, which is used to compensate the system's preference for short output sentences;
- a **source-to-target lexicon model** and a **target-to-source lexicon model**, these models use word-to-word IBM Model 1 probabilities (Och and Ney, 2004) to estimate the lexical weights for each tuple in the translation table.

Decisions on the particular LM configuration and smoothing technique were taken on the minimal-perplexity and maximal-BLEU bases.

The decoder (called MARIE), an open source tool[2], implementing a beam search strategy with distortion capabilities was used in the translation system.

Given the development set and references, the log-linear combination of weights was adjusted using a simplex optimization method (with the optimization criteria of the highest BLEU score) and an n-best re-ranking just as described in *http://www.statmt.org/jhuws/*. This strategy allows for a faster and more efficient adjustment of model weights by means of a double-loop optimization, which provides significant reduction of the number of translations that should be carried out.

3 Reordering framework

For a great number of translation tasks a certain reordering strategy is required. This is especially important when the translation is performed between pairs of languages with non-monotonic word order. There are various types of distortion models, simplifying bilingual translation. In our system we use an extended monotone reordering model based on automatically learned reordering rules. A detailed description can be found in Crego and Mariño (2006).

[1] http://www.speech.sri.com/projects/srilm/
[2] http://gps-tsc.upc.es/veu/soft/soft/marie/

Apart from that, tuples were extracted by an unfolding technique: this means that the tuples are broken into smaller tuples, and these are sequenced in the order of the target words.

3.1 Reordering patterns

Word movements are realized according to the reordering rewrite rules, which have the form of:

$$t_1, ..., t_n \mapsto i_1, ..., i_n$$

where $t_1, ..., t_n$ is a sequence of POS tags (relating a sequence of source words), and $i_1, ..., i_n$ indicates which order of the source words generate monotonically the target words.

Patterns are extracted in training from the crossed links found in the word alignment, in other words, found in translation tuples (as no word within a tuple can be linked to a word out of it (Crego and Mariño, 2006)).

Having all the instances of rewrite patterns, a score for each pattern on the basis of relative frequency is calculated as shown below:

$$p(t_1, ..., t_n \mapsto i_1, ..., i_n) = \frac{N(t_1, ..., t_n \mapsto i_1, ..., i_n)}{NN(t_1, ..., t_n)}$$

3.2 Search graph extension and source POS model

The monotone search graph is extended with reorderings following the patterns found in training. Once the search graph is built, the decoder traverses the graph looking for the best translation. Hence, the winning hypothesis is computed using all the available information (the whole SMT models).

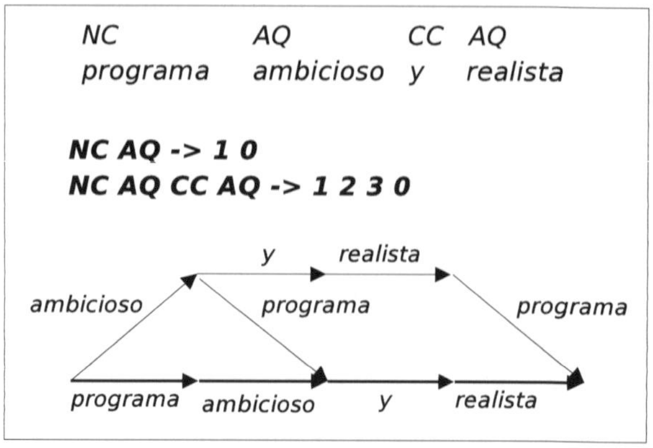

Figure 1: Search graph extension. *NC, CC and AQ stand respectively for name, conjunction and adjective.*

The procedure identifies first the sequences of words in the input sentence that match any available pattern. Then, each of the matchings implies the addition of an arc into the search graph (encoding the reordering learned in the pattern). However, this addition of a new arc is not

Task	BL		BL+SPOS	
	Europarl	News	Europarl	News
es2en	32.79	36.09	32.88	36.36
en2es	32.05	33.91	32.10	33.63

Table 1: BLEU comparison demonstrating the impact of the source-side POS tags model.

performed if a translation unit with the same source-side words already exists in the training. Figure 1 shows how two rewrite rules applied over an input sentence extend the search graph given the reordering patterns that match the source POS tag sequence.

The reordering strategy is additionally supported by a *4-gram language model* (estimated with *Good-Turing smoothing*) of reordered **source POS tags** (SPOS). In training, POS tags are reordered according with the extracted reordering patterns and word-to-word links. The resulting sequence of source POS tags is used to train the Ngram LM.

Table 1 presents the effect of the source POS LM introduction to the reordering module of the Ngram-based SMT. As it can be seen, the impactya le h of the source-side POS LM is minimal, however we decided to consider the model aiming at improving it in future. The reported results are related to the *Europarl* and News Commentary (*News*) development sets. BLEU calculation is case insensitive and insensitive to tokenization. *BL* (baseline) refers to the presented Ngram-based system considering all the features, apart from the target and source POS models.

4 WMT 2008 Evaluation Framework

4.1 Corpus

An extraction of the official transcriptions of the 3rd release of the European Parliament Plenary Sessions[3] was provided for the ACL WMT 2008 shared translation task. About 40 times smaller corpus from news domain (called News Commentary) was also available. For both tasks, our training corpus was the catenation of the Europarl and News Commentary corpora.

TALP UPC participated in the constraint to the provided training data track for Spanish-English and English-Spanish translation tasks. We used the same training material for the traditional and challenging tasks, while the development sets used to tune the system were distinct (**2000** sentences for **Europarl task** and **1057** for **News Commentary**, **one reference translation** for each of them). A brief training and development corpora statistics is presented in Table 2.

[3] http://www.statmt.org/wmt08/shared-task.html

	Spanish	English
Train		
Sentences	1.3 M	1.3 M
Words	38.2 M	35.8 K
Vocabulary	156 K	120 K
Development Europarl		
Sentences	2000	2000
Words	61.8 K	58.7 K
Vocabulary	8 K	6.5 K
Development News Commentary		
Sentences	1057	1057
Words	29.8 K	25.8 K
Vocabulary	5.4 K	4.9 K

Table 2: Basic statistics of ACL WMT 2008 corpus.

4.2 Processing details

The training data was preprocessed by using provided tools for tokenizing and filtering.

POS tagging. POS information for the source and the target languages was considered for both translation tasks that we have participated. The software tools available for performing POS-tagging were Freeling (Carreras et al., 2004) for Spanish and TnT (Brants, 2000) for English. The number of classes for English is 44, while Spanish is considered as a more inflectional language, and the tag set contains 376 different tags.

Word Alignment. The word alignment is automatically computed by using GIZA++[4](Och and Ney, 2000) in both directions, which are symmetrized by using the union operation. Instead of aligning words themselves, stems are used for aligning. Afterwards case sensitive words are recovered.

Spanish Morphology Reduction. We implemented a morphology reduction of the Spanish language as a preprocessing step. As a consequence, training data sparseness due to Spanish morphology was reduced improving the performance of the overall translation system. In particular, the pronouns attached to the verb were separated and contractions as *del* or *al* were splitted into *de el* or *a el*. As a post-processing, in the En2Es direction we used a POS target LM as a feature (instead of the target language model based on classes) that allowed to recover the segmentations (de Gispert, 2006).

4.3 Experiments and Results

In contrast to the last year's system where statistical classes were used to train the target-side tags LM, this year we used **linguistically motivated word classes**

[4] http://code.google.com/p/giza-pp/

Task	BL+SPOS		BL+SPOS+TPOS (UPC 2008)	
	Europarl	News	Europarl	News
es2en	32.88	36.36	32.89	36.31
en2es	31.52	34.13	30.72	32.72
en2es "clean"[5]	32.10	33.63	32.09	35.04

Table 3: BLEU scores for Spanish-English and English-Spanish 2008 development corpora (Europarl and News Commentary).

Task	UPC 2008	
	Europarl	News
es2en	32.80	19.61
en2es	31.31	19.28
en2es "clean"[5]	32.34	20.05

Table 4: BLEU scores for official tests 2008.

(POS) which were considered to train the POS target LM and extract the reordering patterns. Other characteristics of this year's system are:

- **reordering patterns** technique;
- **source POS model**, supporting word reordering;
- **no LM interpolation**. For this year's evaluation, we trained two separate LMs for each domain-specific corpus (i.e., Europarl and News Commentary tasks).

It is important to mention that 2008 training material is identical to the one provided for the 2007 shared translation task.

Table 3 presents the *BLEU* score obtained for the 2008 development data sets and shows the impact of the target-side POS LM introduction, which can be characterized as highly corpus- and language-dependent feature. *BL* refers to the same system configuration as described in subsection 3.2. The computed *BLEU* scores are case insensitive, insensitive to tokenization and use one translation reference.

After submitting the systems we discovered a bug related to incorrect implementation of the target LMs of words and tags for Spanish, it caused serious reduction of translation quality (1.4 BLEU points for development set in case of English-to-Spanish Europarl task and 2.3 points in case of the corresponding News Commentary task). The last raw of table 3 (*en2es "clean"*) represents the results corresponding to the UPC 2008 post-evaluation system, while the previous one (*en2es*) refers to the "bugged" system submitted to the evaluation.

The experiments presented in Table 4 correspond to the 2008 test evaluation sets.

[5]Corrected post-evaluation results (see subsection 4.3.)

5 Conclusions

In this paper we introduced the TALP UPC Ngram-based SMT system participating in the WMT08 evaluation. Apart from briefly summarizing the decoding and optimization processes, we have presented the feature models that were taken into account, along with the bilingual Ngram translation model. A reordering strategy based on linguistically-motivated reordering patterns to harmonize the source and target word order has been presented in the framework of the Ngram-based system.

6 Acknowledgments

This work has been funded by the Spanish Government under grant TEC2006-13964-C03 (AVIVAVOZ project). The authors want to thank Adrià de Gispert (Cambridge University) for his contribution to this work.

References

T. Brants. 2000. TnT – a statistical part-of-speech tagger. In *Proceedings of the 6th Applied Natural Language Processing (ANLP-2000)*.

P. Brown, J. Cocke, S. Della Pietra, V. Della Pietra, F. Jelinek, J. D. Lafferty, R. Mercer, and P. S. Roossin. 1990. A statistical approach to machine translation. *Computational Linguistics*, 16(2):79–85.

C. Callison-Burch, C. Fordyce, P. Koehn, C. Monz, and J. Schroeder. 2007. (Meta-) evaluation of machine translation. In *Proceedings of the ACL 2007 Workshop on Statistical and Hybrid methods for Machine Translation (WMT)*, pages 136–158.

X. Carreras, I. Chao, L. Padró, and M. Padró. 2004. Freeling: An open-source suite of language analyzers. In *Proceedings of the 4th Int. Conf. on Language Resources and Evaluation (LREC'04)*.

J. M. Crego and J. B. Mariño. 2006. Improving statistical MT by coupling reordering and decoding. *Machine Translation*, 20(3):199–215.

A. de Gispert. 2006. *Introducing linguistic knowledge into statistical machine translation*. Ph.D. thesis, Universitat Politècnica de Catalunya, December.

P. Koehn and C. Monz. 2006. Manual and automatic evaluation of machine translation between european languages. In *Proceedings of the ACL 2006 Workshop on Statistical and Hybrid methods for Machine Translation (WMT)*, pages 102–121.

J. B. Mariño, R. E. Banchs, J. M. Crego, A. de Gispert, P. Lambert, J. A. R. Fonollosa, and M. R. Costa-jussà. 2006. N-gram based machine translation. *Computational Linguistics*, 32(4):527–549, December.

F. J. Och and H. Ney. 2000. Improved statistical alignment models. In *Proceedings of the the 38th Annual Meeting on Association for Computational Linguistics (ACL)*, pages 440–447.

F. Och and H. Ney. 2004. The alignment template approach to statistical machine translation. 30(4):417 – 449, December.

European Language Translation with Weighted Finite State Transducers: The CUED MT System for the 2008 ACL Workshop on SMT

Graeme Blackwood, Adrià de Gispert, Jamie Brunning, William Byrne
Machine Intelligence Laboratory
Department of Engineering, Cambridge University
Trumpington Street, Cambridge, CB2 1PZ, U.K.
{gwb24|ad465|jjjb2|wjb31}@cam.ac.uk

Abstract

We describe the Cambridge University Engineering Department phrase-based statistical machine translation system for Spanish-English and French-English translation in the ACL 2008 Third Workshop on Statistical Machine Translation Shared Task. The CUED system follows a generative model of translation and is implemented by composition of component models realised as Weighted Finite State Transducers, without the use of a special-purpose decoder. Details of system tuning for both Europarl and News translation tasks are provided.

1 Introduction

The Cambridge University Engineering Department statistical machine translation system follows the Transducer Translation Model (Kumar and Byrne, 2005; Kumar et al., 2006), a phrase-based generative model of translation that applies a series of transformations specified by conditional probability distributions and encoded as Weighted Finite State Transducers (Mohri et al., 2002).

The main advantages of this approach are its modularity, which facilitates the development and evaluation of each component individually, and its implementation simplicity which allows us to focus on modeling issues rather than complex decoding and search algorithms. In addition, no special-purpose decoder is required since standard WFST operations can be used to obtain the 1-best translation or a lattice of alternative hypotheses. Finally, the system architecture readily extends to speech translation, in which input ASR lattices can be translated in the same way as for text (Mathias and Byrne, 2006).

This paper reviews the first participation of CUED in the ACL Workshop on Statistical Machine Translation in 2008. It is organised as follows. Firstly, section 2 describes the system architecture and its main components. Section 3 gives details of the development work conducted for this shared task and results are reported and discussed in section 4. Finally, in section 5 we summarise our participation in the task and outline directions for future work.

2 The Transducer Translation Model

Under the Transducer Translation Model, the generation of a target language sentence t_1^J starts with the generation of a source language sentence s_1^I by the source language model $P_G(s_1^I)$. Next, the source language sentence is segmented into phrases according to the unweighted uniform phrasal segmentation model $P_W(u_1^K, K|s_1^I)$. This source phrase sequence generates a reordered target language phrase sequence according to the phrase translation and reordering model $P_R(x_1^K|u_1^K)$. Next, target language phrases are inserted into this sequence according to the insertion model $P_\Phi(v_1^R|x_1^K, u_1^K)$. Finally, the sequence of reordered and inserted target language phrases are transformed to word sequences t_1^J under the target phrasal segmentation model $P_\Omega(t_1^J|v_1^R)$. These component distributions together form a joint distribution over the source and target language sentences and their possible intermediate phrase sequences as $P(t_1^J, v_1^R, x_1^K, u_1^K, s_1^I)$.

In translation under the generative model, we start with the target sentence t_1^J in the foreign language

Proceedings of the Third Workshop on Statistical Machine Translation, pages 131–134,
Columbus, Ohio, USA, June 2008.

and search for the best source sentence $\hat{s}_1^I$. Encoding each distribution as a WFST leads to a model of translation as the series of compositions

$$L = G \circ W \circ R \circ \Phi \circ \Omega \circ T \quad (1)$$

in which T is an acceptor for the target language sentence and L is the word lattice of translations obtained during decoding. The most likely translation $\hat{s}_1^I$ is the path in L with least cost.

2.1 TTM Reordering Model

The TTM reordering model associates a jump sequence with each phrase pair. For the experiments described in this paper, the jump sequence is restricted such that only adjacent phrases can be swapped; this is the MJ1 reordering model of (Kumar and Byrne, 2005). Although the reordering probability for each pair of phrases could be estimated from word-aligned parallel data, we here assume a uniform reordering probability p tuned as described in section 3.1. Figure 1 shows how the MJ1 reordering model for a pair of phrases **x1** and **x2** is implemented as a WFST.

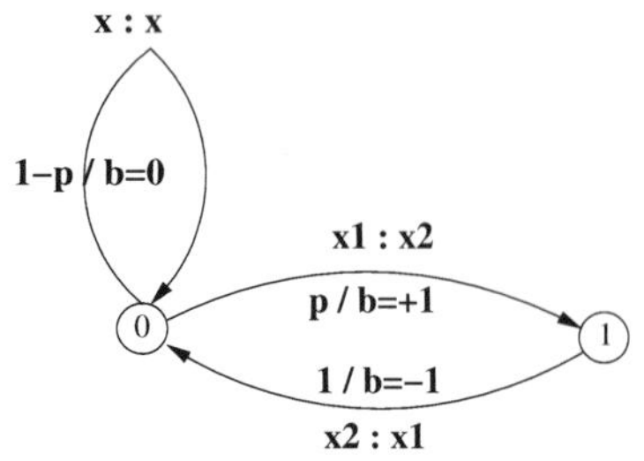

Figure 1: *The uniform MJ1 reordering transducer.*

3 System Development

CUED participated in two of the WMT shared task tracks: French→English and Spanish→English. For both tracks, primary and contrast systems were submitted. The primary submission was restricted to only the parallel and language model data distributed for the shared task. The contrast submission incorporates large additional quantities of English monolingual training text for building the second-pass language model described in section 3.2.

Table 1 summarises the parallel training data, including the total number of sentences, total number of words, and lower-cased vocabulary size. The Spanish and French parallel texts each contain approximately 5% News Commentary data; the rest is Europarl data. Various single-reference development and test sets were provided for each of the tracks. However, the 2008 evaluation included a new News task, for which no corresponding development set was available.

	sentences	words	vocab
FR	1.33M	39.9M	124k
EN		36.4M	106k
ES	1.30M	38.2M	140k
EN		35.7M	106k

Table 1: *Parallel corpora statistics.*

All of the training and system tuning was performed using lower-cased data. Word alignments were generated using GIZA++ (Och and Ney, 2003) over a stemmed version of the parallel text. Stems for each language were obtained using the Snowball stemmer[1]. After unioning the Viterbi alignments, the stems were replaced with their original words, and phrase-pairs of up to five foreign words in length were extracted in the usual fashion (Koehn et al., 2003).

3.1 System Tuning

Minimum error training (Och, 2003) under BLEU (Papineni et al., 2001) was used to optimise the feature weights of the decoder with respect to the *dev2006* development set. The following features are optimized:

- Language model scale factor
- Word and phrase insertion penalties
- Reordering scale factor
- Insertion scale factor
- Translation model scale factor: u-to-v
- Translation model scale factor: v-to-u
- Three phrase pair count features

The phrase-pair count features track whether each phrase-pair occurred once, twice, or more than twice

[1]Available at http://snowball.tartarus.org

in the parallel text (Bender et al., 2007). All decoding and minimum error training operations are performed with WFSTs and implemented using the OpenFST libraries (Allauzen et al., 2007).

3.2 English Language Models

Separate language models are used when translating the Europarl and News sets. The models are estimated using SRILM (Stolcke, 2002) and converted to WFSTs for use in TTM translation. We use the offline approximation in which failure transitions are replaced with epsilons (Allauzen et al., 2003).

The Europarl language model is a Kneser-Ney (Kneser and Ney, 1995) smoothed default-cutoff 5-gram back-off language model estimated over the concatenation of the Europarl and News language model training data. The News language model is created by optimising the interpolation weights of two component models with respect to the News Commentary development sets since we believe these more closely match the *newstest2008* domain. The optimised interpolation weights were 0.44 for the Europarl corpus and 0.56 for the much smaller News Commentary corpus. For our contrast submission, we rescore the first-pass translation lattices with a large zero-cutoff stupid-backoff (Brants et al., 2007) language model estimated over approximately five billion words of newswire text.

4 Results and Discussion

Table 2 reports lower-cased BLEU scores for the French→English and Spanish→English Europarl and News translation tasks. The NIST scores are also provided in parentheses. The row labelled "TTM+MET" shows results obtained after TTM translation and minimum error training, i.e. our primary submission constrained to use only the data distributed for the task. The row labelled "+5gram" shows translation results obtained after rescoring with the large zero-cutoff 5-gram language model described in section 3.2. Since this includes additional language model data, it represents the CUED contrast submission.

Translation quality for the ES→EN task is slightly higher than that of FR→EN. For Europarl translation, most of the additional English language model training data incorporated into the 5-gram rescoring step is out-of-domain and so does not substantially improve the scores. Rescoring yields an average gain of just +0.5 BLEU points.

Translation quality is significantly lower in both language pairs for the new *news2008* set. Two factors may account for this. The first is the change in domain and the fact that no training or development set was available for the News translation task. Secondly, the use of a much freer translation in the single News reference, which makes it difficult to obtain a good BLEU score. However, the second-pass 5-gram language model rescoring gains are larger than those observed in the Europarl sets, with approximately +1.7 BLEU points for each language pair. The additional in-domain newswire data clearly helps to improve translation quality.

Finally, we use a simple 3-gram casing model trained on the true-case workshop distributed language model data, and apply the SRILM `disambig` tool to restore true-case for our final submissions. With respect to the lower-cased scores, true-casing drops around 1.0 BLEU in the Europarl task, and around 1.7 BLEU in the News Commentary and News tasks.

5 Summary

We have reviewed the Cambridge University Engineering Department first participation in the workshop on machine translation using a phrase-based SMT system implemented with a simple WFST architecture. Results are largely competitive with the state-of-the-art in this task.

Future work will examine whether further improvements can be obtained by incorporating additional features into MET, such as the word-to-word Model 1 scores or phrasal segmentation models. The MJ1 reordering model could also be extended to allow for longer-span phrase movement. Minimum Bayes Risk decoding, which has been applied successfully in other tasks, could also be included.

The difference in the gains from 5-gram lattice rescoring suggests that, particularly for Europarl translation, it is important to ensure the language model data is in-domain. Some form of count mixing or alternative language model adaptation techniques may prove useful for unconstrained Europarl translation.

Task		dev2006	devtest2006	test2007	**test2008**	**newstest2008**
FR→EN	TTM+MET	31.92 (7.650)	32.51 (7.719)	32.94 (7.805)	32.83 (7.799)	19.58 (6.108)
	+5gram	32.51 (7.744)	32.96 (7.797)	33.33 (7.880)	33.03 (7.856)	21.22 (6.311)
ES→EN	TTM+MET	33.11 (7.799)	32.25 (7.649)	32.90 (7.766)	33.11 (7.859)	20.99 (6.308)
	+5gram	33.30 (7.835)	32.96 (7.740)	33.55 (7.857)	33.47 (7.893)	22.83 (6.513)

Table 2: *Translation results for the Europarl and News tasks for various dev sets and the 2008 test sets.*

Acknowledgements

This work was supported in part under the GALE program of the Defense Advanced Research Projects Agency, Contract No. HR0011-06-C-0022.

References

Cyril Allauzen, Mehryar Mohri, and Brian Roark. 2003. Generalized algorithms for constructing statistical language models. In *Proceedings of the 41st Meeting of the Association for Computational Linguistics*, pages 557–564.

Cyril Allauzen, Michael Riley, Johan Schalkwyk, Wojciech Skut, and Mehryar Mohri. 2007. OpenFST: a general and efficient weighted finite-state transducer library. In *Proceedings of the 9th International Conference on Implementation and Application of Automata*, pages 11–23. Springer.

Oliver Bender, Evgeny Matusov, Stefan Hahn, Sasa Hasan, Shahram Khadivi, and Hermann Ney. 2007. The RWTH Arabic-to-English spoken language translation system. In *Proceedings of the 2007 Automatic Speech Understanding Workshop*, pages 396–401.

Thorsten Brants, Ashok C. Popat, Peng Xu, Franz J. Och, and Jeffrey Dean. 2007. Large language models in machine translation. In *Proceedings of the 2007 Joint Conference on Empirical Methods in Natural Language Processing and Computational Natural Language Learning*, pages 858–867.

R. Kneser and H. Ney. 1995. Improved backing-off for m-gram language modeling. In *Acoustics, Speech, and Signal Processing*, pages 181–184.

Philipp Koehn, Franz Josef Och, and Daniel Marcu. 2003. Statistical phrase-based translation. In *Proceedings of the 2003 Conference for Computational Linguistics on Human Language Technology*, pages 48–54, Morristown, NJ, USA.

Shankar Kumar and William Byrne. 2005. Local phrase reordering models for statistical machine translation. In *Proceedings of the conference on Human Language Technology and Empirical Methods in Natural Language Processing*, pages 161–168.

Shankar Kumar, Yonggang Deng, and William Byrne. 2006. A weighted finite state transducer translation template model for statistical machine translation. *Natural Language Engineering*, 12(1):35–75.

Lambert Mathias and William Byrne. 2006. Statistical phrase-based speech translation. In *2006 IEEE International Conference on Acoustics, Speech and Signal Processing*.

Mehryar Mohri, Fernando Pereira, and Michael Riley. 2002. Weighted finite-state transducers in speech recognition. In *Computer Speech and Language*, volume 16, pages 69–88.

Franz Josef Och and Hermann Ney. 2003. A systematic comparison of various statistical alignment models. *Computational Linguistics*, 29(1):19–51.

Franz Josef Och. 2003. Minimum error rate training in statistical machine translation. In *Proceedings of the 41st Meeting of the Association for Computational Linguistics*, pages 160–167, Morristown, NJ, USA.

Kishore Papineni, Salim Roukos, Todd Ward, and Wei-Jing Zhu. 2001. BLEU: a method for automatic evaluation of machine translation. In *Proceedings of the 40th Meeting of the Association for Computational Linguistics*, pages 311–318, Morristown, NJ, USA.

Andreas Stolcke. 2002. SRILM – an extensible language modeling toolkit. In *Proceedings of International Conference on Spoken Language Processing*.

Effects of Morphological Analysis in Translation between German and English

Sara Stymne, Maria Holmqvist and Lars Ahrenberg
Department of Computer and Information Science
Linköping University, Sweden
{sarst,marho,lah}@ida.liu.se

Abstract

We describe the LIU systems for German-English and English-German translation submitted to the Shared Task of the Third Workshop of Statistical Machine Translation. The main features of the systems, as compared with the baseline, is the use of morphological pre- and post-processing, and a sequence model for German using morphologically rich parts-of-speech. It is shown that these additions lead to improved translations.

1 Introduction

Research in statistical machine translation (SMT) increasingly makes use of linguistic analysis in order to improve performance. By including abstract categories, such as lemmas and parts-of-speech (POS), in the models, it is argued that systems can become better at handling sentences for which training data at the word level is sparse. Such categories can be integrated in the statistical framework using factored models (Koehn et al., 2007). Furthermore, by parsing input sentences and restructuring based on the result to narrow the structural difference between source and target language, the current phrase-based models can be used more effectively (Collins et al., 2005).

German differs structurally from English in several respects (see e.g. Collins et al., 2005). In this work we wanted to look at one particular aspect of restructuring, namely splitting of German compounds, and evaluate its effect in both translation directions, thus extending the initial experiments reported in Holmqvist et al. (2007). In addition, since German is much richer in morphology than English, we wanted to test the effects of using a sequence model for German based on morphologically subcategorized parts-of-speech. All systems have been specified as extensions of the Moses system provided for the Shared Task.

2 Part-of-speech and Morphology

For both English and German we used the part-of-speech tagger TreeTagger (Schmid, 1994) to obtain POS-tags.

The German POS-tags from TreeTagger were refined by adding morphological information from a commercial dependency parser, including case, number, gender, definiteness, and person for nouns, pronouns, verbs, adjectives and determiners in the cases where both tools agreed on the POS-tag. If they did not agree, the POS-tag from TreeTagger was chosen. This tag set seemed more suitable for SMT, with tags for proper names and foreign words which the commercial parser does not have.

3 Compound Analysis

Compounding is common in many languages, including German. Since compounding is highly productive it increases vocabulary size and leads to sparse data problems.

Compounds in German are formed by joining words, and in addition filler letters can be inserted or letters can be removed from the end of all but the last word of the compound (Langer, 1998). We have chosen to allow simple additions of letter(s) (*-s, -n, -en, -nen, -es, -er, -ien*) and simple truncations (*-e,*

Proceedings of the Third Workshop on Statistical Machine Translation, pages 135–138,
Columbus, Ohio, USA, June 2008. ©2008 Association for Computational Linguistics

-en, -n). Example of compounds with additions and truncations can be seen in (1).

(1) a. Staatsfeind (Staat + Feind)
public enemy

b. Kirchhof (Kirche + Hof)
graveyard

3.1 Splitting compounds

Noun and adjective compounds are split by a modified version of the corpus-based method presented by Koehn and Knight (2003). First the German language model data is POS-tagged and used to calculate frequencies of all nouns, verbs, adjectives, adverbs and the negative particle. Then, for each noun and adjective all splits into these known words from the corpus, allowing filler additions and truncations, are considered, choosing the splitting option with the highest arithmetic mean[1] of the frequencies of its parts.

A length limit of each part was set to 4 characters. For adjectives we restrict the number of parts to maximum two, since they do not tend to have multiple parts as often as nouns. In addition we added a stop list with 14 parts, often mistagged, that gave rise to wrong adjective splits, such as *arische* ('Aryan') in *konsularische* ('consular').

As Koehn and Knight (2003) points out, parts of compounds do not always have the same meaning as when they stand alone, e.g. *Grundrechte* ('basic rights'), where the first part, *Grund*, usually translates as *foundation*, which is wrong in this compound. To overcome this we marked all compound parts but the last, with the symbol '#'. Thus they are handled as separate words. Parts of split words also receive a special POS-tag, based on the POS of the last word of the compound, and the last part receives the same POS as the full word.

We also split words containing hyphens based on the same algorithm. Their parts receive a different POS-tag, and the hyphens are left at the end of all but the last part.

[1]We choose the arithmetic mean over the geometric mean used by Koehn and Knight (2003) in order to increase the number of splits.

3.2 Merging compounds

For translation into German, the translation output contains split compounds, which need to be merged. An algorithm for merging has been proposed by Popović et al. (2006) using lists of compounds and their parts. This method cannot merge unseen compounds, however, so instead we base merging on POS. If a word has a compound-POS, and the following word has a matching POS, they are merged. If the next POS does not match, a hyphen is added to the word, allowing for coordinated compounds as in (2).

(2) Wasser- und Bodenqualität
water and soil quality

4 System Descriptions

The main difference of our system in relation to the baseline system of the Shared Task[2] is the pre- and post-processing described above, the use of a POS factor, and an additional sequence model on POS. We also modified the tuning to include compound merging, and used a smaller corpus, 600 sentences picked evenly from the dev2006 corpus, for tuning. We use the Moses decoder (Koehn et al., 2007) and SRILM language models (Stolcke, 2002).

4.1 German ⇒ English

We used POS as an output factor, as can be seen in Figure 1. Using additional factors only on the target side means that only the training data need to be POS-tagged, not the tuning data or translation input. However, POS-tagging is still performed for German as input to the pre-processing step. As Figure 1 shows we have two sequence models. A 5-gram language model based on surface form using Kneser-Ney smoothing and in addition a 7-gram sequence model based on POS using Witten-Bell[3] smoothing.

The training corpus was filtered to sentences with 2–40 words, resulting in a total of 1054688 sentences. Training was done purely on Europarl data, but results were submitted both on Europarl and

[2]`http://www.statmt.org/wmt08/baseline.html`

[3]Kneser-Ney smoothing can not be used for the POS sequence model, since there were counts-of-counts of zero. However, Witten-Bell smoothing gives good results when the vocabulary is small.

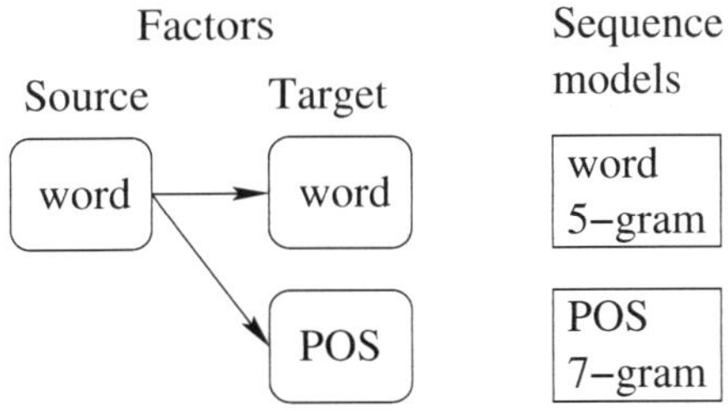

Figure 1: Architecture of the factored system

News data. The news data were submitted to see how well a pure out-of-domain system could perform.

In the pre-processing step compounds were split. This was done for training, tuning and translation. In addition German contracted prepositions and determiners, such as *zum* from *zu dem* ('to the'), when identified as such by the tagger, were split.

4.2 English ⇒ German

All features of the German to English system were used, and in addition more fine-grained German POS-tags that were sub-categorized for morphological features. This was done for training, tuning and sequence models. At translation time no pre-processing was needed for the English input, but a post-processing step for the German output is required, including the merging of compounds and contracted prepositions and determiners. The latter was done in connection with uppercasing, by training an instance of Moses on a lower cased corpus with split contractions and an upper-cased corpus with untouched contractions. The tuning step was modified so that merging of compounds were done as part of the tuning.

4.3 Baseline

For comparison, we constructed a baseline according to the shared-task description, but with smaller tuning corpus, and the same sentence filtering for the translation model as in the submitted system, using only sentences of length 2-40.

In addition we constructed a factored baseline system, with POS as an output factor and a sequence model for POS. Here we only used the original POS-tags from TreeTagger, no additional morphology was added for German.

	De-En	En-De
Baseline	26.95	20.16
Factored baseline	27.43	20.27
Submitted system	27.63	20.46

Table 1: Bleu scores for Europarl (test2007)

	De-En	En-De
Baseline	19.54	14.31
Factored baseline	20.16	14.37
Submitted system	20.61	14.77

Table 2: Bleu scores for News Commentary (nc-test2007)

5 Results

Case-sensitive Bleu scores[4] (Papineni et al., 2002) for the Europarl devtest set (test2007) are shown in table 1. We can see that the submitted system performs best, and that the factored baseline is better than the pure baseline, especially for translation into English.

Bleu scores for News Commentary[5] (nc-test2007) are shown in Table 2. Here we can also see that the submitted system is the best. As expected, Bleu is much lower on out-of-domain news text than on the Europarl development test set.

5.1 Compounds

The quality of compound translations were analysed manually. The first 100 compounds that could be found by the splitting algorithm were extracted from the Europarl reference text, test2007, together with their English translations[6].

System translations were compared to the annotated compounds and classified into seven categories: correct, alternative good translation, correct but different form, part of the compound translated, no direct equivalent, wrong and untranslated. Out of these the first three categories can be considered good translations.

We performed the error analysis for the submitted and the baseline system. The result can be seen in

[4]The %Bleu notation is used in this report

[5]No development test set for News test were provided, so we present result for the News commentary, which can be expected to give similar results.

[6]The English translations need not be compounds. Compounds without a clear English translation were skipped.

	De ⇒ En		En ⇒ De	
	Subm	Base	Subm	Base
Correct	50	46	40	39
Alternative	36	26	32	29
Form	5	7	6	8
Part	2	5	10	15
No equivalent	6	2	8	5
Wrong	1	7	1	1
Untranslated	–	7	3	3

Table 3: Results of the error analysis of compound translations

Table 3. For translation into English the submitted system handles compound translations considerably better than the baseline with 91% good translations compared to 79%. In the submitted system all compounds have a translation, compared to the baseline system which has 7% of the compounds untranslated. In the other translation direction the difference is smaller, the biggest difference is that the submitted system has fewer cases of partial translation.

5.2 Agreement in German NPs

To study the effects of using fine-grained POS-tags in the German sequence model, a similar close study of German NPs was performed. 100 English NPs having at least two dependents of the head noun were selected from a randomly chosen subsection of the development test set. Their translations in the baseline and submitted system were then identified. Translations that were not NPs were discarded. In about two thirds (62 out of 99) of the cases, the translations were identical. For the remainder, 12 translations were of equal quality, the submitted system had a better translation in 17 cases (46%), and a worse one in 8 cases (22%). In the majority of cases where the baseline was better, this was due to word selection, not agreement.

6 Conclusions

Adding morphological processing improved translation results in both directions for both text types. Splitting compounds gave a bigger effect for translation from German. Marking of compound parts worked well, with no untranslated parts left in the sample used for evaluation. The mini-evaluation of German NPs in English-German translation indicates that the morphologically rich POS-based sequence model for German also had a positive effect.

Acknowledgement

We would like to thank Joe Steinhauer for help with the evaluation of German output.

References

M. Collins, P. Koehn, and I. Kučerová. 2005. Clause restructuring for statistical machine translation. In *Proceedings of the 43rd Annual Meeting of the ACL*, pages 531–540, Ann Arbor, Michigan.

M. Holmqvist, S. Stymne, and L. Ahrenberg. 2007. Getting to know Moses: Initial experiments on German-English factored translation. In *Proceedings of the Second Workshop on Statistical Machine Translation*, pages 181–184, Prague, Czech Republic. Association for Computational Linguistics.

P. Koehn and K. Knight. 2003. Empirical methods for compound splitting. In *Proceedings of the tenth conference of EACL*, pages 187–193, Budapest, Hungary.

P. Koehn, H. Hoang, A. Birch, C. Callison-Burch, M. Federico, N. Bertoldi, B. Cowan, W. Shen, C. Moran, R. Zens, C. Dyer, O. Bojar, A. Constantin, and E. Herbst. 2007. Moses: Open source toolkit for statistical machine translation. In *Proceedings of the 45th Annual Meeting of the ACL, demonstration session*, Prague, Czech Republic.

S. Langer. 1998. Zur Morphologie und Semantik von Nominalkomposita. In *Tagungsband der 4. Konferenz zur Verarbeitung natürlicher Sprache (KONVENS)*, pages 83–97.

K. Papineni, S. Roukos, T. Ward, and W.-J. Zhu. 2002. BLEU: a method for automatic evaluation of machine translation. In *Proceedings of the 40th Annual Meeting of the ACL*, pages 311–318, Philadelphia, Pennsylvania.

M. Popović, D. Stein, and H. Ney. 2006. Statistical machine translation of German compound words. In *Proceedings of FinTAL - 5th International Conference on Natural Language Processing*, pages 616–624, Turku, Finland.

H. Schmid. 1994. Probabilistic part-of-speech tagging using decision trees. In *Preoceedings of the International Conference on New Methods in Language Processing*, Manchester, UK.

A. Stolcke. 2002. SRILM - an extensible language modeling toolkit. In *Proceedings of the International Conference on Spoken Language Processing (ICSLP)*, pages 901–904, Denver, Colorado.

Towards better Machine Translation Quality for the German–English Language Pairs

Philipp Koehn Abhishek Arun Hieu Hoang
School of Informatics
University of Edinburgh
pkoehn@inf.ed.ac.uk a.arun@sms.ed.ac.uk h.hoang@sms.ed.ac.uk

Abstract

The Edinburgh submissions to the shared task of the Third Workshop on Statistical Machine Translation (WMT-2008) incorporate recent advances to the open source Moses system. We made a special effort on the German–English and English–German language pairs, leading to substantial improvements.

1 Introduction

Edinburgh University participated in the shared task of the Third Workshop on Statistical Machine Translation (WMT-2008), which is partly funded by the EUROMATRIX project, which also funds our work. In this project, we set out to build machine translation systems for all language pairs of official EU languages. Hence, we also participated in the shared task in all language pairs.

For all language pairs, we used the Moses decoder (Koehn et al., 2007), which follows the phrase-based statistical machine translation approach (Koehn et al., 2003), with default settings as a starting point. We recently added minimum Bayes risk decoding and reordering constraints to the decoder. We achieved consistent increase in BLEU scores with these improvements, showing gains of up to 0.9% BLEU on the 2008 news test set.

Most of our efforts were focused on the language pairs German–English and English–German. For both language pairs, we explored language-specific and more general improvements, resulting in gains of up to 1.5% BLEU for German–English and 1.4% BLEU for English–German.

2 Recent Improvements

Over the last months, we added minimum Bayes risk decoding and additional reordering constraints to the Moses decoder. The WMT-2008 shared task offered the opportunity to assess these components over a large range of language pairs and tasks.

For all our experiments, we trained solely on the Europarl corpus, which allowed us to treat the 2007 news commentary test set (nc-test2007) as a stand-in for the 2008 news test set (news-2008), for which we have no in-domain training data. This may have resulted in lower performance due to less (and very relevant) training data, but it also allowed us to optimize for a true out-of-domain test set.

The baseline training uses Moses default parameters. We use a maximum sentence length of 80, a phrase translation table with the five traditional features, lexicalized reordering, and lowercase training and test data. All reported BLEU scores are not case-sensitive, computed using the NIST tool.

2.1 Minimum Bayes Risk Decoding

Minimum Bayes risk decoding was proposed by Kumar and Byrne (2004). Instead of selecting the translation with the highest probability, minimum Bayes risk decoding selects the translation that is most similar to the highest scoring translations. Intuitively, this avoid the selection of an outlier as the best translation, since the decision rule prefers translations that are similar to other high-scoring translations.

Minimum Bayes risk decoding is defined as:

$$\mathbf{e}_{\text{MBR}} = \text{argmax}_{\mathbf{e}} \sum_{\mathbf{e}'} L(\mathbf{e}, \mathbf{e}')\ p(\mathbf{e}'|\mathbf{f})$$

As similarity function L, we use sentence-level BLEU with add-one smoothing. As highest scoring translations, we consider the top 100 distinct translations, for which we convert the translation scores into a probability distribution p (with a scaling factor of 1). We tried other n-best list sizes and scaling factors, with very similar outcomes.

Proceedings of the Third Workshop on Statistical Machine Translation, pages 139–142,
Columbus, Ohio, USA, June 2008.

Language Pair	Baseline	MBR	MP	MBR+MP
Spanish–German news	11.7	11.8 (+0.1)	11.9 (+0.2)	12.0 (+0.3)
Spanish–German ep	20.7	21.0 (+0.3)	20.8 (+0.1)	21.0 (+0.3)
German–Spanish news	16.2	16.3 (+0.1)	16.4 (+0.2)	16.6 (+0.4)
German–Spanish ep	28.5	28.6 (+0.1)	28.5 (±0.0)	28.6 (+0.1)
Spanish–English news	19.8	20.2 (+0.4)	20.2 (+0.4)	20.3 (+0.5)
Spanish–English ep	33.6	33.7 (+0.1)	33.6 (±0.0)	33.7 (+0.1)
English–Spanish news	20.1	20.5 (+0.4)	20.5 (+0.4)	20.7 (+0.6)
English–Spanish ep	33.1	33.1 (±0.0)	33.0 (–0.1)	33.1 (±0.0)
French–English news	18.5	19.1 (+0.6)	19.1 (+0.6)	19.2 (+0.7)
French–English ep	33.5	33.5 (±0.0)	33.4 (–0.1)	33.5 (±0.0)
English–French news	17.8	18.0 (+0.2)	18.2 (+0.4)	18.3 (+0.5)
English–French ep	31.1	31.1 (±0.0)	31.1 (±0.0)	31.1 (±0.0)
Czech–English news	14.2	14.4 (+0.2)	14.3 (+0.1)	14.5 (+0.3)
Czech–English nc	22.8	23.0 (+0.2)	22.9 (+0.2)	23.0 (+0.2)
English–Czech news	9.6	9.6 (±0.0)	9.7 (+0.1)	9.6 (±0.0)
English–Czech nc	12.9	13.0 (+0.1)	12.9 (±0.0)	13.0 (+0.1)
Hungarian–English news	7.9	8.3 (+0.4)	8.5 (+0.6)	8.8 (+0.9)
English–Hungarian news	6.1	6.3 (+0.2)	6.4 (+0.3)	6.5 (+0.4)
average news	-	+0.26	+0.33	+0.46
average ep	-	+0.08	–0.02	+0.08

Table 1: Improvements in BLEU on the test sets test2008 (ep), newstest2008 (news) and nc-test2008 (nc) for minimum Bayes risk decoding (MBR) and the monotone-at-punctuation reordering (MP) constraint.

2.2 Monotone at Punctuation

The reordering models in phrase-based translation systems are known to be weak, since they essentially relies on the interplay of language model, a general preference for monotone translation, and (in the case of lexicalized reordering) a local model based on a window of neighboring phrase translations. Allowing any kind of reordering typically reduces translation performance, so reordering is limited to a window of (in our case) six words.

One noticeable weakness is that the current model frequently reorders words beyond clause boundaries, which is almost never well-motivated, and leads to confusing translations. Since clause boundaries are often indicated by punctuation such as comma, colon, or semicolon, it is straight-forward to introduce a reordering constraint that addresses this problem.

Our implementation of a monotone-at-punctuation reordering constraint (Tillmann and Ney, 2003) requires that all input words before clause-separating punctuation have be translated, before words afterwards are covered. Note that this constraint does not limit in any way phrase translations that span punctuation.

2.3 Results

Table 1 summarizes the impact of minimum Bayes risk decoding (MBR) and the monotone-at-punctuation reordering constraint (MP). Scores show higher gains for out-of-domain news test sets (+0.46) than for in-domain Europarl sets (+0.08).

3 German–English

Translating between German and English is surprisingly difficult, given that the languages are closely related. The main sources for this difficulty is the different syntactic structure at the clause level and the rich German morphology, including the merging of noun compounds.

In prior work, we addressed **reordering** with a pre-order model that transforms German for training and testing according to a set of hand-crafted rules (Collins et al., 2005). Employing this method to our baseline system leads to an improvement of +0.8 BLEU on the nc-test2007 set and +0.5 BLEU on the test2007 set.

German–English	nc-test2007	test2007
baseline	20.3	27.6
tokenize hyphens	20.1 (–0.2)	27.6 (±0.0)
tok. hyph. + truecase	20.7 (+0.4)	27.8 (+0.2)

Table 2: Impact of truecasing on case-sensitive BLEU

In a more integrated approach, factored translation models (Koehn and Hoang, 2007) allow us to consider grammatical coherence in form of **part-of-speech language models**. When translating into output words, we also generate a part-of-speech tag along with each output word. Since there are only 46 POS tags in English, we are able to train high-order n-gram models of these sequences. In our experiments, we used a 7-gram model, yielding improvements of +0.2/–0.1. We obtained the POS tags using Brill's tagger (Brill, 1995).

Next, we considered the problem of unknown input words, which is partly due to hyphenated words, noun compounds, and morphological variants. Using the baseline model, 907 words (1.78%) in nc-test2007 and 262 (0.47%) in test2007 are unknown. First we separate our **hyphens** by tokenizing words such as *high-risk* into *high @-@ risk*. This reduces the number of unknown words to 791/224. Unfortunately, it hurts us in terms of BLEU (–0.1/–0.1). Second, we **split compounds** using the frequency-based method (Koehn and Knight, 2003), reducing the number of unknown words to than half, 424/94, improving BLEU on nc-test2007 (+0.5/–0.2).

A final modification to the data preparation is **truecasing**. Traditionally, we lowercase all training and test data, but especially in German, case marks important distinctions. German nouns are capitalized, and keeping case allows us to make the distinction between, say, the noun *Wissen* (*knowledge*) and the verb *wissen* (*to know*). By truecasing, we only change the case of the first word of a sentence to its most common form. This method still needs some refinements, such as the handling of headlines or all-caps text, but it did improve performance over the hyphen-tokenized baseline (+0.3/+0.2) and the original baseline (+0.2/+0.1).

Note that truecasing simplifies the recasing problem, so a better way to gauge its effect is to look at the case-sensitive BLEU score. Here the difference are slightly larger over both the hyphen-tokenized baseline (+0.6/+0.2) and the original baseline (+0.4/+0.2). See the Table 2 for details.

German–English	nc-test2007	test2007
baseline	21.3	28.4
pos lm	21.5 (+0.2)	28.3 (–0.1)
reorder	22.1 (+0.8)	28.9 (+0.5)
tokenize hyphens	21.2 (–0.1)	28.3 (–0.1)
tok. hyph. + split	21.8 (+0.5)	28.2 (–0.2)
tok. hyph. + truecase	21.5 (+0.2)	28.5 (+0.1)
mp	21.6 (+0.3)	28.2 (–0.2)
mbr	21.4 (+0.1)	28.3 (–0.1)
big beam	21.3 (±0.0)	28.3 (–0.1)

Table 3: Impact of individual modifications for German–English, measured in BLEU on the development sets

German–English	nc-test2007	test2007
baseline	21.3	28.4
+ reorder	22.1 (+0.8)	28.9 (+0.5)
+ tokenize hyphens	22.1 (+0.8)	28.9 (+0.5)
+ truecase	22.7 (+1.3)	28.9 (+0.5)
+ split	23.0 (+1.7)	29.1 (+0.7)
+ mbr	23.1 (+1.8)	29.3 (+0.9)
+ mp	23.3 (+2.0)	29.2 (+0.8)

Table 4: Impact of combined modifications for German–English, measured in BLEU on the development sets

As for the other language pairs, using the **monotone-at-punctuation** reordering constraint (+0.3/–0.2) and **minimum Bayes risk decoding** (+0.1/–0.1) mostly helps. We also tried **bigger beam** sizes (stack size 1000, phrase table limit 50), but without gains in BLEU (±0.0/–0.1).

Table 3 summarizes the contributions of the individual modifications we described above. For our final system, we added the improvements one by one (see Table 4), except for the bigger beam size and the POS language model. This led to an overall increase of +2.0/+0.8 over the baseline. Due to a bug in splitting, the system we submitted to the shared task had a score of only +1.5/+0.6 over the baseline.

4 English–German

For English–German, we applied many of the same methods as for the inverse language pair. Tokenizing out **hyphens** has questionable impact (–0.1/+0.1), while **truecasing** shows minor gains (±0.0/+0.1), slightly higher for case-sensitive scoring (+0.2/+0.3). We have not yet developed a method that is the analog of the compound splitting

English–German	nc-test2007	test-2007
baseline	14.6	21.0
tokenize hyphens	14.5 (–0.1)	21.1 (+0.1)
tok. hyph. + truecase	14.6 (±0.0)	21.1 (+0.1)
morph lm	15.7 (+1.1)	21.2 (+0.2)
mbr	14.9 (+0.3)	21.0 (±0.0)
mp	14.8 (+0.2)	20.9 (–0.1)
big beam	14.7 (+0.1)	21.0 (±0.0)

Table 5: Impact of individual modifications for English–German, measured in BLEU on the development sets

method — compound merging. We consider this an interesting challenge for future work.

While the rich German morphology on the source side mostly poses sparse data problems, on the target side it creates the problem of which morphological variant to choose. The right selection hinges on grammatical agreement within noun phrases, the role that each noun phrase plays in the clause, and the grammatical nature of the subject of a verb. We use LoPar (Schmidt and Schulte im Walde, 2000), which gives us **morphological features** such as case, gender, count, although in limited form, it often opts for more general categories such as *not genitive*. We include these features in a sequence model, as we used a sequence model over part-of-speech tags previously. The gains of this method are especially strong for the out-of-domain set (+1.1/+0.2).

Minimum Bayes risk decoding (+0.3/±0.0), the **monotone-at-punctuation** reordering constraint (+0.2/–0.1), and **bigger beam sizes** (+0.1/±0.0) have similar impact as for the other language pairs. See Table 5 for a summary of all modifications. By combining everything except for the bigger beam size, we obtain overall gains of +1.4/+0.4 over the baseline. For details, refer to Table 6.

5 Conclusions

We built Moses systems trained on either only Europarl data or, for Czech and Hungarian, the available training data. We showed gains with minimum Bayes risk decoding and a reordering constraint involving punctuation. For German↔English, we employed further language-specific improvements.

Acknowledgements: This work was supported in part under the EuroMatrix project funded by the European Commission (6th Framework Programme).

English–German	nc-test2007	test2007
baseline	14.6	21.0
+ tokenize hyphens	14.5 (–0.1)	21.1 (+0.1)
+ truecase	14.6 (±0.0)	21.1 (+0.1)
+ morph lm	15.4 (+0.8)	21.3 (+0.3)
+ mbr	15.7 (+1.1)	21.4 (+0.4)
+ mp	16.0 (+1.4)	21.4 (+0.4)

Table 6: Impact of combined modifications for English–German, measured in BLEU on the development sets

References

Brill, E. (1995). Transformation-based error-driven learning and natural language processing: A case study in part of speech tagging. *Computational Linguistics*, 21(4).

Collins, M., Koehn, P., and Kucerova, I. (2005). Clause restructuring for statistical machine translation. In *Proceedings of the 43rd Annual Meeting of the Association for Computational Linguistics (ACL'05)*, pages 531–540, Ann Arbor, Michigan. Association for Computational Linguistics.

Koehn, P. and Hoang, H. (2007). Factored translation models. In *Proceedings of the 2007 Joint Conference on Empirical Methods in Natural Language Processing and Computational Natural Language Learning (EMNLP-CoNLL)*, pages 868–876.

Koehn, P., Hoang, H., Birch, A., Callison-Burch, C., Federico, M., Bertoldi, N., Cowan, B., Shen, W., Moran, C., Zens, R., Dyer, C., Bojar, O., Constantin, A., and Herbst, E. (2007). Moses: Open source toolkit for statistical machine translation. In *Proceedings of the 45th Annual Meeting of the Association for Computational Linguistics Companion Volume Proceedings of the Demo and Poster Sessions*, pages 177–180, Prague, Czech Republic. Association for Computational Linguistics.

Koehn, P. and Knight, K. (2003). Empirical methods for compound splitting. In *Proceedings of Meeting of the European Chapter of the Association of Computational Linguistics (EACL)*.

Koehn, P., Och, F. J., and Marcu, D. (2003). Statistical phrase based translation. In *Proceedings of the Joint Conference on Human Language Technologies and the Annual Meeting of the North American Chapter of the Association of Computational Linguistics (HLT-NAACL)*.

Kumar, S. and Byrne, W. (2004). Minimum bayes-risk decoding for statistical machine translation. In *Proceedings of the Joint Conference on Human Language Technologies and the Annual Meeting of the North American Chapter of the Association of Computational Linguistics (HLT-NAACL)*.

Schmidt, H. and Schulte im Walde, S. (2000). Robust German noun chunking with a probabilistic context-free grammar. In *Proceedings of the International Conference on Computational Linguistics (COLING)*.

Tillmann, C. and Ney, H. (2003). Word reordering and a dynamic programming beam search algorithm for statistical machine translation. *Computational Linguistics*, 29(1).

Phrase-Based and Deep Syntactic English-to-Czech Statistical Machine Translation *

Ondřej Bojar and **Jan Hajič**
Institute of Formal and Applied Linguistics
ÚFAL MFF UK, Malostranské náměstí 25
CZ-11800 Praha, Czech Republic
{bojar,hajic}@ufal.mff.cuni.cz

Abstract

This paper describes our two contributions to WMT08 shared task: factored phrase-based model using Moses and a probabilistic tree-transfer model at a deep syntactic layer.

1 Introduction

Czech is a Slavic language with very rich morphology and relatively free word order. The Czech morphological system (Hajič, 2004) defines 4,000 tags in theory and 2,000 were actually seen in a big tagged corpus while the English Penn Treebank tagset contains just about 50 tags. In our parallel corpus (see below), the English vocabulary size is 148k distinct word forms but more than twice as big in Czech, 343k distinct word forms.

When translating to Czech from an analytic language such as English, target word forms have to be chosen correctly to produce a grammatical sentence and preserve the expressed relations between elements in the sentence, e.g. verbs and their modifiers.

This year, we have taken two radically different approaches to English-to-Czech MT. Section 2 describes our setup of the phrase-based system Moses (Koehn et al., 2007) and Section 3 focuses on a system with probabilistic tree transfer employed at a deep syntactic layer and the new challenges this approach brings.

*The work on this project was supported by the grants FP6-IST-5-034291-STP (EuroMatrix), MSM0021620838, MŠMT ČR LC536, and GA405/06/0589.

2 Factored Phrase-Based MT to Czech

Bojar (2007) describes various experiments with factored translation to Czech aimed at improving target-side morphology. We use essentially the same setup with some cleanup and significantly larger target-side training data:

Parallel data from CzEng 0.7 (Bojar et al., 2008), with original sentence-level alignment and tokenization. The parallel corpus was taken as a monolithic text source disregarding differences between CzEng data sources. We use only 1-1 aligned sentences.

Word alignment using GIZA++ toolkit (Och and Ney, 2000), the default configuration as available in training scripts for Moses. We based the word alignment on Czech and English lemmas (base forms of words) as provided by the combination of taggers and lemmatizers by Hajič (2004) for Czech and Brants (2000) followed by Minnen et al. (2001) for English. We symmetrized the two GIZA++ runs using grow-diag-final heuristic.

Truecasing. We attempted to preserve meaning-bearing case distinctions. The Czech lemmatizer produces case-sensitive lemmas and thus makes it easy to cast the capitalization of the lemma back on the word form.[1] For English we approximate the same effect by a two-step procedure.[2]

[1]We change the capitalization of the form to match the lemma in cases where the lemma is lowercase, capitalized (ucfirst) or all-caps. For mixed-case lemmas, we keep the form intact.

[2]We first collect a lexicon of the most typical "shapes" for each word form (ignoring title-like sentences with most words capitalized and the first word in a sentence). Capitalized and all-caps words in title-like sentences are then changed to their

Proceedings of the Third Workshop on Statistical Machine Translation, pages 143–146,
Columbus, Ohio, USA, June 2008. ©2008 Association for Computational Linguistics

Decoding steps. We use a simple two-step scenario similar to class-based models (Brown and others, 1992): (1) the source English word forms are translated to Czech word forms and (2) full Czech morphological tags are generated from the Czech forms.

Language models. We use the following 6 independently weighted language models for the target (Czech) side:

- 3-grams of word forms based on all CzEng 0.7 data, 15M tokens,
- 3-grams of word forms in Project Syndicate section of CzEng (in-domain for WMT07 and WMT08 NC-test set), 1.8M tokens,
- 4-grams of word forms based on Czech National Corpus (Kocek et al., 2000), version SYN2006, 365M tokens,
- three models of 7-grams of morphological tags from the same sources.

Lexicalized reordering using the monotone/swap/discontinuous bidirectional model based on both source and target word forms.

MERT. We use the minimum-error rate training procedure by Och (2003) as implemented in the Moses toolkit to set the weights of the various translation and language models, optimizing for BLEU.

Final detokenization is a simple rule-based procedure based on Czech typographical conventions. Finally, we capitalize the beginnings of sentences.

See BLEU scores in Table 2 below.

3 MT with a Deep Syntactic Transfer

3.1 Theoretical Background

Czech has a well-established theory of linguistic analysis called Functional Generative Description (Sgall et al., 1986) supported by a big treebanking enterprise (Hajič and others, 2006) and on-going adaptations for other languages including English (Cinková and others, 2004). There are two layers

typical shape. In other sentences we change the case only if a typically lowercase word is capitalized (e.g. at the beginning of the sentence) or if a typically capitalized word is all-caps. Unknown words in title-like sentences are lowercased and left intact in other sentences.

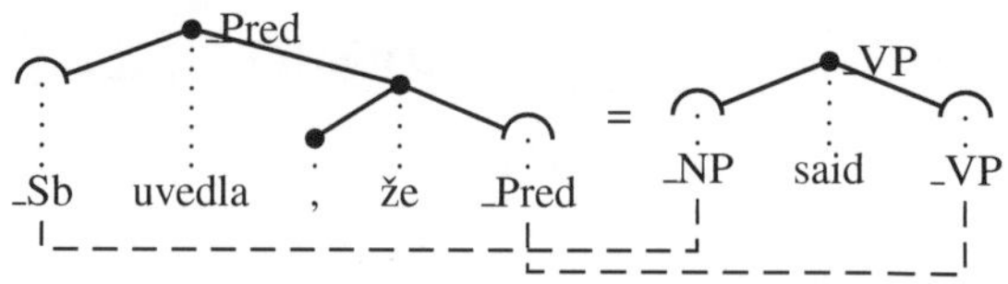

Figure 1: Sample treelet pair, a-layer.

of syntactic analysis, both formally captured as labelled ordered dependency trees: the ANALYTICAL (a-, surface syntax) representation bears a 1-1 correspondence between tokens in the sentence and nodes in the tree; the TECTOGRAMMATICAL (t-, deep syntax) representation contains nodes only for autosemantic words and adds nodes for elements not expressed on the surface but required by the grammar (e.g. dropped pronouns).

We use the following tools to automatically annotate plaintext up to the t-layer: (1) TextSeg (Češka, 2006) for tokenization, (2) tagging and lemmatization see above, (3) parsing to a-layer: Collins (1996) followed by head-selection rules for English, McDonald and others (2005) for Czech, (4) parsing to t-layer: Žabokrtský (2008) for English, Klimeš (2006) for Czech.

3.2 Probabilistic Tree Transfer

The transfer step is based on Synchronous Tree Substitution Grammars (STSG), see Bojar and Čmejrek (2007) for a detailed explanation. The essence is a log-linear model to search for the most likely synchronous derivation $\hat{\delta}$ of the source T_1 and target T_2 dependency trees:

$$\hat{\delta} = \underset{\delta \text{ s.t. source is } T_1}{\text{argmax}} \exp\Big(\sum_{m=1}^{M} \lambda_m h_m(\delta)\Big) \quad (1)$$

The key feature function h_m in STSG represents the probability of attaching pairs of dependency treelets $t^i_{1:2}$ such as in Figure 1 into aligned pairs of frontiers ($\frown$) in another treelet pair $t^j_{1:2}$ given frontier state labels (e.g. _Pred-_VP in Figure 1):

$$h_{STSG}(\delta) = \log \prod_{i=0}^{k} p(t^i_{1:2} \mid \text{frontier states}) \quad (2)$$

Other features include e.g. number of internal nodes (drawn as • in Figure 1) produced, number of treelets produced, and more importantly the traditional n-gram language model if the target (a-)tree is linearized right away or a binode model promoting likely combinations of the governor $g(e)$ and the child $c(e)$ of an edge $e \in T_2$:

$$h_{binode}(\delta) = \log \prod_{e \in T_2} p(c(e) \mid g(e)) \quad (3)$$

The probabilistic dictionary of aligned treelet pairs is extracted from node-aligned (GIZA++ on linearized trees) parallel automatic treebank as in Moses' training: all treelet pairs compatible with the node alignment.

3.2.1 Factored Treelet Translation

Labels of nodes at the t-layer are not atomic but consist of more than 20 attributes representing various linguistic features.[3] We can consider the attributes as individual factors (Koehn and Hoang, 2007). This allows us to condition the translation choice on a subset of source factors only. In order to generate a value for each target-side factor, we use a sequence of mapping steps similar to Koehn and Hoang (2007). For technical reasons, our current implementation allows to generate factored target-side only when translating a single node to a single node, i.e. preserving the tree structure.

In our experiments we used 8 source (English) t-node attributes and 14 target (Czech) attributes.

3.3 Recent Experimental Results

Table 1 shows BLEU scores for various configurations of our decoder. The abbreviations indicate between which layers the tree transfer was employed (e.g. "eact" means English a-layer to Czech t-layer). The "p" layer is an approximation of phrase-based MT: the surface "syntactic" analysis is just a left-to-right linear tree.[4] For setups ending in t-layer, we use a deterministic generation the of Czech sentence by Ptáček and Žabokrtský (2006).

For WMT08 shared task, Table 2, we used a variant of the "etct factored" setup with the annotation pipeline as incorporated in TectoMT (Žabokrtský, 2008) environment and using TectoMT internal rules for t-layer parsing and generation instead of Klimeš (2006) and (Ptáček and Žabokrtský, 2006).

[3]Treated as atomic, t-node labels have higher entropy (11.54) than lowercase plaintext (10.74). The t-layer by itself does not bring any reduction in vocabulary. The idea is that the attributes should be more or less independent and should map easier across languages.

[4]Unlike Moses, "epcp" does not permit phrase reordering.

Tree-based Transfer	LM Type	BLEU
epcp	n-gram	10.9±0.6
eaca	n-gram	8.8±0.6
epcp	none	8.7±0.6
eaca	none	6.6±0.5
etca	n-gram	6.3±0.6
etct factored, preserving structure	binode	5.6±0.5
etct factored, preserving structure	none	5.3±0.5
eact, target side atomic	binode	3.0±0.3
etct, atomic, all attributes	binode	2.6±0.3
etct, atomic, all attributes	none	1.6±0.3
etct, atomic, just t-lemmas	none	0.7±0.2
Phrase-based (Moses) as reported by Bojar (2007)		
Vanilla	n-gram	12.9±0.6
Factored to improve target morphology	n-gram	14.2±0.7

Table 1: English-to-Czech BLEU scores for syntax-based MT on WMT07 DevTest.

	WMT07	WMT08	
	DevTest	NC Test	News Test
Moses	14.9±0.9	16.4±0.6	12.3±0.6
Moses, CzEng data only	13.9±0.9	15.2±0.6	10.0±0.5
etct, TectoMT annotation	4.7±0.5	4.9±0.3	3.3±0.3

Table 2: WMT08 shared task BLEU scores.

3.3.1 Discussion

Our syntax-based approach does not reach scores of phrase-based MT due to the following reasons:

Cumulation of errors at every step of analysis.

Data loss due to incompatible parses and node alignment. Unlike e.g. Quirk et al. (2005) or Huang et al. (2006) who parse only one side and project the structure, we parse both languages independently. Natural divergence and random errors in either of the parses and/or the alignment prevent us from extracting many treelet pairs.

Combinatorial explosion in target node attributes. Currently, treelet options are fully built in advance. Uncertainty in the many t-node attributes leads to too many insignificant variations while e.g. different lexical choices are pushed off the stack. While vital for final sentence generation (see Table 1), fine-grained t-node attributes should be produced only once all key structural, lexical and form decisions have been made. The same sort of explosion makes complicated factored setups not yet feasible in Moses, either.

Lack of n-gram LM in the (deterministic) generation procedures from a t-tree. While we support final LM-based rescoring, there is too little variance in n-best lists due to the explosion mentioned above.

Too many model parameters given our stack limit. We use identical MERT implementation to optimize λ_ms but in the large space of hypotheses, MERT does not converge.

3.3.2 Related Research

Our approach should not be confused with the TectoMT submission by Zdeněk Žabokrtský with a deterministic transfer: heuristics fully exploiting the similarity of English and Czech t-layers.

Ding and Palmer (2005) improve over word-based MT baseline with a formalism very similar to STSG. Though not explicitly stated, they seem not to encode frontiers in the treelets and allow for adjunction (adding siblings), like Quirk et al. (2005), which significantly reduces data sparseness.

Riezler and III (2006) report an improvement in MT grammaticality on a very restricted test set: short sentences parsable by an LFG grammar without back-off rules.

4 Conclusion

We have presented our best-performing factored phrase-based English-to-Czech translation and a highly experimental complex system with tree-based transfer at a deep syntactic layer. We have discussed some of the reasons why the phrase-based MT currently performs much better.

References

Ondřej Bojar and Martin Čmejrek. 2007. Mathematical Model of Tree Transformations. Project EuroMatrix - Deliverable 3.2, ÚFAL, Charles University, Prague.

Ondřej Bojar, Zdeněk Žabokrtský, Pavel Češka, Peter Beňa, and Miroslav Janíček. 2008. CzEng 0.7: Parallel Corpus with Community-Supplied Translations. In *Proc. of LREC 2008*. ELRA.

Ondřej Bojar. 2007. English-to-Czech Factored Machine Translation. In *Proc. of ACL Workshop on Statistical Machine Translation*, pages 232–239, Prague.

Thorsten Brants. 2000. TnT - A Statistical Part-of-Speech Tagger . In *Proc. of ANLP-NAACL*.

Peter F. Brown et al. 1992. Class-based n-gram models of natural language. *Computational Linguistics*, 18(4):467–479.

Pavel Češka. 2006. Segmentace textu. Bachelor's Thesis, MFF, Charles University in Prague.

Silvie Cinková et al. 2004. Annotation of English on the tectogrammatical level. Technical Report TR-2006-35, ÚFAL/CKL, Prague, Czech Republic.

Michael Collins. 1996. A New Statistical Parser Based on Bigram Lexical Dependencies. In *Proc. of ACL*.

Yuan Ding and Martha Palmer. 2005. Machine Translation Using Probabilistic Synchronous Dependency Insertion Grammars. In *Proc. of ACL*.

Jan Hajič. 2004. *Disambiguation of Rich Inflection (Computational Morphology of Czech)*. Nakladatelství Karolinum, Prague.

Jan Hajič et al. 2006. Prague Dependency Treebank 2.0. LDC2006T01, ISBN: 1-58563-370-4.

Liang Huang, Kevin Knight, and Aravind Joshi. 2006. Statistical Syntax-Directed Translation with Extended Domain of Locality. In *Proc. of AMTA*, Boston, MA.

Václav Klimeš. 2006. *Analytical and Tectogrammatical Analysis of a Natural Language*. Ph.D. thesis, ÚFAL, MFF UK, Prague, Czech Republic.

Jan Kocek, Marie Kopřivová, and Karel Kučera, editors. 2000. *Český národní korpus - úvod a příručka uživatele*. FF UK - ÚČNK, Praha.

Philipp Koehn and Hieu Hoang. 2007. Factored Translation Models. In *Proc. of EMNLP*.

Philipp Koehn, Hieu Hoang, et al. 2007. Moses: Open Source Toolkit for Statistical Machine Translation. In *Proc. of ACL Demo and Poster Sessions*.

Ryan McDonald et al. 2005. Non-Projective Dependency Parsing using Spanning Tree Algorithms. In *Proc. of HLT/EMNLP 2005*.

Guido Minnen, John Carroll, and Darren Pearce. 2001. Applied morphological processing of English. *Natural Language Engineering*, 7(3):207–223.

Franz Josef Och and Hermann Ney. 2000. A Comparison of Alignment Models for Statistical Machine Translation. In *Proc. of COLING*, pages 1086–1090.

Franz Josef Och. 2003. Minimum Error Rate Training in Statistical Machine Translation. In *Proc. of ACL*.

Jan Ptáček and Zdeněk Žabokrtský. 2006. Synthesis of Czech Sentences from Tectogrammatical Trees. In *Proc. of TSD*, pages 221–228.

Chris Quirk, Arul Menezes, and Colin Cherry. 2005. Dependency Treelet Translation: Syntactically Informed Phrasal SMT. In *Proc. of ACL*, pages 271–279.

Stefan Riezler and John T. Maxwell III. 2006. Grammatical Machine Translation. In *Proc. of HLT/NAACL*.

Petr Sgall, Eva Hajičová, and Jarmila Panevová. 1986. *The Meaning of the Sentence and Its Semantic and Pragmatic Aspects*. Academia, Prague.

Zdeněk Žabokrtský. 2008. Tecto MT. Technical report, ÚFAL/CKL, Prague, Czech Republic. In prep.

Improving English-Spanish Statistical Machine Translation: Experiments in Domain Adaptation, Sentence Paraphrasing, Tokenization, and Recasing

Preslav Nakov*
EECS, CS division
University of California at Berkeley
Berkeley, CA 94720
nakov@cs.berkeley.edu

Abstract

We describe the experiments of the UC Berkeley team on improving English-Spanish machine translation of news text, as part of the WMT'08 Shared Translation Task. We experiment with domain adaptation, combining a small in-domain news bi-text and a large out-of-domain one from the Europarl corpus, building two separate phrase translation models and two separate language models. We further add a third phrase translation model trained on a version of the news bi-text augmented with monolingual sentence-level syntactic paraphrases on the source-language side, and we combine all models in a log-linear model using minimum error rate training. Finally, we experiment with different tokenization and recasing rules, achieving 35.09% Bleu score on the WMT'07 news test data when translating from English to Spanish, which is a sizable improvement over the highest Bleu score achieved on that dataset at WMT'07: 33.10% (in fact, by our system). On the WMT'08 English to Spanish news translation, we achieve 21.92%, which makes our team the second best on Bleu score.

1 Introduction

Modern Statistical Machine Translation (SMT) systems are trained on sentence-aligned bilingual corpora, typically from a single domain. When tested on text from that same domain, they demonstrate state-of-the art performance, but on out-of-domain test data the results can get significantly worse. For example, on the WMT'06 Shared Translation Task, the scores for French to English translation dropped from about 30 to about 20 Bleu points for nearly all systems when tested on *News Commentary* rather than *Europarl* text, which was used on training (Koehn and Monz, 2006).

Therefore, in 2007 the Shared Task organizers provided 1M words of bilingual *News Commentary* training data in addition to the 30M *Europarl* data, thus inviting interest in domain adaptation experiments. Given the success of the idea, the same task was offered this year with slightly larger training bi-texts: 1.3M and 32M words, respectively.

2 System Parameters

The team of the University of California at Berkeley (ucb) participated in the WMT'08 Shared Translation Task with two systems, English→Spanish and Spanish→English, applied to translating *News Commentary* text, for which a very limited amount of training data was provided. We experimented with domain adaptation, combining the provided small in-domain bi-text and the large out-of-domain one from the *Europarl* corpus, building two phrase translation models and two language models. We further added a third phrase translation model trained on a version of the news bi-text augmented with monolingual sentence-level syntactic paraphrases on the source-language side, and we combined all models in one big log-linear model using minimum error rate training. We also experimented with different tokenization and recasing ideas.

*After January 2008 at the Linguistic Modeling Department, Institute for Parallel Processing, Bulgarian Academy of Sciences, nakov@lml.bas.bg

Proceedings of the Third Workshop on Statistical Machine Translation, pages 147–150,
Columbus, Ohio, USA, June 2008.

2.1 Sentence-Level Syntactic Paraphrases

The idea of using paraphrases is motivated by the observation that, in many cases, the testing text contains pieces that are equivalent, but syntactically different from the phrases learned on training, which might result in missing the opportunity for a high-quality translation. For example, an English→Spanish SMT system could have an entry in its phrase table for *inequality of income*, but not for *income inequality*. Note that the latter phrase is hard to translate into Spanish where noun compounds are rare: the correct translation in this case requires a suitable Spanish preposition and a reordering, which are hard for the system to realize and do properly. We address this problem by generating nearly-equivalent syntactic paraphrases of the source-side training sentences, targeted at noun compounds. We then pair each paraphrased sentence with the foreign translation associated with the original sentence in the training data. The resulting augmented bi-text is used to train an SMT system, which learns many useful new phrases. The idea was introduced in (Nakov and Hearst, 2007), and is described in more detail in (Nakov, 2007).

Unfortunately, using multiple paraphrased versions of the same sentence changes the word frequencies in the training bi-text, thus causing worse maximum likelihood estimates, which results in bad system performance. However, real improvements can still be achieved by merging the phrase tables of the two systems, giving priority to the original.

2.2 Domain Adaptation

In our previous findings (Nakov and Hearst, 2007), we found that using in-domain and out-of-domain language models is the best way to perform domain adaptation. Following (Koehn and Schroeder, 2007), we further used two phrase tables.

2.3 Improving the Recaser

One problem we noticed with the default recasing is that unknown words are left in lowercase. However, many unknown words are in fact named entities (persons, organization, or locations), which should be spelled capitalized. Therefore, we prepared a new recasing script, which makes sure that all unknown words keep their original case.

2.4 Changing Tokenization/Detokenization

We found the default tokenizer problematic: it keeps complex adjectives as one word, e.g., *well-rehearsed*, *self-assured*, *Arab-Israeli*. While linguistically correct, this is problematic for machine translation due to data sparsity. For example, the SMT system might know how to translate into Spanish both *well* and *rehearsed*, but not *well-rehearsed*, and thus at translation time it would be forced to handle it as an unknown word. A similar problem is related to double dashes '--', as illustrated by the following training sentence: "*So the question now is what can China do to freeze--and, if possible, to reverse--North Korea's nuclear program.*"

Therefore, we changed the tokenizer, so that it puts a space around '-' and '--'. We also changed the detokenizer accordingly, adding some rules for fixing erroneous output, e.g., making sure that in Spanish text ¿ and ?, ¡ and ! match. We also added some rules for numbers, e.g., the English 1,185.32 should be spelled as 1.185,32 in Spanish.

3 The UCB System

As Table 1 shows, we performed many experiments varying different parameters of the system. Due to space limitations, here we will only describe our best system, $\text{news}_{10} \prec \text{euro}_{10} \prec \text{par}_{10}$.

To build the system, we trained three separate phrase-based SMT systems (max phrase lengths 10): on the original *News Commentary* corpus (*news*), on the paraphrased version of *News Commentary* (*par*), and on the *Europarl* dataset (*euro*). As a result, we obtained three phrase tables, T_{news}, T_{par}, and T_{euro}, and three lexicalized reordering models, R_{news}, R_{par}, and R_{euro}, which we had to merge.

First, we kept all phrase pairs from T_{news}. Then we added those phrase pairs from T_{euro} which were not present in T_{news}. Finally, we added to them those from T_{par} which were not in T_{news} nor in T_{euro}. For each phrase pair added, we retained its associated features: forward phrase translation probability, reverse phrase translation probability, forward lexical translation probability, reverse lexical translation probability, and phrase penalty. We further added three new features – P_{news}, P_{euro}, and P_{par} – each of them was 1 if the phrase pair came from that system, and 0.5 otherwise.

Model	BLEU DR	BLEU IR	Tokenizer	News Comm. slen	News Comm. plen	News Comm. LM	Europarl slen	Europarl plen	Europarl LM	Tuning #iter	Tuning score
1	2	3	4	5	6	7	8	9	10	11	12
I. Original Tokenizer											
news$_{7}$ (baseline)	32.04	32.30	def.	40	7	3	–	–	–	8	33.51
news$_{7}$	31.98	32.21	def.	100	7	3	–	–	–	19	33.95
news$_{10}$	32.43	32.67	def.	100	10	3	–	–	–	13	34.50
II. New Tokenizer											
- II.1. Europarl only											
euro$_{7}$	29.92	30.19	new	–	–	–	40	7	5	10	33.02
euro$_{10}$	30.14	30.36	new	–	–	–	40	10	5	10	32.86
- II.2. News Commentary only											
par$_{10}$	31.17	31.44	new	100	10	3	–	–	–	8	33.91
news$_{10}$	32.27	32.53	new	100	10	3	–	–	–	12	34.49
news$_{10}$$\prec$par$_{10}$	32.09	32.34	new	100	10	3	–	–	–	24	34.63
- II.3. News Commentary + Europarl											
-- II.3.1. using Europarl LM											
par$_{10}$	32.88	33.16	new	100	10	3	–	–	5	11	35.54
news$_{10}$	33.99	34.26	new	100	10	3	–	–	5	8	36.16
news$_{10}$$\prec$par$_{10}$	34.42	34.71	new	100	10	3	–	–	5	17	36.41
-- II.3.2. using Europarl LM & Phrase Table (max phrase length 7)											
$\star$news$_{10}$+euro$_{7}$+par$_{10}$	32.75	32.96	new	100	10	3	40	7	5	27	35.28
$\star$news$_{10}$+euro$_{7}$	34.06	34.32	new	100	10	3	40	7	5	28	36.82
news$_{10}$$\prec$euro$_{7}$	34.05	34.31	new	100	10	3	40	7	5	9	36.71
news$_{10}$$\prec$par$_{10}$$\prec$euro$_{7}$	34.25	34.52	new	100	10	3	40	7	5	14	36.88
news$_{10}$$\prec$euro$_{7}$$\prec$par$_{10}$	34.69	34.97	new	100	10	3	40	7	5	10	37.01
-- II.3.3. using Europarl LM & Phrase Table (max phrase length 10)											
$\star$news$_{10}$+euro$_{10}$+par$_{10}$	32.74	33.02	new	100	10	3	40	10	5	36	35.60
news$_{10}$$\prec$euro$_{10}$$\prec$par$_{10}$	**34.85**	**35.09**	**new**	**100**	**10**	**3**	**40**	**10**	**5**	**12**	**37.13**

Table 1: **English→Spanish translation experiments with the WMT'07 data: training on *News Commentary* and *Europarl*, and evaluating on *News Commentary*.** Column 1 provides a brief description of the model used. Here we use *euro*, *news* and *par* to refer to using phrase tables extracted from the *Europarl*, the *News Commentary*, or the *Paraphrased News Commentary* training bi-text; the index indicates the maximum phrase length allowed. The $\prec$ operation means the phrase tables are merged, giving priority to the left one and using additional features indicating where each phrase pair came from, while the $+$ operation indicates the phrase tables are used together without priorities. The models using the $+$ operation are marked with a $\star$ as a reminder that the involved phrase tables are used together, as opposed to being priority-merged. Note also that the models from II.3.1. only use the Spanish part of the *Europarl* training data to build an out-of-domain language model; this is not indicated in column 1, but can be seen in column 10. Columns 2 and 3 show the testing Bleu score after applying the Default Recaser (*DR*) and the Improved Recaser (*IR*), respectively. Column 4 shows whether the default or the new tokenizer was used. Columns 5, 6 and 7 contain the parameters of the *News Commentary* training data: maximum length of the training sentences used (*slen*), maximum length of the extracted phrases (*plen*), and order of the language model (*LM*), respectively. Columns 8, 9 and 10 contain the same parameters for the *Europarl* training data. Column 11 shows the number of iterations the MERT tuning took, and column 12 gives the corresponding tuning Bleu score achieved. Finally, for the WMT'08 competition, we used the system marked in bold.

We further merged R_{news}, R_{euro}, and R_{par} in a similar manner: we first kept all phrases from R_{news}, then we added those from R_{euro} which were not present in R_{news}, and finally those from R_{par} which were not in R_{news} nor in R_{euro}.

We used two language models with Kneser-Ney smoothing: a 3-gram model trained on *News Commentary*, and a 5-gram model trained on *Europarl*.

We then trained a log-linear model using the following feature functions: language model probabilities, word penalty, distortion cost, and the parameters from the phrase table. We set the feature weights by optimizing the *Bleu* score directly using minimum error rate training (Och, 2003) on the development set. We used these weights in a beam search decoder to produce translations for the test sentences, which we compared to the WMT'07 gold standard using *Bleu* (Papineni et al., 2002).

4 Results and Discussion

Table 1 shows the evaluation results using the WMT'07 *News Commentary* test data. Our best English→Spanish system $news_{10} \prec euro_{10} \prec par_{10}$ (see the table caption for explanation of the notation), which is also our submission, achieved 35.09 Bleu score with the improved recaser; with the default recaser, the score drops to 34.85.

Due to space limitations, our Spanish→English results are not in Table 1. This time, we did not use paraphrases, and our best system $news_{10} \prec euro_{10}$ achieved 35.78 and 35.17 Bleu score with the improved and the default recaser, respectively.

As the table shows, using the improved recaser yields consistent improvements by about 0.3 Bleu points. Using an out-of-domain language model adds about 2 additional Bleu points, e.g., $news_{10}$ improves from 32.53 to 34.26, and $news_{10} \prec par_{10}$ improves from 32.34 to 34.71. The impact of also adding an out-of-domain phrase table is tiny: $news_{10} \prec euro_7$ improves on $news_{10}$ by 0.05 only. Adding paraphrases however can yield an absolute improvement of about 0.6, e.g., 34.31 vs. 34.97 for $news_{10} \prec euro_7$ and $news_{10} \prec euro_7 \prec par_{10}$. Interestingly, using an out-of-domain phrase table has a bigger impact when paraphrases are used, e.g., for $news_{10} \prec par_{10}$ and $news_{10} \prec euro_7 \prec par_{10}$ we have 34.71 and 34.97, respectively. Finally, we were surprised to find out that using the new tokenizer does not help: for $news_{10}$ the default tokenizer yields 32.67, while the new one only achieves 32.53. This is surprising for us, since the new tokenizer used to help consistent on the WMT'06 data.

5 Conclusions and Future Work

We described the UCB system for the WMT'08 Shared Translation Task. By combining in-domain and out-of-domain data, and by using sentence-level syntactic paraphrases and a better recaser, we achieved an improvement of almost 2 Bleu points[1] over the best result on the WMT'07 test data[2], and the second best Bleu score for this year's English→Spanish translation of news text.

In future work, we plan a deeper analysis of the obtained results. First, we would like to experiment with new ways to combine data from different domains. We also plan to further improve the recaser, and to investigate why the new tokenizer did not help for the WMT'07 data.

References

Philipp Koehn and Christof Monz. 2006. Manual and automatic evaluation of machine translation between european languages. In *Proceedings on the Workshop on Statistical Machine Translation*, pages 102–121.

Philipp Koehn and Josh Schroeder. 2007. Experiments in domain adaptation for statistical machine translation. In *Proceedings of the Second Workshop on Statistical Machine Translation*, pages 224–227. Association for Computational Linguistics.

Preslav Nakov and Marti Hearst. 2007. UCB system description for the WMT 2007 shared task. In *Workshop on Statistical Machine Translation*, pages 212–215.

Preslav Nakov. 2007. *Using the Web as an Implicit Training Set: Application to Noun Compound Syntax and Semantics*. Ph.D. thesis, EECS Department, University of California, Berkeley, UCB/EECS-2007-173.

Franz Josef Och. 2003. Minimum error rate training in statistical machine translation. In *Proceedings of ACL*, pages 160–167.

Kishore Papineni, Salim Roukos, Todd Ward, and Wei-Jing Zhu. 2002. Bleu: a method for automatic evaluation of machine translation. In *Proceedings of ACL*, pages 311–318.

[1] Note however that this year we had more training data compared to last year: 1.3M vs. 1M words for *News Commentary*, and 32M vs. 30M words for *Europarl*.

[2] In fact, achieved by our system at WMT'07.

Improving Word Alignment with Language Model Based Confidence Scores

Nguyen Bach, Qin Gao, Stephan Vogel
InterACT, Language Technologies Institute
Carnegie Mellon University
Pittsburgh, PA 15213, USA
{nbach, qing, vogel+}@cs.cmu.edu

Abstract

This paper describes the statistical machine translation systems submitted to the ACL-WMT 2008 shared translation task. Systems were submitted for two translation directions: English→Spanish and Spanish→English. Using sentence pair confidence scores estimated with source and target language models, improvements are observed on the News-Commentary test sets. Genre-dependent sentence pair confidence score and integration of sentence pair confidence score into phrase table are also investigated.

1 Introduction

Word alignment models are a crucial component in statistical machine translation systems. When estimating the parameters of the word alignment models, the sentence pair probability is an important factor in the objective function and is approximated by the empirical probability. The empirical probability for each sentence pair is estimated by maximum likelihood estimation over the training data (Brown et al., 1993). Due to the limitation of training data, most sentence pairs occur only once, which makes the empirical probability almost uniform. This is a rather weak approximation of the true distribution.

In this paper, we investigate the methods of weighting sentence pairs using language models, and extended the general weighting method to genre-dependent weight. A method of integrating the weight directly into the phrase table is also explored.

2 The Baseline Phrase-Based MT System

The ACL-WMT08 organizers provided Europarl and News-Commentary parallel corpora for English ↔ Spanish. Detailed corpus statistics is given in Table 1. Following the guidelines of the workshop we built baseline systems, using the lower-cased Europarl parallel corpus (restricting sentence length to 40 words), GIZA++ (Och and Ney, 2003), Moses (Koehn et al., 2007), and the SRI LM toolkit (Stolcke, 2002) to build 5-gram LMs. Since no News development sets were available we chose News-Commentary sets as replacements. We used test-2006 (E06) and nc-devtest2007 (NCd) as development sets for Europarl and News-Commentary; test-2007 (E07) and nc-test2007 (NCt) as held-out evaluation sets.

	English	Spanish
Europarl (E)		
sentence pairs	1,258,778	
unique sent. pairs	1,235,134	
avg. sentence length	27.9	29.0
# words	35.14 M	36.54 M
vocabulary	108.7 K	164.8 K
News-Commentary (NC)		
sentence pairs	64,308	
unique sent. pairs	64,205	
avg. sentence length	24.0	27.4
# words	1.54 M	1.76 M
vocabulary	44.2 K	56.9 K

Table 1: Statistics of English↔Spanish Europarl and News-Commentary corpora

To improve the baseline performance we trained systems on all true-cased training data with sentence length up to 100. We used two language models, a 5-gram LM build from the Europarl corpus and a 3-gram LM build from the News-Commentary data. Instead of interpolating the two language models, we explicitly used them in the decoder and optimized their weights via minimum-error-rate (MER) training (Och, 2003). To shorten the training time, a multi-threaded GIZA++ version was used to utilize multi-processor servers (Gao and Vogel, 2008). Other parameters were the same as the baseline system. Table 2 shows results in lowercase BLEU (Papineni et al., 2002) for both the baseline (B) and the improved baseline systems (B5) on development and held-

Proceedings of the Third Workshop on Statistical Machine Translation, pages 151–154,
Columbus, Ohio, USA, June 2008.

out evaluation sets. We observed significant gains for the News-Commentary test sets. Our improved baseline systems obtained a comparable performance with the best English↔Spanish systems in 2007 (Callison-Burch et al., 2007).

Pairs		Europarl		NC	
		E06	E07	NCd	NCt
En→Es	B	33.00	32.21	31.84	30.56
	B5	33.33	32.25	35.10	34.08
Es→En	B	33.08	33.23	31.18	31.34
	B5	33.26	33.23	36.06	35.56

Table 2: NIST-BLEU scores of baseline and improved baseline systems experiments on English↔Spanish

3 Weighting Sentence Pairs

3.1 Problem Definition

The quality of word alignment is crucial for the performance of the machine translation system.

In the well-known so-called IBM word alignment models (Brown et al., 1993), re-estimating the model parameters depends on the empirical probability $\hat{P}(e^k, f^k)$ for each sentence pair (e^k, f^k). During the EM training, all counts of events, e.g. word pair counts, distortion model counts, etc., are weighted by $\hat{P}(e^k, f^k)$. For example, in IBM Model 1 the lexicon probability of source word **f** given target word **e** is calculated as (Och and Ney, 2003):

$$p(\mathbf{f}|\mathbf{e}) = \frac{\sum_k c(\mathbf{f}|\mathbf{e}; e^k, f^k)}{\sum_{k,\mathbf{f}} c(\mathbf{f}|\mathbf{e}; e^k, f^k)} \quad (1)$$

$$c(\mathbf{f}|\mathbf{e}; e^k, f^k) = \sum_{e^k, f^k} \hat{P}(e^k, f^k) \sum_a P(a|e^k, f^k) \cdot \sum_j \delta(\mathbf{f}, f_j^k)\delta(\mathbf{e}, e_{a_j}^k) \quad (2)$$

Therefore, the distribution of $\hat{P}(e^k, f^k)$ will affect the alignment results. In Eqn. 2, $\hat{P}(e^k, f^k)$ determines how much the alignments of sentence pair (e^k, f^k) contribute to the model parameters. It will be helpful if the $\hat{P}(e^k, f^k)$ can approximate the true distribution of $P(e^k, f^k)$.

Consider that we are drawing sentence pairs from a given data source, and each *unique* sentence pair (e^k, f^k) has a probability $P(e^k, f^k)$ to be observed. If the training corpora size is infinite, the normalized frequency of each unique sentence pair will converge to $P(e^k, f^k)$. In that case, equally assigning a number to each occurrence of (e^k, f^k) and normalizing it will be valid. However, the assumption is invalid if the data source is finite. As we can observe in the training corpora, most sentences occur only one time, and thus $\hat{P}(e^k, f^k)$ will be uniform.

To get a more informative $\hat{P}(e^k, f^k)$, we explored methods of weighting sentence pairs. We investigated three sets of features: sentence pair confidence (sc), genre-dependent sentence pair confidence ($gdsc$) and phrase alignment confidence (pc) scores. These features were calculated over an entire training corpus and could be easily integrated into the phrase-based machine translation system.

3.2 Sentence Pair Confidence

We can hardly compute the joint probability of $P(e^k, f^k)$ without knowing the conditional probability $P(e^k|f^k)$ which is estimated during the alignment process. Therefore, to estimate $P(e^k, f^k)$ before alignment, we make an assumption that $\hat{P}(e^k, f^k) = P(e^k)P(f^k)$, which means the two sides of sentence pair are independent of each other. $P(e^k)$ and $P(f^k)$ can be obtained by using language models. $P(e^k)$ or $P(f^k)$, however, can be small when the sentence is long. Consequently, long sentence pairs will be assigned low scores and have negligible effect on the training process. Given limited training data, ignoring these long sentences may hurt the alignment result. To compensate this, we normalize the probability by the sentence length. We propose the following method to weighting sentence pairs in the corpora. We trained language models for source and target language, and the average log likelihood (AVG-LL) of each sentence pair was calculated by applying the corresponding language model. For each sentence pair (e^k, f^k), the AVG-LL $\mathcal{L}(e^k, f^k)$ is

$$\begin{aligned} \mathcal{L}(e^k) &= \tfrac{1}{|e^k|} \textstyle\sum_{e_i^k \in e^k} \log P(e_i^k|h) \\ \mathcal{L}(f^k) &= \tfrac{1}{|f^k|} \textstyle\sum_{f_j^k \in f^k} \log P(f_j^k|h) \\ \mathcal{L}(e^k, f^k) &= [\mathcal{L}(e^k) + \mathcal{L}(f^k)]/2 \end{aligned} \quad (3)$$

where $P(e_i^k|h)$ and $P(f_j^k|h)$ are ngram probabilities. The sentence pair confidence score is then given by:

$$sc(e^k, f^k) = \exp(\mathcal{L}(e^k, f^k)). \quad (4)$$

3.3 Genre-Dependent Sentence Pair Confidence

Genre adaptation is one of the major challenges in statistical machine translation since translation models suffer from data sparseness (Koehn and Schroeder, 2007). To overcome these problems previous works have focused on explicitly modeling topics and on using multiple language and translation models. Using a mixture of topic-dependent Viterbi alignments was proposed in (Civera and Juan, 2007). Language and translation model adaptation to Europarl and News-Commentary have been explored in (Paulik et al., 2007).

Given the sentence pair weighting method, it is possible to adopt genre-specific language models into the weighting process. The genre-dependent sentence pair confidence $gdsc$ simulates weighting the training sentences again from different data sources, thus, given genre g, it can be formulated as:

$$gdsc(e^k, f^k) = sc(e^k, f^k|g) \quad (5)$$

where $P(e_i^k|h)$ and $P(f_j^k|h)$ are estimated by genre-specific language models.

The score generally represents the likelihood of the sentence pair to be in a specific genre. Thus, if both sides of the sentence pair show a high probability according to the genre-specific language models, alignments in the pair should be more possible to occur in that particular domain, and put more weight may contribute to a better alignment for that genre.

3.4 Phrase Alignment Confidence

So far the confidence scores are used only in the training of the word alignment models. Tracking from which sentence pairs each phrase pair was extracted, we can use the sentence level confidence scores to assign confidence scores to the phrase pairs. Let $S(\tilde{e}, \tilde{f})$ denote the set of sentences pairs from which the phrase pair $(\tilde{e}, \tilde{f})$ was extracted. We calculate then a phrase alignment confidence score pc as:

$$pc(\tilde{e}, \tilde{f}) = \exp \frac{\sum_{(e^k, f^k) \in S(\tilde{e}, \tilde{f})} \log sc(e^k, f^k)}{|S(\tilde{e}, \tilde{f})|} \quad (6)$$

This score is used as an additional feature of the phrase pair. The feature weight is estimated in MER training.

4 Experimental Results

The first step in validating the proposed approach was to check if the different language models do assign different weights to the sentence pairs in the training corpora. Using the different language models NC (News-Commentary), EP (Europarl), NC+EP (both NC and EP) the genre-specific sentence pair confidence scores were calculated. Figure 1 shows the distributions of the differences in these scores across the two corpora. As expected, the language model build from the NC corpus assigns - on average - higher weights to sentence pairs in the NC corpus and lower weights to sentence pairs in the EP corpus (Figure 1a). The opposite is true for the EP LM. When comparing the scores calculated from the NC LM and the combined NC+EP LM we still see a clear separation (Figure 1b). No marked difference can be seen between using the EP LM and the NC+EP LM (Figure 1c), which again is expected, as the NC corpus is very small compared to the EP corpus.

The next step was to retrain the word alignment models using sentences weights according to the various confidence scores. Table 3 shows training and test set perplexities for IBM model 4 for both training directions. Not only do we see a drop in training set perplexities, but also in test set perplexities. Using the genre specific confidence scores leads to lower perplexities on the corresponding test set, which means that using the proposed method does lead to small, but consistent adjustments in the alignment models.

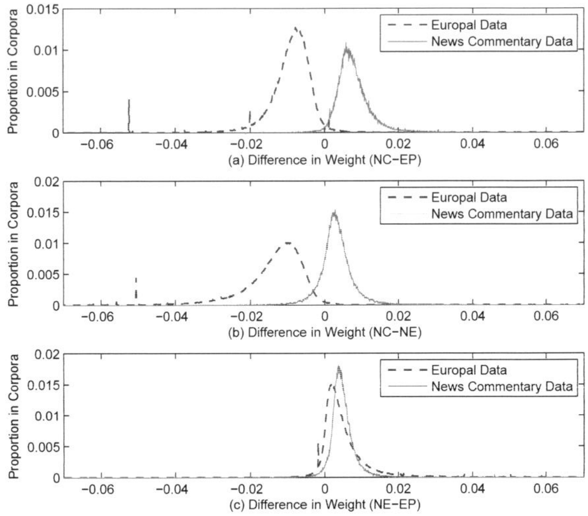

Figure 1: Histogram of weight differences genre specific confidence scores on NC and EP training corpora

		Uniform	NC+EP	NC	EP
train	En→Es	46.76	**42.36**	42.97	44.47
	Es→En	70.18	**62.81**	62.95	65.86
test	NC(En→Es)	53.04	53.44	**51.09**	55.94
	EP(En→Es)	91.13	90.89	91.84	**90.77**
	NC(Es→En)	81.39	81.28	**78.23**	80.33
	EP(Es→En)	126.56	125.96	123.23	**122.11**

Table 3: IBM model 4 training and test set perplexities using genre specific sentence pair confidence scores.

In the final step the specific alignment models were used to generate various phrase tables, which were then used in translation experiments. Results are shown in Table 4. We report lower-cased Bleu scores. We used nc-dev2007 (NCt1) as an additional held-out evaluation set. Bold cells indicate highest scores.

As we can see from the results, improvements are obtained by using sentence pair confidence scores. Using confidence scores calculated from the EP LM gave overall the best performance. While we observe only a small improvement on Europarl sets, improvements on News-Commentary sets are more pronounced, especially on held-out evaluation sets NCt and NCt1. The experiments do not give evidence that genre-dependent confidence can improve over using the general confidence

	Test Set				
	E06	E07	NCd	NCt	NCt1
			Es→En		
B5	33.26	33.23	36.06	35.56	35.64
NC+EP	33.23	32.29	36.12	35.47	35.97
NC	**33.43**	**33.39**	36.14	35.27	35.68
EP	33.36	**33.39**	**36.16**	**35.63**	**36.17**
			En→Es		
B5	**33.33**	32.25	35.10	34.08	34.43
NC+EP	33.23	**32.29**	**35.12**	34.56	34.89
NC	33.30	32.27	34.91	34.07	34.29
EP	33.08	**32.29**	35.05	**34.52**	**35.03**

Table 4: Translation results (NIST-BLEU) using *gdsc* with different genre-specific language models for Es↔En systems

score. As the News-Commentary language model was trained on a very small amount of data further work is required to study this in more detail.

	Test Set				
	E06	E07	NCd	NCt	NCt1
			Es→En		
B5	33.26	33.23	36.06	35.56	35.64
NC+EP+*pc*	**33.54**	**33.39**	36.07	35.38	35.85
NC+*pc*	33.17	33.31	35.96	**35.74**	36.04
EP+*pc*	33.44	32.87	**36.22**	35.63	**36.09**
			En→Es		
B5	**33.33**	32.25	**35.10**	34.08	34.43
NC+EP+*pc*	33.28	32.45	34.82	33.68	33.86
NC+*pc*	33.13	**32.47**	34.01	**34.34**	**34.98**
EP+*pc*	32.97	32.20	34.26	33.99	34.34

Table 5: Translation results (NIST-BLEU) using *pc* with different genre-specific language models for Es↔En systems

Table 5 shows experiments results in NIST-BLEU using *pc* score as an additional feature on phrase tables in Es↔En systems. We observed that across development and held-out sets the gains from *pc* are inconsistent, therefore our submissions are selected from the B5+EP system.

5 Conclusion

In the ACL-WMT 2008, our major innovations are methods to estimate sentence pair confidence via language models. We proposed to use source and target language models to weight the sentence pairs. We developed sentence pair confidence (*sc*), genre-dependent sentence pair confidence (*gdsc*) and phrase alignment confidence (*pc*) scores. Our experimental results shown that we had a better word alignment and translation performance by using *gdsc*. We did not observe consistent improvements by using phrase pair confidence scores in our systems.

Acknowledgments

This work is in part supported by the US DARPA under the GALE program. Any opinions, findings, and conclusions or recommendations expressed in this material are those of the authors and do not necessarily reflect the views of DARPA.

References

Peter F. Brown, Stephen A. Della Pietra, Vincent J. Della Pietra, and Robert L. Mercer. 1993. The mathematics of statistical machine translation: Parameter estimation. In *Computational Linguistics*, volume 19(2), pages 263–331.

Chris Callison-Burch, Cameron Fordyce, Philipp Koehn, Christof Monz, and Josh Schroeder. 2007. (Meta-) evaluation of machine translation. In *Proc. of the ACL 2007 Second Workshop on Statistical Machine Translation*, Prague, Czech Republic.

Jorge Civera and Alfons Juan. 2007. Domain adaptation in statistical translation with mixture modelling. In *Proc. of the ACL 2007 Second Workshop on Statistical Machine Translation*, Prague, Czech Republic.

Qin Gao and Stephan Vogel. 2008. Parallel implementations of word alignment tool. In *Proc. of the ACL 2008 Software Engineering, Testing, and Quality Assurance Workshop*, Columbus, Ohio, USA.

Philipp Koehn and Josh Schroeder. 2007. Experiments in domain adaptation for statistical machine translation. In *Proc. of the ACL 2007 Second Workshop on Statistical Machine Translation*, Prague, Czech Republic.

Philipp Koehn, Hieu Hoang, Alexandra Birch, Chris Callison-Burch, Marcello Federico, Nicola Bertoldi, Brooke Cowan, Wade Shen, Christine Moran, Richard Zens, Chris Dyer, Ondrej Bojar, Alexandra Constantin, and Evan Herbst. 2007. Moses: Open source toolkit for statistical machine translation. In *Proc. of the 45th Annual Meeting of the Association for Computational Linguistics, demo sessions*, pages 177–180, Prague, Czech Republic, June.

Franz J. Och and Hermann Ney. 2003. A systematic comparison of various statistical alignment models. In *Computational Linguistics*, volume 1:29, pages 19–51.

Franz Josef Och. 2003. Minimum error rate training in statistical machine translation. In Erhard Hinrichs and Dan Roth, editors, *Proceedings of the 41st Annual Meeting of the Association for Computational Linguistics*, pages 160–167.

Kishore Papineni, Salim Roukos, Todd Ward, and Wei-Jing Zhu. 2002. Bleu: a method for automatic evaluation of machine translation. In *Proc. of the 40th Annual Conf. of the Association for Computational Linguistics (ACL 02)*, pages 311–318, Philadelphia, PA, July.

Matthias Paulik, Kay Rottmann, Jan Niehues, Silja Hildebrand, and Stephan Vogel. 2007. The ISL phrase-based mt system for the 2007 ACL workshop on statistical machine translation. In *In Proc. of the ACL 2007 Second Workshop on Statistical Machine Translation*, Prague, Czech Republic.

Andreas Stolcke. 2002. SRILM – An extensible language modeling toolkit. In *Proc. Intl. Conf. on Spoken Language Processing*, volume 2, pages 901–904, Denver.

Kernel Regression Framework for Machine Translation: UCL System Description for WMT 2008 Shared Translation Task

Zhuoran Wang
University College London
Dept. of Computer Science
Gower Street, London, WC1E 6BT
United Kingdom
z.wang@cs.ucl.ac.uk

John Shawe-Taylor
University College London
Dept. of Computer Science
Gower Street, London, WC1E 6BT
United Kingdom
jst@cs.ucl.ac.uk

Abstract

The novel kernel regression model for SMT only demonstrated encouraging results on small-scale toy data sets in previous works due to the complexities of kernel methods. It is the first time results based on the real-world data from the shared translation task will be reported at ACL 2008 Workshop on Statistical Machine Translation. This paper presents the key modules of our system, including the kernel ridge regression model, retrieval-based sparse approximation, the decoding algorithm, as well as language modeling issues under this framework.

1 Introduction

This paper follows the work in (Wang et al., 2007; Wang and Shawe-Taylor, 2008) which applied the kernel regression method with high-dimensional outputs proposed originally in (Cortes et al., 2005) to statistical machine translation (SMT) tasks. In our approach, the machine translation problem is viewed as a string-to-string mapping, where both the source and the target strings are embedded into their respective kernel induced feature spaces. Then kernel ridge regression is employed to learn the mapping from the input feature space to the output one. As a kernel method, this model offers the potential advantages of capturing very high-dimensional correspondences among the features of the source and target languages as well as easy integration of additional linguistic knowledge via selecting particular kernels. However, unlike the sequence labeling tasks such as optical character recognition in (Cortes et al., 2005), the complexity of the SMT problem itself together with the computational complexities of kernel methods significantly complicate the implementation of the regression technique in this field.

Our system is actually designed as a hybrid of the classic phrase-based SMT model (Koehn et al., 2003) and the kernel regression model as follows: First, for each source sentence a small relevant set of sentence pairs are retrieved from the large-scale parallel corpus. Then, the regression model is trained on this small relevant set only as a sparse approximation of the regression hyperplane trained on the entire training set, as proposed in (Wang and Shawe-Taylor, 2008). Finally, a beam search algorithm is utilized to decode the target sentence from the very noisy output feature vector we predicted, with the support of a pre-trained phrase table to generate possible hypotheses (candidate translations). In addition, a language model trained on a monolingual corpus can be integrated either directly into the regression model or during the decoding procedure as an extra scoring function.

Before describing each key component of our system in detail, we give a block diagram overview in Figure 1.

2 Problem Formulation

Concretely, the machine translation problem in our method is formulated as follows. If we define a feature space $\mathcal{H}_x$ of our source language $\mathcal{X}$, and define the mapping $\Phi : \mathcal{X} \rightarrow \mathcal{H}_x$, then a sentence $\mathbf{x} \in \mathcal{X}$ can be expressed by its feature vector $\Phi(\mathbf{x}) \in \mathcal{H}_x$. The definition of the feature space $\mathcal{H}_y$ of our target language $\mathcal{Y}$ can be made in a similar way, with cor-

Proceedings of the Third Workshop on Statistical Machine Translation, pages 155–158,
Columbus, Ohio, USA, June 2008.

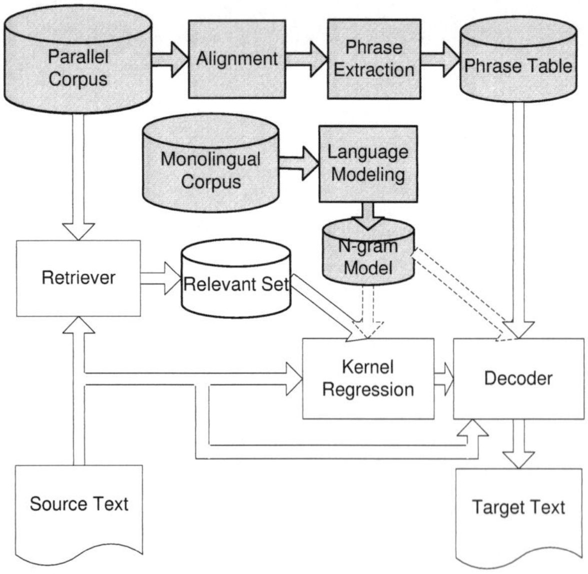

Figure 1: System overview. The processes in gray blocks are pre-performed for the whole system, while the white blocks are online processes for each input sentence. The two dash-line arrows represent two possible ways of language model integration in our system described in Section 6.

responding mapping $\Psi : \mathcal{Y} \rightarrow \mathcal{H}_y$. Now in the machine translation task, we are trying to seek a matrix represented linear operator $\mathbf{W}$, such that:

$$\Psi(\mathbf{y}) = \mathbf{W}\Phi(\mathbf{x}) \qquad (1)$$

to predict the translation $\mathbf{y}$ for an arbitrary source sentence $\mathbf{x}$.

3 Kernel Ridge Regression

Based on a set of training samples, i.e. bilingual sentence pairs $S = \{(\mathbf{x}_i, \mathbf{y}_i) : \mathbf{x}_i \in \mathcal{X}, \mathbf{y}_i \in \mathcal{Y}, i = 1, \ldots, m.\}$, we use ridge regression to learn the $\mathbf{W}$ in Equation (1), as:

$$\min \quad \|\mathbf{W}\mathbf{M}_\Phi - \mathbf{M}_\Psi\|_F^2 + \nu\|\mathbf{W}\|_F^2 \qquad (2)$$

where $\mathbf{M}_\Phi = [\Phi(\mathbf{x}_1), ..., \Phi(\mathbf{x}_m)]$, $\mathbf{M}_\Psi = [\Psi(\mathbf{y}_1), ..., \Psi(\mathbf{y}_m)]$, $\|\cdot\|_F$ denotes the Frobenius norm that is a matrix norm defined as the square root of the sum of the absolute squares of the elements in that matrix, and ν is a regularization coefficient.

Differentiating the expression and setting it to zero gives the explicit solution of the ridge regression problem:

$$\mathbf{W} = \mathbf{M}_\Psi(\mathbf{K}_\Phi + \nu\mathbf{I})^{-1}\mathbf{M}_\Phi^\top \qquad (3)$$

where $\mathbf{I}$ is the identity matrix, and $\mathbf{K}_\Phi = \mathbf{M}_\Phi^\top\mathbf{M}_\Phi = (\kappa_\Phi(\mathbf{x}_i, \mathbf{x}_j)_{1\leq i,j\leq m})$. Note here, we use the kernel function:

$$\kappa_\Phi(\mathbf{x}_i, \mathbf{x}_j) = \langle\Phi(\mathbf{x}_i), \Phi(\mathbf{x}_j)\rangle = \Phi(\mathbf{x}_i)^\top\Phi(\mathbf{x}_j) \qquad (4)$$

to denote the inner product between two feature vectors. If the feature spaces are properly defined, the 'kernel trick' will allow us to avoid dealing with the very high-dimensional feature vectors explicitly (Shawe-Taylor and Cristianini, 2004).

Inserting Equation (3) into Equation (1), we obtain our prediction as:

$$\Psi(\mathbf{y}) = \mathbf{M}_\Psi(\mathbf{K}_\Phi + \nu\mathbf{I})^{-1}\mathbf{k}_\Phi(\mathbf{x}) \qquad (5)$$

where $\mathbf{k}_\Phi(\mathbf{x}) = (\kappa_\Phi(\mathbf{x}, \mathbf{x}_i)_{1\leq i\leq m})$ is an $m \times 1$ column matrix. Note here, we will use the exact matrix inversion instead of iterative approximations.

3.1 N-gram String Kernel

In the practical learning and prediction processes, only the inner products of feature vectors are required, which can be computed with the kernel function implicitly without evaluating the explicit coordinates of points in the feature spaces. Here, we define our features of a sentence as its word n-gram counts, so that a blended n-gram string kernel can be used. That is, if we denote by $\mathbf{x}^{i:j}$ a substring of sentence $\mathbf{x}$ starting with the ith word and ending with the jth, then for two sentences $\mathbf{x}$ and $\mathbf{z}$, the blended n-gram string kernel is computed as:

$$\kappa(\mathbf{x}, \mathbf{z}) = \sum_{p=1}^{n} \sum_{i=1}^{|\mathbf{x}|-p+1} \sum_{j=1}^{|\mathbf{z}|-p+1} [\![\mathbf{x}^{i:i+p-1} = \mathbf{z}^{j:j+p-1}]\!] \qquad (6)$$

Here, $|\cdot|$ denotes the length of the sentence, and $[\![\cdot]\!]$ is the indicator function for the predicate. In our system, the blended tri-gram kernel is used, which means we count the n-grams of length up to 3.

4 Retrieval-based Sparse Approximation

For SMT, we are not able to use the entire training set that contains millions of sentences to train our regression model. Fortunately, it is not necessary either. Wang and Shawe-Taylor (2008) suggested that a small set of sentences whose source is relevant to the input can be retrieved, and the regression model can be trained on this small-scale relevant set only.

Src	*n' y a-t-il pas ici deux poids , deux mesures*
Rlv	pourquoi *y a-t-il deux poids , deux mesures*
	pourquoi *deux poids* et *deux mesures*
	peut-être *n' y a-t-il pas* d' épidémie non plus
	pourquoi *n' y a-t-il pas* urgence
	cette directive doit exister d' *ici deux* mois

Table 1: A sample input (Src) and some of the retrieved relevant examples (Rlv).

In our system, we take each sentence as a document and use the *tf-idf* metric that is frequently used in information retrieval tasks to retrieve the relevant set. Preliminary experiments show that the size of the relevant set should be properly controlled, as if many sentences that are not very close to the source text are involved, they will correspond to adding noise. Hence, we use a threshold of the *tf-idf* score to filter the relevant set. On average, around 1500 sentence pairs are extracted for each source sentence. Table 1 shows a sample input and some of its top relevant sentences retrieved.

5 Decoding

After the regression, we have a prediction of the target feature vector as in Equation (1). To obtain the target sentence, a decoding algorithm is still required to solve the pre-image problem. This is achieved in our system by seeking the sentence $\hat{\mathbf{y}}$ whose feature vector has the minimum Euclidean distance to the prediction, as:

$$\hat{\mathbf{y}} = \arg \min_{\mathbf{y} \in \mathcal{Y}(\mathbf{x})} \|\mathbf{W}\Phi(\mathbf{x}) - \Psi(\mathbf{y})\| \quad (7)$$

where $\mathcal{Y}(\mathbf{x}) \subset \mathcal{Y}$ denotes a finite set covering all potential translations for the given source sentence $\mathbf{x}$. To obtain a smaller search space and more reliable translations, $\mathcal{Y}(\mathbf{x})$ is generated with the support of a phrase table extracted from the whole training set. Then a modified beam search algorithm is employed, in which we restricted the distortion of the phrases by only allowing adjacent phrases to exchange their positions, and rank the search states in the beams according to Equation (7) but applied directly to the partial translations and their corresponding source parts. A more detailed explanation of the decoding algorithm can be found in (Wang et al., 2007). In addition, Wang and Shawe-Taylor (2008) further showed that the search error rate of this algorithm is acceptable.

6 Language Model Integration

In previous works (Wang et al., 2007; Wang and Shawe-Taylor, 2008), there was no language model utilized in the regression framework for SMT, as similar function can be achieved by the correspondences among the n-gram features. It was demonstrated to work well on small-scale toy data, however, real-world data are much more sparse and noisy, where a language model will help significantly.

There are two ways to integrate a language model in our framework. First, the most straightforward solution is to add a weight to adjust the strength of the regression based translation scores and the language model score during the decoding procedure. Alternatively, as language model is n-gram-based which matches the definition of our feature space, we can add a langauge model loss to the objective function of our regression model as follows. We define our language score for a target sentence $\mathbf{y}$ as:

$$\text{LM}(\mathbf{y}) = \mathbf{V}^\top \Psi(\mathbf{y}) \quad (8)$$

where $\mathbf{V}$ is a vector whose components $\mathbf{V}_{y''y'y}$ will typically be log-probabilities $\log P(y|y''y')$, and y, y' and y'' are arbitrary words. Note here, in order to match our blended tri-gram induced feature space, we can make $\mathbf{V}$ of the same dimension as $\Psi(\mathbf{y})$, while zero the components corresponding to uni-grams and bi-grams. Then the regression problem can be defined as:

$$\min \|\mathbf{W}\mathbf{M}_\Phi - \mathbf{M}_\Psi\|_F^2 + \nu_1 \|\mathbf{W}\|_F^2 - \nu_2 \mathbf{V}^\top \mathbf{W}\mathbf{M}_\Phi \mathbf{1} \quad (9)$$

where ν_2 is a coefficient balancing between the prediction being close to the target feature vector and being a fluent target sentence, and $\mathbf{1}$ denotes a vector with components 1. By differentiating the expression with respect to $\mathbf{W}$ and setting the result to zero, we can obtain the explicit solution as:

$$\mathbf{W} = (\mathbf{M}_\Psi + \nu_2 \mathbf{V}\mathbf{1}^\top)(\mathbf{K}_\Phi + \nu_1 \mathbf{I})^{-1}\mathbf{M}_\Phi^\top \quad (10)$$

7 Experimental Results

Preliminary experiments are carried out on the French-English portion of the Europarl corpus. We

System	BLEU (%)	NIST	METEOR (%)	TER (%)	WER (%)	PER (%)
Kernel Regression	26.59	7.00	52.63	55.98	60.52	43.20
Moses	31.15	7.48	56.80	55.14	59.85	42.79

Table 3: Evaluations based on different metrics with comparison to Moses.

train our regression model on the training set, and test the effects of different language models on the development set (test2007). The results evaluated by BLEU score (Papineni et al., 2002) is shown in Table 2.

It can be found that integrating the language model into the regression framework works slightly better than just using it as an additional score component during decoding. But language models of higher-order than the n-gram kernel cannot be formulated to the regression problem, which would be a drawback of our system. Furthermore, the BLEU score performance suggests that our model is not very powerful, but some interesting hints can be found in Table 3 when we compare our method with a 5-gram language model to a state-of-the-art system Moses (Koehn and Hoang, 2007) based on various evaluation metrics, including BLEU score, NIST score (Doddington, 2002), METEOR (Banerjee and Lavie, 2005), TER (Snover et al., 2006), WER and PER. It is shown that our system's TER, WER and PER scores are very close to Moses, though the gaps in BLEU, NIST and METEOR are significant, which suggests that we would be able to produce accurate translations but might not be good at making fluent sentences.

	no-LM	LM^1_{3gram}	LM^2_{3gram}	LM^1_{5gram}
BLEU	23.27	25.19	25.66	26.59

Table 2: BLEU score performance of different language models. LM^1 denotes adding the language model during decoding process, while LM^2 represents integrating the language model into the regression framework as described in Problem (9).

8 Conclusion

This work is a novel attempt to apply the advanced kernel method to SMT tasks. The contribution at this stage is still preliminary. When applied to real-world data, this approach is not as powerful as the state-of-the-art phrase-based log-linear model. However, interesting prospects can be expected from the shared translation task.

Acknowledgements

This work is supported by the European Commission under the IST Project SMART (FP6-033917).

References

Satanjeev Banerjee and Alon Lavie. 2005. METEOR: An automatic metric for MT evaluation with improved correlation with human judgments. In *Proceedings of the ACL Workshop on Intrinsic and Extrinsic Evaluation Measures for Machine Translation and/or Summarization*, pages 65–72.

Corinna Cortes, Mehryar Mohri, and Jason Weston. 2005. A general regression technique for learning transductions. In *Proc. of ICML'05*.

George Doddington. 2002. Automatic evaluation of machine translation quality using n-gram co-occurrence statistics. In *Proc. of HLT'02*, pages 138–145.

Philipp Koehn and Hieu Hoang. 2007. Factored translation models. In *Proc. of EMNLP-CoNLL'07*.

Philipp Koehn, Franz Josef Och, and Daniel Marcu. 2003. Statistical phrase-based translation. In *Proc. of HAACL-HLT'03*, pages 48–54.

Kishore Papineni, Salim Roukos, Todd Ward, and Wei-Jing Zhu. 2002. Bleu: A method for automatic evaluation of machine translation. In *Proc. of ACL'02*.

John Shawe-Taylor and Nello Cristianini. 2004. *Kernel Methods for Pattern Analysis*. Cambridge University Press.

Matthew Snover, Bonnie Dorr, Richard Schwartz, Linnea Micciulla, and John Makhoul. 2006. A study of translation edit rate with targeted human annotation. In *Proc. of AMTA'06*.

Zhuoran Wang and John Shawe-Taylor. 2008. Kernel-based machine translation. In Cyril Goutte, Nicola Cancedda, Marc Dymetman, and George Foster, editors, *Learning Machine Translation*. MIT Press, to appear.

Zhuoran Wang, John Shawe-Taylor, and Sandor Szedmak. 2007. Kernel regression based machine translation. In *Proc. of NAACL-HLT'07, Short Paper Volume*, pages 185–188.

Using syntactic coupling features for discriminating phrase-based translations (WMT-08 Shared Translation Task)

Vassilina Nikoulina and Marc Dymetman
Xerox Research Centre Europe
Grenoble, France
{nikoulina,dymetman}@xrce.xerox.com

Abstract

Our participation in the shared translation task at WMT-08 focusses on news translation from English to French. Our main goal is to contrast a baseline version of the phrase-based MATRAX system, with a version that incorporates syntactic "coupling" features in order to discriminate translations produced by the baseline system. We report results comparing different feature combinations.

1 Introduction

Our goal is to try to improve the fluency and adequacy of a baseline phrase-based SMT system by using a variety of "syntactic coupling features", extracted from parses for the source and target strings. These features are used for reranking the n-best candidates of the baseline system.

The phrase-based SMT system MATRAX, developed at XRCE, is used as the baseline in the experiments. MATRAX is based on a fairly standard log-linear model, but one original aspect of the system is the use of non-contiguous bi-phrases such as *ne ... plus / not ... anymore*, where words in the source and target phrases may be separated by gaps, to be filled at translation time by lexical material provided by some other such pairs (Simard et al., 2005).

For parsing, we use the *Xerox Incremental Parser* XIP (Aït-Mokhtar et al., 2002), which is a robust dependency parser developed at the Xerox Research Centre Europe. XIP is fast (around 2000 words per second for English) and is well adapted to a situation, like the one we have here, were we need to parse on the order of a few hundred target candidates on the fly. Also of interest to us is the fact that XIP produces labelled dependencies, a feature that we use in some of our experiments.

1.1 Decoding and Training

We resort to a standard reranking approach in which we produce an n-best list of MATRAX candidate translations (with n = 100 in our experiments), and then rerank this list with a linear combination of our parse-dependent features. In order to train the feature weights, we use an averaged structured perceptron approach (Roark et al., 2004), where we try to learn weights such that the first candidate to emerge is equal to the "oracle" candidate, that is, the candidate that is closest to the reference in terms of NIST score.

1.2 Coupling Features

Our general approach to computing coupling features between the dependency structure of the source and that of a candidate translation produced by MATRAX is the following: we start by aligning the words between the source and the candidate translation, we parse both sides, and we count (possibly according to a weighting scheme) the number of configurations ("rectangles") that are of the following type: $((s_1, s_{12}, s_2), (t_1, t_{12}, t_2))$, where s_{12} is an edge between s_1 and s_2, t_{12} is an edge between t_1 and t_2, s_1 is aligned with t_1 and s_2 is aligned with t_2. We implemented several variants of this basic scheme.

We start by describing different "generic" coupling functions derived from the basic scheme, as-

Proceedings of the Third Workshop on Statistical Machine Translation, pages 159–162,
Columbus, Ohio, USA, June 2008. ©2008 Association for Computational Linguistics

suming that word alignments have been already determined, then we describe the option of taking into account specific dependency labels when counting rectangles, and finally we describe two options for computing the word alignments.

1.2.1 Generic features

The first measure of coupling is based on simple, non-weighted, word alignments. Here we simply consider that a word of the source and a word of the target are aligned or not aligned, without any intermediary degree, and consider that a rectangle exists on the quadruple of words s_1, s_2, t_1, t_2 iff s_i is aligned to t_i, s_1 and s_2 have a dependency link between them (in whatever direction) and similarly for t_1 and t_2. The first feature that we introduce, *Coupling-Count*, is simply the count of all such rectangles between the source and the target.

We note that the value of this feature tends to be correlated with the size of the source and target dependency trees. We therefore introduce some normalized variants of the feature:

- *Coupling-Recall.* We compute the number of source edges for which there exists a projection in the target. More formally, the number of edges between two words s_1, s_2 such that there exist two words t_1, t_2 with s_i aligned to t_i and such that t_1, t_2 have an edge between them. We then divide this number by the total number of edges in the source.

- *Coupling-Precision.* We do the same thing this time starting from the target.

- *Coupling-F-measure.* This is defined as the harmonic mean of the two previous features.

1.2.2 Label-specific features

The features previously defined do not take into account the labels associated with edges in the dependency trees. However, while rectangles of the form $((s_1, \text{subj}, s_2), (t_1, \text{subj}, t_2))$ may be rather systematic between such languages as English and French, other rectangles may be much less so, due on the one hand to actual linguistic divergences between the two languages, but also, as importantly in practice, to different representational conventions used by different grammar developers for the two languages.[1]

In order to control this problem, we introduce a collection of *Label-Specific-Coupling* features, each for a specific pair of source label and target label. The values of a label-specific feature are the number of occurrences for this specific label pair. We use only label pairs that have been observed to be aligned in the training corpus (that is, that participate in observed rectangles). In one version of that approach, we use all such pairs found in the corpus, in another version only the pairs above a certain frequency threshold in the corpus.

1.2.3 Alignment

In order to compute the features described above, a prerequisite is to be able to determine a word alignment between the source and a candidate translation. Our first approach is to use GIZA++ (corresponding roughly to IBM Model 4) to create these alignments, by producing for a given source and a given candidate translation n-best alignment lists in both directions and applying standard techniques of symmetrization to produce a bidirectional alignment.

Another way to find word alignments is to use the information provided by the baseline system. Since MATRAX is a phrase-based system, it has access to the bi-phrases (aligned by definition) that are used in order to generate a candidate translation. However note that when we use a bi-phrase based alignment, there will be differences from the word alignment that we discussed before, and we need to adapt our coupling functions.

1.2.4 Related approaches

There is a growing body of work on the use of syntax for improving the quality of SMT systems. Our approach is closest to the line taken in (Och et al., 2003), where syntactic features are also used for discriminating between candidates produced by a phrase-based system, but here we introduce and compare results for a wider variety of coupling features, taking into account different combinations involving normalization of the counts, symmetrized features between the source and target, labelled de-

[1] Although the XIP formalism is shared between grammar developers of French and English, the grammars do sometimes follow different conventions.

pendencies, and also consider several ways for computing the word alignment on the basis of which edge couplings are determined.

2 Experiments

2.1 Description

Our participation concerns the English to French News translation task. To train our baseline system we used the News Commentary corpus, namely the training ($\sim$ 1M words) and development (1057 sentences) sets proposed for the shared translation task. The same development set was used for the MERT training procedure of the baseline system, as well as for learning the parameters of the reranking procedure. Note that the test data on which we report our experimental results here is the one proposed as development test set for the News translation task (1064 sentences, nc-devtest2007).

Using MATRAX as the baseline system we generate 100-best lists of candidate translations for all source sentences of the test set, we rerank these candidates using our features, and we output the top candidate. We present our results in Table 1, distinguished according to the actual combination of features used in each experiment.

- The *Baseline* entry in the table corresponds to MATRAX results on the test set, without the use of any of the coupling features.
- We distinguish two sub-tables, according to whether Giza-based alignments or phrase-based alignments were used.
- The *Generic* keyword corresponds to the coupling features introduced in section 1.2.1, based on rectangle counts, independent of the labels of the edges.
- The *Matrax* keyword corresponds to using MATRAX "internal" features as reranking features, along with the coupling features. These MATRAX features are pretty standard phrase-based features, apart from some features dealing explicitly with gapped phrases, and are described in detail in (Simard et al., 2005).
- The *Labels* and *Frequent Labels* keywords corresponds to using label-specific features. In the first case (Labels) we extracted all of the aligned label pairs (label pair associated with a coupling rectangle) found in a training set, while in the second case (Frequent Labels), we only kept the most frequently observed among these label pairs.
- When several keywords appear on a line, we used the union of the corresponding features, and in the last line of the table, we show a combination involving at the same time some features computed on the basis of Giza-based alignments and of phrase-based alignments.
- Along with the NIST and BLEU scores of each combination, we also conducted an informal manual assessment of the quality of the results relative to the MATRAX baseline. We took a random sample of 100 source sentences from the test set and for each sentence, assessed whether the first candidate produced by reranking was better, worse, or indistinguishable in terms of quality relative to the baseline translation. We report the number of improvements (+) and deteriorations (-) among these 100 samples as well as their difference.[2]

3 Discussion

While the overall results in terms of Bleu and Nist do not show major improvements relative to the baseline, there are several interesting observations to make. First of all, if we focus on feature combinations in which MATRAX features are included (shown in italics in the table), we see that there is a general tendency for the results, both in terms of automatic and human evaluations, to be better than for the same combination without the MATRAX features; the explanation seems to be that if we do not use the MATRAX features during reranking, but consider the 100 candidates in the n-best list to be equally valuable from the viewpoint of MATRAX features, we lose essential information that cannot

[2]All the results reported here correspond to our own evaluations, prior to the WMT evaluations. Given time constraints, we focussed more on contrasting the baseline with the baseline + coupling features, than in tuning the baseline itself for the task at hand. After the submission deadline, we were able to improve the baseline for this task.

	NIST	BLEU	-	+	Diff
Baseline	6.4093	0.2034	0	0	0
Giza-based alignments					
Generic	6.3383	0.2043	15	17	2
Generic, Matrax	*6.3782*	*0.2083*	*4*	*18*	*14*
Labels	6.3483	0.1963	12	18	6
Labels, Generic	6.3514	0.2010	3	18	15
Labels, Generic, Matrax	*6.4016*	*0.2075*	*3*	*20*	*17*
Frequent Labels	6.3815	0.2054	7	11	4
Frequent Labels, Generic	6.3826	0.2044	6	18	12
Frequent Labels, Generic, Matrax	*6.4177*	*0.2100*	*2*	*16*	*14*
Phrase-based alignments					
Generic	6.2869	0.1964	12	14	2
Generic, Matrax	*6.3972*	*0.2031*	*4*	*11*	*7*
Labels	6.3677	0.1995	16	15	-1
Labels, Generic	6.3567	0.1977	8	15	7
Labels, Generic, Matrax	*6.4269*	*0.2049*	*4*	*17*	*13*
Frequent Labels	6.3701	0.1998	3	15	12
Frequent Labels, Generic	6.3846	0.2013	7	16	9
Frequent Labels, Generic, Matrax	*6.4160*	*0.2049*	*4*	*16*	*12*
Giza Generic, Phrase Generic, Giza Labels, Matrax	*6.4351*	*0.2060*	*7*	*22*	*15*

Table 1: Reranking results.

be recovered simply by appeal to the syntactic coupling features.

If we now concentrate on the lines which do include MATRAX features and compare their results with the baseline, we see a trend for these results to be better than the baseline, both in terms of automatic measures as (more strongly) in terms of human evaluation. Taken individually, perhaps the improvements are not very clear, but *collectively*, a trend does seem to appear in favor of syntactic coupling features generally, although we have not conducted formal statistical tests to validate this impression. A more detailed comparison between individual lines, inside the class of combinations that include MATRAX features, appears however difficult to make on the basis of the reported experiments.

References

Salah Aït-Mokhtar, Jean-Pierre Chanod, and Claude Roux. 2002. Robustness beyond shallowness: incremental deep parsing. *Natural Language Engineering*, 8(3):121–144.

Franz Josef Och, Daniel Gildea, Sanjeev Khudanpur, Anoop Sarkar, Kenji Yamada, Alex Fraser, Shankar Kumar, Libin Shen, David Smith, Katherine Eng, Viren Jain, Zhen Jin, and Dragomir Radev. 2003. Syntax for Statistical Machine Translation: Final report of John Hopkins 2003 Summer Workshop. Technical report, John Hopkins University.

B. Roark, M. Saraclar, M. Collins, and M. Johnson. 2004. Discriminative language modeling with conditional random fields and the perceptron algorithm. In *Proceedings of the 42nd Annual Meeting of the Association for Computational Linguistics (ACL'04)*, July.

Michel Simard, Nicola Cancedda, Bruno Cavestro, Marc Dymetman, Éric Gaussier, Cyril Goutte, Kenji Yamada, Philippe Langlais, and Arne Mauser. 2005. Translating with non-contiguous phrases. In *HLT/EMNLP*.

Statistical Transfer Systems for French–English and German–English Machine Translation

Greg Hanneman and **Edmund Huber** and **Abhaya Agarwal** and **Vamshi Ambati** and **Alok Parlikar** and **Erik Peterson** and **Alon Lavie**
Language Technologies Institute
Carnegie Mellon University
Pittsburgh, PA 15213 USA
{ghannema, ehuber, abhayaa, vamshi, aup, eepeter, alavie}@cs.cmu.edu

Abstract

We apply the Stat-XFER statistical transfer machine translation framework to the task of translating from French and German into English. We introduce statistical methods within our framework that allow for the principled extraction of syntax-based transfer rules from parallel corpora given word alignments and constituency parses. Performance is evaluated on test sets from the 2007 WMT shared task.

1 Introduction

The Carnegie Mellon University statistical transfer (Stat-XFER) framework is a general search-based and syntax-driven framework for developing MT systems under a variety of data conditions (Lavie, 2008). At its core is a transfer engine using two language-pair-dependent resources: a grammar of weighted synchronous context-free rules (possibly augmented with unification-style feature constraints), and a probabilistic bilingual lexicon of syntax-based word- and phrase-level translations. The Stat-XFER framework has been used to develop research MT systems for a number of language pairs, including Chinese–English, Hebrew–English, Urdu–English, and Hindi–English.

In this paper, we describe our use of the framework to create new French–English and German–English MT systems for the 2008 Workshop on Statistical Machine Translation shared translation task. We first describe the acquisition and processing of resources for each language pair and the roles of those resources within the Stat-XFER system (Section 2); we then report results on common test sets (Section 3) and share some early analysis and future directions (Section 4).

2 System Description

Building a new machine translation system under the Stat-XFER framework involves constructing a bilingual translation lexicon and a transfer grammar. Over the past six months, we have developed new methods for extracting syntax-based translation lexicons and transfer rules fully automatically from parsed and word-aligned parallel corpora. These new methods are described in detail by Lavie et al. (2008). Below, we detail the statistical methods by which these resources were extracted for our French–English and German–English systems.

2.1 Lexicon

The bilingual lexicon is automatically extracted from automatically parsed and word-aligned parallel corpora. To obtain high-quality statistical word alignments, we run GIZA++ (Och and Ney, 2003) in both the source-to-target and target-to-source directions, then combine the resulting alignments with the Sym2 symmetric alignment heuristic of Ortiz-Martínez et al. (2005)[1]. From this data, we extract a lexicon of both word-to-word and syntactic phrase-to-phrase translation equivalents.

The word-level correspondences are extracted directly from the word alignments: parts of speech for these lexical entries are obtained from the preter-

[1]We use Sym2 over more well-known heuristics such as "grow-diag-final" because Sym2 has been shown to give the best results for the node-alignment subtask that is part of our processing chain.

Proceedings of the Third Workshop on Statistical Machine Translation, pages 163–166,
Columbus, Ohio, USA, June 2008.

w_s	c_s	w_t	c_t	r
paru	V	appeared	V	0.2054
paru	V	seemed	V	0.1429
paru	V	found	V	0.0893
paru	V	published	V	0.0804
paru	V	felt	V	0.0714
⋮		⋮		⋮
paru	V	already	ADV	0.0089
paru	V	appear	V	0.0089
paru	V	authoritative	ADJ	0.0089

Table 1: Part of the lexical entry distribution for the French (source) word *paru*.

minal nodes of parse trees of the source and target sentences. If parsers are unavailable for either language, we have also experimented with determining parts of speech with independent taggers such as TreeTagger (Schmid, 1995). Alternatively, parts of speech may be projected through the word alignments from one language to the other if the information is available on at least one side. Syntactic phrase-level correspondences are extracted from the parallel data by applying the PFA node alignment algorithm described by Lavie et al. (2008). The yields of the aligned parse tree nodes are extracted as constituent-level translation equivalents.

Each entry in the lexicon is assigned a rule score, r, based on its source-side part of speech c_s, source-side text w_s, target-side part of speech c_t, and target-side text w_t. The score is a maximum-likelihood estimate of the distribution of target-language translation and source- and target-language parts of speech, given the source word or phrase.

$$r = p(w_t, c_t, c_s \mid w_s) \quad (1)$$

$$\approx \frac{\#(w_t, c_t, w_s, c_s)}{\#(w_s) + 1} \quad (2)$$

We employ add-one smoothing in the denominator of Equation 2 to counteract overestimation in the case that $\#(w_s)$ is small. Rule scores provide a way to promote the more likely translation alternatives while still retaining a high degree of diversity in the lexicon. Table 1 shows part of the lexical distribution for the French (source) word *paru*.

The result of the statistical word alignment process and lexical extraction is a bilingual lexicon containing 1,064,755 entries for French–English and 1,111,510 entries for German–English. Sample lexical entries are shown in Figure 1.

2.2 Grammar

Transfer grammars for our earlier statistical transfer systems were manually created by in-house experts of the languages involved and were therefore small. The Stat-XFER framework has since been extended with procedures for automatic grammar acquisition from a parallel corpus, given constituency parses for source or target data or both. Our French and German systems used the context-free grammar rule extraction process described by Lavie et al. (2008). For French, we used 300,000 parallel sentences from the Europarl training data parsed on the English side with the Stanford parser (Klein and Manning, 2003) and on the French side with the Xerox XIP parser (Aït-Mokhtar et al., 2001). For German, we used 300,000 Europarl sentence pairs parsed with the English and German versions of the Stanford parser[2].

The set of rules extracted from the parsed corpora was filtered down after scoring to improve system performance and run time. The final French rule set was comprised of the 1500 most frequently occurring rules. For German, rules that occurred less than twice were filtered out, leaving a total of 16,469. In each system, rule scores were again calculated by Equation 2, with w_s and w_t representing the full right-hand sides of the source and target grammar rules.

A secondary version of our French system used a word-level lexicon extracted from the intersection, rather than the symmetricization, of the GIZA++ alignments in each direction; we hypothesize that this tends to improve precision at the expense of recall. The word-level lexicon was supplemented with syntax-based phrase-level entries obtained from the PFA node alignment algorithm. The grammar contained the 700 highest-frequency and the 500 highest-scoring rules extracted from the parallel parsed corpus. This version had a total lexicon size of 2,023,531 entries and a total grammar of 1034 rules after duplicates were removed. Figure 2 shows

[2]Due to a combination of time constraints and paucity of computational resources, only a portion of the Europarl parallel corpus was utilized, and none of the supplementary news commentary training data was integrated.

```
{VS,248840}
V::V |: ["paru"] -> ["appeared"]
(
  (*score* 0.205357142857143)
)
```

```
{NP,2000012}
NP::NP |: ["ein" "Beispiel"] -> ["an" "example"]
(
  (*score* 0.763636363636364)
)
```

Figure 1: Sample lexical entries for French and German.

sample grammar rules automatically learned by the process described above.

2.3 Transfer Engine

The Stat-XFER transfer engine runs in a two-stage process, first applying the grammar and lexicon to an input sentence, then running a decoder over the resulting lattice of scored translation pieces. Scores for each translation piece are based on a log-linear combination of several features: language model probability, rule scores, source-given-target and target-given-source lexical probabilities, parse fragmentation, and length. For more details, see Lavie (2008). The use of a German transfer grammar an order of magnitude larger than the corresponding French grammar was made possible due to a recent optimization made in the engine. When enabled, it constrains the search of translation hypotheses to the space of hypotheses whose structure satisfies the consituent structure of a source-side parse.

3 Evaluation

We trained our model parameters on a subset of the provided "dev2006" development set, optimizing for case-insensitive IBM-style BLEU (Papineni et al., 2002) with several iterations of minimum error rate training on n-best lists. In each iteration's list, we also included the lists from previous iterations in order to maintain a diversity of hypothesis types and scores. The provided "test2007" and "nc-test2007" data sets, identical with the test data from the 2007 Workshop on Statistical Machine Translation shared task, were used as internal development tests.

Tables 2, 3, and 4 report scores on these data sets for our primary French, secondary French, and German systems. We report case-insensitive scores for version 0.6 of METEOR (Lavie and Agarwal, 2007) with all modules enabled, version 1.04 of IBM-style BLEU (Papineni et al., 2002), and version 5 of TER (Snover et al., 2006).

Data Set	METEOR	BLEU	TER
dev2006	0.5332	0.2063	64.81
test2007	0.5358	0.2078	64.75
nc-test2007	0.5369	0.1719	69.83

Table 2: Results for the primary French–English system on provided development and development test sets.

Data Set	METEOR	BLEU	TER
dev2006	0.5330	0.2086	65.02
test2007	0.5386	0.2129	64.29
nc-test2007	0.5311	0.1680	70.90

Table 3: Results for the secondary French–English system on provided development and development test sets.

4 Analysis and Conclusions

From the development test results in Section 3, we note that the Stat-XFER systems' performance currently lags behind the state-of-the-art scores on the 2007 test data[3]. This may be in part due to the low volume of training data used for rule learning. A key research question in our approach is how to distinguish low-frequency correct and useful transfer rules from "noisy" rules that are due to parser errors and incorrect word alignments. We believe that learning rules from more data will help alleviate this problem by proportionally increasing the counts of good rules compared to incorrect ones. We also plan to study methods for more effective rule set pruning, regardless of the volume of training data used.

The difference in metric scores between in-domain and out-of-domain data is partly due to effects of reference length on the metrics used. Detailed output from METEOR and BLEU shows that the reference translations for the test2007 set are about 94% as long as the primary French–English

[3]Top scores on the 2007 test data are approximately 0.60 METEOR, 0.33 BLEU, and 57.6 TER. See Callison-Burch et al. (2007) for full results.

```
{PP,1627955}
(X1::Y1)
  (X4::Y3)
)
(
  (*score* 0.866050808314088 )
```

```
{PP,3000085}
PP:ADVP ["vor" CARD "Monaten"] -> [NUM "months" "ago"]
(
  (*score* 0.9375)
  (X2::Y1)
)
```

Figure 2: Sample grammar rules for French and German.

Data Set	METEOR	BLEU	TER
dev2006	0.4967	0.1794	68.68
test2007	0.5052	0.1878	67.94
nc-test2007	0.4939	0.1347	74.38

Table 4: Results for the German–English system on provided development and development test sets.

system's translations. On this set, our system has approximately balanced precision (0.62) and recall (0.66). However, the nc-test2007 references are only 84% as long as our output, a situation that hurts our system's precision (0.57) but boosts its recall (0.68). METEOR, as a metric that favors recall, shows a negligible increase in score between these two test sets, while BLEU and TER report significant relative drops of 17.3% and 7.8%. This behavior appears to be consistent on the test2007 and nc-test2007 data sets across systems (Callison-Burch et al., 2007).

Acknowledgments

This research was supported in part by NSF grants IIS-0121631 (AVENUE) and IIS-0534217 (LETRAS), and by the DARPA GALE program. We thank the members of the Parsing and Semantics group at Xerox Research Centre Europe for assisting in parsing the French data using their XIP parser.

References

Salah Aït-Mokhtar, Jean-Pierre Chanod, and Claude Roux. 2001. A multi-input dependency parser. In *Proceedings of the Seventh International Workshop on Parsing Technologies*, Beijing, China, October.

Chris Callison-Burch, Cameron Fordyce, Philipp Koehn, Christof Monz, and Josh Schroeder. 2007. (Meta-) evaluation of machine translation. In *Proceedings of the Second Workshop on Statistical Machine Translation*, pages 136–158, Prague, Czech Republic, June.

Dan Klein and Christopher D. Manning. 2003. Fast exact inference with a factored model for natural language parsing. In *Advances in Neural Information Processing Systems 15*, pages 3–10. MIT Press, Cambridge, MA.

Alon Lavie and Abhaya Agarwal. 2007. METEOR: An automatic metric for MT evaluation with high levels of correlation with human judgments. In *Proceedings of the Second Workshop on Statistical Machine Translation*, pages 228–231, Prague, Czech Republic, June.

Alon Lavie, Alok Parlikar, and Vamshi Ambati. 2008. Syntax-driven learning of sub-sentential translation equivalents and translation rules from parsed parallel corpora. In *Proceedings of the Second Workshop on Syntax and Structure in Statistical Translation*, Columbus, OH, June. To appear.

Alon Lavie. 2008. Stat-XFER: A general search-based syntax-driven framework for machine translation. In *Computational Linguistics and Intelligent Text Processing*, Lecture Notes in Computer Science, pages 362–375. Springer.

Franz Josef Och and Hermann Ney. 2003. A systematic comparison of various statistical alignment models. *Computational Linguistics*, 29(1):19–51.

Daniel Ortiz-Martínez, Ismael García-Varea, and Francisco Casacuberta. 2005. Thot: A toolkit to train phrase-based models for statistical machine translation. In *Proceedings of the 10th Machine Translation Summit*, pages 141–148, Phuket, Thailand, September.

Kishore Papineni, Salim Roukos, Todd Ward, and Wei-Jing Zhu. 2002. BLEU: A method for automatic evalution of machine translation. In *Proceedings of the 40th Annual Meeting of the Association for Computational Linguistics*, pages 311–318, Philadelphia, PA, July.

Helmut Schmid. 1995. Improvements in part-of-speech tagging with an application to German. In *Proceedings of the ACL SIGDAT Workshop*.

Matthew Snover, Bonnie Dorr, Richard Schwartz, Linnea Micciulla, and John Makhoul. 2006. A study of translation edit rate with targeted human annotation. In *Proceedings of the Seventh Conference of the Association for Machine Translation in the Americas*, pages 223–231, Cambridge, MA, August.

TectoMT: Highly Modular MT System with Tectogrammatics Used as Transfer Layer*

Zdeněk Žabokrtský, Jan Ptáček, Petr Pajas
Institute of Formal and Applied Linguistics
Charles University, Prague, Czech Republic
{zabokrtsky,ptacek,pajas}@ufal.mff.cuni.cz

Abstract

We present a new English→Czech machine translation system combining linguistically motivated layers of language description (as defined in the Prague Dependency Treebank annotation scenario) with statistical NLP approaches.

1 Introduction

We describe a new MT system (called TectoMT) based on the conventional analysis-transfer-synthesis architecture. We use the layers of language description defined in the Prague Dependency Treebank 2.0 (PDT for short, (Hajič and others, 2006)), namely (1) *word layer* – raw text, no linguistic annotation, (2) *morphological layer* – sequence of tagged and lemmatized tokens, (3) *analytical layer* – each sentence represented as a surface-syntactic dependency tree, and (4) *tectogrammatical layer* – each sentence represented as a deep-syntactic dependency tree in which only autosemantic words do have nodes of their own; prefixes w-, m-, a-, or t- will be used for denoting these layers.[1]

We use 'Praguian' tectogrammatics (introduced in (Sgall, 1967)) as the transfer layer because we believe that, first, it largely abstracts from language-specific (inflection, agglutination, functional words...) means of expressing non-lexical meanings, second, it allows for a natural transfer factorization, and third, local tree contexts in t-trees carry more information (esp. for lexical choice) than local linear contexts in the original sentences.

In order to facilitate separating the transfer of lexicalization from the transfer of syntactization, we introduce the concept of *formeme*. Each t-node's has a formeme attribute capturing which morphosyntactic form has been (in the case of analysis) or will be (synthesis) used for the t-node in the surface sentence shape. Here are some examples of formemes we use for English: n:subj (semantic noun (sn) in subject position), n:for+X (sn with preposition *for*), n:X+ago (sn with postposition *ago*), n:poss (possessive form of sn), v:because+fin (semantic verb (sv) as a subordinating finite clause introduced by *because*), v:without+ger (sv as a gerund after *without*), adj:attr (semantic adjective (sa) in attributive position), adj:compl (sa in complement position).

The presented system intensively uses the PDT technology (data formats, software tools). Special attention is paid to modularity: the translation is implemented (in Perl) as a long sequence of processing modules (called blocks) with relatively tiny, well-defined tasks, so that each module is independently testable, improvable, or substitutable. TectoMT allows to easily combine blocks based on different approaches, from blocks using complex probabilistic solutions (e.g., B2, B6, B35, see the next section), through blocks applying simpler Machine Learning techniques (e.g., B69) or empirically based heuristics (e.g., B7, B25, B36, B71), to blocks implementing 'crisp' linguistic rules (e.g., B48-B51, B59). There are also blocks for trivial technical tasks (e.g., B33, B72).

*The research reported in this paper is financially supported by grants GAAV ČR 1ET101120503 and MSM0021620838.

[1] In addition, we use also p-layer (phrase structures) as an a-layer alternative, the only reason for which is that we do not have a working a-layer parser for English at this moment.

Proceedings of the Third Workshop on Statistical Machine Translation, pages 167–170,
Columbus, Ohio, USA, June 2008. ©2008 Association for Computational Linguistics

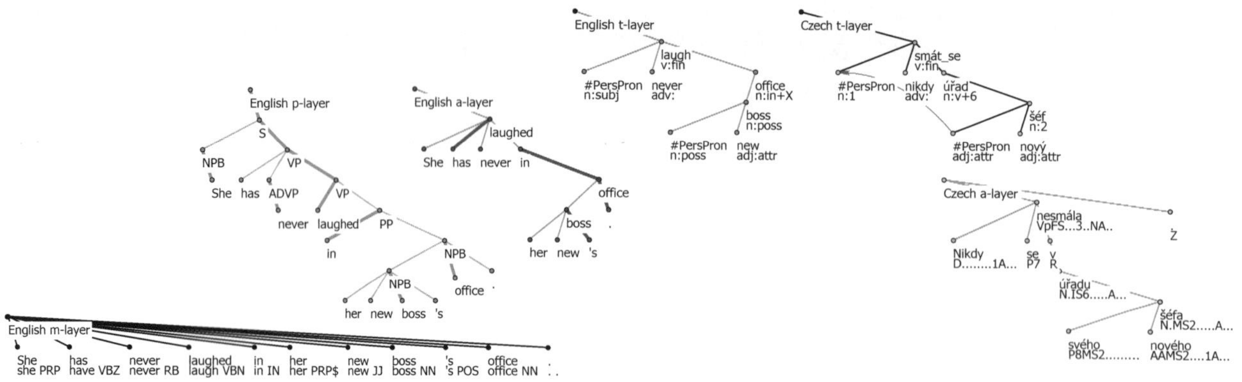

Figure 1: MT 'pyramid' as implemented in TectoMT. All the representations are rooted with artificial nodes, serving only as labels. Virtually, the pyramid is bottomed with the input sentence on the source side (*She has never laughed in her new boss's office.*) and its automatic translation on the target side (*Nikdy se nesmála v úřadu svého nového šéfa.*).

2 Translation Procedure

The structure of this section directly renders the sequence of blocks currently used for English-Czech translation in TectoMT. The intermediate stages of the translation process are illustrated in Figure 1; identifiers of the blocks affecting on the translation of the sample sentence are typeset in bold.

2.1 From English w-layer to English m-layer

B1: Segment the source English text into sentences. **B2**: Split the sentences into sequences of tokens, roughly according to Penn Treebank (PTB for short; (Marcus et al., 1994)) conventions. **B3**: Tag the tokens with PTB-style POS tags using a tagger (Brants, 2000). B4: Fix some tagging errors systematically made by the tagger using a rule-based corrector. **B5**: Lemmatize the tokens using `morpha`, (Minnen et al., 2000).

2.2 From English m-layer to English p-layer

B6: Build PTB-style phrase-structure tree for each sentence using a parser (Collins, 1999).

2.3 From English p-layer to English a-layer

B7: In each phrase, mark the head node (using a set of heuristic rules). **B8**: Convert phrase-structure trees to a-trees. B9: Apply some heuristic rules to fix apposition constructions. B10: Apply another heuristic rules for reattaching incorrectly positioned nodes. B11: Unify the way in which multiword prepositions (such as *because of*) and subordinating conjunctions (such as *provided that*) are treated. B12: Assign analytical functions (only if necessary for a correct treatment of coordination/apposition constructions).

2.4 From English a-layer to English t-layer

B13: Mark a-nodes which are auxiliary (such as prepositions, subordinating conjunctions, auxiliary verbs, selected types of particles, etc.) **B14**: Mark *not* as an auxiliary node too (but only if it is connected to a verb form). **B15**: Build t-trees. Each a-node cluster formed by an autosemantic node and possibly several associated auxiliary nodes is 'collapsed' into a single t-node. T-tree dependency edges are derived from a-tree edges connecting the a-node clusters. B16: Explicitely distinguish t-nodes that are members of coordination (conjuncts) from shared modifiers. It is necessary as they all are attached below the coordination conjunction t-node. **B17**: Modify t-lemmas in specific cases. E.g., all kinds of personal pronouns are represented by the 'artificial' t-lemma #PersPron. B18: Assign functors that are necessary for proper treatment of coordination and apposition constructions. B19: Distribute shared auxiliary words in coordination constructions. **B20**: Mark t-nodes that are roots of t-subtrees corresponding to finite verb clauses. B21: Mark passive verb forms. B22: Assign (a subset of) functors. B23: Mark t-nodes corresponding to infinitive verbs. B24: Mark t-nodes which are roots of t-subtrees corresponding to relative clauses. B25: Identify coreference links between relative pronouns (or other relative pronominal word) and their nominal antecedents. B26: Mark t-nodes that are the roots of t-subtrees corresponding to direct speeches. B27: Mark t-nodes that are the roots of t-subtrees corresponding to parenthesized expressions. **B28**: Fill the nodetype attribute (rough classification of t-nodes). **B29**: Fill the sempos attribute (fine-grained classification of t-nodes). **B30**: Fill the grammateme attributes (semantically indispensable morphological categories, such as number for nouns, tense for verbs). **B31**: Determine the formeme of each t-node. B32: Mark personal names, distinguish male and female first names if possible.

2.5 From English t-layer to Czech t-layer

B33: Initiate the target-side t-trees, simply by cloning the source-side t-trees. **B34**: In each t-node, translate its formeme.[2] **B35**: Translate t-lemma in each t-node as its most probable target-language counterpart (which is compliant with the previously chosen formeme), according to a probabilistic dictionary.[3] B36: Apply manual rules for fixing the formeme and lexeme choices, which are otherwise systematically wrong and are reasonably frequent. **B37**: Fill the gender grammateme in t-nodes corresponding to denotative nouns (it follows from the chosen t-lemma).[4] **B38**: Fill the aspect grammateme in t-nodes corresponding to verbs. Information about aspect (perfective/imperfective) is necessary for making decisions about forming complex future tense in Czech. B39: Apply rule-based correction of translated date/time expressions (several templates such as *1970's*, *July 1*, etc.). B40: Fix grammateme values in places where the English-Czech grammateme correspondence is not trivial (e.g., if an English gerund expression is translated using Czech subordinating clause, the tense grammateme has to be filled). **B41**: Negate verb forms where some arguments of the verbs bear negative meaning (double negation in Czech). B42: Verb t-nodes in active voice that have transitive t-lemma and no accusative object, are turned to reflexives. **B43**: The t-nodes with genitive formeme or prepositional-group formeme, whose counterpart English t-nodes are located in pre-modification position, are moved to post-modification position. B44: Reverse the dependency orientation between numeric expressions and counted nouns, if the value of the numeric expression is greater than four and the noun without the numeral would be expressed in nominative or accusative case. **B45**: Find coreference links from personal pronouns to their antecedents, if the latter are in subject position (needed later for reflexivization).

2.6 From Czech t-layer to Czech a-layer

B46: Create initial a-trees by cloning t-trees. **B47**: Fill the surface morphological categories (gender, number, case, negation, etc.) with values derived from values of grammatemes, formeme, semantic part of speech etc. B48: Propagate the values of gender and number of relative pronouns from their antecedents (along the coreference links). **B49**: Propagate the values of gender, number and person according to the subject-predicate agreement (i.e., from subjects to the finite verbs). **B50**: Resolve agreement of adjectivals in attributive positions (copying gender/number/case from their governing nouns). B51: Resolve complement agreement (copying gender/number from subject to adjectival complement). **B52**: Apply pro-drop – deletion of personal pronouns in subject positions. **B53**: Add preposition a-nodes (if implied by the t-node's formeme). B54: Add a-nodes for subordinating conjunction (if implied by the t-node's formeme). **B55**: Add a-nodes corresponding to reflexive particles for reflexiva tantum verbs. B56: Add an a-node representing the auxiliary verb *být* (to be) in the case of compound passive verb forms. B57: Add a-nodes representing modal verbs, accordingly to the deontic modality grammateme. B58: Add the auxiliary verb *být* in imperfective future-tense complex verb forms. B59: Add verb forms such as *by/bys/bychom* expressing conditional verb modality. B60: Add auxiliary verb forms such as *jsem/jste* in past-tense complex verb forms. B61:

[2] The translation mapping from English formemes to Czech formemes was obtained as follows: we analyzed 10,000 sentence pairs from the WMT'08 training data up to the t-layer (using a tagger shipped with the PDT and parser (McDonald et al., 2005) for Czech), added formemes to t-trees on both sides, aligned the t-trees (using a set of weighted heuristic rules, similarly to (Menezes and Richardson, 2001)), and from the aligned t-node pairs extracted for each English formeme its most frequent Czech counterpart.

[3] The dictionary was created by merging the translation dictionary from PCEDT ((Cuřín and others, 2004)) and a translation dictionary extracted from a part of the parallel corpus Czeng ((Bojar and Žabokrtský, 2006)) aligned at word-level by Giza++ ((Och and Ney, 2003)).

[4] Czech nouns have grammatical gender which is (among others) important for resolving grammatical agreement.

Partition a-trees into finite clauses (a-nodes belonging to the same clause are coindexed). **B62**: In each clause, a-nodes which represent clitics are moved to the so called second position in the clause (according to Wackernagel's law). **B63**: Add a-nodes corresponding to sentence-final punctuation mark. B64: Add a-nodes corresponding to commas on boundaries between governing and subordinated clauses. B65: Add a-nodes corresponding to commas in front of conjunction *ale* and also commas in multiple coordinations. B66: Add pairs of parenthesis a-nodes. **B67**: Choose morphological lemmas in a-nodes corresponding to personal pronouns. **B68**: Generate the resulting word forms (derived from lemmas and tags) using Czech word form generator described in (Hajič, 2004). B69: Vocalize prepositions *k*, *s*, *v*, and *z* (accordingly to the prefix of the following word). **B70**: Capitalize the first word in each sentence as well as in each direct speech.

2.7 From Czech a-layer to Czech w-layer

B71: Create the resulting sentences by flattening the a-trees. Heuristic rules for proper spacing around punctuation marks are used. B72: Create the resulting text by concatenating the resulting sentences.

3 Final remarks

We believe that the potential contribution of tectogrammatical layer of language representation for MT is the following: it abstracts from many language-specific phenomena (which could reduce the notorious data-sparsity problem) and offers a natural factorization of the translation task (which could be useful for formulating independence assumptions when building probabilistic models). Of course, the question naturally arises whether these properties can ever outbalance the disadvantages, especially cumulation and interference of errors made on different layers, considerable technical complexity, and the need for detailed linguistic insight. In our opinion, this question still remains open. On one hand, the translation quality offered now by TectoMT is below the state-of-the-art system according to the preliminary evaluation of the WMT08 Shared Task. But on the other hand, the potential of tectogrammatics has not been used fully, and moreover there are still many components with only pilot heuristic implementation which increase the number of translation errors and which can be relatively easily substituted by corpus-based solutions. In the near future, we plan to focus especially on the transfer blocks, which are currently based on the naive assumption of isomorphism of the source and target t-trees and which do not make use of the target language model, so far.

References

Ondřej Bojar and Zdeněk Žabokrtský. 2006. CzEng: Czech-English Parallel Corpus, Release version 0.5. *Prague Bulletin of Mathematical Linguistics*, 86:59–62.

Thorsten Brants. 2000. TnT - A Statistical Part-of-Speech Tagger . pages 224–231, Seattle.

Michael Collins. 1999. *Head-driven Statistical Models for Natural Language Parsing*. Ph.D. thesis, University of Pennsylvania, Philadelphia.

Jan Cuřín et al. 2004. Prague Czech - English Dependency Treebank, Version 1.0. CD-ROM, Linguistics Data Consortium, LDC Catalog No.: LDC2004T25, Philadelphia.

Jan Hajič et al. 2006. Prague Dependency Treebank 2.0. CD-ROM, Linguistic Data Consortium, LDC Catalog No.: LDC2006T01, Philadelphia.

Jan Hajič. 2004. *Disambiguation of Rich Inflection – Computational Morphology of Czech*. Charles University – The Karolinum Press, Prague.

Mitchell P. Marcus, Beatrice Santorini, and Mary Ann Marcinkiewicz. 1994. Building a Large Annotated Corpus of English: The Penn Treebank. *Computational Linguistics*, 19(2):313–330.

Ryan McDonald, Fernando Pereira, Kiril Ribarov, and Jan Hajič. 2005. Non-Projective Dependency Parsing using Spanning Tree Algorithms. In *Proceedings of HTL/EMNLP*, pages 523–530, Vancouver, Canada.

Arul Menezes and Stephen D. Richardson. 2001. A best-first alignment algorithm for automatic extraction of transfer mappings from bilingual corpora. In *Proceedings of the workshop on Data-driven methods in machine translation*, volume 14, pages 1–8.

Guido Minnen, John Carroll, and Darren Pearce. 2000. Robust Applied Morphological Generation. In *Proceedings of the 1st International Natural Language Generation Conference*, pages 201–208, Israel.

Franz Josef Och and Hermann Ney. 2003. A Systematic Comparison of Various Statistical Alignment Models. *Computational Linguistics*, 29(1):19–51.

Petr Sgall. 1967. *Generativní popis jazyka a česká deklinace*. Academia, Prague.

MATREX: the DCU MT System for WMT 2008

John Tinsley, Yanjun Ma, Sylwia Ozdowska, Andy Way
National Centre for Language Technology
Dublin City University
Dublin 9, Ireland
{jtinsley, yma, sozdowska, away}@computing.dcu.ie

Abstract

In this paper, we give a description of the machine translation system developed at DCU that was used for our participation in the evaluation campaign of the Third Workshop on Statistical Machine Translation at ACL 2008.

We describe the modular design of our data-driven MT system with particular focus on the components used in this participation. We also describe some of the significant modules which were unused in this task.

We participated in the *EuroParl* task for the following translation directions: Spanish–English and French–English, in which we employed our hybrid EBMT-SMT architecture to translate. We also participated in the Czech–English *News* and *News Commentary* tasks which represented a previously untested language pair for our system. We report results on the provided development and test sets.

1 Introduction

In this paper, we present the Data-Driven MT systems developed at DCU, MATREX (Machine Translation using Examples). This system is a hybrid system which exploits EBMT and SMT techniques to build a combined translation model.

We participated in both the French–English and Spanish–English EuroParl tasks. In these two tasks, we monolingually chunk both source and target sides of the dataset using a marker-based chunker (Gough and Way, 2004). We then align these chunks using a dynamic programming, edit-distance-style algorithm and combine them with phrase-based SMT-style chunks into a single translation model.

We also participated in the Czech–English News Commentary and News tasks. This language pair represents a new challenge for our system and provides a good test of its flexibility.

The remainder of this paper is organised as follows: Section 2 details the various components of our system, in particular the chunking and chunk alignment strategies used for the shared task. In Section 3, we outline the complete system setup for the shared task, and in Section 4 we give some results and discussion thereof.

2 The MATREX System

The MATREX system is a modular hybrid data-driven MT system, built following established Design Patterns, which exploits aspects of both the EBMT and SMT paradigms. It consists of a number of extendible and re-implementable modules, the most significant of which are:

- *Word Alignment Module*: outputs a set of word alignments given a parallel corpus,
- *Chunking Module*: outputs a set of chunks given an input corpus,
- *Chunk Alignment Module*: outputs aligned chunk pairs given source and target chunks extracted from comparable corpora,
- *Decoder*: returns optimal translation given a set of aligned sentence, chunk/phrase and word pairs.

In some cases, these modules may comprise wrappers around pre-existing software. For example, our system configuration for the shared task incorporates a wrapper around GIZA++ (Och and Ney, 2003) for word alignment and a wrapper around Moses (Koehn et al., 2007) for decoding. It

Proceedings of the Third Workshop on Statistical Machine Translation, pages 171–174,
Columbus, Ohio, USA, June 2008.

should be noted, however, that the complete system is not limited to using only these specific module choices. The following subsections describe those modules unique to our system.

2.1 Marker-Based Chunking

The chunking module used for the shared task is based on the Marker Hypothesis, a psycholinguistic constraint which posits that all languages are marked for surface syntax by a specific closed set of lexemes or morphemes which signify context. Using a set of closed-class (or "marker") words for a particular language, such as determiners, prepositions, conjunctions and pronouns, sentences are segmented into chunks. A chunk is created at each new occurrence of a marker word with the restriction that each chunk must contain at least one content (or non-marker) word. An example of this chunking strategy for English and Spanish is given in Figure 1.

2.2 Chunk Alignment

In order to align the chunks obtained by the chunking procedures described in Section 2.1, we make use of an "edit-distance-style" dynamic programming alignment algorithm.

In the following, a denotes an alignment between a target sequence e consisting of I chunks and a source sequence f consisting of J chunks. Given these sequences of chunks, we are looking for the most likely alignment $\hat{a}$:

$$\hat{a} = \operatorname*{argmax}_a \mathbb{P}(a|e,f) = \operatorname*{argmax}_a \mathbb{P}(a,e|f).$$

We first consider alignments such as those obtained by an edit-distance algorithm, i.e.

$$a = (t_1, s_1)(t_2, s_2)\dots(t_n, s_n),$$

with $\forall k \in [\![1,n]\!]$, $t_k \in [\![0,I]\!]$ and $s_k \in [\![0,J]\!]$, and $\forall k < k'$:

$$t_k \leq t_{k'} \text{ or } t_{k'} = 0,$$
$$s_k \leq s_{k'} \text{ or } s_{k'} = 0,$$

where $t_k = 0$ (resp. $s_k = 0$) denotes a non-aligned target (resp. source) chunk.

We then assume the following model:

$$\mathbb{P}(a,e|f) = \Pi_k \mathbb{P}(t_k, s_k, e|f) = \Pi_k \mathbb{P}(e_{t_k}|f_{s_k}),$$

where $\mathbb{P}(e_0|f_j)$ (resp. $\mathbb{P}(e_i|f_0)$) denotes an "insertion" (resp. "deletion") probability.

Assuming that the parameters $\mathbb{P}(e_{t_k}|f_{s_k})$ are known, the most likely alignment is computed by a simple dynamic-programming algorithm.[1]

Instead of using an Expectation-Maximization algorithm to estimate these parameters, as commonly done when performing word alignment (Brown et al., 1993; Och and Ney, 2003), we directly compute these parameters by relying on the information contained within the chunks. The conditional probability $\mathbb{P}(e_{t_k}|f_{s_k})$ can be computed in several ways. In our experiments, we have considered three main sources of knowledge: (i) word-to-word translation probabilities, (ii) word-to-word cognates, and (iii) chunk labels. These sources of knowledge are combined in a log-linear framework. The weights of the log-linear model are not optimised; we experimented with different sets of parameters and did not find any significant difference as long as the weights stay in the interval $[0.5 - 1.5]$. Outside this interval, the quality of the model decreases. More details about the combination of knowledge sources can be found in (Stroppa and Way, 2006).

2.3 Unused Modules

There are numerous other features available in our system which, due to time constraints, were not exploited for the purposes of the shared task. They include:

- *Word packing* (Ma et al., 2007): a bilingually motivated packing of words that changes the basic unit of the alignment process in order to simplify word alignment.
- *Supertagging* (Hassan et al., 2007b): incorporating lexical syntactic descriptions, in the form of supertags, to the language model and target side of the translation model in order to better inform decoding.
- *Source-context features* (Stroppa et al., 2007): use memory-based classification to incorporate context-informed features on the source side of the translation model.
- *Treebank-based phrase extraction* (Tinsley et al., 2007): extract word and phrase alignments based on linguistically informed sub-sentential alignment of the parallel data.

[1]This algorithm is actually a classical edit-distance algorithm in which distances are replaced by opposite-log-conditional probabilities.

English: *[I voted] [in favour] [of the strategy presented] [by the council] [concerning relations] [with Mediterranean countries]*
Spanish: *[He votado] [a favor] [de la estrategia presentada] [por el consejo] [relativa las relaciones] [con los países mediterranéos]*

Figure 1: English and Spanish Marker-Based chunking

Filter criteria	es–en	fr–en	cz–en
Initial Total	1258778	1288074	1096941
Blank Lines	5632	4200	2
Length	6794	8361	2922
Fertility	120	82	1672
Final Total	1246234	1275432	1092345

Table 1: Summary of pre-processing on training data.

System	BLEU (-EBMT)	BLEU (+EBMT)
es–en	0.3283	0.3287
fr–en	0.2768	0.2770
cz–en	0.2235	-

Table 2: Summary of results on developments sets *devtest2006* for EuroParl tasks and *nc-test2007* for cz–en tasks.

System	BLEU (-EBMT)	BLEU (+EBMT)
es–en	0.3274	0.3285
fr–en	0.3163	0.3174
cz–en (news)	0.1458	-
cz–en (nc)	0.2217	-

Table 3: Summary of results on 2008 test data.

3 Shared Task Setup

The following section describes the system setup using the Spanish–English and French–English *EuroParl*, and Czech–English *CzEng* training data.

3.1 Pre-processing

For all tasks we initially tokenised the data (Czech data was already tokenised) and removed blank lines. We then filtered out sentence pairs based on length (>100 words) and fertility (9:1 word ratio). Finally we lowercased the data. Details of this pre-processing are given in Table 1.

3.2 System Configuration

As mentioned in Section 2, our word alignment module employs a wrapper around GIZA++.

We built a 5-gram language model based the target side of the training data. This was done using the SRI Language Modelling toolkit (Stolcke, 2002) employing linear interpolation and modified Kneser-Ney discounting (Chen and Goodman, 1996).

Our phrase-table comprised a combination of marker-based chunk pairs[2], extracted as described in Sections 2.1 and 2.2, and word-alignment-based phrase pairs extracted using the "*grow-diag-final*" method of Koehn et al. (2003), with a maximum phrase length of 7 words. Phrase translation probabilities were estimated by relative frequency over all phrase pairs and were combined with other features, such as a reordering model, in a log-linear combination of functions.

We tuned our system on the development set *devtest2006* for the EuroParl tasks and on *nc-test2007* for Czech–English, using minimum error-rate training (Och, 2003) to optimise BLEU score.

Finally, we carried out decoding using a wrapper around the Moses decoder.

3.3 Post-processing

Case restoration was carried out by training the system outlined above - without the EBMT chunk extraction - to translate from the lowercased version of the applicable target language training data to the truecased version. We have previously shown this approach to be very effective for both case and punctuation restoration (Hassan et al., 2007a). The translations were then detokenised.

4 Results

The system output is evaluated with respect to BLEU score. Results on the development sets and test sets for each task are given in Tables 2 and 3 respectively, where "-EBMT" indicates that EBMT chunk modules were not used, and "+EBMT" indicates that they were used.

[2]This module was omitted from the Czech–English system as we have yet to verify whether marker-based chunking is appropriate for Czech.

4.1 Discussion

Those configurations which incorporated the EBMT chunks improved slightly over those which did not. Groves (2007) has shown previously that combining EBMT and SMT translation models can lead to considerable improvement over the baseline systems from which they are derived. The results achieved here lead us to believe that on such a large scale there may be a more effective way to incorporate the EBMT chunks.

Previous work has shown the EBMT chunks to have higher precision than their SMT counterparts, but they lack sufficient recall when used in isolation (Groves, 2007). We believe that increasing their influence in the translation model may lead to improved translation accuracy. One experiment to this effect would be to add the EBMT chunks as a separate phrase table in the log-linear model and allow the decoder to chose when to use them.

Finally, we intend to exploit the unused modules of the system in future experiments to investigate their effects on the tasks presented here.

Acknowledgments

This work is supported by Science Foundation Ireland (grant nos. 05/RF/CMS064 and OS/IN/1732). Thanks also to the reviewers for their insightful comments and suggestions.

References

Brown, P. F., Pietra, S. A. D., Pietra, V. J. D., and Mercer, R. L. (1993). The mathematics of statistical machine translation: Parameter estimation. *Computational Linguistics*, 19(2):263–311.

Chen, S. F. and Goodman, J. (1996). An Empirical Study of Smoothing Techniques for Language Modeling. In *Proceedings of the Thirty-Fourth Annual Meeting of the Association for Computational Linguistics*, pages 310–318, San Francisco, CA.

Gough, N. and Way, A. (2004). Robust Large-Scale EBMT with Marker-Based Segmentation. In *Proceedings of the 10th International Conference on Theoretical and Methodological Issues in Machine Translation (TMI-04)*, pages 95–104, Baltimore, MD.

Groves, D. (2007). *Hybrid Data-Driven Models of Machine Translation*. PhD thesis, Dublin City University, Dublin, Ireland.

Hassan, H., Ma, Y., and Way, A. (2007a). MATREX: the DCU Machine Translation System for IWSLT 2007. In *Proceedings of the International Workshop on Spoken Language Translation*, pages 69–75, Trento, Italy.

Hassan, H., Sima'an, K., and Way, A. (2007b). Supertagged Phrase-based Statistical Machine Translation. In *Proceedings of the 45th Annual Meeting of the Association for Computational Linguistics (ACL'07)*, pages 288–295, Prague, Czech Republic.

Koehn, P., Hoang, H., Birch, A., Callison-Burch, C., Federico, M., Bertoldi, N., Cowan, B., Shen, W., Moran, C., Zens, R., Dyer, C., Bojar, O., Constantin, A., and Herbst, E. (2007). Moses: Open Source Toolkit for Statistical Machine Translation. In *Annual Meeting of the Association for Computational Linguistics (ACL), demonstration session*, pages 177–180, Prague, Czech Republic.

Koehn, P., Och, F. J., and Marcu, D. (2003). Statistical Phrase-Based Translation. In *Proceedings of the 2003 Conference of the North American Chapter of the Association for Computational Linguistics on Human Language Technology (NAACL '03)*, pages 48–54, Edmonton, Canada.

Ma, Y., Stroppa, N., and Way, A. (2007). Boostrapping Word Alignment via Word Packing. In *Proceedings of the 45th Annual Meeting of the Association for Computational Linguistics (ACL'07)*, pages 304–311, Prague, Czech Republic.

Och, F. (2003). Minimum error rate training in statistical machine translation. In *Proceedings of the 41st Annual Meeting of the Association for Computational Linguistics (ACL), pages 160–167, Sapporo, Japan.*, Sapporo, Japan.

Och, F. J. and Ney, H. (2003). A Systematic Comparison of Various Statistical Alignment Models. *Computational Linguistics*, 29(1):19–51.

Stolcke, A. (2002). SRILM - An Extensible Language Modeling Toolkit. In *Proceedings of the International Conference Spoken Language Processing*, Denver, CO.

Stroppa, N., van den Bosch, A., and Way, A. (2007). Exploiting Source Similarity for SMT using Context-Informed Features. In *Proceedings of the 11th International Conference on Theoretical and Methodological Issues in Machine Translation (TMI-07)*, pages 231–240, Skövde, Sweden.

Stroppa, N. and Way, A. (2006). MaTrEx: the DCU machine translation system for IWSLT 2006. In *Proceedings of the International Workshop on Spoken Language Translation*, pages 31–36, Kyoto, Japan.

Tinsley, J., Hearne, M., and Way, A. (2007). Exploiting Parallel Treebanks to Improve Phrase-Based Statistical Machine Translation. In *Proceedings of the Sixth International Workshop on Treebanks and Linguistic Theories (TLT-07)*, pages 175–187, Bergen, Norway.

Can we relearn an RBMT system?

Loïc Dugast (1,2) **Jean Senellart** (1) **Philipp Koehn** (2)
dugast@systran.fr senellart@systran.fr pkoehn@inf.ed.ac.uk

(1) SYSTRAN S.A.
La Grande Arche
1, Parvis de la Défense
92044 Paris
La Défense Cedex
France

(2) School of Informatics
University of Edinburgh
2 Buccleuch Place
Edinburgh, EH8 9LW
United Kingdom

Abstract

This paper describes SYSTRAN submissions for the shared task of the third Workshop on Statistical Machine Translation at ACL. Our main contribution consists in a French-English statistical model trained without the use of any human-translated parallel corpus. In substitution, we translated a monolingual corpus with SYSTRAN rule-based translation engine to produce the parallel corpus. The results are provided herein, along with a measure of error analysis.

1 Introduction

Current machine translation systems follow two different lines of research: (1) manually written rules associated with bilingual dictionaries (rule-based systems), (2) a statistical framework (statistical machine translation) based on large amount of monolingual and parallel corpora. The first line uses linguistically generalized information based on what humans understand from what happens in a given language (source and target) and what happens in the translation process. The translation process is *building* a translation from a given source sentence based on this knowledge. The second line exploits implicit information present in already translated corpora and more generally any text production in the target language to automatically *find* the most likely translation for a given source sentence. This approach has proven to be competitive with the rule-based approach when provided with enough resources on a specific domain. Though based on fundamentally different paradigms and exploiting different types of information, these two research lines are not in opposition and may be combined to produce improved results. For instance, serial combination of the two approaches has produced very good results in WMT07 (Simard, 2007), (Dugast, 2007) and NIST07 (Ueffing, 2008). (Schwenk et al., 2008) also combines both approaches and resources to build a better system.

The SYSTRAN's R&D team actually works to merge these two approaches, drawing benefit from their respective strengths. Initially, the SYSTRAN system was a pure rule-based system that in recent years began integrating statistical features and corpus-based model (Senellart, 2006). It must be noted that, for sake of simplification of the experiment and its interpretation, the base system mentioned in this paper is a purely rule-based version. In the framework of this research effort, various exploratory experiments are being run which aim both at finding efficient combination setups and at discriminating strengths and weaknesses of rule-based and statistical systems.

We had performed a first analysis on a statistical post-editing system (Dugast, 2007). The system submitted for Czech-English follows this setup. We present also here an original French-English statistical model which doesn't make use of the target side of the parallel data to train its phrase-table, but rather uses the rule-based translation of the source side. We call this system "SYSTRAN Relearnt" because, as far as the translation model is concerned, this system is a statistical model of the rule-based engine. In addition to the submitted system which only makes use of the Europarl monolingual data, we present additional results

Proceedings of the Third Workshop on Statistical Machine Translation, pages 175–178,
Columbus, Ohio, USA, June 2008.

using unrelated monolingual data in the news domain. Though human evaluation of these systems will provide additional insight, we try here to start analyzing the specificities of those systems.

2 Training without any human reference translation

If the need in terms of monolingual corpus to build language models can most of the time be fulfilled without much problem, the reliance of statistical models on parallel corpora is much more problematic. Work on domain adaptation for statistical machine translation (Koehn and Schroeder, 2007) tries to bring solutions to this issue. Statistical Post-Editing may well be another way to perform efficient domain-adaptation, but still requires parallel corpora. We try here to open a new path. Our submitted system for French-English on the Europarl task is a phrase based system, whose phrase table was trained on the rule based translation of the French Europarl corpus. The French side of the Europarl parallel corpus was translated with the baseline rule-based translation engine to produce the target side of the training data. However, the language model was trained on the real English Europarl data provided for the shared task. Training was otherwise performed according to baseline recommendations.

Corpus	Size (sentences)	Size (words)
Parallel FR-EN	0.94 M	21 M
Monolingual EN (LM)	1.4 M	38 M

Table 1: Corpus sizes for the submitted Europarl-domain translation

An additional (non-submitted) system was trained using two monolingual news corpora of approximately a million sentences. The French corpus was built from a leading French newspaper, the English from a leading American newspaper, both of the same year (1995). In the previous model, the English corpus used to train the language model actually contained the reference translations of the source corpus. This is not the case here. As for the previous model, the French corpus was translated by the rule-based system to produce the parallel training data, while the English corpus was used to train a language model,. This same language model is used in both statistical models: a *relearnt* system and a baseline phrase-based model whose phrase table was learnt from the Europarl parallel data. Both trainings followed the baseline recommendations of the shared task.

Corpus	Size (sentences)	Size (words)
Parallel FR-EN (Europarl v3)	0.94M	21M
Monolingual FR (Le Monde 1995)	0.96M	18M
Monolingual EN (NYT 1995)	3.8M	19M

Table 2: Corpus sizes for the additional model, trained on news domain

3 Results for the SYSTRAN-relearnt systems

We provide here results on evaluation metrics, an initial error analysis and results on the additional *relearnt* model.

Table 3 provides metrics results for four different systems : purely rule based, purely statistical, and the *relearnt* systems: Relearnt-0 is a plain statistical model of systran, while Relearnt uses a real English language model and is tuned on real English.

Model	BLEU(tuning, dev2006)	BLEU (test, devtest2006)
Baseline SYSTRAN	n.a.	21.27
Relearnt-0, with SYSTRAN English LM, tuned on SYSTRAN English	20.54	20.92
Relearnt	26.74	26.57
Baseline Moses	29.98	29.86

Table 3: Results of systems on Europarl task, trained (when relevant) on Europarl-only data

The score of the Relearnt-0 model is slightly lower than the rule-based original (absence of morphological analysis and some non-local rules which failed to be modelled may explain this). The use of a real English language model and tuning set gives a more than 5 BLEU points improvement, which is only 3 BLEU points below the Moses baseline, which uses the Europarl phrase table.

Comparing these three systems may help us discriminate between the statistical nature of a translation system and the fact it was trained on the relevant domain. For this purpose, we defined 11 error types and counted occurrences for 100 random-picked sentences of the devtest2006 test corpus for the three following systems : a baseline phrase-based system, a SYSTRAN relearnt phrase-based system and the baseline SYSTRAN rule-based system. Results are displayed in tables 5.a and 5.b.

MC	Missing Content
MO	Missing Other
TCL	Translation Choice (content, lemma)
TCI	Translation Choice (content, inflection)
TCO	Translation Choice (other)
EWC	Extra Word Content
EWO	Extra Word Other
UW	Unknown word
WOS	Word Order, short
WOL	Word Order, long (distance>=3 words)
PNC	Punctuation

Table 4 : Short definition of error types

System	MC	MO	TCL	TCI	TCO
SYSTRAN	**0.02**	**0.2**	1.11	**0.14**	0.48
Relearnt	0.22	0.39	0.77	0.22	0.38
Moses	0.35	0.46	**0.63**	0.27	**0.25**

Table 5.a : Average number of errors/sentence

System	EWC	EW0	UW	WOS	WOL	PNC
SYSTRAN	**0**	0.72	**0.06**	0.41	**0.02**	**0**
Relearnt	0.05	**0.35**	0.09	0.41	0.05	**0**
Moses	0.17	0.4	0.12	**0.3**	0.08	0.02

Table 5.b : Average number of errors/sentence

Such results lead us to make the following comments, regarding the various error types:

- Missing words

This type of error seems to be specific to statistical systems (counts are close between *relearnt* and baseline Moses) . Although we do not have evidence for that, we guess that it is especially impairing adequacy when content words are concerned.

- Extra words

Obviously, the rule-based output produces many useless functional words (determiners, prepositions…) while statistical systems do not have this problem that much. However, they may also produce extra content words..

- Unknown words

Few words are out of the rule-based dictionaries' vocabulary. Morphological analysis may explain at least part of this.

- Translation choice

Translation choice is the major strength of the statistical model. Note that the *relearnt* system gains a great deal of the difference between Systran and Moses in this category. We would expect the remaining difference to require more translation choices (which may be learnt from a parallel corpus). Inflection errors remain low for the rule-based system only, thanks to its morphological module.

- Word Order

The language model couldn't lower the number of short-distance word-order errors (no difference between SYSTRAN and SYSTRAN relearnt). Long-distance word order is, as expected, better for the rule-based output, though French-English is not known to be especially sensitive to this issue.

Additionally, table 6 shows the results of the *relearnt* system we trained using only monolingual corpus. It performed better than both the europarl-trained phrase-based model and the baseline rule-based engine. Table 7 shows the three different translations of a same example French sentence.

Model	BLEU (tuning, nc-dev2007)	BLEU (test, nctest2007)
SYSTRAN	n.a.	21.32
Relearnt	22.8	23.15
Baseline Moses	22.7	22.19

Table 6 : Results of systems on News task

SOURCE	Ces politiques sont considérées comme un moyen d'offrir des réparations pour les injustices du passé et, plus important, de créer des modèles de rôle et de surmonter la discrimination restante et peut-être involontaire.
SYSTRAN	These policies are regarded as a means of offering repairs for the injustices of the past and, more important, of creating models of role and of overcoming remaining and perhaps involuntary discrimination.
Moses	these policies are regarded as a way to offer of repairs for past injustices and , more important , to create a role models and remaining discrimination and perhaps involuntary .
Relearnt	these policies are regarded as a means to offer repairs for the past injustices and , more important , creating role models and overcome remaining discrimination and perhaps involuntary .
REF	These policies are seen as a way of offering reparation for past injustices and, more importantly, for creating role models and for overcoming residual and perhaps involuntary discrimination.

Table 7 : Example outputs for the news domain models (example taken from the **nc-test2007** corpus)

4 Conclusion

The *relearnt* experiment primary goal was to set-up a comparison between three different systems, with equivalent resources. This experiment showed that a statistical translation system may be granted a high BLEU score, even if its translation model was not extracted from corpus. It remains to be seen how this correlates with human judgment (Callison-Burch, 2006), but the detailed error analysis we performed already shows improvements for important categories of errors.

This experiment provided us with some new insight on the strengths and weaknesses of rule-based and phrase-based systems. As an intermediate between a purely corpus-based statistical system and a rule-based system, this setup could benefit from some of the strengths of a phrase-based statistical system, though at the expense of its known drawbacks.

As future work, we may pursue in this direction by exploring the effect of the size of the monolingual corpus used for training the translation model. We may also refine the model by using the target side of the parallel training data when building the language model corpus (to avoid a mismatch of vocabularies) and also combine such a model with the translation model(s) trained on whatever parallel data is available. This would then be interesting to compare this strategy with the corpus-based-only strategies that make use of smaller in-domain parallel corpora.

References

Chris Callison-Burch, Miles Osborne and Philipp Koehn, 2006. *Re-evaluating the Role of Bleu in Machine Translation Research.* In Proceedings of EACL-2006

L. Dugast, J. Senellart and P. Koehn. *Statistical Post-Editing on SYSTRAN's Rule-Based Translation System. Proc. 2nd ACL Workshop on Statistical Machine Translation*, pp. 220-223, June 2007.

Philipp Koehn &al. *Moses: Open Source Toolkit for Statistical Machine Translation*, ACL 2007, demonstration session

Philipp Koehn and Josh Schroeder. Experiments in Domain Adaptation for Statistical Machine Translation, ACL Workshop on Statistical Machine Translation 2007

Holger Schwenk, Jean-Baptiste Fouet and Jean Senellart. *First Steps towards a general purpose French/English Statistical Machine Translation System.* Submitted at the 3rd ACL Workshop on Statistical Machine Translation, 2008

Jean Senellart. 2006. *Boosting linguistic rule-based MT system with corpus-based approaches.* In Presentation. GALE PI Meeting, Boston, MA

M. Simard, C. Goutte, and P. Isabelle. *Statistical Phrase-based Post-Editing. Proc. HLT-NAACL*, pp. 508-515, April 2007.

Simard Michel & al. 2007. *Rule-based Translation With Statistical Phrase-based Post-editing.* In Proceedings of WMT07

Nicola Ueffing, Jens Stephan, Evgeny Matusov, Loïc Dugast, George Foster, Roland Kuhn, Jean Senellart, and Jin Yang *Tighter Integration of Rule-based and Statistical MT in Serial System Combination.* Submitted

Using Moses to Integrate Multiple Rule-Based Machine Translation Engines into a Hybrid System

Andreas Eisele[1,2], **Christian Federmann**[2], **Hervé Saint-Amand**[1], **Michael Jellinghaus**[1], **Teresa Herrmann**[1], **Yu Chen**[1]
1: Saarland University, Saarbrücken, Germany
2: DFKI GmbH, Saarbrücken, Germany

Abstract

Based on an architecture that allows to combine statistical machine translation (SMT) with rule-based machine translation (RBMT) in a multi-engine setup, we present new results that show that this type of system combination can actually increase the lexical coverage of the resulting hybrid system, at least as far as this can be measured via BLEU score.

1 Introduction

(Chen et al., 2007) describes an architecture that allows to combine statistical machine translation (SMT) with one or multiple rule-based machine translation (RBMT) systems in a multi-engine setup. It uses a variant of standard SMT technology to align translations from one or more RBMT systems with the source text and incorporated phrases extracted from these alignments into the phrase table of the SMT system. Using this approach it is possible to employ a vanilla installation of the open-source decoder Moses[1] (Koehn et al., 2007) to find good combinations of phrases from SMT training data with the phrases derived from RBMT. A similar method was presented in (Rosti et al., 2007).

This setup provides an elegant solution to the fairly complex task of integrating multiple MT results that may differ in word order using only standard software modules, in particular GIZA++ (Och and Ney, 2003) for the identification of building blocks and Moses for the recombination, but the authors were not able to observe improvements in terms of BLEU score. A closer investigation revealed that the experiments had suffered from a couple of technical difficulties, such as mismatches in character encodings generated by different MT engines and similar problems. This motivated us to re-do these experiments in a somewhat more systematic way for this year's shared translation task, paying the required attention to all the technical details and also to try it out on more language pairs.

2 System Architecture

For conducting the translations, we use a multi-engine MT approach based on a "vanilla" Moses SMT system with a modified phrase table as a central element. This modification is performed by augmenting the standard phrase table with entries obtained from translating the data with several rule-based MT systems. The resulting phrase table thus combines statistically gathered phrase pairs with phrase pairs generated by linguistic rules.

Basing its decision about the final translation on the obtained "combined" phrase table, the SMT decoder searches for the best translation by recombining the building blocks that have been contributed by the different RBMT systems and the original SMT system trained on Europarl data.

A sketch of the overall architecture is given in Fig. 1, where the lighter parts represent the modules and data sets used in purely statistical MT, and the darker parts are the additional modules and data sets derived from the rule-based engines. The last word in the proposed setup is thus given to the SMT decoder, which can recombine (and potentially also tear apart) linguistically well-formed constructs

[1] see http://www.statmt.org/moses/

Proceedings of the Third Workshop on Statistical Machine Translation, pages 179–182,
Columbus, Ohio, USA, June 2008.

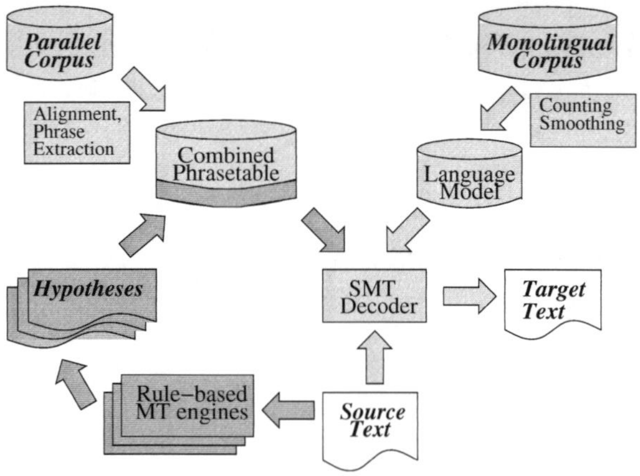

Figure 1: Hybrid architecture of the system

from the rule-based engines' output.

2.1 The Combined Phrase Table

The combined phrase table is built from the original Moses phrase table and separate phrase tables for each of the RBMT systems that are used in our setup. Since the original phrase table is created during the training process of the Moses decoder with the Europarl bilingual corpus as training material, it comprises general knowledge about typical constructions and vocabulary from the Europarl domain. Therefore, a standard Moses SMT system is, in principle, well adapted for input from this domain. However, it will have problems in dealing with vocabulary and structures that did not occur in the training data. The additional phrase tables are generated separately for each RBMT system from the source text and its translation by the respective system. By using a combined phrase table that includes the original Moses phrase table as well as the phrase tables from the RBMT systems, the hybrid system can both handle a wider range of syntactic constructions and exploit knowledge that the RBMT systems possess about the particular vocabulary of the source text.

3 Implementation

3.1 MT Systems and Knowledge Sources

Apart from the Moses SMT system, we used a set of six rule-based MT engines that are partly available via web interfaces and partly installed locally. The web interfaces are provided by Altavista Babelfish (based on Systran), SDL, ProMT and Lucy (a recent offspring of METAL). All of them deliver significantly different output translations. Locally installed systems are OpenLogos (for German↔English, English→Spanish and English→French) and translatePro by lingenio (for German↔English). The language model for our primary setup is based on the Europarl corpus whereas the English Gigaword corpus served as training data for a contrastive setup that was created for the translation direction German→English only.

3.2 Alignment of RBMT output

As already mentioned above, the construction of the RBMT system specific phrase tables is a major part of the overall system architecture. Such an RBMT phrase table is generated from a bilingual corpus consisting of the input text and its translation by the respective RBMT system. Because this corpus has the mere size of the text to be translated, it usually is not big enough to ensure the statistical methods for phrase table building of the Moses system to work. Therefore, we create the alignments between the RBMT input and output with help of another tool (Theison, 2007) that is based on knowledge learned in a previously conducted training phase with an appropriately bigger corpus. On the basis of the alignments created in this manner, the Moses training script provides a phrase table that consists of the source text vocabulary. These steps are carried out for each one of the six RBMT systems leading to six source text specific phrase tables which are then combined with the original Moses phrase table.

3.3 Combination of Phrase Tables

The combination process basically consists of the concatenation of the Moses phrase table and the previously created RBMT phrase tables with one minor adjustment: The phrase table resulting from this combination now also features additional columns indicating which system each phrase table entry originated from. For each new source text, the RBMT phrase tables have to be created from scratch and incorporated into a new combined phrase table.

3.4 Tuning

The typical process for creating an SMT system with the Moses toolkit includes a tuning step in which

	Europarl						NewsCommentary					
	de-en	en-de	fr-en	en-fr	es-en	en-es	de-en	en-de	fr-en	en-fr	es-en	en-es
SMT	22.81	19.78	24.18	21.62	31.68	24.46	14.24	9.75	11.60	12.24	17.27	14.48
Hybrid	**27.85**	**20.75**	**28.12**	**28.82**	**33.15**	**32.31**	17.36	13.57	17.66	20.71	**22.16**	**22.55**
RBMT1*	13.34	11.09	——	17.19	——	18.63	14.90	12.34	——	15.11	——	17.13
RBMT2	16.19	12.06	——	——	——	——	16.66	13.64	——	——	——	——
RBMT3	16.32	10.88	18.18	20.38	19.32	20.89	16.88	12.53	17.20	18.82	19.00	19.98
RBMT4	15.58	12.09	19.00	22.20	18.99	21.69	**17.41**	**13.93**	17.73	**20.85**	19.14	21.70
RBMT5	15.58	9.54	21.36	12.98	18.47	20.59	15.99	11.05	**18.65**	19.49	20.50	20.02
RBMT6	13.96	9.44	17.16	18.91	18.01	19.18	15.08	10.41	16.86	17.82	18.70	19.97

Table 1: Performance of baseline SMT system, our system and RBMT systems (BLEU scores)

the system searches for the best weight configuration for the columns in the phrase table while given a development set to be translated, and corresponding reference translations. In our hybrid setup, it is equally essential to conduct tuning since the combined phrase table we use contains 7 more columns than the original Moses phrase table. All these columns are given the same default weight initially and thus still need be to be tuned to more meaningful values. From this year's Europarl development data the first 200 sentences of each of the data sets dev2006, test2006, test2007 and devtest2006 were concatenated to build our development set. This set of 800 sentences was used for Minimum Error Rate Training (Och, 2003) to tune the weights of our system with respect to BLEU score.

4 Results

In order to be able to evaluate our hybrid approaches in contrast to stand-alone rule-based approaches, we also calculated BLEU scores for the translations conducted by the RBMT systems used in the hybrid setup. Our hybrid system is compared to a SMT baseline and all the 6 RBMT systems that we used. Table 1 shows the evaluation of all the systems in terms of BLEU score (Papineni et al., 2002) with the best score highlighted. The empty cells in the table indicate the language pairs which are not available in the corresponding systems[2]. The SMT system is the one upon which we build the hybrid system. According to the scores, the hybrid system produces better results than the baseline SMT system in all cases. The difference between our system and the baseline is more significant for out-of-domain tests, where gaps in the lexicon tend to be more severe.

Figure 2 illustrates an example of how the hybrid system differs from the baseline SMT system and how it benefits from the RBMT systems. The example lists the English translations of the same German sentence (from News Commentary test set) from different systems involved in our experiment. Neither the word "Pentecost" nor its German translation "Pfingsten" has appeared in the training corpus. Therefore, the SMT baseline system cannot translate the word and chooses to leave the word as it is whereas all the RBMT systems translate the word correctly. The hybrid system appears to have the corresponding lexicon gap covered by the extra entries produced by the RBMT systems. On the other side, these additional entries may not always be helpful. The errors in RBMT outputs can be significant noise that destroys the correct information in the SMT system. In the example translation produced by the hybrid system, there is a comma missing after "in addition", which appears to be frequent in the RBMT outputs.

5 Outlook

The results reported in this paper are still somewhat preliminary in the sense that many possible (including some desirable) variants of the setup could not be tried out due to lack of time. In particular, we think that the full power of our approach on out-of-domain test data can only be exploited with the help of large language models trained on out-of-domain text, but could not yet try this systematically. Furthermore, the presence of multiple instances of

[2]The identities of respective RBMT systems are not revealed in this paper. RBMT1 is evaluated on the partial results produced due to some technical problems.

Source	Darüber hinaus gibt es je zwei Feiertage zu Ostern, Pfingsten, und Weihnachten.
Reference	In addition, Easter, Pentecost, and Christmas are each two-day holidays.
Moses	In addition, there are two holidays, pfingsten to Easter, and Christmas.
Hybrid	In addition there are the two holidays to Easter, Pentecost and Christmas.
RBMT1	Furthermore there are two holidays to Easter, Pentecost and Christmas .
RBMT2	Furthermore there are two holidays each at Easter, Pentecost and Christmas.
RBMT3	In addition there are each two holidays to Easters, Whitsun, and Christmas.
RBMT4	In addition, there is two holidays to Easter, Pentecost, and Christmas.
RBMT5	Beyond that there are ever two holidays to Easter, Whitsuntide, and Christmas.
RBMT6	In addition it gives two holidays apiece to easter, Pentecost, and Christmas.

Figure 2: German-English translation examples

the same phrase pair (with different weight) in the combined phrase table causes the decoder to generate many instances of identical results in different ways, which increases computational effort and significantly decreases the number of distinct cases that are considered during MERT. We suspect that a modification of our scheme that avoids this problem will be able to achieve better results, but experiments in this direction are still ongoing.

The approach presented here combines the strengths of multiple systems and is different from recent work on post-correction of RBMT output as presented in (Simard et al., 2007; Dugast et al., 2007), which focuses on the improvement of a single RBMT system by correcting typical errors via SMT techniques. These ideas are independent and a suitable combination of them could give rise to even better results.

Acknowledgments

This work was supported by the EuroMatrix project funded by the European Commission (6th Framework Programme). We thank Martin Kay, Hans Uszkoreit, and Silke Theison for interesting discussions and practical help, and two anonymous reviewers for hints to improve the paper.

References

Yu Chen, Andreas Eisele, Christian Federmann, Eva Hasler, Michael Jellinghaus, and Silke Theison. 2007. Multi-engine machine translation with an open-source SMT decoder. In *Proceedings of WMT07*, pages 193–196, Prague, Czech Republic, June. Association for Computational Linguistics.

Loïc Dugast, Jean Senellart, and Philipp Koehn. 2007. Statistical post-editing on SYSTRAN's rule-based translation system. In *Proceedings of WMT07*, pages 220–223, Prague, Czech Republic, June. Association for Computational Linguistics.

Philipp Koehn, Hieu Hoang, Alexandra Birch, Chris Callison-Burch, Marcello Federico, Nicola Bertoldi, Brooke Cowan, Wade Shen, Christine Moran, Richard Zens, Chris Dyer, Ondrej Bojar, Alexandra Constantin, and Evan Herbst. 2007. Moses: Open source toolkit for statistical machine translation. In *Proc. of ACL Demo and Poster Sessions*, pages 177–180, Jun.

Franz Josef Och and Hermann Ney. 2003. A systematic comparison of various statistical alignment models. *Computational Linguistics*, 29(1):19–51, Mar.

Franz Josef Och. 2003. Minimum error rate training for statistical machine translation. In *Proceedings of ACL*, Sapporo, Japan, July.

Kishore Papineni, Salim Roukos, Todd Ward, and Wei-Jing Zhu. 2002. Bleu: A method for automatic evaluation of machine translation. In *Proceedings of ACL*.

Antti-Veikko Rosti, Necip Fazil Ayan, Bing Xiang, Spyros Matsoukas, Richard Schwartz, and Bonnie J. Dorr. 2007. Combining translations from multiple machine translation systems. In *Proceedings of the Conference on Human Language Technology and North American chapter of the Association for Computational Linguistics Annual Meeting (HLT-NAACL'2007)*, pages 228–235, Rochester, NY, April 22-27.

Michel Simard, Nicola Ueffing, Pierre Isabelle, and Roland Kuhn. 2007. Rule-based translation with statistical phrase-based post-editing. In *Proceedings of WMT07*, pages 203–206, Prague, Czech Republic, June. Association for Computational Linguistics.

Silke Theison. 2007. Optimizing rule-based machine translation output with the help of statistical methods. Diploma thesis, Saarland University.

Incremental Hypothesis Alignment for Building Confusion Networks with Application to Machine Translation System Combination

Antti-Veikko I. Rosti and **Bing Zhang** and **Spyros Matsoukas** and **Richard Schwartz**
BBN Technologies, 10 Moulton Street, Cambridge, MA 02138
{arosti,bzhang,smatsouk,schwartz}@bbn.com

Abstract

Confusion network decoding has been the most successful approach in combining outputs from multiple machine translation (MT) systems in the recent DARPA GALE and NIST Open MT evaluations. Due to the varying word order between outputs from different MT systems, the hypothesis alignment presents the biggest challenge in confusion network decoding. This paper describes an incremental alignment method to build confusion networks based on the translation edit rate (TER) algorithm. This new algorithm yields significant BLEU score improvements over other recent alignment methods on the GALE test sets and was used in BBN's submission to the WMT08 shared translation task.

1 Introduction

Confusion network decoding has been applied in combining outputs from multiple machine translation systems. The earliest approach in (Bangalore et al., 2001) used edit distance based multiple string alignment (MSA) (Durbin et al., 1988) to build the confusion networks. The recent approaches used pair-wise alignment algorithms based on symmetric alignments from a HMM alignment model (Matusov et al., 2006) or edit distance alignments allowing shifts (Rosti et al., 2007). The alignment method described in this paper extends the latter by incrementally aligning the hypotheses as in MSA but also allowing shifts as in the TER alignment.

The confusion networks are built around a "skeleton" hypothesis. The skeleton hypothesis defines the word order of the decoding output. Usually, the 1-best hypotheses from each system are considered as possible skeletons. Using the pair-wise hypothesis alignment, the confusion networks are built in two steps. First, all hypotheses are aligned against the skeleton independently. Second, the confusion networks are created from the union of these alignments. The incremental hypothesis alignment algorithm combines these two steps. All words from the previously aligned hypotheses are available, even if not present in the skeleton hypothesis, when aligning the following hypotheses. As in (Rosti et al., 2007), confusion networks built around all skeletons are joined into a lattice which is expanded and rescored with language models. System weights and language model weights are tuned to optimize the quality of the decoding output on a development set.

This paper is organized as follows. The incremental TER alignment algorithm is described in Section 2. Experimental evaluation comparing the incremental and pair-wise alignment methods are presented in Section 3 along with results on the WMT08 Europarl test sets. Conclusions and future work are presented in Section 4.

2 Incremental TER Alignment

The incremental hypothesis alignment is based on an extension of the TER algorithm (Snover et al., 2006). The extension allows using a confusion network as the reference. First, the algorithm finds the minimum edit distance between the hypothesis and the reference network by considering all word arcs between two consecutive nodes in the reference network as possible matches for a hypothesis word at

Proceedings of the Third Workshop on Statistical Machine Translation, pages 183–186,
Columbus, Ohio, USA, June 2008.

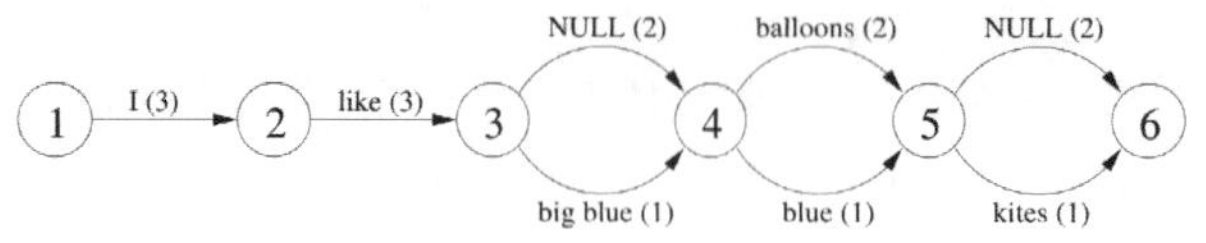

Figure 1: Network after pair-wise TER alignment.

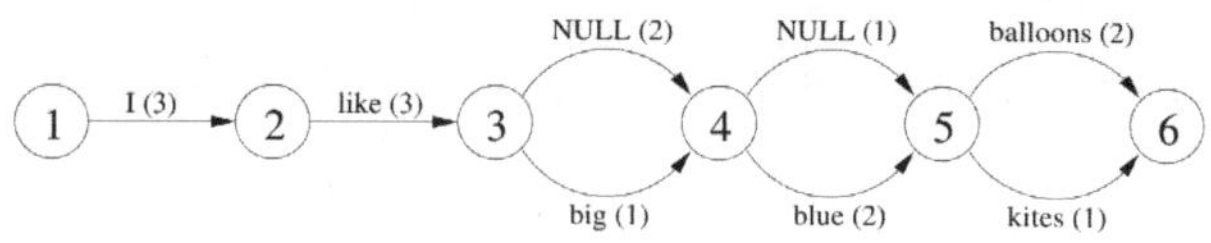

Figure 2: Network after incremental TER alignment.

that position. Second, shifts of blocks of words that have an exact match somewhere else in the network are tried in order to find a new hypothesis word order with a lower TER. Each shifted block is considered a single edit. These two steps are executed iteratively as a greedy search. The final alignment between the re-ordered hypothesis and the reference network may include matches, substitutions, deletions, and insertions.

The confusion networks are built by creating a simple confusion network from the skeleton hypothesis. If the skeleton hypothesis has N words, the initial network has N arcs and $N + 1$ nodes. Each arc has a set of system specific confidence scores. The score for the skeleton system is set to $1/2$ and the confidences for other systems are set to zeros. For each non-skeleton hypothesis, a TER alignment against the current network is executed as described above. Each match found will increase the system specific word arc confidence by $1/(1 + k)$ where k is the rank of the hypothesis in that system's N-best list. Each substitution will generate a new word arc at the corresponding position in the network. The word arc confidence for the system is set to $1/(1+k)$ and the confidences for other systems are set to zeros. Each deletion will generate a new NULL word arc unless one exists at the corresponding position in the network. The NULL word arc confidences are adjusted as in the case of a match or a substitution depending on whether the NULL word arc exists or not. Finally, each insertion will generate a new node and two word arcs at the corresponding position in the network. The first word arc will have the inserted word with the confidence set as in the case of a substitution and the second word arc will have a NULL word with confidences set by assuming all previously aligned hypotheses and the skeleton generated the NULL word arc.

After all hypotheses have been added into the confusion network, the system specific word arc confidences are scaled to sum to one over all arcs between each set of two consecutive nodes. Other scores for the word arc are set as in (Rosti et al., 2007).

2.1 Benefits over Pair-Wise TER Alignment

The incremental hypothesis alignment guarantees that insertions between a hypothesis and the current confusion network are always considered when aligning the following hypotheses. This is not the case in any pair-wise hypothesis alignment algorithm. During the pair-wise hypothesis alignment, an identical word in two hypotheses may be aligned as an insertion or a substitution in a different position with respect to the skeleton. This will result in undesirable repetition and lower confidence for that word in the final confusion network. Also, multiple insertions are not handled implicitly.

For example, three hypotheses "I like balloons", "I like big blue balloons", and "I like blue kites" might be aligned by the pair-wise alignment, assuming the first as the skeleton, as follows:

I	like	NULL	balloons	NULL
I	like	big blue	balloons	NULL

I	like	NULL	balloons	NULL
I	like	NULL	blue	kites

which results in the confusion network shown in Figure 1. The number of hypotheses proposing each word is shown in parentheses. The alignment between the skeleton and the second hypothesis has two consecutive insertions "big blue" which are not available for matching when the third hypothesis is aligned against the skeleton. Therefore, the word "blue" appears twice in the confusion network. If many hypotheses have multiple insertions at the same location with respect to the skeleton, they have to be treated as phrases or a secondary alignment process has to be applied.

Assuming the same hypotheses as above, the incremental hypothesis alignment may yield the following alignment:

System	TER	BLEU	MTR
worst	53.26	33.00	63.15
best	42.30	48.52	67.71
syscomb pw	39.85	52.00	68.73
syscomb giza	40.01	52.24	68.68
syscomb inc	39.25	52.73	68.97
oracle	21.68	64.14	78.18

Table 1: Results on the Arabic GALE Phase 2 system combination tuning set with four reference translations.

System	TER	BLEU	MTR
worst	59.09	20.74	57.24
best	48.18	31.46	62.61
syscomb pw	46.31	33.02	63.18
syscomb giza	46.03	33.39	63.21
syscomb inc	45.45	33.90	63.45
oracle	27.53	49.10	71.81

Table 2: Results on the Arabic GALE Phase 2 evaluation set with one reference translation.

I	like	NULL	NULL	balloons
I	like	big	blue	balloons
I	like	NULL	blue	kites

which results in the confusion network shown in Figure 2. In this case the word "blue" is available for matching when the third hypothesis is aligned. It should be noted that the final confusion network depends on the order in which the hypotheses are added. The experiments so far have indicated that different alignment order does not have a significant influence on the final combination results as measured by the automatic evaluation metrics. Usually, aligning the system outputs in the decreasing order of their TER scores on the development set yields the best scores.

2.2 Confusion Network Oracle

The extended TER algorithm can also be used to estimate an oracle TER in a confusion network by aligning the reference translations against the confusion network. The oracle hypotheses can be extracted by finding a path with the maximum number of matches. These hypotheses give a lower bound on the TER score for the hypotheses which can be generated from the confusion networks.

3 Experimental Evaluation

The quality of the final combination output depends on many factors. Combining very similar outputs does not yield as good gains as combining outputs from diverse systems. It is also important that the development set used to tune the combination weights is as similar to the evaluation set as possible. This development set should be different from the one used to tune the individual systems to avoid bias toward any system that may be over-tuned. Due to the tight schedule for the WMT08, there was no time to experiment with many configurations. As more extensive experiments have been conducted in the context of the DARPA GALE program, results on the Arabic GALE Phase 2 evaluation setup are first presented. The translation quality is measured by three MT evaluation metrics: TER (Snover et al., 2006), BLEU (Papineni et al., 2002), and METEOR (Lavie and Agarwal, 2007).

3.1 Results on Arabic GALE Outputs

For the Arabic GALE Phase 2 evaluation, nine systems were combined. Five systems were phrase-based, two hierarchical, one syntax-based, and one rule-based. All statistical systems were trained on common parallel data, tuned on a common genre specific development set, and a common English tokenization was used. The English bi-gram and 5-gram language models used in the system combination were trained on about 7 billion words of English text. Three iterations of bi-gram decoding weight tuning were performed followed by one iteration of 5-gram re-scoring weight tuning. All weights were tuned to minimize the sum of TER and 1-BLEU. The final 1-best outputs were true-cased and detokenized before scoring.

The results on the newswire system combination development set and the GALE Phase 2 evaluation set are shown in Tables 1 and 2. The first two rows show the worst and best scores from the individual systems. The scores may be from different systems as the best performing system in terms of TER was not necessarily the best performing system in terms of the other metrics. The following three rows show the scores of three combination outputs where the only difference was the hypothesis alignment method. The first, `syscomb pw`, corresponds

	BLEU	
System	de-en	fr-en
worst	11.84	16.31
best	28.30	33.13
syscomb	29.05	33.63

Table 3: NIST BLEU scores on the German-English (de-en) and French-English (fr-en) Europarl test2008 set.

to the pair-wise TER alignment described in (Rosti et al., 2007). The second, `syscomb giza`, corresponds to the pair-wise symmetric HMM alignments from GIZA++ described in (Matusov et al., 2006). The third, `syscomb inc`, corresponds to the incremental TER alignment presented in this paper. Finally, `oracle` corresponds to an estimate of the lower bound on the translation quality obtained by extracting the TER oracle output from the confusion networks generated by the incremental TER alignment. It is unlikely that there exists a set of weights that would yield the oracle output after decoding, though. The incremental TER alignment yields significant improvements over all individual systems and the combination outputs using the pair-wise alignment methods.

3.2 Results on WMT08 Europarl Outputs

On the WMT08 shared translation task, translations for two language pairs and two tasks were provided for the system combination experiments. Twelve systems participated in the German-English and fourteen in the French-English translation tasks. The translations of the Europarl test (test2008) were provided as the development set outputs and the translations of the News test (newstest2008) were provided as the evaluation set outputs. An English bi-gram, 4-gram, and true-caser language models were trained by using all English text available for the WMT08 shared task, including Europarl monolingual and news commentary parallel training sets. The outputs were tokenized and lower-cased before combination, and the final combination output was true-cased and detokenized.

The results on the Europarl test set for both language pairs are shown in table 3. The first two rows have the NIST BLEU scores of the worst and the best individual systems. The last row, `syscomb`, corresponds to the system combination using the incremental TER alignment. The improvements in the NIST BLEU scores are fairly modest which is probably due to low diversity of the system outputs. It is also unlikely that these weights are optimal for the out-of-domain News test set outputs.

4 Conclusions

This paper describes a novel hypothesis alignment algorithm for building confusion networks from multiple machine translation system outputs. The algorithm yields significant improvements on the Arabic GALE evaluation set outputs and was used in BBN's submission to the WMT08 shared translation task. The hypothesis alignment may benefit from using stemming and synonymy in matching words. Also, special handling of punctuation may improve the alignment further. The future work will investigate the influence of better alignment to the final combination outputs.

Acknowledgments

This work was supported by DARPA/IPTO Contract No. HR0011-06-C-0022 under the GALE program.

References

S. Bangalore, G. Bordel, and G. Riccardi. 2001. Computing consensus translation from multiple machine translation systems. In *Proc. ASRU*, pages 351–354.

R. Durbin, S.R. Eddy, A. Krogh, and G. Mitchison. 1988. *Biological Sequence Analysis: Probabilistic Models of Proteins and Nucleic Acids*. Cambridge Univ. Press.

A. Lavie and A. Agarwal. 2007. METEOR: An automatic metric for MT evaluation with high levels of correlation with human judgments. In *Proc. ACL/WMT*, pages 228–231.

E. Matusov, N. Ueffing, and H. Ney. 2006. Computing consensus translation from multiple machine translation systems using enhanced hypotheses alignment. In *Proc. EACL*, pages 33–40.

K. Papineni, S. Roukos, T. Ward, and W.-J. Zhu. 2002. BLEU: a method for automatic evaluation of machine translation. In *Proc. ACL*, pages 311–318.

A.-V.I. Rosti, S. Matsoukas, and R. Schwartz. 2007. Improved word-level system combination for machine translation. In *Proc. ACL 2007*, pages 312–319.

M. Snover, B. Dorr, R. Schwartz, L. Micciula, and J. Makhoul. 2006. A study of translation edit rate with targeted human annotation. In *Proc. AMTA*, pages 223–231.

The Role of Pseudo References in MT Evaluation

Joshua S. Albrecht and **Rebecca Hwa**
Department of Computer Science
University of Pittsburgh
{jsa8,hwa}@cs.pitt.edu

Abstract

Previous studies have shown automatic evaluation metrics to be more reliable when compared against many human translations. However, multiple human references may not always be available. It is more common to have only a single human reference (extracted from parallel texts) or no reference at all. Our earlier work suggested that one way to address this problem is to train a metric to evaluate a sentence by comparing it against *pseudo references*, or imperfect "references" produced by off-the-shelf MT systems. In this paper, we further examine the approach both in terms of the training methodology and in terms of the role of the human and pseudo references. Our expanded experiments show that the approach generalizes well across multiple years and different source languages.

1 Introduction

Standard automatic metrics are *reference-based*; that is, they compare system-produced translations against human-translated references produced for the same source. Since there is usually no single best way to translate a sentence, each MT output should be compared against many references. On the other hand, creating multiple human references is itself a costly process. For many naturally occurring datasets (e.g., parallel corpora) only a single reference is readily available.

The focus of this work is on developing automatic metrics for sentence-level evaluation with *at most one human reference*. One way to supplement the single human reference is to use *pseudo references*, or sentences produced by off-the-shelf MT systems, as stand-ins for human references. However, since pseudo references may be imperfect translations themselves, the comparisons cannot be fully trusted. Previously, we have taken a learning-based approach to develop a composite metric that combines measurements taken from multiple pseudo references (Albrecht and Hwa, 2007). Experimental results suggested the approach to be promising; but those studies did not consider how well the metric might generalize across multiple years and different languages. In this paper, we investigate the applicability of the pseudo-reference metrics under these more general conditions.

Using the WMT06 Workshop shared-task results (Koehn and Monz, 2006) as training examples, we train a metric that evaluates new sentences by comparing them against pseudo references produced by three off-the-shelf MT systems. We apply the learned metric to sentences from the WMT07 shared-task (Callison-Burch et al., 2007b) and compare the metric's predictions against human judgments. We find that additional pseudo references improve correlations for automatic metrics.

2 Background

The ideal evaluation metric reports an accurate distance between an input instance and its gold standard, but even when comparing against imperfect standards, the measured distances may still convey some useful information – they may help to triangulate the input's position relative to the true gold standard.

In the context of sentence-level MT evaluations,

Proceedings of the Third Workshop on Statistical Machine Translation, pages 187–190,
Columbus, Ohio, USA, June 2008.

the challenges are two-fold. First, the ideal quantitative distance function between a translation hypothesis and the proper translations is not known; current automatic evaluation metrics produce approximations to the true translational distance. Second, although we may know the qualitative goodness of the MT systems that generate the pseudo references, we do not know how imperfect the pseudo references are. These uncertainties make it harder to establish the true distance between the input hypothesis and the (unobserved) acceptable gold standard translations.

In order to combine evidence from these uncertain observations, we take a learning-based approach. Each hypothesis sentence is compared with multiple pseudo references using multiple metrics. Representing the measurements as a set of input features and using human-assessed MT sentences as training examples, we train a function that is optimized to correlate the features with the human assessments in the training examples. Specifically, for each input sentence, we compute a set of 18 kinds of reference-based measurements for each pseudo reference as well as 26 monolingual fluency measurements. The full set of measurements then serves as the input feature vector into the function, which is trained via support vector regression. The learned function can then be used as an evaluation metric itself: it takes the measurements of a new sentence as input and returns a composite score for that sentence.

The approach is considered successful if the metric's predictions on new test sentences correlate well with quantitative human assessments. Like other learned models, the metric is expected to perform better on data that are more similar to the training instances. Therefore, a natural question that arises with a metric developed in this manner is: how well does it generalize?

3 Research Questions

To better understand the capability of metrics that compare against pseudo-references, we consider the following aspects:

The role of learning Standard reference-based metrics can also use pseudo references; however, they would treat the imperfect references as gold standard. In contrast, the learning process aims to determine how much each comparison with a pseudo reference might be trusted. To observe the role of learning, we compare trained metrics against standard reference-based metrics, all using pseudo references.

The amount vs. types of training data The success of any learned model depends on its training experiences. We study the trade-off between the size of the training set and the specificity of the training data. We perform experiments comparing a metric trained from a large pool of heterogeneous training examples that include translated sentences from multiple languages and individual metrics trained from particular source languages.

The role of a single human reference Previous studies have shown the importance of comparing against multiple references. The approach in this paper attempts to approximate multiple human references with machine-produced sentences. Is a single trust-worthy translation more useful than multiple imperfect translations? To answer this question, we compare three different reference settings: using just a single human reference, using just the three pseudo references, and using all four references.

4 Experimental Setup

For the experiments reported in this paper, we used human-evaluated MT sentences from past shared-tasks of the WMT 2006 and WMT 2007. The data consists of outputs from German-English, Spanish-English, and French-English MT systems. The outputs are translations from two corpora: *Europarl* and *news commentary*. System outputs have been evaluated by human judges on a 5-point scale (Callison-Burch et al., 2007a). We have normalized scores to reduce biases from different judges (Blatz et al., 2003).

We experimented with using four different subsets of the WMT2006 data as training examples: only German-English, only Spanish-English, only French-English, all 06 data. The metrics are trained using support vector regression with a Gaussian kernel as implemented in the SVM-Light package (Joachims, 1999). The SVM parameters are tuned via grid-search on development data, 20% of the full training set that has been reserved for this purpose.

We used three MT systems to generate pseudo references: Systran[1], GoogleMT [2], and Moses (Koehn et al., 2007). We chose these three systems because they are widely accessible and because they take relatively different approaches. Moreover, although they have not all been human-evaluated in the past WMT shared tasks, they are well-known for producing good translations.

A metric is evaluated based on its Spearman rank correlation coefficient between the scores it gave to the evaluative dataset and human assessments for the same data. The correlation coefficient is a real number between -1, indicating perfect negative correlations, and +1, indicating perfect positive correlations.

Two standard reference-based metrics, BLEU (Papineni et al., 2002) and METEOR (Banerjee and Lavie, 2005), are used for comparisons. BLEU is smoothed (Lin and Och, 2004), and it considers only matching up to bigrams because this has higher correlations with human judgments than when higher-ordered n-grams are included.

5 Results

The full experimental comparisons are summarized in Table 1. Each cell shows the correlation coefficient between the human judgments and a metric (column) that uses a particular kind of references (row) for some evaluation data set (block row).

The role of learning With the exception of the German-English data, the learned metrics had higher correlations with human judges than the baselines, which used standard metrics with a single human reference. On the other hand, results suggest that pseudo references often also improve correlations for standard metrics. This may seem counter-intuitive because we can easily think of cases in which pseudo references hurt standard metrics (e.g., use poor outputs as pseudo references). We hypothesize that because the pseudo references came from high-quality MT systems and because standard metrics are based on simple word matches, the chances for bad judgments (input words matched against pseudo reference, but both are wrong) are relatively small compared to chances for good judgments. We further hypothesize that the learned metrics would be robust against the qualities of the pseudo reference MT systems.

The amount vs. types of training data Comparing the three metrics trained from single language datasets against the metric trained from all of WMT06 dataset, we see that the learning process benefitted from the larger quantity of training examples. It may be the case that the MT systems for the three language pairs are at a similar stage of maturity such that the training instances are mutually helpful.

The role of a single human reference Our results reinforce previous findings that metrics are more reliable when they have access to more than a single human reference. Our experimental data suggests that a single human reference often may not be as reliable as using three pseudo references alone. Finally, the best correlations are achieved by using both human and pseudo references.

6 Conclusion

We have presented an empirical study on automatic metrics for sentence-level MT evaluation with at most one human reference. We show that pseudo references from off-the-shelf MT systems can be used to augment the single human reference. Because they are imperfect, it is important to weigh the trustworthiness of these references through a training phase. The metric seems robust even when the applied to sentences from different systems of a later year. These results suggest that multiple imperfect translations make informative comparison points in supplement to human references.

Acknowledgments

This work has been supported by NSF Grants IIS-0612791.

[1] Available from http://www.systransoft.com/. We note that Systran is also a participating system under evaluation. Although Sys-Test will be deemed to be identical to Sys-Ref, it will not automatically receive a high score because the measurement is weighted by whether Sys-Ref was reliable during training. Furthermore, measurements between Sys-Test and other pseudo-references will provide alternative evidences for the metric to consider.

[2] http://www.google.com/language_tools/

Eval. Data	Ref Type	METEOR	BLEU	SVM(de06)	SVM(es06)	SVM(fr06)	SVM(wmt06)
de	1HR	0.458	*0.471*				
europarl	3PR	0.521*	0.527*	0.422	0.403	0.480*	0.467
07	1HR+3PR	0.535*	0.547*	0.471	0.480*	0.477*	0.523*
de	1HR	0.290	*0.333*				
news	3PR	0.400*	0.400*	0.262	0.279	0.261	0.261
07	1HR+3PR	0.432*	0.417*	0.298	0.321	0.269	0.330
es	1HR	0.377	*0.412*				
europarl	3PR	0.453*	0.483*	0.336	0.453*	0.432*	0.456*
07	1HR+3PR	0.491*	0.503*	0.405	0.513*	0.483*	0.510*
es	1HR	0.317	*0.332*				
news	3PR	0.320	0.317	0.393*	0.381*	0.426*	0.426*
07	1HR+3PR	0.353*	0.325	0.429*	0.427*	0.380*	0.486*
fr	1HR	*0.265*	0.246				
europarl	3PR	0.196	0.285*	0.270*	0.284*	0.355*	0.366*
07	1HR+3PR	0.221	0.290*	0.277*	0.324*	0.304*	0.381*
fr	1HR	0.226	*0.280*				
news	3PR	0.356*	0.383*	0.237	0.252	0.355*	0.373*
07	1HR+3PR	0.374*	0.394*	0.272	0.339*	0.319*	0.388*

Table 1: Correlation comparisons of metrics (columns) using different references (row): a single human reference (1HR), 3 pseudo references (3PR), or all (1HR+3PR). The type of training used for the regression-trained metrics are specified in parentheses. For each evaluated corpus, correlations higher than *standard metric using one human reference* are marked by an asterisk(*).

References

Joshua S. Albrecht and Rebecca Hwa. 2007. Regression for sentence-level MT evaluation with pseudo references. In *Proceedings of the 45th Annual Meeting of the Association for Computational Linguistics (ACL-2007)*.

Satanjeev Banerjee and Alon Lavie. 2005. Meteor: An automatic metric for MT evaluation with improved correlation with human judgments. In *ACL 2005 Workshop on Intrinsic and Extrinsic Evaluation Measures for Machine Translation and/or Summarization*, June.

John Blatz, Erin Fitzgerald, George Foster, Simona Gandrabur, Cyril Goutte, Alex Kulesza, Alberto Sanchis, and Nicola Ueffing. 2003. Confidence estimation for machine translation. Technical Report Natural Language Engineering Workshop Final Report, Johns Hopkins University.

Chris Callison-Burch, Cameron Fordyce, Philipp Koehn, Christof Monz, and Josh Schroeder. 2007a. (meta-) evaluation of machine translation. In *Proceedings of the Second Workshop on Statistical Machine Translation*, pages 136–158, Prague, Czech Republic, June. Association for Computational Linguistics.

Chris Callison-Burch, Philipp Koehn, Cameron Shaw Fordyce, and Christof Monz, editors. 2007b. *Proceedings of the Second Workshop on Statistical Machine Translation*. Association for Computational Linguistics, Prague, Czech Republic, June.

Thorsten Joachims. 1999. Making large-scale SVM learning practical. In Bernhard Schöelkopf, Christopher Burges, and Alexander Smola, editors, *Advances in Kernel Methods - Support Vector Learning*. MIT Press.

Philipp Koehn and Christof Monz, editors. 2006. *Proceedings on the Workshop on Statistical Machine Translation*. Association for Computational Linguistics, New York City, June.

P. Koehn, H. Hoang, A. Birch, C. Callison-Burch, M. Federico, N. Bertoldi, B. Cowan, W. Shen, C. Moran, R. Zens, et al. 2007. Moses: Open source toolkit for statistical machine translation. *Proceedings of ACL, Demonstration Session*.

Chin-Yew Lin and Franz Josef Och. 2004. Orange: a method for evaluating automatic evaluation metrics for machine translation. In *Proceedings of the 20th International Conference on Computational Linguistics (COLING 2004)*, August.

Kishore Papineni, Salim Roukos, Todd Ward, and Wei-Jing Zhu. 2002. Bleu: a method for automatic evaluation of machine translation. In *Proceedings of the 40th Annual Meeting of the Association for Computational Linguistics*, Philadelphia, PA.

Ranking vs. Regression in Machine Translation Evaluation

Kevin Duh*
Dept. of Electrical Engineering
University of Washington
Seattle, WA 98195
kevinduh@u.washington.edu

Abstract

Automatic evaluation of machine translation (MT) systems is an important research topic for the advancement of MT technology. Most automatic evaluation methods proposed to date are score-based: they compute scores that represent translation quality, and MT systems are compared on the basis of these scores.

We advocate an alternative perspective of automatic MT evaluation based on ranking. Instead of producing scores, we directly produce a ranking over the set of MT systems to be compared. This perspective is often simpler when the evaluation goal is system comparison. We argue that it is easier to elicit human judgments of ranking and develop a machine learning approach to train on rank data. We compare this ranking method to a score-based regression method on WMT07 data. Results indicate that ranking achieves higher correlation to human judgments, especially in cases where ranking-specific features are used.

1 Motivation

Automatic evaluation of machine translation (MT) systems is an important research topic for the advancement of MT technology, since automatic evaluation methods can be used to quickly determine the (approximate) quality of MT system outputs. This is useful for tuning system parameters and for comparing different techniques in cases when human judgments for each MT output are expensivie to obtain.

Many automatic evaluation methods have been proposed to date. Successful methods such as BLEU (Papineni et al., 2002) work by comparing MT output with one or more human reference translations and generating a similarity score. Methods differ by the definition of similarity. For instance, BLEU and ROUGE (Lin and Och, 2004) are based on n-gram precisions, METEOR (Banerjee and Lavie, 2005) and STM (Liu and Gildea, 2005) use word-class or structural information, Kauchak (2006) leverages on paraphrases, and TER (Snover et al., 2006) uses edit-distances. Currently, BLEU is the most popular metric; it has been shown that it correlates well with human judgments on the corpus level. However, finding a metric that correlates well with human judgments on the sentence-level is still an open challenge (Blatz and others, 2003).

Machine learning approaches have been proposed to address the problem of sentence-level evaluation. (Corston-Oliver et al., 2001) and (Kulesza and Shieber, 2004) train classifiers to discriminate between human-like translations and automatic translations, using features from the aforementioned metrics (e.g. n-gram precisions). In contrast, (Albrecht and Hwa, 2007) argues for a regression approach that directly predicts human adequecy/fluency scores.

All the above methods are score-based in the sense that they generate a score for each MT system output. When the evaluation goal is to compare multiple MT systems, scores are first generated independently for each system, then systems are ranked by their respective scores. We think that this two-step process may be unnecessarily complex. Why solve a more difficult problem of predicting the quality of MT system outputs, when the goal is simply

*Work supported by an NSF Graduate Research Fellowship.

Proceedings of the Third Workshop on Statistical Machine Translation, pages 191–194,
Columbus, Ohio, USA, June 2008.

to compare systems? In this regard, we propose a ranking-based approach that directly ranks a set of MT systems without going through the intermediary of system-specific scores. Our approach requires (a) training data in terms of human ranking judgments of MT outputs, and (b) a machine learning algorithm for learning and predicting rankings.[1]

The advantages of a ranking approach are:

- It is often easier for human judges to rank MT outputs by preference than to assign absolute scores (Vilar et al., 2007). This is because it is difficult to quantify the quality of a translation accurately, but relative easy to tell which one of several translations is better. Thus human-annotated data based on ranking may be less costly to acquire.

- The inter- and intra-annotator agreement for ranking is much more reasonable than that of scoring. For instance, Callison-Burch (2007) found the inter-annotator agreement (Kappa) for scoring fluency/adequency to be around .22-.25, whereas the Kappa for ranking is around .37-.56. Thus human-annotated data based on ranking may be more reliable to use.

- As mentioned earlier, when the final goal of the evaluation is comparing systems, ranking more directly solves the problem. A scoring approach essentially addresses a more difficult problem of estimating MT output quality.

Nevertheless, we note that score-based approaches remain important in cases when the absolute difference between MT quality is desired. For instance, one might wonder *by how much* does the top-ranked MT system outperform the second-ranked system, in which case a ranking-based approach provide no guidance.

In the following, Section 2 formulates the sentence-level MT evaluation problem as a ranking problem; Section 3 explains a machine learning approach for training and predicting rankings; this is our submission to the WMT2008 Shared Evaluation task. Ranking vs. scoring approaches are compared in Section 4.

2 Formulation of the Ranking Problem

We formulate the sentence-level MT evaluation problem as follows: Suppose there are T source sentences to be translated. Let $r_t, t = 1..T$ be the set of references[2]. Corresponding to each source sentence, there are N MT system outputs $o_t^{(n)}$, $n = 1..N$ and M_t ($M_t \leq N$) human evaluations. The evaluations are represented as M_t-dimensional label vectors y_t. In a scoring approach, the elements of y_t may correspond to, e.g. a fluency score on a scale of 1 to 5. In a ranking approach, they may correspond to relative scores that are used to represent ordering (e.g. $y_t = [6; 1; 3]$ means that there are three outputs, and the first is ranked best, followed by third, then second.)

In order to do machine learning, we extract feature vectors $x_t^{(n)}$ from each pair of r_t and $o_t^{(n)}$.[3] The set $\{(x_t^{(n)}, y_t)\}_{t=1..T}$ forms the training set. In a scoring approach, we train a function f with $f(x_t^{(n)}) \approx y^{(n)}$. In a ranking approach, we train f such that higher-ranked outputs have higher function values. In the example above, we would want: $f(x_t^{(n=1)}) > f(x_t^{(n=3)}) > f(x_t^{(n=2)})$. Once f is trained, it can be applied to rank any new data: this is done by extracting features from references/outputs and sorting by function values.

3 Implementation

3.1 Sentence-level scoring and ranking

We now describe the particular scoring and ranking implementations we examined and submitted to the WMT2008 Shared Evaluation task. In the scoring approach, f is trained using RegressionSVM (Drucker and others, 1996); in the ranking approach, we examined RankSVM (Joachims, 2002) and RankBoost (Freund et al., 2003). We used only linear kernels for RegressionSVM and RankSVM, while allowed RankBoost to produce non-linear f based on a feature thresholds.

[1]Our ranking approach is similar to Ye et. al. (2007), who was the first to advocate MT evaluation as a ranking problem. Here we focus on comparing ranking vs. scoring approaches, which was not done in previous work.

[2]Here we assume single reference for ease of notation; this can be easily extended for multiple reference

[3]Only M_t (not N) features vectors are extracted in practice.

ID	Description
1-4	log of ngram precision, n=1..4
5	ratio of hypothesis and reference length
6-9	ngram precision, n=1..4
10-11	hypothesis and reference length
12	BLEU
13	Smooth BLEU
14-20	Intra-set features for ID 5-9, 12,13

Table 1: Feature set: Features 1-5 can be combined (with uniform weights) to form the log(BLEU) score. Features 6-11 are redundant statistics, but scaled differently. Feature 12 is sentence-level BLEU; Feature 13 is a modified version with add-1 count to each ngram precision (this avoids prevalent zeros). Features 14-20 are only available in the ranking approach; they are derived by comparing different outputs within the same set to be ranked.

The complete feature set is shown in Table 1. We restricted our feature set to traditional BLEU statistics since our experimental goal is to directly compare regression, ranking, and BLEU. Features 14-20 are the only novel features proposed here. We wanted to examine features that are enabled by a ranking approach, but not possible for a scoring approach. We thus introduce "intra-set features", which are statistics computed by observing the entire set of existing features $\{x_t^{(n)}\}_{n=1..M_t}$.

For instance: We define Feature 14 by looking at the relative 1-gram precision (Feature 1) in the set of M_t outputs. Feature 14 is set to value 1 for the output which has the best 1-gram precision, and value 0 otherwise. Similarly, Feature 15 is a binary variable that is 1 for the output with the best 2-gram precision, and 0 for all others. The advantage of intra-set features is calibration. e.g. If the outputs for $r_{t=1}$ all have relatively high BLEU compared to those of $r_{t=2}$, the basic BLEU features will vary widely across the two sets, making it more difficult to fit a ranking function. On the other hand, intra-set features are of the same scale ($[0, 1]$ in this case) across the two sets and therefore induce better margins.

While we have only explored one particular instantiation of intra-set features, many other definitions are imaginable. Novel intra-set features is a promising research direction; experiments indicate that they are most important in helping ranking outperform regression.

3.2 Corpus-level ranking

Sentence-level evaluation generates a ranking for each source sentence. How does one produce an overall corpus-level ranking based on a set of sentence-level rankings? This is known as the "consensus ranking" or "rank aggregation" problem, which can be NP-hard under certain formulations (Meilă et al., 2007). We use the FV heuristic (Fligner and Verducci, 1988), which estimates the empirical probability P_{ij} that system i ranks above system j from sentence-level rankings (i.e. P_{ij} = number of sentences where i ranks better than j, divided by total number of sentences). The corpus-level ranking of system i is then defined as $\sum_{j'} P_{ij'}$.

4 Experiments

For experiments, we split the provided development data into train, dev, and test sets (see Table 2). The data split is randomized at the level of different evaluation tracks (e.g. en-es.test, de-en.test are different tracks) in order to ensure that dev/test are sufficiently novel with respect to the training data. This is important since machine learning approaches have the risk of overfitting and spreading data from the same track to both train and test could lead to overoptimistic results.

	Train	Dev	Test
# tracks	8	3	3
# sets	1504 (63%)	514 (21%)	390 (16%)
# sent	6528 (58%)	2636 (23%)	2079 (19%)

Table 2: Data characteristics: the training data contains 8 tracks, which contained 6528 sentence evaluations or 1504 sets of human rankings ($T = 1504$).

In the first experiment, we compared Regression SVM and Rank SVM (both used Features 1-12) by training on varying amounts of training data. The sentence-level rankings produced by each are compared to human judgments using the Spearman rank correlation coefficient (see Figure 1).

In the second experiment, we compared all ranking and scoring methods discussed thus far. The full training set is used; the dev set is used to tune the cost parameter for the SVMs and number of iterations for RankBoost, which is then applied without modification to the test set. Table 3 shows the aver-

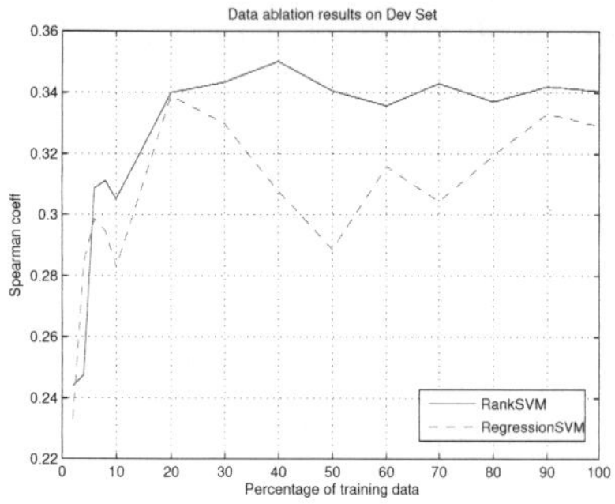

Figure 1: Ranking slightly outperforms Regression for various amounts of training data. Regression results appear to be less stable, with a rise/fall in average Spearman coefficent around 20%, possibly because linear regression functions become harder to fit with more data.

	Feature	Dev	Test
BLEU	1-5	.14	.05
Smoothed BLEU	1-5	.19	.24
Regression SVM	1-12	.33	.24
RankSVM	1-12	.34	.25
RankBoost	1-12	.29	.22
RankSVM	1-20	**.52**	**.42**
RankBoost	1-20	.51	.38

Table 3: Average Spearman coefficients on Dev/Test. The intra-set features gave the most significant gains (e.g. .42 on test of RankSVM). Refer to Table 1 to see what features are used in each row. The SVM/RankBoost results for features 1-12 and 1-5 are similar; only those of 1-12 are reported.

age Spearman coefficient for different methods and different feature sets. There are several interesting observations:

1. BLEU performs poorly, but SmoothedBLEU is almost as good as the machine learning methods that use same set of basic BLEU features.
2. Rank SVM slightly outperforms RankBoost.
3. Regression SVM and Rank SVM gave similar results under the same feature set. However, Rank SVM gave significant improvements when intra-set features are incorporated.

The last observation is particularly important: it shows that the training criteria differences between the ranking and regression is actually not critical. Ranking can outperform regression, but only when ranking-specific features are considered. Without intra-set features, ranking methods may be suffering the same calibration problems as regression.

References

J. Albrecht and R. Hwa. 2007. A re-examination of machine learning approaches for sentence-level MT evaluation. In *ACL*.

S. Banerjee and A. Lavie. 2005. Meteor: An automatic metric for mt evaluation with improved correlation with human judgments. In *ACL 2005 Wksp on Intrinsic/Extrinsic Evaluation for MT/Summarization*.

J. Blatz et al. 2003. Confidence estimation for machine translation. Technical report, Johns Hopkins University, Natural Language Engineering Workshop.

C. Callison-Burch et al. 2007. (meta-) evaluation of machine translation. In *ACL2007 SMT Workshop*.

S. Corston-Oliver, M. Gamon, and C. Brockett. 2001. A machine learning approach to the automatic evaluation of machine translation. In *ACL*.

H. Drucker et al. 1996. Support vector regression machines. In *NIPS*.

M. Fligner and J. Verducci. 1988. Multistage ranking models. *Journal of American Statistical Assoc.*, 88.

Y. Freund, R. Iyer, R. Schapire, and Y. Singer. 2003. An efficient boosting method for combining preferences. *JMLR*, 4.

T. Joachims. 2002. Optimizing search engines using clickthrough data. In *KDD*.

D. Kauchak and R. Barzilay. 2006. Paraphrasing for automatic evaluation. In *NAACL-HLT*.

A. Kulesza and S. Shieber. 2004. A learning approach to improving sentence-level mt evaluation. In *TMI*.

C.-Y. Lin and F. Och. 2004. Automatic evaluation of machine translation quality using longest common subsequence and skip-bigram statistics. In *ACL*.

D. Liu and D. Gildea. 2005. Syntactic features for evaluation of machine translation. In *ACL 2005 Wksp on Intrinsic/Extrinsic Evaluation for MT/Summarization*.

M. Meilă, K. Phadnis, A. Patterson, and J. Bilmes. 2007. Consensus ranking under the exponential model. In *Conf. on Uncertainty in Artificial Intelligence (UAI)*.

K. Papineni, S. Roukos, T. Ward, and W.-J. Zhu. 2002. Bleu: a method for automatic evaluation of machine translation. In *ACL*.

M. Snover, B. Dorr, R. Schwartz, L. Micciulla, and J. Makhoul. 2006. A study of translation edit rate with targeted human annotation. In *Conf. of Assoc. for Machine Translation in the Americas (AMTA-2006)*.

D. Vilar, G. Leusch, H. Ney, and R. Banchs. 2007. Human evaluation of machine translation through binary system comparisons. In *ACL2007 SMT Workshop*.

Y. Ye, M. Zhou, and C.-Y. Lin. 2007. Sentence level machine translation evaluation as a ranking problem. In *ACL2007 Wksp on Statistical Machine Translation*.

A Smorgasbord of Features for Automatic MT Evaluation

Jesús Giménez and **Lluís Màrquez**
TALP Research Center, LSI Department
Universitat Politècnica de Catalunya
Jordi Girona Salgado 1–3, E-08034, Barcelona
{jgimenez,lluism}@lsi.upc.edu

Abstract

This document describes the approach by the NLP Group at the Technical University of Catalonia (UPC-LSI), for the shared task on Automatic Evaluation of Machine Translation at the ACL 2008 Third SMT Workshop.

1 Introduction

Our proposal is based on a rich set of individual metrics operating at different linguistic levels: lexical (i.e., on word forms), shallow-syntactic (e.g., on word lemmas, part-of-speech tags, and base phrase chunks), syntactic (e.g., on dependency and constituency trees), shallow-semantic (e.g., on named entities and semantic roles), and semantic (e.g., on discourse representations). Although from different viewpoints, and based on different similarity assumptions, in all cases, translation quality is measured by comparing automatic translations against human references. Extensive details on the metric set may be found in the IQMT technical manual (Giménez, 2007).

Apart from individual metrics, we have also applied a simple integration scheme based on uniformly-averaged linear metric combinations (Giménez and Màrquez, 2008a).

2 What is new?

The main novelty, with respect to the set of metrics presented last year (Giménez and Màrquez, 2007), is the incorporation of a novel family of metrics at the properly semantic level. *DR* metrics analyze similarities between automatic and reference translations by comparing their respective discourse representation structures (DRS), as provided by the the C&C Tools (Clark and Curran, 2004). DRS are essentially a variation of first-order predicate calculus which can be seen as semantic trees. We use three different kinds of metrics:

DR-STM Semantic Tree Matching, a la Liu and Gildea (2005), but over DRS instead of over constituency trees.

DR-O_r-$\star$ Lexical overlapping over DRS.

DR-O_{rp}-$\star$ Morphosyntactic overlapping on DRS.

Further details on DR metrics can be found in (Giménez and Màrquez, 2008b).

2.1 Improved Sentence Level Behavior

Metrics based on deep linguistic analysis rely on automatic processors trained on out-domain data, which may be, thus, prone to error. Indeed, we found out that in many cases, metrics are unable to produce a result due to the lack of linguistic analysis. For instance, in our experiments, for SR metrics, we found that the semantic role labeler was unable to parse 14% of the sentences. In order to improve the recall of these metrics, we have designed two simple variants. Given a linguistic metric x, we define:

- x_b $\longrightarrow$ by backing off to lexical overlapping, O_l, only when the linguistic processor is not able to produce a linguistic analysis. Otherwise, x score is returned. Lexical scores are conveniently scaled so that they are in a similar range to scores of x. Specifically, we multiply

Proceedings of the Third Workshop on Statistical Machine Translation, pages 195–198,
Columbus, Ohio, USA, June 2008.

them by the average x score attained over all other test cases for which the parser succeeded.

- $x_i \longrightarrow$ by linearly interpolating x and O_l scores for all test cases, via the arithmetic mean.

In both cases, system scores are calculated by averaging over all sentence scores. Currently, these variants are applied only to SR and DR metrics.

2.2 Uniform Linear Metric Combinations

We have simulated a non-parametric combination scheme based on human acceptability by working on uniformly averaged linear combinations (ULC) of metrics (Giménez and Màrquez, 2008a). Our approach is similar to that of Liu and Gildea (2007) except that in our case the contribution of each metric to the overall score is not adjusted.

Optimal metric sets are determined by maximizing the correlation with human assessments, either at the document or sentence level. However, because exploring all possible combinations was not viable, we have used a simple algorithm which performs an approximate search. First, metrics are ranked according to their individual quality. Then, following that order, metrics are added to the optimal set only if in doing so the global quality increases.

3 Experimental Work

We use all into-English test beds from the 2006 and 2007 editions of the SMT workshop (Koehn and Monz, 2006; Callison-Burch et al., 2007). These include the translation of three different language-pairs: German-to-English (de-en), Spanish-to-English (es-en), and French-to-English (fr-en), over two different scenarios: in-domain (European Parliament Proceedings) and out-of-domain (News Commentary Corpus)[1]. In all cases, a single reference translation is available. In addition, human assessments on adequacy and fluency are available for a subset of systems and sentences. Each sentence has been evaluated at least by two different judges. A brief numerical description of these test beds is available in Table 1.

[1]We have not used the out-of-domain Czech-to-English test bed from the 2007 shared task because it includes only 4 systems, and only 3 of them count on human assessments.

	WMT 2006			
	in-domain		**out-of-domain**	
	2,000 cases		1,064 cases	
	#snt	**#sys**	**#snt**	**#sys**
de-en	2,281	10/12	1,444	10/12
es-en	1,852	11/15	1,008	11/15
fr-en	2,268	11/14	1,281	11/14

	WMT 2007			
	in-domain		**out-of-domain**	
	2,000 cases		2,007 cases	
	#snt	**#sys**	**#snt**	**#sys**
de-en	956	7/8	947	5/6
es-en	812	8/10	675	7/9
fr-en	624	7/8	741	7/7

Table 1: Test bed description. '#snt' columns show the number of sentences assessed (considering all systems). '#sys' columns shows the number of systems counting on human assessments with respect to the total number of systems which participated in each task.

Metrics are evaluated in terms of human acceptability, i.e., according to their ability to capture the degree of acceptability to humans of automatic translations. We measure human acceptability by computing Pearson correlation coefficients between automatic metric scores and human assessments of translation quality both at document and sentence level. We use the sum of adequacy and fluency to simulate a global assessment of quality. Assessments from different judges over the same test case are averaged into a single score.

3.1 Individual Performance

In first place, we study the behavior of individual metrics. Table 2 shows meta-evaluation results, over into-English WMT 2007 test beds, in-domain and out-of-domain, both at the system and sentence levels, for a set of selected representatives from several linguistic levels.

At the system level (columns 1-6), corroborating previous findings by Giménez and Màrquez (2007), highest levels of correlation are attained by metrics based on deep linguistic analysis (either syntactic or semantic). In particular, two kinds of metrics, respectively based on head-word chain matching over grammatical categories and relations ('DP-

Level	Metric	System Level de-en in	System Level de-en out	System Level es-en in	System Level es-en out	System Level fr-en in	System Level fr-en out	Sentence Level de-en in	Sentence Level de-en out	Sentence Level es-en in	Sentence Level es-en out	Sentence Level fr-en in	Sentence Level fr-en out
Lexical	1-TER	0.64	0.41	0.83	0.58	0.72	0.47	0.43	0.29	0.23	0.23	0.29	0.20
	BLEU	0.87	0.76	0.88	0.70	0.74	0.54	0.46	0.27	0.33	0.20	0.20	0.12
	GTM ($e = 2$)	0.82	0.69	0.93	0.71	0.76	0.60	**0.56**	0.36	**0.43**	0.33	0.27	0.18
	ROUGE$_W$	0.87	0.91	0.96	0.78	0.85	0.83	**0.58**	**0.40**	**0.43**	**0.35**	0.30	**0.31**
	METEOR$_{wn}$	0.83	0.92	0.96	0.74	0.91	0.86	0.53	**0.41**	0.35	0.28	**0.33**	**0.32**
	O_l	0.79	0.75	0.91	0.55	0.81	0.66	0.48	0.33	0.35	0.30	0.30	0.21
Syntactic	CP-O_c-⋆	0.84	0.88	0.95	0.62	0.84	0.76	0.49	0.37	0.38	0.33	**0.32**	0.25
	DP-HWC$_w$-4	0.85	0.93	0.96	0.68	0.84	0.80	0.31	0.26	0.33	0.07	0.10	0.14
	DP-HWC$_c$-4	**0.91**	**0.98**	0.96	**0.90**	**0.98**	**0.95**	0.30	0.25	0.23	0.06	0.13	0.12
	DP-HWC$_r$-4	0.89	**0.97**	0.97	**0.92**	**0.97**	**0.95**	0.33	0.28	0.29	0.08	0.16	0.16
	DP-O_r-⋆	0.88	0.96	0.97	0.84	0.89	0.89	**0.57**	**0.41**	**0.44**	**0.36**	**0.33**	**0.30**
	CP-STM-4	0.88	**0.97**	0.97	0.79	0.89	0.89	0.49	0.39	0.40	**0.37**	**0.32**	0.26
Shallow Semantic	NE-M_e-⋆	*-0.13*	0.79	0.95	0.68	0.87	0.92	*-0.03*	*0.07*	*0.07*	*-0.05*	*0.05*	*0.06*
	NE-O_e-⋆⋆	*-0.18*	0.78	0.95	0.58	0.81	0.71	0.32	0.26	0.37	0.26	0.31	0.20
	SR-O_r-⋆	0.55	0.96	0.94	0.69	0.89	0.85	0.26	0.14	0.30	0.11	0.08	0.19
	SR-O_r-⋆$_b$	0.24	**0.98**	0.94	0.68	0.92	0.87	0.33	0.21	0.35	0.15	0.18	0.24
	SR-O_r-⋆$_i$	0.51	0.95	0.93	0.67	0.88	0.83	0.37	0.26	0.38	0.19	0.24	0.27
	SR-M_r-⋆	0.38	0.95	0.96	0.83	0.79	0.75	0.32	0.18	0.28	0.18	0.08	0.14
	SR-M_r-⋆$_b$	0.14	**0.98**	0.97	0.82	0.84	0.79	0.37	0.23	0.32	0.21	0.15	0.17
	SR-M_r-⋆$_i$	0.38	0.94	0.96	0.80	0.79	0.74	0.40	0.27	0.36	0.24	0.20	0.20
	SR-O_r	0.73	**0.99**	0.94	0.66	0.97	0.93	0.12	0.09	0.16	0.07	-0.04	0.17
	SR-O_{ri}	0.66	**0.99**	0.94	0.64	**0.95**	0.89	0.29	0.25	0.29	0.19	0.15	0.28
Semantic	DR-O_r-⋆	0.87	0.89	0.96	0.71	0.78	0.75	0.50	**0.40**	0.37	**0.35**	0.27	0.28
	DR-O_r-⋆$_b$	0.91	0.93	0.97	0.72	0.83	0.80	0.52	**0.41**	0.38	**0.34**	0.28	0.27
	DR-O_r-⋆$_i$	0.87	0.87	0.96	0.68	0.79	0.74	0.53	**0.42**	0.39	**0.35**	0.30	0.28
	DR-O_{rp}-⋆	**0.92**	**0.98**	**0.99**	0.81	0.91	0.89	0.42	0.32	0.29	0.25	0.21	**0.30**
	DR-O_{rp}-⋆$_b$	**0.93**	**0.98**	**0.99**	0.81	**0.94**	**0.91**	0.45	0.34	0.32	0.22	0.22	**0.30**
	DR-O_{rp}-⋆$_i$	**0.91**	0.95	**0.98**	0.75	0.89	0.85	0.50	0.38	0.36	0.28	0.27	**0.33**
	DR-STM-4	0.89	0.95	**0.98**	0.79	0.85	0.87	0.28	0.29	0.25	0.21	0.15	0.22
	DR-STM-4$_b$	**0.92**	**0.97**	**0.98**	0.80	0.90	**0.91**	0.36	0.31	0.29	0.21	0.19	0.23
	DR-STM-4$_i$	0.91	0.94	0.97	0.74	0.87	0.86	0.43	0.35	0.34	0.26	0.24	0.27
ULC	Optimal$_{07}$	0.93	1.00	0.99	0.92	0.98	0.95	0.60	0.46	0.47	0.42	0.36	0.39
	Optimal$_{06}$	*0.01*	0.95	0.96	0.75	0.97	0.87	0.50	0.41	0.40	0.20	0.27	0.30
	Optimal⋆$_{07}$	0.93	0.98	0.99	0.81	0.94	0.91	0.58	0.45	0.46	0.39	0.35	0.34
	Optimal⋆$_{06}$	*0.34*	0.96	0.98	0.82	0.92	0.93	0.54	0.41	0.42	0.32	0.32	0.34
	Optimal$_h$	0.87	0.98	0.97	0.79	0.91	0.89	0.56	0.44	0.43	0.32	0.31	0.35

Table 2: Meta-evaluation results based on human acceptability for the WMT 2007 into-English translation tasks

HWC$_c$-4', 'DP-HWC$_r$-4'), and morphosyntactic overlapping over discourse representations ('DR-O_{rp}-⋆'), are consistently among the top-scoring in all test beds. At the lexical level, variants of ROUGE and METEOR attain the best results, close to the performance of syntactic and semantic features. It can also be observed that metrics based on semantic roles and named entities have serious troubles with the German-to-English in-domain test bed (column 1).

At the sentence level, the highest levels of correlation are attained by metrics based on lexical similarity alone, only rivaled by lexical overlapping over dependency relations ('DP-O_r-⋆') and discourse representations ('DR-O_r-⋆'). We speculate the underlying cause might be on the side of parsing errors. In that respect, lexical back-off strategies report in all cases a significant improvement.

It can also be observed that, over these test beds, metrics based on named entities are completely useless at the sentence level, at least in isolation. The reason is that they capture a very partial aspect of quality which may be not relevant in many cases. This has been verified by computing the 'NE-O_e-⋆⋆' variant which considers also lexical overlapping over regular items. Observe how this metric attains a much higher correlation with human assessments.

3.2 Metric Combinations

We also study the behavior of metric combinations under the ULC scheme. Last 5 rows in Table 2 shows meta-evaluation results following 3 different optimization strategies:

Optimal: the metric set is optimized for each test bed (language-pair and domain) individually.

Optimal$\star$: the metric set is optimized over the union of all test beds.

Optimal$_h$: the metric set is heuristically defined so as to include several of the top-scoring representatives from each level: Optimal$_h$ = { ROUGE$_W$, METEOR$_{wnsyn}$, DP-HWC$_c$-4, DP-HWC$_r$-4, DP-O_r-$\star$, CP-STM-4, SR-M_r-$\star_i$, SR-O_r-$\star_i$, SR-O_{ri}, DR-O_r-$\star_i$, DR-O_{rp}-$\star_b$ }.

We present results optimizing over the 2006 and 2007 data sets. Let us provide, as an illustration, Optimal$\star_{07}$ sets. For instance, at the system level, no combination improved the isolated global performance of the 'DR-O_{rp}-$\star_b$' metric (R=0.94). In contrast, at the sentence level, the optimal metric set contains several metrics from each linguistic level: Optimal$\star_{07}$ = { ROUGE$_W$, DP-O_r-$\star$, CP-STM-4, SR-O_r-$\star_i$, SR-M_r-$\star_i$, DR-O_r-$\star_i$ }. A similar pattern is observed for all test beds, both at the system and sentence levels, although with different metrics.

The behavior of optimal metric sets is in general quite stable, except for the German-to-English in-domain test bed which presents an anomalous behavior when meta-evaluating WMT 2006 optimal metric sets at the system level. The reason for this anomaly is in the 'NE-M_e-$\star$' metric, which is included in the 2006 optimal set: { 'NE-M_e-$\star$', 'SR-O_{ri}' }. 'NE-M_e-$\star$' is based on lexical matching over named entities, and attains in the 2006 German-to-English in-domain test bed a very high correlation of 0.95 with human assessments. This partial aspect of quality seems to be of marginal importance in the 2007 test bed. We have verified this hypothesis by computing optimal metrics sets without considering NE variants. Correlation increases to more reasonable values (e.g., from 0.01 to 0.66 and from 0.34 to 0.91. This result suggests that more robust metric combination schemes should be pursued.

For future work, we plan to apply parametric combination schemes based on human likeness classifiers, as suggested by Kulesza and Shieber (2004). We must also further investigate the impact of parsing errors on the performance of linguistic metrics.

Acknowledgments

This research has been funded by the Spanish Ministry of Education and Science (OpenMT, TIN2006-15307-C03-02). Our group is recognized by DURSI as a Quality Research Group (2005 SGR-00130).

References

Chris Callison-Burch, Cameron Fordyce, Philipp Koehn, Christof Monz, and Josh Schroeder. 2007. (Meta-) Evaluation of Machine Translation. In *Proceedings of the ACL Second SMT Workshop*, pages 136–158.

Stephen Clark and James R. Curran. 2004. Parsing the WSJ using CCG and Log-Linear Models. In *Proceedings of the 42nd Annual Meeting of the Association for Computational Linguistics (ACL)*, pages 104–111.

Jesús Giménez and Lluís Màrquez. 2007. Linguistic Features for Automatic Evaluation of Heterogeneous MT Systems. In *Proceedings of the ACL Second SMT Workshop*, pages 256–264.

Jesús Giménez and Lluís Màrquez. 2008a. Heterogeneous Automatic MT Evaluation Through Non-Parametric Metric Combinations. In *Proceedings of IJCNLP*, pages 319–326.

Jesús Giménez and Lluís Màrquez. 2008b. On the Robustness of Linguistic Features for Automatic MT Evaluation. To be published.

Jesús Giménez. 2007. IQMT v 2.1. Technical Manual (LSI-07-29-R). Technical report, TALP Research Center. LSI Department. http://www.lsi.upc.edu/ nlp/IQMT/IQMT.v2.1.pdf.

Philipp Koehn and Christof Monz. 2006. Manual and Automatic Evaluation of Machine Translation between European Languages. In *Proceedings of the Workshop on Statistical Machine Translation*, pages 102–121.

Alex Kulesza and Stuart M. Shieber. 2004. A learning approach to improving sentence-level MT evaluation. In *Proceedings of the 10th TMI*, pages 75–84.

Ding Liu and Daniel Gildea. 2005. Syntactic Features for Evaluation of Machine Translation. In *Proceedings of ACL Workshop on Intrinsic and Extrinsic Evaluation Measures for MT and/or Summarization*.

Ding Liu and Daniel Gildea. 2007. Source-Language Features and Maximum Correlation Training for Machine Translation Evaluation. In *Proceedings of NAACL*, pages 41–48.

Fast, Easy, and Cheap: Construction of Statistical Machine Translation Models with MapReduce

Christopher Dyer, Aaron Cordova, Alex Mont, Jimmy Lin
Laboratory for Computational Linguistics and Information Processing
University of Maryland
College Park, MD 20742, USA
redpony@umd.edu

Abstract

In recent years, the quantity of parallel training data available for statistical machine translation has increased far more rapidly than the performance of individual computers, resulting in a potentially serious impediment to progress. Parallelization of the model-building algorithms that process this data on computer clusters is fraught with challenges such as synchronization, data exchange, and fault tolerance. However, the MapReduce programming paradigm has recently emerged as one solution to these issues: a powerful functional abstraction hides system-level details from the researcher, allowing programs to be transparently distributed across potentially very large clusters of commodity hardware. We describe MapReduce implementations of two algorithms used to estimate the parameters for two word alignment models and one phrase-based translation model, all of which rely on maximum likelihood probability estimates. On a 20-machine cluster, experimental results show that our solutions exhibit good scaling characteristics compared to a hypothetical, optimally-parallelized version of current state-of-the-art single-core tools.

1 Introduction

Like many other NLP problems, output quality of statistical machine translation (SMT) systems increases with the amount of training data. Brants et al. (2007) demonstrated that increasing the quantity of training data used for language modeling significantly improves the translation quality of an Arabic-English MT system, even with far less sophisticated backoff models. However, the steadily increasing quantities of training data do not come without cost. Figure 1 shows the relationship between the amount of parallel Arabic-English training data used and both the translation quality of a state-of-the-art phrase-based SMT system and the time required to perform the training with the widely-used Moses toolkit on a commodity server.[1] Building a model using 5M sentence pairs (the amount of Arabic-English parallel text publicly available from the LDC) takes just over two days.[2] This represents an unfortunate state of affairs for the research community: excessively long turnaround on experiments is an impediment to research progress.

It is clear that the needs of machine translation researchers have outgrown the capabilities of individual computers. The only practical recourse is to distribute the computation across multiple cores, processors, or machines. The development of parallel algorithms involves a number of tradeoffs. First is that of cost: a decision must be made between "exotic" hardware (e.g., large shared memory machines, InfiniBand interconnect) and commodity hardware. There is significant evidence (Barroso et al., 2003) that solutions based on the latter are more cost effective (and for resource-constrained academic institutions, often the only option).

Given appropriate hardware, MT researchers must still contend with the challenge of developing software. Quite simply, parallel programming is difficult. Due to communication and synchronization

[1] http://www.statmt.org/moses/

[2] All single-core timings reported in this paper were performed on a 3GHz 64-bit Intel Xeon server with 8GB memory.

Proceedings of the Third Workshop on Statistical Machine Translation, pages 199–207,
Columbus, Ohio, USA, June 2008.

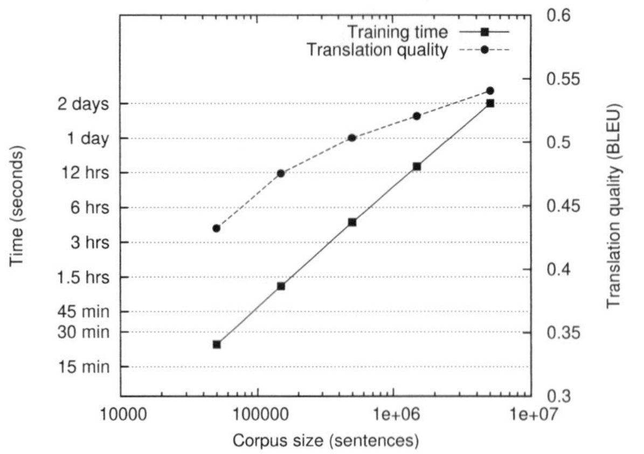

Figure 1: Translation quality and training time as a function of corpus size.

issues, concurrent operations are notoriously challenging to reason about. In addition, fault tolerance and scalability are serious concerns on commodity hardware prone to failure. With traditional parallel programming models (e.g., MPI), the developer shoulders the burden of handling these issues. As a result, just as much (if not more) effort is devoted to system issues as to solving the actual problem.

Recently, Google's MapReduce framework (Dean and Ghemawat, 2004) has emerged as an attractive alternative to existing parallel programming models. The MapReduce abstraction shields the programmer from having to explicitly worry about system-level issues such as synchronization, data exchange, and fault tolerance (see Section 2 for details). The runtime is able to transparently distribute computations across large clusters of commodity hardware with good scaling characteristics. This frees the programmer to focus on actual MT issues.

In this paper we present MapReduce implementations of training algorithms for two kinds of models commonly used in statistical MT today: a phrase-based translation model (Koehn et al., 2003) and word alignment models based on pairwise lexical translation trained using expectation maximization (Dempster et al., 1977). Currently, such models take days to construct using standard tools with publicly available training corpora; our MapReduce implementation cuts this time to hours. As an benefit to the community, it is our intention to release this code under an open source license.

It is worthwhile to emphasize that we present these results as a "sweet spot" in the complex design space of engineering decisions. In light of possible tradeoffs, we argue that our solution can be considered fast (in terms of running time), easy (in terms of implementation), and cheap (in terms of hardware costs). Faster running times could be achieved with more expensive hardware. Similarly, a custom implementation (e.g., in MPI) could extract finer-grained parallelism and also yield faster running times. In our opinion, these are not worthwhile tradeoffs. In the first case, financial constraints are obvious. In the second case, the programmer must explicitly manage all the complexities that come with distributed processing (see above). In contrast, our algorithms were developed within a matter of weeks, as part of a "cloud computing" course project (Lin, 2008). Experimental results demonstrate that MapReduce provides nearly optimal scaling characteristics, while retaining a high-level problem-focused abstraction.

The remainder of the paper is structured as follows. In the next section we provide an overview of MapReduce. In Section 3 we describe several general solutions to computing maximum likelihood estimates for finite, discrete probability distributions. Sections 4 and 5 apply these techniques to estimate phrase translation models and perform EM for two word alignment models. Section 6 reviews relevant prior work, and Section 7 concludes.

2 MapReduce

MapReduce builds on the observation that many tasks have the same basic structure: a computation is applied over a large number of records (e.g., parallel sentences) to generate partial results, which are then aggregated in some fashion. The per-record computation and aggregation function are specified by the programmer and vary according to task, but the basic structure remains fixed. Taking inspiration from higher-order functions in functional programming, MapReduce provides an abstraction at the point of these two operations. Specifically, the programmer defines a "mapper" and a "reducer" with the following signatures (square brackets indicate a list of elements):

map: $\langle k_1, v_1 \rangle \rightarrow [\langle k_2, v_2 \rangle]$
reduce: $\langle k_2, [v_2] \rangle \rightarrow [\langle k_3, v_3 \rangle]$

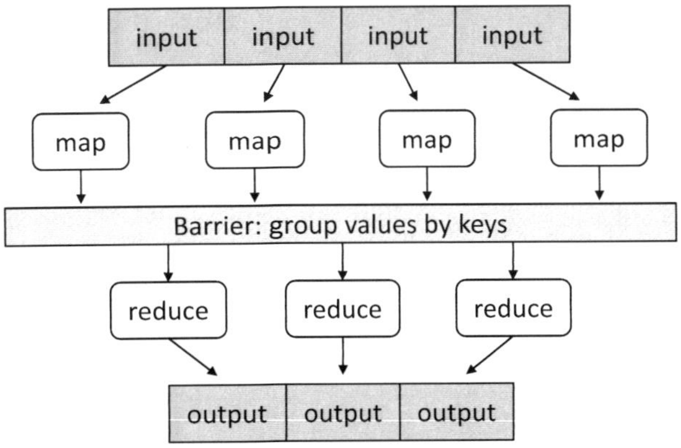

Figure 2: Illustration of the MapReduce framework: the "mapper" is applied to all input records, which generates results that are aggregated by the "reducer".

Key/value pairs form the basic data structure in MapReduce. The "mapper" is applied to every input key/value pair to generate an arbitrary number of intermediate key/value pairs. The "reducer" is applied to all values associated with the same intermediate key to generate output key/value pairs. This two-stage processing structure is illustrated in Figure 2.

Under this framework, a programmer need only provide implementations of map and reduce. On top of a distributed file system (Ghemawat et al., 2003), the runtime transparently handles all other aspects of execution, on clusters ranging from a few to a few thousand workers on commodity hardware assumed to be unreliable, and thus is tolerant to various faults through a number of error recovery mechanisms. The runtime also manages data exchange, including splitting the input across multiple map workers and the potentially very large sorting problem between the map and reduce phases whereby intermediate key/value pairs must be grouped by key.

For the MapReduce experiments reported in this paper, we used Hadoop version 0.16.0,[3] which is an open-source Java implementation of MapReduce, running on a 20-machine cluster (1 master, 19 slaves). Each machine has two processors (running at either 2.4GHz or 2.8GHz), 4GB memory (map and reduce tasks were limited to 768MB), and 100GB disk. All software was implemented in Java.

[3]http://hadoop.apache.org/

Method 1

Map_1	$\langle A, B\rangle \rightarrow \langle\langle A, B\rangle, 1\rangle$
Reduce_1	$\langle\langle A, B\rangle, c(A, B)\rangle$
Map_2	$\langle\langle A, B\rangle, c(A, B)\rangle \rightarrow \langle\langle A, ^*\rangle, c(A, B)\rangle$
Reduce_2	$\langle\langle A, ^*\rangle, c(A)\rangle$
Map_3	$\langle\langle A, B\rangle, c(A, B)\rangle \rightarrow \langle A, \langle B, c(A, B)\rangle\rangle$
Reduce_3	$\langle A, \langle B, \frac{c(A,B)}{c(A)}\rangle\rangle$

Method 2

Map_1	$\langle A, B\rangle \rightarrow \langle\langle A, B\rangle, 1\rangle; \langle\langle A, ^*\rangle, 1\rangle$
Reduce_1	$\langle\langle A, B\rangle, \frac{c(A,B)}{c(A)}\rangle$

Method 3

Map_1	$\langle A, B_i\rangle \rightarrow \langle A, \langle B_i : 1\rangle\rangle$
Reduce_1	$\langle A, \langle B_1 : \frac{c(A,B_1)}{c(A)}\rangle, \langle B_2 : \frac{c(A,B_2)}{c(A)}\rangle \cdots\rangle$

Table 1: Three methods for computing $P_{MLE}(B|A)$. The first element in each tuple is a key and the second element is the associated value produced by the mappers and reducers.

3 Maximum Likelihood Estimates

The two classes of models under consideration are parameterized with conditional probability distributions over discrete events, generally estimated according to the maximum likelihood criterion:

$$P_{MLE}(B|A) = \frac{c(A,B)}{c(A)} = \frac{c(A,B)}{\sum_{B'} c(A,B')} \quad (1)$$

Since this calculation is fundamental to both approaches (they distinguish themselves only by where the counts of the joint events come from—in the case of the phrase model, they are observed directly, and in the case of the word-alignment models they are the number of expected events in a partially hidden process given an existing model of that process), we begin with an overview of how to compute conditional probabilities in MapReduce.

We consider three possible solutions to this problem, shown in Table 1. Method 1 computes the count for each pair $\langle A, B\rangle$, computes the marginal $c(A)$, and then groups all the values for a given A together, such that the marginal is guaranteed to be first and then the pair counts follow. This enables Reducer_3 to only hold the marginal value in memory as it processes the remaining values. Method 2 works similarly, except that the original mapper emits *two* values for each pair $\langle A, B\rangle$ that is encountered: one that will be the marginal and one that contributes to the pair count. The reducer groups all pairs together by the A value, processes the marginal first, and, like Method 1, must only keep this value in memory as it processes the remaining pair counts. Method 2 requires more data to be processed by the MapReduce framework, but only requires a single sort operation (i.e., fewer MapReduce iterations).

Method 3 works slightly differently: rather than computing the pair counts independently of each other, the counts of *all* the B events jointly occurring with a particular $A = a$ event are stored in an associative data structure in memory in the reducer. The marginal $c(A)$ can be computed by summing over all the values in the associative data structure and then a second pass normalizes. This requires that the conditional distribution $P(B|A = a)$ not have so many parameters that it cannot be represented in memory. A potential advantage of this approach is that the MapReduce framework can use a "combiner" to group many $\langle A, B\rangle$ pairs into a single value before the key/value pair leaves for the reducer.[4] If the underlying distribution from which pairs $\langle A, B\rangle$ has certain characteristics, this can result in a significant reduction in the number of keys that the mapper emits (although the number of statistics will be identical). And since all keys must be sorted prior to the reducer step beginning, reducing the number of keys can have significant performance impact.

The graph in Figure 3 shows the performance of the three problem decompositions on two model types we are estimating, conditional phrase translation probabilities (1.5M sentences, max phrase length=7), and conditional lexical translation probabilities as found in a word alignment model (500k sentences). In both cases, Method 3, which makes use of more memory to store counts of all B events associated with event $A = a$, completes at least 50% more quickly. This efficiency is due to the Zipfian distribution of both phrases and lexical items in our corpora: a few frequent items account for a large portion of the corpus. The memory requirements were also observed to be quite reasonable for the models in question: representing $P(B|A = a)$ in the phrase model required at most 90k parameters, and in the lexical model, 128k parameters (i.e., the size of the vocabulary for language B). For the remainder of the experiments reported, we confine ourselves to the use of Method 3.

[4]Combiners operate like reducers, except they run directly on the output of a mapper before the results leave memory. They can be used when the reduction operation is associative and commutative. For more information refer to Dean and Ghemawat (2004).

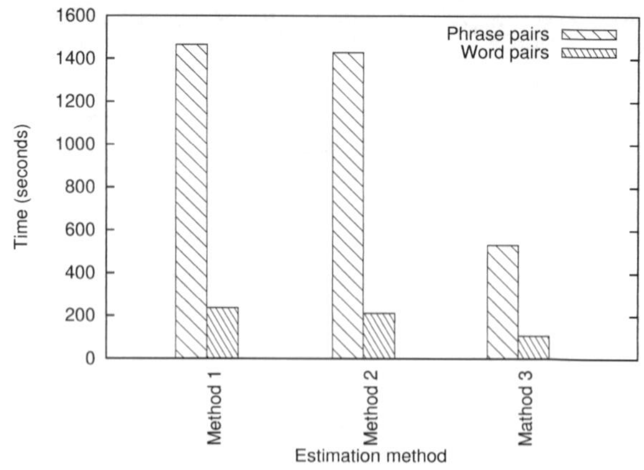

Figure 3: P_{MLE} computation strategies.

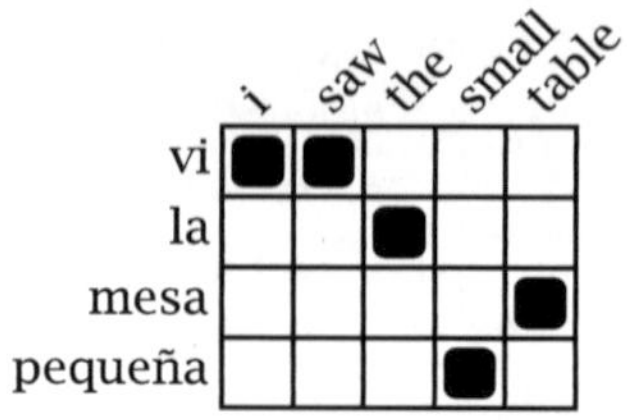

Figure 4: A word-aligned sentence. Examples of consistent phrase pairs include $\langle vi,\ i\ saw\rangle$, $\langle la\ mesa\ pequeña,\ the\ small\ table\rangle$, and $\langle mesa\ pequeña,\ small\ table\rangle$; but, note that, for example, it is not possible to extract a consistent phrase corresponding to the foreign string *la mesa* or the English string *the small*.

4 Phrase-Based Translation

In phrase-based translation, the translation process is modeled by splitting the source sentence into phrases (a contiguous string of words) and translating the phrases as a unit (Och et al., 1999; Koehn et al., 2003). Phrases are extracted from a word-aligned parallel sentence according to the strategy proposed by Och et al. (1999), where every word in a phrase is aligned only to other words in the phrase, and not to any words outside the phrase bounds. Figure 4 shows an example aligned sentence and some of the consistent subphrases that may be extracted.

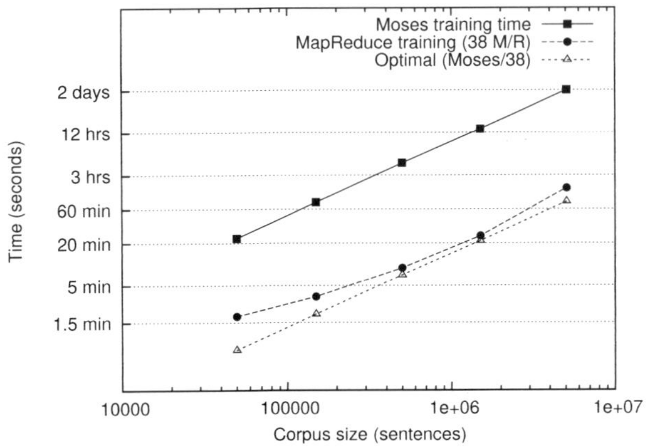

Figure 5: Phrase model extraction and scoring times at various corpus sizes.

Constructing a model involves extracting all the phrase pairs $\langle \overline{e}, \overline{f} \rangle$ and computing the conditional phrase translation probabilities in both directions.[5] With a minor adjustment to the techniques introduced in Section 3, it is possible to estimate $P(B|A)$ and $P(A|B)$ concurrently.

Figure 5 shows the time it takes to construct a phrase-based translation model using the Moses tool, running on a single core, as well as the time it takes to build the same model using our MapReduce implementation. For reference, on the same graph we plot a hypothetical, optimally-parallelized version of Moses, which would run in $\frac{1}{38}$ of the time required for the single-core version on our cluster.[6]

Although these represent completely different implementations, this comparison offers a sense of MapReduce's benefits. The framework provides a conceptually simple solution to the problem, while providing an implementation that is both scalable and fault tolerant—in fact, transparently so since the runtime hides all these complexities from the researcher. From the graph it is clear that the overhead associated with the framework itself is quite low, especially for large quantities of data. We concede that it may be possible for a custom solution (e.g., with MPI) to achieve even faster running times, but we argue that devoting resources to developing such a solution would not be cost-effective.

Next, we explore a class of models where the standard tools work primarily in memory, but where the computational complexity of the models is greater.

5 Word Alignment

Although word-based translation models have been largely supplanted by models that make use of larger translation units, the task of generating a *word alignment*, the mapping between the words in the source and target sentences that are translationally equivalent, remains crucial to nearly all approaches to statistical machine translation.

The IBM models, together with a Hidden Markov Model (HMM), form a class of generative models that are based on a lexical translation model $P(f_j|e_i)$ where each word f_j in the foreign sentence f_1^m is generated by precisely one word e_i in the sentence e_1^l, independently of the other translation decisions (Brown et al., 1993; Vogel et al., 1996; Och and Ney, 2000). Given these assumptions, we let the sentence translation probability be mediated by a latent alignment variable (a_1^m in the equations below) that specifies the pairwise mapping between words in the source and target languages. Assuming a given sentence length m for f_1^m, the translation probability is defined as follows:

$$\begin{aligned} P(f_1^m|e_1^l) &= \sum_{a_1^m} P(f_1^m, a_1^m|e_1^l) \\ &= \sum_{a_1^m} P(a_1^m|e_1^l, f_1^m) \prod_{j=1}^{m} P(f_j|e_{a_j}) \end{aligned}$$

Once the model parameters have been estimated, the single-best word alignment is computed according to the following decision rule:

$$\hat{a}_1^m = \arg\max_{a_1^m} P(a_1^m|e_1^l, f_1^m) \prod_{j=1}^{m} P(f_j|e_{a_j})$$

In this section, we consider the MapReduce implementation of two specific alignment models:

1. IBM Model 1, where $P(a_1^m|e_1^l, f_1^m)$ is uniform over all possible alignments.

2. The HMM alignment model where $P(a_1^m|e_1^l, f_1^m) = \prod_{j=1}^{m} P(a_j|a_{j-1})$.

[5] Following Och and Ney (2002), it is customary to combine both these probabilities as feature values in a log-linear model.

[6] In our cluster, only 19 machines actually compute, and each has two single-core processors.

Estimating the parameters for these models is more difficult (and more computationally expensive) than with the models considered in the previous section: rather than simply being able to count the word pairs and alignment relationships and estimate the models directly, we must use an existing model to compute the *expected counts* for all possible alignments, and then use these counts to update the new model.[7] This training strategy is referred to as expectation-maximization (EM) and is guaranteed to always improve the quality of the prior model at each iteration (Brown et al., 1993; Dempster et al., 1977).

Although it is necessary to compute a sum over all possible alignments, the independence assumptions made in these models allow the total probability of generating a particular observation to be efficiently computed using dynamic programming.[8] The HMM alignment model uses the forward-backward algorithm (Baum et al., 1970), which is also an instance of EM. Even with dynamic programming, this requires $\mathcal{O}(Slm)$ operations for Model 1, and $\mathcal{O}(Slm^2)$ for the HMM model, where m and l are the average lengths of the foreign and English sentences in the training corpus, and S is the number of sentences. Figure 6 shows measurements of the average iteration run-time for Model 1 and the HMM alignment model as implemented in Giza++ (Och and Ney, 2003), a state-of-the-art C++ implementation of the IBM and HMM alignment models that is widely used. Five iterations are generally necessary to train the models, so the time to carry out full training of the models is approximately *five times* the per-iteration run-time.

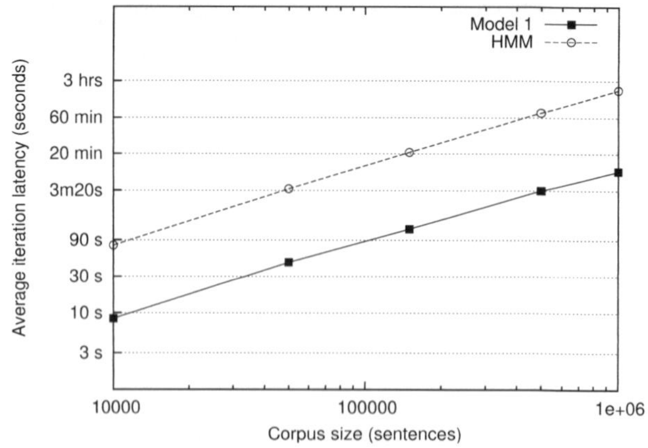

Figure 6: Per-iteration average run-times for Giza++ implementations of Model 1 and HMM training on corpora of various sizes.

5.1 EM with MapReduce

Expectation-maximization algorithms can be expressed quite naturally in the MapReduce framework (Chu et al., 2006). In general, for discrete generative models, mappers iterate over the training instances and compute the partial expected counts for all the unobservable events in the model that should be associated with the given training instance. Reducers aggregate these partial counts to compute the total expected joint counts. The updated model is estimated using the maximum likelihood criterion, which just involves computing the appropriate marginal and dividing (as with the phrase-based models), and the same techniques suggested in Section 3 can be used with no modification for this purpose. For word alignment models, Method 3 is possible since word pairs distribute according to Zipf's law (meaning there is ample opportunity for the combiners to combine records), and the number of parameters for $P(e|f_j = f)$ is at most the number of items in the vocabulary of E, which tends to be on the order of hundreds of thousands of words, even for large corpora.

Since the alignment models we are considering are fundamentally based on a lexical translation probability model, i.e., the conditional probability distribution $P(e|f)$, we describe in some detail how EM updates the parameters for this model.[9] Using the model parameters from the previous iteration (or starting from an arbitrary or heuristic set of parameters during the first iteration), an expected count is computed for every $l \times m$ pair $\langle e_i, f_j \rangle$ for each parallel sentence in the training corpus. Figure 7 illus-

[7] For the first iteration, when there is no prior model, a heuristic, random, or uniform distribution may be chosen.

[8] For IBM Models 3-5, which are not our primary focus, dynamic programming is not possible, but the general strategy for computing expected counts from a previous model and updating remains identical and therefore the techniques we suggest in this section are applicable to those models as well.

[9] Although computation of expected count for a word pair in a given training instance obviously depends on which model is being used, the set of word pairs for which partial counts are produced for each training instance, as well as the process of aggregating the partial counts and updating the model parameters, is identical across this entire class of models.

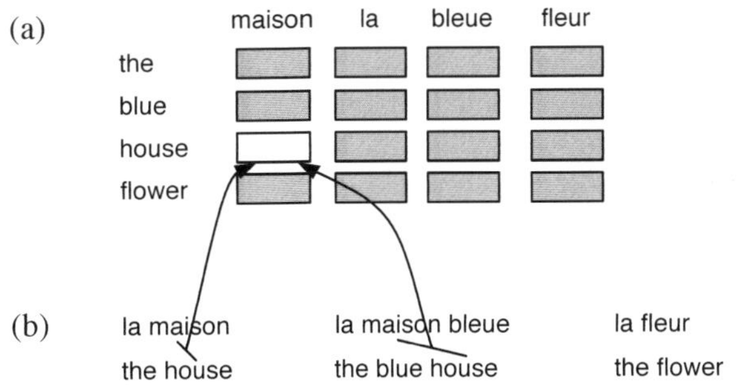

Figure 7: Each cell in (a) contains the expected counts for the word pair $\langle e_i, f_j \rangle$. In (b) the example training data is marked to show which training instances contribute partial counts for the pair $\langle house,\ maison \rangle$.

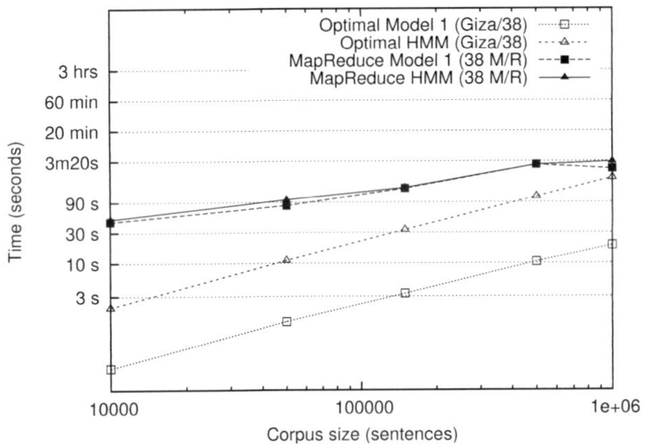

Figure 8: Average per-iteration latency to train HMM and Model 1 using the MapReduce EM trainer, compared to an optimal parallelization of Giza++ across the same number of processors.

trates the relationship between the individual training instances and the global expected counts for a particular word pair. After collecting counts, the conditional probability $P(f|e)$ is computed by summing over all columns for each f and dividing. Note that under this training regime, a non-zero probability $P(f_j|e_i)$ will be possible only if e_i and f_j co-occur in at least one training instance.

5.2 Experimental Results

Figure 8 shows the timing results of the MapReduce implementation of Model 1 and the HMM alignment model. Similar to the phrase extraction experiments, we show as reference the running time of a hypothetical, optimally-parallelized version of Giza++ on our cluster (i.e., values in Figure 6 divided by 38). Whereas in the single-core implementation the added complexity of the HMM model has a significant impact on the per-iteration running time, the data exchange overhead dominates in the performance of both models in a MapReduce environment, making running time virtually indistinguishable. For these experiments, after each EM iteration, the updated model parameters (which are computed in a distributed fashion) are compiled into a compressed representation which is then distributed to all the processors in the cluster at the beginning of the next iteration. The time taken for this process is included in the iteration latencies shown in the graph. In future work, we plan to use a distributed model representation to improve speed and scalability.

6 Related work

Expectation-maximization algorithms have been previously deployed in the MapReduce framework in the context of several different applications (Chu et al., 2006; Das et al., 2007; Wolfe et al., 2007). Wolfe et al. (2007) specifically looked at the performance of Model 1 on MapReduce and discuss how several different strategies can minimize the amount of communication required but they ultimately advocate abandoning the MapReduce model. While their techniques do lead to modest performance improvements, we question the cost-effectiveness of the approach in general, since it sacrifices many of the advantages provided by the MapReduce environment. In our future work, we instead intend to make use of an approach suggested by Das et al. (2007), who show that a distributed database running in tandem with MapReduce can be used to provide the parameters for very large mixture models efficiently. Moreover, since the database is distributed across the same nodes as the MapReduce jobs, many of the same data locality benefits that Wolfe et al. (2007) sought to capitalize on will be available without abandoning the guarantees of the MapReduce paradigm.

Although it does not use MapReduce, the MTTK tool suite implements distributed Model 1, 2 and HMM training using a "home-grown" parallelization scheme (Deng and Byrne, 2006). However, the tool relies on a cluster where all nodes have access to the same shared networked file storage, a restriction that MapReduce does not impose.

There has been a fair amount of work inspired by the problems of long latencies and excessive space requirements in the construction of phrase-based and hierarchical phrase-based translation models. Several authors have advocated indexing the training data with a suffix array and computing the necessary statistics during or immediately prior to decoding (Callison-Burch et al., 2005; Lopez, 2007). Although this technique works quite well, the standard channel probability $P(\overline{f}|\overline{e})$ cannot be computed, which is not a limitation of MapReduce.[10]

7 Conclusions

We have shown that an important class of model-building algorithms in statistical machine translation can be straightforwardly recast into the MapReduce framework, yielding a distributed solution that is cost-effective, scalable, robust, and exact (i.e., doesn't resort to approximations). Alternative strategies for parallelizing these algorithms either impose significant demands on the developer, the hardware infrastructure, or both; or, they require making unwarranted independence assumptions, such as dividing the training data into chunks and building separate models. We have further shown that on a 20-machine cluster of commodity hardware, the MapReduce implementations have excellent performance and scaling characteristics.

Why does this matter? Given the difficulty of implementing model training algorithms (phrase-based model estimation is difficult because of the size of data involved, and word-based alignment models are a challenge because of the computational complexity associated with computing expected counts), a handful of single-core tools have come to be widely used. Unfortunately, they have failed to scale with the amount of training data available. The long latencies associated with these tools on large datasets imply that any kind of experimentation that relies on making changes to variables upstream of the word alignment process (such as, for example, altering the training data $f \rightarrow f'$, building a new model $P(f'|e)$, and reevaluating) is severely limited by this state of affairs. It is our hope that by reducing the cost of this these pieces of the translation pipeline, we will see a greater diversity of experimental manipulations. Towards that end, we intend to release this code under an open source license.

For our part, we plan to continue pushing the limits of current word alignment models by moving towards a distributed representation of the model parameters used in the expectation step of EM and abandoning the compiled model representation. Furthermore, initial experiments indicate that reordering the training data can lead to better data locality which can further improve performance. This will enable us to scale to larger corpora as well as to explore different uses of translation models, such as techniques for processing comparable corpora, where a strict sentence alignment is not possible under the limitations of current tools.

Finally, we note that the algorithms and techniques we have described here can be readily extended to problems in other areas of NLP and beyond. HMMs, for example, are widely used in ASR, named entity detection, and biological sequence analysis. In these areas, model estimation can be a costly process, and therefore we believe this work will be of interest for these applications as well. It is our expectation that MapReduce will also provide solutions that are fast, easy, and cheap.

[10]It is an open question whether the channel probability and inverse channel probabilities are both necessary. Lopez (2008) presents results suggesting that $P(\overline{f}|\overline{e})$ is not necessary, whereas Subotin (2008) finds the opposite.

Acknowledgments

This work was supported by the GALE program of the Defense Advanced Research Projects Agency, Contract No. HR0011-06-2-0001. We would also like to thank the generous hardware support of IBM and Google via the Academic Cloud Computing Initiative. Specifically, thanks go out to Dennis Quan and Eugene Hung from IBM for their tireless support of our efforts. Philip Resnik and Miles Osborne provided helpful comments on an early draft. The last author would like to thank Esther and Kiri for their kind support.

References

Luiz André Barroso, Jeffrey Dean, and Urs Hölzle. 2003. Web search for a planet: The Google cluster architecture. *IEEE Micro*, 23(2):22–28.

Leonard E. Baum, Ted Petrie, George Soules, and Norman Weiss. 1970. A maximization technique occurring in the statistical analysis of probabilistic functions of Markov chains. *Annals of Mathematical Statistics*, 41(1):164–171.

Thorsten Brants, Ashok C. Popat, Peng Xu, Franz J. Och, and Jeffrey Dean. 2007. Large language models in machine translation. In *Proceedings of the 2007 Joint Conference on Empirical Methods in Natural Language Processing and Computational Natural Language Learning*, pages 858–867, Prague, Czech Republic.

Peter F. Brown, Vincent J. Della Pietra, Stephen A. Della Pietra, and Robert L. Mercer. 1993. The mathematics of statistical machine translation: parameter estimation. *Computational Linguistics*, 19(2):263–311.

Chris Callison-Burch, Colin Bannard, and Josh Schroeder. 2005. Scaling phrase-based statistical machine translation to larger corpora and longer phrases. In *Proceedings of the 43rd Annual Meeting of the Association for Computational Linguistics (ACL 2005)*, pages 255–262, Ann Arbor, Michigan.

Cheng T. Chu, Sang K. Kim, Yi A. Lin, Yuanyuan Yu, Gary R. Bradski, Andrew Y. Ng, and Kunle Olukotun. 2006. Map-Reduce for machine learning on multicore. In *Advances in Neural Information Processing Systems 19 (NIPS 2006)*, pages 281–288, Vancouver, British Columbia, Canada.

Abhinandan S. Das, Mayur Datar, Ashutosh Garg, and Shyam Rajaram. 2007. Google news personalization: scalable online collaborative filtering. In *Proceedings of the 16th International Conference on World Wide Web (WWW 2007)*, pages 271–280, Banff, Alberta, Canada.

Jeffrey Dean and Sanjay Ghemawat. 2004. MapReduce: Simplified data processing on large clusters. In *Proceedings of the 6th Symposium on Operating System Design and Implementation (OSDI 2004)*, pages 137–150, San Francisco, California.

Arthur Dempster, Nan Laird, and Donald Rubin. 1977. Maximum likelihood from incomplete data via the EM algorithm. *Journal of the Royal Statistics Society*, 39(1):1–38.

Yonggang Deng and William J. Byrne. 2006. MTTK: An alignment toolkit for statistical machine translation. In *Proceedings of the 2006 Human Language Technology Conference of the North American Chapter of the Association for Computational Linguistics (HLT/NAACL 2006), Companion Volume*, pages 265–268, New York, New York.

Sanjay Ghemawat, Howard Gobioff, and Shun-Tak Leung. 2003. The Google File System. In *Proceedings of the 19th ACM Symposium on Operating Systems Principles (SOSP-03)*, pages 29–43, Bolton Landing, New York.

Philipp Koehn, Franz Josef Och, and Daniel Marcu. 2003. Statistical phrase-based translation. In *Proceedings of the 2003 Human Language Technology Conference of the North American Chapter of the Association for Computational Linguistics (HLT/NAACL 2003)*, pages 48–54, Edmonton, Alberta, Canada.

Jimmy Lin. 2008. Exploring large-data issues in the curriculum: A case study with MapReduce. In *Proceedings of the Third Workshop on Issues in Teaching Computational Linguistics at ACL 2008*, Columbus, Ohio.

Adam Lopez. 2007. Hierarchical phrase-based translation with suffix arrays. In *Proceedings of the 2007 Joint Conference on Empirical Methods in Natural Language Processing and Computational Natural Language Learning*, pages 976–985, Prague, Czech Republic.

Adam Lopez. 2008. *Machine Translation by Pattern Matching*. Ph.D. dissertation, University of Maryland, College Park, MD.

Franz Josef Och and Hermann Ney. 2000. A comparison of alignment models for statistical machine translation. In *Proceedings of the 18th International Conference on Computational Linguistics (COLING 2000)*, pages 1086–1090, Saarbrucken, Germany.

Franz Josef Och and Hermann Ney. 2002. Discriminitive training and maximum entropy models for statistical machine translation. In *Proceedings of the 40th Annual Meeting of the Association for Computational Linguistics (ACL 2002)*, pages 295–302, Philadelphia, Pennsylvania.

Franz Josef Och and Hermann Ney. 2003. A systematic comparison of various statistical alignment models. *Computational Linguistics*, 29(1):19–51.

Franz Josef Och, Christoph Tillmann, and Hermann Ney. 1999. Improved alignment models for statistical machine translation. In *Proceedings of the 1999 Joint SIGDAT Conference on Empirical Methods in Natural Language Processing and Very Large Corpora*, pages 20–28, College Park, Maryland.

Michael Subotin. 2008. Exponential models for machine translation. Master's thesis, University of Maryland, College Park, MD.

Stephan Vogel, Hermann Ney, and Christoph Tillmann. 1996. HMM-based word alignment in statistical translation. In *Proceedings of the 16th conference on Computational linguistics (COLING 1996)*, pages 836–841, Copenhagen, Denmark.

Jason Wolfe, Aria Delier Haghighi, and Daniel Klein. 2007. Fully distributed EM for very large datasets. Technical Report UCB/EECS-2007-178, EECS Department, University of California, Berkeley.

Dynamic Model Interpolation for Statistical Machine Translation

Andrew FINCH
NICT[†]-ATR[‡]
Kyoto, Japan
andrew.finch@atr.jp

Eiichiro SUMITA
NICT[†]-ATR[‡]
Kyoto, Japan
eiichiro.sumita@atr.jp

Abstract

This paper presents a technique for class-dependent decoding for statistical machine translation (SMT). The approach differs from previous methods of class-dependent translation in that the class-dependent forms of all models are integrated directly into the decoding process. We employ probabilistic mixture weights between models that can change dynamically on a segment-by-segment basis depending on the characteristics of the source segment. The effectiveness of this approach is demonstrated by evaluating its performance on travel conversation data. We used the approach to tackle the translation of questions and declarative sentences using class-dependent models. To achieve this, our system integrated two sets of models specifically built to deal with sentences that fall into one of two classes of dialog sentence: *questions* and *declarations*, with a third set of models built to handle the general class. The technique was thoroughly evaluated on data from 17 language pairs using 6 machine translation evaluation metrics. We found the results were corpus-dependent, but in most cases our system was able to improve translation performance, and for some languages the improvements were substantial.

1 Introduction

Topic-dependent modeling has proven to be an effective way to improve quality the quality of models in speech recognition (Iyer and Osendorf, 1994; Carter, 1994). Recently, experiments in the field of machine translation (Hasan and Ney, 2005; Yamamoto and Sumita, 2007; Finch et al. 2007, Foster and Kuhn, 2007) have shown that class-specific models are also useful for translation.

In the method proposed by Yamamoto and Sumita (2007), topic dependency was implemented by partitioning the data into sets before the decoding process commenced, and subsequently decoding these sets independently using different models that were specific to the class predicted for the source sentence by a classifier that was run over the source sentences in a pre-processing pass. Our approach is in many ways a generalization of this work. Our technique allows the use of multiple-model sets within the decoding process itself. The contributions of each model set can be controlled dynamically during the decoding through a set of interpolation weights. These weights can be changed on a sentence-by-sentence basis. The previous approach is, in essence, the case where the interpolation weights are either 1 (indicating that the source sentence is the same topic as the model) or 0 (the source sentence is a different topic). One advantage of our proposed technique is that it is a soft approach. That is, the source sentence can belong to multiple classes to varying degrees. In this respect our approach is similar to that of Foster and Kuhn (2007), however we used a probabilistic classifier to determine a vector of probabilities representing class-membership, rather than distance-based weights. These probabilities were used directly as the mixture weights for the respective models in an interpolated model-set. A second difference between our approach and that of Foster and Kuhn, is that we include a general model built from all of the data along with the set of class-specific models.

Our approach differs from all previous approaches in the models that are class-dependent. Hasan and Ney (2005) used only a class-dependent language model. Both Yamamoto and Sumita (2007) and Foster and Kuhn (2007), extended this to include the translation model. In our approach we combine all of the models, including the distortion and target length models, in the SMT system within a single framework.

The contribution of this paper is two-fold. The first is the proposal of a technique for combining

† National Institute for Science and Technology
‡ Advanced Telecommunications Research Laboratories

Proceedings of the Third Workshop on Statistical Machine Translation, pages 208–215,
Columbus, Ohio, USA, June 2008. ©2008 Association for Computational Linguistics

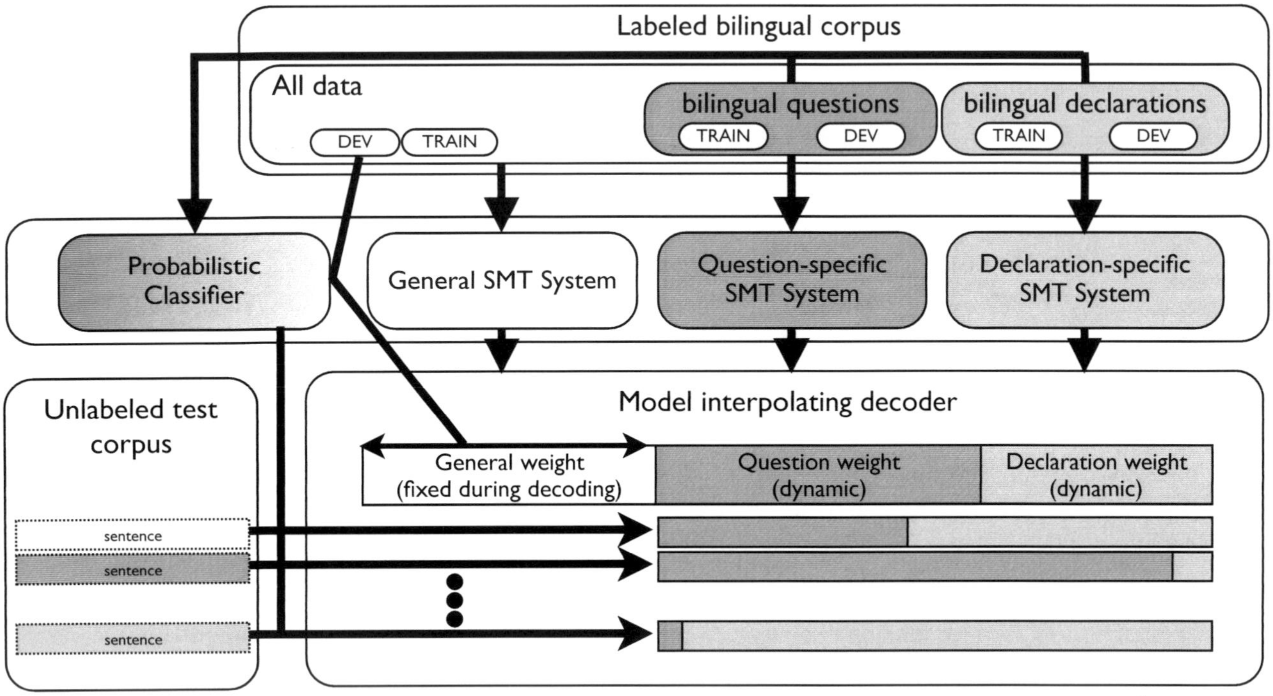

Figure 1. The architecture of the class-based SMT system used in our experiments

multiple SMT systems in a weighted manner to allow probabilistic soft weighting between topic-dependent models for all models in the system. The second is the application of this technique to improve the quality of dialog systems by building and combing class-based models for interrogative and declarative sentences.

For the purposes of this paper, we wish to make the distinction between interrogative sentences and those which are not. For the sake of simplicity of expression we will call those sentences which are interrogative, *questions* and those which are not, *declarations* for the remainder of this article.

The techniques proposed here were evaluated on a variety of different languages. We enumerate them below as a key: Arabic (ar), Danish (da), German (de), English (en), Spanish (es), French (fr), Indonesian (Malay) (id), Italian (it), Japanese (ja), Korean (ko), Malaysian (Malay) (ms), Dutch (nl), Portugese (pt), Russian (ru), Thai (th), Vietnamese (vi) and Chinese (zh).

2 System Overview

2.1 Experimental Data

To evaluate the proposed technique, we conducted experiments on a travel conversation corpus. The experimental corpus was the travel arrangement task of the BTEC corpus (Kikui et al., 2003) and used English as the target and each of the other languages as source languages. The training, development, and evaluation corpus statistics are shown in Table 1. The evaluation corpus had sixteen reference translations per sentence. This training corpus was also used in the IWSLT06 Evaluation Campaign on Spoken Language Translation (Paul 2006) J-E open track, and the evaluation corpus was used as the IWSLT05 evaluation set.

2.2 System Architecture

Figure 1 shows the overall structure of our system. We used punctuation (a sentence-final '?' character) on the target-side as the ground truth as to the class of the target sentence. Neither punctuation nor case information was used for any other purpose in the experiments. The data were partitioned into classes, and further sub-divided into training and development sets for each class. 1000 sentences were set aside as development data, and the remainder was used for training. Three complete SMT systems were built: one for each class, and one on the data from both classes. A probabilistic classifier (described in the next section) was also trained from the full set of training data.

The machine translation decoder used is able to linearly interpolate all of the models models from

	Questions + Decls.		Questions		Declarations		Test
	Train	Dev	Train	Dev	Train	Dev	
Sentences	161317	1000	69684	1000	90633	1000	510
Words	1001671	6112	445676	6547	549375	6185	3169

Table 1. The corpus statistics of the target language corpus (en). The number of sentences is the same as these values for all source languaes. The number of words in the source language differs, and depends on the segmentation granularity.

all of the sub-systems according to a vector of interpolation weights supplied for each source word sequence to be decoded. To do this, prior to the search, the decoder must first merge the phrase-tables from each sub-system. Every phrase from all of the phrase-tables is used during the decoding. Phrases that occur in one sub-system's table, but do not occur in another sub-system's table will be used, but will receive no support (zero probability) from those sub-systems that did not acquire this phrase during training. The search process proceeds as in a typical multi-stack phrase-based decoder. The weight for the general model was set by tuning the parameter on the general development set in order to maximize performance in terms of BLEU score. This weight determines the amount of probability mass to be assigned to the general model, and it remains fixed during the decoding of all sentences. The remainder of the probability mass is divided among the class-specific models dynamically sentence-by-sentence at run-time. The proportion that is assigned to each class is simply the class membership probability of the source sequence assigned by the classifier.

3 Question Prediction

3.1 Outline of the Problem

Given a source sentence of a particular class (interrogative or declarative in our case), we wish to ensure that the target sentence generated is of an appropriate class. Note that this does not necessarily mean that given a question in the source, a question should be generated in the target. However, it seems reasonable to assume that, intuitively at least, one should be able to generate a target question from a source question, and a target declaration from a source declaration. This is reasonable because the role of a machine translation engine is not to be able to generate every possible translation from the source, but to be able to generate one acceptable translation. This assumption leads us to two plausible ways to proceed.

1. To predict the class of the source sentence, and use this to constrain the decoding process used to generate the target
2. To predict the class of the target

In our experiments, we chose the second method, as it seemed the most correct, but feel there is some merit in both strategies.

3.2 The Maximum Entropy Classifier

We used a Maximum Entropy (ME) classifier to determine which class to which the input source sentence belongs using a set of lexical features. That is, we use the classifier to set the mixture weights of the class-specific models. In recent years such classifiers have produced powerful models utilizing large numbers of lexical features in a variety of natural language processing tasks, for example Rosenfeld (1996). An ME model is an exponential model with the following form:

$$p(t,c) = \gamma \prod_{k=0}^{K} \alpha_k^{f_k(c,t)} p_0$$

where:

t	is the class being predicted;
c	is the context of t;
γ	is a normalization coefficient;
K	is the number of features in the model;
α_k	is the weight of feature f_k;
f_k	are binary feature functions;
p_0	is the default model

<s> where
<s> where is
<s> where is the
is
the
is the
is the station </s>
the station </s>
station </s>

Figure 2. The set of n-gram ($n \leq 3$) features extracted from the sentence <s> where is the station </s> for use as predicates in the ME model to predict target sentence class.

We used the set of all n-grams ($n \leq 3$) occurring in the source sentences as features to predict the sentence's class. Additionally we introduced beginning of sentence tokens (<s>) and end of sentence tokens into the word sequence to distinguish n-grams occurring at the start and end of sentences from those occurring within the sentence. This was based on the observation that "question words" or words that indicate that the sentence is a question will frequently be found either at the start of the sentence (as in the wh- <what, where, when> words in English or the -kah words in Malay <apakah, dimanakah, kapankah>), or at the end of the sentence (for example the Japanese "ka" or the Chinese "ma"). In fact, in earlier models we used features consisting of n-grams occurring only at the start and end of the source sentence. These classifiers performed quite well (approximately 4% lower than the classifiers that used features from all of the n-grams in the source), but an error analysis showed that n-grams from the interior of the sentence were necessary to handle sentences such as "excuse me please where is ...". A simple example sentence and the set of features generated from the sentence is shown in Figure 2.

We used the ME modeling toolkit of (Zhang, 2004) to implement our ME models. The models were trained by using L-BFGS parameter estimation, and a Gaussian prior was used for smoothing during training.

3.3 Forcing the target to conform

Before adopting the mixture-based approach set out in this paper, we first pursued an obvious and intuitively appealing way of using this classifier. We applied it as a filter to the output of the decoder, to force source sentences that the classifier predicts should generate questions in the target to actually generate questions in the target. This approach was unsuccessful due to a number of issues.

Source Language	English Punctuation	Own Punctuation
ar	98.0	N/A
da	97.3	98.0
de	98.1	98.6
en	98.9	98.9
es	96.3	96.7
fr	97.7	98.7
id	97.9	98.5
it	94.9	95.4
ja	94.1	N/A
ko	94.2	99.4
ms	98.1	99.0
nl	98.1	99.0
pt	96.2	96.0
ru	95.9	96.6
th	98.2	N/A
vi	97.7	98.0
zh	93.2	98.8

Table 2. The classifcation accuracy (%) of the classifier used to predict whether or not an input sentence either is or should give rise to a question in the target.

We took the n-best output from the decoder and selected the highest translation hypothesis on the list that had agreement on class according to source and target classifiers. The issues we encountered included, too much similarity in the n-best hypotheses, errors of the MT system were correlated with errors of the classifier, and the number of cases that were corrected by the system was small <2%. As a consequence, the method proposed in this paper was preferred.

4 Experiments

4.1 Experimental Conditions

Decoder

The decoder used to in the experiments, CleopATRa is an in-house phrase-based statistical decoder that can operate on the same principles as the PHARAOH (Koehn, 2004) and MOSES (Koehn et

Source	BLEU	NIST	WER	PER	GTM	METEOR
ar	0.4457 (0.00)	8.9386 (0.00)	0.4458 (0.00)	0.3742 (0.00)	0.7469 (0.00)	0.6766 (0.00)
da	0.6640 (0.64)	11.4500 (1.64)	0.2560 (0.08)	0.2174 (2.42)	0.8338 (0.68)	0.8154 (1.23)
de	0.6642 (0.79)	11.4107 (0.44)	0.2606 (2.18)	0.2105 (0.14)	0.8348 (-0.13)	0.8132 (-0.07)
es	0.7345 (0.00)	12.1384 (0.00)	0.2117 (0.00)	0.1668 (0.00)	0.8519 (0.00)	0.8541 (0.00)
fr	0.6666 (0.95)	11.7443 (0.63)	0.2548 (4.82)	0.2172 (6.50)	0.8408 (0.48)	0.8293 (1.29)
id	0.5295 (9.56)	10.3459 (4.11)	0.3899 (21.17)	0.3239 (4.65)	0.7960 (1.35)	0.7521 (2.35)
it	0.6702 (1.01)	11.5604 (0.41)	0.2590 (3.25)	0.2090 (0.62)	0.8351 (0.36)	0.8171 (0.05)
ja	0.5971 (3.47)	10.6346 (2.56)	0.3779 (5.53)	0.2842 (2.80)	0.8125 (0.74)	0.7669 (0.67)
ko	0.5898 (1.78)	10.2151 (1.31)	0.3891 (0.74)	0.3138 (-0.10)	0.7880 (0.36)	0.7397 (0.35)
ms	0.5102 (10.19)	9.9775 (2.75)	0.4058 (18.53)	0.3355 (3.59)	0.7815 (0.18)	0.7247 (2.49)
nl	0.6906 (2.55)	11.9092 (1.47)	0.2415 (3.21)	0.1872 (1.73)	0.8548 (0.39)	0.8399 (0.36)
pt	0.6623 (0.35)	11.6913 (0.26)	0.2549 (2.52)	0.2110 (2.68)	0.8396 (0.02)	0.8265 (-0.07)
ru	0.5877 (0.34)	10.1233 (-1.10)	0.3447 (1.99)	0.2928 (1.71)	0.7900 (0.15)	0.7537 (-0.40)
th	0.4857 (1.50)	9.5901 (1.17)	0.4883 (-0.23)	0.3579 (2.03)	0.7608 (0.45)	0.7104 (1.23)
vi	0.5118 (0.67)	9.8588 (1.85)	0.4274 (-0.05)	0.3301 (0.12)	0.7806 (1.05)	0.7254 (0.43)
zh	0.5742 (0.00)	10.1263 (0.00)	0.3937 (0.00)	0.3172 (0.00)	0.7936 (0.00)	0.7343 (0.00)

Table 3. Performance results translating from a number of source languages into English. Figures in parentheses are the percentage improvement in the score relative to the original score. Bold-bordered cells indicate those conditions where performance degraded. White cells indicate the proposed system's performance is significanly different from the baseline (using 2000-sample bootstrap resampling with a 95% confidence level). TER scores were not tested for significance due to technical difficulties. ar, es and zh were also omitted since the systems were identical.

al, 2007) decoders. The decoder was configured to produce near-identical output to MOSES for these experiments. The decoder was modified in order to handle multiple-sets of models, accept weighted input, and to incorporate the dynamic interpolation process during the decoding.

Practical Issues

Perhaps the largest concerns about the proposed approach come from the heavy resource requirements that could potentially occur when dealing with large numbers of models. However, one important characteristic of the decoder used in our experiments is its ability to leave its models on disk, loading only the parts of the models neces-

Source	Baseline	No Classifier	Hard	Proposed
ar	0.4457 (0.00)	0.4457 (0.00)	0.4457 (0.00)	0.4457
da	0.6598 (0.64)	0.6647 (-0.11)	0.6591 (0.74)	0.664
de	0.6590 (0.79)	0.6651 (-0.14)	0.6634 (0.12)	0.6642
es	0.7345 (0.00)	0.7345 (0.00)	0.7345 (0.00)	0.7345
fr	0.6603 (0.95)	0.6594 (1.09)	0.6605 (0.92)	0.6666
id	0.4833 (9.56)	0.5029 (5.29)	0.5276 (0.36)	0.5295
it	0.6635 (1.01)	0.6660 (0.63)	0.6644 (0.87)	0.6702
ja	0.5771 (3.47)	0.5796 (3.02)	0.5667 (5.36)	0.5971
ko	0.5795 (1.78)	0.5837 (1.05)	0.5922 (-0.41)	0.5898
ms	0.4630 (10.19)	0.5015 (1.73)	0.5057 (0.89)	0.5102
nl	0.6734 (2.55)	0.6902 (0.06)	0.6879 (0.39)	0.6906
pt	0.6600 (0.35)	0.6643 (-0.30)	0.6598 (0.38)	0.6623
ru	0.5857 (0.34)	0.5885 (-0.14)	0.5844 (0.56)	0.5877
th	0.4785 (1.50)	0.4815 (0.87)	0.4831 (0.54)	0.4857
vi	0.5084 (0.67)	0.5095 (0.45)	0.5041 (1.53)	0.5118
zh	0.5742 (0.00)	0.5742 (0.00)	0.5742 (0.00)	0.5742

Table 4. Performance results comaparing our proposes method with other techniques. The column labeled 'Baseline' is the same as in Table 3, for reference. The column lableled 'No Classifier', is the same system as our proposed method, except that the classifier was replaced with a default model that assigned a class membership probability of 0.5 in every case. The column labeled 'Hard' corresponds to a system that used hard weights (either 1 or 0) for the class-dependent models. The column labeled 'Proposed' are the results from our proposed method. Figures in parentheses represent the percentage improvement of the proposed method's score relative to the alternative method. Cells with bold borders indicate those conditions where performance was degraded.

sary to decode the sentence in hand. This reduced the memory overhead considerably when loading multiple models, without noticeably affecting decoding time. Moreover, it is also possible to precompute the interpolated probabilities for most of the models for each sentence before the search commences, reducing both search memory and processing time.

Decoding Conditions

For tuning of the decoder's parameters, minimum error training (Och 2003) with respect to the BLEU score using was conducted using the respective development corpus. A 5-gram language model, built using the SRI language modeling toolkit (Stolcke, 1999) with Witten-Bell smoothing was used. The model included a length model, and also the simple distance-based distortion model used by the PHARAOH decoder (Koehn, 2004).

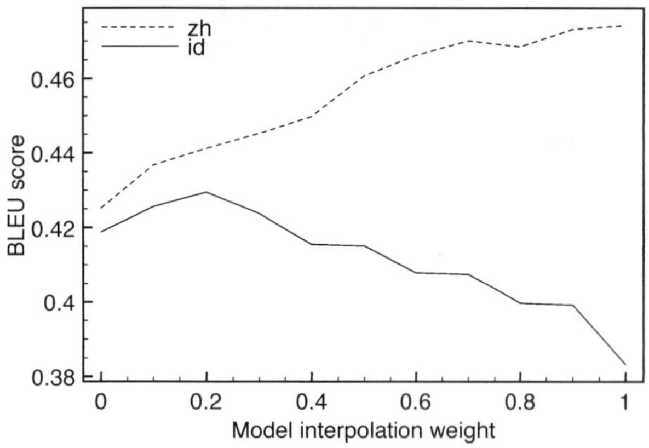

Figure 3. Graph showing the BLEU score on the developmment set plotted against the general model's interpolation weight (a weight of 0 meaning no contribution from the general model) for two systems in our experiments.

Tuning the interpolation weights

The interpolation weights were tuned by maximizing the BLEU score on the development set over a set of weights ranging from 0 to 1 in increments of 0.1. Figure 1 shows the behavior of two of our models with respect to their weight parameter.

Evaluation schemes

To obtain a balanced view of the merits of our proposed approach, in our experiments we used 6 evaluation techniques to evaluate our systems. These were: BLEU (Papineni, 2001), NIST (Doddington, 2002), WER (Word Error Rate), PER (Position-independent WER), GTM (General Text Matcher), and METEOR (Banerjee and Lavie, 2005).

4.2 Classification Accuracy

The performance of the classifier (from 10-fold cross-validation on the training set) is shown in Table 2. We give classification accuracy figures for predicting both source (same language) and target (English) punctuation. Unsurprisingly, all systems were better at predicting their own punctuation. The poorer scores in the table might reflect linguistic characteristics (perhaps questions in the source language are often expressed as statements in the target), or characteristics of the corpus itself. For all languages the accuracy of the classifier seemed satisfactory, especially considering the possibility of inconsistencies in the corpus itself (and therefore our test data for this experiment).

4.3 Translation Quality

The performance of the SMT systems are shown in Table 3. It is clear from the table that for most of the experimental conditions evaluated the system outperformed a baseline system that consisted of an SMT system trained on all of the data. For those metrics in which performance degraded, in all-but-one the results were statistically insignificant, and in all cases most of the other MT evaluation metrics showed an improvement. Some of the language pairs showed striking improvements, in particular both of the Malay languages id and ms improved by over 3.5 BLEU points each using our technique. Interestingly Dutch, a relative of Malay, also improved substantially. This evidence points to a linguistic explanation for the gains. Malay has very simple and regular question structure, the question words appear at the front of question sentences (in the same way as the target language) and do not take any other function in the language (unlike the English "do" for example). Perhaps this simplicity of expression allowed our class-specific models to model the data well in spite of the reduced data caused by dividing the data. Another factor might be the performance of the classifier which was high for all these languages (around 98%). Unfortunately, it is hard to know the reasons behind the variety of scores in the table. One large factor is likely to be differences in corpus quality, and also the relationship between the source and target corpus. Some corpora are direct translations of each other, whereas others are translated through another language. Chinese was one such language, and this may explain why we were unable to improve on the baseline for this language even though we were very successful for both Japanese and Thai, which are relatives of Chinese.

4.4 Comparison to Previous Methods

We ran an experiment to compare our proposed method to an instance of our system that used hard weights. The aim was to come as close as possible within our framework to the system proposed by Yamamoto and Sumita (2007). We used weights of 1 and 0, instead of the classification probabilities to weight the class-specific models. To achieve this, we thresholded the probabilities from the classifier such that probabilities >0.5 gave a weight of 1, otherwise a weight of 0 was used. The performance of this system is shown in Table 4 under the column heading 'Hard'. In all-but-one of the conditions this system was outperformed by or equal to the proposed approach.

The column labeled "No Classifier" in Table 4 illustrates the effectiveness of the classifier in our system. These results show the effect of using equal weights (0.5) to interpolate between the Question and Declaration models. This system, although not as effective as the system with the classifier, gave a respectable performance.

5 Conclusion

In this paper we have presented a technique for combining all models from multiple SMT engines into a single decoding process. This technique allows for topic-dependent decoding with probabilistic soft weighting between the component models. We demonstrated the effectiveness of our approach on conversational data by building class-specific models for interrogative and declarative sentence classes. We carried out an extensive evaluation of the technique using a large number of language pairs and MT evaluation metrics. In most cases we were able to show significant improvements over a system without model interpolation, and for some language pairs the approach excelled. The best improvement of all the language pairs was for Malaysian (Malay)-English which outperformed the baseline system by 4.7 BLEU points (from 0.463 to 0.510). In future research we would like to try the approach with larger sets of models, and also (possibly overlapping) subsets of the data produced using automatic clustering methods.

References

Satanjeev Banerjee and Alon Lavie. 2005. METEOR: an automatic metric for MT evaluation with improved correlation with human judgments. *ACL-2005: Workshop on Intrinsic and Extrinsic Evaluation Measures for Machine Translation and/or Summarization*, pp. 65-72.

David Carter, 1994. Improving Language Models by Clustering Training Sentences, *Proc. ACL*, pp. 59-64.

J. Civera and A. Juan. Domain adaptation in statistical machine translation with mixture modelling. *In Proceedings of the Second Workshop on ACL Statistical Machine Translation*, pp. 177-180, Prague,

Czech Republic, June 2007.Andrew Finch, Etienne Denoual, Hideo Okuma, Michael Paul, Hirofumi Yamamoto, Keiji Yasuda, Ruiqiang Zhang, and Eiichiro Sumita. 2007. The NICT/ATR speech translation system for IWSLT 2007. *IWSLT 2007*, Trento, Italy.

George Doddington. 2002 Automatic evaluation of machine translation quality using n-gram co-occurrence statistics. *Proc. of Human Language Technology Conference*, San Diego, California, pp. 138-145.

George Foster and Roland Kuhn. 2007. Mixture-model adaptation for SMT. *In Proceedings of the Second Workshop on Statistical Machine Translation*, ACL, pp. 128-135, Prague, Czech Republic,

Sasa Hasan and Hermann Ney. 2005. Clustered Language Models Based on Regular Expressions for SMT, *Proc. EAMT*, Budapest, Hungary.

Rukmini Iyer and Mari Ostendorf. 1994. Modeling Long Distance Dependence in Language: Topic mixture versus dynamic cache models, *IEEE Transactions on Speech and Audio Processing*.

Philipp Koehn, Franz Josef Och, and Daniel Marcu. 2003. Statistical Phrase-Based Translation. *In Proceedings of the Human Language Technology Conference 2003*, Edmonton, Canada.

Philipp Koehn. 2004. Pharaoh: a beam search decoder for phrase-based statistical machine translation models. Machine translation: from real users to research: *6th conference of AMTA*, Washington, DC, Springer Verlag, pp. 115-124.

Philipp Koehn, Hieu Hoang, Alexandra Birch, Chris Callison-Burch, Marcello Federico, Nicola Bertoldi, Brooke Cowan, Wade Shen, Christine Moran, Richard Zens, Chris Dyer, Ondřej Bojar, Alexandra Constantin, Evan Herbst. 2007. Moses: open source toolkit for statistical machine translation, *ACL 2007: proceedings of demo and poster sessions*, Prague, Czech Republic, pp. 177-180.

Franz J. Och, Hermann Ney, 2003. A Systematic Comparison of Various Statistical Alignment Models, *Computational Linguistics*, No. 1, Vol. 29, pp. 19-51.

Franz J. Och, 2003. Minimum error rate training for statistical machine trainslation, *Proc. ACL*.

Michael Paul, 2006. Overview of the IWSLT 2006 Evaluation Campaign, *IWSLT 2006*.

Kishore Papineni, Salim Roukos, Todd Ward, & Wei-Jing Zhu. 2001. Bleu: a method for automatic evaluation of machine translation. *IBM Research Report, RC22176*, September 17.

Ronald Rosenfeld. 1996. A maximum entropy approach to adaptive statistical language modeling. *Computer Speech and Language*, 10:187–228.

Matthew Snover, Bonnie Dorr, Richard Schwartz, Linnea Micciulla, and John Makhoul. 2006. A Study of Translation Edit Rate with Targeted Human Annotation, *Proceedings of Association for Machine Translation in the Americas*.

Andreas Stolcke. 1999. SRILM - An Extensible Language Model Toolkit. http://www.speech.sri.com/projects/srilm/

Hirofumi Yamamoto and Eiichiro Sumita. 2007. Bilingual cluster based models for statistical machine translation. *EMNLP-CoNLL-2007*, Prague, Czech Republic; pp. 514-523.

Le Zhang. 2004. Maximum Entropy Modeling Toolkit for Python and C++, [On-line].

Improved Statistical Machine Translation by Multiple Chinese Word Segmentation

Ruiqiang Zhang[1,2] and **Keiji Yasuda**[1,2] and **Eiichiro Sumita**[1,2]
[1]National Institute of Information and Communications Technology
[2]ATR Spoken Language Communication Research Laboratories
2-2-2 Hikaridai, Science City, Kyoto, 619-0288, Japan
{ruiqiang.zhang,keiji.yasuda,eiichiro.sumita}@atr.jp

Abstract

Chinese word segmentation (CWS) is a necessary step in Chinese-English statistical machine translation (SMT) and its performance has an impact on the results of SMT. However, there are many settings involved in creating a CWS system such as various *specifications* and *CWS methods*. This paper investigates the effect of these settings to SMT. We tested dictionary-based and CRF-based approaches and found there was no significant difference between the two in the qualty of the resulting translations. We also found the correlation between the CWS F-score and SMT BLEU score was very weak. This paper also proposes two methods of combining advantages of different specifications: a simple concatenation of training data and a feature interpolation approach in which the same types of features of translation models from various CWS schemes are linearly interpolated. We found these approaches were very effective in improving quality of translations.

1 Introduction

Chinese word segmentation (CWS) is a necessary step in Chinese-English statistical machine translation (SMT). The research on CWS independently from SMT has been conducted for decades. As an evidence, the CWS evaluation campaign, the Sighan Bakeoff (Emerson, 2005),[1], has been held four times since 2004. However, works on relations between CWS and SMT are scarce.

Generally, two factors need to be considered in constructing a CWS system. The first one is the *specifications* for CWS, i.e., the rules or guidelines for word segmentation, and the second one is the *CWS methods*. There are many CWS specifications used by different organizations. Unfortunately, these organizations do not seem to have any intention of reaching a unified specification. More than five or six specifications have been used in the four Sighan Bakeoffs. There is also significant disagreement on the specifications, although much of their contents is the same. One of the aims of this work was therefore to establish whether inconsistencies in specifications significantly affect the quality of SMT.

The second factor is CWS methods. We grouped all of the CWS methods into two classes: the class without out-of-vocabulary (OOV) recognition and the class with OOV recognition, represented by the dictionary-based CWS and the CRF-based CWS, respectively. Out-of-vocabulary recognition may have two-sided effects on SMT performance. The CRF-based CWS that supports OOV recognition produces word segmentations with a higher F-score, but a huge number of new words recognized correctly and incorrectly that can incur data sparseness in training the SMT models. On the other hand, the dictionary-based approach that does not support OOV recognition produced a lower F-score, but with a relatively weak data spareness problem. Which approach pro-

[1]A CWS competition organized by the ACL special interest group on Chinese.

Proceedings of the Third Workshop on Statistical Machine Translation, pages 216–223,
Columbus, Ohio, USA, June 2008.

Table 1: Examples of disagreement in segmentation guidelines

	ChineseName	EnglishName	Time
AS	DENGXIAOPING	*GEORGE BUSH*	1997YEAR 7MONTH 1DAY
CITYU	DENGXIAOPING	GEORGEBUSH	1997 YEAR 7 MONTH 1 DAY
MSR	DENGXIAOPING	GEORGEBUSH	1997YEAR7MONTH1DAY
PKU	*DENG XIAOPING*	GEORGEBUSH	1997YEAR 7MONTH 1DAY

Table 2: A second example of disagreement in segmentation guidelines

	Composite words	Composite words
AS	FUJITSUCOMPANY	EUROZONE
CITYU	*FUJITSU COMPANY*	EUROZONE
MSR	FUJITSUCOMPANY	*EURO ZONE*
PKU	*FUJITSU COMPANY*	EUROZONE

duces a better SMT result is our research interest in this work.

The performance of CWS is usually measured by the F-score, while that of SMT is measured using the BLEU score. Does a CWS with a higher F-score produce a better translation? In this paper we answer this question by comparing F-scores with BLEU scores.

In this work, we also propose approaches to make use of all the Sighan training data regardless of the specifications. Two methods are proposed: (1) a simple combination of all the training data, and (2) implementing linear interpolation of multiple translation models. Linear interpolation is widely used in language modeling for speech recognition. We interpolated multiple translation models generated by the CWS schemes and found our approaches were very effective in improving the translations.

2 CWS specifications and corpora from the second Sighan Bakeoff

A Chinese word is composed of one or more characters. There are no spaces between the words. Automatic word segmentation is required for machine translation. Usually a specification is needed to carry out word segmentation. Unfortunately, there are many different versions of specifications. Different tasks give rise to different requirements and the CWS specifications must be adjusted accordingly. For example, shorter segmentation has been shown to be better for speech recognition. A composite word (numbers, dates, times, etc.) is split into characters even if it is one word defined by linguists. In contrast, longer segmentation is preferred for named entity recognition consisting of longer character sequences, such as the name of people, places, and organizations.

This work investigated four well-known specifications created by four different organizations: Academia Sinica (AS), City University of Hong Kong (CITYU), Microsoft Research (Beijing) (MSR), and Beijing University (PKU). These specs were used in the second Sighan Bakeoff (Emerson, 2005). When we compared the four specifications and the manual segmentations in the Sighan Bakeoff training data, we found there were many inconsistencies among the four specifications. Some examples are shown in Table 1 and 2. For instance, the AS and PKU specifications are distinct in splitting both Chinese and English names. We also found the MSR specification generated more composite words and grouped longer character sequences into a word. Using this specification could generate tens of thousands of new words, which can cause data sparseness for SMT.

In addition to using the four specifications, we also downloaded the training and test corpora of the second Sighan Bakeoff. We used each of the training corpora provided to create a CWS scheme and evaluated the performance of the schemes on our test data. This enabled us to examine the effect of CWS specifications on SMT.

We used a Chinese word segmentation tool, Achilles, to implement word segmentation. Part of the work using this tool was described by (Zhang et al., 2006). The approach was reported to achieve the highest word segmentation accuracy using the data from the second Sighan Bakeoff. Moreover, this tool meets our need to test the effect of the two kinds of CWS approaches for SMT. We can easily train a dictionary-based and a CRF-based CWS by using this tool. By turning the program's option for the CRF model on and off, we can use the Achilles as a dictionary-based approach and as a CRF-based CWS. In fact, the dictionary-based approach is the default approach for Achilles.

3 Experiments

3.1 SMT resources

We followed the instructions for the 2005 NIST MT evaluation campaign. Training the translation models for our SMT system used the available LDC parallel data except the UN corpus. To train the language models for English, we used all the available English parallel data plus Xinhua News of the LDC Gigaword English corpus, LDC2005T12. In summary, we used 2.4 million parallel sentences for training the translation model. We used the test data defined in the NIST MT05 evaluation which is defined in the LDC corpus as LDC2006E38. We used the corpus, LDC2006E43, as the development data for loglinear model optimization.

We used a phrase-based SMT system that is based on a log-linear model incorporating multiple features. The training and decoding system of our SMT used the publicly available Pharaoh (Koehn et al., 2003)[2]. GIZA++ was used for word alignment.

The Pharaoh decoder was used exclusively in all the experiments. No additional features but the defaults defined by Pharaoh were used. The feature weights were optimized against the BLEU scores (Och, 2003).

We chose automatic metrics to evaluate CWS and SMT. We used the F-score for CWS and BLEU for SMT. The BLEU is BLEU4, computed using the NIST-provided "mt-eval" script.

[2]http://www.iccs.informatics.ed.ac.uk/~pkoehn

3.2 Implementation of CWS schemes

To determine the effect of CWS on SMT, we created 14 CWS schemes which are shown in Table 3. Schemes 1 to 12 were implemented using the in-house tool, Achilles, and schemes 13 and 14 using off-the-shelf tools. The CWS schemes are named according to the specifications (AS, CITYU, MSR, PKU), implementing methods (CRF-based or dictionary-based), and lexicon sources (Sighan or LDC corpus). The table also shows the results of segmentation on the SMT training and test data, i.e., number of total tokens, unique words, and OOV words.

We divided the schemes into two groups for simplicity. The first group includes schemes 1 to 12, which were trained using a specific Sighan corpus. For example, schemes 1 to 3 were trained using the AS corpus, schemes 4 to 6 using the CITYU corpus, and so on. The meaning of the name of the CWS scheme can be derived from the table – the name is defined by specifications, methods and lexicon sources. For example, the CRF-AS scheme performs CRF-based segmentation; and its lexicon is from the AS corpus provided by the Sighan. The CRF-AS segmenter can be easily trained, as described by Achilles.

The second group contains two schemes 13 and 14. The ICTCLAS is a HHMM-based hierarchical HMM segmenter (Zhang et al., 2003) that uses the specifications of PKU. This segmenter incorporates parts-of-speech information in the probability models and generates multiple HMM models for solving segmentation ambiguities. The MSRSEG was developed by Gao et al. (Gao et al., 2004). This segmenter is based on the MSR specifications. It uses a log-linear model that integrates multiple features.

The segmenters of the first group, dict-AS and dict-LDC-AS, are two dictionary-based CWS schemes. They differ in lexicon size and lexicon extracting source. The former used a lexicon extracted directly from the Sighan AS training data while the latter used a lexicon from LDC parallel corpora. It took some efforts to get the lexicon. First, we used the CRF-AS to segment the LDC corpora. We extracted a unique word list from the segmented data and sorted it in decreasing order according to word frequency. Because OOV was recognized by

Table 3: Analysis of results of segmentation on LDC training and test data for all CWS schemes

No.	CWS schemes	Specifications	Methods	Lexicon	Tokens	Unique words	OOVs
1	CRF-AS	AS	CRF	Sighan	47,934,088	413,588	1,193
2	dict-AS	AS	Dict	Sighan	51,664,675	89,346	237
3	dict-LDC-AS	AS	Dict	LDC	48,665,364	102,919	273
4	CRF-CITYU	CITYU	CRF	Sighan	47,963,541	426,273	1,155
5	dict-CITYU	CITYU	Dict	Sighan	51,251,729	56,996	362
6	dict-LDC-CITYU	CITYU	Dict	LDC	48,787,154	102,754	217
7	CRF-MSR	MSR	CRF	Sighan	46,483,923	523,788	1,297
8	dict-MSR	MSR	Dict	Sighan	51,302,509	60,247	248
9	dict-LDC-MSR	MSR	Dict	LDC	47,469,271	102,390	217
10	CRF-PKU	PKU	CRF	Sighan	48,022,697	440,114	1,136
11	dict-PKU	PKU	Dict	Sighan	52,721,809	47,176	211
12	dict-LDC-PKU	PKU	Dict	LDC	48,721,795	102,213	256
13	ICTCLAS	PKU	HHMM	-	50,751,402	162,222	835
14	MSRSEG	MSR	-	-	48,734,113	274,411	1,443

the CRF-AS, a huge word list was generated(see Table 3). We chose the most frequent 100,000 words as the dictionary for the dict-LDC-AS [3]. The LM for the dict-AS was trained using the AS corpus while the LM for the dict-LDC-AS was trained using the segmented SMT training corpus.

Therefore, the dict-LDC-AS used a larger lexicon than the dict-AS. This lexicon contained the most frequent OOV words recognized by the CRF-AS. Our aim was to investigate whether the dict-LDC-AS, whose lexicon consisted of the lexicon of dict-AS and new words recognized by CRF-AS, could improve SMT.

As shown in Table 3, using CRF-AS generated a huge number of unique words for the training data and OOV words for the test data. We found that the CRF-AS generated three times more OOVs for the test data than the dictionary-based CWS,dict-AS (see OOVs in Table 3).

Other schemes in the first group were implemented similarly to the "AS".

Table 3 lists the segmentation statistics for the training and test data of all the tested CWS schemes, where "Tokens" indicates the total number of words in the training data. "Unique words" and "OOVs" mean the lexicon size of the segmented training data and the unknown words in the test data, respectively.

[3]Only those words that appeared at least five times in the lexicon were considered.

Table 4: BLEU scores for CWS schemes

CWS	AS	CITYU	MSR	PKU
CRF	23.70	23.55	22.50	23.61
dict	23.46	23.72	23.33	23.61
dict-LDC	23.52	23.36	23.16	23.74
ICTCLAS	-	-	-	24.12
MSRSEG	-	-	19.72	-
BEST	23.70	23.72	23.33	23.74 (24.12)

3.3 Effect of CWS specifications on SMT

Our first concern was the effect of CWS specifications on SMT. The results in Table 4 show the relationships that were found. The last row gives the best BLEU scores obtained for each of the CWS specifications. The scores for AS, CITYU, MSR and PKU were 23.70 (CRF-AS), 23.72 (dict-CITYU), 23.33 (dict-MSR) and 23.74 (dict-PKU-LDC), respectively. We found there were no observable differences between AS, CITYU, and PKU. However, the specification that produced the worst translations was the MSR. The MSR specification appears to have been designed for recognizing named entities (NE) (See the examples of segmentation in Table 1). Many NEs are regarded as words by MSR, while they are more appropriately split into separate words by other specifications. For example, the long word, "1997YEAR7MONTH1DAY" ("July 1, 1997"). As a result, the CRF-MSR generated 20% more words in the vocabulary than the other CWS schemes in segmenting the SMT training data. The larger vocabulary can trigger data sparseness problems and result in SMT degradation. The segmenter, MSRSEG, produced an even lower BLEU score (19.72) than the Achilles.

The results were verified by significance test (Zhang et al., 2004). We found the systems with the BLEU scores higher than 23.70 were significantly better than those lower than 23.70.

3.4 Correlation between BLEU score and F-score

The values of the F-scores and BLEU scores are listed in parallel in Table 5. We tied the F-scores and specifications together because comparing the value of the F-score across specs is meaningless. We separated the F-score and BLEU score for different corpus. The F-score was calculated using the Sighan test data. The CRF-based approach usually gives a higher F-score, but its corresponding BLEU scores were not always higher. The F-score and BLEU score correlated well for ICTCLAS and CRF-AS but less well for CRF-CITYU, CRF-PKU and CRF-MSR. Obviously, there is no strong correlation between the F-score and BLEU score.

4 Effect of combining multiple CWS schemes

We used the Sighan Bakeoff corpora of different CWS specifications separately in the previous experiments. Here, we propose two approaches to using all the resources combined. The first approach is to concatenate all the training data of the Sighan Bakeoff, regardless of the specifications and training a new CWS for segmenting SMT training data. The second approach involves linear integration of translation models. We found that both approaches produced an improvement in translation quality.

4.1 Effect of combining training data from multiple CWS specifications

The CWS specifications are very different and the corresponding Sighan training data are segmented in different ways. We used these data separately in the previous work as if they were incompatible. However, creating data manually is laborious and costly. It would therefore be a significant advantage if all the data could be used, regardless of the different specifications. We therefore created a new CWS scheme, called "dict-hybrid". This CWS was trained by concatenating all the Sighan Bakeoff corpora regardless of the different specifications. The "dict-hybrid" was trained using Achilles. It uses a dictionary-based approach, and its lexicon and language model were obtained as follows.

First, we created a hybrid corpus by combining all the Sighan training corpora: AS, CITYU, MSR, PKU. The hybrid corpus was used to train a CRF-based CWS. This CWS was then used to segment the SMT training corpus and then we extracted a lexicon of 100,000 from the top frequent words of the segmented SMT corpus. This lexicon was used as the lexicon of the "dict-hybrid." The LM of "dict-hybrid" was also trained on the segmented corpus. Note a lexicon and a LM are the only needed resources for building a dictionary-based CWS, like the "dict-hybrid." (Zhang et al., 2006)

We used the "dict-hybrid" to segment the SMT training corpus and test data. This segmentation generated 49,546,231 tokens, 112,072 unique words for the training data and 693 OOVs for the test data.

The segmentation data were used for training a new SMT model. We tested the model using the same approach and found the BLEU score obtained by this CWS scheme was 23.91. This score was better than those in Table 4 obtained by any of the Achilles CWS schemes except ICTCLAS. Therefore, the CWS scheme "dict-hybrid" produced better translations than other schemes implemented using Achilles, indicating that using multiple CWS corpora can improve SMT even if their specifications are different.

Significance testing also showed that the results for ICTCLAS and "dict-hybrid" were not significantly different. The results of "dict-hybrid" are significantly better than those in the Table 4 which have

Table 5: Correlation between F-score and BLEU

PKU		
	F-score	BLEU
CRF	0.939	23.61
dict	0.930	23.61
dict-LDC	0.931	23.74
ICTCLAS	0.948	24.12

MSR		
	F-score	BLEU
CRF	0.954	22.50
dict	0.947	23.22
dict-LDC	0.928	23.16
MSRSEG	0.969	19.72

CITYU		
	F-score	BLEU
CRF	0.920	23.55
dict	0.873	23.72
dict-LDC	0.886	23.36

AS		
	F-score	BLEU
CRF	0.922	23.70
dict	0.896	23.46
dict-LDC	0.878	23.52

a BLEU score lower than 23.70.

4.2 Effect of feature interpolation of translation models

We investigated the effect of linearly integrating multiple features of the same type. We generated multiple translation models by using different word segmenters. Each translation model corresponded to a word segmenter. The same type of features as in the log-linear model were added linearly. For example, the phrase translation model $p(e|f)$ can be linearly interpolated as, $p(e|f) = \sum_{i=1}^{S} \alpha_i p_i(e|f)$ where $p_i(e|f)$ is the phrase translation model corresponding to the i-th CWSs. α_i is the weight, and S is the total number of models. $\sum_{i=1}^{S} \alpha_i = 1$.

αs can be obtained by maximizing the likelihood or BLEU scores of the development data. Optimizing the α has been described elsewhere (Foster and Kuhn, 2007). $p(e|f)$ is the phrase translation model generated.

In addition to the phrase translation model, we used the same approach to integrate three other features: phrase inverse probability $p(f|e)$, lexical probability $lex(e|f,a)$, and lexical inverse probability $lex(f|e,a)$.

We integrated the CWS schemes ranked in the top five in Table 4: ICTCLAS, dict-hybrid, dict-LDC-PKU, dict-CITYU, and CRF-AS. We labeled the five schemes A, B, C, D, and E, respectively, as shown in Table 6. The first line of Table 6 represents the test data segmented by the five CWS schemes. "tst-A" means the test data was segmented by ICTCLAS. "tst-B" means the test data segmented by "dict-hybrid", and so on. The second line gives baseline results showing the original results without the use of feature integration. For different test data, the baseline is different. The baseline of ICTCLAS was tested on "tst-A" only. The baseline of "dict-hybrid" was tested on "tst-B" only. From the third line we gradually added a translation model to the models used in the baseline. For example, "A+B" integrates models made using ICTCLAS and "dict-hybrid." Each integration models were tested only on the test data participated in the integration. Hence, some slots in Table 6 are blank.

We did not carry out parameter optimization with regards to the αs. Instead, we used equal αs for all the features. For example, all αs equal 0.5 for A+B, and 0.25 for A+B+C+D. Each cell in Table 6 indicates the BLEU score of the integration in relation to the test data. We found our approach improved the baseline results significantly. The more models integrated, the better the results. The improvement was positive for all of the test data. With regards to the integration, if a phrase pair exists in one model only, we suppose the values of probabilities are zero in other models.

To better understand the effects of feature interpolation, we blended the features of the translation models, as shown in Table 7, by simply combining the phrase pairs without probability interpolation. When we merged two models, we defined one model as the master model and the other as the supplementary model. Only phrase pairs that were in the supplementary models but not in the master model were appended to the master model. Their feature probabilities were not changed. Hence, the combined model was a blend of phrase pairs from the master model and supplementary model. There was no probability integration, that was significantly different from the feature interpolation approach. For each set of test data in Table 7, the master model was the model using the same CWS as the test data. While there was one row for each type of combination, the cells in the row contained different models. For example, "A+B" for test data "A" uses "A" as the master model and "B" as the supplementary model, while the opposite holds for test data "B".

Comparing Table 6 and 7 showed that feature interpolation outperformed feature blending. Feature interpolation yielded surprisingly good results. The performance consistently improved when more models were integrated, but this was not the case for feature blending. This shows that probability integration is very effective. Increasing the size of phrase pairs, as feature blending does, is not as effective.

We used equal values for the αs. Optimal values may be obtained using the optimization approach of maximizing BLEU or the likelihood of development data as has been reported previously (Foster and Kuhn, 2007). However, optimization is computationally expensive and the effect was not satisfactory. Therefore, we decided not optimizing the αs in this work.

5 Related work and Discussions

CWS has been the subject of intensive research in recent years, as is evident from the last four international evaluations, the Sighan Bakeoffs, and many approaches have been proposed over the past decade. Segmentation performance has been improved significantly, from the earliest maximal match (dictionary-based) approaches to CRF (Peng and McCallum, 2004) approach. We used dictionary-based and CRF-based CWS approaches to demonstrate the effect of CWS on SMT, both without and with OOV recognition.

SMT is a very complicated system to study. Its response to CWS schemes is intractable and it is very hard to use one or two measures to describe the relationship between CWS and SMT, in a similar way to describing the relationship between the alignment error rate (AER) and SMT (Fraser and Marcu, 2007). The CWS and SMT are related by a series of factors such as the specifications, OOVs, lexicons, and F-scores. None of these factors can be directly related to the SMT. While we have completed many experiments, based on changing the CWS specifications and methods used, to determine the relationship between CWS and SMT, we have not established any overwhelming rules. However, we believe the following guidelines are appropriate in considering a CWS system for SMT. Firstly, the F-score is not a reliable guide to SMT quality. A very high F-score may produce the lowest quality translations, as was found for the MSRSEG. Secondly, it is better to design a specification with smaller word units to reduce data sparseness. Specifications like those for MSR will produce an inferior translation. Thirdly, do not use a huge lexicon for word segmentation. A huge lexicon will result in data sparseness and segmentation complexity. And lastly, using multiple word segmentation results and approaches does work. We used two approaches that combined multiple word segmentation - dict-hybrid and feature integration - and both improved the translations significantly.

The BLEU scores in our experiments were relatively low in comparison with current state-of-the art results. However, our system was very similar to the system (Koehn et al., 2005) that gave a BLEU score of 24.3, comparable to ours. The BLEU score can be raised if we do post-editing, use more data for language modeling and other methods.

6 Conclusions

We investigated the effect of CWS on SMT from two points of view. Firstly, we analyzed multiple CWS specifications and built a CWS for each one to examine how they affected translations. Secondly, we investigated the advantages and disadvantages of various CWS approaches, both dictionary-based and CRF-based, and built CWSs using these approaches to examine their effect on translations.

We proposed a new approach to linear interpolation of translation features. This approach produced a significant improvement in translation and

Table 6: Feature interpolation of translation models: A=ICTCLAS, B=dict-hybrid, C=dict-PKU-LDC, D=dict-CITYU, E=CRF-AS

Model	tst-A	tst-B	tst-C	tst-D	tst-E
Baseline	24.12	23.91	23.74	23.72	23.70
A+B	24.25	24.20			
A+B+C	24.49	24.31	23.84		
A+B+C+D	24.60	24.43	24.05	24.27	
A+B+C+D+E	24.61	24.55	24.16	24.39	24.17

Table 7: Feature blending of translation models

Model	tst-A	tst-B	tst-C	tst-D	tst-E
Baseline	24.12	23.91	23.74	23.72	23.70
A+B	24.20	24.24			
A+B+C	24.27	24.14	23.69		
A+B+C+D	23.92	24.29	23.61	24.00	
A+B+C+D+E	23.86	24.31	23.69	24.05	23.76

achieved the best BLEU score of all the CWS schemes.

We have published a much more detailed paper (Zhang et al., 2008) to describe the relations between CWS and SMT.

References

Thomas Emerson. 2005. The second international chinese word segmentation bakeoff. In *Proceedings of the Fourth SIGHAN Workshop on Chinese Language Processing*, Jeju, Korea.

George Foster and Roland Kuhn. 2007. Mixture-model adaptation for SMT. In *Proceedings of the Second Workshop on Statistical Machine Translation*, pages 128–135, Prague, Czech Republic, June. Association for Computational Linguistics.

Alexander Fraser and Daniel Marcu. 2007. Measuring word alignment quality for statistical machine translation. In *Computational linguistics, Squibs Discussion*, volume 33 of *3*, pages 293–303, September.

Jianfeng Gao, Andi Wu, Mu Li, Chang-Ning Huang, Hongqiao Li, Xinsong Xia, and Haowei Qin. 2004. Adaptive chinese word segmentation. In *ACL-2004*, pages 462–469, Barcelona, July.

Philipp Koehn, Franz J. Och, and Daniel Marcu. 2003. Statistical phrase-based translation. In *HLT-NAACL 2003: Main Proceedings*, pages 127–133.

Philipp Koehn, Amittai Axelrod, Alexandra Birch Mayne, Miles Osborne Chris Callison-Burch, David Talbot, and Michael White. 2005. Edinburgh system description for the 2005 nist mt evaluation. In *Proceedings of Machine Translation Evaluation Workshop*.

Franz Josef Och. 2003. Minimum error rate training in statistical machine translation. In *Proc. of the 41st Annual Meeting of the Association for Computational Linguistics (ACL)*, pages 160–167.

Fuchun Peng and Andrew McCallum. 2004. Chinese segmentation and new word detection using conditional random fields. In *Proc. of Coling-2004*, pages 562–568, Geneva, Switzerland.

Huaping Zhang, HongKui Yu, Deyi xiong, and Qun Liu. 2003. HHMM-based Chinese lexical analyzer ICTCLAS. In *Proceedings of the Second SIGHAN Workshop on Chinese Language Processing*, pages 184–187.

Ying Zhang, Stephan Vogel, and Alex Waibel. 2004. Interpreting BLEU/NIST scores: How much improvement do we need to have a better system? In *Proceedings of the LREC*.

Ruiqiang Zhang, Genichiro Kikui, and Eiichiro Sumita. 2006. Subword-based tagging by conditional random fields for chinese word segmentation. In *Proceedings of the HLT-NAACL, Companion Volume: Short Papers*, pages 193–196, New York City, USA, June.

Ruiqiang Zhang, Keiji Yasuda, and Eiichiro Sumita. 2008. Chinese word segmentation and statistical machine translation. *ACM Trans. Speech Lang. Process.*, 5(2), May.

Optimizing Chinese Word Segmentation for Machine Translation Performance

Pi-Chuan Chang, Michel Galley, and **Christopher D. Manning**
Computer Science Department, Stanford University
Stanford, CA 94305
pichuan,galley,manning@cs.stanford.edu

Abstract

Previous work has shown that Chinese word segmentation is useful for machine translation to English, yet the way different segmentation strategies affect MT is still poorly understood. In this paper, we demonstrate that optimizing segmentation for an existing segmentation standard does not always yield better MT performance. We find that other factors such as segmentation consistency and granularity of Chinese "words" can be more important for machine translation. Based on these findings, we implement methods inside a conditional random field segmenter that directly optimize segmentation granularity with respect to the MT task, providing an improvement of 0.73 BLEU. We also show that improving segmentation consistency using external lexicon and proper noun features yields a 0.32 BLEU increase.

1 Introduction

Word segmentation is considered an important first step for Chinese natural language processing tasks, because Chinese words can be composed of multiple characters but with no space appearing between words. Almost all tasks could be expected to benefit by treating the character sequence "天花" together, with the meaning *smallpox,* rather than dealing with the individual characters "天" (*sky*) and "花" (*flower*). Without a standardized notion of a word, traditionally, the task of Chinese word segmentation starts from designing a segmentation standard based on linguistic and task intuitions, and then aiming to building segmenters that output words that conform to the standard. One widely used standard is the Penn Chinese Treebank (CTB) Segmentation Standard (Xue et al., 2005).

It has been recognized that different NLP applications have different needs for segmentation. Chinese information retrieval (IR) systems benefit from a segmentation that breaks compound words into shorter "words" (Peng et al., 2002), paralleling the IR gains from compound splitting in languages like German (Hollink et al., 2004), whereas automatic speech recognition (ASR) systems prefer having longer words in the speech lexicon (Gao et al., 2005). However, despite a decade of very intense work on Chinese to English machine translation (MT), the way in which Chinese word segmentation affects MT performance is very poorly understood. With current statistical phrase-based MT systems, one might hypothesize that segmenting into small chunks, including perhaps even working with individual characters would be optimal. This is because the role of a phrase table is to build domain and application appropriate larger chunks that are semantically coherent in the translation process. For example, even if the word for *smallpox* is treated as two one-character words, they can still appear in a phrase like "天 花→*smallpox*", so that *smallpox* will still be a candidate translation when the system translates "天" "花". Nevertheless, Xu et al. (2004) show that an MT system with a word segmenter outperforms a system working with individual characters in an alignment template approach. On different language pairs, (Koehn and Knight, 2003) and (Habash and Sadat, 2006) showed that data-driven methods for splitting and preprocessing can improve Arabic-English and German-English MT.

Beyond this, there has been no finer-grained analysis of what style and size of word segmentation is optimal for MT. Moreover, most discussion of segmentation for other tasks relates to the size units to identify in the segmentation standard: whether to join or split noun compounds, for instance. People

Proceedings of the Third Workshop on Statistical Machine Translation, pages 224–232,
Columbus, Ohio, USA, June 2008. ©2008 Association for Computational Linguistics

generally assume that improvements in a system's word segmentation accuracy will be monotonically reflected in overall system performance. This is the assumption that justifies the concerted recent work on the independent task of Chinese word segmentation evaluation at SIGHAN and other venues. However, we show that this assumption is false: aspects of segmenters other than error rate are more critical to their performance when embedded in an MT system. Unless these issues are attended to, simple baseline segmenters can be more effective inside an MT system than more complex machine learning based models, with much lower word segmentation error rate.

In this paper, we show that even having a basic word segmenter helps MT performance, and we analyze why building an MT system over individual characters doesn't function as well. Based on an analysis of baseline MT results, we pin down four issues of word segmentation that can be improved to get better MT performance. *(i)* While a feature-based segmenter, like a support vector machine or conditional random field (CRF) model, may have very good aggregate performance, inconsistent context-specific segmentation decisions can be quite harmful to MT system performance. *(ii)* A perceived strength of feature-based systems is that they can generate out-of-vocabulary (OOV) words, but these can hurt MT performance, when they could have been split into subparts from which the meaning of the whole can be roughly compositionally derived. *(iii)* Conversely, splitting OOV words into non-compositional subparts can be very harmful to an MT system: it is better to produce such OOV items than to split them into unrelated character sequences that are known to the system. One big source of such OOV words is named entities. *(iv)* Since the optimal granularity of words for phrase-based MT is unknown, we can benefit from a model which provides a knob for adjusting average word size.

We build several different models to address these issues and to improve segmentation for the benefit of MT. First, we emphasize lexicon-based features in a feature-based sequence classifier to deal with segmentation inconsistency and over-generating OOV words. Having lexicon-based features reduced the MT training lexicon by 29.5%, reduced the MT test data OOV rate by 34.1%, and led to a 0.38 BLEU point gain on the test data (MT05). Second, we extend the CRF label set of our CRF segmenter to identify proper nouns. This gives 3.3% relative improvement on the OOV recall rate, and a 0.32 improvement in BLEU. Finally, we tune the CRF model to generate shorter or longer words to directly optimize the performance of MT. For MT, we found that it is preferred to have words slightly shorter than the CTB standard.

The paper is organized as follows: we describe the experimental settings for the segmentation task and the task in Section 2. In Section 3.1 we demonstrate that it is helpful to have word segmenters for MT, but that segmentation performance does not directly correlate with MT performance. We analyze what characteristics of word segmenters most affect MT performance in Section 3.2. In Section 4 and 5 we describe how we tune a CRF model to fit the "word" granularity and also how we incorporate external lexicon and information about named entities for better MT performance.

2 Experimental Setting

2.1 Chinese Word Segmentation

For directly evaluating segmentation performance, we train each segmenter with the SIGHAN Bakeoff 2006 training data (the UPUC data set) and then evaluate on the test data. The training data contains 509K words, and the test data has 155K words. The percentage of words in the test data that are unseen in the training data is 8.8%. Detail of the Bakeoff data sets is in (Levow, 2006). To understand how each segmenter learns about OOV words, we will report the F measure, the in-vocabulary (IV) recall rate as well as OOV recall rate of each segmenter.

2.2 Phrase-based Chinese-to-English MT

The MT system used in this paper is Moses, a state-of-the-art phrase-based system (Koehn et al., 2003). We build phrase translations by first acquiring bidirectional GIZA++ (Och and Ney, 2003) alignments, and using Moses' grow-diag alignment symmetrization heuristic.[1] We set the maximum phrase length to a large value (10), because some segmenters described later in this paper will result in shorter

[1]In our experiments, this heuristic consistently performed better than the default, grow-diag-final.

words, therefore it is more comparable if we increase the maximum phrase length. During decoding, we incorporate the standard eight feature functions of Moses as well as the lexicalized reordering model. We tuned the parameters of these features with Minimum Error Rate Training (MERT) (Och, 2003) on the NIST MT03 Evaluation data set (919 sentences), and then test the MT performance on NIST MT03 and MT05 Evaluation data (878 and 1082 sentences, respectively). We report the MT performance using the original BLEU metric (Papineni et al., 2001). All BLEU scores in this paper are uncased.

The MT training data was subsampled from GALE Year 2 training data using a collection of character 5-grams and smaller n-grams drawn from all segmentations of the test data. Since the MT training data is subsampled with character n-grams, it is not biased towards any particular word segmentation. The MT training data contains 1,140,693 sentence pairs; on the Chinese side there are 60,573,223 non-whitespace characters, and the English sentences have 40,629,997 words.

Our main source for training our five-gram language model was the English Gigaword corpus, and we also included close to one million English sentences taken from LDC parallel texts: GALE Year 1 training data (excluding FOUO data), Sinorama, AsiaNet, and Hong Kong news. We restricted the Gigaword corpus to a subsample of 25 million sentences, because of memory constraints.

3 Understanding Chinese Word Segmentation for Phrase-based MT

In this section, we experiment with three types of segmenters – character-based, lexicon-based and feature-based – to explore what kind of characteristics are useful for segmentation for MT.

3.1 Character-based, Lexicon-based and Feature-based Segmenters

The training data for the segmenter is two orders of magnitude smaller than for the MT system, it is not terribly well matched to it in terms of genre and variety, and the information an MT system learns about alignment of Chinese to English might be the basis for a task appropriate segmentation style for Chinese-English MT. A phrase-based MT system like Moses can extract "phrases" (sequences of tokens) from a word alignment and the system can construct the words that are useful. These observations suggest the first hypothesis.

Segmentation Performance			
Segmenter	F measure	OOV Recall	IV Recall
CharBased	0.334	0.012	0.485
MaxMatch	0.828	0.012	0.951
MT Performance			
Segmenter	MT03 (dev)	MT05 (test)	
CharBased	30.81	29.36	
MaxMatch	31.95	30.73	

Table 1: CharBased vs. MaxMatch

Hypothesis 1. *A phrase table should capture word segmentation. Character-based segmentation for MT should not underperform a lexicon-based segmentation, and might outperform it.*

Observation In the experiments we conducted, we found that the phrase table cannot capture everything a Chinese word segmenter can do, and therefore having word segmentation helps phrase-based MT systems. [2]

To show that having word segmentation helps MT, we compare a lexicon-based maximum-matching segmenter with character-based segmentation (treating each Chinese character as a word). The lexicon-based segmenter finds words by greedily matching the longest words in the lexicon in a left-to-right fashion. We will later refer to this segmenter as MaxMatch. The MaxMatch segmenter is a simple and common baseline for the Chinese word segmentation task.

The segmentation performance of MaxMatch is not very satisfying because it cannot generalize to capture words it has never seen before. However, having a basic segmenter like MaxMatch still gives the phrase-based MT system a win over the character-based segmentation (treating each Chinese character as a word). We will refer to the character-based segmentation as CharBased.

In Table 1, we can see that on the Chinese word segmentation task, having MaxMatch is obviously better than not trying to identify Chinese words at all (CharBased). As for MT performance, in Table 1 we see that having a segmenter, even as sim-

[2]Different phrase extraction heuristics might affect the results. In our experiments, grow-diag outperforms both one-to-many and many-to-one for both MaxMatch and CharBased. We report the results only on grow-diag.

Reference translation: scientists complete sequencing of the chromosome linked to early dementia
CharBased segmented input: 科␣学␣家␣为␣攸␣关␣初␣期␣失␣智␣症␣的␣染␣色␣体␣完␣成␣定␣序
MaxMatch segmented input: 科学家␣为␣攸关␣初期␣失␣智␣症␣的␣染色␣体␣完成␣定␣序
Translation with CharBased segmentation: scientists at the beginning of the stake of chile lost the genome sequence completed
Translation with MaxMatch segmentation: scientists at stake for the early loss of intellectual syndrome chromosome completed sequencing

Table 2: An example showing that character-based segmentation provides weaker ability to distinguish character with multiple unrelated meanings.

ple as MaxMatch, can help phrase-based MT system by about 1.37 BLEU points on all 1082 sentences of the test data (MT05). Also, we tested the performance on 828 sentences of MT05 where all elements are in vocabulary[3] for both MaxMatch and CharBased. MaxMatch achieved 32.09 BLEU and CharBased achieved 30.28 BLEU, which shows that on the sentences where all elements are in vocabulary, there MaxMatch is still significantly better than CharBased. Therefore, Hypothesis 1 is refuted.

Analysis We hypothesized in Hypothesis 1 that the phrase table in a phrase-based MT system should be able to capture the meaning by building "phrases" on top of character sequences. Based on the experimental result in Table 1, we see that using character-based segmentation (CharBased) actually performs reasonably well, which indicates that the phrase table does capture the meaning of character sequences to a certain extent. However, the results also show that there is still some benefit in having word segmentation for MT. We analyzed the decoded output of both systems (CharBased and MaxMatch) on the development set (MT03). We found that the advantage of MaxMatch over CharBased is two-fold, *(i)* lexical: it enhances the ability to disambiguate the case when a character has very different meaning in different contexts, and *(ii)* reordering: it is easier to move one unit around than having to move two consecutive units at the same time. Having words as the basic units helps the reordering model.

For the first advantage, one example is the character "智", which can both mean "intelligence", or an abbreviation for Chile (智利). The comparison between CharBased and MaxMatch is listed in Table 2. The word 失智症 (dementia) is unknown for both segmenters. However, MaxMatch gave a better translation of the character 智. The issue here is not that the "智"→"intelligence" entry never appears in the phrase table of CharBased. The real issue is, when 智 means Chile, it is usually followed by the character 利. So by grouping them together, MaxMatch avoided falsely increasing the probability of translating the stand-alone 智 into Chile. Based on our analysis, this ambiguity occurs the most when the character-based system is dealing with a rare or unseen character sequence in the training data, and also occurs more often when dealing with transliterations. The reason is that characters composing a transliterated foreign named entity usually doesn't preserve their meanings; they are just used to compose a Chinese word that sounds similar to the original word – much more like using a character segmentation of English words. Another example of this kind is "阿耳滋海默氏症" (Alzheimer's disease). The MT system using CharBased segmentation tends to translate some characters individually and drop others; while the system using MaxMatch segmentation is more likely to translate it right.

The second advantage of having a segmenter like the lexicon-based MaxMatch is that it helps the reordering model. Results in Table 1 are with the linear distortion limit defaulted to 6. Since words in CharBased are inherently shorter than MaxMatch, having the same distortion limit means CharBased is limited to a smaller context than MaxMatch. To make a fairer comparison, we set the linear distortion limit in Moses to unlimited, removed the lexicalized reordering model, and retested both systems. With this setting, MaxMatch is 0.46 BLEU point better than CharBased (29.62 to 29.16) on MT03. This result suggests that having word segmentation does affect how the reordering model works in a phrase-based system.

Hypothesis 2. *Better Segmentation Performance Should Lead to Better MT Performance*

Observation We have shown in Hypothesis 1 that it is helpful to segment Chinese texts into words first. In order to decide a segmenter to use, the most intuitive thing to do is to find one that gives higher F measure on segmentation. Our experiments show that higher F measure does not necessarily

[3]Except for dates and numbers.

lead to higher BLEU score. In order to contrast with the simple maximum matching lexicon-based model (MaxMatch), we built another segmenter with a CRF model. CRF is a statistical sequence modeling framework introduced by Lafferty et al. (2001), and was first used for the Chinese word segmentation task by Peng et al. (2004), who treated word segmentation as a binary decision task. We optimized the parameters with a quasi-Newton method, and used Gaussian priors to prevent overfitting.

The probability assigned to a label sequence for a particular sequence of characters by a CRF is given by the equation:

$$p_\lambda(\mathbf{y}|\mathbf{x}) = \frac{1}{Z(\mathbf{x})} \exp \sum_{t=1}^{T} \sum_{k=1}^{K} \lambda_k f_k(\mathbf{x}, y_{t-1}, y_t, t) \quad (1)$$

$\mathbf{x}$ is a sequence of T unsegmented characters, $Z(\mathbf{x})$ is the partition function that ensures that Equation 1 is a probability distribution, $\{f_k\}_{k=1}^{K}$ is a set of feature functions, and $\mathbf{y}$ is the sequence of binary predictions for the sentence, where the prediction $y_t = +1$ indicates the t-th character of the sequence is preceded by a space, and where $y_t = -1$ indicates there is none. We trained a CRF model with a set of basic features: character identity features of the current character, previous character and next character, and the conjunction of previous and current characters in the zero-order templates. We will refer to this segmenter as CRF-basic.

Table 3 shows that the feature-based segmenter CRF-basic outperforms the lexicon-based MaxMatch by 5.9% relative F measure. Comparing the OOV recall rate and the IV recall rate, the reason is that CRF-basic wins a lot on the OOV recall rate. We see that a feature-based segmenter like CRF-basic clearly has stronger ability to recognize unseen words. On MT performance, however, CRF-basic is 0.38 BLEU points worse than MaxMatch on the test set. In Section 3.2, we will look at how the MT training and test data are segmented by each segmenter, and provide statistics and analysis for why certain segmenters are better than others.

3.2 Consistency Analysis of Different Segmenters

In Section 3.1 we have refuted two hypotheses. Now we know that: (*i*) phrase table construction does not fully capture what a word segmenter can do. Thus it is useful to have word segmentation for MT. (*ii*) a higher F measure segmenter does not necessarily outperforms on the MT task.

To understand what factors other than segmentation F measure can affect MT performance, we introduce another CRF segmenter CRF-Lex that includes lexicon-based features by using external lexicons. More details of CRF-Lex will be described in Section 5.1. From Table 3, we see that the segmentation F measure is that CRF-Lex > CRF-basic > MaxMatch. And now we know that the better segmentation F measure does not always lead to better MT BLEU score, because of in terms of MT performance, CRF-Lex > MaxMatch > CRF-basic.

In Table 4, we list some statistics of each segmenter to explain this phenomenon. First we look at the lexicon size of the MT training and test data. While segmenting the MT data, CRF-basic generates an MT training lexicon size of 583K unique word tokens, and MaxMatch has a much smaller lexicon size of 39K. CRF-Lex performs best on MT, but the MT training lexicon size and test lexicon OOV rate is still pretty high compared to MaxMatch. Only examining the MT training and test lexicon size still doesn't fully explain why CRF-Lex outperforms MaxMatch. MaxMatch generates a smaller MT lexicon and lower OOV rate, but for MT it wasn't better than CRF-Lex, which has a bigger lexicon and higher OOV rate. In order to understand why MaxMatch performs worse on MT than CRF-Lex but bet-

Segmentation Performance

Segmenter	F measure	OOV Recall	IV Recall
CRF-basic	0.877	0.502	0.926
MaxMatch	0.828	0.012	0.951
CRF-Lex	0.940	0.729	0.970

MT Performance

Segmenter	MT03 (dev)	MT05 (test)
CRF-basic	33.01	30.35
MaxMatch	31.95	30.73
CRF-Lex	32.70	30.95

Table 3: CRF-basic vs MaxMatch

Segmenter	#MT Training Lexicon Size	#MT Test Lexicon Size
CRF-basic	583147	5443
MaxMatch	39040	5083
CRF-Lex	411406	5164
	MT Test Lexicon OOV rate	**Conditional Entropy**
CRF-basic	7.40%	0.2306
MaxMatch	0.49%	0.1788
CRF-Lex	4.88%	0.1010

Table 4: MT Lexicon Statistics and Conditional Entropy of Segmentation Variations of three segmetners

ter than CRF-basic, we use conditional entropy of segmentation variations to measure consistency.

We use the gold segmentation of the SIGHAN test data as a guideline. For every work type w_i, we collect all the different pattern variations v_{ij} in the segmentation we want to examine. For example, for a word "*ABC*" in the gold segmentation, we look at how it is segmented with a segmenter. There are many possibilities. If we use c_x and c_y to indicate other Chinese characters and ␣ to indicate white spaces, "c_x␣ABC␣c_y" is the correct segmentation, because the three characters are properly segmented from both sides, and they are concatenated with each other. It can also be segmented as "c_x␣A␣BC␣c_y", which means although the boundary is correct, the first character is separated from the other two. Or, it can be segmented as "c_xA␣BCc_y", which means the first character was actually part of the previous word, while *BC* are the beginning of the next word. Every time a particular word type w_i appears in the text, we consider a segmenter more consistent if it can segment w_i in the same way every time, but it doesn't necessarily have to be the same as the gold standard segmentation. For example, if "*ABC*" is a Chinese person name which appears 100 times in the gold standard data, and one segmenter segment it as c_x␣A␣BC␣c_y 100 times, then this segmenter is still considered to be very consistent, even if it doesn't exactly match the gold standard segmentation. Using this intuition, the conditional entropy of segmentation variations $H(V|W)$ is defined as follows:

$$\begin{aligned} H(V|W) &= -\sum_{w_i} P(w_i) \sum_{v_{ij}} P(v_{ij}|w_i) \log P(v_{ij}|w_i) \\ &= -\sum_{w_i} \sum_{v_{ij}} P(v_{ij}, w_i) \log P(v_{ij}|w_i) \end{aligned}$$

Now we can look at the overall conditional entropy $H(V|W)$ to compare the consistency of each segmenter. In Table 4, we can see that even though MaxMatch has a much smaller MT lexicon size than CRF-Lex, when we examine the consistency of how MaxMatch segments in context, we find the conditional entropy is much higher than CRF-Lex. We can also see that CRF-basic has a higher conditional entropy than the other two. The conditional entropy $H(V|W)$ shows how consistent each segmenter is, and it correlates with the MT performance in Table 4. Note that consistency is only one of the competing factors of how good a segmentation is for MT performance. For example, a character-based segmentation will always have the best consistency possible, since every word *ABC* will just have one pattern: c_x␣A␣B␣C␣c_y. But from Section 3.1 we see that CharBased performs worse than both MaxMatch and CRF-basic on MT, because having word segmentation can help the granularity of the Chinese lexicon match that of the English lexicon.

In conclusion, for MT performance, it is helpful to have consistent segmentation, while still having a word segmentation matching the granularity of the segmented Chinese lexicon and the English lexicon.

4 Optimal Average Token Length for MT

We have shown earlier that word-level segmentation vastly outperforms character based segmentation in MT evaluations. Since the word segmentation standard under consideration (Chinese Treebank (Xue et al., 2005)) was neither specifically designed nor optimized for MT, it seems reasonable to investigate whether any segmentation granularity in continuum between character-level and CTB-style segmentation is more effective for MT. In this section, we present a technique for directly optimizing a segmentation property—characters per token average—for translation quality, which yields significant improvements in MT performance.

In order to calibrate the average word length produced by our CRF segmenter—i.e., to adjust the rate of word boundary predictions ($y_t = +1$), we apply a relatively simple technique (Minkov et al., 2006) originally devised for adjusting the precision/recall tradeoff of any sequential classifier. Specifically, the weight vector **w** and feature vector of a trained linear sequence classifier are augmented at test time to include new class-conditional feature functions to bias the classifier towards particular class labels. In our case, since we wish to increase the frequency of word boundaries, we add a feature function:

$$f_0(\mathbf{x}, y_{t-1}, y_t, t) = \begin{cases} 1 & \text{if } y_t = +1 \\ 0 & \text{otherwise} \end{cases}$$

Its weight λ_0 controls the extent of which the classifier will make positive predictions, with very large positive λ_0 values causing only positive predictions (i.e., character-based segmentation) and large negative values effectively disabling segmentation boundaries. Table 5 displays how changes of the

λ_0	-1	0	1	2	4	8	32
len	1.64	1.62	1.61	1.59	1.55	1.37	1

Table 5: Effect of the bias parameter λ_0 on the average number of character per token on MT data.

bias parameter λ_0 affect segmentation granularity.[4] Since we are interested in analyzing the different regimes of MT performance between CTB segmentation and character-based, we performed a grid search in the range between $\lambda_0 = 0$ (maximum-likelihood estimate) and $\lambda_0 = 32$ (a value that is large enough to produce only positive predictions). For each λ_0 value, we ran an entire MT training and testing cycle, i.e., we re-segmented the entire training data, ran GIZA++, acquired phrasal translations that abide to this new segmentation, and ran MERT and evaluations on segmented data using the same λ_0 values.

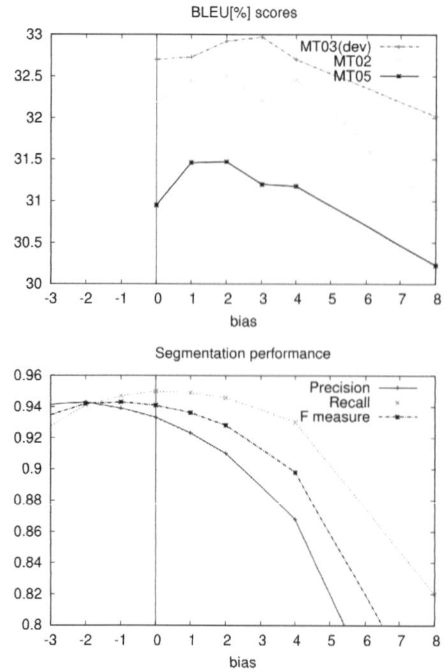

Figure 1: A bias towards more segment boundaries ($\lambda_0 > 0$) yields better MT performance and worse segmentation results.

Segmentation and MT results are displayed in Figure 1. First, we observe that an adjustment of the precision and recall tradeoff by setting negative bias values ($\lambda_0 = -2$) slightly improves segmentation performance. We also notice that raising λ_0 yields relatively consistent improvements in MT performance, yet causes segmentation performance (F measure) to be increasingly worse. While the latter finding is not particularly surprising, it further confirms that segmentation and MT evaluations can yield rather different outcomes. We chose the $\lambda_0 = 2$ on another dev set (MT02). On the test set MT05, $\lambda_0 = 2$ yields 31.47 BLEU, which represents a quite large improvement compared to the unbiased segmenter (30.95 BLEU). Further reducing the average number of characters per token yields gradual drops of performance until character-level segmentation ($\lambda_0 \geq 32$, 29.36 BLEU).

[4]Note that character-per-token averages provided in the table consider each non-Chinese word (e.g., foreign names, numbers) as one character, since our segmentation post-processing prevents these tokens from being segmented.

Here are some examples of how setting $\lambda_0 = 2$ shortens the words in a way that can help MT.

- separating adjectives and pre-modifying adverbs:
  很大(*very big*) → 很(*very*) 大(*big*)
- separating nouns and pre-modifying adjectives:
  高血压(*high blood pressure*)
  → 高(*high*) 血压(*blood pressure*)
- separating compound nouns:
  内政部(*Department of Internal Affairs*)
  → 内政(*Internal Affairs*) 部(*Department*).

5 Improving Segmentation Consistency of a Feature-based Sequence Model for Segmentation

In Section 3.1 we showed that a statistical sequence model with rich features can generalize better than maximum matching segmenters. However, it also inconsistently over-generates a big MT training lexicon and OOV words in MT test data, and thus causes a problem for MT. To improve a feature-based sequence model for MT, we propose 4 different approaches to deal with named entities, optimal length of word for MT and joint search for segmentation and MT decoding.

5.1 Making Use of External Lexicons

One way to improve the consistency of the CRF model is to make use of external lexicons (which are not part of the segmentation training data) to add lexicon-based features. All the features we use are listed in Table 6. Our linguistic features are adopted from (Ng and Low, 2004) and (Tseng et al., 2005). There are three categories of features:

Lexicon-based Features		Linguistic Features	
(1.1)	$L_{Begin}(C_n), n \in [-2,1]$	(2.1)	$C_n, n \in [-2,1]$
(1.2)	$L_{Mid}(C_n), n \in [-2,1]$	(2.2)	$C_{n-1}C_n, n \in [-1,1]$
(1.3)	$L_{End}(C_n), n \in [-2,1]$	(2.3)	$C_{n-2}C_n, n \in [1,2]$
(1.4)	$L_{End}(C_{-1}) + L_{End}(C_0) + L_{End}(C_1)$	(2.4)	$Single(C_n), n \in [-2,1]$
		(2.5)	$UnknownBigram(C_{-1}C_0)$
(1.5)	$L_{End}(C_{-2}) + L_{End}(C_{-1}) + L_{Begin}(C_0) + L_{Mid}(C_0)$	(2.6)	$ProductiveAffixes(C_{-1}, C_0)$
		(2.7)	$Reduplication(C_{-1}, C_n), n \in [0,1]$
(1.6)	$L_{End}(C_{-2}) + L_{End}(C_{-1}) + L_{Begin}(C_{-1}) + L_{Begin}(C_0) + L_{Mid}(C_0)$		

Table 6: Features for CRF-Lex

Segmentation Performance			
Segmenter	F measure	OOV Recall	IV Recall
CRF-Lex-NR	0.943	0.753	0.970
CRF-Lex	0.940	0.729	0.970
MT Performance			
Segmenter	MT03 (dev)	MT05 (test)	
CRF-Lex-NR	32.96	31.27	
CRF-Lex	32.70	30.95	

Table 7: CRF-Lex-NR vs CRF-Lex

character identity n-grams, morphological and character reduplication features. Our lexicon-based features are adopted from (Shi and Wang, 2007), where $L_{Begin}(C_0)$, $L_{Mid}(C_0)$ and $L_{End}(C_0)$ represent the maximum length of words found in a lexicon that contain the current character as either the first, middle or last character, and we group any length equal or longer than 6 together. The linguistic features help capturing words that were unseen to the segmenter; while the lexicon-based features constrain the segmenter with external knowledge of what sequences are likely to be words.

We built a CRF segmenter with all the features listed in Table 6 (CRF-Lex). The external lexicons we used for the lexicon-based features come from various sources including named entities collected from Wikipedia and the Chinese section of the UN website, named entities collected by Harbin Institute of Technology, the ADSO dictionary, EMM News Explorer, Online Chinese Tools, Online Dictionary from Peking University and HowNet. There are 423,224 distinct entries in all the external lexicons.

The MT lexicon consistency of CRF-Lex in Table 4 shows that the MT training lexicon size has been reduced by 29.5% and the MT test data OOV rate is reduced by 34.1%.

5.2 Joint training of Word Segmentation and Proper Noun Tagging

Named entities are an important source for OOV words, and in particular are ones which it is bad to break into pieces (particularly for foreign names). Therefore, we use the proper noun (NR) part-of-speech tag information from CTB to extend the label sets of our CRF model from 2 to 4 ({beginning of a word, continuation of a word} $\times$ {NR, not NR}). This is similar to the "all-at-once, character-based" POS tagging in (Ng and Low, 2004), except that we are only tagging proper nouns. We call the 4-label extension CRF-Lex-NR. The segmentation and MT performance of CRF-Lex-NR is listed in Table 7. With the 4-label extension, the OOV recall rate improved by 3.29%; while the IV recall rate stays the same. Similar to (Ng and Low, 2004), we found the overall F measure only goes up a tiny bit, but we do find a significant OOV recall rate improvement.

On the MT performance, CRF-Lex-NR has a 0.32 BLEU gain on the test set MT05. In addition to the BLEU improvement, CRF-Lex-NR also provides extra information about proper nouns, which can be combined with postprocessing named entity translation modules to further improve MT performance.

6 Conclusion

In this paper, we investigated what segmentation properties can improve machine translation performance. First, we found that neither character-based nor a standard word segmentation standard are optimal for MT, and show that an intermediate granularity is much more effective. Using an already competitive CRF segmentation model, we directly optimize segmentation granularity for translation quality, and obtain an improvement of 0.73 BLEU point on MT05 over our lexicon-based segmentation baseline. Second, we augment our CRF model with lexicon and proper noun features in order to improve segmentation consistency, which provide a 0.32 BLEU point improvement.

7 Acknowledgement

The authors would like to thank Menqgiu Wang and Huihsin Tseng for useful discussions. This paper is based on work funded in part by the Defense Advanced Research Projects Agency through IBM.

References

Jianfeng Gao, Mu Li, Andi Wu, and Chang-Ning Huang. 2005. Chinese word segmentation and named entity recognition: A pragmatic approach. *Computational Linguistics*.

Nizar Habash and Fatiha Sadat. 2006. Arabic preprocessing schemes for statistical machine translation. In *Proceedings of the Human Language Technology Conference of the NAACL, Companion Volume: Short Papers*, pages 49–52, New York City, USA, June. Association for Computational Linguistics.

Vera Hollink, Jaap Kamps, Christof Monz, and Maarten de Rijke. 2004. Monolingual document retrieval for European languages. *Information Retrieval*, 7(1).

Philipp Koehn and Kevin Knight. 2003. Empirical methods for compound splitting. In *EACL '03: Proceedings of the tenth conference on European chapter of the Association for Computational Linguistics*, pages 187–193. Association for Computational Linguistics.

Philipp Koehn, Franz Josef Och, and Daniel Marcu. 2003. Statistical phrase-based translation. In *Proc. of NAACL-HLT*.

John Lafferty, Andrew McCallum, and Fernando Pereira. 2001. Conditional random fields: Probabilistic models for segmenting and labeling sequence data. In *Proc. 18th International Conf. on Machine Learning*.

Gina-Anne Levow. 2006. The third international Chinese language processing bakeoff: Word segmentation and named entity recognition. In *Proc. of the Fifth SIGHAN Workshop on Chinese Language Processing*, July.

Einat Minkov, Richard Wang, Anthony Tomasic, and William Cohen. 2006. NER systems that suit user's preferences: Adjusting the recall-precision trade-off for entity extraction. In *Proc. of NAACL-HLT, Companion Volume: Short Papers*, New York City, USA, June.

Hwee Tou Ng and Jin Kiat Low. 2004. Chinese part-of-speech tagging: One-at-a-time or all-at-once? Word-based or character-based? In *Proc. of EMNLP*.

Franz Josef Och and Hermann Ney. 2003. A systematic comparison of various statistical alignment models. *Computational Linguistics*, 29(1).

Franz Josef Och. 2003. Minimum error rate training for statistical machine translation. In *ACL*.

Kishore Papineni, Salim Roukos, Todd Ward, and Wei-Jing Zhu. 2001. BLEU: a method for automatic evaluation of machine translation. In *ACL*.

Fuchun Peng, Xiangji Huang, Dale Schuurmans, and Nick Cercone. 2002. Investigating the relationship between word segmentation performance and retrieval performance in Chinese IR. In *Proc. of the 19th International Conference on Computational Linguistics*.

Fuchun Peng, Fangfang Feng, and Andrew McCallum. 2004. Chinese segmentation and new word detection using conditional random fields. In *Proc. of COLING*.

Yanxin Shi and Mengqiu Wang. 2007. A dual-layer CRFs based joint decoding method for cascaded segmentation and labeling tasks. In *IJCAI*.

Huihsin Tseng, Pichuan Chang, Galen Andrew, Daniel Jurafsky, and Christopher Manning. 2005. A conditional random field word segmenter for Sighan bakeoff 2005. In *Proc. of the Fourth SIGHAN Workshop on Chinese Language Processing*.

Jia Xu, Richard Zens, and Hermann Ney. 2004. Do we need Chinese word segmentation for statistical machine translation. In *Proc. of the Third SIGHAN Workshop on Chinese Language Learning*.

Nianwen Xue, Fei Xia, Fu dong Chiou, and Martha Palmer. 2005. Building a large annotated Chinese corpus: the Penn Chinese treebank. *Journal of Natural Language Engineering*, 11(2).

Author Index